Modern
RUSSIAN
Grammar

Routledge
Taylor & Francis Group

LONDON AND NEW YORK

Routledge Modern Grammars

Series concept and development – Sarah Butler

Other books in the series:
Modern Mandarin Chinese Grammar
Modern Mandarin Chinese Grammar Workbook

Modern German Grammar, Second Edition
Modern German Grammar Workbook, Second Edition

Modern Spanish Grammar, Second Edition
Modern Spanish Grammar Workbook, Second Edition

Modern Italian Grammar, Second Edition
Modern Italian Grammar Workbook, Second Edition

Modern French Grammar, Second Edition
Modern French Grammar Workbook, Second Edition

Modern
RUSSIAN
Grammar

John Dunn
and Shamil Khairov

First published 2009
by Routledge
2 Park Square, Milton Park, Abingdon, Oxfordshire OX14 4RN

Simultaneously published in the USA and Canada
by Routledge
711 Third Ave, New York, NY 10017

Routledge is an imprint of the Taylor & Francis Group, an informa business

Typeset in Times and Akzidenz Grotesk by
Florence Production Ltd, Stoodleigh, Devon

British Library Cataloguing in Publication Data
A catalogue record for this book is available from the British Library

Library of Congress Cataloging in Publication Data
Dunn, J. A. (John A.), 1949–
  Modern Russian Grammar: a practical guide/John Dunn and Shamil Khairov.
    p.cm. – (Routledge modern grammars)
  Includes bibliographical references and index.
  1. Russian language – Grammar. 2. Russian Language – Textbooks for
foreign speakers – English. I. Khairov, Shamil. II. Title.
PG2112.D86 2008
491.7′82421–dc22   2008019529

ISBN: 978–0–415–42289–5 (hbk)
ISBN: 978–0–415–39750–6 (pbk)
ISBN: 978–0–203–96759–1 (ebk)

Contents

Part A   **Structures**

CONTENTS

CONTENTS

Part B   Functions

CONTENTS

CONTENTS

Introduction

This book is an innovative reference grammar, aimed at meeting the practical needs of English speakers who are learning Russian as a foreign language. It provides the necessary structural and functional information to enable users properly to interpret what they hear and read, and to communicate effectively, both in speech and in writing, in a wide range of situations. Most people who learn Russian start the language at university, and our book is aimed particularly at students in the first two years of a university course. It will, however, also be valuable for more advanced students, as well as for those learning Russian at school or independently. Although not particularly orientated towards 'business Russian', the book will be useful for those whose reasons for learning the language are related to business.

Following the pattern of the previous volumes in this series, the book is divided into two parts. Part A (Chapters 1–11) deals with the structure of the language. This is closer to a traditional grammar, in that attention is focused on the grammatical behaviour of the different parts of speech, as well as on issues that are particularly important to Russian grammar, such as the use of the cases, the aspects of the verb and grammatical agreement. Part B, however, is concerned with functions. This relates to the ways in which language is used in particular contexts and situations, and it is these contexts and situations that determine the way in which the information is presented. From a starting point such as asking questions, giving instructions and making requests or talking about causes and consequences, the user is given the necessary grammatical information to allow successful communication to take place.

It has to be said that writing a grammar of Russian presents a number of interesting challenges. The first is that, for English speakers Russian is from the structural point of view a very complex language. It has a rich system of endings and patterns, embellished by numerous exceptions, that, as is often the way with language, tend to affect words that are in common use. This has inevitably influenced the structure of the book, and Part A is rather more substantial than is the case with the other volumes in the series. It also means that it is impossible to avoid using a certain amount of grammatical terminology. Here we have borne in mind that readers will also be using other course materials, and in order to minimise confusion, our use of terminology is fairly traditional for English-language grammars. We have at the same time taken account of the knowledge of grammar likely to be possessed by native speakers of English starting to learn Russian, and grammatical terms are explained either in the Glossary or in the relevant chapter.

It is also the case that for various linguistic and cultural reasons Russian is a language that tends to 'do things' differently from English. Even such relatively straightforward contexts such as addressing friends, acquaintances and strangers, talking about marital status, indicating possession or describing a journey involve using language in ways bearing little resemblance to those that will be familiar to English speakers. It is this consideration that has determined our choice of structures for Part B and, in particular, explains why we have devoted substantial chapters to such questions as establishing identity, establishing contact, and talking about coming and going.

The political, social and economic changes that have taken place in Russia since 1985 have been matched by changes to the language. Fortunately (for us, at least) grammar moves at a much slower pace than does vocabulary, although we have had to contend with the fact that there is now much less agreement about what constitutes 'good' or 'correct' Russian than used to be the case. We have tried to take due note of linguistic innovations, especially where this is likely to be especially relevant to learners; at the same time, bearing in mind the need for reference grammars to have a certain 'timeless' quality, we have steered clear of matters that are likely to be ephemeral (for this reason we give relatively few examples involving prices!). Above all, we have aimed at following the principle that this book is intended to be a practical guide.

There is a long-standing tradition in the writing of Russian textbooks that the material presented should reflect the notion that 'everything in the garden is rosy'. This can sometimes provoke the reaction of focusing undue attention on the unkempt and weed-choked areas of the linguistic 'garden' that have been previously kept hidden. Here too, we have tried to avoid extreme positions. Most of our recommendations and examples belong to a standard and neutral educated register, but where appropriate we have labelled usages as 'informal' or 'formal': the former are likely to be appropriate in such contexts as conversations between friends or personal letters; the latter would tend to occur in official documents and letters, or be used at meetings or in lectures. With a couple of reasoned exceptions we have avoided extremes of 'high' and 'low' language and have purposely steered clear of vulgar or obscene forms. Mindful of the fact that for Russian perhaps to a greater extent than for other languages learners are not always expected to produce the same language as native speakers, we have issued, where necessary, 'health warnings' about certain usages that will be encountered but which may sound odd, inappropriate or even offensive if uttered by a learner of the language.

Finally, this is a practical guide: we cannot claim to be comprehensive or to have foreseen every eventuality. It will be noticed that many of our recommendations are hedged with words such as 'normally' and 'generally'. What this means is that users should feel free to go ahead and follow these recommendations without trepidation, but should not be unduly surprised and should certainly not be put off if they occasionally encounter something that appears to be a direct contradiction.

Warmest thanks are due to Sarah Butler for her editorial guidance and encouragement during the early stages of writing this book, and to Larisa Stizhko who has read through the text and given us a great many valuable comments on current Russian usage. We would also like to thank the Russian students of Glasgow University who for more than thirty years have acted as unwitting guinea-pigs for much of the material included here, and whose unexpectedly cheerful willingness to engage with the complexities of Russian grammar was a great incentive for us to take up the challenge of writing this book.

John Dunn and Shamil Khairov

How to use this book

Part A of this book is a reference guide to the *structures* of Russian. The individual chapters deal with grammatical categories such as nouns, verbs, adjectives and pronouns. There are also chapters devoted to the use of the cases, to aspects of the verb and to grammatical agreement.

Part B is concerned with communicative *functions*, that is, the uses to which language is put. In this part of the book, therefore, each individual chapter is concerned with a specific function, such as establishing identity, talking about being and becoming, or asking questions. This part also includes chapters on focus and emphasis, and on communication strategies.

Each chapter is divided into sections, and in order to allow the material to be presented in portions of manageable size, most of the latter are divided further into subsections. Each chapter, section and subsection has its own heading, as in the following examples:

> **13 Establishing contact**
> **13.2 Greetings**
> **13.2.2 Informal greetings**

In Part A much of the information is presented in the form of grammatical tables or of lists. Where appropriate, in Part A and throughout Part B the grammatical information is illustrated by copious examples, which are more or less complicated according to the type of information being presented. Many of the examples have been taken from actual printed or Internet sources, but these have mostly been adapted to remove extraneous linguistic complexities or obscure references. Where it was thought helpful, notes are used to provide supplementary grammatical or cultural information.

Russian language material is presented in **bold type**, and in the examples key words are highlighted by the use of *italic*. All examples are translated into English, and a literal version is supplied in those instances where the natural English translation is significantly different from the Russian original.

It is impossible to describe a language such as Russian without using a certain amount of grammatical terminology. We have tried as far as possible to use standard terms, and where necessary, we explain the terms used at the point where they first occur. There is in addition a separate Glossary of grammatical terms at the front of the book.

There are three ways of finding out where a specific topic may be located in the book. At the very beginning of the book the Contents lists what can be found in each chapter in the order in which the material is presented. At the end of the book the main Index lists all the topics covered in English alphabetical order, while a separate Index lists key Russian words in Russian alphabetical order (a table of the Russian alphabet is given at the beginning of Chapter 1). Finally, where an explanation or an example touches on a grammatical point covered elsewhere in the book, this is indicated by means of a cross-reference.

We have tried to keep the use of abbreviations to a minimum, but the following English abbreviations are used to indicate the names of the grammatical cases:

nom.   nominative
gen.   genitive
dat.   dative
acc.   accusative
instr.   instrumental
prep.   prepositional

The following *Russian* abbreviations are used for the aspects of the verb, especially in Chapters 4 and 5:

нсв   **несовершённый**   *imperfective*
св   **совершённый**   *perfective*

The following abbreviations are also used:

sing.   singular
fem.   feminine
masc.   masculine
n.   neuter
pl.   plural

Glossary of grammatical terms

Note: **Bold type** is used to cross-refer to other entries in the Glossary.

Active voice
The category of voice is used to indicate the relationship of **subject** and **object** to the action or state indicated by the **verb**. The **active** voice is used when the **subject** of the **verb** is the performer of the action or the main participant in the state or event; it contrasts with the **passive voice**. *See* **4.14** and **20.2**.

Adjective
An adjective is a word that indicates some attribute or quality and is used to qualify a **noun**; examples are кра́сный 'red' and англи́йский 'English'. Adjectives have distinct sets of endings and normally agree with the nouns they qualify in **number, gender** and **case**. *See* **Chapter 6** and **11.1**.

Adverb
Adverbs are mainly used to qualify a **verb**, although they can also qualify **adjectives** or even other **adverbs**. Examples are бы́стро 'quickly', по-ру́сски 'in Russian' and о́чень 'very'. **Adverbs** never change their endings. *See* **9.1**.

Agreement
One of the two factors that determine which endings are put on **nouns, verbs, adjectives, pronouns** and **numerals** (*see* also **Government**). The principle of **agreement** is that the endings of certain words are determined by the word either that they qualify or to which they refer. The two contexts where **agreement** is particularly important are within the **noun phrase** and between the **grammatical subject** of a sentence and the **verb**. *See* **Chapter 11**.

Article
An **article** is a word used with a **noun** to indicate whether it is definite or indefinite. In English the **articles** are 'the' and 'a/an'. Russian has no **articles** and therefore has to resort to other means to indicate whether a noun is definite or indefinite. *See* **20.4**.

Aspect
A category that refers to the different ways in which the action or state indicated by a verb may be viewed by the speaker. The Russian verb has two **aspects**, imperfective and perfective: in general terms the perfective **aspect** is used when an action or state is considered from the point of view of either one (beginning or end) or both of its boundaries, while the imperfective is used in all other circumstances. Every Russian verb belongs to either the imperfective or the perfective **aspect**, and **aspect** is one of the attributes of a verb given in dictionaries. *See* **4.2** and **Chapter 5**.

Case

Case refers to the different endings assumed by **nouns, adjectives, pronouns** and **numerals** as a means of indicating the particular grammatical function that the word concerned fulfils in a sentence. Russian has six **cases**: nominative, genitive, dative, accusative, instrumental and prepositional. *See* **Chapters 2** and **3**.

Clause

A clause is a unit that contains a **verb**, but which forms part of a larger sentence. A **main clause** is one that is capable of standing on its own, while a **subordinate clause** is one that must be combined with a **main clause**. A **subordinate clause** is most frequently introduced by a subordinating **conjunction**, although they can also be introduced by a relative **pronoun**. *See* **7.5, 9.3** and **Chapter 21**.

Comparative

The **comparative** form of an **adjective** or **adverb** is used when comparing different degrees of the quality indicated by the word in question; examples are **бы́стрее** 'quicker, more quickly' and **гро́мче** 'louder, more loudly'. *See* **6.8.1–6.8.3, 9.1.7** and **21.9.1– 21.9.6**.

Complement

The **complement** is usually the **noun** or **adjective** that completes a sentence containing a verb such as **быть** 'to be' or **станови́ться/стать** 'to become'. In Russian the **complement** is sometimes in the nominative **case** and sometimes in the instrumental. *See* **14.1**.

Conditional mood.

The conditional is the form of the **verb** that is used in a variety of hypothetical situations, such as conditions incapable of being fulfilled and certain kinds of wishes or requests. It is formed by combining the **particle бы** with the past **tense** form of the verb. *See* **4.10, 18.4** and **21.5.2**.

Conjugation

Conjugation is the term used for the changes in the endings of **verbs** to reflect **agreement** with the **subject**. It also the term used for the two regular patterns of verb endings in the present and future perfective. *See* **Chapter 4**, especially **4.3** and **4.6–4.8**.

Conjunctions

Conjunctions are words that join two **clauses** together. Two main **clauses** are joined by co-ordinating **conjunctions**, for example **и** 'and' or **но** 'but'. A main **clause** and a subordinate **clause** are joined by subordinating **conjunctions**, such as **е́сли** 'if', **когда́** 'when' or **потому́ что** 'because'. *See* **9.3** and **Chapter 21**.

Declension

Declension is the term used for the changes in the endings of **nouns, adjectives, pronouns** and **numerals** to reflect different grammatical functions. *See* **Chapters 2, 3, 6, 7, 8**.

Direct object

The **direct object** of a **verb** denotes the principal person or object affected by the action that the **verb** indicates. In Russian the **direct object** is in the accusative **case**, though after a negated verb it is sometimes in the genitive. *See* **3.2** and **15.4**.

Fleeting vowel

This is the term used for a vowel (usually **e, o** or **ë**) that occurs in some forms of a word, but not in others. It is particularly important for the **noun declension** system, although examples occur with other parts of speech as well. *See* especially **2.5**, but also **4.5.3, 4.7.3, 4.7.13, 6.5.1**.

Gender

Gender is a system of classifying **nouns**. Russian has **three** genders – masculine, feminine and neuter – and all nouns that can occur in the singular belong to one or other of these genders. There are no gender distinctions in the plural. **Gender** is mainly indicated through the system of **agreement**: **adjectives**, for example, have separate sets of endings for each of the three **genders**. There is also a very strong correlation between **gender** and **declension** type. *See* **2.3** and **Chapter 11**.

Gerund

Gerund is the term conventionally used in Russian grammar for a form that is at the same time both a part of the **verb** and an **adverb**. The main function of the **gerund** is to form complex sentences, in which a **gerund** is used in place of a **conjunction +** **verb**. *See* **4.11** and **21.10**.

Government

Government is one of the two factors that determine which endings are put on **nouns, adjectives, pronouns** and **numerals** (*see* also **Agreement**). **Government** essentially concerns the rules for selecting which **case** to use in different grammatical circumstances. *See* **Chapter 3** and **9.2**.

Grammatical subject *see* **Subject**.

Imperative mood

This is the form of the **verb** used in commands, prohibitions and certain kinds of requests. *See* **4.9** and **Chapter 18**.

Impersonal predicate forms

These fulfil the same function as **verbs**, but unlike ordinary **verbs** they can never be used along with a **grammatical subject** and they do not change their endings. Some **impersonal predicate forms**, such as хорошо́ 'it is good to', are part of the **adverb** system, while others, such as мо́жно 'one may; one can', are words that are used only in this function. *See* **11.2.2**.

Impersonal verbs

Impersonal verbs are those **verbs** that cannot be used with a **grammatical subject**. **Impersonal verbs** occur only in the third person singular (present and future **tenses**) or the neuter singular (past **tense**). *See* **3.4.3** and **11.2.2**.

Infinitive

This is the form under which verbs are listed in dictionaries. It does not change its ending. Infinitives are normally used in conjunction with other **verbs**, although under certain circumstances they can be used on their own in commands and prohibitions. *See* **4.1** and **18.2.2**.

Part A

Structures

Tense

Tense is the category of the **verb** that relates to time. Russian has a simple system of three **tenses:** present, future and past. *See* **4.3–4.5.**

Transitive verb

Transitive verb is a **verb** that is used with a **direct object**. *See* **14.13.1.**

Uninflected parts of speech

Uninflected parts of speech are those that never change their endings. The principal **uninflected parts of speech** are **adverbs, conjunctions, particles and prepositions.** *See* **Chapter 9.**

Unproductive verb classes

Unproductive verb classes are those to which no new **verbs** can be added. Although many **unproductive verb classes** contain very few **verbs**, there are many **verbs** in common use that belong to one or other of these classes. *See* **4.7.**

Verbs

Verbs are words that denote an action or a state. Examples include **быть**, 'to be', **де́лать** 'to do' and **чита́ть**, 'to read'. *See* **Chapter 4.**

Verbs of motion

Verbs of motion are a special group of **verbs** that have meanings related to movement in one form or another. These verbs have certain special characteristics, the most important being that they come in pairs: one member denotes motion in one direction, while the other denotes motion in more than one direction or in no specific direction. *See* **Chapter 22.**

Vvódnye slová

Vvódnye slová or 'introductory words' are a special group of words and phrases that normally come at or near the beginning of a sentence and that are separated from the rest of the sentence by a comma. They provide extra information that in one way or another qualifies what is said in the rest of the sentence. *See* **23.2.1.**

Prefix

Prefix is a form, usually of one or two syllables, that is attached to the beginning of a word in order to supply additional information relating to grammar or meaning. Russian has a rich range of **prefixes** that can be attached to **verbs** to convey various meanings or nuances. *See* **10.4**.

Preposition

Prepositions are words placed before **nouns** or **noun phrases** to provide additional information about the meaning and function of the noun. Each **preposition** is followed by a **noun** in a particular **case** (part of **government**); some **prepositions** can be followed by more than one **case**, depending on their precise meaning in the particular context in which they are used. *See* **9.2**.

Productive verb classes

Productive verb classes are those classes of verbs to which newly formed **verbs** can in principle be added. The majority of Russian **verbs** belong to one of the four classes of **productive verbs**. *See* **4.6**.

Pronoun

Pronouns are either words used in place of **nouns** or words that serve to qualify **nouns**, usually in a rather more general way than **adjectives**. **Pronouns** are divided into several categories, including personal **pronouns** (e.g. мы 'we'), possessive **pronouns** (e.g. наш 'our'), demonstrative **pronouns** (e.g. э́тот 'this'), interrogative **pronouns** (e.g. что? 'what?'), relative **pronouns** (e.g. кото́рый 'who', 'which', 'that') and indefinite **pronouns** (e.g. кто-то 'someone'). *See* **Chapter 7**.

Reflexive verb

Although **reflexive verbs** do serve certain other functions as well, the main purpose of making a verb **reflexive** is to transform a **transitive verb** into one that is **intransitive**. **Reflexive verbs** are indicated by the presence of the **suffix -ся (-сь** after a vowel) in all forms of the **verb**. *See* **14.3.2**.

Subject

The **subject** of a sentence denotes the person, animal or object that performs the action or is the main participant in the event indicated by the **verb** (**active voice**); in the **passive voice** the **subject** denotes the person, animal or object affected by the action. Russian distinguishes between the **grammatical subject**, which is always in the nominative **case**, and the logical **subject**, which is used with the **infinitive** or with **impersonal verbs** and **predicate forms**, and which is in some other **case**, usually the dative. *See* **3.1, 3.4.3** and **11.2.2**.

Suffix

This is a form, usually of one or two syllables, which is attached to the end of a word in order to supply additional information relating to grammar or meaning. Russian has a rich range of **suffixes** that can be attached to **nouns** to convey various meanings or nuances. *See* **10.1**.

Superlative

The **superlative** is the form of an **adjective** or an **adverb** that is used to indicate the highest possible degree of quality concerned, for example, са́мый высо́кий '(the) highest' or гро́мче всех 'loudest (of all)'. *See* **6.8.4, 6.8.5** and **9.1.7**.

GLOSSARY OF GRAMMATICAL TERMS

Fleeting vowel
This is the term used for a vowel (usually **e, o** or **ë**) that occurs in some forms of a word, but not in others. It is particularly important for the **noun declension** system, although examples occur with other parts of speech as well. *See* especially **2.5**, but also **4.5.3, 4.7.3, 4.7.13, 6.5.1**.

Gender
Gender is a system of classifying **nouns**. Russian has **three** genders – masculine, feminine and neuter – and all nouns that can occur in the singular belong to one or other of these genders. There are no gender distinctions in the plural. **Gender** is mainly indicated through the system of **agreement**: **adjectives**, for example, have separate sets of endings for each of the three **genders**. There is also a very strong correlation between **gender** and **declension** type. *See* **2.3** and **Chapter 11**.

Gerund
Gerund is the term conventionally used in Russian grammar for a form that is at the same time both a part of the **verb** and an **adverb**. The main function of the **gerund** is to form complex sentences, in which a **gerund** is used in place of a **conjunction** + **verb**. *See* **4.11** and **21.10**.

Government
Government is one of the two factors that determine which endings are put on **nouns, adjectives, pronouns** and **numerals** (*see* also **Agreement**). **Government** essentially concerns the rules for selecting which **case** to use in different grammatical circumstances. *See* **Chapter 3** and **9.2**.

Grammatical subject *see* **Subject**.

Imperative mood
This is the form of the **verb** used in commands, prohibitions and certain kinds of requests. *See* **4.9** and **Chapter 18**.

Impersonal predicate forms
These fulfil the same function as **verbs**, but unlike ordinary **verbs** they can never be used along with a **grammatical subject** and they do not change their endings. Some **impersonal predicate forms**, such as хорошо́ 'it is good to', are part of the **adverb** system, while others, such as мо́жно 'one may; one can', are words that are used only in this function. *See* **11.2.2**.

Impersonal verbs
Impersonal verbs are those **verbs** that cannot be used with a **grammatical subject**. **Impersonal verbs** occur only in the third person singular (present and future **tenses**) or the neuter singular (past **tense**). *See* **3.4.3** and **11.2.2**.

Infinitive
This is the form under which verbs are listed in dictionaries. It does not change its ending. Infinitives are normally used in conjunction with other **verbs**, although under certain circumstances they can be used on their own in commands and prohibitions. *See* **4.1** and **18.2.2**.

Intransitive verb
This is any **verb** that is not used with a **direct object**. *See* **4.13.1**.

Noun
A **noun** is a word denoting a living being, an object or a concept. Examples of **nouns** are волк 'wolf', стол 'table' or понятие 'concept'. **Nouns** denoting living beings or physical objects are called concrete **nouns**, while **nouns** denoting concepts are referred to as abstract **nouns**. **Nouns** that function as the names of people, places or organisations are proper **nouns**; all other nouns are common **nouns**. *See* **Chapters 2** and **3**.

Noun phrase
Noun phrase is the term used for a **noun** and any accompanying **adjectives, pronouns** or **numerals**. The phrase эти два молодых студента 'these two young students' is an example of a **noun phrase** that contains all four types of word. *See* **11.1**.

Number
Number as a grammatical category is a part of the **noun** system relating to quantity. There are two **numbers:** singular (relating to one person, animal, object or concept) and plural (relating to more than one of any of the above). Most nouns have both singular and plural forms, although some occur only in the singular and some only in the plural. *See* **2.1**.

Numeral
The **numeral** in Russian is a distinct part of speech, divided into three sub-groups: cardinal **numerals** (**8.1**), collective **numerals** (**8.3**) and ordinal **numerals** (**8.4**). Each of these has its own set(s) of endings and its own rules for combining with **nouns** and **adjectives**. *See* **Chapter 8**.

Participle
Participle is the term conventionally used in Russian grammar for a verbal **adjective,** that is, something at the same time both part of the **verb** and an **adjective**. The forms of the participle are described in **4.12**; its use is described in **4.14** and **23.1.3**.

Particle
Particle is a term used for an additional word providing information that supplements or supports that provided by the main elements of a sentence. Some **particles** have a very specific grammatical or semantic function, while others are used mostly to provide focus and emphasis. *See* **9.4** and **20.3.3**.

Passive voice
The category of voice is used to indicate the relationship of **subject** and **object** to the action or state indicated by the **verb**. The **passive** voice is used when the **subject** of a **verb** is affected by the action, rather than performing it. It contrasts with the **active voice**. *See* **4.14** and **20.2**.

Person
Person indicates the relationship between the verb and the **grammatical subject** of the sentence. There are three **persons**: the first **person** indicates or includes the speaker, the second **person** indicates or includes the addressee(s); the **third person** indicates the person(s), object(s) or concept(s) being referred to. Since each **person** can be singular or plural (*see* **Number**), there are six **person** forms in all.

1

Sounds and spelling

The Russian alphabet

Russian is written in the *Cyrillic* alphabet. This consists of 33 letters: 21 letters represent consonant sounds; 10 letters are used to express vowel sounds, and 2 letters – the soft sign ь and the hard sign ъ – have no sound value of their own.

Unlike English, Russian does not use combinations of letters for denoting a single sound.

Letters in alphabetical order	Pronunciation	Letter name	
А а	as in <u>f</u>ather (but shorter)	а	(a)
Б б	as in <u>b</u>oss	бэ	(be)
В в	as in <u>v</u>ast	вэ	(ve)
Г г	as in <u>g</u>um	гэ	(ge)
Д д	as in <u>d</u>ark	дэ	(de)
Е е	as in <u>ye</u>llow or ch<u>e</u>ck	е	(ye)
Ё ё	as in <u>yo</u>gurt or ch<u>o</u>colate	ё	(yo)
Ж ж	as the s in plea<u>s</u>ure	жэ	(zhe)
З з	as in <u>z</u>one	зэ	(ze)
И и	as in <u>ea</u>st (but shorter)	и	(i)
Й й	as in <u>y</u>es or bo<u>y</u>	и краткое 'short и'	
К к	as in <u>c</u>up	ка	(ka)
Л л	as in <u>l</u>uck	эль	(el)
М м	as in <u>m</u>other	эм	(em)
Н н	as in <u>n</u>o<u>n</u>e	эн	(en)
О о	as in m<u>o</u>ck or t<u>au</u>ght (but shorter)	о	(o)
П п	as in <u>p</u>ark	пэ	(pe)
Р р	as the Scottish rolled <u>r</u> in <u>r</u>ock	эр	(er)
С с	as in <u>s</u>un	эс	(es)
Т т	as in <u>t</u>all	тэ	(te)
У у	as in m<u>oo</u>n (but shorter)	у	(u)
Ф ф	as in <u>f</u>all	эф	(ef)
Х х	as in Scottish lo<u>ch</u>	ха	(kha)
Ц ц	as in nu<u>ts</u>	цэ	(tse)
Ч ч	a in <u>ch</u>ess	че	(che)
Ш ш	as in <u>sh</u>ark	ша	(sha)
Щ щ	as in fre<u>sh sh</u>eets	ща	(shsha)
Ъ ъ	no sound value	твёрдый знак 'hard sign'	

Letters in alphabetical order	Pronunciation	Letter name	
Ы ы	no exact English equivalent; approximately as in th<u>i</u>n	**ы**	(y)
Ь ь	no sound value	**мягкий знак** 'soft sign'	
Э э	as in <u>e</u>gg	**э**	(eh)
Ю ю	as in <u>you</u> or t<u>u</u>na	**ю**	(yu)
Я я	as in <u>y</u>ard	**я**	(ya)

The precise difference between the pronunciation of **и** and **ы** is explained in **1.3.1**. The exact pronunciation of most letters is partly determined by the neighbouring letters in the word or sentence (*see* **1.2.1** and **1.3.1**).

1.2 Consonants

1.2.1 Hard and soft consonants

Most Russian consonant sounds have two pronunciations, which are conventionally described as *hard* and *soft*. The distinguishing feature of soft consonants is that they are *palatalised* – that is, they are pronounced with the middle part of the tongue raised towards the hard palate.

For more on the pronunciation of soft consonants, *see* **1.2.3**.

Whether a consonant is hard or soft in Russian is important because it can serve to distinguish between two otherwise identical words: **был** (hard **б**, hard **л**) 'was', **быль** (hard **б**, soft **л**) 'true story', **бил** (soft **б**, hard **л**) past tense of 'hit' or 'beat'; **мат** (hard **м** , hard **т**) 'checkmate', **мать** (hard **м**, soft **т**) 'mother', **мят** (soft **м**, hard **т**) 'crumpled', **мять** (soft **м**, soft **т**) 'to crumple'.

Not all consonants form hard/soft pairs. The sounds represented by the letters **ж, ц, ш** are always hard, while those represented by **ч, щ** and **й** are always soft.

1.2.2. The pronunciation of hard consonants

Most hard consonants are pronounced in a similar or identical fashion to their English equivalents, as indicated in the table in **1.1**. The following, however, require a more detailed explanation.

The hard **л** is pronounced with the tongue resting against the top teeth. It sounds like the English 'l' in words such as 'film', 'table'.

To pronounce **ж** and **ш**, the middle of the tongue is drawn down to the bottom of the mouth, while the tip of the tongue points upwards towards the area behind the top teeth.

Hard **д, н** and **т** are pronounced with the tip of the tongue resting against the back of the top teeth.

Hard **к, п** and **т** are pronounced without the slight aspiration (expulsion of a breath of air) that usually accompanies the equivalent sounds in English.

1.2.3 The pronunciation of soft consonants

Soft or *palatalised* consonants can be heard in English in the way that many (though not all) English speakers pronounce the initial consonants in words such as 'due', 'new' and 'Tuesday'. In Russian, however, the consonants б, в, г, д, з, к, л, м, н, п, р, с, т, ф, х are all capable of being palatalised, while ч and щ are *always* palatalised. The distinguishing feature of palatalised consonants is that the middle part of the tongue is raised towards the hard palate (the middle part of the top of the mouth). The perception is often of a slight [y] sound pronounced together with the consonant, but some care should be taken not to exaggerate this effect, since in Russian there is a clear distinction between a palatalised consonant and a consonant followed by y:

обе́д [ob'ed] 'dinner' ~ объе́дки [ob'yedk'i] '[food] leftovers'.

NOTE | In transcriptions, the sign ' is used to indicate a palatalised consonant.

For the use of the hard sign (ъ) to indicate the presence of the sound [y] *see* **1.3.2**.

The palatalised consonant щ is pronounced as a long soft 'sh' sound, as in the English sequence 'fre<u>sh sh</u>eets', but without the slight pause between the words. An alternative pronunciation, <u>shch</u>, as in 'A<u>shch</u>urch', is recommended in older text books, but is now falling into disuse.

1.2.4 The representation of hard and soft consonants in writing

The letters б, в, г, д, з, к, л, м, н, п, р, с, т, ф, х are used to represent both hard and soft consonants. The hardness or softness is not denoted by the letters themselves, but is indicated by the letter that immediately follows them (or by the absence of a following letter).

The consonants б, в, г, д, з, к, л, м, н, п, р, с, т, ф, х are pronounced *hard* when they:

(a) occur at the very end of a word:

хо́ди*т* 'he goes (on foot)', глаз 'eye', спор*т* 'sport';

(b) when they are followed immediately by another consonant:

*г*лаз 'eye', знать 'to know', с*п*ор*т* 'sport';

(c) when they are followed by one of the vowel letters from the group а, о, у, э, ы:

*д*а 'yes', *х*о́дит 'he goes [on foot]', *р*ука́ 'hand', 'arm', сэр 'sir', *т*ы 'you'.

The consonants б, в, г, д, з, к, л, м, н, п, р, с, т, ф, х are pronounced *soft* when they are followed by either:

(a) the *soft* sign (ь):

ло́шад*ь* 'horse', возьму́ 'I will take', фил*ь*м 'film', крова́*т*ь 'bed';

(b) one of the vowel letters from the group е, ё, и, ю, я:

*б*е́лый 'white', *т*ётя 'aunt', *в*и́за 'visa', плюс 'plus', *м*я́со 'meat'.

5

1.2.5 ## Voiced and unvoiced consonants

The letters **б, в, г, д, ж, з** normally denote *voiced* consonants – that is, consonants pronounced with a vibration of the vocal cords. The *unvoiced* consonants corresponding to these are indicated respectively by the letters **п, ф, к, т, ш, с**. Voiced consonants are normally *devoiced* – that is, pronounced like their unvoiced counterparts when they occur either at the end of a word or before *another unvoiced consonant*. This change in pronunciation, which can occur across a boundary between two words, is not usually reflected in the spelling:

> зу*б* [p] 'tooth', ле*в* [f] 'lion', фла*г* [k] 'flag', го*д* [t] 'year', му*ж* [sh] 'husband', гла*з* (s) 'eye';

NOTE: | Бог 'God' is pronounced [bokh].

> тру́*б*ка [p] 'pipe', *в*се [f] 'all', но́*г*ти [k] 'nails', во́*д*ка [t] 'vodka', му*ж*ско́й [sh] 'masculine', ска́*з*ка [s] 'fairy tale'; *в* парк [f] 'to the park', и*з* теа́тра [s] 'from the theatre', на*д* столо́м [t] 'above the table', му*ж* сестры́ [sh] 'sister's husband', сне*г* чист [k] 'the snow is clean'.

Unvoiced consonants are pronounced like the corresponding *voiced* consonant when they occur before a *voiced* consonant:

> *с*бить [z] 'to knock down', *к* дру́гу [g] 'to a friend', на*ш* дом [zh] 'our house', о*т*бро́сы [d] 'garbage'.

NOTE: | Unvoiced consonants are *not* voiced when they occur before в: отве́*т* [t] 'answer'.

1.2.6 ## Consonant clusters

When two or more consonants come together, the pronunciation of the resulting cluster may differ from the sum of the original components.

Spelled	Pronounced
чт	шт in что 'what' and что́бы 'in order to', otherwise чт: по́чта 'post office', почти́ 'almost'
чн	шн in certain everyday words: коне́чно 'of course', ску́чно 'boring' (adv.) яи́чница 'fried eggs', and also in female patronymics: **Ники́тична, Ильи́нична** For more on patronymics *see* **12.1.2**. Otherwise чн: начни́ 'start!', очну́ться 'to come to oneself', ве́чный 'eternal', бесконе́чный 'infinite, endless'
лн	н in со́лнце 'sun' Otherwise лн: со́лнечный 'sunny', по́лный 'full'
гк	хк: лёгкий 'light', 'easy', мя́гкий 'soft'
стн	сн: че́стный 'honest', ме́стный 'local'
здн	зн: звёздный 'star' (adj.), по́здно 'late' (adv.)
зж сж	a long ж: е́зжу 'I go', 'I travel', сжа́ть 'to grip'
зч	щ: перево́зчик 'carrier'

Spelled	Pronounced
сч	щ: in the root -чит/чёт-: **счита́ть** 'to count', 'to consider', **расчёт** 'calculation'; also in **сча́стье** 'happiness'; otherwise щч: **исчеза́ть** 'to disappear'
жч	щ: **мужчи́на** 'man'; **перебе́жчик** 'deserter'
сш	a long ш: **сши́ть** 'to sew (together)', **бесшу́мный** 'noiseless', **без шу́ма** 'without noise'
зш	
ться	цца: **мы́ться** 'to wash oneself', **улыба́ться** 'to smile', **мо́ются** 'they wash themselves', **улыба́ются** 'they smile'
тся	

NOTE: The greeting **здра́вствуйте** 'hello' is pronounced as **здра́ствуйте** in formal language, but more informally as **здра́сьте**.

1.3 Vowels

1.3.1 Russian vowel sounds and letters

To indicate the six Russian vowel sounds, ten letters are used: **а, е, ё, и, о, у, ы, э, ю, я.**

The pronunciation of the vowels is indicated in the table in **1.1**. Russian vowels are pronounced as 'pure' vowels with the tongue remaining in a constant position; they do not have the 'diphthong' quality that vowels generally have in most English pronunciations.

For changes to the pronunciation of vowels in unstressed syllables, *see* **1.4**.

The vowel 'o' is an *open* sound – that is, it is closer to the vowel in 'all' or 'taught', than to the vowel in 'hope'.

The vowel **ы** has no direct equivalent in English, although it is not unlike the vowel in the word 'bit' as pronounced by some Scottish speakers. It is a vowel half-way between the 'ee' in f<u>ee</u>l and the 'oo' in f<u>oo</u>l, and a close approximation can be achieved by spreading the lips for the 'ee' sound and then moving the tongue towards the back of the mouth.

1.3.2 The pronunciation of я, е, ё, ю

Four of the letters indicating *vowels* (**я, е, ё, ю**) have two pronunciations, depending on what comes immediately before them. If this is a *consonant*, they are pronounced as the vowels 'a', 'e', 'o', 'u' respectively; at the same time they also indicate that the preceding consonant is *soft*:

мя́со [m'a..] 'meat', **те́ло** [t'e..] 'body', **всё** [fs'o] 'everything', **меню́** [..n'u] 'menu'.

If they (a) occur at the beginning of a word, (b) come immediately after another vowel or (c) come immediately after the soft sign (**ь**) or the hard sign (**ъ**), the letters **я, е, ё, ю** express not one, but two sounds: their normal vowel sound preceded by the sound

[y] – i.e. [ya], [ye], [yo], [yu] respectively:

> **я́щик** [yashshik] 'box', **éду** [yedu] 'I am going [by transport]', **ёлка** [yolka] 'Christmas tree', **юг** [yuk] 'south';

> **шéя** [sheya] 'neck', **уéду** [uyedu] 'I shall go away', **даёт** [dayot] 's/he gives', **мою́** [moyu] 'I wash';

> **статья́** [stat'ya] 'article' **досьé** [dos'ye] 'dossier', **льёт** [l'yot] 's/he pours', **пью** [p'yu] 'I drink'; **разъясни́ть** [..zyas..] 'to clarify', **съéзд** [syest] 'congress'.

NOTES

(i) When и, occurs after a vowel or at the beginning of a word, it is usually pronounced without the preceding (y):

> **наи́вный** [na-iv..] 'naive', **клéнт** [kle-it] 's/he glues', **и́мя** [im'a] 'name'.

After the soft sign (ь), however, the [y] is usually pronounced:

> **статьи́** [stat'yi] 'articles'.

(ii) In the examples given in this section, the function of the hard and soft signs is to indicate the presence of the sound [y] between a consonant and a vowel. This is the sole function of the hard sign in present-day Russian.

In certain names and in foreign words the combination of **й** with **я**, **е**, **о** or even **и** is possible:

> **Ма́йя** 'Maya' (female name), **парано́йя** 'paranoia', **майо́р** 'major' (military rank), **Йéмен** 'Yemen', **Нью-Йо́рк** 'New York', **йо́га** 'yoga', **йо́гурт** 'yogurt'.

1.4 Stress

1.4.0 Introduction

Each Russian word normally has *one stressed* syllable. This syllable is pronounced with greater emphasis, and the vowel in the stressed syllable is longer than other vowels. Stress in Russian is described as being both free and mobile – that is it can fall on *any* syllable in a word and can fall on *different* syllables in different forms of the same word. This principle is illustrated by the following forms of the word **голова́** 'head':

голова́:	nom. sing.
го́лову:	acc. sing.
на́ голову:	acc. sing. after the preposition **на**
голо́в:	gen. pl.

For more on the grammatical terms, *see* **2.2**.

For the rules of stress with prepositions, *see* **9.2.7**.

1.4.1 The importance of stress

The position of the stressed syllable is important for two reasons. The first is that sometimes two otherwise identical words are distinguished only by the place of the stress:

> **му́ка** 'torment', **мука́** 'flour'
> **до́ма** 'at home', **дома́** 'houses'.

The second is that the pronunciation of many vowels depends on whether they appear in a stressed or an unstressed syllable. This question is discussed in detail in **1.4.3**.

1.4.2 The marking of stress

Russian stress is normally marked in textbooks and dictionaries, but is indicated in ordinary text only when it is necessary to avoid misunderstandings (as in the examples quoted in **1.4.1.**). The normal means of indicating stress is the *acute accent* (´).

In this book, with the exception of a few examples (e.g. in **1.6**) which are intended to reproduce as closely as possible the appearance of a normal printed text, stress is indicated throughout by means of the acute accent.

Because the letter **ё** is used only in stressed syllables, stress is not indicated separately for words containing this letter.

For more on the use of **ё** only in stressed syllables *see* **1.5.1**.

Stress is not normally indicated for words of only one syllable. Where stress is indicated on a word of one syllable – for example, the negative particle **не** and certain prepositions – it indicates that this syllable carries the stress for the following word as well. An example is the phrase **на́ го́лову**, quoted in **1.4.0**.

Occasionally, a word will be found with two stress marks. This means that there are alternative stresses: for example, **роди́ла́сь** 'she was born', means that both **роди́лась** and **родила́сь** are possible.

1.4.3 Reduction of unstressed vowels.

When unstressed, the vowels **о**, **а/я**, **е/э** are significantly *reduced* – that is, they become shorter, but also change their quality. The symbols α and ə are used below to denote different levels of vowels reduction: α stands for a sound similar to **а**, but shorter and less distinct, like the vowel in the 'Mac (Mc)' prefix of certain Scottish surnames, or the first vowel in 'candelabra'; ə stands for a short neutral vowel similar to the second and the final vowels in 'candelabra'.

1.4.4 Unstressed a and o

Unstressed **а** and **о** are pronounced as *α* when they occur either in the syllable *immediately before* the stressed syllable or at the *very beginning* of a word:

> **дарю́** [dα-] 'I give', **африка́нец** [αf-] 'African', **ходи́ть** [khα-] 'to go (on foot)', **отказа́ться** [αt-] 'to refuse'.

Unstressed **а** and **о** are pronounced as ə when they occur either two or more syllables before the stressed syllable or in any syllable that comes *after* the stress:

> **дарови́тый** [dər-] 'gifted', **вы́дать** [-dət'] 'to give out', **ходово́й** [khəd-] 'marketable, popular', **вы́ход** [-khət] 'exit'.

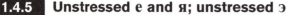

1.4.5 **Unstressed е and я; unstressed э**

Unstressed **е** and **я** are pronounced as a shorter version of **i** when they occur in any syllable *before* the stressed syllable:

> **семьсо́т** [s'im-] 'seven hundred', **пятьсо́т** [p'it-] 'five hundred', **семиле́тний** [s'i-] 'seven years old', **пятьдеся́т** [p'i-] 'fifty'.

Unstressed **е** and **я** are pronounced as **э** when they occur in any syllable that comes *after* the stress:

> **во́семь** [-s'əm'] 'eight', **па́мять** [-m'ət'] 'memory'.

Unstressed **э**, which occurs only at the beginning of a word, is normally pronounced as a shorter version of **i**:

> **эква́тор** [ikv-] 'equator', **эгои́ст** [ig-] 'egoist', **эколо́гия** [ik-] 'ecology'.

1.4.6 **Other unstressed vowels**

The vowels **и, ы, у/ю** in unstressed positions are shorter than when they are stressed, but any change in quality is negligible.

1.4.7 **Stress units of more than one word**

Sometimes a single stress unit is made up of more than one word. This is most commonly the case when nouns are used with prepositions or when a word is preceded or followed by an unstressed particle. In such cases the rules of vowel reduction apply to the stress unit as a whole:

> **за тебя́** [zət-] 'for you', **через де́нь** [chiri'rizd'-] 'after a day', **какие́-то** [-tə] 'some (pl.)', **принеси́-ка** [-kə] 'bring!', **не зна́ешь ли?** [n'iz-] 'don't you know?', **под го́ру** [-gəru] 'downhill'.

1.4.8 **Secondary stress**

Stress units containing a preposition with more than one syllable as well as many compound words may have a weaker *secondary stress*. This is usually indicated by a *grave accent* (`):

> **Во́зле до́ма** 'near the house', **по́сле ма́тча** 'after the match', **литерату́рове́дение** 'literary science', **га́ла-конце́рт** 'gala concert', **те́лесериа́л** 'TV serial', **моро́зоусто́йчивый** 'frost resistant'.

Secondary stress, where it occurs, always *precedes* the main stress.

1.5 # Spelling rules

1.5.0 ## Introduction

Russian spelling is not, strictly speaking, 'phonetic' (as is sometimes claimed), but it is much more predictable than English spelling, and in general there is a reasonably close relationship between spelling and pronunciation. Nevertheless, there are some specific peculiarities which it is useful to bear in mind. These rules are particularly important for determining the spelling of the endings that are attached to *nouns*, *adjectives*, *pronouns*, *numerals and verbs*.

Use of the letter ё

As was noted in **1.4.2**, the letter **ё** occurs only in *stressed* syllables. In *unstressed* syllables it is replaced by **е**:

вошёл 'he went in', *but* вышел 'he went out'; вёл 'he led', *but* вела́ 'she led'.

In addition, the letter **ё** is used consistently only in textbooks, dictionaries and books written for children. Elsewhere it is usually replaced by the letter **е**. This means, for example, that the following words will appear in print as:

ее 'her', еще 'still, more', принес 'he brought', легкий 'light, easy', мед 'honey'.

They should, however, be read as:

её, ещё, принёс, лёгкий, мёд.

In dictionaries and other lists arranged alphabetically, **е** and **ё** are usually treated as being the same letter.

Spelling after ш, ж, ч, щ, ц

As was pointed out in **1.2.4**, one of the functions of the vowel letters is to indicate the hardness or softness of the preceding consonant. Since, however, the consonants **ш, ж, ц** are *always hard* and **ч, щ** are *always soft*, this function becomes redundant, and the choice of vowel letter to follow these consonants is determined instead by special rules.

The letters **ю** and **я** do not occur after these consonants; instead, **у** and **а** are used:

варю́ 'I boil', *but* спешу́ 'I hurry', ви́жу 'I see', лечу́ 'I am flying', пущу́ 'I will let'.
варя́ 'boiling', *but* спеша́ 'hurrying', трево́жа 'worrying', мо́лча 'in silence', мо́рща 'wrinkling'.

For more on these verb forms, *see* **4.6.4**, **4.7.15** and **4.11**.

Exceptions to this spelling rule are found in a few words of foreign origin:

парашю́т 'parachute', жюри́ 'jury'.

The letter **ы** does not occur after **ш, ж, ч, щ**; instead **и** is used:

столы́ 'tables', *but* карандаши́ 'pencils', ножи́ 'knives', врачи́ 'doctors', това́рищи 'comrades'.

For more on these noun forms, *see* **2.6.1** and **2.6.2**.

The letter **ы** is normally used after **ц**, but **и** occurs in some words of foreign origin and in some surnames:

цыплёнок 'chicken', отцы́ 'fathers', *but* цирк 'circus', Е́льцин 'El'tsin'.

NOTE | When **и** is used after **ш, ж** or **ц**, it is pronounced as if it were **ы.**

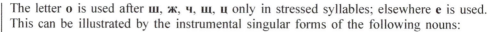

The letter **о** is used after **ш, ж, ч, щ, ц** only in stressed syllables; elsewhere **е** is used. This can be illustrated by the instrumental singular forms of the following nouns:

> каранда́ш 'pencil', – карандашо́м, *but* душ 'shower' – ду́шем
> нож 'knife' – ножо́м, *but* муж 'husband' – му́жем
> врач 'doctor' – врачо́м, *but* матч '(football) match' – ма́тчем
> борщ 'borshch' – борщо́м, *but* това́рищ 'comrade' – това́рищем

For more on these endings *see* **2.6.1** and **2.6.2**.

Exceptions to this rule are found in a few words of foreign origin and in a few surnames:

> шокола́д 'chocolate', жоке́й 'jockey', Шостако́вич 'Shostakovich'.

1.5.3   Use of e and э

The letter **э** is found mostly at the beginning of a word in foreign borrowings and foreign proper names:

> эгои́ст 'egoist', экономи́ст 'economist', эколо́гия 'ecology', Э́мма 'Emma', Эдинбу́рг 'Edinburgh'.

The letter **э** occurs in a small number of native Russian words such as:

> э́то 'this (is)', э́тот 'this', эх 'oh'.

The letter **э** is used after a consonant in only a small number of Russian words of foreign origin and in the transcription of some foreign proper names:

> мэр 'mayor', сэр 'sir', рэп 'rap (music)'; Блэр 'Blair', Тэ́тчер 'Thatcher'.

For the use of **э** to transcribe English **a**, *see* **1.6.5**.

Elsewhere the letter **е** is used even after hard consonants. This sequence occurs only in words recently borrowed from foreign languages and in native Russian words after the consonants **ш, ж, ц**:

> стюарде́сса 'stewardess', ре́гби 'rugby', Се́нт-Луи́с 'Saint-Louis', темп 'pace', же́нщина 'woman', ше́я 'neck', цель 'aim'.

1.5.4   Use of и after к, г, х

The letter **ы** does not occur after the consonants **к, г, х**; instead **и** is used:

> столы́ 'tables', *but* я́щики 'boxes', мозги́ 'brains', духи́ 'perfume'.

1.5.5   The ending -го (vo)

The ending **-го** is pronounced as [vo] when it occurs in the *genitive singular masculine* and *neuter* ending of *adjectives, pronouns* and *certain numeral forms*, such as **оди́н**:

он 'he'	его́ [yivo]
тот 'that'	того́ [tɑvo]
кто 'who?'	кого́ [kɑvo]
что 'what?'	чего́ [chivo]
но́вый 'new'	но́вого [novəvə]
хоро́ший 'good'	хоро́шего [khɑroshəvə]

12

си́ний '(dark) blue'   **си́*него*** [s'in'əvə]
тре́тий 'third'   **тре́тье*го*** [tr'et'yəvə]
оди́н 'one'   **одно*го́*** [ɑdnɑvo]

For more on these endings, *see* **Chapters 6, 7** and **8.**

The same discrepancy between pronunciation and spelling is found in the word **сего́дня** (s'ivodn'ə) 'today'.

The spelling of certain prefixes

Normally the spelling of affixes remains unchanged regardless of the way in which pronunciation is affected by surrounding consonants. The prefixes **без-, вз-, воз-, из-** and **раз-** form, however, an exception, since they are spelled **бес-, вс-, вос-, ис-, рас-** when they occur before an *unvoiced* consonant (**к, п, с, т, ф, ц, ч, ш, щ**):

*без*ду́мный 'thoughtless', *but* *бес*стра́стный 'passionless';
*вз*дремну́ть 'to take a nap', *but* *вс*кипяти́ть 'to boil';
*воз*роди́ть 'to revive', *but* *вос*пита́ть 'to bring up';
*из*да́ть 'to publish', *but* *ис*пра́вить 'to correct';
*раз*буди́ть 'to wake', *but* *рас*сы́пать 'to scatter'.

Use of capital letters

Capital letters in Russian are used in much the same way as they are in English. There are, however, some important differences that it is useful to note. In particular capital letters are not normally used in Russian for:

The first person singular pronoun **я** 'I':

Тру́дно пове́рить, но за́втра *я* уже́ бу́ду в Москве́.
It's hard to believe it, but tomorrow I'll already be in Moscow.

Days of the week and names of months:

Я, наве́рное, прие́ду в *четве́рг*.
I'll probably arrive on Thursday.

В *ию́ле* и в *а́вгусте* здесь быва́ет о́чень жа́рко.
In July and August it can get very hot here.

Adjectives derived from names of countries and nouns denoting nationalities and the inhabitants of towns and cities:

В университе́те я изуча́л *англи́йскую литерату́ру*.
At university I studied English literature.

В на́шей гости́нице мно́го *ру́сских*, но кро́ме нас, ка́жется, нет никаки́х *англича́н*.
There are a lot of Russians in our hotel, but apart from us there don't seem to be any other English people.

Как и мно́гие *москвичи́*, они́ ре́дко по́льзовались свое́й маши́ной в черте́ го́рода.
Like many Muscovites, they rarely used their car within the city limits.

For more on adjectives and nouns denoting nationality, *see* **10.1.8, 10.1.9** and **12.5.**

On the other hand it is customary in letters to use a capital letter for the second person pronouns **Вы** 'you' and **Ваш** 'your' when they are used as *polite singular* forms:

> **Жаль, что в *Ва́шем* письме́ *Вы* не рассказа́ли о *Ва́шей* пое́здке в Кита́й.**
> It's a pity that in your letter you didn't tell me anything about your trip to China.

With titles and names of organisations and institutions of various sorts, books, plays, television programmes and the like, it is usual to use a capital letter only for the first word:

> **Министе́рство культу́ры**
> 'The Ministry of Culture'

> **Моско́вский госуда́рственный университе́т**
> 'Moscow State University'

> **Большо́й теа́тр**
> 'The Bolshoi Theatre'

> **«Незави́симая газе́та»**
> *Nezavisimaia gazeta* (the name of a newspaper)

> **«Кто хо́чет стать миллионе́ром?»**
> *Who Wants to be a Millionaire?*

> **Но́вый год**
> 'New Year'

With geographical names, generic terms such as **мо́ре** 'sea' and **у́лица** 'street' are normally spelled with a small letter:

Чёрное мо́ре	The Black Sea
о́зеро Байка́л	Lake Baikal
у́лица Тверска́я	Tverskaia Street
Кра́сная пло́щадь	Red Square

It is normal to spell with a capital letter all words that form the names of countries, major geographical regions, international organisations and certain titles that are deemed worthy of particular respect:

> **Росси́йская Федера́ция**
> The Russian Federation

> **Се́верная Ирла́ндия**
> Northern Ireland

> **Восто́чная Сиби́рь**
> Eastern Siberia

> **Да́льний Восто́к**
> The Far East

> **Европе́йский Сою́з**
> The European Union

Госуда́рственная Ду́ма Росси́йской Федера́ции
The State Duma of the Russian Federation

День Побе́ды
Victory Day (9 May)

1.5.8 Use of inverted commas

The most common form of inverted commas used in print in Russian is « ... ». In handwriting these usually take the form of „ ... ". In general inverted commas are used more frequently in Russian than in English. In addition to titles of books, films, plays, newspapers, and so on (where italics are often used in English), inverted commas tend to be used for names of companies, rock bands, sports teams, brand names and even the names of the Moscow underground stations:

Лу́чше, коне́чно, чита́ть «Войну́ и мир» в оригина́ле.
It's better, of course, to read *War and Peace* in the original.

За́втра в кинотеа́тре «Иллюзио́н» пока́зывают фильм «Броненосец Потёмкин».
Tomorrow they're showing *Battleship Potemkin* in the *Illuzion* cinema.

Весно́й про́шлого го́да петербу́ргский футбо́льный клуб «Зени́т» факти́чески перешёл под контро́ль компа́нии «Газпром».
In the spring of last year Zenit, the St Petersburg football team was effectively taken over by Gazprom.

В шестидеся́тые го́ды «Битлз» бы́ли о́чень популя́рными в Сове́тском Сою́зе, хотя́ их пласти́нки там не продава́лись.
In the 1960s the Beatles were very popular in the Soviet Union, although their records were not on sale there.

Рестора́н «Пеки́н» нахо́дится недалеко́ от метро́ «Маяко́вская».
The Peking restaurant is near the Mayakovskaia underground station.

On inverted commas in direct speech, *see* **21.8.1**.

For the rules for declining words and phrases in inverted commas, *see* **11.1.3**.

1.6 Transliteration and transcription

1.6.0 Introduction

In circumstances where it is either impossible or undesirable to reproduce Russian words in their original form, it is necessary to resort to *transliteration* or *transcription*. Transliteration means the substitution of Russian letters by their nearest English equivalents in such a way as to allow the reader to reconstruct the spelling of the Russian original. *Transcription* means the use of English letters to reproduce the sounds of the Russian original; its purpose is to enable the reader to reconstruct the pronunciation of the Russian original.

Except in special circumstances – for example, in guides to the pronunciation of Russian (as in the earlier sections of this chapter) – Russian is reproduced in English by means of transliteration. It is recommended that learners of the language adopt a standard system of transliteration and try to use it as consistently as possible.

1.6.1 The Library of Congress system of transliteration

Until quite recently there were several systems of transliteration in common use, but since the 1980s what is known as the *Library of Congress* system has gradually come to be adopted for most purposes throughout the English-speaking world. It is this system that is used wherever transliterated forms appear in this book.

Library of Congress system: Table of transliteration

Russian letter	English equivalent	Russian letter	English equivalent	Russian letter	English equivalent
а	a	к	k	х	kh
б	b	л	l	ц	ts
в	v	м	m	ч	ch
г	g	н	n	ш	sh
д	d	о	o	щ	shch
е	e	п	p	ъ	"
ё	ё	р	r	ы	y
ж	zh	с	s	ь	'
з	z	т	t	э	è
и	i	у	u	ю	iu
й	i	ф	f	я	ia

NOTES

(i) Where the letter **е** is used instead of **ё**, it is usually transliterated as **e**; therefore, **Горбачёв** would be transliterated as **Gorbachëv**, but **Горбачев** would be **Gorbachev.**

(ii) The Library of Congress system has a number of ambiguities. The most important is that the same letter, **i**, is used for both **и** and **й**, so that both **бой** and **бои** are transliterated as **boi.**

For the use of the letter **e** in place of **ё**, *see* **1.5.1.**

1.6.2 Examples of transliteration using the Library of Congress system

The following examples illustrate the Library of Congress system of transliteration:

Дмитрий Анатольевич Медведев	**Dmitrii Anatol'evich Medvedev**
Борис Николаевич Ельцин	**Boris Nikolaevich El'tsin**
Хрущёв	**Khrushchëv**
Толстой	**Tolstoi**
Достоевский	**Dostoevskii**
Чехов	**Chekhov**
Горький	**Gor'kii**
Маяковский	**Maiakovskii**
Татьяна	**Tat'iana**
Анастасия	**Anastasiia**
Владивосток	**Vladivostok**

Ярославль	Iaroslavl'
Нижний Новгород	Nizhnii Novgorod
съезд	s"ezd
сестра	sestra
сёстры	sëstry

1.6.3 Exceptions to the Library of Congress system

In some circumstances – for example, in formal academic writing – it is desirable to follow the Library of Congress system as closely and as consistently as possible. Elsewhere, however, some departures from the system may be admissible or even preferable.

In cases where non-standard characters are impossible or are not wanted ë can be replaced by e or o, and the character ', used to transliterate ь, can be omitted:

Горбачёв would be transliterated as **Gorbachev** or **Gorbachov**.

Горький would be transliterated as **Gorkii**.

With proper names it is sometimes desirable to use an English spelling that represents the pronunciation more closely than does the Library of Congress transliteration. In such cases:

Ельцин might be represented as **Yeltsin**.

Ярославль might be represented as **Yaroslavl**.

Some Russian proper names have an English spelling that has become generally accepted:

Чайковский (the composer) is almost invariably known in English as Tchaikovsky; this spelling is based on a nineteenth-century French transliteration.

1.6.4 The representation of English forms in Russian

Because of the complex and often eccentric relationship between spelling and pronunciation in English, *transliteration* does not really work for representing English words in Russian, and instead a system closer to *transcription* is normally used. There are, however, some points to note:

1 The model of pronunciation used is that of a British film actor of the 1930s. What this means is that **a** is often rendered by **e** or **э**, and **u** is often rendered by **a.**
2 Those who devise the transcription may not be aware of all of the eccentricities of English spelling and may therefore not reflect the exact pronunciation – for example, the name 'Neil' is often rendered as **Нейл.**
3 There may well be variations and inconsistencies. For example, forms used in some official documents, such as visas, may sometimes be closer to a transliteration than those encountered elsewhere.

The following conventions are used for letters indicating sounds that do not occur in Russian:

h (except when silent) is rendered by **г** *or* **x**
j (and the **g** as in **gem**) are rendered by **дж**
th (as in **think**) is rendered by **т**
th (as in **this**) is rendererd by **т** *or* **з**

w is rendered by **в** *or* **у**

(i) The use of **г** for English 'h' is now rather old-fashioned and tends to be restricted to proper names that are well established, such as **Гарольд** for 'Harold'.

(ii) English 'l', when it occurs at the end of a word or before a consonant, is often rendered by **ль**.

(iii) English double letters tend to be rendered by double letters in Russian.

1.6.5 Examples of English names in Russian

Winston Churchill	**Уинстон Черчилль**	Sarah Butler	**Сара Батлер**
John Dunn	**Джон Данн**	Tony Blair	**Тони Блэр**
Harry Potter	**Гарри Поттер**	Anthony	**Антони** *or* **Энтони**
Frank	**Фрэнк**	Heather	**Хезер** *or* **Хизер**
Aberdeen	**Абердин**	Blackpool	**Блэкпул**
Bradford	**Брадфорд**	Edinburgh	**Эдинбург**
Glasgow	**Глазго**	Dublin	**Дублин**
New York	**Нью-Йорк**	Seattle	**Сиэтл**
Washington	**Вашингтон**	Perth	**Перт**
(*The*) *Times*	**«Таймс»**		

2

Nouns

Introduction

The Russian noun contains the following categories.

Number (**2.1**). This is a category that relates to quantity. Russian, like English, has two numbers: *singular* and *plural*.

Case (**2.2**). This category refers to different endings assumed by certain parts of speech as a means of indicating the particular grammatical function that the part of speech fulfils in a sentence. English (although only in certain pronouns) can distinguish three cases: a *subject* case ('he'), an *object* case ('him') and a *possessive* case ('his'); Russian *nouns*, *adjectives*, *pronouns* and *numerals* have six cases: *nominative*, *genitive*, *dative*, *accusative*, *instrumental* and *prepositional*.

Gender (**2.3**). This category is essentially a means of classifying nouns, although there is some link between *grammatical* and *biological* gender. Russian distinguishes three genders: *masculine*, *feminine* and *neuter*, although there are no distinctions of gender in the plural.

Animacy (**2.4**). In some circumstances Russian distinguishes between *animate* nouns, which refer to persons or animals, and *inanimate* nouns (all others).

2.1 Number

2.1.1 Singular and plural

The *singular* is used to denote *one* person, animal, object or concept, while the *plural* is used to indicate *more than one* of any of the above. Most nouns have both singular and plural forms.

2.1.2 Nouns that occur only in the singular

There are quite a few nouns which in Russian are used only in the *singular*. Those that require particular attention are the ones for which the normal English equivalent can occur either in the singular or in the plural. Such nouns include:

Certain *abstract* nouns:

борьба́   struggle   ра́зница   difference

The names of certain vegetables, berries and fruit, for example:

горо́х	peas	**лук**	onion(s)
морко́вь	carrot(s)	**карто́фель, карто́шка**	potatoes
изю́м	raisins	**клубни́ка**	strawberries
мали́на	raspberries	**виногра́д**	grape(s)

NOTE | The word **карто́шка** is characteristic of informal language.

Some nouns that fit into neither of the above categories:

ложь	lie
ору́жие	weapons
пла́мя	flame

2.1.3 Nouns used only in the plural

Some nouns that occur only in the *plural* denote objects that can be thought of as being made up of paired elements:

брю́ки	trousers
штаны́	trousers
трусы́, тру́сики	(under)pants, knickers
шо́рты	shorts
пла́вки	swimming trunks
колго́тки	tights
но́жницы	scissors
щипцы́	tongs, pincers, tweezers

Other nouns that occur only in the plural are, however, less easy to explain:

дрова́	firewood
дро́жжи	yeast
обо́и	wallpaper
поми́нки	wake (for the dead)
са́ни	sledge
сли́вки	cream
су́тки	day, period of 24 hours
счёты	abacus
черни́ла	ink
щи	type of cabbage soup

2.2 Case

2.2.1 The six cases

Although, as was noted above, English has the remains of a case system, the Russian system is much more complicated. Russian has six cases: *nominative, genitive, dative, accusative, instrumental* and *prepositional*. These names are for the most part arbitrary, and each case has in practice a wide range of functions; these are described in detail in **Chapter 3**.

NOTE | There is more than one standard order for listing the different cases. That used above (and in the following sections) is the one preferred for grammars and reference works produced in Russia.

How the cases are indicated

The *case* in which a noun is used is indicated by the *ending*. As there are separate sets of endings for the *singular* and the *plural*, the ending of a noun gives information about both *case* and *number*.

The *nominative singular* (*nominative plural* for nouns that occur only in the plural) is the form under which nouns are listed in dictionaries.

The process of changing the endings associated with each noun in order to indicate the different cases is usually referred to as *declension*. Russian has several standard *declension types*, and the great majority of nouns belong to one or other of these. There are also some non-standard declension types, which group together relatively small numbers of nouns. In most instances (although by no means always), the remaining endings of any noun can be predicted from the *nominative singular*.

The different declension types are described in detail in **2.6–2.11**.

Russian has a number of indeclinable nouns. These have the same ending for all case forms in both singular and plural.

Indeclinable nouns are described in detail in **2.13–2.14**.

2.3 Gender

2.3.0 Introduction

Grammatical *gender* is a means of classifying nouns. Russian has three grammatical genders – *masculine*, *feminine* and *neuter* – and all nouns that can occur in the singular belong to one or other of these genders. There are no gender distinctions in the plural, and nouns that occur only in the plural do not belong to any grammatical gender.

2.3.1 Grammatical and biological gender

There is a partial match between *grammatical* and *biological gender*, in that nouns referring to male persons or animals are generally *masculine*, and nouns referring to female persons or animals tend to be *feminine*. All other nouns, however, can belong to any one of the three genders:

мужчи́на (masc.)	man	брат (masc.)	brother
лев (masc.)	lion	же́нщина (fem.)	woman
сестра́ (fem.)	sister	льви́ца (fem.)	lioness
потоло́к (masc.)	ceiling	дверь (fem.)	door
окно́ (n.)	window	атеи́зм (masc.)	atheism
рели́гия (fem.)	religion	христиа́нство (n.)	Christianity

There are a very small number of neuter nouns that refer or can refer to persons or animals:

живо́тное	animal	лицо́	face; person

2.3.2 Determining grammatical gender

The only absolutely reliable indicator of grammatical gender is the ending of any *adjective* or *pronoun* that may accompany a *noun*:

хоро́ший мужчи́на good man; **-ий** is an ending that indicates *masculine* gender.

хоро́шая же́нщина good woman; **-ая** is an ending that indicates *feminine* gender.

хоро́шее сло́во good word; **-ее** is an ending that indicates *neuter* gender.

хоро́шие мужчи́ны	good men
хоро́шие же́нщины	good women
хоро́шие слова́	good words

In these examples **-ие** is an ending used for all nouns in the *plural*.

The endings of *adjectives* are described in detail in **Chapter 6**.

The endings of *pronouns* are described in detail in **Chapter 7**.

The question of *agreement* between *adjectives*, *pronouns* and *nouns* is examined in detail in **11.1**.

2.3.3 Grammatical gender and declension type

There is a very close relationship between *grammatical gender* and *declension type*:

Nouns which in the *nominative singular* end in a *consonant* or in **-й** are normally *masculine*:

стол	table	**студе́нт**	(male) student
май	May (the month)	**геро́й**	hero

Nouns which in the *nominative singular* end in **-а** or **-я** (except **-мя**) are normally *feminine*:

кни́га	book	**студе́нтка**	(female) student
неде́ля	week	**тётя**	aunt

Nouns which in the *nominative singular* end in **-а** or **-я** and which refer to male persons are *masculine*:

дя́дя	uncle	**мужчи́на**	man
ю́ноша	youth, young man		

Nouns which in the *nominative singular* end in **-а** or **-я** and which can refer either to male or to female persons are *masculine* unless they refer specifically to a woman, in which case they are *feminine*:

левша́	left-hander	**пья́ница**	drunkard

Nouns which in the *nominative singular* end in **-о**, **-е**, **-ё** or **-мя** are normally *neuter*:

окно́	window	**мо́ре**	sea
зда́ние	building	**копьё**	spear
вре́мя	time		

The only nouns that can cause problems are those ending in **-ь**, since some are *masculine*, while others are *feminine*. For some nouns it is possible to work out what the gender will be.

Nouns ending in **-тель** or **-арь** and denoting someone who carries out a particular activity are *masculine*:

писа́тель	writer	председа́тель	chairman
врата́рь	goalkeeper		

Names of months are *masculine*:

янва́рь	January	апре́ль	April
октя́брь	October		

Abstract nouns ending in **-ость** or **-знь** are *feminine*:

ра́дость	joy	ста́рость	old age
боле́знь	illness	жизнь	life

Nouns ending in **-овь**, **-жь**, **-чь**, **-шь** or **-щь** are *feminine*:

кровь	blood	це́рковь	church
рожь	rye	ме́лочь	small change
ро́скошь	luxury	вещь	thing

With other nouns ending in **-ь** there are no reliable ways of predicting the gender. For example, the following are *masculine*:

автомоби́ль	car, motor vehicle	го́лубь	dove, pigeon
гость	guest	гусь	goose
день	day	дождь	rain
ка́мень	stone	карто́фель	potatoes
Кремль	Kremlin	ле́бедь	swan
портфе́ль	briefcase	реме́нь	strap
роя́ль	(grand) piano	рубль	rouble
слова́рь	dictionary	у́голь	coal
шампу́нь	shampoo		

The following nouns are *feminine*:

дверь	door	кость	bone
ло́шадь	horse	ме́бель	furniture
о́чередь	queue	пе́чень	liver
пыль	dust	роль	part, role
соль	salt	степь	steppe
цель	goal, aim	цепь	chain

The rules for determining the gender of *indeclinable* nouns and of *abbreviations* and *acronyms* are given in **2.13.2** and **2.14.2** respectively.

2.4 Animacy

Russian nouns are divided into *animate* and *inanimate* nouns. Animate nouns are those that denote human beings or animals. All other nouns are inanimate.

The importance of the distinction between animate and inanimate nouns is its effect on certain endings for the *accusative* case. In the *singular*, all *animate masculine* nouns ending in a *consonant*, in –й or in -ь have an ending in the *accusative* that is identical to that of the *genitive*; all *inanimate masculine* nouns belonging to these declension types have an ending in the *accusative* that is identical to that of the *nominative*:

Animate

Nom.	Acc.	Gen.
брат 'brother'	бра́та	бра́та
геро́й 'hero'	геро́я	геро́я
коро́ль 'king'	короля́	короля́
тигр 'tiger'	ти́гра	ти́гра
соловей 'nightingale'	соловья́	соловья́
лось 'elk'	ло́ся	ло́ся

Inanimate

Nom.	Acc.	Gen.
стол 'table'	стол	стола́
поцелу́й 'kiss'	поцелу́й	поцелу́я
день 'day'	день	дня

No other nouns are affected in the singular by the distinction between animate and inanimate nouns.

In the *plural* all animate nouns (regardless of the gender and the declension type in the singular) have an ending in the *accusative* that is identical to that of the *genitive*; all inanimate nouns have an ending in the *accusative* that is identical to that of the *nominative*:

Animate

Nom. sing.	Nom. pl.	Acc. pl.	Gen. pl.
тигр 'tiger'	ти́гры	ти́гров	ти́гров
геро́й 'hero'	герои	геро́ев	геро́ев
коро́ль 'king'	короли́	королей	короле́й
му́ха 'fly'	му́хи	мух	мух
судья́ 'judge'	су́дьи	су́дей	су́дей
ло́шадь 'horse'	ло́шади	лошаде́й	лошаде́й
лицо́ 'person'	ли́ца	лиц	лиц

Inanimate

Nom. sing.	Nom. pl.	Acc. pl.	Gen. pl.
стол 'table'	столы́	столы́	столо́в
день 'day'	дни	дни	дней
кни́га 'book'	кни́ги	кни́ги	книг
неде́ля 'week'	неде́ли	неде́ли	неде́ль
кость 'bone'	ко́сти	ко́сти	косте́й
по́ле 'field'	поля́	поля́	поле́й

Nom. sing.	Nom. pl.	Acc. pl.	Gen. pl.
и́мя 'name'	имена́	имена́	имён
лицо́ 'face'	ли́ца	ли́ца	лиц

In the following sections the tables illustrating declension types will, where applicable, contain examples of both animate and inanimate nouns.

(i) The distinction between *animate* and *inanimate* nouns generally follows common-sense principles and presents few difficulties. Nevertheless, it may be noted that while труп 'corpse', is inanimate, мертве́ц 'dead man' is animate; ку́кла 'doll, puppet' is animate. Ферзь 'queen' (in chess) is a masculine animate noun.

(ii) As the example of лицо́ shows, some nouns can be either *animate* or *inanimate*, depending on the meaning: when лицо́ means 'person', it is animate, but when it means 'face', it is inanimate. Similarly, when Спарта́к denotes 'Spartacus' (the leader of the Roman slave rebellion), it is animate; when it denotes 'Spartak' (the sports organisation) it is inanimate (when used in the latter sense it is normally written in inverted commas; *see* **1.5.8**).

2.5 The fleeting vowel

2.5.0 Introduction

An important part in the Russian grammatical system is played by the so-called *fleeting vowel*. This is a vowel that is found in some forms of a word, but not in others. There are occasional exceptions, but normally the only vowels that can be fleeting are **е**, **ё** and **о**. Although examples of the fleeting vowel can be found elsewhere, this phenomenon is particularly important for the noun declension system.

For examples of the fleeting vowel in verbs and adjectives, *see* **4.5.3**, **4.7.3**, **4.7.13**, **6.5.1**.

2.5.1 The fleeting vowel with masculine nouns ending in a consonant, -й or -ь

The fleeting vowel occurs with a large number of masculine nouns ending in a consonant, **-й or -ь**. The vowel is present in the *nominative singular* (and *accusative singular* if the noun is *inanimate*), but absent in all other forms of the noun. The fleeting vowel is particularly likely to occur with nouns ending in **-ец**, **-ок**, **-ёк** or **-ей**, although it is by no means restricted to these nouns:

Nom. sing.	Gen. sing.	Nom. pl.
оте́ц 'father'	отца́	отцы́
огуре́ц 'cucumber'	огурца́	огурцы́
ры́нок 'market'	ры́нка	ры́нки
ту́рок 'Turk'	ту́рка	ту́рки
ве́тер 'wind'	ве́тра	ве́тры
ого́нь 'fire'	огня́	огни́
козёл 'billy-goat'	козла́	козлы́

With nouns ending in **-ёк** (after a consonant) or **-ей**, the fleeting vowel is replaced by a *soft sign* (**ь**):

Nom. sing.	Gen. sing.	Nom. pl.
конёк 'skate'	конька́	коньки́
воробе́й 'sparrow'	воробья́	воробьи́

With nouns ending in **-ёк** (after a vowel) the fleeting vowel is replaced by **-й-**:

Nom. sing.	Gen. sing.	Nom. pl.
паёк 'ration'	пайка́	пайки́

With the noun **за́яц** 'hare' in all forms except the nominative singular **-я-** is replaced by **-й-**:

Nom. sing.	Gen. sing.	Nom. pl.
за́яц	за́йца	за́йцы

2.5.2 The fleeting vowel with nouns ending in -а, -я, -о, -е, -ё

With nouns ending in **-а, -я, -о, -е, -ё**, a *fleeting vowel* sometimes appears in the *genitive plural*. This occurs with most (though not all) nouns which have a series of *two or more* consonants immediately preceding the ending:

Nom. sing.	Nom. pl.	Gen. pl.
ло́жка 'spoon'	ло́жки	ло́жек
ку́хня 'kitchen'	ку́хни	ку́хонь
окно́ 'window'	о́кна	о́кон
се́рдце 'heart'	сердца́	серде́ц

In some instances, the sequence of two consonants may be separated by **-ь-**:

Nom. sing.	Nom. pl.	Gen. pl.
тюрьма́ 'prison'	тю́рьмы	тю́рем
письмо́ 'letter'	пи́сьма	пи́сем

The rules for determining which vowel is used are as follows:

(i) After **к, г, х** only **-о-** is used; for examples, *see* **ку́хня** and **окно́** above.

(ii) The vowel **-о-** is used before **-к, -г, -х** unless the preceding consonant is **ж, ц, ч,** or **ш**:

Nom. sing.	Nom. pl.	Gen. pl.
ска́зка 'fairy tale'	ска́зки	ска́зок
ру́чка 'handle', 'pen'	ру́чки	ру́чек

(*See also* ло́жка above.)

(iii) In all other instances either -е- or -ё- is used, depending on the stress; -ё- is used when the stress is on the fleeting vowel:

Nom. sing.	Nom. pl.	Gen. pl.
сестра́ 'sister'	сёстры	сестёр
серьга́ 'earring'	се́рьги	серёг
кре́сло 'armchair'	кре́сла	кре́сел

NOTE: The vowel -е- is used before -ц even in stressed syllables; see the example се́рдце above.

A *soft sign* (ь) before я, е or ё is usually replaced by -е- or -и-; the former normally occurs under stress:

Nom. sing.	Nom. pl.	Gen. pl.
статья́ 'article'	статьи́	стате́й
свинья́ 'pig'	сви́ньи	свине́й
сиде́нье 'seat'	сиде́нья	сиде́ний
копьё 'spear'	ко́пья	ко́пий

When -й- appears before the last consonant it is usually replaced by -е-:

Nom. sing.	Nom. pl.	Gen. pl.
копе́йка 'kopeck'	копе́йки	копе́ек

NOTE: The genitive plural of яйцо́ 'egg' is яи́ц; the genitive plural of война́ 'war' is войн.

Not all nouns in these classes with a sequence of consonants immediately before the ending have the fleeting vowel in the genitive plural. Nouns that do not have the fleeting vowel include those ending in -ство, -сто, -та, -да as well as some others that are less predictable:

Nom. sing.	Nom. pl.	Gen. pl.
вещество́ 'substance'	вещества́	веще́ств
ме́сто 'place'	места́	мест
ка́рта 'map'	ка́рты	карт
звезда́ 'star'	звёзды	звёзд
со́лнце 'sun'	со́лнца	солнц

2.5.3 The fleeting vowel with feminine nouns ending in -ь

Some nouns, for example, **ложь** 'lie', **рожь** 'rye', **любовь** 'love' and **церковь** 'church', have a *fleeting vowel* that is present in the *nominative, accusative* and *instrumental singular*, but absent in all other forms:

Nom./acc. sing	ложь	рожь	любовь	церковь
Gen./dat./prep. sing.	лжи	ржи	любви	церкви
Instr. sing.	ложью	рожью	любовью	церковью
Nom./acc. pl.	—	—	любви	церкви

NOTE   When **Любовь** occurs as a *forename*, it does not have a *fleeting vowel*:

Nom./acc. sing.   **Любовь**   Gen./dat./prep. sing.   **Любови**

Examples of nouns containing a fleeting vowel will be included in the tables in the following sections.

2.6 Masculine nouns ending in a consonant, -й or -ь

2.6.1 Masculine nouns ending in a consonant other than -к, -г, -х, -ц, -ж, -ч, -ш, -щ

The following tables give examples of:
an *inanimate* noun (**стол** 'table');
an *animate* noun (**слон** 'elephant');
a noun with a *fleeting vowel* (**осёл** 'donkey').

	Singular	Plural
Nom.	стол	столы́
Gen.	стола́	столо́в
Dat.	столу́	стола́м
Acc.	стол	столы́
Inst.	столо́м	стола́ми
Prep.	столе́	стола́х

	Singular	Plural
Nom.	слон	слоны́
Gen.	слона́	слоно́в
Dat.	слону́	слона́м
Acc.	слона́	слоно́в
Inst.	слоно́м	слона́ми
Prep.	слоне́	слона́х

	Singular	Plural
Nom.	осёл	ослы́
Gen.	осла́	осло́в
Dat.	ослу́	осла́м

	Singular	*Plural*
Acc.	осла́	осло́в
Instr.	осло́м	осла́ми
Prep.	осле́	осла́х

2.6.2   Masculine nouns ending in -к, -г, -х, -ц, -ж, -ч, -ш, -щ: application of the spelling rules given in 1.5.2 and 1.5.4

The application of the spelling rules given in **1.5.2** and **1.5.4** means that the *nominative plural* of masculine nouns ending in -г, -к, -х, -ж, -ч, ш, -щ ends in **-и**:

Nom. sing.	*Nom. pl.*
враг 'enemy'	враги́
волк 'wolf'	во́лки
слух 'rumour'	слу́хи
нож 'knife'	ножи́
врач 'doctor'	врачи́
каранда́ш 'pencil'	карандаши́
плащ 'raincoat'	плащи́

The application of the spelling rules given in **1.5.2** means that the *instrumental singular* of nouns ending in -ц, -ж, -ч, -ш, -щ is **-ом** only when the ending is *stressed*, otherwise it is **-ем**:

Nom. sing.	*Instr. sing.*
оте́ц 'father'	отцо́м
нож	ножо́м
врач	врачо́м
каранда́ш	карандашо́м
плащ	плащо́м
ме́сяц 'month', 'moon'	ме́сяцем
муж 'husband'	му́жем
плач 'weeping'	пла́чем
душ 'shower'	ду́шем
това́рищ 'comrade'	това́рищем

Following the same rule the *genitive plural* of masculine nouns ending in **-ц** ends in **-ов** only when the ending is *stressed*; otherwise the ending is **-ев**:

Nom. sing.	*Gen. pl.*
коне́ц 'end'	концо́в
па́лец 'finger'	па́льцев

This rule does not, apply, however to the *genitive plural* of *masculine nouns* ending in -ж, -ч, -ш, -щ, this ending is always **-ей** regardless of the stress:

Nom. sing.	*Gen. pl.*
нож	ножей
пляж 'beach'	пляжей
врач	врачей
карандаш	карандашей
товарищ	товарищей

2.6.3 Masculine nouns ending in -й

The endings of masculine nouns ending in **-й** are affected by the spelling rule given in **1.5.1**. In the *instrumental singular* and the *genitive plural* the respective endings **-ём** and **-ёв** occur only when the stress is on the ending; otherwise, the corresponding endings are **-ем** and **-ев**.

The first of the following tables gives an example of an *inanimate* noun with stress not on the ending (**поцелуй** 'kiss'); the second table gives an example of an *animate* noun with stress not on the ending (**герой** 'hero'); the third table gives an example of a noun both with a *fleeting vowel* and with stress on the ending (**ручей** 'stream').

	Singular	*Plural*
Nom.	поцелуй	поцелуи
Gen.	поцелуя	поцелуев
Dat.	поцелую	поцелуям
Acc.	поцелуй	поцелуи
Instr.	поцелуем	поцелуями
Prep.	поцелуе	поцелуях

	Singular	*Plural*
Nom.	герой	герои
Gen.	героя	героев
Dat.	герою	героям
Acc.	героя	героев
Instr.	героем	героями
Prep.	герое	героях

	Singular	*Plural*
Nom.	ручей	ручьи
Gen.	ручья	ручьёв
Dat.	ручью	ручьям
Acc.	ручей	ручьи
Instr.	ручьём	ручьями
Prep.	ручье	ручьях

NOTE | Nouns ending in **-ий** have the ending **-ии** in the *prepositional singular*:

Nom. sing.	Prep. sing.
ка́льций 'calcium'	ка́льции
ге́ний 'genius'	ге́нии

Masculine nouns ending in -ь

The endings of masculine nouns ending in **-ь** are also affected by the spelling rule given in **1.5.1**. In the *instrumental singular* the ending **-ём** occurs only when the stress is on the ending; otherwise the corresponding ending is **-ем**.

The *genitive plural* ending for these nouns is **-ей**.

The following tables give examples of:

(a) an *inanimate* noun which also has stress on the ending (**рубль** 'rouble');
(b) an *animate* noun which also has stress not on the ending (**гость** 'guest');
(c) a noun with a *fleeting vowel* (**ого́нь** 'fire').

	Singular	Plural
Nom.	рубль	рубли́
Gen.	рубля́	рубле́й
Dat.	рублю́	рубля́м
Acc.	рубль	рубли́
Instr.	рублём	рубля́ми
Prep.	рубле́	рубля́х

The noun **путь** 'way, track, path' has the irregular form **пути́** in the *genitive, dative* and *prepositional singular*.

	Singular	Plural
Nom.	гость	го́сти
Gen.	го́стя	госте́й
Dat.	го́стю	гостя́м
Acc.	го́стя	госте́й
Instr.	го́стем	гостя́ми
Prep.	го́сте	гостя́х

	Singular	Plural
Nom.	ого́нь	огни́
Gen.	огня́	огне́й
Dat.	огню́	огня́м
Acc.	ого́нь	огни́
Instr.	огнём	огня́ми
Prep.	огне́	огня́х

Non-standard endings for masculine nouns ending in a consonant, -й or -ь

The second genitive in -у/-ю

Some nouns belonging to the classes described in **2.6** have a second form of the *genitive singular* ending in **-у/-ю**. This second form of the genitive singular can serve two functions.

With nouns denoting uncountable substances, the *second genitive* has a *partitive* function and is used in a range of quantity expressions. In practice, this *partitive genitive* tends to be used only with a small number of nouns indicating substances in common use, and in most instances it is an optional alternative to the normal genitive singular ending in **-а/-я**:

Дай мне, пожа́луйста, ча́шку ча́ю (ча́я).
Would you mind giving me a cup of tea.

К сожале́нию у меня́ нет са́хару (са́хара).
Unfortunately, I haven't got any sugar.

Чай о́чень кре́пкий, подле́й в ча́йник кипятку́ (кипятка́).
This tea is very strong; pour some boiling water into the teapot.

Мо́жет, к ко́фе вы́пьем по рю́мке коньяку́ (коньяка́)?
How about having a glass of brandy with our coffee?

For the use of the preposition **по** in constructions indicating '(so many), each', *see* **19.1.4**.

The use of the partitive genitive is obligatory in the common set phrases **мно́го наро́ду** 'a lot of people', and **ма́ло наро́ду** 'not many people', used in the context of whether a location is crowded or not:

Когда́ они́ пришли́ в кафе́, там уже́ бы́ло *мно́го наро́ду*, и они́ с трудо́м нашли́ свобо́дный сто́лик.
When they arrived at the café, there were already a lot of people there [*or* it was already very busy], and they had some difficulty finding a free table.

В про́шлом году́ мы отдыха́ли на се́вере А́нглии: там *ма́ло наро́ду* и це́ны не сли́шком высо́кие.
Last year we went on holiday to the North of England: there are not many people there [*or* it's quiet] and the prices are reasonable.

For more on the use of the genitive in quantity expressions, *see* **3.3.2**.

The other use of the *second genitive* in **-у** is in various set expressions, for the most part in constructions involving a *negative* or after certain *prepositions*. Perhaps the most useful of these is the phrase **ни ра́зу** 'not (even) once' (*see also* **15.3.4**); with others it is probably more important to recognise them than to be able to use them:

Я *ни ра́зу* не ста́лкивался с э́той пробле́мой.
Not once have I encountered this problem.

С тех пор, как он уе́хал за грани́цу, от него́ *ни слу́ху ни ду́ху*.
Since he went abroad we haven't heard a thing from him.

Он рассказа́л нам тако́й смешно́й анекдо́т, что мы чуть не у́мерли *со́ сме́ху.*

He told us such a funny joke that we almost died of laughter.

For more on negative constructions using **ни**, *see* **15.3.4**.

For more on the preposition **с/со** used to indicate cause, *see* **21.4.4**.

2.7.2 The second prepositional in -у́/-ю́

Some nouns belonging to the classes described in **2.6** have a second form of the *prepositional singular* ending in -у́/-ю́. This form is used only after the prepositions **в/ во** 'in, at', and **на** 'on, at', when these are used to indicate location; after other prepositions (such as **о(б)** 'about, concerning') the normal prepositional form is used. This form is found mainly (though not exclusively) with monosyllabic nouns, and when it occurs, this ending is always stressed and its use is obligatory.

For more on the use of prepositions with the prepositional case, *see* **9.2.6**.

For more on the use of the prepositions **в/во** and **на** to indicate location, *see* sections **21.2.1–21.2.10**.

Examples of nouns that have a *second prepositional* form include the following:

Nom. sing.	Meaning	Normal prep. sing.	Second prep. sing.
аэропо́рт	airport	об аэропо́рте	в аэропорту́
бал	ball, dance	о ба́ле	на балу́
бе́рег	shore	о бе́реге	на берегу́
бой	battle	о бо́е	в бою́
глаз	eye	о гла́зе	в глазу́
год	year	о го́де	в году́
лес	wood, forest	о ле́се	в лесу́
лёд	ice	о льде	на льду́
мех	fur	о ме́хе	в/на меху́
нос	nose	о но́се	в/на носу́
плен	captivity	о пле́не	в плену́
пол	floor	о по́ле	на полу́
порт	port	о по́рте	в порту́
рай	paradise	о ра́е	в раю́
рот	mouth	о рте	во рту́
угол	corner	об угле́	в/на углу́
шкаф	cupboard	о шка́фе	в шкафу́

2.7.3 The nominative plural in -а́/-я́

Some nouns belonging to the classes described in **2.6** have a *nominative plural* that ends in -а́/-я́. This ending is always stressed, and nouns that take this ending have the stress on the ending in all forms of the plural.

This ending is particularly likely to be found with nouns denoting objects that usually come in pairs:

Nom. sing.	Nom. pl.
бе́рег 'shore', 'bank' (of a river)	берега́
бок 'side'	бока́
глаз 'eye'	глаза́
рог 'horn'	рога́
рука́в 'sleeve'	рукава́

Other nouns that take this ending include the following:

Nom. sing.	Nom. pl.
а́дрес 'address'	адреса́
век 'century'	века́
ве́чер 'evening'	вечера́
го́лос 'voice'	голоса́
го́род 'town', 'city'	города́
дире́ктор 'boss', 'director'	директора́
до́ктор 'doctor'	доктора́
дом 'house', 'block of flats'	дома́
ко́локол 'bell'	колокола́
край 'edge'	края́
но́мер 'number', 'hotel room'	номера́
о́круг 'district'	округа́
о́стров 'island'	острова́
па́рус 'sail'	паруса́
па́спорт 'passport'	паспорта́
по́вар 'cook'	повара́
по́езд 'train'	поезда́
профе́ссор 'professor'	профессора́
сорт 'sort, 'type'	сорта́
том 'volume'	тома́

Some nouns have alternative endings in **-ы (-и)** and **-а́ (-я́)**. Where this occurs, the latter ending tends to be more characteristic of informal language:

Nom. sing.	Nom. pl.
бухга́лтер 'accountant'	бухга́лтеры *or* бухгалтера́
догово́р 'contract', 'treaty'	догово́ры *or* договора́
тра́ктор 'tractor'	тра́кторы *or* трактора́

A number of nouns have endings in **-ы (-и)** and **-а́ (-я́)** which are not interchangeable, but which are selected according to the precise meaning of the word concerned:

Nom. sing.	Meaning	Nom. pl. in ы (-и)	Meaning	Nom. pl. in а (-я)	Meaning
о́браз	image; icon	о́бразы	images	образа́	icons
про́пуск	omission; pass	про́пуски	omissions	пропуска́	passes (documents)

The following may also be noted:

Nom. sing.	Nom. pl.
цвет 'colour'	цвета́
цвето́к 'flower'	цветы́
счёт 'account', 'score'	счета́, *but also* счёты (no sing.) 'abacus'
про́вод 'wire'	провода́, *but also* про́воды (no sing.) 'farewell party'

NOTE
It is often difficult to predict which nouns will have a *nominative plural* in **-а́/-я́**, but a useful hint is that a noun of more than one syllable, which has stress on the final syllable in the *nominative singular*, will normally not have this ending. The only exception in common use is **рука́в** 'sleeve' (see above).

2.7.4   The 'zero ending' in the genitive plural

Some nouns belonging to the classes described in **2.6** have a so-called *zero ending* in the *genitive plural*; this means that the *genitive plural* is identical to the *nominative singular*. This ending is found with the following:

(1) Many nouns denoting weights, measures and other units, as well as some other words that occur mainly after numerals:

Nom. sing.	Nom. pl.	Gen. pl.
ватт 'watt'	ва́тты	ватт
герц 'hertz'	ге́рцы	герц
раз 'time', 'occasion'	разы́	раз

NOTES

(i) The nouns **грамм** 'gram', **килогра́мм** 'kilogram' have alternative forms **грамм**, **килогра́мм** and **гра́ммов**, **килогра́ммов**. The latter sometimes occur in formal contexts, but are rarely used in ordinary speech.

(ii) The nouns **байт** 'byte', **килоба́йт** 'kilobyte' have alternative forms **байт**, **килоба́йт** and **ба́йтов**, **килоба́йтов**. The former are particularly likely to be used after a numeral.

For the use of the genitive plural after certain numerals, *see* **8.2.3** and **8.2.4**.

(2) Some nouns indicating nationalities and ethnic groups:

Nom. sing.	Nom. pl.	Gen. pl.
башки́р 'Bashkir'	башки́ры	башки́р
грузи́н 'Georgian'	грузи́ны	грузи́н
ту́рок 'Turk'	ту́рки	ту́рок

The noun **цыга́н** 'gypsy', has an irregular nominative plural **цыга́не**:

Nom. sing.	Nom. pl.	Gen. pl.
цыга́н	цыга́не	цыга́н

For the use of small letters with nouns indicating nationalities and ethnic groups, *see* **1.5.7**.

(3) Some nouns indicating military terms:

Nom. sing.	Nom. pl.	Gen. pl.
партиза́н 'partisan'	партиза́ны	партиза́н
солда́т 'soldier'	солда́ты	солда́т

(4) Some nouns denoting objects that tend to come in pairs:

Nom. sing.	Nom. pl.	Gen. pl.
боти́нок 'shoe'	боти́нки	боти́нок
глаз 'eye'	глаза́	глаз
сапо́г '(high) boot'	сапоги́	сапо́г
чуло́к 'stocking'	чулки́	чуло́к

NOTES

(i) For nouns in groups (2) and (3) the *genitive plural* with a *zero ending* is more likely to be used with nouns, which in the nominative singular, end in -н, -р or -т.

(ii) Some nouns denoting the names of fruit have alternative forms in -ов and with a zero ending. Examples include: помидо́р 'tomato' (помидо́ров and помидо́р) and баклажа́н 'aubergine', 'egg-plant' (баклажа́нов and баклажа́н).

(iii) The noun во́лос 'hair' has a zero ending in the genitive plural, but with a different stress: воло́с.

2.8 Neuter nouns ending in -о, -е, -ё, -мя

2.8.1 Nouns ending in -о:

The first table gives an example of the standard declension pattern (ме́сто 'place'); the second table gives an example of a noun with a *fleeting vowel* (письмо́ 'letter'):

	Singular	Plural
Nom.	ме́сто	места́
Gen.	ме́ста	мест
Dat.	ме́сту	места́м
Acc.	ме́сто	места́
Instr.	ме́стом	места́ми
Prep.	ме́сте	места́х

	Singular	Plural
Nom.	письмо́	пи́сьма
Gen.	письма́	пи́сем
Dat.	письму́	пи́сьмам
Acc.	письмо́	пи́сьма
Instr.	письмо́м	пи́сьмами
Prep.	письме́	пи́сьмах

Nouns ending in -e

The following tables give examples of:

(a) the standard declension pattern (кла́дбище 'cemetery');
(b) a noun ending in -e with a *fleeting vowel* (се́рдце 'heart');
(c) a noun ending in -ье (уще́лье 'ravine', 'gorge')
(d) a noun ending in -ие (зда́ние 'building').

	Singular	Plural
Nom.	кла́дбище	кла́дбища
Gen.	кла́дбища	кла́дбищ
Dat.	кла́дбищу	кла́дбищам
Acc.	кла́дбище	кла́дбища
Instr.	кла́дбищем	кла́дбищами
Prep.	кла́дбище	кла́дбищах

NOTE   The nouns мо́ре 'sea' and по́ле 'field' have the *nominative plural* ending **-я** and the *genitive plural* ending **-ей**:

Nom. sing.	Nom. pl.	Gen. pl.
мо́ре	моря́	море́й
по́ле	поля́	поле́й

	Singular	Plural
Nom.	се́рдце	сердца́
Gen.	се́рдца	серде́ц
Dat.	се́рдцу	сердца́м
Acc.	се́рдце	сердца́
Instr.	се́рдцем	сердца́ми
Prep.	се́рдце	сердца́х

	Singular	Plural
Nom.	уще́лье	уще́лья
Gen.	уще́лья	уще́лий
Dat.	уще́лью	уще́льям
Acc.	уще́лье	уще́лья
Instr.	уще́льем	уще́льями
Prep.	уще́лье	уще́льях

NOTE   Nouns ending in -ье have the *fleeting vowel* -и- in the *genitive plural*.

	Singular	*Plural*
Nom.	зда́ние	зда́ния
Gen.	зда́ния	зда́ний
Dat.	зда́нию	зда́ниям
Acc.	зда́ние	зда́ния
Instr.	зда́нием	зда́ниями
Prep.	зда́нии	зда́ниях

NOTE | The *prepositional singular* of these nouns ends in **-ии**; the *genitive plural* ends in **-ий**.

2.8.3 Nouns ending in -ё

	Singular	*Plural*
Nom.	копьё	ко́пья
Gen.	копья́	ко́пий
Dat.	копью́	ко́пьям
Acc.	копьё	ко́пья
Instr.	копьём	ко́пьями
Prep.	копье́	ко́пьях

NOTE | The noun **ружьё** 'gun' has the *genitive plural* **ру́жей**. Almost all other nouns ending in **-ё** occur in the singular only.

2.8.4 Nouns ending in -мя

	Singular	*Plural*
Nom.	и́мя	имена́
Gen.	и́мени	имён
Dat.	и́мени	имена́м
Acc.	и́мя	имена́
Instr.	и́менем	имена́ми
Prep.	и́мени	имена́х

2.8.5 Non-standard endings for nouns ending in -о or -е: nominative plural in -и

Almost all nouns (except surnames) ending in **-ко** have a *nominative plural* ending in **-ки**:

Nom. sing.	*Nom. pl.*
ве́ко 'eyelid'	ве́ки
очко́ 'point (in a game)'	очки́
я́блоко 'apple'	я́блоки

NOTES

(i) There is one exception to the above rule:

Nom. sing. о́блако 'cloud'   Nom. pl. облака́

(ii) The noun очки́ (in the plural only) has the additional meaning of 'spectacles'.

For surnames ending in **-ко**, *see* **2.13.1**.

Two further nouns, both denoting parts of the body, have a *nominative plural* ending in **-и**:

Nom. sing.	Nom. pl.
коле́но 'knee'	коле́ни
плечо́ 'shoulder'	пле́чи

For examples where a *nominative plural* in **-и** is combined with other non-standard endings, *see* **2.11.6**.

2.8.6 Non-standard endings for nouns ending in -о or -е: genitive plural ending in -ов or -ев

Some nouns ending in **-ко** have a *genitive plural* ending in **-ков**; examples include:

Nom. sing.	Gen. pl.
очко́	очко́в
о́блако	облако́в

Some nouns ending in **-ье** have a *genitive plural* ending in **-ьев**; the only example in common use is:

Nom. sing.	Gen. pl.
пла́тье 'dress'	пла́тьев

2.9 Nouns, mostly feminine, ending in -а or -я

2.9.1 Nouns ending in -а

The following tables give examples of:

(a) an *inanimate* noun (берёза 'birch');
(b) an *animate* noun (коро́ва 'cow');
(c) a noun with a *fleeting vowel* (сестра́ 'sister').

	Singular	*Plural*
Nom.	берёза	берёзы
Gen.	берёзы	берёз

	Singular	Plural
Dat.	берёзе	берёзам
Acc.	берёзу	берёзы
Instr.	берёзой	берёзами
Prep.	берёзе	берёзах

	Singular	Plural
Nom.	коро́ва	коро́вы
Gen.	коро́вы	коро́в
Dat.	коро́ве	коро́вам
Acc.	коро́ву	коро́в
Instr.	коро́вой	коро́вами
Prep.	коро́ве	коро́вах

	Singular	Plural
Nom.	сестра́	сёстры
Gen.	сестры́	сестёр
Dat.	сестре́	сёстрам
Acc.	сестру́	сестёр
Instr.	сестро́й	сёстрами
Prep.	сестре́	сёстрах

2.9.2 Application of the spelling rules given in 1.5.2 and 1.5.4

Application of the spelling rules given in **1.5.2** and **1.5.4** means that nouns ending in -га, -ка, -ха, -жа, -ча, -ша, or ща have the *genitive singular* and the *nominative plural* ending in -и:

Nom. sing.	Gen. sing.	Nom. pl.
кни́га 'book'	кни́ги	кни́ги
рука́ 'arm', 'hand'	руки́	ру́ки
му́ха 'fly'	му́хи	му́хи
кра́жа 'theft'	кра́жи	кра́жи
да́ча 'dacha'	да́чи	да́чи
ю́ноша 'youth', 'young man'	ю́ноши	ю́ноши
тёща 'mother-in-law' (wife's mother)	тёщи	тёщи

Application of the spelling rule given in **1.5.2** means that nouns ending in -жа, -ца, -ча, -ша or -ща and having the stress not on the ending, have an *instrumental singular* ending in -ей:

Nom. sing.	Instr. sing.
са́жа 'soot'	са́жей
яи́чница 'fried eggs'	яи́чницей
да́ча 'dacha'	да́чей
ю́ноша 'youth', 'young man'	ю́ношей
тёща 'mother-in-law' (wife's mother)	тёщей

2.9.3 ### Nouns ending in -я

The following tables give examples of:

(a) an inanimate noun (неде́ля, 'week');
(b) an animate noun (ня́ня, 'nanny');
(c) a noun with a fleeting vowel (земля́, 'land', 'earth').

	Singular	*Plural*
Nom.	неде́ля	неде́ли
Gen.	неде́ли	неде́ль
Dat.	неде́ле	неде́лям
Acc.	неде́лю	неде́ли
Inst.	неде́лей	неде́лями
Prep.	неде́ле	неде́лях

	Singular	*Plural*
Nom.	ня́ня	ня́ни
Gen.	ня́ни	нянь
Dat.	ня́не	ня́ням
Acc.	ня́ню	нянь
Instr.	ня́ней	ня́нями
Prep.	ня́не	ня́нях

	Singular	*Plural*
Nom.	земля́	зе́мли
Gen.	земли́	земе́ль
Dat.	земле́	зе́млям
Acc.	зе́млю	зе́мли
Instr.	землёй	зе́млями
Prep.	земле́	зе́млях

NOTES

(i) As is shown in the above tables, the ending in the *instrumental singular* is **-ёй** when the stress is on the ending; otherwise it is **-ей**.

(ii) Nouns ending in **-ия** have the ending **-ии** in the *dative* and *prepositional* singular:

Nom. sing.	*Dat. sing.*	*Prep. sing.*
А́нглия 'England'	А́нглии	А́нглии

(iii) Nouns in which the final **-я** follows a vowel have a *genitive plural* ending in **-й**:

Nom. sing.	*Gen. pl.*
ста́я 'flock' (of birds)	стай
ли́ния 'line'	ли́ний

(iv) Most nouns ending in **-ья** have a *genitive plural* ending in **-ей**:

Nom. sing.	*Gen. pl.*
статья́ 'article'	стате́й
судья́ 'judge', 'referee'	суде́й

2.9.4   **Non-standard endings with nouns ending in -a or -я**

Some nouns ending in **-ча**, **-ша** or **-я** have a *genitive plural* ending in **-ей**. This ending is particularly likely to occur with nouns that are (or can be) *masculine*:

Nom. sing.	Gen. pl.
левша́ 'left-hander'	левше́й
ю́ноша 'youth', 'young man'	ю́ношей
дя́дя 'uncle'	дя́дей

Examples of *feminine* nouns with this ending include the following (in some instances the ending in **-ей** is optional):

Nom. sing.	Gen. pl.
до́ля 'share'	доле́й
ноздря́ 'nostril'	ноздре́й
простыня́ 'sheet'	простыне́й/простны́нь
свеча́ 'candle'	свече́й
тётя 'aunt'	тётей/тёть

Most nouns ending in **-ня**, and having a fleeting vowel in the genitive plural, have a genitive plural ending in **-н**:

Nom. sing.	Gen. pl.
ба́сня 'fable'	ба́сен
пе́сня 'song'	пе́сен

Exceptions are:

Nom. sing.	Gen. pl.
дере́вня 'village', 'countryside'	дереве́нь
ку́хня 'kitchen'	ку́хонь

2.10   Feminine nouns ending in -ь

2.10.1   **Standard endings**

The following tables give an example of:

(a) an inanimate noun (**роль** 'role', 'part');
(b) an animate noun (**свекро́вь** 'mother-in-law' (husband's mother)).

For examples with a 'fleeting vowel', *see* **2.5.3**.

	Singular	Plural
Nom.	ро́ль	ро́ли
Gen.	ро́ли	роле́й
Dat.	ро́ли	роля́м
Acc.	ро́ль	ро́ли
Instr.	ро́лью	роля́ми
Prep.	ро́ли	роля́х

	Singular	Plural
Nom.	свекро́вь	свекро́ви
Gen.	свекро́ви	свекрове́й
Dat.	свекро́ви	свекро́вям
Acc.	свекро́вь	свекрове́й
Instr.	свекро́вью	свекро́вями
Prep.	свекро́ви	свекро́вях

2.10.2 ## Application of the spelling rule given in 1.5.2

Nouns ending in **-жь**, **-чь**, **-шь** or **-щь** have the endings **-ам**, **-ами**, **-ах** in the *dative, instrumental* and *prepositional* plural respectively:

Nom. sing.	Dat. pl.	Instr. pl.	Prep. pl.
ночь 'night'	**ноча́м**	**ноча́ми**	**ноча́х**
мышь 'mouse'	**мыша́м**	**мыша́ми**	**мыша́х**
вещь 'thing'	**веща́м**	**веща́ми**	**веща́х**

2.10.3 ## Non-standard endings: мать, дочь

The nouns **мать** 'mother' and **дочь** 'daughter' insert **-ер-** before all endings except the *nominative* and *accusative singular*:

	Singular		Plural	
Nom.	ма́ть	до́чь	ма́тери	до́чери
Gen.	ма́тери	до́чери	матере́й	дочере́й
Dat.	ма́тери	до́чери	матеря́м	дочеря́м
Acc.	ма́ть	до́чь	матере́й	дочере́й
Instr.	ма́терью	до́черью	матеря́ми	дочерьми́ *or* дочеря́ми
Prep.	ма́тери	до́чери	матеря́х	дочеря́х

2.10.4 ## Non-standard endings: instrumental plural in -ьми

The nouns **дверь** 'door', **дочь** 'daughter' and **ло́шадь** 'horse' have alternative endings for the *instrumental plural* in **-ьми** and **-ями**:

двери́ми/дверя́ми дочерьми́/дочеря́ми   лошадьми́/лошадя́ми

2.11 Non-standard declension types

2.11.0 Introduction

There are a number of *non-standard declension types*. These are generally characterised by the presence in the *plural* of a set of endings that cannot be predicted from the *nominative singular*.

2.11.1 Nouns ending in a consonant and having a nominative plural in -ья

A number of masculine nouns ending in a consonant have a *nominative plural* ending in **-ья**. These decline according to the following patterns. It will be noticed that the ending in the *genitive plural* depends on the stress: when the stress is on the ending, it is **-ей** (with no soft sign!), otherwise it is **-ьев**. The tables give examples of:

(a) *animate* nouns (**муж** 'husband', **брат** 'brother');
(b) an *inanimate* noun (**стул**, 'chair').

	Singular	Plural	Singular	Plural
Nom.	муж	мужья́	брат	бра́тья
Gen.	му́жа	муже́й	бра́та	бра́тьев
Dat.	му́жу	мужья́м	бра́ту	бра́тьям
Acc.	му́жа	муже́й	бра́та	бра́тьев
Instr.	му́жем	мужья́ми	бра́том	бра́тьями
Prep.	му́же	мужья́х	бра́те	бра́тьях

	Singular	Plural
Nom.	стул	сту́лья
Gen.	сту́ла	сту́льев
Dat.	сту́лу	сту́льям
Acc.	стул	сту́лья
Instr.	сту́лом	сту́льями
Prep.	сту́ле	сту́льях

There are no inanimate nouns with a genitive plural ending in **-ей**.

In some instances nouns belonging to this group have an additional complication, involving either a *change of consonant* or the insertion of an *extra syllable* in all endings of the *plural*:

Nom. sing.	Nom. pl.	Gen. pl.
клок 'shred', 'patch'	кло́чья	кло́чьев
друг 'friend'	друзья́	друзе́й
сын 'son'	сыновья́	сынове́й

Some nouns have two different plural forms with different meanings:

Nom. sing.	Meaning	Nom. pl. in ы (-и)	Meaning	Nom. pl. in -ья	Meaning
зуб	tooth; cog	зу́бы	teeth	зу́бья	cogs
ко́рень	root	ко́рни	roots (general)	коре́нья	roots (used in cooking or traditional medicine)
лист	leaf; sheet of paper	листы́	sheets of paper	ли́стья	leaves
по́вод	cause; rein	по́воды	causes	пово́дья	reins

2.11.2 **Nouns ending in -о and having a nominative plural in -ья**

Some neuter nouns ending in **-о** have a *nominative plural* in **-ья**. These decline according to the following pattern:

	Singular	Plural
Nom.	де́рево 'tree'	дере́вья
Gen.	де́рева	дере́вьев
Dat.	де́реву	дере́вьям
Acc.	де́рево	дере́вья
Instr.	де́ревом	дере́вьями
Prep.	де́реве	дере́вьях

Other examples include:

Nom. sing.	Nom. pl.
крыло́ 'wing'	кры́лья
перо́ 'feather'	пе́рья

2.11.3 **Masculine nouns in -анин (-янин)**

Masculine nouns ending in **-анин** or **-янин**, many of which denote the inhabitants of certain cities or countries, or the members of certain religions or social classes, lose the **-ин-** in the *plural* and have non-standard endings in the *nominative* and *genitive plural*:

	Singular	Plural
Nom.	англича́нин 'Englishman'	англича́не
Gen.	англича́нина	англича́н
Dat.	англича́нину	англича́нам
Acc.	англича́нина	англича́н
Inst.	англича́нином	англича́нами
Prep.	англича́нине	англича́нах

For the use of small letters with nouns indicating the inhabitants of cities and countries, *see* **1.5.7**.

For more examples of nouns belonging to this declension type, *see* **10.1.8**.

2.11.4 Masculine nouns in -ёнок (-о́нок)

Masculine nouns ending in **-ёнок (-о́нок)** decline according to the following pattern. Almost all of these nouns in common use denote the young of animals.

	Singular	*Plural*
Nom.	котёнок 'kitten'	котя́та
Gen.	котёнка	котя́т
Dat.	котёнку	котя́там
Acc.	котёнка	котя́т
Instr.	котёнком	котя́тами
Prep.	котёнке	котя́тах

NOTES:

(i) The spelling **-онок** occurs after the consonants **-ж, -ч** and **-ш**. In accordance with the spelling rule given in **1.5.2** the plural forms are spelled **-ата**, etc.:

Nom. sing.	*Nom. pl.*	*Gen. pl.*
медвежо́нок 'bear-cub'	медвежа́та	медвежа́т

(ii) The noun **щено́к** 'puppy' has alternative forms in the plural:

Nom. pl.	*Gen. pl.*	*Dat. pl.*
щенки́/щеня́та	щенко́в/щеня́т	щенка́м/щеня́там

For **ребёнок** and **ребя́та**, which form a special case, *see* **2.11.7**.

2.11.5 Other non-standard masculine nouns

The nouns **чёрт** 'devil' and **сосе́д** 'neighbour', 'room-mate' decline as follows:

	Singular	*Plural*	*Singular*	*Plural*
Nom.	чёрт	че́рти	сосе́д	сосе́ди
Gen.	чёрта	черте́й	сосе́да	сосе́дей
Dat.	чёрту	чертя́м	сосе́ду	сосе́дям
Acc.	чёрта	черте́й	сосе́да	сосе́дей
Instr.	чёртом	чертя́ми	сосе́дом	сосе́дями
Prep.	чёрте	чертя́х	сосе́де	сосе́дях

The nouns **хозя́ин** 'master', 'owner' and **господи́н** 'gentleman', 'Mr' decline as follows:

	Singular	*Plural*	*Singular*	*Plural*
Nom.	хозя́ин	хозя́ева	господи́н	господа́
Gen.	хозя́ина	хозя́ев	господи́на	госпо́д

	Singular	Plural	Singular	Plural
Dat.	хозя́ину	хозя́евам	господи́ну	господа́м
Acc.	хозя́ина	хозя́ев	господи́на	госпо́д
Instr.	хозя́ином	хозя́евами	господи́ном	господа́ми
Prep.	хозя́ине	хозя́евах	господи́не	господа́х

For the use of **господи́н** and **господа́** in forms of address, *see* **13.4.3** and **13.5.2**.

2.11.6 Other non-standard neuter nouns

The nouns **у́хо** 'ear' and **о́ко** 'eye' have a change of consonant in the *plural* as well as non-standard endings in the *nominative* and *genitive plural*:

	Singular	Plural	Singular	Plural
Nom.	у́хо	у́ши	о́ко	о́чи
Gen.	у́ха	уше́й	о́ка	оче́й
Dat.	у́ху	уша́м	о́ку	оча́м
Acc.	у́хо	у́ши	о́ко	о́чи
Instr.	у́хом	уша́ми	о́ком	оча́ми
Prep.	у́хе	уша́х	о́ке	оча́х

NOTE The normal word for 'eye' is **глаз**; **о́ко** is mostly used in poetic and high-flown language; it is found, for example, in the title of the well-known song **«О́чи чёрные»** 'Black eyes'.

The noun **су́дно** 'vessel', 'ship' declines as follows:

	Singular	Plural
Nom.	су́дно	суда́
Gen.	су́дна	судо́в
Dat.	су́дну	суда́м
Acc.	су́дно	суда́
Instr.	су́дном	суда́ми
Prep.	су́дне	суда́х

The nouns **не́бо** 'sky', 'heaven' and **чу́до** 'miracle' insert **-ec-** before the endings in the plural:

	Singular	Plural
Nom.	не́бо	небеса́
Gen.	не́ба	небе́с
Dat.	не́бу	небеса́м
Acc.	не́бо	небеса́
Instr.	не́бом	небеса́ми
Prep.	не́бе	небеса́х

Nouns where the singular and plural forms are totally different

The noun **челове́к** 'man', 'person', has no plural forms of its own. Instead, **лю́ди** (which in turn has no corresponding singular form) is used:

	Singular	Plural
Nom.	челове́к	лю́ди
Gen.	челове́ка	люде́й
Dat.	челове́ку	лю́дям
Acc.	челове́ка	люде́й
Instr.	челове́ком	людьми́
Prep.	челове́ке	лю́дях

For the use of **челове́к** as a special *genitive plural* form after certain numerals, *see* **8.2.3.**

The position with **ребёнок** 'child' is a little more complicated. An associated plural form **ребя́та** does exist, but this normally has the meaning of 'lads', 'guys' and is a sort of collective noun used to refer to groups of young men or mixed groups of young people. Instead, to indicate the plural 'children' the unrelated form **де́ти** is used. The declension of **ребёнок** and **ребя́та** follows the pattern given in **2.11.4**; **де́ти** declines as follows:

Nom.	де́ти
Gen.	дете́й
Dat.	де́тям
Acc.	дете́й
Instr.	детьми́
Prep.	де́тях

The declension of nouns that exist in only the plural

It will be noted from the tables of declensions given in the preceding sections that with a minute handful of exceptions, such as the instrumental forms **людьми́, детьми́**, the endings for the *dative, instrumental* and *prepositional plural* all follow the regular patterns **-ам, -ами, -ах** or **-ям, -ями, -ях**, with the choice between **-а-** and **-я-** being determined by the spelling rules given in **1.2.4** and **1.5.2**. Therefore, with nouns that exist in only the plural, the sole form that is not immediately unpredictable from the *nominative* is the *genitive*. Below we give the *genitive* and *dative* forms of the nouns listed above in **2.1.3**:

Nom.	Gen.	Dat.
брю́ки 'trousers'	брюк	брю́кам
штаны́ 'trousers'	штано́в	штана́м
трусы́ '(under)pants', 'knickers'	трусо́в	труса́м
шо́рты 'shorts'	шорт/шо́ртов	шо́ртам
пла́вки 'swimming trunks'	пла́вок	пла́вкам
колго́тки 'tights'	колго́ток	колго́ткам
но́жницы 'scissors'	но́жниц	но́жницам
щипцы́ 'tongs', 'pincers', 'tweezers'	щипцо́в	щипца́м
дрова́ 'firewood'	дров	дрова́м

Nom.	Gen.	Dat.
дро́жжи 'yeast'	дрожже́й	дрожжа́м
обо́и 'wallpaper'	обо́ев	обо́ям
поми́нки 'wake'	поми́нок	поми́нкам
са́ни 'sledge'	сане́й	саня́м
сли́вки 'cream'	сли́вок	сли́вкам
су́тки 'day', 'period of 24 hours'	су́ток	су́ткам
счёты 'abacus'	счётов	счётам
черни́ла 'ink'	черни́л	черни́лам
щи 'type of cabbage soup'	щей	щам

2.12 Declension of surnames

2.12.1 Russian surnames ending in -ов, -ев, -ёв, -ин, -ын

The most widely occurring endings for Russian surnames are **-ов**, **-ев**, **-ёв**, **-ин**, **-ын**, – for example, **Петро́в**, **Бре́жнев**, **Горбачёв**, **Пу́шкин**, **Солжени́цын**. These surnames, which have *masculine*, *feminine* and *plural* forms, have a special declension pattern that combines a mixture of *noun* and *adjective* endings.

Information on the declension of adjectives is given in **Chapter 6**.

	Masculine	*Feminine*	*Plural*
Nom.	**Петро́в**	**Петро́ва**	**Петро́вы**
Gen.	**Петро́ва**	**Петро́вой**	**Петро́вых**
Dat.	**Петро́ву**	**Петро́вой**	**Петро́вым**
Acc.	**Петро́ва**	**Петро́ву**	**Петро́вых**
Instr.	**Петро́вым**	**Петро́вой**	**Петро́выми**
Prep.	**Петро́ве**	**Петро́вой**	**Петро́вых**

	Masculine	*Feminine*	*Plural*
Nom.	**Пу́шкин**	**Пу́шкина**	**Пу́шкины**
Gen.	**Пу́шкина**	**Пу́шкиной**	**Пу́шкиных**
Dat.	**Пу́шкину**	**Пу́шкиной**	**Пу́шкиным**
Acc.	**Пу́шкина**	**Пу́шкину**	**Пу́шкиных**
Instr.	**Пу́шкиным**	**Пу́шкиной**	**Пу́шкиными**
Prep.	**Пу́шкине**	**Пу́шкиной**	**Пу́шкиных**

NOTE Place names ending in **-ов**, **-ев**, **-ёв**, **-ин**, **-ын** decline like ordinary masculine nouns ending in a consonant:

> **У него́ да́ча где́-то под *Пу́шкином*.**
> He has a dacha somewhere near (the town of) Pushkin.

2.12.2 **Other surnames ending in a consonant or -ь**

Other surnames ending in a consonant or in -ь (including foreign surnames that happen to end in -ов, -ев or -ин) decline in the *masculine* and in the *plural* like other masculine nouns ending in a consonant or in -ь. The *feminine* form, which in the nominative is identical to the masculine, is always *indeclinable*.

For more on indeclinable nouns, *see* **2.13.**

2.13 **Indeclinable nouns**

2.13.1 **Which nouns are indeclinable?**

Russian has a fairly large number of *indeclinable* nouns, that is, nouns that have the same ending for all cases and (where relevant) in both singular and plural. For the most part it is relatively simple to predict which nouns do not decline; specifically, nouns belonging to the following categories are indeclinable:

(i) All nouns which in the *nominative singular* end in -и, -у, -ю, -э or -ы:

такси́ 'taxi'	кенгуру́ 'kangaroo'
меню́ 'menu'	каноэ́ 'canoe'

In practice, there are no nouns in common use that have a nominative singular ending in -ы.

(ii) *All feminine* nouns ending in a *consonant*:

мада́м 'madam(e)'	мисс 'miss'
ми́ссис 'Mrs'	

By far the largest group of nouns belonging to this category is made up of women's forenames and surnames.

Forenames (mostly of foreign origin):

Ма́ргарет 'Margaret'	Эли́забет 'Elizabeth'

Surnames (of any origin):

Кли́нтон 'Clinton'	Тэ́тчер 'Thatcher'
Абрамо́вич 'Abramovich'	Жук 'Zhuk'

(iii) Borrowed or newly coined words ending in -о or -е:

депо́ 'depôt'	кило́ 'kilo(gram)'
кино́ 'cinema'	метро́ 'metro', 'underground railway'
пальто́ (cf. French *paletot*) 'overcoat'	кафе́ 'café'
ко́фе 'coffee'	купе́ 'compartment' (in a railway carriage)

Surnames (of whatever origin) ending in -о or -е also belong to this category:

Кличко́ 'Klichko'	Ю́щенко 'Iushchenko' (Yushchenko)
Гюго́ '(Victor) Hugo'	Пиранде́лло 'Pirandello'
Гёте 'Goethe'	Ви́тте 'Witte'

(iv) Some borrowed nouns and foreign surnames ending in **-a**. There is no hard-and-fast rule about this, but nouns are more likely not to be declined if the final **-a** is preceded by a vowel or if the word is borrowed from a French word with a silent final consonant:

бо́а 'boa' буржуа́ 'bourgeois'
Дюма́ 'Dumas'

(v) Words ending in a consonant and occurring only in the plural:

кома́ндос 'commandos' пра́ймериз 'primaries' (in an election campaign)
«Би́тлз» 'The Beatles'

(vi) Surnames ending in **-ых** or **-их** and looking like the genitive plural forms of adjectives:

Седы́х
Козло́вских

The declension of adjectives is described in **Chapter 6**.

NOTE │ Place names ending in **-ино**, **-ово/-ево** can decline like other neuter nouns ending in **-о**, but there is a tendency to make these nouns indeclinable.

2.13.2 The gender of indeclinable nouns

Special rules exist for determining the gender of *indeclinable* nouns. If an indeclinable noun denotes a person or an animal, it will normally be *masculine*, although if it explicitly denotes a woman or a female animal it will be *feminine*. All other indeclinable nouns are *neuter*.

There are, however, some exceptions to this rule. The noun **ко́фе** 'coffee' is according to all dictionaries and reference books masculine, but in informal speech it will sometimes be neuter. Conversely, some other nouns denoting drinks, such as **ви́ски** 'whisk(e)y' or **пе́пси** 'Pepsi', are normally listed as neuter, but in informal speech can be masculine. The noun **е́вро** 'euro' (the currency unit), can be either masculine or neuter, although the former is more common.

NOTE │ Although it is a form that is frequently encountered, many speakers of Russian consider treating **ко́фе** as a neuter noun to be unacceptable. In cases of doubt it is probably safer for learners to follow the recommendations of dictionaries and other reference works.

2.14 Abbreviations and acronyms

2.14.1 Declension of abbreviations and acronyms

Modern Russian, both spoken and written, contains a large number of *abbreviations* and *acronyms*. Frequently encountered examples include the following:

КВН (Клуб весёлых и нахо́дчивых)
A Club for the Merry and the Resourceful (a popular and long-running television programme)

МВД (Министе́рство вну́тренних дел)
Ministry of the Interior

МГУ (Моско́вский госуда́рственный университе́т)
Moscow State University

МЧС (Министе́рство по чрезвыча́йным ситуа́циям)
Ministry for Emergencies

НА́ТО
NATO

РФ (Росси́йская Федера́ция)
The Russian Federation

СНГ (Содру́жество незави́симых госуда́рств)
CIS (The Commonwealth of Independent States)

США (Соединённые Шта́ты Аме́рики)
USA

чп (чрезвыча́йное происше́ствие)
emergency

In general, abbreviations and acronyms are indeclinable. If, however, an acronym takes the form of a masculine noun ending in an consonant, it can be declined like other masculine nouns ending in a consonant. Whether these forms are declined is largely a matter of custom and practice and even personal preference, but they are more likely to be declined in informal language. Examples include:

ГУМ (Госуда́рственный универса́льный магази́н)
GUM (a large department store, now more a collection of independent trading outlets, located in the centre of Moscow)

МИД (Министе́рство иностра́нных дел)
Ministry of Foreign Affairs

В *ГУ́Ме* откры́лся бути́к «Iceberg».
Iceberg have opened a boutique in GUM.

Профессиона́льный у́ровень перево́дчиков *МИ́Да* исключи́тельно высо́к.
The level of professionalism of the translators who work for the Ministry of Foreign Affairs is exceptionally high.

Those acronyms that are no longer perceived as such and which are (or can be) written with small letters tend to be declined as a matter of course:

ВУЗ/вуз (вы́сшее уче́бное заведе́ние)
higher education institution, university

ЖЭК/жэк (жили́щно-эксплуатацио́нная конто́ра)
district housing office

ЗАГС/загс (за́пись а́ктов гражда́нского состоя́ния)
Register Office

С нача́ла но́вого уче́бного го́да повыша́ются стипе́ндии *во всех ву́зах* Росси́и.
Student grants in all Russian universities are being increased from the start of the coming academic year.

Через па́ру ме́сяцев яви́лись *из ЖЭ́Ка* и сказа́ли, что за́втра начну́т ремо́нт.
A few months later someone came round from the housing office and said that the repairs would begin the next day.

Церемо́ния регистра́ции бра́ка *в ЗА́ГСе* незате́йлива и коротка́.
The wedding ceremony in a Register Office is short and simple.

2.14.2 The gender of abbreviations and acronyms

The general rule for establishing the gender of abbreviations and acronyms is that the gender is the same as it would be if the abbreviation or acronym were written out in full. According to this rule (in each instance the word that establishes the gender has been italicised)

МГУ (Моско́вский госуда́рственный *университе́т*) is *masculine*;
РФ (Росси́йская *Федера́ция*) is *feminine*;
СНГ (*Содру́жество* незави́симых госуда́рств) is *neuter*;
США (Соединённые *Шта́ты* Аме́рики) is *plural*.

Regardless of this rule, acronyms that take the form of a masculine noun ending in a consonant and which are capable of being declined tend to be treated as masculine:

В Гро́зном откры́лся пе́рвый госуда́рственный духо́вный вуз – Чече́нский исла́мский институ́т.
The first state-owned theological college – the Chechen Islamic Institute – has opened in Groznyi.

The masculine adjective endings used in this example are explained in **6.1.**

3

Case

Introduction

The use of the *case system* to indicate different grammatical functions can be illustrated by the three different forms of the English pronoun 'he'. The form 'he' is used to indicate the *subject* of a sentence:

> *He* can see me.

The form 'him' is used among other functions to indicate either the direct or the indirect object of a verb. It is also used after prepositions:

> I can see *him*.

> I gave *him* the book.

> I haven't heard from *him* for a long time.

The form 'his' is used to indicate possession:

> I have borrowed *his* book.

The Russian case system is much more complicated. As noted in **Chapter 2**, there are six cases: *nominative, genitive, dative, accusative, instrumental* and *prepositional*. In addition, the case system encompasses not only *nouns*, but also *adjectives, pronouns* and *numerals*.

The declension of adjectives, pronouns and numerals is described in Chapters 6, 7 and 8 respectively.

A further complication is that almost all of the cases are used in a wide variety of functions and the relationship between these different functions is in many instances neither obvious nor logical. The aim of this chapter is to examine the principal functions of each of the cases in turn.

There are two points to note here. The first is that this chapter concentrates on the principal functions of the cases; further illustrations of the different ways in which they are used will be given in **Part B** of this book. The second is that each of the cases can be used after prepositions: a list of prepositions and the cases they are used with is given in **9.2**.

3.1 The nominative

3.1.1 Dictionaries and vocabularies

The *nominative* is the form under which *nouns*, *adjectives*, *pronouns* and *numerals* are listed in dictionaries, vocabularies and other word lists. Nouns are listed under the *nominative singular* (*nominative plural* if they have no singular form), while adjectives, pronouns and the numeral **один** 'one' are listed under the *nominative singular masculine*.

3.1.2 The use of the nominative to indicate the subject of finite verbs

The *nominative* is the case used to indicate the *subject* of a *finite verb*:

> ***Мой брат*** то́лько что верну́лся из Великобрита́нии.
> My brother has just returned from Great Britain.

> Ро́вно сто де́сять лет наза́д в Санкт-Петербу́рге состоя́лся *пе́рвый* в
> Росси́и *футбо́льный матч*.
> Russia's first football match took place in St Petersburg exactly 110 years ago.

NOTE: In Russian it is not necessary for the subject of a sentence to precede the verb. For more on word order, *see* **20.1**.

For a description of which verb forms are finite and which are non-finite, *see* **4.0**.

3.1.3 The use of the nominative to indicate the complement

In certain circumstances the *nominative* case is used for the *complement* in sentences containing definitions or statements of equivalence. The nominative is always used in present-tense constructions where there is no explicit verb form (corresponding to the present tense of the verb 'to be' in English) and is sometimes used in sentences containing different forms of the verb **быть**, especially if the complement takes the form of an adjective:

> Говоря́т, её оте́ц – *изве́стный поли́тик*.
> They say her father is a well-known politician.

> Пессими́ст счита́ет, что стака́н *полупусто́й*, тогда́ как оптими́ст
> полага́ет, что он наполови́ну *по́лон*.
> A pessimist thinks that the glass is half-empty, while an optimist assumes that it is half-full.

> Как оказа́лось, она была́ соверше́нно *права́*.
> As it turned out, she was absolutely right.

For more on the complement of **быть** and other verbs with a related meaning, *see* **3.5** and **14.1**.

3.1.4 ## The use of the nominative in forms of address

The *nominative* is the case that is used when addressing people:

> **Джон, мо́жно вас на мину́точку?**
> John, can I have a word with you? *or* John, can I borrow you for a minute?

> **Тётя Ната́ша, а у вас в де́тстве была́ ве́рная подру́га?**
> Auntie Natasha, did you have a best (*literally*, a faithful) friend when you were a child?

> **А тебе́, *малы́ш*, давно́ пора́ спать.**
> And you, young man, should have been in bed a long time ago.

3.2 ## The accusative

The main use of the *accusative* case is to indicate the *direct object* of a verb:

> **Я давно́ зна́ю *ва́шего му́жа*: мы учи́лись вме́сте в шко́ле.**
> I've known your husband for a long time: we were at school together.

> **Она́ написа́ла о́чень *хоро́шую кни́гу* о жи́зни в постсове́тской Росси́и.**
> She's written a very good book on life in post-Soviet Russia.

> **Исто́рия пока́зывает, что искорени́ть *корру́пцию* по́лностью и навсегда́ невозмо́жно.**
> History shows that it is impossible permanently and totally to eradicate corruption.

When ordering food and drink in a bar or restaurant, or when asking for someone on the telephone, it is normal to use the accusative, even though no verb may be present in the sentence:

> **Мне, пожа́луйста, *соля́нку*, а на второ́е *котле́ту* по-ки́евски.**
> I'll have the solianka (a thick soup with meat or fish and vegetables) and for my main course chicken Kiev.

> **Алло́, до́брый день. Мо́жно *Алекса́ндра Никола́евича* к телефо́ну?**
> Hello. May I speak to Aleksandr Nikolaevich, please?

For more on Russian names and forms of address, *see* **12.1** and **13.4**.

For more on using the telephone, *see* **13.6.2**.

For the use of the accusative in time expressions, *see* **21.1.3**.

3.3 ## The genitive

3.3.1 ## The use of the genitive in constructions involving two nouns

The genitive is used in a wide range of constructions involving two nouns that are placed adjacent to each other. Most of these correspond to constructions where English would use the preposition 'of' or the possessive form in -'s (-s'):

The genitive indicates *possession* in the strict sense of the word:

маши́на Та́ни	Tania's car
рюкза́к сы́на	(my) son's rucksack
иму́щество олига́рхов	the oligarchs' property
да́ча друзе́й	(our) friends' dacha

Мы договори́лись встре́титься через неде́лю на кварти́ре *его́ бра́та*.
We agreed to meet a week later in his brother's flat.

Вообще́-то, э́то моби́льник *жены́*; свой я забы́л до́ма.
This is really my wife's mobile; I've left mine at home.

For more on the absence of the possessive pronoun in constructions involving close relatives and the like, *see* **7.2.4**.

The genitive is also used to indicate *relationships between people*:

подру́га до́чери	(our) daughter's friend
учи́тель сы́на	(our) son's teacher
помо́щник президе́нта	the president's assistant

В ру́сском языке́ англи́йскому 'brother-in-law' соотве́тствуют три сло́ва: зять – э́то муж *сестры́*, шу́рин – э́то брат *жены́*, а де́верь – э́то брат *му́жа*.
Russian has three words that correspond to English 'brother-in-law': **ziat'** means 'the husband of one's sister', **shurin**, 'the brother of one's wife' and **dever'**, 'the brother of one's husband'.

The genitive is used in constructions indicating functions, positions and titles:

Глава́ прави́тельства	the head of the government
Геро́й Росси́и	Hero of Russia (an official title)
води́тель тролле́йбуса	trolleybus driver
нача́льник отде́ла	head of a department
чемпио́н ми́ра	world champion

Л.А. Верби́цкая – ре́ктор *Са́нкт-Петербу́ргского университе́та* и президе́нт *Росси́йского о́бщества* преподава́телей ру́сского языка́ и литерату́ры.
L.A. Verbitskaia is the Rector of St Petersburg University and President of the Russian Society of Russian Language and Literature Teachers.

The genitive is also used in constructions indicating the part of a whole:

кусо́к пирога́	a piece of the pie
часть кла́сса	part of the class
оста́тки обе́да	the leftovers from the dinner
коне́ц фи́льма	the end of the film

Они́ купи́ли себе́ кварти́ру в о́чень прести́жном райо́не *Москвы́*.
They have bought themselves a flat in a very prestigious area of Moscow.

In constructions containing two nouns the genitive can indicate (a) the *performer* of an action:

ле́кция профе́ссора	the professor's lecture
вопро́сы студе́нтов	the students' questions
колеба́ния ма́ятника	the swing of the pendulum
фотогра́фия до́чери	the daughter's photograph
	[i.e. one that she has taken]

Изверже́ние *вулка́на* заста́ло жи́телей доли́ны враспло́х.
The eruption of the volcano caught the valley dwellers unawares.

А вот э́та фотогра́фия *до́чери* получи́ла приз на ко́нкурсе.
And that photograph taken by our daughter won a prize at the competition.

(b) the *object* of an action:

чте́ние стихо́в	the reading of poetry
ограбле́ние ба́нка	a bank robbery
приготовле́ние у́жина	making supper
фотогра́фия до́чери	a photograph of (our) daughter [i.e. one that depicts her]

Укрепле́ние *ку́рса* рубля́ – одна́ из гла́вных зада́ч Центроба́нка.
Strengthening the exchange rate of the rouble is one of the main tasks of the Central Bank.

Фотогра́фию *до́чери* он пове́сил у себя́ в каю́те.
He put up a photograph of his daughter in his cabin.

3.3.2 The use of the genitive in quantity expressions

The *genitive* is used in constructions indicating the *quantity* of a particular substance:

Я купи́л две буха́нки *хле́ба*, литр *молока́*, па́чку *ма́сла*, ба́нку *майоне́за*, пучо́к *петру́шки*, килогра́мм *мя́са* и две́сти грамм *колба́сы*.
I've bought two loaves of bread, a litre of milk, a packet of butter, a jar of mayonnaise, a bunch of parsley, a kilo of meat and 200 grams of salami.

Он вдруг почу́вствовал, что ему́ ну́жен глото́к *све́жего во́здуха*.
He suddenly felt that he needed a breath of fresh air.

The genitive is also used in *partitive* constructions, that is, when it indicates an unspecified quantity of a substance (i.e. where English uses, for example, 'some'):

Спаси́бо, я пи́ва не пью, а вот *ча́ю* вы́пью с удово́льствием, е́сли дади́те.
No thank you, I don't drink beer, but I would like some tea, if you're offering it.

Тебе́ *де́нег* на доро́гу дать, или не на́до?
Do you want me to give you some money for the journey, or are you all right?

For the use of the genitive after certain numerals and in other quantity expressions, *see* **8.2** and **8.6.3**

3.3.3 The use of the genitive in negative constructions

The *genitive* is used with *negative* forms of the verb **быть** (and other verbs with a related meaning) to indicate absence or non-existence:

Президе́нта сейча́с нет в Москве́: он отдыха́ет в Со́чи.
The President is not in Moscow at the moment; he's on holiday in Sochi.

Таки́х лека́рств про́сто не существу́ет.
That kind of medicine simply doesn't exist.

For more on the form **нет**, *see* **4.8**.

For more on the use of the genitive to indicate absence or non-existence, *see* **15.1.2**.

The genitive is also used sometimes instead of the accusative to indicate the *direct object* of a *negated verb*:

> **Обы́чно она́ не де́лает *оши́бок*, но в э́том дикта́нте их це́лых пять.**
> She doesn't usually make mistakes, but there are no fewer than five in this dictation.

> **Спаси́бо, я *пи́ва* не пью, а вот ча́ю вы́пью с удово́льствием, е́сли дади́те.**
> No thank you, I don't drink beer, but I would like some tea, if you're offering it.

For more on the use of the accusative and the genitive to indicate the direct object of a negated verb, *see* **15.5**.

3.3.4 | Verbs that take an object in the genitive

The following verbs are normally used with an object in the genitive.

NOTE: In the following and in subsequent lists verbs will normally be given in pairs separated by a slash (/). In such cases the verb to the left of the slash is imperfective and the verb to the right is perfective. Verbs separated by a comma are alternative forms. For an explanation of imperfective and perfective verbs, *see* **4.2**.

боя́ться	to fear, be frightened
держа́ться	to keep to
добива́ться/доби́ться	to strive for, to attain
достига́ть/дости́гнуть, дости́чь	to achieve
жела́ть/пожела́ть	to wish, to desire
избега́ть/избежа́ть, избе́гнуть	to avoid
лиша́ться/лиши́ться	to be deprived of, to lose
каса́ться/косну́ться	to touch, to concern
ослу́шиваться/ослу́шаться	to disobey
приде́рживаться	to hold to, to keep to
слу́шаться/послу́шаться	to obey

> **Я не люблю́ находи́ться на у́лице по́здно ве́чером: глу́по, но *бою́сь темноты́*.**
> I don't like to be out in the streets late at night, it's stupid, but I'm afraid of the dark.

> **На про́шлой неде́ле це́ны на нефть *дости́гли истори́ческого ма́ксимума*.**
> Last week oil prices reached an all-time high.

> **Жела́ю вам *кре́пкого здоро́вья*, *успе́хов* в рабо́те и *сча́стья* в ли́чной жи́зни.**
> I wish you good health, success in your work and happiness in your personal life.

> **Что *каса́ется ва́шего вопро́са*, то обеща́ю вам, что он не оста́нется без отве́та.**
> As far as your question is concerned, I promise you that it will not remain unanswered.

Спуска́ясь на эскала́торе, *держи́тесь пра́вой стороны́.*
Keep to the right when coming down the escalator.

In some salutations that are in the genitive case the verb **жела́ю** 'I wish' is understood:

всего́ до́брого, всего́ хоро́шего
good-bye, all the best

до́брого вре́мени су́ток
good whatever time of day it is (a semi-humorous greeting frequently used in e-mails and on the Internet)

споко́йной но́чи
good night

NOTE | In more informal language the verbs **боя́ться** and **(по)слу́шаться** can sometimes be found with an object in the *accusative*, especially if the object is *animate* and/or a *proper name*.

Че́стно говоря́, мы все бои́мся на́шу но́вую нача́льницу.
To be honest, we're all frightened of our new boss.

The title of Edward Albee's play *Who's Afraid of Virginia Woolf?* can be translated either as **«Кто бои́тся Вирджи́нии Вулф»** (genitive) or as **«Кто бои́тся Вирджи́нию Вулф»** (accusative).

3.3.5 Verbs that can take an object either in the accusative or in the genitive

The following verbs can be used with an object either in the *accusative* or in the *genitive*:

ждать   to wait (for)
ожида́ть   to wait for, to expect

With these verbs the accusative tends to be used if the object is *definite* (and especially if the object is *animate*), while the genitive tends to be used if the object is *indefinite*:

Ждём пи́сем **от тех, кто нужда́ется в на́шей по́мощи.**
We await letters from those who need our help.

Обеща́ли присла́ть письмо́ с приглаше́нием, и тепе́рь *жду э́то письмо́* **с больши́м нетерпе́нием.**
They promised to send a letter with an invitation, and now I'm desperately waiting for that letter to arrive.

—**Почему́ не е́дем?**
—*Ждём Ва́ню,* **он пошёл покупа́ть минера́лку.**
—Why don't we go?
—We're waiting for Vania, he's gone off to buy some mineral water.

For more on the formation **минера́лка,** *see* **10.1.11.**

проси́ть/попроси́ть   to ask for

Here, if the object is the *item* asked for, it tends to be in the *genitive* when it is abstract or indefinite; otherwise, it is mostly in the *accusative*. If, however, the object is the *person* to whom the request is made, it is in the *accusative* provided that there is no other object; if there is another object, the person asked is indicated using the *preposition* **y** (+ gen.):

> **Прошу́ проще́ния**: я был непра́в.
> I apologise; I was wrong.

> **Я попроси́л у него́ видеока́меру** на́ день; ты представля́ешь, он отказа́л.
> I asked to borrow his video-camera for a day, and can you imagine? He refused.

> **Он попроси́л жену́** перезвони́ть ему́ через час.
> He asked his wife to phone him back in an hour.

> **сто́ить**
> to cost

The accusative is used if the object is a sum of money, but in other contexts the genitive is used:

> **Э́тот га́лстук сто́ит *ты́сячу* рубле́й.**
> This tie costs 1,000 roubles.

> **Чемпио́нство сто́ило ему́ *сло́манного ребра́*.**
> Winning the championship cost him a broken rib.

> **иска́ть**
> to look for

> **хоте́ть/захоте́ть**
> to want

> **тре́бовать/потре́бовать**
> to demand

With these verbs the object is usually in the accusative, but the genitive is sometimes used if the object is *general and abstract*:

> ***Что*** ты хо́чешь – чай или ко́фе?
> What do you want – tea or coffee?

> Ну, ***чего́*** же ты хо́чешь от жи́зни?
> Well, then, what do you want from life?

> У нас не рабо́тал душ, так что потре́бовали *друго́й но́мер*.
> The shower wasn't working where we were, so we demanded a different room.

> Мы потре́бовали *объясне́ний*.
> We demanded explanations.

3.4 The dative

3.4.1 The use of the dative for the indirect object

The *dative* is used for the *indirect object* of a verb. This is the recipient of something that is given or the person to whom something is communicated in one form or another:

> Ка́ждый ме́сяц я даю́ *свое́й бы́вшей жене́* пять ты́сяч рубле́й.
> Every month I give my former wife 5,000 roubles.

Передайте привет *сестре́.*
Pass on my regards to your sister.

Я пишу́ *бабушке* **неча́сто, приме́рно три ра́за в год.**
I don't write to my grandmother often, about three times a year.

Президе́нт сообщи́л *собра́вшимся журнали́стам* **о том, что он не наме́рен баллоти́роваться на тре́тий срок.**
The President told the assembled jounalists that he had no intention of standing for a third term.

Мы посла́ли *всем на́шим чита́телям* **анке́ту по электро́нной по́чте в фо́рме вложе́ния.**
We've sent all our readers a questionnaire in the form of an e-mail attachment.

The dative is also used to indicate the person to whom permission is given or refused:

Вла́сти разреши́ли *организа́торам* **провести́ свою́ а́кцию то́лько на окра́ине го́рода.**
The authorities allowed the organisers to hold their event, but only on the outskirts of the city.

Пассажи́рам **запрещено́ проноси́ть в сало́н самолёта жи́дкости и ре́жущие предме́ты.**
Passengers are forbidden from carrying liquids and sharp objects onto the plane.

The use of the dative to indicate the logical subject of an infinitive

The *infinitive*, being by definition a *non-finite* form of the verb, never occurs with a *subject* in the *nominative*. Instead, in sentences where the *main verb* is an *infinitive*, any logical subject is in the *dative*.

For more on the infinitive, *see* **4.1**.

Тебе́ **бы** *отдохну́ть* **как сле́дует!**
You should get a proper rest!

У университе́та не хвата́ет общежи́тий, и *иногоро́дним студе́нтам* **не́где** *жить.* **Что** *бе́дному студе́нту* **де́лать в таки́х обстоя́тельствах?**
The university does not have enough hostel accommodation and students from out of town have nowhere to live. What is a poor student to do in such circumstances?

For more on the constructions used in these examples, *see* **15.5** and **18.4**.

The use of the dative in impersonal constructions

The *dative* is used to indicate the main participant in a wide range of *impersonal* constructions. In such constructions the verb (if there is one) is the *third person singular* (present and future tenses) or in the *neuter singular* (past tense); there is no subject in the nominative.

For more on these verb forms, *see* **4.3.1** and **4.5.1**.

For more on impersonal constructions, *see* **11.2.2**.

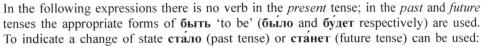

In the following expressions there is no verb in the *present* tense; in the *past* and *future* tenses the appropriate forms of **быть** 'to be' (**бы́ло** and **бу́дет** respectively) are used. To indicate a change of state **ста́ло** (past tense) or **ста́нет** (future tense) can be used:

мне хо́лодно	I am cold
мне тепло́	I am warm
мне жа́рко	I am hot
мне лу́чше	I feel better, it's better for me
мне ху́же	I feel worse, it's worse for me
мне ве́село	I feel cheerful
мне гру́стно	I feel sad
мне интере́сно	it's interesting for me
мне ску́чно	I am bored
мне удо́бно	I feel comfortable
мне неудо́бно	I feel uncomfortable/awkward/embarrassed
мне жаль	I feel sorry (for)
мне жа́лко	I feel sorry (for), I begrudge
мне сты́дно	I feel ashamed
мне всё равно́	I couldn't care less, it's all the same to me
мне безразли́чно	it's all the same to me, it's a matter of indifference
мне на́до	I have to, I must
мне ну́жно	I have to, I must
мне необходи́мо	I have to, I cannot avoid (doing)

На про́шлой неде́ле *всем москвича́м бы́ло хо́лодно*: сли́шком ра́но отключи́ли отопле́ние в э́том году́.
Last week all the inhabitants of Moscow were feeling cold: the (district) heating was switched off too early this year.

К ве́черу *больно́му ста́ло лу́чше*: он уже́ не ка́шлял, и температу́ра спа́ла.
By evening the patient started to feel better; he was no longer coughing and his temperature had gone down.

Мне, как че́стному челове́ку, сты́дно за госуда́рство, где происхо́дят таки́е ве́щи.
As an honest man I feel ashamed on behalf of a state where such things happen.

Де́вочке бы́ло *жаль* ко́шку, но она́ понима́ла, что котя́т на́до бу́дет разда́ть.
The girl felt sorry for her cat, but she understood that the kittens would have to be given away.

Ты пойми́, *мне не жа́лко де́нег*, но я зна́ю, к чему́ э́то приведёт.
It's not that I begrudge the money, you understand, but I know what it will lead to.

NOTE When **жаль** and the more informal **жа́лко** mean 'to feel sorry for', they are used with an object in the *accusative*. When **жа́лко** means 'to begrudge', it is used with an object either in the *genitive* or in the *accusative*.

For more on **мне на́до** and **мне ну́жно**, *see* **18.1.1**.

The following verbs are *impersonal*:

> везти́/повезти́: мне везёт
> I am lucky

> приходи́ться/прийти́сь: мне прихо́дится
> I have to (by force of circumstances)

> хоте́ться/захоте́ться: мне хо́чется
> I feel like, I would like

> спа́ться: мне не спи́тся
> I can't sleep

> *На́шей кома́нде повезло́*: нам доста́лся сла́бый сопе́рник.
> Our team was lucky: we were drawn against a weak opponent.

> Из-за нелётной пого́ды *Аэрофло́ту пришло́сь* отмени́ть бо́лее
> пяти́десяти ре́йсов.
> Because of the bad weather Aeroflot had to cancel over fifty flights.

> *Ка́ждой же́нщине хо́чется*, чтобы её счита́ли осо́бенной.
> Every woman would like to be considered special.

NOTE | The verb pair **везти́/повезти́** is *impersonal* only in this meaning; when it means 'to convey (by transport)', it is used in normal *personal* constructions.

For more on the use of **везти́/повезти́**, *see* **22.1**.

The following verbs can be used in either *impersonal* or *personal* constructions:

каза́ться/показа́ться: мне ка́жется	I think
надоеда́ть/надое́сть: мне надое́ло	I'm fed up (of)
нра́виться/понра́виться: мне нра́вится	I like
сни́ться/присни́ться: мне присни́лось	I dreamt
удава́ться/уда́ться: мне удаётся	I succeed (in doing something)

Examples of *impersonal* constructions:

> *Нам ка́жется*, что *на́шим зри́телям надое́ло* ви́деть одни́ и те же ли́ца,
> слы́шать одни́ и те же шу́тки.
> We think that our viewers are fed up of seeing the same faces and hearing the
> same jokes all the time.

> *Президе́нту не нра́вится*, когда́ ему́ задаю́т вопро́сы о ситуа́ции в Чечне́.
> The President doesn't like being asked questions about the situation in Chechnya.

> *Мне присни́лось*, бу́дто ты ста́ла у нас пе́рвой же́нщиной-президе́нтом.
> I dreamt you became our first woman president.

> *Сестре́ удало́сь* найти́ просто́рную кварти́ру в са́мом це́нтре го́рода.
> My sister has succeeded in finding a spacious flat in the very centre of the city.

Examples of *personal* constructions:

> *Тако́й исхо́д собы́тий каза́лся большинству́* коммента́торов
> маловероя́тным.
> Most commentators thought that this development of events was unlikely.

Тури́стам надое́ли бесконе́чные дожди́, и мно́гие ста́ли уезжа́ть домо́й
до сро́ка.
The tourists had got fed up of the ceaseless rain, and many decided to go home
ahead of schedule.

Мои́ фи́льмы нра́вятся не всем зри́телям.
Not all audiences like my films.

Вчера́ мне присни́лся стра́шный сон.
I had a terrible dream last night.

Пе́рвые щи, кото́рые удаю́тся молодо́му по́вару, всегда́ са́мые вку́сные.
The first *shchi* that a young cook makes successfully is always the tastiest.

For an explanation of *shchi*, see **2.1.3**.

3.4.4 Verbs that take an object in the dative

The following verbs are used with an *object* in the *dative* case:

ве́рить/пове́рить	to believe (someone or something)
вреди́ть/навреди́ть	to harm
доверя́ть/дове́рить	to trust
изменя́ть/измени́ть	to betray
меша́ть/помеша́ть	to disturb, to hinder
обуча́ться/обучи́ться	to learn, to study
помога́ть/помо́чь	to help
предше́ствовать	to precede
принадлежа́ть	to belong
равня́ться	to be equal to (*see* **19.1.2**)
ра́доваться/обра́доваться	to be pleased (about something)
соболе́зновать	to commiserate with
соде́йствовать	to further
соотве́тствовать	to correspond to
сопротивля́ться	to resist, to oppose
сочу́вствовать	to sympathise (with)
угожда́ть/угоди́ть	to please, to oblige
удивля́ться/удиви́ться	to be surprised (at *or* by something)
учи́ться/научи́ться	to learn

А ты ве́ришь его́ расска́зам о том, как он обща́лся с инопланетя́нами?
Do you believe his stories about talking to aliens from another planet?

У нас по э́тому вопро́су о́чень твёрдая пози́ция, и изменя́ть свои́м
при́нципам мы не наме́рены.
We have adopted a very firm line on this question and we do not intend to
betray our principles.

На пе́рвом ку́рсе все студе́нты обуча́ются осно́вам информа́тики.
In the first year all students study basic IT.

Э́ти стари́нные кни́ги принадлежа́ли моему́ де́душке.
These old books belonged to my grandfather.

Роди́тели помога́ли молодожёнам как могли́.
Their parents helped the young (married) couple as best they could.

(i) When **ве́рить/пове́рить** means 'to believe in something or someone', it is followed by the preposition **в** (+ acc.).

> **Он никогда́ не** *ве́рил в Бо́га* **и остава́лся убеждённым атеи́стом до конца́ свои́х дней.**
> He never believed in God and remained a convinced atheist to the end of his days.

(ii) When **доверя́ть/дове́рить** means 'to entrust something into someone's care', the thing entrusted is a *direct object* in the *accusative* case, while the person to whom it is entrusted is an *indirect object* in the dative.

> **Я про́сто не зна́ю, могу́ ли я** *дове́рить маши́ну сы́ну.*
> I simply don't know if I can trust my son with my car.

(iii) When **изменя́ть/измени́ть** means 'to change', it is followed by a *direct object* in the *accusative.*

> **С года́ми она́** *измени́ла свои́ взгля́ды* **на воспита́ние дете́й.**
> Over the years she has changed her views on how to bring up children.

(iv) When **принадлежа́ть** means 'to belong to a category of a group' it is followed by the preposition **к** (+ dat.).

> **И́менно э́ти лю́ди** *принадлежа́т к гру́ппе* **ри́ска.**
> It is precisely these people who belong to the group most at risk.

With the verbs **учи́ть/научи́ть** and **обуча́ть/обучи́ть** 'to teach, to instruct' the person being instructed is indicated using the accusative case, while the subject being taught is indicated using the dative:

> **По-мо́ему, хорошо́, что** *на́ших дете́й у́чат осно́вам* **би́знеса.**
> In my opinion it's a good thing that our children are taught the rudiments of business.

3.5 The instrumental

3.5.1 The use of the instrumental to indicate the instrument or means with which an action is carried out or accomplished

The *instrumental* is used to indicate the *instrument* with which an action is carried out or the *means* by which an action is accomplished:

> **На вся́кий слу́чай запо́лните анке́ту** *карандашо́м*: **ле́гче бу́дет испра́вить оши́бки.**
> To be on the safe side, fill in the form in pencil; it will be easier to correct any mistakes.

> **Серьёзные поку́пки она́ предпочита́ла опла́чивать** *креди́тной ка́рточкой.*
> She preferred to pay for her more serious purchases with a credit card.

> **Посу́ду из-под молока́ сле́дует мыть снача́ла** *холо́дной*, **а зате́м** *горя́чей водо́й.*
> Crockery that has had milk in it should be washed in cold water first and then in hot water.

> *Ни угро́зами, ни угово́рами* **подейство́вать на него́ невозмо́жно.**
> It's impossible to move him with either threats or persuasion.

3.5.2 **The use of the instrumental to indicate the agent in a passive construction**

The *instrumental* is used to indicate the *agent* in a *passive* construction (that is, the person, or less often, the object responsible for carrying out the action indicated by the passive verb or participle).

For more on passive verbs and participles, *see* **4.14** and **23.1.3**:

> **Э́та кни́га была́ напи́сана *мои́м де́душкой*.**
> This book was written by my grandfather.

> **Э́то не помеша́ло ей поби́ть реко́рд, устано́вленный её**
> ***соотéчественницей* де́сять лет наза́д.**
> This did not stop her from breaking the record established by her compatriot ten years ago.

3.5.3 **The use of the instrumental to indicate the complement**

The *instrumental* is very frequently used to indicate the *complement* of the verb **быть**, especially if the complement is a *noun*:

> **Когда́ я *был студе́нтом*, у меня́ не бы́ло де́нег, чтобы регуля́рно ходи́ть**
> **в теа́тр.**
> When I was a student, I didn't have the money to go to the theatre regularly.

> **Его́ происхожде́ние не име́ет значе́ния. Гла́вное, чтобы он был *че́стным***
> ***челове́ком*.**
> His origins are irrelevant. The main thing is that he should be an honest man.

For more on the complement of **быть**, *see* **3.1** and **14.1**.

In addition, the instrumental is normally used to indicate the complement of the following verbs:

вы́глядеть	to look
де́латься/сде́латься	to become
каза́ться/показа́ться	to seem
ока́зываться/оказа́ться	to (turn out to) be
остава́ться/оста́ться	to remain
станови́ться/стать	to become, to be
явля́ться	to be

> **В э́той шля́пе я *вы́гляжу по́лным идио́том*.**
> I look (like) a total idiot in this hat.

> **Его́ назначе́ние *оказа́лось* для всех нас *больши́м сюрпри́зом*.**
> His appointment came as a surprise to everyone.

> ***Остаётся зага́дкой*, как не́которым се́мьям удаётся своди́ть концы́ с**
> **конца́ми.**
> It remains a mystery how some families make ends meet.

> **Он *явля́ется Но́белевским лауреа́том* в о́бласти медици́ны.**
> He's a Nobel prize-winner for medicine.

For more on verbs that can correspond to English 'to be', *see* **14.1.5**.

3.5.4 The use of the instrumental to indicate a predicate with a transitive verb

There are in Russian a number of *transitive* verbs, corresponding to English 'to call', 'to consider', 'to elect as', 'to appoint (as)' and other verbs with a similar meaning which are used with the *instrumental*; the form in the instrumental indicates what the *direct object* is called, considered to be, elected or appointed as, and so on. Verbs in this category include the following:

выбира́ть/вы́брать	to choose, to elect
избира́ть/избра́ть	to elect (to high office)
назнача́ть/назна́чить	to appoint
называ́ть/назва́ть	to call, to name
счита́ть/счесть	to consider
чу́вствовать себя́/почу́вствовать себя́	to feel (ill, etc.)

В апре́ле 1995 го́да Миро́нова *избра́ли пе́рвым замести́телем* **председа́теля законода́тельного собра́ния Санкт-Петербу́рга.**
In April 1995 Mironov was elected first deputy chairman of the St Petersburg city council.

В Росси́и по́льзователи Интерне́та *называ́ют* **си́мвол «@»** *«соба́кой».*
In Russia, Internet users call the @ symbol a 'dog'.

Ско́лько на́до зараба́тывать, что́бы *чу́вствовать себя́ счастли́вым?*
How much do you need to earn in order to feel happy?

NOTES

(i) The verbs называ́ть and счита́ть are often used in the *imperfective passive* forms называ́ться and счита́ться respectively.

Он *счита́ется веду́щим специали́стом* **в э́той о́бласти.**
He is considered to be a leading specialist in this area.

For more on passive verbs, *see* **4.14**.

(ii) The verbs называ́ть and называ́ться are often used with a *predicate* in the nominative, especially if the predicate is a proper name and/or it appears in inverted commas:

Он когда́-то был веду́щим о́чень популя́рной програ́ммы, кото́рая *называ́лась* *«Взгляд».*
He was once a presenter on a very popular (televison) programme called *Vzgliad (View)*.

3.5.5 The use of the instrumental to indicate state or capacity

The instrumental is often used to indicate the *state* or *capacity* in which someone carries out a particular action:

Тогда́ он рабо́тал *гла́вным инжене́ром* **на одно́м из кру́пных заво́дов Петербу́рга.**
At that time he was working as the chief engineer of a large factory in St Petersburg.

В да́нном слу́чае на́ша о́бласть мо́жет служи́ть *приме́ром* **для всей Росси́и.**
In this case our region can serve as an example for the whole of Russia.

Чтóбы бежáть из осаждённого гóрода, емý пришлóсь переодéться *жéнщиной.*
The only way he could escape from the besieged city was to dress up as a woman.

Похóже, что он опя́ть вы́шел *сухи́м* **из воды́.**
It looks as if he's got off scot-free again (*literally*, 'as if he's come out of the water dry').

Онá вернýлась из óтпуска *свéжей и отдохнýвшей.*
She returned from her holidays fresh and relaxed.

The use of the instrumental in adverbial functions

The instrumental is used in a variety of adverbial constructions, indicating, for example, the manner in which, the place where or the time when something is done:

Развернýться в э́том дворé бы́ло невозмóжно, и пришлóсь выезжáть *зáдним хóдом.*
It was impossible to turn round in the yard and we had to drive out backwards.

Я отпрáвлю вам э́тот журнáл *заказнóй бандерóлью.*
I'll send you the magazine as a registered package.

Нóвое прави́тельство *пéрвым дéлом* **займётся бюджéтом на слéдующий год.**
The first task of the new government will be to sort out the budget for next year (*literally*, '… will as its first task …'].

В Прáге онá люби́ла *часáми* **броди́ть** *ýлочками* **Стáрого гóрода.**
When she was in Prague she could spend hours wandering through the narrow streets of the old town.

For more on the use of the instrumental in time expressions, *see* **21.1.1**.

Verbs that take an object in the instrumental

A large number of verbs are used with an object in the *instrumental*; for convenience, these can be divided into groups according their meaning.

(a) Verbs indicating *activities* or *interests*:

занимáться/заня́ться
to occupy oneself with

интересовáться/заинтересовáться
to be interested in

увлекáться/увлéчься
to be keen on, to be carried away by

К сожалéнию, нáши дéти всё мéньше *занимáются спóртом.*
Unfortunately, our children do less and less sport.

(b) Verbs referring to *control*, *use* and *ownership*:

владéть	to own
злоупотребля́ть/злоупотреби́ть	to abuse, to misuse
пóльзоваться/воспóльзоваться	to use, to take advantage of

пра́вить	to rule
распола́гать	to have at one's disposal
руководи́ть	to be in charge of, to manage
управля́ть	to manage, to run

Здесь запрещено́ *по́льзоваться мобильны́ми телефо́нами*.
It's forbidden to use mobile phones here.

Мы не *располага́ем информа́цией* о том, кто владе́л *э́той карти́ной* по́сле войны́.
We have no information about who owned this picture after the war.

(c) Verbs expressing an *attitude*, especially one of *admiration* or *scorn*:

бре́зговать/побре́зговать	to be fastidious *or* squeamish about
восхища́ться/восхити́ться	to admire (e.g. a person)
горди́ться	to be proud of
любова́ться	to admire (e.g. a view)
наслажда́ться	to enjoy, to delight in
пренебрега́ть/пренебре́чь	to scorn, to disregard, to neglect

Мы все *восхища́емся* его *достиже́ниями*.
We all admire his achievements.

Не сто́ит *пренебрега́ть здоро́вьем*.
It's not worth neglecting your health.

(d) Some verbs are used with an *object* in the *instrumental* when they refer to movements made by parts of the body:

кача́ть/покача́ть голово́й	to shake one's head
кива́ть/кивну́ть голово́й	to nod one's head
маха́ть/махну́ть руко́й	to wave one's hand
морга́ть/моргну́ть гла́зом	to blink, to wink
пожима́ть/пожа́ть плеча́ми	to shrug one's shoulders
то́пать нога́ми/то́пнуть ного́й	to stamp one's feet/foot

Он не отве́тил на мой вопро́с, лишь *пожа́л плеча́ми* и вы́шел из ко́мнаты.
He didn't answer my question, but merely shrugged his shoulders and left the room.

(e) Some miscellaneous verbs:

па́хнуть	to smell of
обме́ниваться/обменя́ться	to exchange
рискова́ть/рискну́ть	to risk
торгова́ть	to trade in

Не люблю́, когда́ в о́фисе *па́хнет сигаре́тами*.
I don't like it when the office smells of cigarettes.

NOTE | The verb **па́хнуть** is often used impersonally (as in the above example). For more on impersonal constructions, *see* **11.2.2**.

3.6 The prepositional

The *prepositional* case is used only after *prepositions*. A list of the prepositions that are used with the prepositional case is given in **9.2.6**.

4

Verbs

4.0 ## Introduction

The Russian *verb* is a grammatically complex part of speech: if the most complex English verb ('to be') has eight separate forms ('am', 'is', 'are', 'was', 'were', 'be', 'being', 'been'), most Russian verbs have fifty or more separate forms. Moreover, the Russian verb contains a large number of categories, many of which are either unimportant or do not exist at all in English.

Finite and *non-finite verbs*. *Non-finite* verbs are those that are incapable of being combined with a *grammatical subject*. In Russian, there are three non-finite forms: the *infinitive* (**4.1**), *the gerund* (**4.11**) and the *participle* (**4.12**). All the remaining forms are *finite*.

Aspect (**4.2**) refers to the different ways in which the action or state indicated by the verb may be viewed by the speaker. The Russian verb has two aspects, *imperfective* and *perfective*.

Tense is used to situate the action or state indicated by the verb in a particular time. The Russian verb has a simple system of three tenses: *present* (**4.3**), *future* (**4.4**) and *past* (**4.5**).

Person indicates the relationship between the verb and the *grammatical subject* of the sentence. There are three persons: the *1st person* indicates or includes the speaker ('I', 'we'), the *2nd person* indicates or includes the addressee(s) ('you'); the *3rd person* indicates the person(s), object(s) or concept(s) being referred to ('he', 'she', 'it', 'they'). Since each person can be *singular* or *plural* (see **2.1**), there are six forms in all.

Mood indicates the attitude of the speaker towards the state or action. Straightforward statements or questions are in the *indicative* mood; the *imperative* (**4.9**) is used for commands or prohibitions, and the *conditional* or *subjunctive* (**4.10**) is used for hypothetical statements.

Transitive and *intransitive verbs* (**4.13.1**): a transitive verb is one that is used with a direct object in the accusative case; all other verbs are intransitive.

Reflexive verbs (**4.13.2**): although reflexive verbs do serve certain other functions as well, the main purpose of making a verb reflexive is to transform a transitive verb into one that is intransitive.

NOTE | Reflexive verbs are indicated by the suffix **-ся** (**-сь** after a vowel), which is attached to all forms of the verb.

Voice (**4.14**) is the category used to indicate the relationship of *subject* and *object* to the action or state indicated by the verb. The *active* voice is used when the subject of the verb is the performer of the action or the main participant in the state; the *passive* voice is used when the subject is on the receiving end of the action.

4.1 The infinitive

The *infinitive* is the form by which a verb is listed in dictionaries. It most frequently ends in **-ть**:

чита́ть	to read
писа́ть	to write
говори́ть	to say, to speak

A few verbs have an infinitive ending in **-ти́** (with stress always on the ending), for example:

грести́	to row (i.e. a boat)
вести́	to (be) lead(ing)
везти́	to (be) convey(ing)
изобрести́	to invent

A small number of verbs have an infinitive ending in **-чь**, for example:

мочь	to be able
печь	to bake

The ending of the infinitive never changes.

For more on the meaning of **вести́, нести́, идти́** (and other verbs indicating movement), *see* **22.1**.

As suggested in the glosses above, the *infinitive* of the Russian verb corresponds approximately to the 'to' form of the English verb. It is most often used together with another verb, as in the following examples:

Я не *хоте́л* вас *оби́деть*.
I didn't want to offend you.

Вы *мо́жете приходи́ть* в любо́е вре́мя.
You can come any time you like.

Он не *успе́л предупреди́ть* меня́.
He didn't have time to warn me.

On its own the infinitive can sometimes be used to express *commands* and *prohibitions*; *see* **18.2.2**.

4.2 Aspects of the verb

4.2.1 Imperfective and perfective aspects

Although it is arguable that *aspects* are a feature of the English verb (e.g. the difference between 'I do' and 'I am doing'), the Russian verbal aspect differs greatly from the English in both form and function.

The Russian verb system has two aspects: *imperfective* and *perfective*. As may be imagined, each aspect covers a wide range of functions, but in general terms it may be stated that the perfective aspect is used when an action or state is considered from the point of view of either one (beginning or end) or both of its boundaries, while the imperfective is used in all other circumstances (if there is a 'default' aspect in Russian, it is the imperfective).

Every Russian verb belongs to one or the other of these aspects, which means that one English verb will normally correspond to a pair of verbs in Russian, one of which is imperfective and the other perfective:

to give	дава́ть (imperfective)	дать (perfective)
to read	чита́ть (imperfective)	прочита́ть (perfective)
to write	писа́ть (imperfective)	написа́ть (perfective)

In Russian dictionaries the aspect of each verb is indicated, usually by the abbreviations **нсв** (**несоверше́нный** = imperfective) and **св** (**соверше́нный** = perfective). For the remainder of this chapter and in the following chapter the aspect of all verbs used in examples will be indicated by these same abbreviations.

This section is concerned with the *formation* of *aspect pairs*; the use of the two aspects will be examined in detail in **Chapter 5**.

As the examples listed above suggest, in most pairs of verbs the imperfective and perfective partners are closely related, with the relationship normally conforming to one of three basic patterns.

4.2.2 Imperfective and perfective verbs are both unprefixed

In the following examples both the *imperfective* and the *perfective* verb are *unprefixed*:

броса́ть (нсв)	бро́сить (св)	to throw
дава́ть (нсв)	дать (св)	to give
конча́ть (нсв)	ко́нчить (св)	to finish
пуска́ть (нсв)	пусти́ть (св)	to let
толка́ть (нсв)	толкну́ть (св)	to push

4.2.3 The imperfective is unprefixed and the perfective verb is prefixed

In the following examples the *imperfective* verb has no prefix, but the *perfective* is *prefixed*. It will be seen from the list that follows that a number of different prefixes can be used to form the perfective partner of an unprefixed imperfective. There is no easy way of predicting which prefix will be found with any given verb, although the most common prefixes used in this way are **по-**, **с-** and **за-**:

ве́рить (нсв)	пове́рить (св)	to believe
де́лать (нсв)	сде́лать (св)	to do
есть (нсв)	съесть (св)	to eat
жела́ть (нсв)	пожела́ть (св)	to wish
красть (нсв)	укра́сть (св)	to steal
ночева́ть (нсв)	переночева́ть (св)	to spend the night
печь (нсв)	испе́чь (св)	to bake

писа́ть (нсв)	написа́ть (св)	to write
пить (нсв)	вы́пить (св)	to drink
ста́вить (нсв)	поста́вить (св)	to put (standing)
стро́ить (нсв)	постро́ить (св)	to build
хоте́ть (нсв)	захоте́ть (св)	to want
чита́ть (нсв)	прочита́ть (св)	to read

The following two verbs deviate from this pattern:

па́дать (нсв)	упа́сть (св)	to fall

The perfective verb also has a change of suffix:

покупа́ть (нсв)	купи́ть (св)	to buy

Here, uniquely, the imperfective verb has a prefix which is lost in the perfective.

4.2.4 Both imperfective and perfective verbs have the same prefix

In the following examples both *imperfective* and *perfective* verbs have the same prefix:

запи́сывать (нсв)	записа́ть (св)	to record, to write down
подпи́сывать (нсв)	подписа́ть (св)	to sign
припи́сывать (нсв)	приписа́ть (св)	to ascribe
спи́сывать (нсв)	списа́ть (св)	to write off, to copy
доверя́ть (нсв)	дове́рить (св)	to trust
распека́ть (нсв)	распе́чь (св)	to tear a strip off someone
допива́ть (нсв)	допи́ть (св)	to drink something up
спра́шивать (нсв)	спроси́ть (св)	to ask (about something)
представля́ть (нсв)	предста́вить (св)	to present, to introduce
устра́ивать (нсв)	устро́ить (св)	to arrange

In the above examples, the *perfective* partner is formed by adding a *prefix* directly to the *unprefixed* verb; unlike the prefixes used to form the perfective in the examples in **4.2.3**, these prefixes also change the meaning of the verb. The *imperfective* partner is formed from the *perfective* by changing the *suffix* and sometimes by also changing the *vowel* and/or *consonant* in the stem. Unfortunately, it is difficult to give precise rules for forming the imperfective from the perfective, but all the principal patterns are illustrated here:

выбра́сывать (нсв)	вы́бросить (св)	to throw out
продава́ть (нсв)	прода́ть (св)	to sell
допуска́ть (нсв)	допусти́ть (св)	to allow

In these examples, the *perfective* partner is formed by adding a *prefix* to the *perfective* partner of a pair of *unprefixed* verbs; here, too, there are different patterns for forming the imperfective partner:

защища́ть (нсв)	защити́ть (св)	to defend
исчеза́ть (нсв)	исче́знуть (св)	to disappear
продолжа́ть (нсв)	продо́лжить (св)	to continue
убежда́ть (нсв)	убеди́ть (св)	to convince
успева́ть (нсв)	успе́ть (св)	to have time

There are no unprefixed forms of the verbs listed in the above examples.

Note on stress: Where a prefix is added to an unprefixed verb, the stress normally remains unchanged. The exception is where a perfective verb has the prefix вы-: here the stress is on the prefix in all forms of the verb. **N.B:** *This rule applies to perfective verbs only.*

For more on verbal prefixes, *see* **10.4**.

4.2.5 Pairs of verbs where the perfective and imperfective partners are unrelated

There are a few pairs of verbs where the *perfective* and *imperfective* partners are unrelated:

брать (нсв)	взять (св)	to take
говори́ть (нсв)	сказа́ть (св)	to say (but *see* **4.2.6** below)
класть (нсв)	положи́ть (св)	to put (lying)
лови́ть (нсв)	пойма́ть (св)	to catch

4.2.6 Exceptions to the principle of 'paired' verbs

Not all verbs come in neat *imperfective/perfective* pairs.

Some *unprefixed* verbs have more than one perfective partner, the choice of which depends on the precise meaning of the verb.

The verb **бить (нсв)** has perfective partners **поби́ть** 'to beat', 'hit someone or something' and **проби́ть** 'to strike' (of a clock).

The verb **говори́ть (нсв)** has perfective partners **поговори́ть** 'to talk', 'to speak' and **сказа́ть** 'to say'.

The verb **есть (нсв)** has perfective partners **съесть** 'to eat something up' (transitive) and **пое́сть** 'to do some eating' (intransitive).

A number of imperfective verbs have no commonly used perfective partner. These include:

выть	to howl
дружи́ть	to be friends with
знать	to know
состоя́ть	to consist of/in
сочу́вствовать	to sympathise
уча́ствовать	to take part in

Examples of perfective verbs without imperfective partners are much less common, but the following may be noted:

ри́нуться	to rush
состоя́ться	to take place (cf. **состоя́ть** above)

NOTE | The **-ся** suffix indicates that the verb is reflexive (*see* **4.13.2**).

Finally, some verbs are *bi-aspectual*, i.e. the same verb is used for both imperfective and perfective aspects; these include:

жени́ться	to get married (of a man)	испо́льзовать	to use
казни́ть	to execute	обеща́ть(ся)	to promise
организова́ть	to organise		

4.3 Present tense

4.3.1 The endings of present tense

Russian has only one *present tense*, which is formed from *imperfective* verbs only. The endings used for the present tense give information about the *person* and *number* of the subject.

The present tense of the verb де́лать 'to do':

1st person sing.	я де́лаю	I do (*or* am doing)
2nd person sing.	ты де́лаешь	you (sing.) do (*or* are doing)
3rd person sing.	он/она́/оно́ де́лает	he/she/it does (*or* is doing)
1st person pl.	мы де́лаем	we do (*or* are doing)
2nd person pl.	вы де́лаете	you (pl.) do (*or* are doing)
3rd person pl.	они́ де́лают	they do (*or* are doing)

NOTE: я де́лаю corresponds to both 'I do' and 'I am doing'.

There are two separate sets of endings for the present tense, as follows:

1	*2*
-ю/у	-ю/-у
-ешь/-ёшь	-ишь
-ет/-ёт	-ит
-ем/-ём	-им
-ете/-ёте	-ите
-ют/-ут	-ят/-ат

Verbs with the endings in column 1 are described as belonging to the *first conjugation*; verbs with the endings in column 2 are described as belonging to the *second conjugation*.

The first conjugation endings -ю, -ют are used after a vowel, the endings -у, -ут after a consonant; the endings with -e- occur when the stress is on any syllable other than the ending.

The second conjugation endings -у, -ат occur only after those consonants which, according to the spelling rules given in **1.5.2**, cannot be followed by я or ю.

NOTE There are a few first conjugation verbs where the endings -ю, -ют occur after the consonants л, н or р. *See* **4.7.1** and **4.7.8** for examples.

Examples of present tense endings

The following tables give examples of present tense endings:

First conjugation verbs

читáть (нсв) 'to read'	писáть (нсв) 'to write'
читáю	пишý
читáешь	пи́шешь
читáет	пи́шет
читáем	пи́шем
читáете	пи́шете
читáют	пи́шут

брать (нсв) 'to take'	давáть (нсв) 'to give'
берý	даю́
берёшь	даёшь
берёт	даёт
берём	даём
берёте	даёте
берýт	даю́т

пить (нсв) 'to drink'	целовáть (нсв) 'to kiss'
пью	целýю
пьёшь	целýешь
пьёт	целýет
пьём	целýем
пьёте	целýете
пьют	целýют

Second conjugation verbs

говори́ть (нсв) 'to say', 'to speak'	кричáть (нсв) 'to shout'
говорю́	кричý
говори́шь	кричи́шь
говори́т	кричи́т
говори́м	кричи́м
говори́те	кричи́те
говоря́т	кричáт

Three observations are prompted by these tables:

(1) Three *stress patterns* are found in the present tense: (a) the stress is always on the stem, e.g. **читáть**; (b) the stress is always on the ending, e.g. **говори́ть**; (c) the stress is on the ending in the 1st person singular, but on the stem in all other forms, e.g. **писáть**. All of these stress patterns can be found with verbs of either conjugation.

(2) In order to work out the full set of endings (including stress) in the present tense, it is both necessary and sufficient to know the 1st and 2nd person singular forms; all other forms can be worked out from these two endings.

(3) Although the endings themselves are regular (see **4.8** for the handful of exceptions), it is not possible to work out the present tense of a verb from the infinitive. From the point of view of the relationship between infinitive and present tense, Russian verbs fall into about twenty classes, which are described below in **4.6** and **4.7**.

4.4 Future tense

4.4.0 Introduction

The *future tense* in Russian is formed from both *imperfective* and *perfective* verbs, although the means of forming the future is different for each aspect.

4.4.1 Imperfective verbs

There is one *imperfective* verb that has a special form for the *future tense*. This is **быть** 'to be', and the future is formed by attaching present tense endings to the stem **буд-**:

бу́ду	I will be	бу́дем	we will be
бу́дешь	you will be	бу́дете	you will be
бу́дет	he/she/it will be	бу́дут	they will be

The future tense of all other imperfective verbs is formed using **бу́ду**, etc. and the infinitive:

читáть (нсв) 'to read'	говори́ть (нсв) 'to say', 'to speak'
бу́ду читáть	бу́ду говори́ть
бу́дешь читáть	бу́дешь говори́ть
бу́дет читáть	бу́дет говори́ть
бу́дем читáть	бу́дем говори́ть
бу́дете читáть	бу́дете говори́ть
бу́дут читáть	бу́дут говори́ть

4.4.2 Perfective verbs

The future tense of all *perfective* verbs is formed in exactly the same way as the present tense of *imperfective* verbs.

прочитáть (св) 'to read'	написáть (св) 'to write'
прочитáю	напишу́
прочитáешь	напи́шешь
прочитáет	напи́шет
прочитáем	напи́шем
прочитáете	напи́шете
прочитáют	напи́шут

вы́пить (св) 'to drink'	поцеловáть (св) 'to kiss'
вы́пью	поцелу́ю
вы́пьешь	поцелу́ешь
вы́пьет	поцелу́ет
вы́пьем	поцелу́ем
вы́пьете	поцелу́ете
вы́пьют	поцелу́ют

поговори́ть (св) 'to speak', 'to have a conversation'	закричáть (св) 'to shout'
поговорю́	закричу́
поговори́шь	закричи́шь
поговори́т	закричи́т
поговори́м	закричи́м
поговори́те	закричи́те
поговоря́т	закричáт

NOTE | The three observations made above at the end of section **4.3** apply equally to the *future perfective*. For this reason in sections **4.6–4.8** the term 'non-past' will be used to refer to both the present tense of imperfective verbs and the future tense of perfective verbs.

4.5 Past tense

4.5.1 The formation of the past tense

Russian has only one *past tense*, but it is formed from both *imperfective* and *perfective* verbs. The formation of the past tense is one of the simpler and more regular features of Russian grammar: for the vast majority of verbs the past tense is formed by removing the final **-ть** of the infinitive and adding the appropriate endings (**-л, -ла, -ло, -ли**) to the stem that remains.

The past tense behaves as if it were a *short form* of adjective (see **6.5**). The endings give information about the gender and number of the subject, but not about the person. This means that each verb has four endings: *masculine singular*, *feminine singular*, *neuter singular* and *plural* (remember that Russian has no gender distinctions in the plural):

Быть (нсв) 'to be':

> **Я/ты/он/Серге́й** *был* **здесь.**
> I (masc.)/you (masc. sg.)/he/Sergei was here.

> **Я/ты/она́/А́нна** *была́* **здесь.**
> I (fem.)/you (fem. sg.)/she/Anna was here.

> **Оно́/окно́** *бы́ло* **откры́то.**
> It/the window was open.

> **Мы/вы/они́/А́нна и Серге́й** *бы́ли* **здесь.**
> We/you (pl.)/Anna and Sergei were here.

For the use of the second person plural pronoun **вы** as a formal means of addressing one person, *see* **13.1**; for the use of the plural verb in such circumstances, *see* **11.2.1**.

Other examples:

Говори́ть (нсв) 'to say', 'to speak':

> **говори́л, говори́ла, говори́ло, говори́ли**

Сказа́ть (св) 'to say':

> **сказа́л, сказа́ла, сказа́ло, сказа́ли**

Писа́ть (нсв) 'to write':

> **писа́л, писа́ла, писа́ло, писа́ли**

Написа́ть (св) 'to write':

> **написа́л, написа́ла, написа́ло, написа́ли**

Дава́ть (нсв) 'to give':

> дава́л, дава́ла, дава́ло, дава́ли

Дать (св) 'to give':

> дал, дала́, да́ло́, да́ли

The past tense of verbs with a stem ending in a consonant

Some verbs form their past tense by adding the endings onto a stem that ends in a *consonant*, in which case the -л in the *masculine* is omitted.

лезть (нсв) 'to (be) climb(ing)':

> лез, ле́зла, ле́зло, ле́зли

нести́ (нсв) 'to (be) carry(ing)':

> нёс, несла́, несло́, несли́

исче́знуть (св) 'to disappear':

> исче́з, исче́зла, исче́зло, исче́зли

мочь (нсв) 'to be able':

> мог, могла́, могло́, могли́

умере́ть (св) 'to die':

> у́мер, умерла́, у́мерло, у́мерли

More detailed information on which classes of verbs form the past tense in this way is given in **4.7**.

An irregular past tense form

Only one verb has a completely *irregular past tense*:

идти́ (нсв) 'to (be) go(ing)':

> шёл, шла, шло, шли

Prefixed forms of идти́ form the *past tense* in the same way:

войти́ (св) 'to enter'

> вошёл, вошла́, вошло́, вошли́

4.6 | **The classification of verbs: productive verb classes**

4.6.0 | **Introduction**

Although there are approximately twenty classes of Russian verbs, the overwhelming majority belong to one of four *productive* classes. This term means that when new verbs are formed (other than by prefixing), they are added to one or other of these classes.

4.6.1 | **First productive class of first conjugation verbs**

This class consists of *first* conjugation verbs following one of the following patterns:

(a)   Infinitive **-ать**   Non-past **-аю, -аешь**, etc.
(b)   Infinitive **-ять**   Non-past **-яю, -яешь**, etc.
(c)   Infinitive **-еть**   Non-past **-ею, -еешь**, etc.

(a)   **де́лать** (нсв) 'to do'   **чита́ть** (нсв) 'to read'
      де́лаю   **чита́ю**
      де́лаешь   **чита́ешь**
      де́лает   **чита́ет**
      де́лаем   **чита́ем**
      де́лаете   **чита́ете**
      де́лают   **чита́ют**

(b)   **позволя́ть** (нсв) 'to permit'   (c)   **уме́ть** (нсв) 'to know how to'
      позволя́ю   **уме́ю**
      позволя́ешь   **уме́ешь**
      позволя́ет   **уме́ет**
      позволя́ем   **уме́ем**
      позволя́ете   **уме́ете**
      позволя́ют   **уме́ют**

4.6.2 | **Second productive class of first conjugation verbs**

This class is made up of *first* conjugation verbs following the pattern:

Infinitive **-овать/-евать**   Non-past **-ую, -уешь (-уёшь)/-юю, -юешь (-юёшь)**, etc.

целова́ть (нсв) 'to kiss'   **танцева́ть** (нсв) 'to dance'   **плева́ть** (нсв) 'to spit'
целу́ю   **танцу́ю**   **плюю́**
целу́ешь   **танцу́ешь**   **плюёшь**
целу́ет   **танцу́ет**   **плюёт**
целу́ем   **танцу́ем**   **плюём**
целу́ете   **танцу́ете**   **плюёте**
целу́ют   **танцу́ют**   **плюю́т**

NOTES

(i) The spelling of the various forms of **танцева́ть** is determined by the rules given in **1.5.2**.

(ii) In spite of appearances, this pattern is perfectly regular and is the one followed by the vast majority of newly formed verbs, for example:

интересова́ть (нсв) 'to interest'	**интересу́ю**	**интересу́ешь**
организова́ть (нсв/св) 'to organise'	**организу́ю**	**организу́ешь**
приватизи́ровать (нсв/св) 'to privatise'	**приватизи́рую**	**приватизи́руешь**
цити́ровать (нсв) 'to quote'	**цити́рую**	**цити́руешь**

4.6.3 **Third productive class of first conjugation verbs**

This class consists of *first* conjugation verbs following the pattern:

Infinitive **-нуть**	Non-past **-ну, -нешь/-нёшь**, etc.
кри́кнуть (св) 'to shout'	толкну́ть (св) 'to push'
кри́кну	толкну́
кри́кнешь	толкнёшь
кри́кнет	толкнёт
кри́кнем	толкнём
кри́кнете	толкнёте
кри́кнут	толкну́т

NOTES

(i) These verbs form the *past tense* from the *infinitive* in the normal way (cf. **4.7.10**):

толкну́л, толкну́ла, толкну́ло, толкну́ли

(ii) With the exception of **гну́ть (нсв)** 'to bend' (transitive), all verbs in this class are perfective.

4.6.4 **The productive class of second conjugation verbs**

The verbs in this class belong to the *second* conjugation verbs and follow the pattern:

Infinitive **-ить**	Non-past **-ю/у, -ишь**, etc.	
говори́ть (нсв)	отве́тить (св)	проси́ть (нсв)
'to speak', 'to say'	'to answer'	'to ask (someone to do something)'
говорю́	отве́чу	прошу́
говори́шь	отве́тишь	про́сишь
говори́т	отве́тит	про́сит
говори́м	отве́тим	про́сим
говори́те	отве́тите	про́сите
говоря́т	отве́тят	про́сят

In the *non-past* of many verbs of this class there is a *consonant alternation* in the *first person singular* only. The alternations are as follows:

с ~ ш, з ~ ж, т ~ ч/щ, д ~ ж, п ~ пл, б ~ бл, ф ~ фл, в ~ вл, м ~ мл.

Except for verbs with a stem ending in **-т**, these alternations are perfectly regular and consistent. The alternation **т ~ ч** is somewhat more common than the alternation **т ~ щ**; with some *prefixed perfective* verbs the appropriate alternation is indicated by the paired *imperfective*:

отве́тить (св) 'to answer' ~ отве́чу	отвеча́ть (нсв)
освети́ть (св) 'to illuminate' ~ освещу́	освеща́ть (нсв)

Examples of the other consonant alternations:

проси́ть (нсв) 'to ask (someone to do something)'	прошу́, про́сишь
сни́зить (св) 'to lower'	снижу́, сни́зишь
ходи́ть (нсв) 'to go (on foot)'	хожу́, хо́дишь
купи́ть (св) 'to buy'	куплю́, ку́пишь
люби́ть (нсв) 'to love'	люблю́, лю́бишь
графи́ть (нсв) 'to rule (paper)'	графлю́, графи́шь
лови́ть (нсв) 'to catch'	ловлю́, ло́вишь
корми́ть (нсв) 'to feed'	кормлю́, ко́рмишь

4.7 Unproductive verbs

4.7.0 Introduction

Although the overwhelming majority of Russian verbs belong to one of the four *productive* classes of verbs described in the preceding section, the unproductive classes include a large number of verbs that are in common use.

4.7.1 First unproductive class of first conjugation verbs

The verbs in this class are *first* conjugation verbs with an infinitive in **-ать** and a *consonant alternation* in the *non-past*:

писа́ть (нсв)	сказа́ть (св)	пла́кать (нсв)	сы́пать (нсв)
'to write'	'to say'	'to cry', 'to weep'	'to pour (dry goods)'
пишу́	скажу́	пла́чу	сы́плю
пи́шешь	ска́жешь	пла́чешь	сы́плешь
пи́шет	ска́жет	пла́чет	сы́плет
пи́шем	ска́жем	пла́чем	сы́плем
пи́шете	ска́жете	пла́чете	сы́плете
пи́шут	ска́жут	пла́чут	сы́плют

The consonant alternations are:

с ~ ш, з ~ ж, т ~ ч, к ~ ч, г ~ ж, х ~ ш, ск ~ щ, п ~ пл, б ~ бл, м~ мл.

Some of these alternations are restricted to a very small number of verbs.

Additional examples to those given above are:

хохота́ть (нсв) 'to laugh (loudly)'	хохочу́, хохо́чешь
маха́ть (нсв) 'to wave'	машу́, ма́шешь
	(but *see* note (i) below)
иска́ть (нсв) 'to look for'	ищу́, и́щешь
колеба́ть (нсв) 'to shake'	колеблю́, коле́блешь
дрема́ть (нсв) 'to doze'	дремлю́, дре́млешь

NOTES (i) Some verbs belonging to this class have an alternative set of endings that follow the pattern of the first class of productive verbs (**4.6.1**):

ка́пать (нсв) 'to drip'	ка́плет *or* ка́пает
маха́ть (нсв) 'to wave'	ма́шет *or* маха́ет

Generally speaking, the forms with the consonant alternation are more old-fashioned and more likely to occur in formal or elevated language.

(ii) The verb **посла́ть** and other *prefixed* verbs with the same root have the alternation **сл ~ шл**:

посла́ть (св) 'to send'   пошлю́, пошлёшь

4.7.2 Second unproductive class of first conjugation verbs

This class is made up of *first* conjugation verbs following the patterns:

(a) Infinitive in **-ать**   Non-past in **-му, мешь/-мёшь**, etc.
(b) Infinitive in **-ать**   Non-past in **-ну, -нешь/-нёшь**, etc.
(c) Infinitive in **-ять**   Non-past in **-му, -мёшь**, etc.

(a) **жать (нсв)**   (b) **нача́ть (св)**   (c) **взять (св)**
'to squeeze'   'to begin'   'to take'
жму   **начну́**   **возьму́**
жмёшь   **начнёшь**   **возьмёшь**
жмёт   **начнёт**   **возьмёт**
жмём   **начнём**   **возьмём**
жмёте   **начнёте**   **возьмёте**
жмут   **начну́т**   **возьму́т**

NOTES

(i) Alongside the verb **жать, жму, жмёшь,** etc. there is an unrelated (and less common) verb **жать (нсв), жну, жнёшь,** etc. 'to reap'.

(ii) The verbs with an infinitive in **-ять** form the *future tense* (all are *perfective*) in slightly different ways:

поня́ть (св) to understand   **пойму́, поймёшь**
снять (св) to take off   **сниму́, сни́мешь**

4.7.3 Third unproductive class of first conjugation verbs

These are *first* conjugation verbs following the pattern:

Infinitive in **-ать**   Non-past in **-у, -ешь/-ёшь**, etc.

жда́ть (нсв) 'to wait'   **стона́ть (нсв)** 'to moan', 'to groan'
жду   **стону́**
ждёшь   **сто́нешь**
ждёт   **сто́нет**
ждём   **сто́нем**
ждёте   **сто́нете**
ждут   **сто́нут**

брать (нсв) 'to take'   **звать (нсв)** 'to call'
беру́   **зову́**
берёшь   **зовёшь**
берёт   **зовёт**
берём   **зовём**
берёте   **зовёте**
беру́т   **зову́т**

NOTE

The verbs **брать, драть (нсв)** (**деру́, дерёшь** etc.) 'to tear' and **звать** have a *fleeting vowel* in the *present tense*.

For more on the fleeting vowel, *see* **2.5**.

4.7.4 Fourth unproductive class of first conjugation verbs

This class consists of *first* conjugation verbs following the pattern:

Infinitive in **-авать**   Non-past in **-аю, -аёшь**, etc.

дава́ть (нсв)   **встава́ть (нсв)**   **узнава́ть (нсв)**
'to give'   'to stand up', 'to get up'   'to recognise'
даю́   **встаю́**   **узнаю́**
даёшь   **встаёшь**   **узнаёшь**
даёт   **встаёт**   **узнаёт**

даём	встаём	узнаём
даёте	встаёте	узнаёте
даю́т	встаю́т	узнаю́т

NOTE The *imperfective* verb узнава́ть is to be distinguished from its *perfective* partner узна́ть. The latter has the *future* tense узна́ю, узна́ешь, etc.

4.7.5 ## Fifth unproductive class of first conjugation verbs

These are *first* conjugation verbs following the pattern:

Infinitive in **-ять**	Non-past in **-ю**, **-ешь/-ёшь**, etc.
ла́ять (нсв) 'to bark'	смея́ться (нсв) 'to laugh'
ла́ю	смею́сь
ла́ешь	смеёшься
ла́ет	смеётся
ла́ем	смеёмся
ла́ете	смеётесь
ла́ют	смею́тся

NOTE смея́ться occurs only as a reflexive verb (*see* **4.13.2**).

4.7.6 ## Sixth class of unproductive verbs of first conjugation verbs

This class is made up of *first* conjugation verbs following the patterns:

(a)	Infinitive in **-ить**	Non-past in **-ью**, **-ьёшь**, etc.
(b)	Infinitive in **-ыть**	Non-past in **-ою**, **-оешь**, etc.
(c)	Infinitive in **-ить**	Non-past in **-ею**, **-еешь**, etc.
(d)	Infinitive in **-еть**	Non-past in **-ою**, **-оёшь**, etc.

(a) **бить (нсв)** 'to beat', 'to hit', 'to strike'	(b) **мыть (нсв)** 'to wash'	(c) **брить (нсв)** 'to shave'	(d) **петь (нсв)** 'to sing'
бью	мо́ю	бре́ю	пою́
бьёшь	мо́ешь	бре́ешь	поёшь
бьёт	мо́ет	бре́ет	поёт
бьём	мо́ем	бре́ем	поём
бьёте	мо́ете	бре́ете	поёте
бьют	мо́ют	бре́ют	пою́т

NOTES: (i) All *unprefixed* verbs in this class have only one syllable in the infinitive.

(ii) **Брить** and **петь** are the only verbs to follow their respective patterns.

4.7

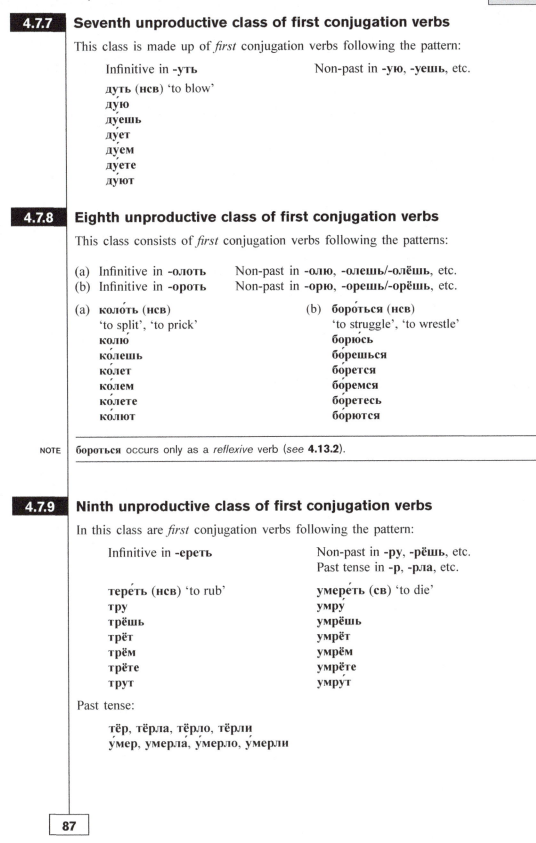

4.7.7

Seventh unproductive class of first conjugation verbs

This class is made up of *first* conjugation verbs following the pattern:

Infinitive in **-уть**   Non-past in **-ую, -уешь**, etc.

дуть (нсв) 'to blow'
ду́ю
ду́ешь
ду́ет
ду́ем
ду́ете
ду́ют

4.7.8

Eighth unproductive class of first conjugation verbs

This class consists of *first* conjugation verbs following the patterns:

(a) Infinitive in **-олоть**   Non-past in **-олю, -олешь/-олёшь**, etc.
(b) Infinitive in **-ороть**   Non-past in **-орю, -орешь/-орёшь**, etc.

(a) коло́ть (нсв)   (b) боро́ться (нсв)
'to split', 'to prick'   'to struggle', 'to wrestle'
колю́   борю́сь
ко́лешь   бо́решься
ко́лет   бо́рется
ко́лем   бо́ремся
ко́лете   бо́ретесь
ко́лют   бо́рются

NOTE   боро́ться occurs only as a *reflexive* verb (*see* **4.13.2**).

4.7.9

Ninth unproductive class of first conjugation verbs

In this class are *first* conjugation verbs following the pattern:

Infinitive in **-ереть**   Non-past in **-ру, -рёшь**, etc.
                                  Past tense in **-р, -рла**, etc.

тере́ть (нсв) 'to rub'   умере́ть (св) 'to die'
тру   умру́
трёшь   умрёшь
трёт   умрёт
трём   умрём
трёте   умрёте
трут   умру́т

Past tense:

тёр, тёрла, тёрло, тёрли
у́мер, умерла́, у́мерло, у́мерли

4.7.10 **Tenth unproductive class of first conjugation verbs**

This class contains *first* conjugation verbs following the pattern:

Infinitive in **-нуть**   Non-past in **-ну, -нешь/-нёшь**, etc.

The past tense is formed without the **-ну-**.

мёрзнуть (нсв) 'to freeze'	**привы́кнуть (св)** 'to get used to'
мёрзну	привы́кну
мёрзнешь	привы́кнешь
мёрзнет	привы́кнет
мёрзнем	привы́кнем
мёрзнете	привы́кнете
мёрзнут	привы́кнут

Past tense:

мёрз, мёрзла, мёрзло, мёрзли
привы́к, привы́кла, привы́кло, привы́кли

NOTES
(i) This class differs from the *third* class of *productive* verbs only in the past tense. It contains both *imperfective* and *perfective* verbs.

(ii) **дости́гнуть (св)** 'to reach', 'to achieve' has an alternative infinitive **дости́чь**.

4.7.11 **Eleventh unproductive class of first conjugation verbs**

This class consists of *first* conjugation verbs following the patterns:

(a) Infinitive in **-ить**   Non-past in **-иву, -ивёшь**, etc.
(b) Infinitive in **-ыть**   Non-past in **-ыву, -ывёшь**, etc.

(a) **жить (нсв)** 'to live'	(b) **плыть (нсв)** 'to (be) swim(ming)'
живу́	плыву́
живёшь	плывёшь
живёт	плывёт
живём	плывём
живёте	плывёте
живу́т	плыву́т

4.7.12 **Twelfth unproductive class of first conjugation verbs**

This class is made up of *first* conjugation verbs following these patterns:

(a) Infinitive in **-зть/-зти**   Non-past in **-зу, -зешь/-зёшь**, etc.
(b) Infinitive in **-сти**   Non-past in **-су, -сёшь**, etc.
(c) Infinitive in **-сти**   Non-past in **-ту, -тёшь**, etc.
(d) Infinitive in **-сть/-сти**   Non-past in **-ду, -дешь/-дёшь**, etc.
(e) Infinitive in **-сти**   Non-past in **-бу, -бёшь**, etc.

(a) **ползти́ (нсв)**	(b) **нести́ (нсв)**	(c) **изобрести́ (св)**
'to (be) crawl(ing)'	'to (be) carrying)'	'to invent'
ползу́	несу́	изобрету́
ползёшь	несёшь	изобретёшь

ползёт	несёт	изобретёт
ползём	несём	изобретём
ползёте	несёте	изобретёте
ползу́т	несу́т	изобрету́т

(d) класть (нсв)   вести́ (нсв)   (e) грести́ (нсв)
    'to put (lying)'   'to (be) lead(ing)'   'to rake', 'to row (a boat)'

кладу́	веду́	гребу́
кладёшь	ведёшь	гребёшь
кладёт	ведёт	гребёт
кладём	ведём	гребём
кладёте	ведёте	гребёте
кладу́т	веду́т	гребу́т

These verbs form the *past tense* as follows:

(a) полз, ползла́, ползло́, ползли́
(b) нёс, несла́, несло́, несли́
(c) изобрёл, изобрела́, изобрело́, изобрели́
(d) вёл, вела́, вело́, вели́
(e) грёб, гребла́, гребло́, гребли́

NOTES

(i) сесть (св) 'to sit down' has the *future tense* ся́ду, ся́дешь, etc. (*past tense* сел, се́ла, се́ло, се́ли).

(ii) расти́ (нсв) 'to grow' (intransitive) has *present tense* расту́, растёшь, etc., but *past tense* рос, росла́, росло́, росли́.

4.7.13   Thirteenth unproductive class of first conjugation verbs

The verbs in this class are *first* conjugation verbs following the patterns:

(a) Infinitive in -чь   Non-past in -гу, -жешь/-жёшь, etc.
(b) Infinitive in -чь   Non-past in -ку, -чешь/-чёшь, etc.

(a) мочь (нсв) 'to be able' (b) жечь (нсв) 'to burn' (c) печь (нсв) 'to bake'

могу́	жгу	пеку́
мо́жешь	жжёшь	печёшь
мо́жет	жжёт	печёт
мо́жем	жжём	печём
мо́жете	жжёте	печёте
мо́гут	жгут	пеку́т

These verbs form the *past tense* as follows:

(a) мог, могла́, могло́, могли́; жёг, жгла, жгло, жгли
(b) пёк, пекла́, пекло́, пекли.

4.7.14 | **Miscellaneous first conjugation verbs**

There are a few *first* conjugation verbs that fall into none of the above classes:

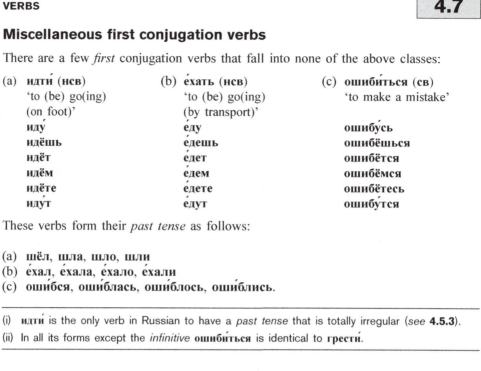

(a) идти́ (нсв)	(b) е́хать (нсв)	(c) ошиби́ться (св)
'to (be) go(ing) (on foot)'	'to (be) go(ing) (by transport)'	'to make a mistake'
иду́	е́ду	ошибу́сь
идёшь	е́дешь	ошибёшься
идёт	е́дет	ошибётся
идём	е́дем	ошибёмся
идёте	е́дете	ошибётесь
иду́т	е́дут	ошибу́тся

These verbs form their *past tense* as follows:

(a) шёл, шла, шло, шли
(b) е́хал, е́хала, е́хало, е́хали
(c) оши́бся, оши́блась, оши́блось, оши́блись.

NOTES | (i) идти́ is the only verb in Russian to have a *past tense* that is totally irregular (*see* **4.5.3**).

(ii) In all its forms except the *infinitive* ошиби́ться is identical to грести́.

4.7.15 | **First unproductive class of second conjugation verbs**

This class consists of *second conjugation* verbs with an *infinitive* in -еть:

ви́деть (нсв)	висе́ть (нсв)	смотре́ть (нсв)
'to see'	'to hang' (intransitive)	'to look at'
ви́жу	вишу́	смотрю́
ви́дишь	виси́шь	смо́тришь
ви́дит	виси́т	смо́трит
ви́дим	виси́м	смо́трим
ви́дите	виси́те	смо́трите
ви́дят	вися́т	смо́трят

NOTE | The same rules concerning *consonant alternations* in the *first person singular* of the *non-past* as were described above (**4.6.4**) for the *productive* class of *second* conjugation verbs also apply to these verbs.

4.7.16 | **Second unproductive class of second conjugation verbs**

These are *second* conjugation verbs with an *infinitive* in -ать/-ять:

спать (нсв)	держа́ть (нсв)	стоя́ть (нсв)
'to sleep'	'to hold'	'to stand'
сплю	держу́	стою́
спишь	де́ржишь	стои́шь
спит	де́ржит	стои́т
спим	де́ржим	стои́м
спи́те	де́ржите	стои́те
спят	де́ржат	стоя́т

NOTES

(i) **Спать** is the only verb in this class where there is a *consonant alternation* in the *first person singular* of the *non-past*. Almost all other verbs in this class with an *infinitive* ending in **-ать** have a stem ending in **ж, ч, ш** or **щ**, and the endings in the *non-past* are subject to the spelling rules described in **1.5.2**.

(ii) The *infinitive* ending **-ять** occurs after a *vowel*.

4.8 Irregular verbs

Russian has only a handful of verbs that are totally irregular.

Two verbs have a mixture of *first* and *second* conjugation endings in the *non-past*:

хоте́ть (нсв) 'to want'	бежа́ть (нсв) 'to (be) run(ning)'
хочу́	бегу́
хо́чешь	бежи́шь
хо́чет	бежи́т
хоти́м	бежи́м
хоти́те	бежи́те
хотя́т	бегу́т

Two verbs have endings in the *non-past* that belong to neither conjugation:

дать (св) 'to give'	есть (нсв) 'to eat'
дам	ем
дашь	ешь
даст	ест
дади́м	еди́м
дади́те	еди́те
даду́т	едя́т

NOTES

(i) These two verbs, though otherwise identical, have different endings in the *third person plural*.

(ii) The past tense of **дать** is perfectly regular; the past tense of **есть** follows the pattern ел, е́ла, е́ло, е́ли.

Although it is an *imperfective* verb, **быть** 'to be' has no *present tense*. The only form that survives is the *third person* (*singular* and *plural*) form **есть**; this is most often used to indicate the presence or existence of something:

> Здесь *есть* одна́ ма́ленькая пробле́ма.
> There is a small problem here.

The *negative* form of **есть** is **нет** (this is the only special negative form in Russian, *see* **15.1**):

> Здесь *нет* пробле́м.
> There are no problems here.

The use of **есть** and **нет** and the ways in which Russian compensates for the otherwise missing *present tense* of **быть** are explained in **14.1**, **14.2**, **14.3** and **15.1**.

4.9 The imperative

4.9.0 Introduction

The *imperative* is used for giving commands and instructions or (in the negative) prohibitions and warnings; it can also be used for making requests (*see* **Chapter 18**). It is formed from both *imperfective* and *perfective* verbs. Special endings exist only for the *second person singular* and *plural*.

4.9.1 Second person singular

This is formed by taking the *second person singular* of the *non-past* and removing the ending (-ешь/-ёшь/-ишь).

If the stem that remains ends in a *vowel*, add **-й**:

де́лать (нсв) 'to do'	де́лаешь	де́лай
танцева́ть (нсв) 'to dance'	танцу́ешь	танцу́й
стреля́ть (нсв) 'to shoot'	стреля́ешь	стреля́й
стоя́ть (нсв) 'to stand'	стои́шь	стой

If the stem that remains ends in a *consonant* and the stress of the verb is either always on the ending or is mobile, add **-и**:

брать (нсв) 'to take'	берёшь	бери́
взять (св) 'to take'	возьмёшь	возьми́
писа́ть (нсв) 'to write'	пи́шешь	пиши́
сказа́ть (св) 'to say'	ска́жешь	скажи́
нести́ (нсв) 'to be carrying'	несёшь	неси́
говори́ть (нсв) 'to say', 'to speak'	говори́шь	говори́
смотре́ть (нсв) 'to look'	смо́тришь	смотри́

If the stem that remains ends in a *consonant* and the stress of the verb is never on the ending, add **-ь**:

пла́кать (нсв) 'to cry'	пла́чешь	плачь
лезть (нсв) 'to climb'	ле́зешь	лезь
сесть (св) 'to sit down'	ся́дешь	сядь
оста́вить (св) 'to leave'	оста́вишь	оста́вь

If, however, the remaining stem ends in *two consonants* or if the verb is a *perfective* verb with the *prefix* **вы-** and the *imperative* of the corresponding unprefixed verb ends in **-и**, then **-и** is added:

кри́кнуть (св) 'to shout'	кри́кнешь	кри́кни
вы́нести (св) 'to carry out'	вы́несешь	вы́неси
(cf. нести́ above)		

The following verbs do not form their *imperative* according to any of the above patterns:

(a) Verbs of class **4.7.4**:

дава́ть (нсв) 'to give'	даёшь	дава́й
встава́ть (нсв) 'to stand up'	встаёшь	встава́й

(b) Verbs of sub-class **4.7.6** (a):

ли́ть (нсв) 'to pour'	льёшь	лей
пи́ть (нсв) 'to drink'	пьёшь	пей

(c) Verbs of class **4.7.13**:

бере́чь (нсв) 'to save'	бережёшь	береги́
печь (нсв) 'to bake'	печёшь	пеки́

The final consonant is the same as in the *first person singular* of the *non-past*.

(d) Other miscellaneous verbs:

бы́ть (нсв) 'to be'	—	будь
лечь (св) 'to lie down'	ля́жешь	ляг
сы́пать (нсв) 'to pour (solids)'	сы́плешь	сыпь

4.9.2 Second person plural

This is formed by adding **-те** to the second person singular. There are no exceptions to this rule:

де́лать (нсв) 'to do'	де́лай	де́лайте
танцева́ть (нсв) 'to dance'	танцу́й	танцу́йте
взять (св) 'to take'	возьми́	возьми́те
писа́ть (нсв) 'to write'	пиши́	пиши́те
говори́ть (нсв) 'to say, to speak'	говори́	говори́те
пла́кать (нсв) 'to cry'	плачь	пла́чьте
оста́вить (св) 'to leave'	оста́вь	оста́вьте
дава́ть (нсв) 'to give'	дава́й	дава́йте
пить (нсв) 'to drink'	пей	пе́йте
бы́ть (нсв) 'to be'	будь	бу́дьте

4.9.3 The third person imperative

The *third person imperative* is formed by using the *particle* **пусть** (less often **пуска́й**) with the *third person singular* or plural of the *future perfective* or *present imperfective*:

войти́ (св) 'to enter'	пусть войдёт	пусть войду́т
говори́ть (нсв) 'to say', 'to speak'	пусть говори́т	пусть говоря́т

Мы гото́вы нача́ть собесе́дование; пусть он войдёт.
We're ready to begin the interview; let him come in.

Пу́сть говоря́т; мы не бои́мся пра́вды.
Let them speak; we're not afraid of the truth.

4.10 The conditional (or subjunctive)

In Russian the terms *conditional* and *subjunctive* are used interchangeably, although the former is more common and is preferred here. The conditional is used for all sorts of hypothetical situations, for example, conditions incapable of being fulfilled or when giving advice (*see* **18.4** and **21.5**).

The conditional can be formed from both *imperfective* and *perfective* verbs. It is formed with the *enclitic particle* **бы** (*see* **9.4**) and the *past tense* of the verb:

говори́ть (нсв) 'to say', 'to speak':

    говори́л бы, говори́ла бы, говори́ло бы, говори́ли бы

сказа́ть (св) 'to say':

    сказа́л бы, сказа́ла бы, сказа́ло бы, сказа́ли бы

писа́ть (нсв) 'to write':

    писа́л бы, писа́ла бы, писа́ло бы, писа́ли бы

написа́ть (св) 'to write':

    написа́л бы, написа́ла бы, написа́ло бы, написа́ли бы

дава́ть (нсв) 'to give':

    дава́л бы, дава́ла бы, дава́ло бы, дава́ли бы

дать (св) 'to give':

    дал бы, дала́ бы, да́ло́ бы, да́ли бы

4.11   Gerunds

4.11.0   Introduction

Gerunds are *verbal adverbs*, which means they are at the same time both a part of the *verb* and an *adverb*. Although they can sometimes be used alongside other adverbs, their main function is to form complex sentences, in which a *gerund* is used in place of a *conjunction* + *verb*.

The use of gerunds is described in detail in **21.10**.

Gerunds are rare in speech, but they are widely used in all forms of writing. There are *imperfective* (or *present*) gerunds and *perfective* (or *past*) gerunds.

4.11.1   The imperfective gerund

The *imperfective gerund* is formed from the present tense of *imperfective* verbs. The easiest way to form this gerund is to take the *third person plural*, remove the final two letters and add **-я**:

чита́ть (нсв) 'to read'	**чита́ют**	**чита́я**
позволя́ть (нсв) 'to allow'	**позволя́ют**	**позволя́я**
целова́ть (нсв) 'to kiss'	**целу́ют**	**целу́я**
идти́ (нсв) 'to (be) go(ing)'	**иду́т**	**идя́**
говори́ть (нсв) 'to say, to speak'	**говоря́т**	**говоря́**
крича́ть (нсв) 'to shout'	**крича́т**	**крича́**

NOTE | The spelling of **крича́** is determined by the spelling rule that prevents the letter **я** occurring after **ж, ц, ч, ш, щ** (*see* **1.5.2**).

The following verbs have an irregular *imperfective gerund*:

дава́ть (нсв) 'to give'	даю́т	дава́я

The same rule applies to all other verbs in class **4.7.4**.

быть (нсв) 'to be'	—	бу́дучи
е́хать (нсв) 'to (be) go(ing) (by transport)'	е́дут	е́дучи

NOTES

(i) It is not normally possible to form *imperfective gerunds* from most *unproductive* classes of *first conjugation* verbs (exceptions are **4.7.4**, **4.7.5**, **4.7.6(c)**, **4.7.7**, **4.7.8** and **4.7.11**).

(ii) Some *imperfective gerund* forms have been transformed into other parts of speech and are no longer used as gerunds:

хотя́ 'although' is a conjunction (*see* **21.6.3**);
смотря́ 'depending (on)' is an adverb used with a question word or the preposition по (+ dat.) (*see* **16.5.3**).

4.11.2 The perfective gerund

The *perfective gerund* is formed from the *past tense* of *perfective* verbs. Where the *masculine singular* form of the *past tense* ends in -л, this is removed and replaced by -в:

прочита́ть (св) 'to read'	прочита́л	прочита́в
написа́ть (св) 'to write'	написа́л	написа́в
взять (св) 'to take'	взял	взяв
поджа́рить (св) 'to fry'	поджа́рил	поджа́рив

Note that *reflexive* verbs (**4.13.2**) form the *perfective gerund* by inserting -ши- between the normal gerund and the *reflexive particle* -сь:

верну́ться (св) 'to return'	верну́лся	верну́вшись

If the *masculine singular* form of the *past tense* ends in a consonant other than -л, then -ши is added:

вы́расти 'to grow up'	вы́рос	вы́росши
испе́чь 'to bake'	испёк	испёкши

Verbs belonging to classes **4.7.9** and **4.7.10** have alternative forms of the perfective gerund:

умере́ть (св) 'to die'	у́мер	умере́в/у́мерши
замёрзнуть (св) 'to freeze' (intransitive)	замёрз	замёрзнув/замёрзши

NOTE

The only perfective gerund formed from исче́знуть (св) 'to disappear' is исче́знув.

Prefixed perfective verbs based on везти́, вести́, идти́ and нести́ form their perfective gerunds according to the rules for forming imperfective gerunds:

ввезти́ (св) 'to import'	ввезу́т	ввезя́
провести́ (св) 'to conduct, to spend (time)'	проведу́т	проведя́
уйти́ (св) 'to go away'	уйду́т	уйдя́
вы́нести (св) 'to carry out'	вы́несут	вы́неся

4.12 Participles

4.12.0 Introduction

The *participle* in Russian is a *verbal adjective*, which means that it is at the same time both part of the *verb* and an *adjective*. There are four participles: *present active*, *past active*, *present passive* and *past passive*. The first three of these have only a *long form*, but the *past passive participle* has both *long* and *short* forms.

For more on the long and short forms of adjectives, *see* **6.1** and **6.5**.

Long form participles are not normally found in speech or in informal writing, but they are a characteristic feature of formal written Russian, where they are used to form clauses similar in function to *relative clauses*.

The use of long form participles is discussed in **23.1.3**.

The *short form* of the *past passive participle* is used to form the *passive voice* of *perfective* verbs (**4.14**) and therefore occurs in both spoken and written language of all types.

The declension of *present* and *past* active participles follows the pattern described in **6.1.5**. The declension of present and past passive participles (in the long form) follows the pattern described in **6.1.1**.

4.12.1 The present active participle

The *present active participle* is formed from *imperfective* verbs. It is most easily formed by taking the *third person plural* of the *present tense*, removing the last letter, adding **-щ-** and the appropriate *adjective* endings:

чита́ть (нсв) 'to read'	чита́ют	чита́ющий, -щая, -щее
писа́ть (нсв) 'to write'	пи́шут	пи́шущий, -щая, -щее
танцева́ть (нсв) 'to dance'	танцу́ют	танцу́ющий, -щая, -щее
пить (нсв) 'to drink'	пьют	пью́щий, -щая, -щее
уходи́ть (нсв) 'to go away'	ухо́дят	уходя́щий, -щая, щее
крича́ть (нсв) 'to shout'	крича́т	крича́щий, -щая, -щее

4.12.2 The past active participle

The *past active participle* is formed from both *imperfective* and *perfective* verbs. It is formed from the *masculine singular* of the *past tense*: if this ends in **-л**, the final consonant is removed and replaced by **-вш-** and the appropriate *adjective* endings:

чита́ть (нсв) 'to read'	чита́л	чита́вший, -шая, -шее
написа́ть (св) 'to write'	написа́л	написа́вший, -шая, -шее
целова́ть (нсв) 'to kiss'	целова́л	целова́вший, -шая, -шее
взять (св) 'to take'	взял	взя́вший, -шая, -шее
сесть (св) 'to sit down'	сел	се́вший, -шая, -шее

If the *masculine singular* of the *past tense* ends in a *consonant* other than **-л**, then **-ш-** and the appropriate *adjective* endings are added to this form:

замёрзнуть (св) 'to freeze'	замёрз	замёрзший, -шая, -шее
умере́ть (св) 'to die'	у́мер	у́мерший, -шая, -шее
нести́ (нсв) 'to (be) carry(ing)'	нёс	нёсший, -шая, -шее

The following *past active participles* are formed irregularly:

вести́ (нсв) 'to (be) lead(ing)'	вёл	ве́дший, -шая, -шее
идти́ (нсв) 'to (be) go(ing)'	шёл	ше́дший, -шая, -шее
обрести́ (св) 'to find', 'to obtain'	обрёл	обре́тший, -шая, -шее

NOTE When *present* or *past active participles* are formed from *reflexive* verbs, the *reflexive suffix* takes the form **-ся** regardless of whether the preceding letter is a *vowel* or a *consonant* (see **4.13.2**):

боя́ться (нсв) 'to be afraid of':

| Present active: | боя́щийся | боя́щаяся | боя́щееся |
| Past active: | боя́вшийся | боя́вшаяся | боя́вшееся |

4.12.3 The present passive participle

The *present passive participle* is the least used of all participles; it is formed from some *imperfective transitive* verbs only. It is formed by adding the appropriate *adjective* endings to the *first person plural* of the present tense:

выбра́сывать (нсв) 'to throw out'	выбра́сываем	выбра́сываемый, -мая, -мое
повторя́ть (нсв) 'to repeat'	повторя́ем	повторя́емый, -мая, -мое
цити́ровать (нсв) 'to quote'	цити́руем	цити́руемый, -мая, -мое
проводи́ть (нсв) 'to conduct, to spend (time)'	прово́дим	проводи́мый, -мая, -мое

Verbs of class **4.7.4** keep the **-ва-** infix from the *infinitive* in the *present passive participle*: past

| признава́ть (нсв) 'to recognise, to admit' | признаём | *but* признава́емый, -мая, -мое |

In practice, the *present passive participle* is formed only from verbs belonging to the classes represented in the examples (**4.6.1**, **4.6.2**, **4.6.4** and all classes of *second* conjugation verbs), and then from not all of these. It is difficult to give precise rules, but generally speaking, *present passive participles* are more likely to be formed from *prefixed imperfective* verbs or from verbs with a more abstract or literary meaning.

4.12.4 The past passive participle

The past passive participle is formed from all *perfective transitive* verbs. The great majority of verbs form this participle with the suffix **-н(н)-**.

Important note: This is the only participle with both *long* and *short* forms. The spelling **-нн-** is used throughout the long form; the spelling **-н(-)** is used throughout the short form.

If the infinitive ends in **-ать**, **-ять** (classes **4.6.1**, **4.6.2**, **4.7.1**, **4.7.3** and **4.7.16**), the *participle* is formed from the *infinitive* by removing the **-ть** and replacing it with the *participle suffix* and the appropriate *adjective* endings:

прочита́ть (св) 'to read'	прочи́танный, -нная, -нное
написа́ть (св) 'to write'	напи́санный, -нная, -нное
нарисова́ть (св) 'to draw'	нарисо́ванный, -нная, -нное
порва́ть (св) 'to tear'	по́рванный, -нная, -нное

Verbs belonging to classes **4.7.12** and **4.7.13** form the *past passive participle* from the *non-past (future)* tense; the *consonant* to which the ending is added is that found in the *first person plural*:

принести́ (св) 'to bring'	принесём	принесённый, -нная, -нное
ввести́ (св) 'to lead in'	введём	введённый, -нная, -нное
изобрести́ (св) 'to invent'	изобретём	изобретённый, -нная, -нное
испе́чь (св) 'to bake'	испечём	испечённый, -нная, -нное
сбере́чь (св) 'to save'	сбережём	сбережённый, -нная, -нное

Prefixed forms of **идти́** follow this pattern:

найти́ (св) 'to find'	найдём	на́йденный, -нная, -нное

Second conjugation verbs with an infinitive in **-ить**, **-еть** have the *suffix* **-енн-/-ённ-** and the same *consonant alternation* as in the *first person singular* of the *future tense*:

Without *consonant alternation*:

поджа́рить (св) 'to fry'	поджа́рю	поджа́ренный, -нная, -нное
реши́ть (св) 'to decide'	решу́	решённый, -нная, -нное

With *consonant alternation*:

пове́сить (св) 'to hang'	пове́шу	пове́шенный, -нная, -нное
сни́зить (св) 'to lower'	сни́жу	сни́женный, -нная, -нное
оплати́ть (св) 'to pay for'	оплачу́	опла́ченный, -нная, -нное
освети́ть (св) 'to illuminate'	освещу́	освещённый, -нная, -нное
оби́деть (св) 'to offend'	оби́жу	оби́женный, -нная, -нное
огра́бить (св) 'to rob'	огра́блю	огра́бленный, -нная, -нное
купи́ть (св) 'to buy'	куплю́	ку́пленный, -нная, -нное
прояви́ть (св) 'to show (a quality), to develop (photographs)'	проявлю́	проя́вленный, -нная, -нное
накорми́ть (св) 'to feed'	накормлю́	нако́рмленный, -нная, -нное

NOTES

(i) Some *second* conjugation verbs with an *infinitive* in **-дить**, **-деть** change the *consonant* to **-жд-** in the *past passive participle*:

утверди́ть (св)	to state, to affirm	утвержу́	утверждённый, -нная, -нное
убеди́ть (св)	to convince	—	убеждённый, -нная, -нное

In the case of *paired imperfective* and *perfective* verbs, these verbs can be identified from the *imperfective*:

утверди́ть (св) ~ утвержда́ть (нсв).
убеди́ть (св) ~ убежда́ть (нсв)

The *first person singular* of the *future tense* of **убеди́ть** (and also of **победи́ть** 'to defeat') is never used.

(ii) The *past passive participle* of **уви́деть** (**св**) 'to see' does not have the expected *consonant alternation*:

уви́деть	уви́жу	уви́денный, -нная, -нное

Verbs belonging to classes **4.6.3, 4.7.2, 4.7.6, 4.7.7, 4.7.8, 4.7.9, 4.7.10, 4.7.11** and *prefixed perfectives* formed from **быть** have a *past passive participle* in **-т-**:

обману́ть (св) 'to deceive'	обма́нутый, -тая, -тое
взять (св) 'to take'	взя́тый, -тая, -тое
спеть (св) 'to sing'	спе́тый, -тая, -тое
разду́ть (св) 'to blow, to inflate'	разду́тый, -тая, -тое
приколо́ть (св) 'to pin up'	приколо́тый, -тая, -тое
запере́ть (св) 'to lock'	за́пертый, -тая, -тое
све́ргнуть (св) 'to overthrow'	све́ргнутый, -тая, -тое
прожи́ть (св) 'to live (a certain length of time somewhere)'	про́житый, -тая, -тое
забы́ть (св) 'to forget'	забы́тый, -тая, -тое

Examples of *short forms*:

прочита́ть (св) 'to read'	прочи́тан, -тана, -тано, -таны
написа́ть (св) 'to write'	напи́сан, -сана, -сано, -саны
принести́ (св) 'to bring'	принесён, -сена́, -сено́, -сены́
испе́чь (св) 'to bake'	испечён, -чена́, -чено́, -чены́
пове́сить (св) 'to hang'	пове́шен, -шена, -шено, -шены
освети́ть (св) 'to illuminate'	освещён, -щена́, -щено́, -щены́
оби́деть (св) 'to offend'	оби́жен, -жена, -жено, -жены
взять (св) 'to take'	взят, взята́, взя́то, взя́ты
забы́ть (св) 'to forget'	забы́т, -та́, -то́, -ты

4.13 Transitive, intransitive and reflexive verbs

4.13.1 Transitive and intransitive verbs

Transitive verbs are those used with a *direct object* in the *accusative* case. In both of the following sentences the verb is *transitive*, since the pronoun **что** and the noun **кни́гу** are both *direct objects* in the *accusative*:

Что́ он де́лает?
What is he doing?

Он чита́ет кни́гу.
He is reading a book.

In the following examples, the verbs are *intransitive*, since they are not used with a *direct object* in the *accusative* case. In the last two examples, the verbs are used with *objects*, but in the *instrumental* and the *dative* cases respectively:

Она́ живёт в Москве́.
She lives in Moscow.

Я уже́ *ходи́л* **за хле́бом**.
I've already been for the bread.

Он *сиде́л* **за столо́м**.
He was sitting at the table.

Мои́ глаза́ ещё не *привы́кли* **к темноте́**.
My eyes still haven't got used to the darkness.

Как *по́льзоваться* **э́тим словарём**.
Guide to the use of this dictionary [*literally*, How to use this dictionary].

Вам *помо́чь?*
Can I help you?

For more on the use of different cases to indicate the object of a verb, *see* **3.2**, **3.3.4**, **3.3.5**, **3.4.4** and **3.5.7**.

In English, the difference between *transitive* and *intransitive* verbs is of little or no importance, and a great many verbs can be used either transitively or intransitively:

| She *walks* to school every day. | *Intransitive* |
| She *walks* the dog every day. | *Transitive* |

| Why not *hang* this picture on the wall? | *Transitive* |
| The picture *is* already *hanging* on the wall. | *Intransitive* |

In Russian, only a very small number of verbs denoting simple actions, such as **чита́ть** 'to read', **писа́ть** 'to write' and **есть** 'to eat', can be used either transitively or intransitively:

| **Что он де́лает? Он** *чита́ет кни́гу.* | *Transitive* |
| What is he doing? He is reading a book. | |

| **Что он де́лает? Он** *чита́ет.* | *Intransitive* |
| What is he doing? He is reading. | |

Even here, however, there is a complication, since the *perfective* partners of these verbs depend on whether the verb is transitive or intransitive: **прочита́ть**, **написа́ть** and **съесть** are normally used if the respective verbs are transitive, while **почита́ть**, **пописа́ть** and **пое́сть** are used if the respective verbs are intransitive.

The vast majority of Russian verbs are either transitive or intransitive; it is virtually impossible for an intransitive verb to be used transitively, and very rare for a transitive verb to be used intransitively. It follows from this that where in English the same verb can be used either transitively or intransitively, different verbs will be required in Russian:

| **Она́ ка́ждый день** *хо́дит* **в шко́лу пешко́м**. | *Intransitive* |
| She *walks* to school every day. | |

| **Она́ ка́ждый день** *выгу́ливает соба́ку.* | *Transitive* |
| She *walks* the dog every day. | |

| **Почему́ не** *пове́сить э́ту карти́ну* **на сте́ну?** | *Transitive* |
| Why not *hang* this picture on the wall? | |

| **Карти́на уже́** *виси́т* **на стене́**. | *Intransitive* |
| The picture *is* already *hanging* on the wall. | |

The verb **ходи́ть (нсв)** 'to go somewhere regularly on foot' is intransitive, whereas **выгу́ливать (нсв)/вы́гулять (св)** 'to take a dog for a walk' is transitive. Similarly, **ве́шать (нсв)/пове́сить (св)** 'to hang something somewhere' is transitive, while **висе́ть (нсв)/повисе́ть (св)** 'to be hanging somewhere' is intransitive.

Sometimes adding a prefix can make an intransitive verb transitive or vice versa: **выгу́ливать** is derived from **гуля́ть (нсв)** 'to walk, 'to stroll', which is intransitive; **плати́ть (нсв)/заплати́ть (св)** 'to pay' is usually intransitive, while **опла́чивать (нсв)/оплати́ть (св)** 'to pay for' is transitive.

> **По́сле обе́да она́ *гуля́ет* в па́рке.**
> After lunch she goes for a walk in the park.

> **Почему́ вы не *заплати́ли за* прое́зд?**
> Why haven't you paid your fare?

> **Почему́ вы не *оплати́ли* прое́зд?**
> Why haven't you paid your fare?

The last two examples have the same meaning and are interchangeable.

4.13.2 Reflexive verbs

Reflexive verbs are formed with the suffix **-ся**. This suffix, which except in *participles* (see **4.12.2**) is shortened to **-сь** after a vowel, appears in all forms of the verb. The various forms of a reflexive verb can be illustrated by **смея́ться (нсв)/засмея́ться (св)** 'to laugh'.

Non-past

(a) *Present imperfective*	(b) *Future perfective*
смею́сь	засмею́сь
смеёшься	засмеёшься
смеётся	засмеётся
смеёмся	засмеёмся
смеётесь	засмеётесь
смею́тся	засмею́тся

Future imperfective:	**бу́ду смея́ться**, etc.
Past tense:	**(за)смея́лся, (за)смея́лась, (за)смея́лось, (за)смея́лись**
Imperative:	**(за)сме́йся, (за)сме́йтесь**
Imperfective gerund:	**смея́сь**
Perfective gerund:	**засмея́вшись**
Present participle:	**смею́щийся, смею́щаяся, смею́щееся**
Past participle:	**(за)смея́вшийся, (за)смея́вшаяся, (за)смея́вшееся**

Reflexive verbs are by definition intransitive, and the main purpose of making a verb reflexive is to turn a transitive verb into an intransitive verb:

> **Я уже́ *верну́л* э́ту кни́гу в библиоте́ку.**

> I've already returned this book to the library.

> **Я *верну́лся* домо́й позавчера́.**
> I returned home the day before yesterday.

Не *открыва́йте* э́ту дверь!
Don't open that door!

Две́ри *открыва́ются* автомати́чески.
The doors open automatically.

За́втра *начина́ю* рабо́ту над кни́гой.
Tomorrow I'm beginning work on the book.

Конце́рт *начина́ется* в во́семь часо́в.
The concert begins at eight o'clock.

Осторо́жно! На́ша соба́ка иногда́ *куса́ет* незнако́мых.
Careful! Our dog sometimes bites strangers.

Осторо́жно! *На́ша соба́ка куса́ется.*
Careful! Our dog bites.

Не *высо́вывайте* го́лову в окно́.
Don't stick your head out of the window.

Не *высо́вываться!*
(Please) do not lean out of the window (as used on notices in railway carriages).

In each of the above pairs of examples the verb in the first sentence is used with a *direct object* in the *accusative* and so is *transitive*, while the verb in the second sentence is *reflexive* and *intransitive*.

There are a number of verbs in Russian that occur only as *reflexive* verbs. Common examples include the following:

боро́ться (нсв)	to struggle, to wrestle
боя́ться (нсв)	to be afraid of
наде́яться (нсв)	to hope, to rely on
напива́ться (нсв)/напи́ться (св)	to get drunk
появля́ться (нсв)/появи́ться (св)	to appear
смея́ться (нсв)/засмея́ться (св)	to laugh

Another function of reflexive verbs is discussed in the following section.

4.14 Active and passive verbs

4.14.1 The active and the passive voices

In all the sentences quoted so far in this section, the verbs have been in the *active* voice, that is to say, the performer of the action or the main participant in the state is the *subject* of the *verb*. When it is necessary to make the recipient of the action the subject of the verb, the *passive* voice is used:

Мой де́душка *написа́л* э́ту кни́гу.   *Active*
My grandfather wrote this book.

Э́та кни́га *была́ напи́сана* мои́м де́душкой.   *Passive*
This book was written by my grandfather.

Мой де́душка *написа́л* э́ту кни́гу в 1931 г.   *Active*
My grandfather wrote this book in 1931.

> **Э́та кни́га *была́ напи́сана* в 1931 г.**   *Passive*
> This book was written in 1931.

When a passive verb is used, what would have been the *direct object* of the corresponding *active verb* becomes the *subject* of the sentence in the *nominative* case. It follows from this that the *passive voice* can be formed only from *transitive* verbs. In a passive sentence, the performer of the action is known as the *agent* and is in the *instrumental* case (as in the first pair of examples). As the second pair of examples shows, it is not necessary for the agent to be present.

For more on the use of the instrumental for the agent of a passive verb, *see* **3.5.2**.

4.14.2 The passive of imperfective verbs

The formation of the passive voice depends on the aspect of the verb. With *imperfective* verbs the *reflexive* is used for the passive:

> **Мы *счита́ем* его́ кру́пным специали́стом в э́той о́бласти.**   *Active*
> We consider him (to be) a great specialist in this area.

> **Он *счита́ется* кру́пным специали́стом в э́той о́бласти.**   *Passive*
> He is considered (to be) a great specialist in this area.

> **На́до *сохраня́ть* таможенную деклара́цию на весь
> пери́од вре́менного въе́зда/вы́езда и *предъявля́ть* её
> таможенным о́рганам при возвраще́нии.**   *Active*
> You should retain your customs declaration for the whole duration
> of your visit and present it to the customs authorities on your return.

> **Таможенная деклара́ция *сохраня́ется* на весь пери́од
> вре́менного въе́зда/вы́езда и *предъявля́ется* таможенным
> о́рганам при возвраще́нии.**   *Passive*
> The customs declaration is retained for the duration of the whole
> visit and is presented to the customs authorities on your return.

As this last example, quoted almost word for word from a Russian customs declaration form, indicates, the use of the *imperfective passive* is often a distinguishing feature of formal and official language.

4.14.3 The passive of perfective verbs

The *passive voice* of *perfective* verbs is formed using the *short form* of the *past passive participle* and the appropriate form of the verb **быть** 'to be':

> **Здесь *был постро́ен* но́вый дом.**
> A new building was put up here.

> **Здесь *постро́ен* но́вый дом.**
> A new building has been put up here.

> **Здесь *бу́дет постро́ен* но́вый дом.**
> A new building will be put up here.

> **Э́та кни́га *была́ напи́сана* на ру́сском языке́.**
> This book was written in Russian.

> **Э́та кни́га *напи́сана* на ру́сском языке́.**
> This book is written in Russian.

Э́та кни́га *бу́дет напи́сана* на ру́сском языке́.
This book will be written in Russian.

There are no stylistic restrictions on the use of perfective passive, but in general passive verbs are used rather less frequently in Russian than in English. More information on the use of passive verbs and the means that exist for avoiding them is given in **20.2**.

5

Aspects of the verb

Introduction

In the previous chapter (*see* **4.2**) it was pointed out that the Russian verb was characterised by the presence of two aspects – *imperfective* and *perfective* – and that every Russian verb (with a handful of exceptions) belongs to one or other of these aspects. In this chapter it is intended to examine in some detail the use of the two aspects, although it may be noted that whole books have been written on this topic, and it will therefore not be possible here to discuss every circumstance in which a decision on aspectual usage has to be made.

It is usually reckoned that aspects of the verb present a particularly tough challenge to speakers of English attempting to learn Russian. There are perhaps three reasons for this.

First, with the exception of the *present tense*, which is formed only from *imperfective verbs*, the aspect system extends to all parts of the verb, including *gerunds* and (at least in some circumstances) *participles*. It is therefore necessary to make a decision about aspects almost every time a verb is used.

Second, differences in meaning between the aspects of the Russian verb tend not to correspond to differences in meaning between English verb forms. For example, in English it is possible to talk about 'reading' in the past using the following forms:

    I read
    I have read
    I did read
    I had read
    I was reading
    I used to read
    I would read

In Russian, an *imperfective* verb (**я чита́л**), depending on the context, might be the equivalent of any of those forms; a *perfective* verb (**я прочита́л**), depending on the context, might be the equivalent of any of the first four forms.

Third, although numerous attempts have been made, it is extremely difficult to come up with a brief account of the differences between the aspects that can serve as a practical guide for all occasions. In section **4.2** it was suggested that each aspect covers a wide range of functions, but in general terms the perfective aspect is used when an action or state is considered from the point of view of its boundaries (beginning, end or both), while the imperfective is used in all other circumstances (if there is a 'default' aspect in Russian, it is the imperfective). The authors of this volume consider this to be as good a single-sentence statement of the difference between the aspects as any other, but we readily accept that there will be many circumstances where it will be of no help at all and that there will even be occasions where the choice of aspect appears to be (or can be interpreted as being) in direct contradiction with it.

Nevertheless, the difficulties should not be overstated. Although a choice of aspect has to be made almost every time a verb is used, not all choices are equally important. The situations where questions of aspect arise can be divided into four categories:

1   Only one aspect is grammatically possible.
2   Either aspect can be used and the meaning of the sentence is affected by the aspect used.
3   One aspect is preferable, but the use of the other aspect will not lead to a misunderstanding.
4   Either aspect can be used without there being any significant difference.

It follows from this that only in the first two situations is there a danger of producing a sentence that is either grammatically unacceptable or likely to be misunderstood. In other situations it is possible that the Russian will not 'sound quite right', but no real problems of communication will arise.

In this chapter the first section will be devoted to those situations where only one aspect is grammatically possible, while examples of the other three situations will be found at different points throughout the remaining sections. The second section will enumerate some general principles that can be applied to most verb forms where there is choice of aspects, while in the remaining sections there will be an examination of the issues relating to the specific meanings of particular groups of verbs (**5.3**), single completed actions (**5.4**), questions (**5.5**), commands and invitations (**5.6**) and negated sentences (**5.7**); the final section (**5.8**) contains a description of a construction that allows both aspects to be used in the same verb phrase. As in the previous chapter, the aspect of each of the relevant verbs used in the examples will be indicated by the abbreviations **нсв** (=**несовершённый** *imperfective*) and **св** (=**совершённый** *perfective*).

5.1   Situations where there is no choice

5.1.0   Introduction

In a number of instances involving the *infinitive*, only one aspect is grammatically possible.

For more on the infinitive, *see* **4.1**.

5.1.1   Only the imperfective is possible

A verb in the *infinitive* must be in the *imperfective* aspect when it is used in conjunction with one of the following:

1 A verb conveying the idea of *beginning*, *continuing* or *stopping* an action, for example:

начина́ть (нсв)/нача́ть (св)	to begin
продолжа́ть (нсв)	to continue
конча́ть (нсв)/ко́нчить (св)	to finish
перестава́ть (нсв)/переста́ть (св)	to cease
прекраща́ть (нсв)/прекрати́ть (св)	to cease
броса́ть (нсв)/бро́сить (св)	to give up

Он *на́чал расска́зывать (нсв)* о том, где он был и что он де́лал.
He began to talk about where he had been and what he had been doing.

Она́ прервала́ свой расска́з, но сле́дователь ничего́ не говори́л и *продолжа́л смотре́ть (нсв)* на неё с ирони́ческой улы́бкой на лице́.
She broke off her account, but the investigating officer said nothing and continued to look at her with an ironic smile on his face.

Он *ко́нчил счита́ть (нсв)* де́ньги и вы́писал квита́нцию.
He finished counting the money and wrote out a receipt.

По́сле пе́рвого ку́рса он *переста́л ходи́ть (нсв)* на ле́кции, но стал проводи́ть бо́льше вре́мени в библиоте́ке.
After first year he stopped going to lectures and spent more time in the library.

Специали́сты пришли́ к вы́воду, что с 1997 го́да озо́новый слой, за исключе́нием простра́нства над по́люсами, *прекрати́л уменьша́ться (нсв)*.
Scientists have come to the conclusion that from 1997 onwards the ozone layer, with the exception of the area above the poles, has stopped diminishing.

Я не знал, что вы *бро́сили кури́ть (нсв)*.
I didn't know you'd given up smoking.

2 A verb or another predicate form indicating the undesirability or the pointlessness of an action, for example:

не на́до	don't, you shouldn't
не ну́жно	don't, you shouldn't
не сто́ит	it's not worth
бесполе́зно	it's pointless
не́зачем	there's no point in
нет смы́сла, не име́ет смы́сла	it makes no sense to

Не на́до звони́ть (нсв) так ра́но: я ещё не просну́лся как сле́дует.
Don't phone so early, I haven't woken up properly yet.

Не ну́жно говори́ть (нсв) таки́е ве́щи вслух.
You shouldn't say such things aloud.

Не сто́ит писа́ть (нсв) жа́лобу: всё равно́ ничего́ не изме́нится.
It's not worth writing a complaint, nothing's going to change anyway.

С ним *бесполе́зно спо́рить (нсв)*: он всё зна́ет и никого́ не слу́шает.
It's pointless arguing with him, he knows everything and doesn't listen to anyone.

Не́зачем идти́ (нсв) так ра́но: в э́то вре́мя никого́ там не бу́дет.
There's no point in going so early; at this time of day there'll be nobody there.

Так по́здно *е́хать* (нсв) на авто́бусе *не име́ет смы́сла*; лу́чше я вы́зову такси́.
It doesn't make sense to go by bus when it's this late; it'll be better if I call a taxi.

3 The following verbs:

запреща́ть (нсв)/запрети́ть (св)	to forbid
уме́ть (нсв)	to know how to do something
учи́ться (нсв)/научи́ться (св)	to learn how to do something

Здесь *запрещено́ по́льзоваться* (нсв) моби́льными телефо́нами.
It's forbidden to use mobile phones here.

Она́ *уме́ет* так краси́во *излага́ть* (нсв) свои́ мы́сли.
She knows how to express her thoughts so beautifully.

Я в шко́ле *учи́лся игра́ть* (нсв) в ша́хматы, но ничего́ не получи́лось.
I tried to learn how to play chess at school, but never got anywhere with it.

5.1.2 Only the perfective is possible

An *infinitive* verb must be in the *perfective* aspect if it is used with any of the following *perfective* verbs:

вы́йти (св)	to pop out (to do something)
зайти́ (св)	to drop in (to do something)
уда́ться (св)	to succeed
успе́ть (св)	to succeed, to have time (to do something)
суме́ть (св)	to be clever enough, to be able (to do something)

Дава́й *вы́йдем* (св) *покури́ть* (св).
Let's go out for a smoke.

Е́сли мо́жно, я *зайду́* (св) за́втра *поговори́ть* (св) о на́ших пла́нах.
If it's all right, I'll call in tomorrow to talk about our plans.

Ему́ *удало́сь* (св) *найти́* (св) кварти́ру в са́мом це́нтре го́рода.
He managed to find a flat in the very centre of town.

Сего́дня я не *успе́ю* (св) *сде́лать* (св) э́тот перево́д.
I won't have time to do the translation today.

Письмо́ напи́сано ме́лким, неразбо́рчивым по́черком, но мы всё же *суме́ли* (св) его́ *прочита́ть* (св).
The letter was written in small, illegible handwriting, but none the less we managed to read it.

NOTE The verb **удава́ться (нсв)/уда́ться (св)**, when used with an *infinitive*, is an *impersonal* verb, and the *dative* case is used to indicate the person who succeeds in doing something.

For more on impersonal verbs, *see* **3.4.3** and **11.2.2**.

5.2 Some general principles

5.2.1 Incomplete actions

When a verb is used to indicate an incomplete action, it is in the *imperfective* aspect. Such actions can be interrupted by some event or can be going on the background while something else happens.

> **Она** *сиде́ла* (*нсв*) **в о́фисе и** *разбира́ла* (*нсв*) **каки́е-то фина́нсовые докуме́нты, когда́ вдруг разда́лся стук в дверь.**
> She was sitting in the office and going through some financial documents, when suddenly there was a knock at the door.

> **Когда́ он вошёл в ко́мнату, его́ нача́льник** *разгова́ривал* (*нсв*) **по телефо́ну.**
> When he came into the room, his boss was talking on the telephone.

> **Он** *спеши́л*, **потому́ что** *опа́здывал* (*нсв*) **на по́езд.**
> He was hurrying because he was late for the train.

In the last example, the second verb is *imperfective* because the action of being late is not completed until the person arrives at the station and discovers that the train has already left. In many instances the incompleteness is implied by the general situation or context:

> —**Что вы** *де́лали* (*нсв*) **вчера́ ве́чером?**
> —**Ничего́ интере́сного: я** *чита́л* (*нсв*) **кни́гу,** *реша́л* (*нсв*) **кроссво́рд в вече́рней газе́те и** *смотре́л* (*нсв*) **телеви́зор.**

> —What did you do yesterday evening?
> —Nothing interesting: I read a book, had a go at crossword in the evening paper, watched television.

If, however, specific accomplishments are mentioned, the *perfective* is more likely to be used:

> **У меня́ вчера́ был тако́й насы́щенный ве́чер: я** *прочита́л* (*св*) **де́сять студе́нческих рабо́т,** *реши́л* (*св*) **кроссво́рд в вече́рней газе́те и наконе́ц** *посмотре́л* (*св*) **ту переда́чу, кото́рую ты всё вре́мя рекоменду́ешь.**
> I had a very full evening yesterday; I read ten student essays, solved the crossword in the evening paper and eventually watched that programme you're always recommending.

Another type of incomplete action is one that is in process and is to be continued:

> *Чита́йте* (*нсв*), *чита́йте* (*нсв*); **не обраща́йте внима́ния на шум в коридо́ре.**
> Carry on reading; don't pay any attention to the noise in the corridor.

5.2.2 Focusing on the process

On meeting a friend or colleague on Monday morning, you may be asked one of the following questions:

> **Как вы** *провели́* (*св*) **суббо́ту-воскресе́нье?**
> **Как вы** *проводи́ли* (*нсв*) **суббо́ту-воскресе́нье?**

Both sentences mean essentially the same thing:

> How did you spend the weekend?

They are, however, asking for different information. When the question is asked using the *perfective* verb (**прове́ли**), you are being invited to sum up your weekend, and an appropriate answer might be:

О́чень хорошо́, спаси́бо.
Very well, thank you.

If the question is asked using the *imperfective* verb (**проводи́ли**), you are being to invited to say what you did to fill up the weekend, i.e. the focus is on the *process* of spending the weekend. Here an appropriate answer might be:

В суббо́ту я ходи́л на футбо́л, а в воскресе́нье съе́здил домо́й к роди́телям.
On Saturday I went to a football match and on Sunday went home to see my parents.

NOTE   The word **уик-э́нд** 'weekend' is known and used by many Russians, although others prefer the the more traditional **суббо́та-воскресе́нье** 'Saturday and Sunday' or **выходны́е** 'days off'.

Хорошо́, что меня́ *встреча́ли* (нсв) на вокза́ле, а то не зна́ю, как бы я добра́лся до гости́ницы.
It's a good job I was met at the station, or else I don't know how I would have got to the hotel.

The idea of meeting someone off a train or an aeroplane is thought of as a process, involving going to the station or the airport, finding the right place to wait and delivering the person to their destination. When, however, the reference is to a simple encounter, the perfective is more likely to be used:

Он до́лго броди́л по у́лицам, пока́, наконе́ц, он не *встре́тил* (св) кого́-то из знако́мых.
He wandered the streets for a long time until at last he met someone he knew.

Пока́ не зна́ю, кто её уби́л. Могу́ то́лько *дога́дываться* (нсв).
At the moment I don't know who killed her. I can only make guesses.

The *imperfective* **дога́дываться** implies that the speaker is in a position to go through the process of making guesses; the *perfective* (**догада́ться**) would imply that the speaker is already in a position to guess the right answer, something that is contradicted by the previous sentence.

Я пойду́ *узнава́ть* (нсв), когда́ отправля́ется по́езд.
I'll go and find out what time the train leaves.

Here the focus is on the process of finding out: going to the station, asking the necessary question and returning with the information. The perfective is used when the focus is on the information itself:

Я то́лько что *узна́л* (св), что наш по́езд отменён; сле́дующий бу́дет то́лько че́рез два часа́.
I've just found out that our train has been cancelled; the next one won't be for another two hours.

Мне не сто́ило большо́го труда́ опрове́ргнуть всю напра́слину, возведённую на меня́, но *опроверга́ть* (нсв) её всё-таки пришло́сь.
It didn't cost me a lot of trouble to refute all the tissue of lies that were told about me, but nevertheless I had to do it.

The *imperfective* **опроверга́ть** is used because the speaker is thinking of himself having to go through the process of refutation.

The focus is on process in contexts relating to the possibility or desirability of starting an action which is already understood to be due to take place at some time:

> **Ита́к, тре́тий ра́унд око́нчен; *мо́жно остана́вливать* (*нсв*) секундоме́р.**
> So, the third round is over; you can stop the stop-watch.

> **Уже́ по́здно; нам, наве́рно, *на́до идти́* (*нсв*), а то не успе́ем на после́дний авто́бус.**
> It's already late; we ought to be going, or else we'll miss the last bus.

> **Ка́жется, *пора́ зака́нчивать* (*нсв*) диску́ссию: лю́ди уже́ ста́ли смотре́ть на часы́.**
> I think it's time we were bringing the discussion to an end; people are already starting to look at their watches.

5.2.3 Repetition

The *imperfective* aspect is normally used to indicate *repeated* actions.

> **Она́ всерьёз следи́ла за свои́м здоро́вьем и регуля́рно *посеща́ла* (*нсв*) тренажёрный зал, бассе́йн и те́ннисный корт.**
> She took a serious interest in her health and paid regular visits to the gym, the swimming baths and the tennis court.

> **Ло́ндонский футбо́льный клуб «Че́лси» с но́вого сезо́на *бу́дет проводи́ть* (*нсв*) выездны́е ма́тчи в я́рких футбо́лках кисло́тно-лимо́нного цве́та.**
> From next season Chelsea, the London football team, will play their away matches in a bright acid-lemon strip.

> **В жа́ркую пого́ду сле́дует поча́ще *пить* (*нсв*) минера́льную во́ду или други́е прохлади́тельные напи́тки.**
> In hot weather you should drink more mineral water or other cooling drinks.

> ***Чита́йте* (*нсв*) на́шу газе́ту ка́ждый день!**
> Read our newspaper every day!

This principle normally applies to statements or instructions that have general significance, even if repetition is not specifically mentioned:

> **Мы бу́дем *пресле́довать* (*нсв*) террори́стов всю́ду.**
> We will pursue terrorists everywhere.

> **По́льзуясь эскала́тором, *сто́йте* (*нсв*) спра́ва, *держи́тесь* (*нсв*) за по́ручень.**
> When using the escalator, stand on the right and keep hold of the handrail.

Where both a *finite verb* and an *infinitive* are used together in a sentence in a context relating to a repeated action, the choice of aspect will be determined by which of the two verbs denotes the action being repeated:

> **Я то́лько что был у врача́; он *посове́товал* (*св*) мне *выпива́ть* (*нсв*) по ли́тру минера́льной воды́ в день.**
> I've just been to the doctor; he's advised me to drink a litre of mineral water a day.

> **При ка́ждой на́шей встре́че он *сове́товал* (нсв) мне *написа́ть* (св) автобиогра́фию.**
> Every time we met he advised me to write my autobiography.

In the first sentence the advice was given once, but is to be followed every day; consequently, the finite verb ('advised') is *perfective* and the infinitive ('to drink') is *imperfective*. In the second sentence the advice was given regularly, but would have been followed only once; here it is the finite verb that is *imperfective* and the infinitive that is *perfective*.

A perfective verb tends to be used when a series of repeated actions is seen as a single event. This occurs, for example, when a series of actions is repeated in quick succession as part of a chain of events:

> **Мы се́ли за стол, *вы́пили* (св) по три ча́шки ча́я и *съе́ли* (св) по по́рции моро́женого.**
> We sat down at the table, drank three cups of tea and ate a portion of icecream each.

> **Пе́ред тем, как поки́нуть зал, он успе́л не́сколько раз *вы́крикнуть* (св) како́й-то непоня́тный ло́зунг.**
> Before leaving the hall he managed several times to shout out some incomprehensible slogan.

The same principle applies when the totality of what has been achieved over a certain period is being summed up:

> **Он про́жил прекра́сную жизнь и *написа́л* (св) прекра́сные кни́ги.**
> He lived a fine life and wrote fine books.

> **За после́дние де́сять лет она́ *опубликова́ла* (св) бо́лее двухсо́т стате́й на ра́зные те́мы.**
> In the last ten years she has published over 200 articles on different topics.

5.2.4   Focusing on completion

The *perfective* aspect is normally used when the focus is on the *completion* of an action:

> **Никто́ отсю́да не уйдёт, пока́ я не *получу́* (св) отве́ты на все мои́ вопро́сы.**
> No one will leave here until I receive answers to all my questions.

> **Кто его́ оби́дит, тот дня *не прожи́вёт* (св).**
> Anyone who offends him won't live to see the end of the day.

The first example talks about an action that cannot take place until another is completed; the second talks about circumstances that will lead to an action in process not being completed.

The focus is on *completion* in many sentences where an *infinitive* is used:

> **Мне не сто́ило большо́го труда́ *опрове́ргнуть* (св) всю напра́слину, возведённую на меня́, но опроверга́ть её всё-таки пришло́сь.**
> It didn't cost me a lot of trouble to refute all the tissue of lies that were told about me, but nevertheless I had to do it.

The second infinitive in this sentence focuses on the process, as was explained above in **5.2.2**; the first infinitive, however, focuses on the *result*, in this case the successful refutation of the tissue of lies. Following the same logic, *perfective* infinitives tend to be used in conjunction with the following:

легко́	it is easy to
тру́дно	it is difficult to
сто́ит	one only has to
стара́ться (нсв)/постара́ться (св)	to try to
пыта́ться (нсв)/попыта́ться	to try to
что́бы	in order to

Ду́маю, что с тако́й информа́цией нам *легко́* бу́дет *докопа́ться* (св) до и́стины.
I think that with this information it will be easy for us to dig down to the truth.

***Тру́дно сказа́ть* (св), когда́ вы смо́жете получи́ть ваш зака́з.**
It's difficult to say when we will be able to get your order to you.

Но *сто́ило ему́ почу́вствовать* (св), что его́ хотя́т обману́ть, как он начина́л зли́ться.
But he only had to feel that someone was trying to deceive him for him to start to get angry.

Я постара́юсь *прийти́* (св) домо́й не по́зже десяти́.
I'll try to come home no later than ten o'clock.

В самолёте он безуспе́шно *пыта́лся засну́ть* (св).
In the aeroplane he tried in vain to fall asleep.

Он взя́лся за э́то де́ло то́лько ра́ди того́, *что́бы зарабо́тать* (св) де́нег для семьи́.
He only took on this task in order to earn some money for his family.

In some instances the aspect of the infinitive affects the meaning of the sentence. In **5.3.2** an example was given of **пора́** used with an *imperfective* infinitive; the meaning was 'It's time' (to be doing something). When **пора́** is used with a *perfective* infinitive, the meaning is 'It's (high) time' (to have done something), i.e. with a focus on *completion*, rather than on *process*:

Нам давно́ *пора́ уйти́* (св) со сце́ны росси́йской поли́тики и *уступи́ть* (св) ме́сто молоды́м.
It's high time we had left the stage of Russian politics and given way to the young.

Хва́тит and **доста́точно** both mean '(it's) enough'; when **доста́точно** is followed by a *perfective* infinitive, it means 'it's enough to', 'all one has to do is . . .':

Доста́точно *прочесть* (св) пе́рвую страни́цу его́ биогра́фии, что́бы поня́ть, почему́ его́ не лю́бят в Кремле́.
It's enough to read the first page of his biography to understand why he's not liked in the Kremlin.

When used with an *imperfective* infinitive, both **доста́точно** and **хва́тит** mean 'that's enough of that', i.e. they form an instruction to stop doing something:

Всё, *хва́тит валя́ть* (нсв) дурака́. Éсли не хо́чешь вести́ серьёзный разгово́р, я уйду́.
Right, that's enough of playing the fool. If you don't want to hold a serious conversation with me, I'm going.

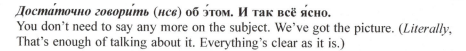

Доста́точно говори́ть (нсв) об э́том. И так всё я́сно.
You don't need to say any more on the subject. We've got the picture. (*Literally,* That's enough of talking about it. Everything's clear as it is.)

5.3 The specific meaning of the verb

5.3.0 Introduction

In many instances the details of aspect usage are determined by specific meaning of the verb concerned.

For specific issues relating to the use of aspects with unprefixed verbs of motion, *see* **22.1**.

5.3.1 Verbs that cannot indicate an action in process in both Russian and English

There are many verbs which, because of their precise meaning, cannot normally indicate *action in process*. With such verbs, however, the usual English meaning does not necessarily indicate whether or not a particular Russian verb belongs to this category.

Examples of where neither a Russian verb nor its English equivalent can normally indicate an action in process:

находи́ть (нсв)/найти́ (св) 'to find'

NOTE | This restriction does not apply in either language when the verb is used in the sense of 'form a particular opinion of something':

Я *нахожу́* (нсв) ва́ши слова́ неуме́стными.
I find your words inappropriate.

5.3.2 Verbs that can indicate an action in process in Russian, but not in English

There are quite a few examples where the Russian verb can indicate an action in process, but where the normal English translation of the Russian *perfective* cannot. In such instances the Russian *imperfective* will usually be translated either by a different verb or by 'try to . . .':

добива́ться (нсв) 'to strive for', 'to try to attain'
добиться (св) 'to attain'

лечи́ть (нсв) 'to treat (a patient)'
вы́лечить (св) 'to cure'

лови́ть (нсв) 'to try to catch'
пойма́ть (св) 'to catch'

реша́ть (нсв) 'to try to decide, to try to solve'
реши́ть (св) 'to decide, to solve'

убежда́ть (нсв) 'to try to convince'
убеди́ть (св) 'to convince'

угова́ривать (нсв) 'to try to persuade'
уговори́ть (св) 'to persuade'

Челове́к до́лжен *добива́ться* (нсв) в своём де́ле соверше́нства.
A person should strive to achieve perfection in whatever activity they are pursuing.

В после́дние го́ды на́ши учёные *доби́лись* (св) потряса́ющих результа́тов в э́той сфе́ре.
In recent years our scientists have achieved amazing results in this field.

В про́шлом году́ меня́ *лечи́ли* (нсв) от радикули́та. Ка́жется, *вы́лечили* (св), но по́лной уве́ренности нет, коне́чно.
Last year I was treated for back pain. I think I'm cured but, of course, you can never be totally sure.

***Лови́ть* (нсв) такси́ лу́чше всего́ на углу́. Там всегда́ большо́е движе́ние.**
The best place to try to catch a taxi is on the corner. There is always a lot of traffic there.

На осно́ве достове́рной информа́ции, полу́ченной из ра́зных исто́чников, сотру́дники мили́ции смогли́ устро́ить заса́ду и *пойма́ть* (св) престу́пников.
On the basis of reliable information received from different sources the police were able to set a trap and catch the criminals.

Вчера́ ве́чером я чита́л кни́гу, *реша́л* (нсв) кроссво́рд в вече́рней газе́те и смотре́л телеви́зор.
Yesterday evening I read a book, had a go at a crossword in the evening paper and watched television.

У меня́ вчера́ был тако́й насы́щенный ве́чер: я прочита́л де́сять студе́нческих рабо́т, *реши́л* (св) кроссво́рд в вече́рней газе́те и наконе́ц посмотре́л ту переда́чу, кото́рую ты всё вре́мя рекоменду́ешь.
I had a very full evening yesterday; I read ten student essays, solved the crossword in the evening paper and eventually watched that programme you're always recommending.

Он о́чень стра́нный челове́к: мо́жет це́лый ве́чер *убежда́ть* (нсв) тебя́, что два́жды два – пять, а не четы́ре, как тебе́ почему́-то всегда́ каза́лось.
He's a very strange man: he can spend a whole evening trying to convince you that two and two are five and not, as for some reason you've always thought, four.

Я зна́ю все ва́ши аргуме́нты наизу́сть, и вы никогда́ не *убеди́те* (св) меня́, что вы пра́вы.
I know all your arguments by heart, and you'll never convince me that you're right.

Я то́лько что был у ше́фа. Он *угова́ривал* (нсв) меня́ возгла́вить на́ше представи́тельство на Се́верном Кавка́зе. Но не *уговори́л* (св)!
I've just been to see the boss. He was trying to persuade me to take over our office in the North Caucasus. But he didn't succeed! (*Literally*, he didn't persuade me.)

NOTE | The phrase **лови́ть (нсв) ры́бу** means 'to go fishing'.

5.3.3

Verbs that can indicate an action in process in English, but not in Russian

There are some verbs where the Russian *imperfective* cannot be used to indicate an action in process, but where no such restriction applies to the English equivalent:

случа́ться (нсв)/случи́ться (св)	to happen
приходи́ть (нсв)/прийти́ (св)	to come, to arrive

In such instances the Russian imperfective can be used to indicate repeated action, but to indicate process an alternative verb with a closely related meaning is used:

происходи́ть (нсв)/произойти́ (св)	to happen
идти́ (нсв)	to be going/coming
прибыва́ть (нсв)/прибы́ть (св)	to arrive

Посмотри́ в окно́ и скажи́ нам, что *происхо́дит* (нсв) на у́лице.
Look out of the window and tell us what's happening outside.

Ти́ше! *Идёт* (нсв) учи́тель.
Quiet! The teacher's coming.

Наш по́езд *прибыва́ет* (нсв) на коне́чную ста́нцию. Выходя́ из ваго́на, пожа́луйста, не забыва́йте свои́ ве́щи.
Our train is coming into the terminus. When leaving the carriage, please remember to take all items of luggage with you (*Literally*, please don't forget your things.)

NOTE | The verb **прибыва́ть (нсв)/прибы́ть (св)** is somewhat associated with official contexts and tends to be used in notices and announcements relating to public transport (*see* **22.4.3**).

5.3.4

Verbs indicating an action that by definition cannot be completed

There are some verbs that indicate actions that by definition cannot be completed. Some of these verbs occur in the *imperfective* only; a list of such verbs was given in **4.2.6**. Others have *perfective* partners which have special connotations. Many of these have a *perfective* partner with the prefix **по-**. This has the connotation of 'doing the action for a while and then doing something else':

лежа́ть (нсв)/полежа́ть (св)	to lie (down), to be lying (down)
сиде́ть (нсв)/посиде́ть (св)	to (be) sit(ting)
стоя́ть (нсв)/постоя́ть (св)	to (be) stand(ing)
говори́ть (нсв)/поговори́ть (св)	to talk
молча́ть (нсв)/помолча́ть (св)	to be silent
пла́кать (нсв)/попла́кать (св)	to cry
рабо́тать (нсв)/порабо́тать (св)	to work

Сейча́с сде́лаем переры́в на ко́фе; *посиди́м* (св) немно́жко, *поговори́м* (нсв), а мину́т че́рез пятна́дцать продо́лжим на́шу рабо́ту.
We'll break for coffee now; we'll sit for a short while and talk, and then after about 15 minutes we'll resume our work.

Услы́шав отве́т, он не́сколько секу́нд *помолча́л* (св), пото́м взял под козырёк, поверну́лся и вы́шел из ко́мнаты.

Having heard the answer, he remained silent for a few seconds, then saluted, turned round and marched out of the room.

NOTE	When **говори́ть** means 'to say', its perfective partner is **сказа́ть**.

Some of these verbs have a second *perfective* partner with the **за-** prefix. This has the connotation of 'beginning the action':

заговори́ть (св)	to (start to) talk
замолча́ть (св)	to fall silent
запла́кать (св)	to (start to) cry

Я о́чень удиви́лся, когда́ он вдруг *заговори́л* (св) по-ру́сски. Но по́сле двух-трёх предложе́ний он *замолча́л* (св). По-ви́димому, не знал, что сказа́ть да́льше.

I was very surprised when he suddenly started speaking Russian. But after two or three sentences he fell silent. Evidently he didn't know what to say next.

Прочита́в письмо́, она́ *запла́кала* (св) и вы́бежала из ко́мнаты.

Having read the letter, she started crying and ran out of the room.

5.3.5 'Semelfactive' perfectives

A special group of *perfective* verbs is made up of the so-called 'semelfactive' verbs. These verbs, all of which belong to class **4.6.3**, denote a single, instaneous action. Examples (given here with their *imperfective* partners) include:

а́хать (нсв)/а́хнуть (св)	to say 'akh', to give a shout of joy, surprise or sadness
вздыха́ть (нсв)/вздохну́ть (св)	to sigh
кива́ть (нсв)/кивну́ть (св)	to nod
кида́ть (нсв)/ки́нуть (св)	to throw
крича́ть (нсв)/кри́кнуть (св)	to shout
лопа́ться (нсв)/ло́пнуть (св)	to burst
маха́ть (нсв)/махну́ть (св)	to wave
о́хать (нсв)/о́хнуть (св)	to say 'okh', to groan
пина́ть (нсв)/пну́ть (св)	to kick
пры́гать (нсв)/пры́гнуть (нсв)	to jump
сверка́ть (нсв)/сверкну́ть (св)	to sparkle, to flash
стреля́ть (нсв)/стрельну́ть (св)	to shoot
стуча́ть (нсв)/сту́кнуть (св)	to knock
толка́ть (нсв)/толкну́ть (св)	to push
хихи́кать (нсв)/хихи́кнуть (св)	to giggle
чиха́ть (нсв)/чихну́ть (св)	to sneeze
шага́ть (нсв)/шагну́ть (св)	to stride

Мир *вздохну́л* (св) с облегче́нием, услы́шав об освобожде́нии зало́жников.

The world gave a sigh of relief when it heard about the release of the hostages.

Ско́ро бу́дет дождь: то́лько что *сверкну́ла* (св) мо́лния.

It's going to rain soon; there's just been a flash of lightning.

5.4 **Single completed actions**

5.4.0 **Introduction**

Because the *imperfective* aspect is normally used for *repeated* actions, and because the *perfective* aspect is used when the focus is on the *completion* of an event, it is tempting to conclude that the perfective is the aspect to be used when describing single completed actions in the past. Unfortunately, it is not as simple as that: although the perfective aspect is indeed used on very many occasions, the imperfective is by no means infrequent. The principle to follow is that given at the beginning of this chapter: the imperfective is the default aspect and should be used unless there is a particular reason for using the perfective. And the reason that is most commonly found for using the perfective is that the event is placed in one of a limited number of specific contexts.

5.4.1 **The context of other actions**

One context that normally requires the use of the *perfective* is that of *preceding* and/or *following* actions – in other words, where an action forms part of a sequence of events. This use of the perfective is found especially frequently in *narratives* of one sort or another:

> **На сле́дующее у́тро он** *проснулся (св)* **в прекра́сном настрое́нии,** *встал (св)***,** *при́нял (св)* **душ,** *побри́лся (св)***,** *позавтракал (св)* **и** *усе́лся (св)* **за рабо́ту.**
> The next day he woke up in an excellent mood, got up, had a shower, shaved, had breakfast and sat down to work.

Sometimes gerunds or conjunctions such as **когда́** 'when' are used to indicate that two or more events occur in sequence:

> *Оде́вшись (св)***, он** *положи́л (св)* **ве́щи в огро́мную су́мку и** *спусти́лся (св)* **вниз.**
> Having got dressed, he put his things in an enormous bag and went downstairs.

> **Он** *успе́л (св)* **прочита́ть де́сять страни́ц,** *когда́* **телефо́нный звоно́к** *заста́вил (св)* **его́ отложи́ть кни́гу.**
> He had managed to read ten pages when a telephone call forced him to put aside his book.

For more on the use of conjunctions and gerunds in time expressions, *see* **21.1** and **21.10**.

The same principle applies to a sequence of events that is expected to take place in the future:

> **Я** *пришлю́ (св)* **тебе́ приглаше́ние, и ты** *офо́рмишь (св)* **туристи́ческую ви́зу и** *прие́дешь (св)* **на неде́лю. Пото́м** *вернёшься (св)* **домо́й,** *ула́дишь (св)* **все форма́льности и** *прие́дешь (св)* **уже́ оконча́тельно.**
> I'll send you an invitation, and you can get a tourist visa and come for a week. Then you'll go home, sort out all the formalities and move here permanently.

A repeated action, an incomplete action or a continuing action taking place in the background of a sequence of events will be indicated by an *imperfective* verb according to the principles discussed in **5.2.1** and **5.2.3**:

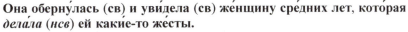

> **Она оберну́лась (св) и уви́дела (св) же́нщину сре́дних лет, кото́рая** *дела́ла (нсв)* **ей каки́е-то же́сты.**
> She turned round and saw a middle-aged woman who was gesturing to her.

The making of the gestures is a repeated action that is going on in the background and is indicated by the imperfective verb **дела́ла**.

> **Я реши́л (св) пое́хать домо́й на метро́. На «Ки́евской», где я** *де́лал (нсв)* **переса́дку на Кольцеву́ю ли́нию, меня́ удиви́ла (св) толпа́ люде́й, стоя́щих на платфо́рме.**
> I decided to go home by metro. At Kievskaia station, where I changed onto the Circle Line, I was surprised by the crowd of people standing on the platform.

Here the verb **де́лал** is imperfective because the narrator had not completed the process of changing from one train to another at the time when he was surprised by the crowd of people on the platform.

The imperfective is also used for whole sequences of repeated actions:

> **У него́ был о́чень стра́нный рабо́чий день: он** *появля́лся (нсв)* **в о́фисе по́зже всех,** *выпива́л (нсв)* **ча́шку ко́фе,** *просма́тривал (нсв)* **электро́нную по́чту и пото́м** *исчеза́л (нсв)* **на весь день.**
> His working day was a very strange one: he would appear in the office later than everyone else, drink a cup of coffee, look through his e-mails and then disappear for the rest of the day.

5.4.2 The context of the present

The *perfective* aspect is used when the focus is on the fact that the consequences of the action continue to be felt at the present time:

> **Я** *разби́л (св)* **очки́ и не зна́ю, как я без них доберу́сь до до́ма.**
> I have broken my glasses and I don't know how I'm going to get home without them.

> **Я то́лько что узна́л (св), что наш по́езд** *отменён (св)***; сле́дующий бу́дет то́лько че́рез два часа́.**
> I've just found out that our train has been cancelled; the next one won't be for another two hours.

In the first example the focus is on the consequences of the speaker breaking his glasses, namely, the difficulty of getting home without them; with the first verb in the second example the focus is on the consequence of finding out, namely, the possession of new information, while with the second verb the focus is on the consequences of the train being cancelled, namely, that the speaker and his companion are stuck in the station for another two hours.

Where the consequences of a past action do not extend into the present, the *imperfective* is more likely to be used. In many instances this use of the imperfective denotes an action that has, so to speak, been 'reversed' by later events:

> **Ты во́время пришёл. Только что** *зашла́ (св)* **твоя́ сестра́; она́ ждёт тебя́ на ку́хне.**
> You've come at just the right time. Your sister has just dropped in; she's waiting for you in the kitchen.

Жаль, что ты пришёл домо́й так по́здно. *Заходи́ла (нсв)* твоя́ сестра́; она́ хоте́ла о чём-то поговори́ть с тобо́й.
It's a pity you've come home so late. Your sister called (and has gone away again); she wanted to talk to you about something.

К сожале́нию я весь день за́нят: *прие́хала (св)* делега́ция из А́нглии, и я до́лжен показа́ть им всё, что мы здесь де́лаем.
Unfortunately, I'm busy all day; a delegation has arrived from England and I have to show them everything that we are doing here.

В про́шлом году́ *приезжа́ла (нсв)* делега́ция из А́нглии. Мы показа́ли им всё, что здесь де́лаем, и в ито́ге был подпи́сан протоко́л о наме́рениях.
Last year a delegation came out from England. We showed them everything that we are doing here and as a result a joint statement of intent was signed.

Although this usage is perhaps most common with prefixed verbs of motion, it can be found with other verbs as well:

Здесь хо́лодно. А-а, вот почему́: кто-то *откры́л (св)* окно́.
It's cold in here. Ah, that's why; somebody has opened the window (and it is still open).

Здесь хо́лодно, как бу́дто кто-то *открыва́л (нсв)* окно́.
It's cold in here, as if somebody had opened the window (but now it's shut).

In the sentences below, the action of summoning the speaker to see the boss is not 'reversed' as such, but once the visit to the boss is over, the direct consequence of the act of summoning (rushing to his office, sitting there and being given instructions, etc.) no longer applies, which is why the *imperfective* is used in the second example:

Я сейча́с иду́ к ше́фу. Меня́ *вы́звали (св)*.
I'm on the way to the boss('s office). I've been summoned to see him.

Я то́лько что был у ше́фа. Меня́ *вызыва́ли (нсв)*.
I've just been with the boss. I'd been summoned to see him.

5.4.3   The context of a specific occasion

The third type of context is that of a specific and explicitly mentioned occasion:

Одна́жды, на исхо́де ле́та про́шлого го́да мне *позвони́л (св)* ста́рый друг и *сказа́л (св)*, что сде́лает мне предложе́ние, от кото́рого я не могу́ отказа́ться.
Once, towards the end of last summer, I was phoned by an old friend, who said he was going to make me an offer I can't refuse.

В про́шлом году́ приезжа́ла делега́ция из А́нглии. Мы *показа́ли (св)* им всё, что здесь де́лаем, и в ито́ге был подпи́сан протоко́л о наме́рениях.
Last year a delegation came out from England. We showed them everything that we are doing here and as a result a joint statement of intent was signed.

If no explicit context is given, the *imperfective* is more likely to be used, even if it is clear that the event occurred only once:

Они́ учи́лись в одно́й шко́ле, но в ра́зных кла́ссах: ви́дели друг дру́га на переме́нах, вме́сте *выступа́ли* (*нсв*) одна́жды на шко́льной сце́не – вот и всё знако́мство.

They had gone to the same school, but were in different classes; they had seen each other at break times and had once performed together on the school stage, but that was the full extent of their acquaintance.

Она́, коне́чно, зна́ет отве́т, но кто-то, ви́димо, *проси́л* (*нсв*) её не говори́ть об э́том.

Of course, she knows the answer, but somebody must have asked her not to talk about it.

The imperfective is even more likely to be used if there is nothing to indicate whether the action took place on one occasion or was repeated:

Припо́мните, мо́жет быть, она́ *расска́зывала* (*нсв*) вам о свое́й рабо́те, куда́ е́здила, с кем встреча́лась.

Try to remember; perhaps she told you about her work, where she travelled to, who she met.

Ты действи́тельно меня́ *предупрежда́л,* (*нсв*), но тепе́рь уже́ по́здно: что сде́лано – то сде́лано.

You did indeed warn me, but it's too late now; what's done is done.

Пове́рьте мне, я зна́ю, как э́ти лю́ди рабо́тают. Я уже́ *ста́лкивался* (*нсв*) с ни́ми.

Believe me, I know how these people work. They've already crossed my path.

One apparent exception to the principles described here occurs when quoting words that were written in the past. In these circumstances the verb **писа́ть** is normally in the imperfective, even though it would seem that a precise context is mentioned:

В отве́тном письме́ (от 24 декабря́ 1876 г.) Чайко́вский *писа́л* (*нсв*): «Как я рад, что ве́чер в консервато́рии оста́вил в вас хоро́шее воспомина́ние!»

In his reply (written on 24 December 1876) Tchaikovsky wrote: 'How glad I am that the evening at the Conservatory has left you with such warm memories.'

5.5 Asking questions

5.5.0 Introduction

Asking questions involves for the most part applying the general principles outlined in **5.2**. There are, however, some specific points to note.

5.5.1 Questions about the past

In general, when asking about a single event in the past, it is possible to follow the principles described in **5.4**. When one is merely making a general enquiry about whether an event has taken place or not, the *imperfective* is normally used:

Вы *чита́ли* (*нсв*) «Войну́ и мир»?
Have you read *War and Peace*?

Я когда́-нибудь *расска́зывал* (*св*) вам о мое́й встре́че с премье́р-мини́стром?
Have I ever told you about the time I met the Prime Minister?

The *perfective* is used when one is enquiring about an event that was expected to take place at a particular time. For example, if you know that someone has been trying to make an international telephone call, you may ask them:

Вы *дозвони́лись* (*св*)?
Did you get through?

Similarly:

Когда́ вы встре́тились в аэропорту́, он *сказа́л* (*св*) вам, куда́ улета́ет?
When you met in the airport, did he tell you where he was flying to?

The perfective is also used when asking about a past event from the point of view of its effect on the present. After making an arrangement to meet someone, you may conclude by saying:

***Договори́лись* (*св*)?**
Is that agreed, then?

When entering a room that is in a state of chaos, you might say:

Что здесь *случи́лось* (*св*)? Отку́да тако́й беспоря́док?
What's happened here? What caused all this chaos?

Questions about the future

When asking about someone's wishes or intentions, the *imperfective* is normally used:

Ты *бу́дешь пить* (*нсв*) ко́фе?
Are you going to have some coffee? *Or*
Would you like a cup of coffee?

In informal speech, this is often shortened to:

Ко́фе бу́дешь?

Где ты *бу́дешь ночева́ть* (*нсв*)?
Where are you going to spend the night?

The *perfective* is more likely to be used in questions relating to matters of fact, especially if there is a specific context or if the focus is on completion:

Когда́ мы *уви́димся* (*св*)?
When will we see each other?

Ты *прие́дешь* (*св*) за́втра или послеза́втра?
Are you arriving tomorrow or the day after?

Мне придётся тебя́ оста́вить на па́ру дней. Ты как, *спра́вишься* (*св*) оди́н? *Смо́жешь* (*св*) себя́ прокорми́ть?
I'm going to have to leave you for a couple of days or so. Will you cope on your own? Will you manage to feed yourself?

5.6 The imperative

5.6.0 Introduction

In general, the use of the aspects with the *imperative* follows the principles outlined in **5.2**. This section is concerned with certain specific issues.

For more on using the imperative, *see* **18.2.1** and **18.3.1**.

5.6.1 Giving instructions

The *perfective* is normally used when giving an instruction that is to be carried out once and where there is no focus on the process:

> *Скажи́те (св), пожа́луйста, ско́лько вре́мени?*
> Could you tell me what time it is, please?

> *Войди́те (св)!*
> Come in!

> *Позвони́ (св) мне сего́дня ве́чером, часо́в в де́сять.*
> Phone me this evening at about ten o'clock.

5.6.2 Issuing an invitation

Following the principle outlined in **5.2.2**, the *imperfective* is used when indicating that the time has now come to carry out an action that is either explicitly or implicitly understood to be appropriate. This includes the issuing of what are in effect *invitations*, a use of the imperfective that is limited to certain specific situations. For example, when visiting someone at their home you may receive all or some of the following invitations:

> *Заходи́те (нсв).*
> Come in.

> *Раздева́йтесь (нсв).*
> Take off your hat and coat.

> *Проходи́те (нсв).*
> Come through into the flat.

> *Сади́тесь (нсв).*
> Sit down.

NOTE | The verb **раздева́ться (нсв)/разде́ться (св)** normally means 'to get undressed'. In this context the invitation does not extend beyond the outer garments.

If, when seated at table, you display a hesitancy in attacking your plate of food, you may be encouraged with the words:

> *Е́шьте, е́шьте (нсв)! Or sometimes Ку́шайте, ку́шайте (нсв)!*
> Do start eating!

NOTE | The verb **ку́шать** is a synonym of **есть** (both mean 'to eat'), but its use is very restricted; it is normally used only in the *second person* (especially the *imperative*) and the infinitive and is principally associated with the issuing of polite invitations to start eating.

A waiter or waitress waiting to take your order may say:

> *Говори́те (нсв).*
> Can I take your order? (*Literally*, Speak.)

5.6.3   Being impatient

Another application of the same principle results in the use of the imperfective when an instruction is repeated. If someone knocks at your door, you will normally respond by saying **Войди́те** (*see* **5.6.2**). If the person, instead of coming in, half-opens the door and looks nervously into the room, you may well go on to say in a tone that, according to the circumstances, can vary from the encouraging to the impatient:

> **Ну**, *входи́те (нсв)* же!
> Well, come in if you're going to.

5.6.4   Other uses of the imperfective

The *imperfective* is also used to express indifference or a challenge to someone to carry out a threat. This usage can correspond to something like the English 'go ahead':

> —**Мы должны́ прове́рить всё, что здесь напи́сано.**
> —**Ну, что ж, *проверя́йте (нсв).***

> —We have to check everything that's written here.
> —Go ahead and check if you want to.

> —**Е́сли не прекрати́тся э́тот шум, мы вы́зовем мили́цию.**
> —**Здесь нет никако́го шу́ма. *Вызыва́йте (нсв).***

> —If this noise doesn't stop, we'll call the police.
> —There's no noise here. Go ahead and call them.

5.7   Negation

5.7.0   Introduction

In general, sentences with *negation* are rather more likely to contain an *imperfective* verb than are sentences where there is no negation. It is probably useful to follow the principle that in sentences with negation the imperfective should be used unless there is a good reason for selecting the perfective.

5.7.1   Negation in the past

A verb in the past tense will be in the *perfective* aspect when it refers to an action that could have taken place on a specific occasion in the past, did not take place and can now no longer take place:

> **Он нажа́л пе́рвую кно́пку, но ничего́ *не произошло́ (св)*. Он нажа́л втору́ю, и дверь откры́лась.**
> He pressed the first button, but nothing happened. He pressed the second, and the door opened.

> **Укра́ли все де́ньги и креди́тные карто́чки, но, к сча́стью, па́спорт и докуме́нты *не взя́ли (св)*.**
> They stole all (my) money and credit cards, but fortunately didn't take (my) passport and other documents.

Sometimes the verb in such sentences is reinforced by the phrase **так и**, corresponding approximately to the English 'never did':

> **Я *так и не узна́л* (св) его́ и́мя.**
> I never did find out his name.

The perfective is also used when the focus is on the implications for the present of the fact that the action has not taken place:

> **Она́ хо́чет показа́ть тебе́, что *не испуга́лась* (св).**
> She wants to show you that she hasn't been frightened *or* that she isn't frightened.

> **Жаль, что мы *не дости́гли* (св) взаимопонима́ния.**
> It's a pity that we haven't reached a mutual understanding.

When an action is expected, but has not yet taken place, either aspect is possible. The perfective is more likely to be used when the focus is on completion, if the action has already started or if the action does not involve intention on the part of the subject:

> **Я то́лько что посмотре́л в я́щик. По́чта ещё *не пришла́* (св).**
> I've just looked in the box. The post hasn't arrived yet.

> **К сожале́нию, я ещё *не сдал* (св) все необходи́мые экза́мены.**
> Unfortunately, I still haven't passed all the necessary examinations.

The *imperfective* is more likely to be used if the focus is on the process, if the action has not started or if the action involves intention on the part of the subject:

> **К сожале́нию, я ещё *не сдава́л* (нсв) все необходи́мые экза́мены.**
> Unfortunately, I still haven't taken all the necessary examinations.

> **Европе́йский суд ещё *не приступа́л* (нсв) к рассмотре́нию э́того и́ска.**
> The European Court (of Human Rights) has not begun its examination of this case.

In some instances of this sort, however, either aspect can be used, without there being any significant difference between them:

> **Госуда́рственная Ду́ма ещё *не рассма́тривала* (нсв) бюдже́т на сле́дующий год.**
> The State Duma has not yet examined the budget for next year.

> **Госуда́рственная Ду́ма ещё *не рассмотре́ла* (св) бюдже́т на сле́дующий год.**
> The State Duma has not yet examined the budget for next year.

In all other circumstances the imperfective will normally be used:

> **Как ни стра́нно, я *не чита́л* (нсв) «Войну́ и мир».**
> Strange as it may seem, I haven't read *War and Peace*.

> **Я могу́ подтверди́ть, что он из ко́мнаты *не выходи́л* (нсв).**
> I can confirm that he didn't leave the room.

> **Пове́рьте мне, я *не убива́л* (нсв) его́.**
> Believe me, I didn't kill him.

> **Ты никогда́ *не расска́зывал* (нсв) мне об э́том.**
> You never told me about that.

5.7.2 ## Negation in the future

In general, the use of aspects with *negated future tense* verbs is not significantly different from that which occurs in *questions* and which is described in **5.5.2**. The *imperfective* tends to be used when referring to intentions:

> **Я прошу́ проще́ния, но я *не бу́ду отвеча́ть* (нсв) на э́тот вопро́с: для э́того ну́жно мно́го вре́мени.**
> I apologise, but I will not answer that question, because it would take up a lot of time.

The *perfective* tends to be used to make factual statements about events that might have occurred, but which will not happen, especially in relation to a specific set of circumstances:

> **Не сто́ит спра́шивать об э́том: никто́ вам ничего́ *не ска́жет* (св), ни здесь, ни в прокурату́ре.**
> It's not worth asking about it; nobody will tell you anything, either here or at the prosecutor's office.

5.7.3 ## Negation with the imperative

Negated imperative verbs are almost invariably in the *imperfective*:

> ***Не подходи́* (нсв) ко мне. У меня́ грипп.**
> Don't come near me. I've got the flu.

> **Ремо́нт бу́дет сде́лан, е́сли не за́втра, то послеза́втра. *Не беспоко́йтесь* (нсв).**
> The repair work will be carried out if not tomorrow, then the day after. Don't worry.

> ***Не покупа́й* (нсв) э́тот сыр. Срок го́дности уже́ истёк.**
> Don't buy that cheese. It's past its sell-by date.

The *perfective* is used only on rare occasions, when the verb serves as a warning to avoid some inadvertant event:

> ***Не потеря́й* (св) ру́чку, а то не́чем бу́дет запо́лнить анке́ту.**
> Don't lose the pen, or you'll have nothing to fill the form in with.

Sometimes these forms are used in conjunction with **смотри́** 'watch', 'mind out':

> ***Смотри́, не разбе́й* (св) э́тот стака́н!**
> Watch you don't break that glass.

5.7.4 ## Negation with infinitives

Infinitive verbs in a sentence with *negation* are most commonly *imperfective*. This applies whether it is the main verb or the infinitive that is negated:

> **Я *не сове́тую* вам *чита́ть* (нсв) «Евге́ния Оне́гина» в перево́де.**
> I don't advise you to read *Evgenii Onegin* in translation.

> **Ребёнку ста́ло лу́чше, так что они́ реши́ли *не вызыва́ть* (нсв) врача́.**
> Their child felt better, so they decided not to ask the doctor to call round.

> **Я сове́тую вам *не задава́ть* (нсв) ему́ э́тот вопро́с.**
> I advise you not to ask him that question.

A *perfective* infinitive is used after negated forms of the verb **хоте́ть** in sentences containing an apology for the unintended consequences of an action:

> **Извини́те, я *не хоте́л* вас *оби́деть* (нсв).**
> I'm sorry, I didn't mean to offend you.

Impossibility and undesirability

An exception to the above principle occurs in contexts relating to permission and (im)possibility, since here the aspect of the infinitive depends on the meaning of the sentence. In general, an *imperfective infinitive* is used in contexts relating to the giving or refusing of permission, while a *perfective infinitive* is used in contexts relating to the possibility or impossibility of an action.

An imperfective infinitive used on its own in a negated sentence indicates a categorical prohibition. This construction has bureaucratic or military connotations, and sometimes it can be found on notices or official documents:

> **Не кури́ть (нсв)!**
> No smoking!

> **Не писа́ть (нсв) ни́же пункти́рной ли́нии.**
> Do not write beneath the dotted line.

The use of the perfective infinitive in such sentences indicates impossibility. This usage is fairly rare and its presence is indicative of a certain degree of rhetorical flourish:

> **Он зна́ет сто́лько языко́в! Все *не перечи́слить* (св)!**
> There's no end to the number of languages he knows!
> (*Literally*, He knows so many languages! It's impossible to enumerate them all!)

The adverb **лу́чше** is used with a *negated imperfective infinitive* to convey a recommendation not to do something. This construction serves as a mild form of negative command:

> **По-мо́ему, *лу́чше не отвеча́ть* (нсв) на э́тот вопро́с.**
> In my opinion, it would be better not to answer that question.
> *Or* I don't think you should answer that question.

Лу́чше can be used with a negated perfective infinitive, although this occurs much less frequently. This construction is used to bestow high praise; the sense is that the action was performed in such a way that it would have been impossible to improve on it:

> **Ты блестя́ще разобра́лся с его́ ка́верзными вопро́сами: *лу́чше не отве́тить* (св)!**
> You coped brilliantly with his trick questions; you couldn't have come up with better answers!

An imperfective infinitive is used with negated forms of the verb **мочь** 'to be able' and with **нельзя́** 'one cannot' to indicate that an action is not permitted:

NOTE | **Нельзя́** is the negative form of **мо́жно** 'one can', 'one may'.

> **К сожале́нию, я *не могу́ отвеча́ть* (нсв) на э́тот вопро́с.**
> Unfortunately, I cannot (i.e. I am not allowed to) answer that question.

> **Туда́ *нельзя́ входи́ть* (нсв): там идёт како́е-то совеща́ние.**
> You can't go in there; there's a meeting going on.

When a perfective infinitive is used with negated forms of the verb **мочь** or with **нельзя**, the meaning conveyed is that the action is impossible:

> **К сожале́нию, я *не могу́ отве́тить* (*св*) на э́тот вопро́с: у меня́ про́сто нет никако́й информа́ции на э́ту те́му.**
> Unfortunately, I can't answer that question; I just don't have any information on that topic.

> **Нельзя́ *сказа́ть* (*св*) зара́нее, како́й у них бу́дет результа́т.**
> You can't say in advance what sort of result they'll get.

If the verb **мочь** or the form **мо́жно** is used with a negated imperfective infinitive, the meaning conveyed is that of permission not to do something:

> **Е́сли хоти́те, вы *мо́жете не отвеча́ть* (*нсв*) на э́тот вопро́с.**
> If you don't want to, you don't have to answer that question.

> **Е́сли у вас ме́ньше, чем де́сять ты́сяч до́лларов, *мо́жно не заполня́ть* (*нсв*) деклара́цию.**
> If you have less than $10,000, you don't have to fill in a declaration form.

If the verb **мочь** is used with a negated perfective infinitive, the meaning conveyed is the possibility that something may not happen (**мо́жно** is not used in this construction):

> **Он *мо́жет не отве́тить* (*св*) на ваш вопро́с: вре́мени у него́ о́чень ма́ло.**
> It's possible he won't answer your question; he's got very little time left.

> **Но мне *мо́гут не пове́рить* (*св*).**
> But it is possible that they won't believe me. *Or* But I might not be believed.

If **нельзя́** or a negated form of the verb **мочь** is used with a negated infinitive, the two negatives cancel each other out, and the meaning is something like 'it is impossible not to'. In this construction, which is used rather more frequently than the English equivalent, the infinitive is usually perfective:

> **Нельзя́ *не восхити́ться* (*св*) его́ реши́тельностью.**
> It is impossible not to admire his determination. *Or* One cannot help admiring his determination.

> **Он *не мо́жет не отве́тить* (*св*) на ва́ше письмо́.**
> He cannot fail to answer your letter. *Or* He has no choice but to answer your letter.

For more on issuing prohibitions, giving advice and giving permission, *see* **18.2.4**, **18.4**, **18.5**.

5.8 Some practical points

5.8.0 Introduction

Practical problems in the use of aspects can sometimes arise from the fact that the various connotations associated with each of the two aspects are not in all cases mutually exclusive. In some instances there are solutions available that might not be immediately obvious.

5.8.1 Making a 'negative' choice

In the previous sections of this chapter attention has been focused on positive reasons for choosing which aspect to use. In some instances, however, the choice of aspect is determined less by any obvious positive connotations of the preferred form than by the potential for misunderstanding that may arise from the connotations of the alternative:

Вы мо́жете *зайти́* (*св*) ко мне по́сле обе́да.
You can call in and see me after lunch.

Он хо́чет *перее́хать* (*св*) в Москву́.
He wants to move to Moscow.

In these examples, assuming they each refer to a specific occasion, the *perfective* infinitive is used not so much because of any particular connotations of the perfective, but because the respective *imperfectives* (**заходи́ть, переезжа́ть**) might introduce undesirable connotations of either repetition or, in the case of the second example, a focus on the process, rather than the result.

For the use of the imperfective to indicate repeated action, *see* **5.2.3**.

For the use of the imperfective to focus on the process, *see* **5.3.2**.

5.8.2 Having your cake and eating it

There is one construction that makes it possible to use both aspects at the same time. This is when the past or the future tense of the *perfective verb* **стать** is combined with an *imperfective infinitive*. This construction is mostly used to indicate the start of a series of repeated actions or of a single continuing action. It occurs frequently in descriptions of a chain of events, but is not restricted to that type of context. When sentences with this construction are being translated into English, the verb **стать** is sometimes rendered as 'start' or 'begin', although in many instances only the accompanying imperfective verb is translated:

Посели́вшись в гости́нице, располо́женной в са́мом це́нтре Ло́ндона, я *стал* (*св*) *жда́ть* (*нсв*). Бли́же к полу́ночи мне позвони́л незнако́мый мужчи́на с иностра́нным акце́нтом.
Having settled into the hotel, which was located in the very centre of London, I waited. Towards midnight I received a telephone call from an unknown man with a foreign accent.

Я по́днял бума́жник и *стал* (*св*) *проверя́ть* (*нсв*) содержи́мое. Сла́ва Бо́гу, докуме́нты оказа́лись на ме́сте. Де́ньги пропа́ли, но э́то, в конце́ концо́в, не так стра́шно.
I picked up my wallet and checked the contents. Thank goodness, the documents were all present and correct. My money had gone but, when all's said and done, that's not so terrible.

Жара́ расслабля́юще де́йствует на всех, и студе́нты и да́же профессора́ *ста́ли* (*св*) *приходи́ть* (*нсв*) на ле́кции в футбо́лках и шо́ртах.
The heat has had a relaxing effect on everyone, and students and even professors have taken to coming to lectures in T-shirts and shorts.

In the first two of these examples the *perfective* verb **стал** is used to situate the action within a sequence of events. In the first example, the *imperfective infinitive* **жда́ть** is used to indicate a continuing event that cannot lead to a conclusion, while in the second example, the imperfective infinitive **проверя́ть** is used to focus on the process. In the following sentence we are given the narrator's reaction to what he finds during the process of checking. In the third example, the perfective verb **ста́ли** is used to indicate that the consequence of the action in the past still applies in the present, while the imperfective infinitive **приходи́ть** indicates repeated action.

For more uses of the verb **стать**, *see* **14.1.6.**

The future **ста́ну** is used less frequently with an imperfective infinitive. Although it can have the same nuances as the past tense, there is often little or no practical difference between this construction and the ordinary *imperfective future* formed using **бу́ду** and the *imperfective infinitive*:

> **Я, наве́рно, ста́ну (св) приходи́ть (нсв) на рабо́ту то́лько по́сле обе́да, так как мне ле́гче рабо́тать до́ма.**
> I shall probably start coming into work only after lunch, since it's easier for me to work at home.

The use of **бу́ду приходи́ть** would not make a significant difference here.

5.8.3 Не стал, не ста́ну + imperfective infinitive

When negated forms of the verb **стать** are used with an *imperfective infinitive*, the effect is to produce a more categorical negation. In the *past tense* the meaning is often close to 'chose/decided not to':

> **Прокурату́ра не ста́ла (св) возбужда́ть (нсв) де́ло про́тив его́ бра́та.**
> The prosecutor's office has decided not to bring criminal charges against his brother.

In the *future tense* this construction can be an emphatic way of indicating that someone has no intention of doing something:

> **Разгова́ривать (нсв) с тобо́й на э́ту те́му я не ста́ну (св).**
> I have no intention of talking to you on that topic.

6

Adjectives

Introduction

Adjectives are words that are used to *qualify nouns*, usually by the addition of a descriptive term. Adjectives can be used in two ways: *attributive adjectives* form part of a single phrase with the nouns they qualify; *predicative adjectives* form part of the *predicate*, that is, they normally appear in conjunction with the verb **быть** or one of its synonyms. The difference between the two types of adjective can be illustrated by the following two English sentences:

There is a *full* glass on the table.   *Attributive*
The glass is *full*.   *Predicative*

Russian adjectives decline in a similar fashion to nouns, albeit with distinct sets of endings. Attributive adjectives agree with the nouns they qualify in *number*, *gender* and *case*; predicative adjectives agree with the nouns they qualify in *number* and *gender*, but are used only in the *nominative* or *instrumental* cases. Some adjectives have an additional form, known as the *short form*, which is used only in the predicative function and only in the *nominative* case; these are described separately in **6.5**.

Attributive adjectives are normally placed *before* the nouns they qualify. Exceptions to this are discussed in **6.7** and **20.1.3**.

Russian adjectives have *four* sets of endings: one for each gender in the singular and one to serve for all nouns in the plural. Almost all adjectives belong to one of three declension types, and although there are some predictable complications caused by the application of the spelling rules given in **1.5.2**, **1.5.4** and **1.5.5**, there are relatively few irregularities.

6.1 Hard adjectives

6.1.1 The standard declension pattern of hard adjectives

The standard declension pattern of *hard* adjectives can be illustrated by **но́вый** 'new':

	Masculine	Feminine	Neuter	Plural
Nom.	но́вый	но́вая	но́вое	но́вые
Gen.	но́вого	но́вой	но́вого	но́вых
Dat.	но́вому	но́вой	но́вому	но́вым
Acc.	as nom. or gen.	но́вую	но́вое	as nom. or gen.
Instr.	но́вым	но́вой	но́вым	но́выми
Prep.	но́вом	но́вой	но́вом	но́вых

The *accusative* ending in the *masculine singular* and in the *plural* is identical to the respective *nominative* ending when the adjective qualifies an *inanimate* noun and identical to the respective *genitive* ending when the adjective qualifies an *animate* noun. This rule applies to all adjectives:

Я купи́л *но́вый стол* для ку́хни.
I've bought a new table for the kitchen.

Я давно́ зна́ю ва́шего *но́вого дру́га*.
I've known your new friend for a long time.

Тепе́рь на́до купи́ть *но́вые сту́лья*.
Now I have to buy new chairs.

Когда́ я перее́хал в Петербу́рг, я бы́стро приобрёл *но́вых друзе́й*.
When I moved to St Petersburg, I soon made new friends.

For more on animate and inanimate nouns, *see* **2.4**.

6.1.2 Adjectives with stress on the ending

Adjectives that have the stress on the ending, for example:

круто́й	steep, hard, tough, 'cool'
молодо́й	young
тупо́й	blunt, dull, stupid

have a *nominative singular masculine* ending in **-о́й**. All other endings follow the standard pattern:

Nom. sing. masc.	Nom. sing. fem.	Nom. sing. n.	Nom. pl.
круто́й	крута́я	круто́е	круты́е

6.1.3 Application of the spelling rule given in 1.5.5

In accordance with the spelling rule given in **1.5.5**, the ending of the *genitive singular masculine* and *neuter* is spelled **-го**, but is pronounced as if written with the letter **в**. For example, the form written **но́вого** is pronounced [nóvəvə]. This rule applies to all adjectives, as well as to *pronouns* and *numerals* with *genitive singular* endings in **-го**.

For an explanation of the vowel symbols used in the above example, *see* **1.4.3** and **1.4.4**.

6.1

Application of the spelling rule given in 1.5.4

When an adjective has a stem ending in -г-, -к- or -х-, the application of the spelling rule given in **1.5.4** means that any -ы- that would occur in an ending is automatically replaced by -и-. This rule affects the *nominative singular masculine*, the *instrumental singular masculine* and *neuter* and all endings in the plural.

For example, **стро́гий** 'severe', **ру́сский** 'Russian', **ти́хий** 'quiet':

Nom. sing. masc.	стро́гий	ру́сский	ти́хий
Instr. sing. masc. and n.	стро́гим	ру́сским	ти́хим
Nom. pl.	стро́гие	ру́сские	ти́хие
Gen. and prep. pl.	стро́гих	ру́сских	ти́хих

If the stress is on the *ending*, the *nominative singular masculine* ends in **-о́й**, but all other endings follow the above pattern:

Nom. sing. masc.	дорого́й 'dear'
Instr. sing. masc. and n.	дороги́м
Nom. pl.	дороги́е
Gen. and prep. pl.	дороги́х

Application of the spelling rules given in 1.5.2

The effects of the spelling rules given in **1.5.2** on the endings of adjectives are a little more complicated than those mentioned in the previous sections. If an adjective has a stem ending in -ж-, -ч-, -ш- or -щ- and if the stress is not on the ending, any -ы- occurring in the ending is replaced by -и- and any -о- occurring immediately after one of these consonants is replaced by -е-. The results of applying these rules can be illustrated by **хоро́ший** 'good':

	Masculine	*Feminine*	*Neuter*	*Plural*
Nom.	хоро́ший	хоро́шая	хоро́шее	хоро́шие
Gen.	хоро́шего	хоро́шей	хоро́шего	хоро́ших
Dat.	хоро́шему	хоро́шей	хоро́шему	хоро́шим
Acc.	as nom. or gen.	хоро́шую	хоро́шее	as nom. or gen.
Instr.	хоро́шим	хоро́шей	хоро́шим	хоро́шими
Prep.	хоро́шем	хоро́шей	хоро́шем	хоро́ших

NOTE | The very small number of rarely used adjectives in **-цый**, for example, **краснолицый** 'red-faced' and **куцый** 'dock-tailed', 'skimpy', follow the second, but not the first of these rules, i.e. they retain **-ы-**, but replace **-о-** with **-е-**.

The number of adjectives in this category with stress on the ending is also very small, but this group includes the widely used **большо́й** 'big' and **чужо́й** 'someone else's'. These adjectives follow the first of the above rules, but not the second, i.e. **-ы-** is replaced by **-и-**, but **-о-** is retained (and is also found in the *nominative singular masculine*). The results of applying these rules can be illustrated by **большо́й**:

	Masculine	Feminine	Neuter	Plural
Nom.	большо́й	больша́я	большо́е	больши́е
Gen.	большо́го	большо́й	большо́го	больши́х
Dat.	большо́му	большо́й	большо́му	больши́м
Acc.	as nom. or gen.	большу́ю	большо́е	as nom. or gen.
Instr.	больши́м	большо́й	больши́м	больши́ми
Prep.	большо́м	большо́й	большо́м	больши́х

6.2 Soft adjectives (1)

Russian has two groups of adjectives with a soft declension. With the exception of **ка́рий** 'brown' (mostly of eyes); 'chestnut' (of horses), all adjectives belonging to the first group end in **-ний**. Their declension can be illustrated by **си́ний** 'dark blue':

	Masculine	Feminine	Neuter	Plural
Nom.	си́ний	си́няя	си́нее	си́ние
Gen.	си́него	си́ней	си́него	си́них
Dat.	си́нему	си́ней	си́нему	си́ним
Acc.	as nom. or gen.	си́нюю	си́нее	as nom. or gen.
Instr.	си́ним	си́ней	си́ним	си́ними
Prep.	си́нем	си́ней	си́нем	си́них

Other freequently used adjectives belonging to this group include:

ве́рхний	upper	да́льний	distant, far
дре́вний	ancient	за́дний	back, rear
заму́жняя	married (of a woman)	и́скре́нний	sincere
кра́йний	extreme, endmost, last	ли́шний	extra, superfluous
ни́жний	lower	пере́дний	front, forward
по́здний	late	после́дний	last
сре́дний	middle, average		

NOTE | Because of its meaning **заму́жняя** normally occurs only in the *feminine* and *plural* forms.

In addition, there a large number of adjectives formed from *nouns*, *adverbs*, *prepositions* and *phrases* that indicate place or time. Examples include:

зима́	winter	зи́мний	winter (adj.)
ве́чер	evening	вече́рний	evening (adj.)
здесь	here	зде́шний	local'
сего́дня	today	сего́дняшний	today's
в про́шлом году́	last year	прошлого́дний	last year's
со́рок лет	forty years	сорокале́тний	forty years (old)

For more on the formation of adjectives in this way, *see* **10.2.2**.

6.3 Soft adjectives (2)

The adjectives belonging to this group are all formed from animate nouns, although the group also includes the *ordinal numeral* **тре́тий** 'third' and the *pronoun* **чей?** 'whose?'.

For more on ordinal numerals, *see* **8.4**.

For more on the pronoun, **чей** *see* **7.4.2**.

The declension of adjectives belonging to this group is characterised by the presence of a *soft sign* (**ь**) immediately before the ending in all forms except the *nominative singular masculine* and by the fact that, unlike other adjectives, they have *monosyllabic* endings in *nominative* and *accusative singular feminine* and *neuter* and the *nominative plural*. Their declension can be illustrated by **пти́чий** (formed from **пти́ца** 'bird'):

	Masculine	*Feminine*	*Neuter*	*Plural*
Nom.	**пти́чий**	**пти́чья**	**пти́чье**	**пти́чьи**
Gen.	**пти́чьего**	**пти́чьей**	**пти́чьего**	**пти́чьих**
Dat.	**пти́чьему**	**пти́чьей**	**пти́чьему**	**пти́чьим**
Acc.	as nom. or gen.	**пти́чью**	**пти́чье**	as nom. or gen.
Instr.	**пти́чьим**	**пти́чьей**	**пти́чьим**	**пти́чьими**
Prep.	**пти́чьем**	**пти́чьей**	**пти́чьем**	**пти́чьих**

For more on the formation and use of these adjectives, *see* **10.2.5**.

6.4 Nouns that decline like adjectives

6.4.0 Introduction

In Russian there are a number of nouns that were originally adjectives or participles and that decline like adjectives, rather than like ordinary nouns.

Common nouns normally have a fixed gender and decline according to the pattern of that gender in the singular, as well as in the plural. Some nouns referring to people, however, have both masculine and feminine forms, and some occur only in the plural.

Surnames have masculine, feminine and plural forms.

6.4.1 Common nouns

Examples of *masculine* nouns:

водяно́й	water spirit
военноплённый	prisoner-of-war
военнослу́жащий	member of the armed forces
главнокома́ндующий	commander-in-chief
дворе́цкий	butler, major-domo
домово́й	spirit that lives in the house
ле́ший	spirit of the forest

портно́й	tailor
рядово́й	private (soldier)
управля́ющий	manager
часово́й	sentry

Examples of *feminine* nouns:

бу́лочная	baker's	ва́нная	bathroom
го́рничная	(chamber)maid	гости́ная	living-room
заку́сочная	snack-bar	запята́я	comma
крива́я	curve (e.g. on a graph)	набере́жная	embankment
пивна́я	beer bar, pub	пра́чечная	laundry
сбо́рная	national (sports) team	столо́вая	canteen, refectory, dining-room
убо́рная	toilet; dressing room (e.g. in a theatre)	шашлы́чная	shashlik-house, kebab-house

Examples of nouns that can be *masculine* or *feminine*:

больно́й, больна́я	patient (sick person)
вожа́тый, вожа́тая	leader of a youth group (e.g. the Pioneers)
дежу́рный, дежу́рная	person on duty
заключённый, заключённая	prisoner
крепостно́й, крепостна́я	serf
ни́щий, ни́щая	beggar
подсуди́мый, подсуди́мая	accused (in court)
рабо́чий, рабо́чая	worker
ру́сский, ру́сская	Russian (man or woman)
слу́жащий, слу́жащая	white-collar employee
сумасше́дший, сумасше́дшая	mad person

Examples of *neuter* nouns:

бу́дущее	the future	горю́чее	fuel
жарко́е	roast meat, fried meat	живо́тное	animal
лёгкое	lung	млекопита́ющее	mammal
моро́женое	icecream	насеко́мое	insect
настоя́щее	the present (time)	пиро́жное	cake
пресмыка́ющееся	reptile	прилага́тельное	adjective
про́шлое	the past	сказу́емое	predicate
содержи́мое	contents (e.g. of a bottle)	существи́тельное	noun
числи́тельное	numeral	шампа́нское	champagne, sparkling wine

NOTE | The noun **пресмыка́ющееся** declines like the *present participle* of a *reflexive* verb, so that the *genitive singular*, for example, is **пресмыка́ющегося**.

For more on the participles of reflexive verbs, *see* **4.12**, **4.13**.

Examples of nouns that occur only in the *plural*:

да́нные 'data' командиро́вочные 'travelling expenses'
нали́чные 'cash' позывны́е 'call-sign'
чаевы́е 'tip' (e.g. in a restaurant)

NOTE In some instances there exist adjectives or participles identical in form to these nouns. In some instances the meaning of the adjective is closely related to that of the noun, e.g. ру́сский, ру́сская, ру́сское, ру́сские 'Russian' or пивно́й, пивна́я, пивно́е, пивны́е 'relating to beer'; in other instances the adjective has a different meaning, e.g. лёгкий, лёгкая, лёгкое, лёгкие 'light', 'easy' or настоя́щий, настоя́щая, ностоя́щее, настоя́щие 'present', but also 'real', 'authentic'.

6.4.2 Surnames

The adjectival ending that occurs most frequently in surnames is **-ский**, as in **Ольша́нский**, **Достое́вский**, **Маяко́вский** and **Чайко́вский**, but other endings characteristic of adjectives are found as well:

Masculine	Feminine	Plural
Ольша́нский	Ольша́нская	Ольша́нские
Чайко́вский	Чайко́вская	Чайко́вские
Крамско́й	Крамска́я	Крамски́е
Лу́жный	Лу́жная	Лу́жные
Толсто́й	Толста́я	Толсты́е
Непо́мнящий	Непо́мнящая	Непо́мнящие

6.5 The short forms of adjectives

6.5.0 Introduction

Many adjectives have a second set of endings known as *short forms*. These endings occur only in the *nominative* and are used only in the *predicative* function. In contrast, the endings described in sections **6.1–6.3** are sometimes known as *long forms*.

This means that adjectives have three forms that can be used in predicative function: the *nominative long form*, the *instrumental long form* and the *short form*. The use of these different forms is explained in **14.1.4**.

6.5.1 The endings of short adjectives

The endings of *short form* adjectives can be arrived at by removing the final syllable (**-ый/-ой/-ий**, **-я**, **-е**, **-е**) from the nominative ending of the long form. The endings can be illustrated by the following examples:

Nom. sing. masc. (long form)	Masc. sing. (short form)	Fem. sing. (short form)	Neut. sing. (short form)	Pl. (short form)
пра́вый 'right'	прав	права́	пра́во	пра́вы
пья́ный 'drunk'	пьян	пьяна́	пья́но	пьяны́
чи́стый 'clean'	чист	чиста́	чи́сто	чи́сты

Nom. sing. masc. (long form)	Masc. sing. (short form)	Fem. sing. (short form)	Neut. sing. (short form)	Pl. (short form)
высо́кий 'high', 'tall'	высо́к	высока́	высоко́	высо́ки
све́жий 'fresh'	свеж	свежа́	свежо́/све́же	свежи́
пусто́й 'empty'	пуст	пуста́	пу́сто	пусты́

NOTE

The stress on the short form endings often differs from that of long form endings and in some instances alternative stresses are possible. This can affect the application of the spelling rules given in **1.5.2**, as in the example **свежо́/све́же** (long form **све́жее**) above.

If the removal of the masculine singular ending **-ый** etc. would result in two consonants coming together, a *fleeting vowel* is usually inserted.

For more on the fleeting vowel, *see* **2.5.0**.

Nom. sing. masc. (long form)	Masc. sing. (short form)	Fem. sing. (short form)	Neut. sing. (short form)	Pl. (short form)
любе́зный 'kind', 'courteous'	любе́зен	любе́зна	любе́зно	любе́зны
те́сный 'cramped', 'small'	те́сен	тесна́	те́сно	те́сны
лёгкий 'light', 'easy'	лёгок	легка́	легко́	лёгки/легки́
ре́зкий 'sharp', 'abrupt'	ре́зок	резка́	ре́зко	ре́зки
досто́йный 'worthy'	досто́ин	досто́йна	досто́йно	досто́йны

NOTES

(i) The rules for determining which *fleeting vowel* is used are essentially the same as those given in **2.5.2** for the *genitive plural* endings of *feminine* and *neuter* nouns.

(ii) In the masculine singular short form of the adjective **досто́йный** the vowel inserted is **и**, and not the expected **е**.

There are, however, some instances where a fleeting vowel is not inserted. Among these are **пусто́й** and **чи́стый**, mentioned above, and other examples include the following:

Nom. sing. masc. (long form)	Masc. sing. (short form)	Fem. sing. (short form)	Neut. sing. (short form)	Pl. (short form)
бо́дрый 'cheerful'	бодр	бодра́	бо́дро	бо́дры́
до́брый 'good', 'kind'	добр	добра́	добро́	добры́
тре́звый 'sober'	трезв	трезва́	тре́зво	трезвы́

6.5.2 Adjectives with no short forms

A substantial number of adjectives either have no short forms or have short forms that are so rarely used that for all practical purposes they can safely be disregarded. The following fall into this category:

1 All adjectives ending in **-ский** or **-енький** (for the special case of **ма́ленький**, *see* below).

6.6

2   All adjectives belonging to the second group of soft adjectives (described in **6.3**).

3   Almost all adjectives belonging to the first group of soft adjectives (described in **6.2**). The only exception in general use is **и́скренний** 'sincere', which has the following short form endings:

Masc. sing.	**и́скренен**
Fem. sing.	**и́скренна**
N. sing.	**и́скренне/и́скренно**
Pl.	**и́скренни/и́скренны**

4   Adjectives that indicate a quality that is by definition inherent or permanent. Examples include **деревя́нный** 'wooden', **десяти́чный** 'decimal', **трамва́йный** 'relating to trams', **я́блочный** 'relating to *or* made from apples'.

6.5.3   **Irregular forms**

The adjectives **большо́й** 'big' and **ма́ленький** 'small' have short forms that are derived (regularly) from the related adjectives **вели́кий** 'great', 'big' and **ма́лый** 'small' respectively:

> большо́й ~ вели́к, велика́, велико́, велики́
> ма́ленький ~ мал, мала́, ма́ло, малы́

The adjective **рад, ра́да, ра́до, ра́ды** 'pleased about something' exists only in the short form; it tends to be used with an *infinitive* or with a noun in the *dative*:

> Мы о́чень *ра́ды* вас ви́деть.
> We are very pleased to see you.

> Я *рад* ва́шим успе́хам.
> I am pleased about your success(es).

6.6   **Possessive adjectives**

6.6.1   **The formation of possessive adjectives**

In informal language Russian makes wide use of *possessive adjectives*. These are formed from proper names and terms indicating family relations that end in **-а** or **-я** by removing the final vowel and adding **-ин**. They are used instead of the *genitive* of the noun concerned to indicate *possession*.

For the use of the genitive case to indicate possession, *see* **3.3.1**.

The following examples illustrate the formation of *possessive adjectives*. In general, when they are formed from forenames, they are usually based on the *familiar*, rather than the full form, although the latter is used in some contexts, e.g. when indicating saints' days.

For more on the full and the familiar forms of forenames, *see* **12.1.1**.

ма́ма	Mum	**ма́мин**	Mum's
па́па	Dad	**па́пин**	Dad's
тёща	(husband's) mother-in-law	**тёщин**	mother-in-law's
Та́ня	Tat'iana, Tania	**Та́нин**	Tania's
Га́ля	Galina, Galia	**Га́лин**	Galia's

Са́ша	Aleksandr, Aleksandra, Sasha	Са́шин	Sasha's
Ми́ша	Mikhail, Misha	Ми́шин	Misha's

6.6.2 The declension of possessive adjectives

Although many of the endings of *possessive adjectives* are the same as of normal adjectives, there are special endings for the *nominative* and the *accusative*:

	Masculine	*Feminine*	*Neuter*	*Plural*
Nom.	ма́мин	ма́мина	ма́мино	ма́мины
Gen.	ма́миного	ма́миной	ма́миного	ма́миных
Dat.	ма́миному	ма́миной	ма́миному	ма́миным
Acc.	as nom. or gen.	ма́мину	ма́мино	as nom. or gen.
Instr.	ма́миным	ма́миной	ма́миным	ма́миными
Prep.	ма́мином	ма́миной	ма́мином	ма́миных

Possessive adjectives do not have short forms.

6.6.3 The use of possessive adjectives

The following sentences illustrate the use of possessive adjectives:

Вдруг за две́рью он услы́шал *па́пин* го́лос.
Suddenly he heard his father's voice on the other side of the door.

У тебя́ нет случа́йно *Ми́шиного* телефо́на?
You wouldn't happen to have Misha's telephone number, would you?

Э́то *Та́нины* ве́щи: лу́чше их не тро́гать.
Those are Tania's things. I wouldn't touch them if I were you.

In each of these sentences the *possessive adjectives* could be replaced by a noun in the *genitive* or by another construction indicating possession:

Вдруг за две́рью он услы́шал го́лос *па́пы*.
У тебя́ нет случа́йно телефо́на *Ми́ши*?
Э́ти ве́щи *принадлежа́т Та́не*: лу́чше их не тро́гать.
(*Literally*, These things belong to Tania.)

Although possessive adjectives tend to be characteristic of informal language, they can be more generally useful as a means of avoiding a string of nouns in the genitive:

Она́ не́сколько раз быва́ла на кварти́ре *Са́шиной ма́тери*.
She had been to Sasha's mother's flat several times.

It is in principle possible to form possessive adjectives by adding the suffix **-ов/-ев** to masculine nouns; these decline exactly like adjectives in **-ин**, but are much less frequently used. Both types of possessive adjectives are, however, found in a range of set expressions. In such instances there is no option of using another construction instead. Examples include:

ахилле́сова пята́	Achilles' heel
крокоди́ловы слёзы	crocodile tears

ма́менькин сыно́к	Mummy's boy
па́пенькина до́чка	Daddy's girl
Татья́нин день	St Tatiana's day (25 January; this has come to be regarded as a special day for students)

Я вам покажу́ ку́зькину мать!
I'll give you what for! I'll show you a thing or two!

Вообще́ он пи́шет о́чень хорошо́, но его́ ахилле́сова пята́ – э́то же́нские персона́жи.
On the whole he writes very well, but female characters are his Achilles' heel.

Сего́дня *Татья́нин день*: в общежи́тиях пройду́т вечери́нки, во мно́гих ба́рах и клу́бах организо́ваны специа́льные дискоте́ки для студе́нтов.
It's St Tatiana's day today. There will be parties in the student hostels, and many bars and clubs are putting on special discos for students.

6.7 Indeclinable adjectives

Russian has a very small number of *indeclinable* adjectives. Most of these belong to one of a restricted range of semantic categories, and they are noteworthy for the fact that, with certain exceptions, they are placed *after* the nouns they qualify.

Adjectives indicating the colour and style of clothes:

ха́ки	khaki
клёш	flared, bell-bottomed

Culinary terms:

ассорти́	mixed
фри	(deep-)fried

Adjectives indicating ethnic groups or languages:

ко́ми	Komi
хи́нди	Hindi
урду́	Urdu
эспера́нто	Esperanto

NOTE The adjective **ко́ми** can either precede or follow the noun it qualifies.

Other indeclinable adjectives:

пик	peak (used only in the phrase **часы́ пик** 'peak hours')
ми́ни	mini (this usually precedes the noun)
э́кстра	extra (quality)

Заба́вно смотре́ть ста́рые фи́льмы семи́десятых годо́в, где все хо́дят в э́тих стра́шных *брю́ках клёш*.
It's funny watching old films from the 1970s, where everyone's wearing those dreadful flared trousers.

«Та́лун» – э́то ежедне́вная информа́ционная програ́мма *на ко́ми языке́*.
Talun is a daily news programme in (the) Komi (language).

Не люблю́ е́здить в метро́ *в часы́ пик*, тем бо́лее, е́сли на́до де́лать переса́дку в це́нтре го́рода.

I don't like being on the metro during the peak time, especially if I have to change trains in the centre of the city.

In present-day Russian, there are a few recently borrowed words, notably **би́знес** 'business', **интерне́т** 'Internet' and **онла́йн** 'on-line', which are used as if they were indeclinable adjectives. The normal spelling convention, however, is to join them to the following noun with hyphen:

Би́знес-образова́ние она́ получи́ла в одно́м из знамени́тых университе́тов США.

She received her business education at a famous university in the United States.

Ка́жется, я об э́том чита́л в како́м-то *интерне́т-журна́ле*.

I think I read about it in some Internet journal.

Мы провели́ ма́ленький *онла́йн-опро́с*, но результа́ты оказа́лись не о́чень интере́сными.

We carried out a small on-line survey of opinion, but the results weren't very interesting.

6.8 Comparative and superlative forms

6.8.0 Introduction

Comparative adjectives are used when comparing different degrees of the quality indicated by the adjective in question. *Superlative* adjectives are used to indicate the highest possible degree of quality concerned.

There are two ways of forming comparative adjectives in Russian: one, the *short comparative*, is used mostly for *predicative* adjectives, while the other, the *long comparative* is mainly used for *attributive* adjectives.

The use of comparative adjectives is described in **21.9.1–21.9.6**.

There are four ways of forming superlative adjectives, which are differentiated by style and function.

6.8.1 The short comparative

The *short comparative* does not decline and has only one form for all numbers and genders. For the majority of adjectives the short comparative is formed by removing the ending and by adding the suffix **-ee**:

гру́бый	crude, rough	грубе́е	cruder, rougher
дли́нный	long	длинне́е	longer
дре́вний	ancient	древне́е	more ancient
интере́сный	interesting	интере́снее	more interesting
но́вый	new	нове́е	newer
я́сный	clear	ясне́е	clearer

If an adjective has a stem that ends in one of the following consonants or sequences of consonants, the consonant(s) undergo a change according to patterns given below and the ending is **-e**. With some adjectives that end in a consonant followed by **-кий**, the **-к-** is removed and the preceding consonant is changed:

г~ж	дорого́й	dear	доро́же	dearer
д~ж	молодо́й	young	моло́же	younger
	ре́дкий	rare	ре́же	rarer
з~ж	бли́зкий	nearer	бли́же	nearer
	у́зкий	narrow	у́же	narrower
к~ч	кре́пкий	strong	кре́пче	stronger
	лёгкий	light, easy	ле́гче	lighter, easier
	жёсткий	hard	жёстче	harder
ст~щ	чи́стый	clean	чи́ще	cleaner
т~ч	бога́тый	rich	бога́че	richer
	коро́ткий	short	коро́че	shorter
х~ш	ти́хий	quiet	ти́ше	quieter

A number of adjectives, many in common use, have irregular comparatives:

большо́й	big	бо́льше	bigger
высо́кий	high	вы́ше	higher
глубо́кий	deep	глу́бже	deeper
далёкий	far, distant	да́льше	farther, further, more distant
дешёвый	cheap	деше́вле	cheaper
до́лгий	long (of time)	до́льше	longer
ма́ленький	small	ме́ньше	smaller
сла́дкий	sweet	сла́ще	sweeter
ста́рый	old	ста́рше	older
то́нкий	thin	то́ньше	thinner
широ́кий	wide	ши́ре	wider

The adjective **по́здний** 'late' has alternative short comparative forms **поздне́е** and **по́зже** 'later'.

Two adjectives have short comparatives that are totally different from the basic form:

плохо́й	bad	ху́же	worse
хоро́ший	good	лу́чше	better

The adjective **худо́й** 'thin' has the short comparative **худе́е**.

There are many adjectives that do not have short comparative forms. These include:

1 Adjectives denoting a quality that by definition cannot exist in different degrees, for example **двуно́гий** 'two-legged', **босо́й** 'bare-footed', **трамва́йный** 'relating to trams'. This category also includes all adjectives belonging to the second group of soft adjectives.

2 Virtually all adjectives ending in **-ский**, **-ской** or **-енький**.

3 Some miscellaneous adjectives, including **ве́тхий** 'old', 'decrepit', **го́лый** 'bare', 'naked', **го́рдый** 'proud', **ди́кий** 'wild', **ли́пкий** 'sticky' and **наго́й** 'naked'.

Especially in informal language the short comparative is frequently used with the prefix **по-**. The effect of adding the prefix is normally to soften slightly the degree of comparison:

Е́сли бы я был *помоло́же*, я бы уе́хал иска́ть рабо́ту за грани́цей.
If I were (a bit) younger, I would go and look for work abroad.

Не нра́вится э́то шампа́нское? Тогда́ попро́буй друго́е. Вот э́то бу́дет *послаще.*
Don't you like this champagne? Then try another. This one here will be a bit sweeter.

6.8.2 The long comparative

The *long comparative* is formed by placing **бо́лее** before the *long form* of adjective:

дре́вний	ancient	бо́лее дре́вний	more ancient
интере́сный	interesting	бо́лее интере́сный	more interesting
оптимисти́ческий	optimistic	бо́лее оптимисти́ческий	more optimistic
широ́кий	wide	бо́лее широ́кий	wider

The only restriction on the formation of the long comparative is that it is not normally used with adjectives denoting a quality that by definition cannot exist in different degrees.

6.8.3 Declining comparatives

There are in Russian four comparative forms that decline like normal long adjectives. These are:

хоро́ший	good	лу́чший	better
плохо́й	bad	ху́дший	worse
большо́й	big	бо́льший	bigger
ма́ленький	little	ме́ньший	smaller

NOTE   Some of the forms of **бо́льший** (e.g. the nominative singular feminine **бо́льшая**) are identical to the equivalent forms of **большо́й**; in such instances the comparative forms are usually printed with the stress mark.

The above forms are used in the attributive function. For examples, *see* **21.9.5**.

In addition, the adjectives **молодо́й** 'young' and **ста́рый** 'old' have associated forms that look like declinable comparatives, but which are really separate adjectives:

молодо́й	мла́дший	younger, junior
ста́рый	ста́рший	elder, older, senior

These forms are mostly used with reference to siblings or ranks (in either the armed forces or civilian life):

Моя́ ста́ршая сестра́ живёт в Петербу́рге.
My elder sister lives in St Petersburg.

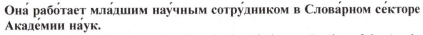

Она́ рабо́тает мла́дшим нау́чным сотру́дником в Слова́рном се́кторе Акаде́мии нау́к.

She works as a junior research officer in the Dictionary Section of the Academy of Sciences.

6.8.4 The superlative with са́мый or наибо́лее

The most common way of forming the *superlative* of adjectives is to place the *pronoun* **са́мый** before the long form of the adjective.

For more on the pronoun **са́мый**, *see* **7.8.2**.

When **са́мый** is used with an adjective, both parts decline and agree with the noun in *number*, *gender* and *case*. **Са́мый** declines like a normal *hard* adjective (*see* **6.1**):

Э́то *са́мая интере́сная* кни́га, кото́рую я когда́-либо чита́л.
This is the most interesting book I have ever read.

Они́ покупа́ют *са́мую сти́льную* оде́жду и едя́т в *са́мых дороги́х* рестора́нах.
They buy the most stylish clothes and eat in the most expensive restaurants.

The *declinable comparative* adjectives **лу́чший** and **ху́дший** can be used either on their own or prefaced by **са́мый** to indicate *superlative* meaning:

У нас ка́ждый год прово́дится ко́нкурс на (*са́мое*) *лу́чшее* стихотворе́ние на те́му «Росси́я».
Every year we hold a competition for the best poem on the topic of 'Russia'.

The adverb **наибо́лее** can be used in place of **са́мый**. **Наибо́лее** is normally found only in written language:

Наибо́лее одарённых дете́й отбира́ют в музыка́льную шко́лу-интерна́т при Моско́вской консервато́рии.
The most talented children are chosen for places at a special (music) boarding-school attached to the Moscow Conservatory.

The opposite of **наибо́лее** is **наиме́нее**:

Ме́тод, кото́рый они́ вы́брали, оказа́лся *наиме́нее эффекти́вным*.
The method they chose proved to be the least effective.

6.8.5 Other forms of the superlative

Some adjectives form a second superlative with the suffix **-ейший** (**-айший** if there is consonant change following the patterns given in **6.8.1** for the short comparative). Examples that are likely to be encountered include:

ва́жный	important	важне́йший	most important
гру́бый	crude, rough	грубе́йший	crudest, roughest
да́льний	far	дальне́йший	furthest, further
интере́сный	interesting	интере́снейший	most interesting
кру́пный	big, large	крупне́йший	biggest, largest
но́вый	new	нове́йший	newest
опа́сный	dangerous	опа́снейший	most dangerous
по́лный	full	полне́йший	fullest

у́мный	clever	умне́йший	most clever
це́нный	valuable	ценне́йший	most valuable

Also:

ма́ленький, ма́лый	small	мале́йший	smallest, slightest

бли́зкий	near	ближа́йший	nearest, next (few)
вели́кий	great	велича́йший	greatest
ме́лкий	small, petty	мельча́йший	smallest, slightest
ре́дкий	rare	редча́йший	rarest
стро́гий	strict, severe	строжа́йший	strictest
ти́хий	quiet	тиша́йший	quietest

Some care is needed in interpreting these forms, since they are potentially ambiguous. While they can be used as true superlatives, they are often used to indicate a very high (but not necessarily the highest) degree of the quality indicated by the adjective:

> **В на́шем регио́не нахо́дится** *крупне́йший в ми́ре заво́д* **по произво́дству тролле́йбусов.**
> Our region is home to the largest trolley-bus factory in the world.

> **Президе́нтские вы́боры – э́то** *крупне́йшее собы́тие* **в жи́зни страны́.**
> The election of a president is a huge event in the life of our country.

For the most part these forms occur in the more formal levels of written language. There are, however, some forms that are used more widely and can even occur in speech. These are **ближа́йший**, both with its spatial meaning ('nearest') and used with **вре́мя** to mean 'in the near future' or with other time-related words to mean 'the next few'; **дальне́йший** with the meaning 'further' (and in the phrase **в дальне́йшем** 'henceforth', 'hereafter'); **мале́йший** with the meaning 'slightest':

> *В ближа́йшее вре́мя* **оса́дков не ожида́ется.**
> No rain or snow is expected in the near future.

> *В ближа́йшие го́ды* **бу́дут снесены́ все пятиэта́жные дома́, постро́енные в хрущёвское вре́мя.**
> During the next few years all the five-storey blocks built in the Khrushchev period will be demolished.

> **Ждём ва́ших** *дальне́йших* **указа́ний.**
> We await your further instructions.

> **Они́ не име́ют ни** *мале́йшего* **представле́ния о том, что мы здесь де́лаем.**
> They haven't even the slightest idea about what we are doing here.

It is also possible to form a superlative by adding the prefix **наи-** either to one of the *declinable comparative* adjectives or to one of the above forms in **-ейший** or **-айший**:

лу́чший	наилу́чший
ху́дший	наиху́дший
бо́льший	наибо́льший
ме́ньший	наиме́ньший
нове́йший	наинове́йший

These forms are also generally characteristic of the more formal levels of written language (including journalism), although **наилу́чший** is often found in expressions of good wishes:

> **Жела́ем здоро́вья, сча́стья и всего́ са́мого *наилу́чшего*.**
> We wish you health, happiness and simply all the very best.

> **Мы счита́ем, что и́менно э́ти но́вые кни́ги должны́ представля́ть *наибо́льший* интере́с для на́ших чита́телей.**
> We think it is these new books that should be of most interest to our readers.

7

Pronouns

7.0 Introduction

Pronouns are often defined as words that can be used in place of nouns, and many of the words that in Russian are conventionally known as pronouns do indeed fulfil this function. Others, however, can serve to *qualify nouns*; the difference between pronouns and adjectives is that the former do not indicate a specific quality, but qualify the noun in a much more general way.

Russian pronouns can be divided into several categories: *personal pronouns* (**7.1**), *possessive pronouns* (**7.2**), *demonstrative pronouns* (**7.3**), *interrogative pronouns* (**7.4**), *relative pronouns* (**7.5**), *indefinite pronouns* (**7.6**) and *pronouns that in one way or another express the idea of totality* (**7.7**); pronouns that fit into none of these categories are dealt with in **7.8**.

Negative pronouns are dealt with in the chapter concerning negation, in sections **15.3.2**, **15.3.3** and **15.5**.

All pronouns decline: some have the same four sets of endings as *adjectives* (masculine, feminine, neuter and plural), while others have only a single set of endings. Indeed, some pronouns have exactly the same endings as adjectives, while others have endings that are peculiar to themselves.

7.1 Personal pronouns

7.1.1 Personal pronouns in Russian

Russian has the following *personal pronouns*:

я	1st person singular: 'I'
ты	2nd person singular (informal): 'you'
он	3rd person singular masculine: 'he (it)'
она́	3rd person singular feminine: 'she (it)'
оно́	3rd person singular neuter: 'it'
мы	1st person plural: 'we'
вы	2nd person singular (formal) and plural: 'you'
они́	3rd person plural: 'they'

There is also a *reflexive* pronoun **себя́**. The use of this pronoun is explained in **7.1.7**.

The choice of which third person pronoun to use is determined by the *grammatical gender* of the noun to which it refers: thus, the masculine form **он** refers to all *masculine* nouns and the feminine form **она́** refers to all *feminine* nouns, regardless of whether they are animate or inanimate:

—**Ты случа́йно не ви́дел** *мою́ ру́чку*?
—**Вот** *она́*, **лежи́т на столе́.**

—You haven't by any chance seen my pen anywhere?
—Here it is, it's on the table.

For more on the gender of nouns, *see* **2.3**.

For more on the use of **ты** and **вы** to address one person, *see* **13.1**.

7.1.2 Declension of the first and second person pronouns and the reflexive pronoun

The *first* and *second person pronouns* and the *reflexive pronoun* decline as follows:

Nom.	я	ты	—
Gen.	меня́	тебя́	себя́
Dat.	мне	тебе́	себе́
Acc.	меня́	тебя́	себя́
Instr.	мной/мно́ю	тобо́й/тобо́ю	собо́й/собо́ю
Prep.	мне	тебе́	себе́

Nom.	мы	вы
Gen.	нас	вас
Dat.	нам	вам
Acc.	нас	вас
Instr.	на́ми	ва́ми
Prep.	нас	вас

NOTES

(i) The *reflexive pronoun* **себя́** has no *nominative* form.

(ii) In the instrumental the forms **мной, тобо́й, собо́й** are more widely used, but the alternatives **мно́ю, тобо́ю, собо́ю** are sometimes preferred for reasons of euphony, especially in *passive constructions*:

Все статьи́, напи́санные *мно́ю* **в про́шлом году́, мо́жно найти́ в Интерне́те.**
All the articles I wrote [*literally*, written by me] last year can be found on the Internet.

For more on passive constructions, *see* **4.14** and **20.2**.

7.1.3 **The declension of the third person pronoun**

The *third person pronoun* declines as follows:

	Masculine	Feminine	Neuter	Plural
Nom.	он	она́	оно́	они́
Gen.	его́	её	его́	их
Dat.	ему́	ей	ему́	им
Acc.	его́	её	его́	их
Instr.	им	ей/е́ю	им	и́ми
Prep.	нём	ней	нём	них

NOTES

(i) The spelling rule given in **1.5.5** applies to the *genitive singular masculine* and *neuter*, i.e. the letter г is pronounced as if it were а **в**.

(ii) The alternative instrumental singular feminine form е́ю is used for euphony and where it is necessary to avoid possible confusion with the dative form ей.

(iii) The *accusative* ending of all personal pronouns is identical to that of the *genitive*.

Immediately after a *preposition* an **н-** is added to the beginning of all relevant forms of the third person pronoun. Because the prepositional case is used only after prepositions, the **н-** is always present in prepositional forms of this pronoun:

Я получи́л *от него́* о́чень стра́нное письмо́.
I've received a very strange letter from him.

Я зайду́ *к нему́* по́сле обе́да.
I'll call in and see him after lunch.

В после́днее вре́мя мы о́чень ма́ло слы́шим *о ней*.
In recent times we've heard very little about her.

Тре́нер извини́лся *перед ни́ми* за плоху́ю игру́ национа́льной сбо́рной.
The coach apologised to them for the poor performance of the national side.

NOTE

Forms without the **н-** are normally preferred after some polysyllabic prepositions, notably **благодаря́** (+ dat.) 'thanks to', **вопреки́** (+ dat.) 'contrary to', **навстре́чу** (+ dat.) 'in the direction of' and **согла́сно** (+ dat.) 'according to'.

7.1.4 **The omission of personal pronouns when they indicate the grammatical subject of a sentence**

In English, the verb does not for the most part give any information about the subject of the sentence, and therefore *personal pronouns* indicating the *grammatical subject* can be omitted only in very restricted circumstances (e.g. after the conjunction 'and'). In Russian, verbs in the *present* and *future* tenses contain information about the subject in the ending, and although this information is not present in the ending of *past* tense verbs, it is nonetheless sometimes possible to omit *subject personal pronouns* in contexts where they would be required in English.

It is difficult to give precise rules for when subject pronouns can be omitted, but in general it occurs more often in speech than in writing. In particular, the subject personal pronoun is often omitted in dialogues of the following sort:

> —*Не по́мните*, во ско́лько начина́ется за́втрашнее совеща́ние?
> —*Не по́мню*, и́ли верне́е, *не зна́ю*.

> —Do you happen to remember what time the meeting starts tomorrow?
> —No, I don't, or rather, I don't know.

The subject personal pronoun tends to be omitted when a sentence is made up of two separate clauses with the same subject:

> Он спеши́л, потому́ что *опа́здывал* на по́езд.
> He was hurrying because he was late for the train.

> В суббо́ту я ходи́л на футбо́л, а в воскресе́нье *съе́здил* домо́й к роди́телям.
> On Saturday I went to a football match and on Sunday I went home to see my parents.

> Мы показа́ли им всё, чем здесь *занима́емся*.
> We showed them everything we're doing here.

The same principle applies when two short sentences follow one another:

> —Но она́ пла́чет. Вдруг *уши́блась*?
> —Е́сли бы *уши́блась*, она́ бы пла́кала намно́го гро́мче.

> —But she's crying. What if she's hurt herself?
> —If she'd hurt herself, she would be crying a lot louder.

7.1.5   The generalised subject

Russian has no special pronoun form to indicate a *generalised subject* (cf. English 'one'). Instead, the most usual way of indicating this is to use the *third person plural* of the verb, but without any explicit noun or pronoun subject:

> *Говоря́т*, её оте́ц – изве́стный поли́тик.
> They say her father is a well-known politician.

> Здесь не *ку́рят*.
> You are requested not to smoke. (*Literally*, One does not smoke here.)

> У нас борщ *гото́вят* по-друго́му.
> Here people make borshch differently.

> В бу́лочную на такси́ не *е́здят*.
> People don't get a taxi to go to the baker's.

This construction is often used in contexts where English would use a *passive verb*:

> Моше́нников *приговори́ли* к разли́чным сро́кам лише́ния свобо́ды.
> The swindlers were sentenced to various terms of imprisonment.

> Нам вчера́ *провели́* скоростно́й интерне́т.
> Yesterday we were connected to broadband. (*Literally*, high-speed Internet.)

For more on the use of the third person plural verb without a pronoun subject in sentences where English would use a passive verb, *see* **20.2.2**.

In more informal language a *second person singular* verb, again without the *pronoun subject*, can be used in a generalised sense (cf. English 'you' used in the same way):

> **Ино́й раз *сиди́шь* до́ма, *смо́тришь* люби́мую переда́чу, и вдруг звони́т телефо́н.**
> Sometimes you can be sitting at home, watching your favourite programme, and suddenly the telephone rings.

In cases other than the *nominative*, the appropriate form of the pronoun **ты** can be used to indicate a generalised person, while the nominative form **ты** is used to indicate a generalised subject in sentences where there is no verb present:

> **Хорошо́, когда́ *ты* нача́льник: *тебя́* все слу́шают, *на тебя́* никто́ не кричи́т.**
> It's good when you're the boss; everybody listens to you and nobody shouts at you.

7.1.6 Multiple persons

In Russian, where there is reference to multiple persons (cf. English 'you and I' or 'you and your sister'), the persons are joined not by a conjunction but by the preposition **c** (+ instr.). In addition, the first (or only) pronoun takes the form of an 'inclusive' plural:

> ***Мы с тобо́й* должны́ обсуди́ть э́тот вопро́с.**
> You and I should discuss this question.

> **А что, ра́зве *вас с сестро́й* не пригласи́ли на сва́дьбу?**
> Were you and your sister not invited to the wedding?

7.1.7 The use of the reflexive pronoun себя́

The *reflexive pronoun* **себя́** has no nominative form. It is used to replace other personal pronouns whenever reference is to the subject of the sentence, and consequently it corresponds to English 'myself', 'yourself', 'ourselves', 'themselves', etc. depending on the context:

> **Е́сли он действи́тельно так счита́ет, он я́вно обма́нывает *себя́*.**
> If he really thinks that, he's clearly deceiving himself.

> **Почему́ ты не ку́пишь *себе́* компью́тер помощне́е?**
> Why don't you buy yourself a more powerful computer?

> **Обяза́тельно принеси́те *с собо́й* все докуме́нты.**
> Don't fail to bring all your documents with you.

> **Мы услы́шали *о себе́* нема́ло ле́стного, но, к сожале́нию, не всё э́то пра́вда.**
> We have heard many flattering things about ourselves, but unfortunately not all of it is true.

The *reflexive pronoun* normally refers to the subject of the nearest verb; in some instances this can be the notional subject of an infinitive:

> **Он посове́товал *нам принести́ с собо́й* все докуме́нты.**
> He advised us to bring all our documents with us.

But:

> **Он посове́товал нам принести́ *ему́* все докуме́нты.**
> He advised us to bring him all our documents.

It is important not to confuse the *reflexive pronoun* **себя́**, which fulfils the function of a *personal pronoun*, with the *reflexive particle* **-ся (-сь)**, used to form *reflexive verbs*.

For more on the formation and function of reflexive verbs, *see* **4.13**, **4.14**.

> **Мой дя́дя *счита́ет себя́* больши́м знатоко́м ма́рочных вин.**
> My uncle considers himself a great connoisseur of fine wines.

> **Мой дя́дя *счита́ется* вели́ким знатоко́м ма́рочных вин.**
> My uncle is considered a great connoisseur of fine wines.

> **Они́ *убеди́ли себя́ в том*, что проти́вник не зна́ет об их за́мыслах.**
> They convinced themselves that their opponent did not know about their plans.

> **Они́ *убеди́лись в том*, что проти́вник не зна́ет об их за́мыслах.**
> They were certain that their opponent did not know about their plans.

The reflexive pronoun **себя́** is used idiomatically in a number of constructions:

вести́/повести́ себя́	to behave
выходи́ть/вы́йти из себя́	to lose one's temper
представля́ть собо́й	to be (formal)
чу́вствовать/почу́вствовать себя́	to feel (ill, happy, etc.)
к себе́, на себя́	pull (on doors)
от себя́	push (on doors)

> **В после́днее вре́мя она́ ста́ла *вести́ себя́* о́чень стра́нно.**
> Recently she has begun to behave very strangely.

For an example of **представля́ть собо́й**, *see* **14.1.5**.

For an example of **чу́вствовать себя́**, *see* **3.5.4**.

More examples of the use of **себя́** are given in **7.8.1**.

7.2 Possessive pronouns

7.2.1 First and second person possessive pronouns

The *first person singular possessive pronoun* is **мой** 'my', 'mine'.

The *second person singular (informal) possessive pronoun* is **твой** 'your', 'yours'.

The *first person plural possessive pronoun* is **наш** 'our', 'ours'.

The *second person singular (formal)* and *plural possessive pronoun* is **ваш** 'your', 'yours'.

These pronouns decline as follows:

	Masculine	Feminine	Neuter	Plural
Nom.	мой	моя́	моё	мои́
Gen.	моего́	мое́й	моего́	мои́х
Dat.	моему́	мое́й	моему́	мои́м
Acc.	as nom. or gen.	мою́	моё	as nom. or gen.
Instr.	мои́м	мое́й	мои́м	мои́ми
Prep.	моём	мое́й	моём	мои́х

	Masculine	Feminine	Neuter	Plural
Nom.	наш	на́ша	на́ше	на́ши
Gen.	на́шего	на́шей	на́шего	на́ших
Dat.	на́шему	на́шей	на́шему	на́шим
Acc.	as nom. or gen.	на́шу	на́ше	as nom. or gen.
Instr.	на́шим	на́шей	на́шим	на́шими
Prep.	на́шем	на́шей	на́шем	на́ших

Твой declines exactly like **мой**.

Ваш declines exactly like **наш**.

The rules for the pronunciation of the *genitive singular masculine* and *neuter* endings and for the use of the different endings for the *accusative singular masculine* and *accusative plural* are the same as those given for adjectives in **6.1.3** and **6.1.1**.

7.2.2   The third person possessive pronouns

The *third person possessive pronouns* are as follows:

> **его́**   his, its (referring to *masculine* and *neuter* nouns)
> **её**   her, its (referring to *feminine* nouns)
> **их**   their (referring to *plural* nouns)

These pronouns are identical to the corresponding *genitive* forms of the third person pronoun (*see* **7.1.3**) and do not decline:

> **Наско́лько я по́мню, я дал ключи́ *её бра́ту*.**
> As far as I remember, I gave the keys to her brother.

> **Я не могу́ не восхища́ться *их успе́хами*.**
> I cannot but admire their success.

Unlike the third person pronoun, however, these *possessive pronouns* never take the **н-** prefix when they follow a preposition:

> **Я забы́л отда́ть ему́ ключи́ *от его́ кварти́ры*.**
> I forgot to give him back the keys to his flat.

> **Да́же в са́мые тру́дные времена́ я всегда́ был *на их стороне́*.**
> Even in the most difficult of times I was always on their side.

The possessive pronoun свой

The *possesive pronoun* **свой**, which declines exactly like **мой** and **твой**, always refers to the subject of the sentence, regardless of the person.

When the subject is in the *first* person, there is usually a choice whether to use **свой** or **мой/наш**:

> **Мы ста́лкиваемся с определёнными тру́дностями в *свое́й/на́шей* рабо́те.**
> We encounter certain difficulties in our work.

> **Гости́ница была́ больша́я, поэ́тому мы не сра́зу смогли́ найти́ *свою́/на́шу* ко́мнату.**
> It was a big hotel, and so we didn't immediately manage to find our room.

In a sentence where the *first person plural* includes both the speaker and the addressee, **наш** tends to be preferred:

> **Послу́шай, ка́жется, мы пропусти́ли *на́шу* о́чередь.**
> Listen, I think we've missed our turn.

When the subject is in the *second* person, **свой** tends to be preferred:

> **Ра́зве *ты* не мо́жешь позвони́ть ему́ *со своего́* моби́льника?**
> Can't you phone him from your mobile?

When the subject is in the *third* person, however, there is a clear distinction between **свой** and **его́/её/их**, and **свой** must be used whenever reference is to the subject of the sentence:

> **На вечери́нке у Ви́ктора Ива́н танцева́л со *свое́й* де́вушкой.**
> At Viktor's party Ivan danced with his (own) girlfriend.

> **На вечери́нке у Ви́ктора Ива́н танцева́л с *его́* де́вушкой.**
> At Viktor's party Ivan danced with his (i.e. Viktor's) girlfriend.

> **Моему́ бра́ту доводи́лось слу́шать, как Бро́дский чита́ет *свои́* стихи́.**
> My brother had occasion to hear Brodsky reading his (own) poetry.

> **Мой брат обожа́ет Бро́дского и ча́сто чита́ет *его́* стихи́ вслух.**
> My brother admires Brodsky and often reads aloud his (i.e. Brodsky's) poetry.

In each of these pairs of examples there is potential for misunderstanding in English, but the fact that **свой** and **его́** would clearly refer to different people means that there is no difficulty in interpreting the Russian correctly.

As with the *reflexive pronoun* **себя́**, **свой** normally relates to the subject of the nearest verb, even when this is the *notional subject* of an *infinitive*:

> **Врач посове́товал *Ивано́ву* поме́ньше по́льзоваться *свое́й* маши́ной.**
> The doctor advised Ivanov not to use his (i.e. Ivanov's) car so much.

> **Козло́в охо́тно позволя́л Ивано́ву по́льзоваться *его́* маши́ной.**
> Kozlov was happy to allow Ivanov to use his (i.e. Kozlov's) car.

Свой cannot normally be used to qualify the subject of a sentence or a clause, nor can it be used or qualify one of two or more joint subjects:

> **Она́ счита́ла, что *её* муж поступи́л о́чень необду́манно.**
> She thought that her husband had acted very precipitately.

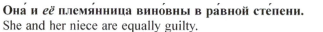

Она́ и *её* племя́нница вино́вны в ра́вной сте́пени.
She and her niece are equally guilty.

Unlike **себя́**, **свой** does have *nominative* case forms. These are used in two sets of circumstances:

1 In sentences indicating possession using the construction with **y** (+ gen.):

Когда́ она́ родила́ пе́рвого ребёнка, у них уже́ была́ *своя́* кварти́ра.
When she gave birth to their first child, they already had their own flat.

For more on the use of this construction to indicate possession, *see* **14.3**.

2 In certain more or less set expressions:

У нас нет от неё секре́тов: она́ здесь *свой* (челове́к).
We don't keep any secrets from her; she's one of us.

Своя́ руба́шка бли́же к те́лу.
Charity begins at home [literally, Ones's own shirt is closer to one's body].

The opposite of **свой** in many instances is the adjective **чужо́й** 'other people's', 'someone else's':

Там нет ничего́ оригина́льного: он то́лько повторя́ет *чужи́е* слова́.
There's nothing original in that; he's simply repeating other people's words.

Чужи́е ве́щи лу́чше не тро́гать.
It's best not to touch someone else's things.

7.2.4 ## The use of possessive pronouns

Russian does not generally use *possessive pronouns* in conjunction with nouns denoting parts of the body, close relatives and in some other contexts where the link between the possessor and the item possessed is obvious:

В отве́т он кивну́л *голово́й*.
He nodded his head in answer.

Я слы́шал, что он ушёл *от жены́* и уе́хал жить куда́-то на Се́вер.
I heard that he's left his wife and gone off to live somewhere in the north.

Ка́жется, пора́ зака́нчивать диску́ссию: лю́ди уже́ ста́ли смотре́ть *на часы́*.
I think it's time we were bringing the discussion to an end; people are already starting to look at their watches.

Она́ допила́ *ко́фе*, попра́вила *причёску*, расплати́лась и вы́шла из кафе́.
She finished her coffee, tidied her hair, paid and left the café.

If someone does something to a part of their (or someone else's) body, the possessor can be indicated by the *dative* form of the appropriate *personal pronoun*:

Они́ в у́жасе: дочь *побри́ла себе́ го́лову*.
They're horrified: their daughter's shaved her head.

Demonstrative pronouns

The declension of the demonstrative pronouns

The two main *demonstrative pronouns* in Russian are э́тот 'this' and тот 'that'. They decline as follows:

	Masculine	Feminine	Neuter	Plural
Nom.	э́тот	э́та	э́то	э́ти
Gen.	э́того	э́той	э́того	э́тих
Dat.	э́тому	э́той	э́тому	э́тим
Acc.	as nom. or gen.	э́ту	э́то	as nom. or gen.
Instr.	э́тим	э́той	э́тим	э́тими
Prep.	э́том	э́той	э́том	э́тих

	Masculine	Feminine	Neuter	Plural
Nom.	тот	та	то	те
Gen.	того́	той	того́	тех
Dat.	тому́	той	тому́	тем
Acc.	as nom. or gen.	ту	то	as nom. or gen.
Instr.	тем	той	тем	те́ми
Prep.	том	той	том	тех

The rules for the pronunciation of the *genitive singular masculine* and *neuter* endings and for the use of the different endings for the *accusative singular masculine* and *accusative plural* are the same as those given for adjectives in **6.1.3** and **6.1.1**.

A third demonstrative pronoun **сей** 'this' is now found only in church language and in the most formal of bureaucratic styles. Relics of it, however, can be found in certain common words and set expressions:

сего́дня [s'ivódn'ə]	today
сейча́с	now, immediately, just a minute
до́ сих пор	up to now
ни то ни сё	neither one thing nor another
ни с того́ ни с сего́	suddenly, without any obvious reason
сию́ мину́ту!	this minute!

A fourth demonstrative pronoun **тако́й** corresponds to English 'such', 'like that/those'. It declines like the adjective **дорого́й** (*see* **6.1.2** and **6.1.4**).

The use of э́тот and тот

In many instances э́тот and тот correspond closely to English 'this' and 'that', except that тот tends to be used only when there is an explicit contrast or when indicating something that is far away:

Э́тот га́лстук мне о́чень нра́вится, а **тот** я скоре́е всего́ отда́м бра́ту.
I like this tie very much, but I'll probably pass that one on to my brother.

Принеси́ мне, пожа́луйста, вон **ту** па́пку.
Could you bring me that folder from over there.

In other contexts, э́тот may be the equivalent of English 'that':

> **Гла́вный реда́ктор заяви́л, что ни́кто с *э́тим* предложе́нием к нему не обраща́лся.**
> The editor-in-chief stated that no one had put that proposal to him.

> **На ва́шем ме́сте я бы *э́того* не де́лал.**
> If I were you, I wouldn't do that.

NOTE In formal language, да́нный (which declines like an adjective) can be used in place of э́тот. It is often found in the phrase в да́нном слу́чае 'in this instance' (for an example, *see* **22.1.3**).

The *neuter* form э́то is used to refer back to general concepts, as well as to whole phrases, clauses or sentences:

> **Он спроси́л меня́ о после́дних собы́тиях на Кавка́зе, но я призна́лся, что ничего́ *об э́том* не зна́ю.**
> He asked me about recent events in the Caucasus, but I admitted that I knew nothing about it.

> **Расскажи́те им о ва́ших моско́вских приключе́ниях; *э́то* бу́дет для них о́чень интере́сно.**
> Tell them about your adventures in Moscow; they'll find it very interesting.

In this usage э́то always refers back to something mentioned. It is not normally used to translate the English 'dummy' subject 'it' in sentences of the following type:

> **Интере́сно бы́ло бы знать, где они́ бы́ли вчера́ ве́чером.**
> *It* would be interesting to know where they got to last night.

> **За́втра у́тром бу́дет я́сно, смо́жем мы вы́ехать или нет.**
> By tomorrow morning *it* will be clear whether we can leave or not.

Э́то is also used for pointing things out and in definitions:

> **—Что *э́то*?**
> **—*Э́то* мой но́вый моби́льник.**

> —What's that?
> —That's my new mobile phone.

> **Э́то – не исто́рия страны́, *э́то* – моя́ ли́чная исто́рия.**
> This is not the history of the nation; it's my personal history.

In sentences of this sort it is the *noun phrase* that is regarded as the subject, and therefore determines the form of any verb that may be present:

> **Э́то была́ для меня́ больша́я *честь*.**
> It was a great honour for me.

Тот is sometimes used as a third person pronoun; it is used in a narrrative sequence when reference is made not to the subject of the preceding sentence, but to someone else involved in the events:

> **Ива́н встреча́л отца́ на вокза́ле. *Он* о́чень уста́л, но тем не ме́нее посчита́л ну́жным это сде́лать.**
> Ivan met his father at the station. He (i.e. Ivan) was very tired, but nonetheless thought it was something he had to do.

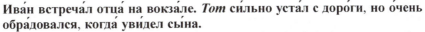
Ива́н встреча́л отца́ на вокза́ле. *Тот си́льно уста́л с доро́ги, но о́чень обра́довался, когда́ уви́дел сы́на.*

Ivan met his father at the station. He/the latter (i.e. the father) was extremely tired after the journey, but was greatly cheered when he saw his son.

The phrase **не тот** means 'the wrong . . .':

У нас пробле́ма: присла́ли *не те* запча́сти.

We have a problem; we've been sent the wrong (spare) parts.

When a preposition is used, it is placed immediately before the *pronoun*:

Он стра́шно расстро́ился, когда́ обнару́жил, что вложи́л письмо́ неве́сте *не в тот* конве́рт.

He was extremely upset when he found out that he had put the letter to his fiancée in the wrong envelope.

For the use of **тот** with relative pronouns, *see* **7.5**.

For the use of **тот** in the phrase **тот же (са́мый)**, *see* **21.9.7**.

7.3.3   The use of тако́й

The *pronoun* **тако́й** means 'such', 'like this', 'like that'. The difference between **тако́й** and **э́тот** can be illustrated by the following pair of examples:

Э́ти фи́льмы я всегда́ смотрю́ с больши́м удово́льствием.

I always enjoy watching these (specific) films.

Таки́е фи́льмы я всегда́ смотрю́ с больши́м удово́льствием.

I always enjoy watching films like these/those.

In some contexts **тако́й** can correspond to English 'that' or 'this' or even the indefinite article:

В *тако́м* слу́чае нам не́зачем продолжа́ть разгово́р.

In that case there's no point in continuing our conversation.

У меня́ *тако́е* предложе́ние: дава́йте устро́им аукцио́н!

I've got a suggestion: let's organise an auction.

Тако́й is also used to qualify *long adjectives* with the meaning 'so':

Ты уме́ешь то́лько критикова́ть. Предложи́ реше́ние, е́сли ты *тако́й* у́мный.

You only know how to criticise. Suggest a solution since you're so clever.

Short adjectives (*see* **6.5**) are qualified by **так**:

Она́ была́ *так хороша́*, *так мила́*, что слов нет.

She was so pretty and so nice that there are no words to describe her.

The pronoun **тако́й-то** means 'such-and-such', i.e. it replaces a specific name when giving general indications:

Здесь на́до указа́ть, что е́дешь в Росси́ю по приглаше́нию *тако́й-то* организа́ции.

Here you have to state that you are travelling to Russia at the invitation of such-and-such an organisation.

7.4 Interrogative pronouns

7.4.1 The interrogative pronouns кто and что

The *interrogative pronouns* кто and что mean 'who' and 'what' respectively. They decline as follows:

Nom.	кто	что
Gen.	кого́	чего́
Dat.	кому́	чему́
Acc.	кого́	что
Instr.	кем	чем
Prep.	ком	чём

The spelling rule given in **1.5.5** applies to the *genitive singular* forms of these pronouns, i.e. the letter г is pronounced as if it were a в.

For examples of the use of кто and что, *see* **12.6.1** and **17.3.1**.

7.4.2 The interrogative pronouns чей, како́й, кото́рый

The *interrogative pronoun* **чей** means 'whose'. It declines like a *soft adjective* of the *second group*, as described in **6.3**, albeit with some slight differences in the *nominative* case. The endings can be illustrated by those of the *nominative* and *genitive* cases:

	Masculine	*Feminine*	*Neuter*	*Plural*
Nom.	чей	чья	чьё	чьи
Gen.	чьего́	чьей	чьего́	чьих

The use of **чей** can be demonstrated by the following examples. In practice, examples of cases other than the nominative are not particularly frequent, especially in speech:

> *Чья* э́та кни́га?
> Whose is that book?

> Есть ли спо́соб узна́ть, с *чьего́* но́мера тебе́ звони́ли?
> Is there a way of finding out from whose number you have been telephoned?

The pronouns **како́й** 'which', 'what kind of' and **кото́рый** 'which' decline like the adjective **дорого́й** and **но́вый** respectively (*see* **6.1.1**, **6.1.2** and **6.1.4**). Examples of their use are given in **17.1.3** and **17.4.1**.

7.5 Relative pronouns

7.5.0 Introduction

The function of a relative pronoun is to serve as a bridge between what would otherwise be two separate sentences. The *interrogative pronouns* **кото́рый**, **кто**, **что**, **чей** and **како́й** can all be used as relative pronouns.

The relative pronoun кото́рый

The most widely used relative pronoun is **кото́рый**, which can correspond to English
'who', 'which' and 'that'. **Кото́рый** is normally used to refer back to a *noun*, and its
ending depends on two factors: the *number* and *gender* are determined by the noun to
which it refers, while the *case* is determined by the *grammatical function* that the pronoun
fulfils in the clause where it appears:

> **Вот но́вая кни́га, *кото́рую* я то́лько что купи́л.**
> Here is a new book that I have just bought.

In the above sentence **кото́рую** is *feminine singular*, agreeing with the feminine singular
noun **кни́га**, but is in the accusative because it functions as the direct object of the
verb **купи́л**.

For more on the use of the accusative case for the direct object of a verb, *see* **3.2**.

In English, it is sometimes possible to join clauses in this way without a relative pronoun;
in Russian, however, the relative pronoun can never be omitted:

> **Кни́га, *кото́рую* я взял в пое́здку, оказа́лась тако́й ску́чной, что я
> наме́ренно оста́вил её в како́м-то кафе́.**
> The book I took with me on my journey was so boring that I deliberately left it
> in a café.

Unlike in English, a relative pronoun cannot be separated from any preposition that may
govern it:

> **Она́ показа́ла мне ста́рую маши́ну, *на кото́рой* её оте́ц е́здил в Росси́ю.**
> She showed me the old car that her father had driven to Russia in.

Nouns used with relative pronouns are frequently qualified by the *demonstrative pronoun*
тот, which can correspond to the English definite article or the demonstrative pronouns
'this' or 'that':

> **Фи́рма несёт юриди́ческую отве́тственность лишь за *те* пу́нкты,
> *кото́рые* перечи́слены в догово́ре.**
> The firm bears legal responsibility only for those matters that are mentioned in
> the agreement.

> **Его́ удиви́ло *то* равноду́шие, *с кото́рым* она́ его́ встре́тила.**
> He was surprised at the indifference with which she greeted him.

The relative pronouns кто and что

When a *relative pronoun* is used to refer back to a pronoun, rather than to a noun, **кто**
'who' or **что** 'that', 'which' is normally used:

> **Он успе́л переки́нуться сло́вом *с ка́ждым, кто* был на приёме.**
> He managed to exchange a few words with everyone who was at the reception.

> **Вы не зна́ете *кого́-нибудь, кто* мог бы перевести́ на ру́сский вот э́тот
> докуме́нт.**
> Do you happen to know anyone who could translate this document into Russian?

> **Это всё, *что* я могу́ сказа́ть по э́тому по́воду.**
> That's everything (that) I can say on the subject.

For more on the pronoun **ка́ждый**, *see* **7.7.2**.

For more on the pronoun **кто́-либо**, *see* **7.6.4**.

For more on the pronoun **весь**, *see* **7.7.1**.

Тот, **кто** can mean 'those who' or 'anyone who'; similarly, **то**, **что** can mean 'that which' or 'what':

> *Тот, кто* быва́л в Росси́и, сра́зу же поймёт, о чём я говорю́.
> Those who have been (*or* Anyone who has been) to Russia will immediately know what I am talking about.

> *То, что* ты говори́шь, меня́ не убежда́ет.
> What you're saying doesn't convince me.

> Не верь *тому́*, *что* он бу́дет сейча́с говори́ть.
> Don't believe what he's about to tell you.

The pronoun **те** is normally followed by **кто**:

> Лу́чше обрати́ться к *тем, кто* уже́ накопи́л како́й-то о́пыт в э́той сфе́ре.
> It's best to approach those who have already gained some experience in this area.

Кото́рые is used, however, if the reference is to inanimate objects:

> Она́ хоте́ла купи́ть себе́ *брю́ки*, но *те, кото́рые* ей понра́вились, оказа́лись малы́.
> She wanted to buy some trousers, but those that she liked were too small.

For the use of the short adjective (**велики́**) meaning 'too big', *see* **14.1.4**.

NOTE | The pronoun **кто** is always followed by a third person *singular* verb (which is *masculine* in the *past tense*), even when it clearly refers to more than one person (*see* **11.2.1**).

Что is used when reference is to a whole clause or sentence or to a general concept not expressed by a specific noun:

> У него́ была́ привы́чка опа́здывать на собра́ния, *что* о́чень раздража́ло его́ колле́г.
> He had the habit of being late for meetings, which greatly irritated his colleagues.

7.5.3 The relative pronouns чей and како́й

The *relative pronoun* **чей** means 'whose':

> Мы ка́ждый день получа́ем бо́лее ста жа́лоб от гра́ждан, *чьи* права́ наруша́ются.
> Every day we receive more than 100 complaints from citizens whose rights are being infringed.

In this sentence it would be possible to replace **чьи** with the *genitive plural* form of **кото́рый**:

> **Мы ка́ждый день получа́ем бо́лее ста жа́лоб от гра́ждан, права́ *кото́рых* наруша́ются.**

When **како́й** is used as a **relative pronoun**, it has the meaning '(of the kind) that'; it tends to be preceded by **тако́й**:

> **Он покупа́ет *таки́е* ви́на, *каки́е* мо́жно найти́ то́лько в са́мых дороги́х магази́нах.**
> He buys wines (of the sort) that you can only find in the most expensive shops.

> **Стоя́ла *така́я* ти́хая и со́лнечная пого́да, *кака́я* обы́чно быва́ет то́лько в середи́не ба́бьего ле́та.**
> There was the calm and sunny weather (of the kind) that you usually only get in the middle of an Indian summer.

7.6   Indefinite pronouns

7.6.1   The formation of indefinite pronouns

By attaching a prefix or suffix to an *interrogative pronoun* Russian forms four separate series of *indefinite pronouns*:

кто́-то	кто́-нибудь	кто́-либо	ко́е-кто́
что́-то	что́-нибудь	что́-либо	ко́е-что́
како́й-то	како́й-нибудь	како́й-либо	ко́е-како́й
че́й-то	че́й-нибудь	че́й-либо	

NOTES

(i) Pronouns formed from **чей** are less widely used that the others, and **ко́е-че́й**, though theoretically possible, is probably best avoided.

(ii) Pronouns with the **ко́е-** prefix can be pronounced either with a secondary stress on the prefix or with two full stresses. Some speakers place a secondary stress on the second syllable of the **-нибудь** suffix.

Although it is possible to give general guidelines on the use of these pronouns, it is worth noting that the boundaries between them are not always easy to draw, and there is a certain amount of overlap in the way they are used.

7.6.2   The -то series

This is probably the most widely used of the four series and the one most likely to encroach on the 'territory' of the others. The basic meaning of this series is 'someone', 'something', 'some (or other)', 'some sort of' – reference is to someone or something specific, the identity of which is either not known or is irrelevant to the speaker:

> **Когда́ тебя́ не́ было до́ма, *кто́-то* тебе́ звони́л.**
> While you weren't here, someone telephoned you.

> **Я слы́шал, как они́ всё вре́мя о *чём-то* перешёптывались.**
> I could hear them whispering about something all the time.

> **Я по́мню то́лько, что на нём была́ *кака́я-то* шля́па.**
> All I remember is that he was wearing some sort of hat.

Его о́чень тру́дно заста́ть на ме́сте: он всё вре́мя за́нят *каки́ми-то* дела́ми.
It's very difficult to find him; he's always busy with some business or other.

Вдруг он услы́шал *чей-то* го́лос.
Suddenly he heard someone's voice.

Кто́-то often has the meaning of 'some people':

По́сле войны́ э́та писа́тельская организа́ция переста́ла существова́ть: *кто-то* у́мер, *кто-то* уе́хал за грани́цу, а *кто-то* вообще́ бро́сил писа́ть.
After the war this writers' organisation ceased to exist; some people died, others went abroad, and some just gave up writing.

Что́-то is often used with neuter singular adjectives:

Наде́юсь, что он принёс с собо́й *что-то съедо́бное*.
I hope he's brought somethig edible with him.

In informal language **что-то** can have the meaning of 'for some reason', 'somehow'; in quantity expressions it can mean 'something over':

Мне *что́-то* не хо́чется идти́ сего́дня на рабо́ту.
Somehow I don't feel like going to work today.

У меня́ с собо́й ты́сяча с *чём-то* рубле́й.
I've got something over a thousand roubles on me.

Како́й-то sometimes serves as the equivalent of an English indefinite article:

Когда́ я откры́л дверь, на поро́ге стоя́л *како́й-то* мужчи́на в чёрном пальто́.
I opened the door to a man in a black overcoat.

Кни́га, кото́рую я взял в пое́здку, оказа́лась тако́й ску́чной, что я наме́ренно оста́вил её в *како́м-то* кафе́.
The book I took with me on my journey was so boring that I deliberately left it in a café.

When used with a long adjective **како́й-то** has the meaning of 'somehow', 'in some way':

Чай сего́дня *како́й-то невку́сный*.
The tea today doesn't taste right somehow.

In informal language **како́й-то** is also used in certain exclamatory set phrases; in these phrases it generally follows the noun:

У́жас *како́й-то*!
It was awful!

Кошма́р *како́й-то*!
It was a nightmare!

По доро́ге в аэропо́рт мы со́рок мину́т проторча́ли в про́бке. *Кошма́р како́й-то*!
We were stuck for 40 minutes in a traffic jam on the way to the airport. It was a nightmare!

The -нибудь series

The **-нибудь** differs from the **-то** series in that it is more indefinite. Here there is no reference to anything specific, and the identity of the person or object in question is unknown to either speaker or addressee. The English equivalents can involve either 'some' or 'any':

Éсли у тебя́ нет открыва́лки, попроси́ у *кого́-нибудь.*
If you don't have a bottle-opener, ask somebody for one.

У нас есть *что́-нибудь* сла́дкое к ча́ю?
Have you anything sweet we can have with our tea?

Есть ко мне *каки́е-нибудь* вопро́сы?
Are there any questions for me?

The boundaries between the **-нибудь** and the **-то** series can be difficult to define. In the following sequence the questioner can use either **что-нибудь** or **что-то**, but the person answering must use **что-то**, since she clearly has something in mind:

—Заче́м ты верну́лась? *Что́-нибудь/что́-то* забы́ла?
—Да, я действи́тельно *что́-то* забы́ла.

—Why have you come back? Have you forgotten something?
—Yes, indeed, I have forgotten something.

In sentences indicating conditions either **-нибудь** or **-то** is possible (cf. English 'someone'/'anyone'):

Éсли *кто́-нибудь/кто́-то* позвони́т с рабо́ты, скажи́, что я за́нят и не могу́ подойти́ к телефо́ну.
If anyone/someone phones from work, tell them I'm busy and can't come to the telephone.

For more on conditions, *see* **21.5**.

In the following pair of sentences **кто́-то** indicates that it was always the same person who asked the question, while **кто́-нибудь** implies that different people asked the first question on different occasions:

В конце́ ка́ждой ле́кции пе́рвый вопро́с всегда́ задава́л *кто́-то* с после́днего ря́да.

В конце́ ка́ждой ле́кции пе́рвый вопро́с всегда́ задава́л *кто́-нибудь* с после́днего ря́да.

Both sentences, however, can be translated into English as:

At the end of each lecture the first question was always asked by someone in the back row.

The **-нибудь** forms can sometimes convey the nuance of English 'any old':

С ва́ми разгова́ривал не *кто́-нибудь*, а сам председа́тель.
That wasn't any old person talking to you, but the chairman himself.

Я не о́чень хочу́ остана́вливаться в *како́й-нибудь* задри́панной гости́нице на окра́ине го́рода.
I don't really want to stay in some miserable hotel on the outskirts of town.

In quantity expressions **какой-нибудь** can convey both approximation and the idea of 'a mere', 'no more than':

> **Через** *каких-нибудь* **два года вы не узнаете наш город.**
> In a mere two years from now you won't recognise our city.

7.6.4 The -либо series

Many dictionaries describe the **-либо** series as being synonymous with the **-нибудь** series, and they are indeed similar in meaning. Nevertheless, there are some contexts where the **-либо** series does seem to be preferred.

Pronouns from the **-либо** series can be used to translate 'any' in a negative construction:

> **Я не могу представить, чтобы** *кто-либо* **сумел его обыграть.**
> I can't imagine that there's anyone capable of beating him.

> **Он заявил, что не планирует приобретать** *какие-либо* **футбольные клубы.**
> He announced that he had no plans to acquire any football clubs.

Pronouns from the **-либо** series are also used in comparisons after **чем**:

> **Он знает об этом больше, чем** *кто-либо* **другой.**
> He knows more about that than anyone else.

For more on comparisons with **чем**, *see* **21.9.2**.

In some contexts pronouns from the **-нибудь** and the **-либо** series are indeed interchangeable. The latter tend to be more characteristic of formal language, but if there is a difference in meaning, it is that the **-либо** pronouns emphasise that it really does not matter who or what is involved:

> **Тебя вполне может временно заменить** *кто-либо/кто-нибудь* **из коллег.**
> You can easily be replaced on a temporary basis by (any)one of your colleagues.

> **А были в вашей библиотеке** *какие-либо/какие-нибудь* **книги по искусству?**
> Did your library have any books on art?

7.6.5 The кое- series

The **кое-** series is the least frequently used of the four series. The meaning of these pronouns is 'some', 'a few', 'one or two', although they can also carry the additional connotation of a slightly dismissive attitude on the part of the speaker:

> **Подозреваю, что** *кое-кому* **наши предложения не понравятся.**
> I suspect that some people won't like our suggestions.

> **Мне уже приходилось** *кое-что* **слышать о нём.**
> I've already had occasion to hear a few things about him.

> **Я тут принёс** *кое-какие* **старые фотографии; посмотрите, может быть, они подойдут для вашей книги.**
> I've brought one or two old photographs with me; have a look and see if they'll do for your book.

Sometimes these pronouns can convey the idea of information that the speaker knows, but does not wish to divulge:

> У меня́ есть для вас *кое-каки́е* пода́рки.
> I've got one or two presents for you (but I'm not telling you what they are).

When these pronouns are used with a *preposition*, the more usual practice is to place the preposition between the *prefix* and the *pronoun*; in this case the different elements are written as three separate words:

> Не тако́й уж я по́лный неве́жда! *Ко́е в чём всё-таки разбира́юсь.*
> I'm not a complete ignoramus, you know! There are one or two things I do know about.

7.7 Pronouns relating to totality

7.7.1 The pronoun весь

The *pronoun* **весь** corresponds to English 'all'. It declines as follows:

	Masculine	Feminine	Neuter
Nom.	весь	вся	всё
Gen.	всего́	всей	всего́
Dat.	всему́	всей	всему́
Acc.	as nom. or gen.	всю	всё
Instr.	всем	всей	всем
Prep.	всём	всей	всём

The rules for the pronunciation of the *genitive singular masculine* and *neuter* endings and for the use of the different endings for the *accusative singular masculine* and *accusative plural* are the same as those given for adjectives in **6.1.3** and **6.1.1**.

The use of **весь** can be illustrated by the following examples:

> Наш рейс отмени́ли, пришло́сь *весь день* просиде́ть в аэропорту́.
> Our flight was cancelled, and we had to spend all day at the airport.

> Я прочита́л не *всю кни́гу*, а то́лько пе́рвые сто страни́ц.
> I haven't read all the book, just the first hundred pages.

> После́дствия глоба́льного потепле́ния тепе́рь ощути́мы на *всех контине́нтах.*
> The consequences of global warming can now be felt in all continents.

Used on their own, the *neuter singular* **всё** means 'everything', and the *plural* **все** 'everyone':

> Скажи́ мне *всё*, что ты зна́ешь.
> Tell me everything you know.

> Не беспоко́йтесь, пи́ва хва́тит *на всех.*
> Don't worry; there'll be enough beer for everybody.

In informal language **всё** can have the meaning 'right', 'that's it!':

> *Всё,* **хва́тит! Я слы́шать э́того бо́льше не могу́.**
> Right, that's enough! I can't listen to any more of this.

Всё is also widely used with the adverbs **ещё** and **равно́**:

> **всё ещё**　　　　　　　　still, even now
> **всё равно́**　　　　　　　still, all the same, nonetheless, anyway

> **Он око́нчил университе́т пять лет наза́д, но** *всё ещё* **живёт у роди́телей.**
> He graduated five years ago, but still lives at home with his parents.

> **Пусть говори́т всё, что уго́дно -** *всё равно́* **ему́ никто́ не пове́рит.**
> Let him say what he likes, (still) nobody will believe him (anyway).

For the use of **всё равно́** to indicate indifference, *see* **16.2.4**.

For the use of **всё** with comparative adjectives and adverbs, *see* **21.9.1**.

The *genitive singular* form **всего́** is used, either on its own or with **лишь**, to mean 'only', 'no more than' in quantity expressions:

> **На ле́кции бы́ло** *всего́ (лишь)* **два́дцать челове́к.**
> There were only twenty people at the lecture.

It is important to distinguish the *pronoun* **весь** 'all', 'the whole' from the *adjective* **це́лый** 'a whole':

> **Не е́шьте** *весь* **арбу́з: оста́вьте хотя́ бы па́ру куско́в на за́втра.**
> Don't eat the whole water-melon; leave at least a couple of portions for tomorrow.

> **Они́ спо́рили о том, мо́жно ли за оди́н раз съесть** *це́лый* **арбу́з.**
> They were debating whether it was possible to eat a whole water-melon at a single sitting.

7.7.2　Other pronouns relating to totality

The other pronouns that relate to totality are **ка́ждый, вся́кий** and **любо́й**. These decline like the adjectives **но́вый, ру́сский** and **молодо́й** respectively (*see* **6.1**).

Ка́ждый corresponds to English 'every'. It is normally used only in the *singular*, although the *plural* forms are used with nouns such as **полчаса́** 'half an hour' and **полго́да** 'half a year', 'six months', which are treated as grammatically plural:

> **Бы́ло ви́дно, что, отвеча́я на вопро́сы, он взве́шивал** *ка́ждое* **сло́во.**
> It was clear that when he answered the questions he was weighing up every word.

> *Ка́ждый* **год он е́здит в Испа́нию на ме́сяц.**
> Every year he goes to Spain for a month.

> *Ка́ждые полчаса́* **в пала́ту загля́дывала медсестра́ – прове́рить, не проснýлся ли он.**
> Every half-hour a nurse looked into the ward to check if he had woken up.

Всякий can also mean 'every', 'all', although nowadays this is most frequently found in certain set phrases, such as **всякий раз** 'every time', **всякий (человек)** 'everybody', **выше всяких похвал** 'beyond all praise'. Its most common meaning is 'all kinds of':

> **В российской истории двоевластие** *всякий раз* **приводило к гражданской войне.**
> In Russian history dual power has led to civil war every time.

> **У него всегда бывают** *всякие* **интересные** *идеи.*
> He always has all sorts of interesting ideas.

> **В жизни** *всякое* **бывает.**
> All sorts of things can happen in life.

Всякий can mean 'any' after the preposition **без** (+ gen) 'without' and in some other constructions with negative implications:

> **Это** *без всякого сомнения* **самый скучный роман, который я когда-либо читал.**
> That is without any doubt the most boring novel I have ever read.

> **Для её гардероба характерно полное отсутствие** *всякого вкуса.*
> Her wardrobe is characterised by the total absence of any taste.

Всякий is also used in a number of set phrases, as shown in the following examples.

на всякий случай and the more informal **на всякий пожарный (случай)** 'just in case':

> **во всяком случае**   in any case
>   at any rate
>   however that may be

> **Возьми зонтик** *на всякий случай.*
> Take an umbrella, just in case.

> **Влияние его идей идёт на убыль,** *во всяком случае* **в России.**
> The influence of his ideas is declining, at any rate in Russia.

> **Экономическая ситуация в наступающем году остаётся нестабильной. Экономисты,** *во всяком случае,* **прогнозируют дальнейший рост инфляции.**
> The economic situation for the coming year remains unstable. At any rate, economists are forecasting a further rise in inflation.

Любой generally corresponds to 'any', especially when used in the sense of 'every':

> **Вы найдёте наши товары в** *любом* **супермаркете.**
> You'll find our goods in any supermarket.

В любом случае means 'in any event', 'whatever happens':

> **В** *любом случае* **я буду ждать вас на вокзале.**
> Whatever happens, I'll be waiting for you at the station.

In some instances the meaning of **любой** is close to, but not identical with that of **кто-нибудь/какой-нибудь**. The difference between them can be illustrated by the following pair of examples:

Éсли ты не знáешь дорóгу, спросú *когó-нибудь*.
If you don't know the way, ask someone [emphasis is on the asking; the person may or may not know the answer].

Доезжáйте до Нéвского проспéкта, а там *любóй* вам скáжет, как пройтú к Рýсскому музéю.
Go to Nevskii Prospekt, and there anyone (you like) (emphasis is on the 'any'; it does not matter who you ask, because everybody knows the answer) will tell you how to get to the Russian Museum.

7.8 Other pronouns

7.8.1 The emphatic pronoun сам

The *emphatic pronoun* **сам** declines as follows:

	Masculine	Feminine	Neuter	Plural
Nom.	**сам**	**самá**	**самó**	**сáми**
Gen.	**самогó**	**самóй**	**самогó**	**самúх**
Dat.	**самомý**	**самóй**	**самомý**	**самúм**
Acc.	as nom. or gen.	**самý (самоё)**	**самó**	as nom. or gen.
Instr.	**самúм**	**самóй**	**самúм**	**самúми**
Prep.	**самóм**	**самóй**	**самóм**	**самúх**

The older *accusative singular feminine* form **самоё** is going out of use. Except for the *nominative plural* the stress is always on the ending.

The rules for the pronunciation of the *genitive singular masculine* and *neuter* endings and for the use of the different endings for the *accusative singular masculine* and *accusative plural* are the same as those given for adjectives in **6.1.3** and **6.1.1**.

The pronoun **сам** adds emphasis to the noun or pronoun with which it is used; **сам** normally follows a pronoun, but tends to precede a noun :

Он отказáлся дéлать какúе-либо комментáрии, заявúв, что у негó *самогó* нет никакóй информáции.
He refused to make any comment, stating that he himself had no information.

Все вáжные решéния, относя́щиеся к сфéре внéшней полúтики, принимáет *сам* Президéнт.
All important decisions on matters concerning foreign policy are taken by the president himself.

Сам can also have the meaning of 'by oneself' in the sense of 'independently':

Спасúбо, но я не нуждáюсь в вáшей пóмощи: я всё сдéлаю *самá*.
Thank you, but I don't need your help; I can do everything myself.

Сам is frequently used with the *reflexive pronoun* **себя́**:

Э́тими дéйствиями онú тóлько вредя́т *самúм себé*.
With these actions they are only damaging themselves.

С течéнием врéмени все полúтики становятся парóдиями *на самúх себя.*

In time all politicians become parodies of themselves.

The following set phrases involving **сам** and **себя** are worth noting:

сам по себé	in itself, independently, separately
самó собóй (разумéется)	of course, obviously, it goes without saying

Идéя *самá по себé* интерéсная, но мóжно ли её применúть на прáктике?
In itself the idea is interesting, but can it be applied in practice?

В их передвижéниях не́ было никакóго взаимодéйствия: кáждый дéйствовал *сам по себé.*
Their movements were totally unco-ordinated with each other; everybody was acting independently.

Самó собóй разумéется, мы бýдем окáзывать необходúмую пóмощь всем пострадáвшим от недáвнего стихúйного бéдствия.
It goes without saying that we will be providing all necessary assistance to the victims of the recent disaster.

The pronoun сáмый

The *pronoun* **сáмый**, which declines like the adjective **нóвый** (*see* **6.1**), is used with nouns indicating place or time to emphasise the precise point where or when something happens; in this sense it usually corresponds to English 'very':

Ей повезлó: онá нашлá квартúру в *сáмом* цéнтре гóрода.
She struck lucky and found a flat in the very centre of the city.

Он затрóнул э́ту тéму тóлько в *сáмом* концé лéкции.
He touched on this topic only at the very end of his lecture.

Сáмый is used in a number of useful set expressions:

в сáмый раз	just right (in terms of time, number or size)
в сáмом дéле	indeed, really, in fact
на сáмом дéле	in actual fact
э́то сáмое	the what's-its-name (used when someone cannot remember the name for something)

Чёрные ботúнки мне великовáты, а вот э́ти корúчневые в *сáмый раз.*
The black boots are a bit big, but the brown ones are just right.

Вы *в сáмом дéле* э́того не знáли?
Did you really not know that?

—Ты зачéм вернýлась? Чтó-нибудь забы́ла?
—Да, я *в сáмом дéле* чтó-то забы́ла.

—Why have you come back? Have you forgotten something?
—Yes, indeed, I have forgotten something.

Он выдаёт себя́ за велúкого колдунá и целúтеля, а *на сáмом дéле* он прóсто шарлатáн.
He claims to be a great magician or healer, but in actual fact he's just a charlatan.

Я принёс тебе́ *э́то са́мое* . . . энциклопе́дию.
I've brought you the what's-its-name, the encyclopedia.

For the use of **са́мый** to form the superlative of adjectives, *see* **6.8.4**.

For the use of **са́мый** in the phrase **тот же (самый)** 'the same', *see* **21.9.7**.

7.8.3 **The reciprocal pronoun друг дру́га**

The pronoun **друг дру́га** means 'each other'; the first part is indeclinable, while the second part declines (in the singular only) according to its function in the sentence and can be used after prepositions:

Вы уже́ зна́ете *друг дру́га*?
Do you already know each other?

Они́ поссо́рились на днях и тепе́рь да́же не здоро́ваются *друг с дру́гом*.
They fell out a few days ago and now aren't even on speaking terms.
(*Literally*, they don't even say 'hello' to each other.)

8
Numerals and other quantity words

Cardinal numerals

Cardinal numerals are those used when counting or indicating quantity.

List of cardinal numerals

0	ноль, нуль	32	три́дцать два, три́дцать две
1	оди́н, одна́, одно́, одни́	38	три́дцать во́семь
2	два, две	40	со́рок
3	три	50	пятьдеся́т
4	четы́ре	60	шестьдеся́т
5	пять	70	се́мьдесят
6	шесть	80	во́семьдесят
7	семь	90	девяно́сто
8	во́семь	100	сто
9	де́вять	101	сто оди́н, сто одна́, сто одно́
10	де́сять	102	сто два, сто две
11	оди́ннадцать	110	сто де́сять
12	двена́дцать	125	сто два́дцать пять
13	трина́дцать	160	сто шестьдеся́т
14	четы́рнадцать	200	две́сти
15	пятна́дцать	300	три́ста
16	шестна́дцать	400	четы́реста
17	семна́дцать	500	пятьсо́т
18	восемна́дцать	600	шестьсо́т
19	девятна́дцать	700	семьсо́т
20	два́дцать	800	восемьсо́т
21	два́дцать оди́н, два́дцать одна́, два́дцать одно́	900	девятьсо́т
		999	девятьсо́т девяно́сто де́вять
22	два́дцать два, два́дцать две	1,000	ты́сяча
		1,001	ты́сяча оди́н, ты́сяча одна́, ты́сяча одно́
23	два́дцать три		
25	два́дцать пять	1,002	ты́сяча два, ты́сяча две
30	три́дцать	1,100	ты́сяча сто
31	три́дцать оди́н, три́дцать одна́, три́дцать одно́	1,211	ты́сяча две́сти оди́ннадцать
		2,000	две ты́сячи

3,000	три ты́сячи	500,000	пятьсо́т ты́сяч
4,000	четы́ре ты́сячи	501,000	пятьсо́т одна́ ты́сяча
5,000	пять ты́сяч	502,000	пятьсо́т две ты́сячи
10,000	де́сять ты́сяч	1,000,000	миллио́н
15,000	пятна́дцать ты́сяч	2,000,000	два миллио́на
40,000	со́рок ты́сяч	5,000,000	пять миллио́нов
41,000	со́рок одна́ ты́сяча	50,000,000	пятьдеся́т миллио́нов
42,000	со́рок две ты́сячи	1,000,000,000	миллиа́рд
100,000	сто ты́сяч		

For the different endings of оди́н, *see* **8.1.2**

For the different endings of два, *see* **8.1.3**

For the different endings of ты́сяча and миллио́н, *see* **8.2**

NOTES

(i) Ноль and нуль are alternative forms. Ноль tends to be preferred in the written language, while нуль is widely used in the spoken language.

(ii) The normal equivalent of (US) billion (i.e. one thousand million) is миллиа́рд; a (US) trillion (i.e. one million million) is, however, триллио́н.

8.1.2 Reading and writing cardinal numbers

The individual elements that are put together to make a large number are written as separate words. Thus, 45 751 384 would be written in full as:

> со́рок пять миллио́нов семьсо́т пятьдеся́т одна́ ты́сяча три́ста во́семьдесят четы́ре

NOTE

As this example shows, no punctuation is used to separate thousands, although a space can be left, especially with very large numbers. A comma is used instead of the decimal point (*see* **8.5.3**).

Sequences of four or more digits are often broken up into units of two or (less often) three digits each, a procedure that is adopted more regularly in speech than in writing. For example, a seven-digit Moscow telephone number is written as:

> 139-92-16 *or* 139 9216

This would normally be read as:

> сто три́дцать де́вять девяно́сто два шестна́дцать

In journalistic and academic writing the following abbreviations are frequently found:

тыс.	ты́сяча (ты́сячи, ты́сяч, etc.)
млн.	миллио́н (миллио́на, миллио́нов, etc.)
млрд.	миллиа́рд (милла́рда, миллиа́рдов, etc.)

Наш заво́д выпуска́ет ежего́дно *400 тыс.* маши́н.
Our factory manufactures 400,000 cars a year.

В Москве́ и её при́городах прожива́ют о́коло *20 млн.* челове́к.
About 20 million people live in Moscow and the surrounding area.

В 2002 году́ вое́нные расхо́ды Росси́и составля́ли о́коло *11 млрд.* **до́лларов.**

In 2002 Russian military expenditure amounted to approximately 11 billion dollars.

8.1.3 Declension of оди́н

The declension of the numeral **оди́н** is similar to that of the pronoun **э́тот**:

For the declension of **э́тот** *see* **7.3.1**.

	Masculine	*Feminine*	*Neuter*	*Plural*
Nom.	оди́н	одна́	одно́	одни́
Gen.	одного́	одно́й	одного́	одни́х
Dat.	одному́	одно́й	одному́	одни́м
Acc.	as nom. or gen.	одну́	одно́	as nom. or gen.
Instr.	одни́м	одно́й	одни́м	одни́ми
Prep.	одно́м	одно́й	одно́м	одни́х

The rules for the *accusative singular masculine* and the *accusative plural* are the same as for *adjectives* and *pronouns*. The form that is identical to the *genitive* is used with *animate* nouns, while the form that is identical to the *nominative* is used with *inanimate* nouns:

For more on animate and inanimate nouns, *see* **2.4**.

Я зна́ю *одного́ челове́ка*, **кото́рый с тобо́й не согласи́тся.**
I know one person who won't agree with you.

Я провёл с ней то́лько *оди́н день*, **но уже́ зна́ю всю исто́рию её семьи́.**
I've only spent one day with her, but I already know the whole history of her family.

Почему́ мужчи́ны лю́бят *одни́х же́нщин*, **а же́нятся на други́х?**
Why do men not marry the women they love?
(*Literally*, Why do men love some women, but marry different ones?)

Я чита́ю *одни́ детекти́вы*.
I read nothing but detective novels.

8.1.4 The plural of оди́н

The plural form of **оди́н** is used in the following ways:

1 To mean 'one' with nouns that denote countable objects and that do not have a singular form, e.g. **су́тки** 'day', 'period of 24 hours', **брю́ки** '(pair of) trousers', **вы́боры** '(political) election(s)':

Он положи́л в чемода́н *одни́ брю́ки* **и** *одну́ руба́шку*.
He put one pair of trousers and one shirt in his suitcase.

2 With the meaning 'only', 'nothing but':

Я чита́ю *одни́ детекти́вы*.
I read nothing but detective novels.

3 With the meaning 'alone', 'on one's own':

Не оставля́йте дете́й до́ма *одни́х*!
Don't leave your children at home on their own.

4 With the meaning 'some' (in contrast to others):

Одни́ **увлека́ются спо́ртом, други́е му́зыкой, а тре́тьи ниче́м не увлека́ются.**
Some people are interested in sport and others in music, but some people aren't interested in anything.

8.1.5 The declension of два, три, четы́ре

The numerals **два** (2), **три** (3) and **четы́ре** (4) follow a declension pattern peculiar to themselves:

	Masculine and neuter	*All genders*	*Feminine*
Nom.	**два**		**две**
Gen.		**двух**	
Dat.		**двум**	
Acc.	as nom. or gen.		as nom. or gen.
Instr.		**двумя́**	
Prep.		**двух**	

	All genders	*All genders*
Nom.	**три**	**четы́ре**
Gen.	**трёх**	**четырёх**
Dat.	**трём**	**четырём**
Acc.	as nom. or gen.	as nom. or gen.
Instr.	**тремя́**	**четырьмя́**
Prep.	**трёх**	**четырёх**

In the *accusative* the form that is identical to the *genitive* is used with *animate* nouns, while the form that is identical to the *nominative* is used with *inanimate* nouns:

Ты заме́тил на углу́ *двух милиционе́ров*?
Did you notice two policemen on the corner?

На э́том сни́мке мы ви́дим всех *четырёх дочере́й* **после́днего царя́.**
On this photograph we can see all four daughters of the last tsar.

Я то́лько что купи́л *две* после́дние *кни́ги* **Бори́са Аку́нина.**
I've just bought Boris Akunin's last two books.

Да́йте, пожа́луйста, три ба́нки пи́ва и *две* **больши́е** *буты́лки* **минера́льной воды́.**
Could you give me three cans of beer and two large bottles of mineral water.

NOTE | **Оди́н** and **два** are the only numerals that distinguish gender; **оди́н, два, три** and **четы́ре** are the only numerals that have different forms in the accusative for animate and inanimate nouns.

8.1.6 The declension of numerals ending in -ь

The numerals 5–20 and 30 all end in **-ь** and have the same endings as *feminine singular nouns* ending in **-ь**:

Nom.	**пять (5)**	**шесть (6)**	**семь (7)**	**во́семь (8)**
Gen.	**пяти́**	**шести́**	**семи́**	**восьми́**
Dat.	**пяти́**	**шести́**	**семи́**	**восьми́**
Acc.	**пять**	**шесть**	**семь**	**во́семь**
Instr.	**пятью́**	**шестью́**	**семью́**	**восемью́** *or* **восьмью́**
Prep.	**пяти́**	**шести́**	**семи́**	**восьми́**

Nom.	**де́вять (9)**	**де́сять (10)**	**двена́дцать (12)**	**два́дцать (20)**
Gen.	**девяти́**	**десяти́**	**двена́дцати**	**двадцати́**
Dat.	**девяти́**	**десяти́**	**двена́дцати**	**двадцати́**
Acc.	**де́вять**	**де́сять**	**двена́дцать**	**два́дцать**
Instr.	**девятью́**	**десятью́**	**двена́дцатью**	**двадцатью́**
Prep.	**девяти́**	**десяти́**	**двена́дцати**	**двадцати́**

NOTE | The numeral **во́семь** has a fleeting vowel, which (optionally) reappears in the *instrumental* case.

The remaining numerals between 11 and 19 follow the same pattern as **двена́дцать**; **три́дцать** (30) follows the same pattern as **два́дцать**.

8.1.7 The declension of со́рок, девяно́сто and сто

The numerals **со́рок** (40), **девяно́сто** (90) and **сто** (100) follow a distinctive, but simple declension pattern:

Nom. and Acc.	*со́рок*	*девяно́сто*	*сто*
All other cases	*сорока́*	*девяно́ста*	*ста*

8.1.8 The declension of the numerals 50–80 and 200–900

The numerals 50–80 and 200–900 follow a complicated declension pattern, in which the forms change both in the *middle* and at the *end* of the word:

Nom.	пятьдеся́т (50)	шестьдеся́т (60)	се́мьдесят (70)	во́семьдесят (80)
Gen.	пяти́десяти	шести́десяти	семи́десяти	восьми́десяти
Dat.	пяти́десяти	шести́десяти	семи́десяти	восьми́десяти
Acc.	пятьдеся́т	шестьдеся́т	се́мьдесят	во́семьдесят
Instr.	пятью́десятью	шестью́десятью	семью́десятью	восемью́десятью *or* восьмью́десятью
Prep.	пяти́десяти	шести́десяти	семи́десяти	восьми́десяти

Nom.	две́сти (200)	три́ста (300)	четы́реста (400)
Gen.	двухсо́т	трёхсо́т	четырёхсо́т
Dat.	двумста́м	трёмста́м	четырёмста́м
Acc.	две́сти	три́ста	четы́реста
Instr.	двумяста́ми	тремяста́ми	четырьмяста́ми
Prep.	двухста́х	трёхста́х	четырёхста́х

Nom.	пятьсо́т (500)	восемьсо́т (800)
Gen.	пятисо́т	восьмисо́т
Dat.	пятиста́м	восьмиста́м
Acc.	пятьсо́т	восемьсо́т
Instr.	пятьюста́ми	восемьюста́ми *or* восьмьюста́ми
Prep.	пятиста́х	восьмиста́х

Шестьсо́т (600), **семьсо́т** (700) and **девятьсо́т** (900) follow the pattern of **пятьсо́т**.

NOTE | In the forms **трёхсо́т, трёмста́м, трёхста́х, четырёхсо́т, четырёмста́м, четырёхста́х** there is a secondary stress on the syllables containing the letter **ё**.

8.1.9 | ## The declension of ноль/нуль, ты́сяча, миллио́н, миллиа́рд

The numerals **ноль/нуль** (0), **ты́сяча** 'thousand', **миллио́н** 'million', **миллиа́рд** '(US) billion' are more like nouns than the other numerals. They have *grammatical gender*, decline like nouns and, unlike other numerals (except **оди́н**), they have both *singular* and *plural* forms.

ноль/нуль is *masculine* and declines like a *masculine noun* ending in **-ь**.

ты́сяча is *feminine* and declines like a *feminine noun* ending in **-ча**.

миллио́н and **миллиа́рд** are *masculine* and decline like *masculine nouns* ending in a *consonant*.

Singular:

Nom.	ноль/нуль	ты́сяча	миллио́н	миллиа́рд
Gen.	ноля́/нуля́	ты́сячи	миллио́на	миллиа́рда
Dat.	нолю́/нулю́	ты́сяче	миллио́ну	миллиа́рду
Acc.	ноль/нуль	ты́сячу	миллио́н	миллиа́рд
Instr.	нолём/нулём	ты́сячей	миллио́ном	миллиа́рдом
Prep.	ноле́/нуле́	ты́сяче	миллио́не	миллиа́рде

Plural:

Nom.	но́ли/нули́	ты́сячи	миллио́ны	миллиа́рды
Gen.	ноле́й/нуле́й	ты́сяч	миллио́нов	миллиа́рдов
Dat.	ноля́м/нуля́м	ты́сячам	миллио́нам	миллиа́рдам
Acc.	но́ли/нули́	ты́сячи	миллио́ны	миллиа́рды
Instr.	ноля́ми/нуля́ми	ты́сячами	миллио́нами	миллиа́рдами
Prep.	ноля́х/нуля́х	ты́сячах	миллио́нах	миллиа́рдах

The plural of **ноль/нуль** is fairly rare, but occurs in such contexts as:

> **Число́ триллио́н изобража́ется на письме́ едини́цей с двена́дцатью нуля́ми.**
> The figure one trillion is written as a one, followed by twelve noughts.

The plural forms of **ты́сяча**, **миллио́н** and **миллиа́рд** occur frequently in combination with other numerals and words indicating quantity. Examples are given in **8.2.5**.

8.1.10 The declension of complex numerals

When two or more numerals are put together to form complex numerals, all parts of the numeral should in principle be declined:

> **На́ша фи́рма име́ет представи́тельства *в двухста́х семи́десяти четырёх города́х* по всему́ ми́ру.**
> Our company has offices in 274 cities throughout the world.

Numerals of this type, although they will sometimes be heard in more formal contexts, are unwieldy and difficult to form spontaneously. In practice, the only case, other than the nominative and the accusative, that is used with any great frequency is the *genitive*, and even here numerals made up of more than two elements can usually be avoided. Examples such as the following are, however, not unusual:

> **В бассе́йн Невы́ вхо́дит *о́коло пяти́десяти ты́сяч озёр и шести́десяти ты́сяч рек*.**
> The basin of the River Neva includes about 50,000 lakes and 60,000 rivers.

> **Доста́вка произво́дится *в тече́ние двадцати́ четырёх часо́в* по́сле получе́ния зака́за.**
> Delivery takes place within 24 hours of our receiving the order.

8.2 Selecting what case to use with cardinal numerals

8.2.0 Introduction

The rules for selecting what case to use with cardinal numerals are complicated and depend both on the numeral concerned and on the case in which the numeral itself is placed.

8.2.1 The cases used with оди́н

The numeral **оди́н** behaves exactly like an *adjective* or a *pronoun*; in other words, it agrees with any noun it is used with in *gender*, *case* and *number*.

For the use of **оди́н** in the plural, *see* **8.1.4**

> **Я купи́л то́лько** *одну́ буха́нку* **чёрного хле́ба.**
> I bought only one loaf of black bread.

> **В сове́тские времена́ иностра́нцы не могли́ е́здить** *из одного́ го́рода* **в**
> **друго́й без разреше́ния мили́ции.**
> In Soviet times foreigners were not able to travel from one town to another
> without the permission of the police.

> **Я чита́ю** *одни́х кла́ссиков;* **в про́шлом году́ я не прочита́л** *ни одного́*
> *совреме́нного рома́на.*
> I only read the classic authors; last year I didn't read a single modern novel.

For the use of **не . . . ни** as an emphatic negative, *see* **15.3.4**.

8.2.2 The cases used with два, три, четы́ре

When the numerals **два**, **три** or **четы́ре** are themselves in the *nominative* or the
(*inanimate*) *accusative*, any noun that is used with them will be in the *genitive
singular*:

> **Я вы́рос в большо́й семье́: у меня́** *три бра́та и две сестры́.*
> I grew up in a big family; I have three brothers and two sisters.

> **Ле́том в на́шем о́фисе о́чень жа́рко: там** *четы́ре окна́,* **и все они́**
> **выхо́дят на юг.**
> In summer it gets very hot in our office; there are four windows and they all
> face south.

A small number of masculine nouns have the stress on the ending when used after **два**,
три, **четы́ре**, but on the stem when used in the genitive case. The most common of
these are **ряд** 'row', **час** 'hour' **шаг** 'pace', 'step':

> **Я ждал его́ на вокза́ле** *три часа́.*
> I waited at the station for him for three hours.

> **Мы проболта́ли** *бо́льше ча́са.*
> We chatted away for more than an hour.

If nouns used after **два**, **три**, **четы́ре** are qualified by an *adjective*, the adjective is in
the *genitive plural*. With *feminine* nouns the adjective can be in either the *genitive plural*
or the *nominative plural*; the genitive tends to be preferred when the stress of the noun
in the *genitive singular* is different from that of the *nominative plural*:

> **У меня́** *два чёрных кота́.*
> I have two black cats.

> **В на́шем о́фисе** *четы́ре больши́х окна́.*
> Our office has four big windows.

> **Мы поста́вили пе́ред собо́й** *три основны́х/основны́е зада́чи.*
> We have set ourselves three main tasks.

> **У меня́** *две ста́рших сестры́.*
> I have two older sisters.

The nominative plural of **зада́ча** is **зада́чи**; the nominative plural of **сестра́** is
сёстры.

A *noun* that takes the endings of an *adjective* (e.g. живо́тное 'animal' or столо́вая 'dining room', 'canteen') behaves like an *adjective*:

> **В на́шем ко́рпусе** *две студе́нческих столо́вых* **и буфе́т для преподава́телей.**
>
> Our building has two student canteens and a snack bar for members of staff.

If an adjective precedes the numeral, it is in the *nominative/accusative plural*:

> **За** *после́дние три го́да* **она́ написа́ла две кни́ги и де́сять нау́чных стате́й.**
>
> In the last three years she has written two books and ten learned articles.

If the numeral is in the (*animate*) accusative, genitive, dative, instrumental or prepositional, then any *noun* and/or *adjective* is in the *plural* and in the *same case* as the numeral:

> **Вы не зна́ете мои́х** *двух мла́дших сестёр?*
>
> Do you know my two younger sisters?

> **Она́ живёт одна́** *с тремя́ огро́мными соба́ками.*
>
> She lives on her own with three enormous dogs.

> **Я смотре́л** *в трёх ра́зных уче́бниках* **и нашёл** *три ра́зных отве́та.*
>
> I looked in three different textbooks and found three different answers.

8.2.3 The cases used with numerals from пять to девятьсо́т

When a numeral between **пять** and **девятьсо́т** is in the *nominative* or the *accusative* case, any following *noun* and/or *adjective* is in the *genitive plural*:

> **Наш по́езд опозда́л** *на пять часо́в.*
>
> Our train was five hours late.

> **За после́дние пять лет она́ написа́ла две кни́ги и** *три́дцать нау́чных стате́й.*
>
> In the last five years she has written two books and thirty learned articles.

> **Тогда́ обе́д в э́том рестора́не сто́ил** *четы́реста рубле́й.*
>
> In those days a meal in this restaurant cost 400 roubles.

The nouns **год** and **челове́к** have special forms that are used after *numerals* instead of the ordinary genitive plural. These forms are respectively **лет** and **челове́к**:

> **За** *после́дние пять лет* **она́ написа́ла две кни́ги и три́дцать нау́чных стате́й.**
>
> In the last five years she has written two books and thirty learned articles.

> **Я насчита́л в за́ле приме́рно** *две́сти челове́к.*
>
> I counted about 200 people in the hall.

As the first of the above examples shows, when an adjective precedes a numeral, it is in the *nominative/accusative plural*.

When one of these numerals is in the *genitive, dative, instrumental* or *prepositional* case, then any accompanying *noun* and/or *adjective* is in the *same case* as the numeral:

> **Наш магази́н рабо́тает** *с семи́ часо́в.*
>
> Our shop is open from seven o'clock.

Он оказа́лся на после́днем ме́сте *со свои́ми ничто́жными пятьюста́ми голоса́ми*.
He ended up in last place with his miserable five hundred votes.

Я побыва́л *в десяти́ ра́зных города́х* и везде́ слы́шал одно́ и то же.
I've been in ten different cities and everywhere I went I heard the same thing.

NOTE | This section applies only to numbers made up of a single element. For complex numerals, *see* **8.2.5**.

8.2.4 | ## The cases used with ноль/нуль, ты́сяча, миллио́н, миллиа́рд

When the numerals **ноль/нуль, ты́сяча, миллио́н** or **миллиа́рд** are followed by a *noun* and/or an *adjective*, these are always in the *genitive plural*, regardless of the case of the numeral itself:

Минима́льная температу́ра но́чью бу́дет *о́коло нуля́ гра́дусов*.
The minimum temperature at night will be around zero degrees.

Таки́е ве́щи мо́жно купи́ть в любо́м магази́не *за ты́сячу рубле́й*.
You can buy things like that in any shop for a thousand roubles.

Оди́н киломе́тр ра́вен (*одно́й*) *ты́сяче ме́тров*.
One kilometre is equal to one thousand metres.

Из окна́ самолёта был ви́ден го́род, кото́рый свети́лся *миллио́ном огне́й*.
From the window of the aeroplane you could see a city lit up by a million lights.

Инвести́ции в э́тот прое́кт соста́вят *о́коло миллиа́рда до́лларов*.
Investment in this project comes to about a billion dollars.

8.2.5 | ## The cases used with complex numerals

When two or more numerals are put together to form complex numerals, the case of any following *nouns* and/or *adjectives* is determined by the *last* numeral in the sequence:

В мое́й кни́ге *две́сти со́рок одна́ страни́ца*.
In my book there are 241 pages.

Моя́ но́вая кни́га соде́ржит *две́сти со́рок одну́ страни́цу*.
My book contains 241 pages.

Он был заде́ржан на грани́це при попы́тке нелега́льно вы́везти из страны́ *се́мьдесят три ре́дкие/ре́дких ико́ны*.
He was arrested at the frontier while trying to take 73 rare icons out of the country illegally.

Оди́н килоба́йт ра́вен (*одно́й*) *ты́сяче двадцати́ четырём ба́йтам*.
One kilobyte is equal to one thousand and twenty-four bytes.

When **ты́сяча, миллио́н** or **миллиа́рд** are used after other numerals, their endings are determined by the rules given in **8.2.1–8.2.3**:

Биле́т до Москвы́ в бизнес-кла́ссе сто́ит *две ты́сячи е́вро*.
A business class ticket to Moscow costs 2,000 euros.

В бассе́йн Невы́ вхо́дит *о́коло пяти́десяти ты́сяч* **озёр и** *шести́десяти ты́сяч* **рек.**

The basin of the River Neva includes about 50,000 lakes and 60,000 rivers.

За э́ти го́ды ву́зы Москвы́ вы́пустили почти́ *два миллио́на* **дипломи́рованных специали́стов.**

In this period almost two million people have graduated from Moscow's higher education institutions.

8.3 Collective numerals

8.3.1 List of collective numerals

Russian has an additional set of numerals, which are known as *collective numerals*.

2	дво́е
3	тро́е
4	че́тверо
5	пя́теро
6	ше́стеро
7	се́меро

Many dictionaries and reference works list collective numerals for 8 (во́сьмеро), 9 (де́вятеро) and 10 (де́сятеро), but these are rarely, if ever, used. There are no collective numerals above 10, and collective numerals cannot be combined with other numeral forms to form complex numerals.

8.3.2 The declension of collective numerals

Collective numerals decline according to the following patterns:

Nom.	дво́е	че́тверо
Gen.	двои́х	четверы́х
Dat.	двои́м	четверы́м
Acc.	as nom. or gen.	as nom. or gen.
Instr.	двои́ми	четверы́ми
Prep.	двои́х	четверы́х

Тро́е follows the pattern of **дво́е**; the remainder follow the pattern of **че́тверо**.

Accusative forms that are the same as the *genitive* are used with *animate nouns*; *accusative forms* that are the same as the *nominative* are used with *inanimate nouns*.

For more on animate and inamimate nouns, *see* **2.4**.

8.3.3 The use of collective numerals

When *collective numerals* are in the *nominative* or *accusative* case, any following *nouns* and/or *adjectives* are in the *genitive plural*. In the *genitive, dative, instrumental* or *prepositional* the numeral and any following nouns and/or adjectives are in the same case. Examples are given below.

Collective numerals are used in the following circumstances:

Дво́е, тро́е, че́тверо are used with nouns that denote countable objects and that do not have a singular form, e.g. **су́тки** 'day', 'period of 24 hours', **брю́ки** 'trousers', **часы́** 'clock', 'watch'; these numerals are also used with **де́ти** 'children':

> **По́сле э́того разгово́ра она́ не спала́ *дво́е су́ток*.**
> After that conversation she didn't sleep for two (whole days and) nights.

> **На туале́тном сто́лике аккура́тно лежа́ли *тро́е но́жниц* и не́сколько расчёсок.**
> On the dressing table were neatly placed three pairs of scissors and several combs.

> **Мое́й до́чери нужна́ кварти́ра побо́льше: у них с му́жем уже́ *че́тверо дете́й*.**
> My daughter needs a bigger flat; she and her husband already have four children.

Any collective numeral can be used with a *masculine noun* referring to a person. In this usage there is little difference between *collective* and ordinary *cardinal* numerals, but *collective numerals* tend to be preferred (1) with masculine nouns that end in the nominative singular in -а or -я (e.g. **мужчи́на** 'man') and (2) when the persons concerned are thought of as a group, rather than as separate individuals:

> **Е́сли встреча́ются *дво́е мужчи́н*, они́ разгова́ривают и́ли о же́нщинах, и́ли о футбо́ле; други́х тем про́сто не существу́ет.**
> If two men meet, they talk about either women or football; there are no other topics of conversation.

> **В на́шем отде́ле *дво́е мужчи́н* и четы́ре же́нщины.**
> In our department there are two men and four women.

> **Победи́телями ко́нкурса при́знаны *тро́е студе́нтов* Новосиби́рского госуда́рственного университе́та.**
> The winners of the competition were three students from Novosibirsk State University.

Collective numerals are used on their own to refer to a group of people; they are mostly used when the group is understood to consist entirely of males or to be mixed:

> **Нас в гру́ппе *че́тверо*.**
> There are four of us in the group.

> **По пя́тницам мы бра́ли в магази́не буты́лку во́дки *на трои́х*, каку́ю-нибу́дь заку́ску и шли к Ива́ну: он жил оди́н.**
> On Fridays we used to go to the shop to buy a bottle of vodka for the three of us and something to eat with it; we went off to Ivan's: he was living alone.

Collective numerals are sometimes used in set phrases, for example:

> **Он ест *за пятеры́х*.**
> He eats enough for five.

> **Не́ было почему́-то трамва́ев, так что она́ пришла́ *на свои́х двои́х*.**
> For some reason there were no trams running, so she came on her own two feet [*or* on Shanks's pony].

When they are used with a noun collective numerals are mostly found in the *nominative* and *accusative* cases. In other cases, they tend to replaced by ordinary cardinal numerals:

> **Она́ прие́хала со свои́ми *двумя́* детьми́.**
> She came with her two children.

> **Ве́треная, моро́зная пого́да сохрани́тся в Москве́, как ми́нимум,**
> ***в тече́ние двух су́ток.***
> The windy and frosty weather in Moscow will continue for at least another 48 hours.

> **Мальчи́шка стоя́л сра́зу *за двумя́ мужчи́нами*, кото́рые гро́мко разгова́ривали между собо́й.**
> The boy stood immediately behind two men who were talking to one another in loud voices.

8.4 Ordinal numerals

8.4.0 Introduction

Ordinal numerals are used to indicate the *order* in which someone or something comes in a sequence. They correspond to English 'first', 'second', 'third', etc. In Russian ordinal numerals are grammatically similar to adjectives.

8.4.1 List of ordinal numerals

1st	пе́рвый, пе́рвая, пе́рвое, пе́рвые	60th	шестидеся́тый
2nd	второ́й, втора́я, второ́е, вторы́е	70th	семидеся́тый
3rd	тре́тий, тре́тья, тре́тье, тре́тьи	80th	восьмидеся́тый
4th	четвёртый, четвёртая, четвёртое, четвёртые	90th	девяно́стый
		100th	со́тый
5th	пя́тый, пя́тая, пя́тое, пя́тые	200th	двухсо́тый
6th	шесто́й, шеста́я, шесто́е, шесты́е	300th	трёхсо́тый
7th	седьмо́й, седьма́я, седьмо́е, седьмы́е	400th	четырёхсо́тый
8th	восьмо́й	500th	пятисо́тый
9th	девя́тый	600th	шестисо́тый
10th	деся́тый	700th	семисо́тый
11th	оди́ннадцатый	800th	восьмисо́тый
15th	пятна́дцатый	900th	девятисо́тый
20th	двадца́тый	1,000th	ты́сячный
30th	тридца́тый	2,000th	двухты́сячный
40th	сороково́й	10,000th	десятиты́сячный
50th	пятидеся́тый	1,000,000th	миллио́нный

When ordinal numbers are made up of more than one element, only the *last* element is in the form of an ordinal numeral; the remaining elements take the form of cardinal numerals:

45th	со́рок пя́тый	150th	сто пятидеся́тый
281st	две́сти во́семьдесят пе́рвый	1975th	ты́сяча девятьсо́т се́мьдесят пя́тый
2007th	две ты́сячи седьмо́й		

8.4.2 Declension of ordinal numerals

The numeral **тре́тий** 'third' declines like one of the second class of *soft adjectives*. Its endings can be illustrated by the following sample:

	Masculine	*Feminine*	*Neuter*	*Plural*
Nom.	тре́тий	тре́тья	тре́тье	тре́тьи
Gen.	тре́тьего	тре́тьей	тре́тьего	тре́тьих

For more detail on the declension of **тре́тий** and other adjectives belonging to the same class, *see* **6.3**.

All other ordinal numerals decline like ordinary *hard* adjectives and follow the pattern of **но́вый** or **молодо́й**, depending on whether the stress is on the *stem* or the *ending*.

For more detail on the declension of adjectives belonging to this class, *see* **6.1**.

Ordinal numerals do not have short forms.

8.4.3 The use of ordinal numerals

In most situations the use of Russian *ordinal numerals* is similar to that of their English equivalents:

> Э́то *втора́я* у́лица нале́во.
> It's the second street on the left.

> *Тре́тье* ма́рта – это мой день рожде́ния.
> The 3rd of March is my birthday.

> Его́ *пе́рвые* три рома́на никто́ не чита́л, но *четвёртый* почему́-то пошёл нарасхва́т.
> Nobody read his first three novels, but the fourth, for some reason, sold like hot cakes.

There are, however, some situations in which a cardinal numeral is used in English, but where an ordinal numeral is preferred in Russian. In particular, ordinal numerals are used (along with the noun **год** 'year') to indicate a calendar year and are used in some constructions for telling the time:

> Она́ родила́сь *в ты́сяча девятьсо́т во́семьдесят второ́м году́.*
> She was born in 1982.

> На́до начина́ть: уже́ де́сять мину́т *шесто́го.*
> We ought to begin; it's already ten past five.

For more on telling the time, *see* **19.2**.

For more on indicating the year in dates, *see* **19.3.2**.

Ordinal numerals also tend to be preferred in a number of circumstances where someone or something is identified by a number. These include members of sports teams, hotel and other rooms, bus and tram routes, railway carriage and seat numbers, chapter and page numbers, and clothes sizes:

> **Знамени́тый хоккеи́ст Вале́рий Харла́мов игра́л под *семна́дцатым но́мером*.**
> The famous ice-hockey player Valerii Kharlamov used to wear the number 17 shirt.

> **Бу́дьте любе́зны, да́йте ключ от *два́дцать пя́того но́мера*.**
> Could I have the key to room 25, please?

> **Прости́те, я дое́ду на *со́рок седьмо́м авто́бусе* до университе́та?**
> Excuse me, will a 47 bus get me to the university?

> **Мне, пожа́луйста, два купе́йных на за́втра до Петрозаво́дска *на шестьсо́т пятьдеся́т седьмо́й (по́езд)*, е́сли мо́жно, *в восьмо́м ваго́не*.**
> Can you give me 2 tickets to Petrozavodsk, for berths in a compartment, travelling tomorrow on train number 657, if possible, in carriage number 8.

> **Я до́лжен вас предупреди́ть, что *на двадца́той страни́це* мое́й статьи́ есть одна́ доса́дная опеча́тка.**
> I ought to warn you that on page 20 of my article there is an annoying misprint.

> **Я обы́чно ношу́ *со́рок тре́тий (разме́р)*, но э́ти ту́фли немно́го теснова́ты.**
> I usually wear size 9 (*literally*, size 43) shoes, but this particular pair feels a little tight.

8.5 Fractions

8.5.1 Special nouns used to indicate fractions

Russian has three special nouns that are used to indicate fractions. These are:

полови́на	half
треть	third
че́тверть	quarter

These nouns are all *feminine* and declined according to the patterns for feminine nouns ending in -**a** or -**ь** given in **2.9** and **2.10**. Their use is illustrated by the following examples:

> **Дава́й разде́лим после́днее я́блоко по́ровну, тебе́ *полови́ну* и мне *полови́ну*.**
> Let's divide the last apple evenly – half for you and half for me.

> **Я прочита́л *две тре́ти* его́ кни́ги, но пото́м бро́сил, так как уже́ разгада́л концо́вку.**
> I read (the first) two-thirds of his book, but then gave up, since I had already guessed the ending.

> ***Три че́тверти* всей недви́жимости в э́той ча́сти го́рода факти́чески принадлежи́т ба́нкам.**
> Three quarters of the property in this part of the city effectively belongs to the banks.

Полови́на can be attached to a numeral by the preposition **с** (+ instr.). When this happens, the case of any following noun and/or adjective is determined by the numeral to which **полови́на** is attached:

> **Мы перее́хали сюда́ *пять с полови́ной ме́сяцев* наза́д.**
> We moved here five and a half months ago.

8.5.2 Ordinary fractions

Other ordinary fractions are indicated by using *ordinal numbers* in the *feminine* (the noun **часть** 'part' is understood):

одна́ пя́тая	one-fifth
две седьмы́х	two-sevenths
три деся́тых	three-tenths

Any following noun and/or adjective is always in the *genitive singular*:

> **Е́сли быть то́чным, то *две пя́тых фи́рмы* принадлежи́т мне, а три пя́тых остальны́м акционе́рам.**
> If we're going to be accurate, two-fifths of the firm belongs to me and three-fifths to the remaining shareholders.

If a fraction follows a whole number, the latter is in the *feminine* and the conjunction **и** is put between the whole number and the fraction:

> **Две и три седьмы́х.**
> Two and three-sevenths.

More examples are given in the following section.

8.5.3 Decimals

As in most other European languages, a comma is used instead of the decimal point in numerals. Unlike most other European languages, however, Russian decimals are not read as they are written but as if they were ordinary fractions. If no noun is present, the *feminine adjective* **це́лая** 'whole' is frequently used between the whole number and the decimal (and is always used after **ноль**):

> **0,5 ноль це́лых, пять деся́тых**
> *literally*, nought and five-tenths

> **7,1 семь (це́лых) (и) одна́ деся́тая**
> *literally*, seven and one-tenth

> **21,43 два́дцать одна́ (це́лая) (и) со́рок три со́тых**
> *literally*, twenty-one and forty-three hundredths

NOTE | **И** tends to be present if **це́лая** is omitted and vice versa.

> **На президе́нтских вы́борах 2004 го́да я́вка избира́телей соста́вила 61,48% (*шестьдеся́т оди́н и со́рок во́семь со́тых проце́нта*).**
> In the 2004 presidential elections the turn-out was 61.48%.

> **Он пробежа́л две́сти ме́тров за *два́дцать одну́ и девяно́сто семь со́тых* секу́нды.**
> He ran 200 metres in 21.97 seconds.

For more on how to read the year, *see* **8.4.3** and **19.3.2**.

NOTES (i) Percentages are indicated by using the masculine noun **проце́нт** 'per cent'.

(ii) This pattern for reading decimal fractions is normally used for figures with one or two places of decimals and is at least in theory possible for three decimal places (**ты́сячная** 'thousandth' would be used). Longer sequences of decimals can be read in the same way as other long sequences of digits; thus, 2,4863 might be read as:

> два и со́рок во́семь шестьдеся́т три.

For more on reading long sequences of digits, *see* **8.1.2**.

8.5.4

Other forms used in fractions

The numeral **полтора́** (feminine **полторы́**) means 'one and a half'. It declines as follows:

	Masc. and n.	*All genders*	*Fem.*
Nom. and Acc.	полтора́		полторы́
All other cases		полу́тора	

The rules for using **полтора́** are the same as for **два, три, четы́ре**: when the numeral is in the *nominative* or the *accusative* any following *noun* is in the *genitive singular* and any following *adjective* is in the *genitive plural*; in all other cases, any following noun or adjective is in the plural and in the same case as the numeral:

> За *полтора́ го́да* я перечита́л всего́ Пу́шкина.
> In eighteen months (*literally*, one and a half years) I reread the whole of Pushkin.

> Текст у меня́ о́чень коро́ткий – не бо́лее *полу́тора страни́ц*.
> My text is very short – no more than one and a half pages.

For more on the rules for using **два, три, четы́ре**, *see* **8.2.2**.

Полтора́ can be combined with other numerals as follows:

полтора́ста	150
полторы́ ты́сячи	1,500
полтора́ миллио́на	1,500,000

> Я по́мню те времена́, когда́ ме́сячная зарпла́та *в полтора́ста рубле́й* счита́лась совсе́м неплохо́й.
> I can remember the days when a monthly salary of 150 roubles was thought to be not at all bad.

> На́ша о́бласть полу́чит *полтора́ миллио́на рубле́й* на борьбу́ с лесны́ми пожа́рами.
> Our region will receive one and a half million roubles to fight forest fires.

The prefix **пол-** 'half-' can be added to a number of nouns. Frequently used examples include the following:

полго́да	half a year, six months
полкило́	half a kilo

пол-ли́тра	half a litre
полчаса́	half an hour

Ка́ждые полчаса́ **она достаёт из су́мочки пома́ду и подкра́шивает гу́бы.**
Every half-hour she gets her lipstick out of her handbag and re-does her lips.

(i) A hyphen is used if the second part of the word begins with a vowel or the letter л.

(ii) When these forms are in the *nominative* or the *accusative*, any adjective or pronoun used with them is in the *plural*.

(iii) When these forms are used in cases other than the *nominative* or the *accusative*, the second part takes the same endings as the unprefixed word; the first part normally changes to полу-.

Мы бы́ли в *полуша́ге* от побе́ды, когда́ прозвуча́л фина́льный свисто́к.
We were within an inch of victory (*literally*, half a step from victory) when the final whistle blew.

Пацие́нтам иногда́ прихо́дится ждать опера́ции до *полуго́да*.
Some patients have to wait for anything up to six months (*literally*, half a year) for their operations.

8.6 Other quantity words

8.6.1 Nouns formed from numerals

The following nouns are derived from numerals:

1	едини́ца	10	деся́тка
2	дво́йка	20	двадца́тка
3	тро́йка	30	тридца́тка
4	четвёрка	40	сороко́вка
5	пятёрка	50	пятидеся́тка
6	шестёрка	60	шестидеся́тка
7	семёрка	70	семидеся́тка
8	восьмёрка	80	восьмидеся́тка
9	девя́тка	100	со́тка

The basic function of these nouns is to indicate the associated digit:

Вы непра́вильно записа́ли мой телефо́н: в нача́ле должна́ быть *дво́йка*.
You've written my telephone number down incorrectly: there should be a '2' at the beginning.

By extension these forms have acquired a number of additional meanings. For example, **дво́йка** and above are used to indicate the face value of playing cards; **дво́йка** (2 = fail), **тро́йка** (3 = satisfactory), **четвёрка** (4 = good), **пятёрка** (5 = excellent) are the standard marks awarded throughout the Russian education system; **тро́йка** can mean 'a team of three horses used to pull a cart or a sledge' and also 'a three-piece suit'; **восьмёрка** can mean 'an eight' (in rowing); **деся́тка** can mean 'a ten-rouble note'. All can be used instead of ordinal numerals to indicate bus or tram routes.

В ка́рты я никогда́ не игра́ю: мне попада́ются одни́ *шестёрки* и *семёрки*.
I never play cards; I only ever get sixes and sevens.

В университе́те она́ учи́лась хорошо́ и получа́ла в основно́м *четвёрки* и *пятёрки*.

She did well at university and mostly got fours and fives.

Отсю́да на́до сесть на *девя́тку* и вы́йти че́рез три остано́вки.

From here you should catch a number nine and get off after three stops.

Гла́вы стран Большо́й *восьмёрки* встреча́ются в э́том году́ в Берли́не.

The heads of government of the G8 countries are meeting this year in Berlin.

Forms other than those listed in the table at the beginning of the section are occasionally found, usually with reference to specific contexts.

В войну́ он был танки́стом: воева́л на знамени́той *три́дцать четвёрке*.

During the war he fought in a tank unit and was in one of the famous T-34 tanks.

The following nouns are used to indicate quantity:

па́ра	pair, couple	**пято́к**	five (of something)
деся́ток	ten (of something)	**дю́жина**	dozen
полсо́тни	fifty (of something)	**со́тня**	hundred (of something)

Вчера́ я купи́л в суперма́ркете *деся́ток* яи́ц, так что на за́втрак мо́жно поджа́рить яи́чницу.

I bought ten eggs at the supermarket yesterday, so we can have fried eggs for breakfast.

NOTES

(i) In Russia, items tend not to be sold in dozens, and **дю́жина** is much less widely used than its English equivalent.

(ii) For the most part these nouns are characteristic of informal language.

8.6.2 ## The numeral о́ба

The numeral **о́ба** (feminine **о́бе**) means 'both'. It declines as follows:

	Masc. and n.	*Fem.*
Nom.	о́ба	о́бе
Gen.	обо́их	обе́их
Dat.	обо́им	обе́им
Acc.	as nom. or gen.	as nom. or gen.
Instr.	обо́ими	обе́ими
Prep.	обо́их	обе́их

In the *accusative* the form that is identical to the *genitive* is used with *animate* nouns, while the form that is identical to the *nominative* is used with *inanimate* nouns.

The rules for using **о́ба** are the same as for **два**, **три**, **четы́ре**: when the numeral is in the *nominative* or the *accusative* any following *noun* is in the *genitive singular* and any following *adjective* is in the *genitive plural*; in all other cases any following *noun* or *adjective* is in the *plural* and in the same case as the numeral.

О́ба мои́х бра́та живу́т в Росси́и.

Both my brothers live in Russia.

Росси́я бу́дет добива́ться тако́го реше́ния, кото́рое прие́млемо *для обе́их сторо́н.*

Russia will strive for a solution that is acceptable to both sides.

The use of **о́ба/о́бе** has an important formal limitation: it can be used only to refer to nouns and to nouns that are both singular and of the same gender. **О́ба/о́бе** cannot refer to two verbs. In cases where nouns are of different genders or plural, or when the reference is made to two verbs the phrase **и то и друго́е/ и те и други́е** is used instead.

Сосе́ди све́рху – пенсионе́ры, сосе́ди по ле́стничной кле́тке – пожило́й инвали́д с до́черью. *И те и други́е* о́чень ми́лые приве́тливые лю́ди.

The upstairs neighbours are pensioners, while those on our landing are an elderly invalid and his daughter. Both sets of people are very nice and friendly.

—Вам гуля́ш и́ли пи́ццу?
—*Мне и то и друго́е.*

—Do you want goulash or pizza?
—Both.

В воскресе́нье я предпочита́ю снача́ла поза́втракать и то́лько пото́м полиста́ть газе́ты, а моя́ жена́ *де́лает и то и друго́е* одновреме́нно.

On Sunday I prefer to have breakfast first and then look at the papers, while my wife does both at the same time.

8.6.3 | Other words used to indicate quantity

The following words are used to indicate quantity:

ско́лько?	how much?, how many?	**сто́лько**	so much, so many
не́сколько	some, several	**мно́го**	much, many
ма́ло	not much, few	**немно́го**	some, a little
мно́гое	much (of)	**мно́гие**	many (of)
немно́гое	a little (of)	**немно́гие**	only a few (of)
не́который	some, a certain	**не́которые**	some, a few (of)

Ско́лько, **сто́лько** and **не́сколко** decline according to the following pattern:

Nom.	**ско́лько**
Gen.	**ско́льких**
Dat.	**ско́льким**
Acc.	**ско́лько**
Instr.	**ско́лькими**
Prep.	**ско́льких**

When **ско́лько** or **сто́лько** is in the *nominative* or the *accusative* case, any following *noun* and/or *adjective* is in the *genitive* (singular or plural); when **не́сколько** is in the *nominative* or the *accusative* case, any following *noun* and/or *adjective* is in the *genitive plural*. When any one of these words is in the *genitive, dative, instrumental* or *prepositional* case, then any accompanying *noun* and/or *adjective* is in the *same case.*

Мно́го, **ма́ло**, **немно́го** do not decline and are used in the *nominative* and *accusative* only. **Мно́го** and **ма́ло** are followed by a noun in the *genitive* (singular or plural); **немно́го** is usually followed by a noun in the *genitive singular*.

Мно́гое and **немно́гое** decline like *adjectives* in the *neuter singular*. **Мно́гие, немно́гие** and **не́которые** decline like *adjectives* in the *plural*. **Не́который** declines like an *adjective*.

For more on the declension of adjectives, *see* **6.1**.

For more on the use of **ско́лько**, *see* **17.3.3** and **19.3.1**.

For more on the use of **сто́лько**, *see* **9.3.5**.

For more on the use of the other words listed here, *see* **19.5**.

9

Uninflected parts of speech

9.0 Introduction

Uninflected parts of speech are those that neither decline nor conjugate. They consist of *adverbs* (**9.1**), *prepositions* (**9.2**), *conjunctions* (**9.3**) and *particles* (**9.4**).

9.1 Adverbs

9.1.0 Introduction

The main function of *adverbs* is to qualify **verbs**, although they can also be used to qualify *adjectives* and even other *adverbs*. An adverb is normally placed *immediately before* the word it qualifies (see **20.1.3**).

9.1.1 Adverbs formed from adjectives: the standard pattern

The standard pattern for forming an adverb from a hard adjective (see **6.1**) is to replace the adjective ending with **-o**:

глу́пый	stupid	глу́по	stupidly
гру́бый	crude, rude	гру́бо	crudely, rudely
дешёвый	cheap	дёшево	cheaply
любе́зный	kind, courteous	любе́зно	kindly, courteously
у́мный	clever	у́мно	cleverly
ча́стый	frequent	ча́сто	frequently
чи́стый	clean	чи́сто	cleanly
дорого́й	dear	до́рого	dearly
ре́дкий	rare	ре́дко	rarely
ти́хий	quiet	ти́хо	quietly
хоро́ший	good	хорошо́	well

Adverbs formed from *soft adjectives* of the *first group* (see **6.2**) and adverbs that are formed from adjectives ending in **-жий**, **-чий**, **-ший** or **-щий** and that do not have stress on the final syllable end in **-e**:

вне́шний	external	вне́шне	externally, on the outside
вну́тренний	internal	вну́тренне	internally
и́скренний	sincere	и́скренне	sincerely
неуклю́жий	clumsy	неуклю́же	clumsily
блестя́щий	brilliant	блестя́ще	brilliantly

194

NOTE Alongside **и́скренне** there is an alternative form **и́скренно** with the same meaning. The adverbs associated with the adjectives **по́здний** 'late' and **ра́нний** 'early' are **по́здно** and **ра́но** respectively.

Adverbs formed from adjectives ending in **-ский** or **-цкий** end in **-ски** or **-цки** respectively:

герои́ческий	heroic	**герои́чески**	heroically
тво́рческий	creative	**тво́рчески**	creatively

Он о́чень *любе́зно* **отве́тил на все мои́ вопро́сы.**
He very kindly answered all my questions.

Она́ *ре́дко* **здесь быва́ет, где́-то два-три ра́за в ме́сяц.**
She rarely comes here, about two or three times a month.

Она́ *блестя́ще* **спра́вилась со все́ми тру́дностями.**
She coped brilliantly with all the difficulties.

Но́вый «Форд» *вне́шне* **похо́ж на ста́рую моде́ль.**
From the outside the new Ford is like the old model.

9.1.2 Adverbs formed from adjectives and pronouns with the prefix по-

A number of adverbs formed from adjectives and pronouns have a hyphenated prefix **по-**. These adverbs can be divided into four groups. The first group is made up of adverbs formed in the usual way from adjectives ending in **-ский** or **-цкий**. These adjectives are in turn mostly formed from nouns, and the adverbs with the **по-** prefix usually refer to doing something or behaving in the manner associated with the noun concerned:

Noun	*Adjective*	*Adverb*
брат 'brother'	**бра́тский** 'fraternal'	**по-бра́тски** 'fraternally'
де́ти 'children'	**де́тский** 'childlike', 'childish'	**по-де́тски** 'in a childlike or a childish manner'
друг 'friend'	**дру́жеский** 'friendly'	**по-дру́жески** 'in a friendly manner', 'like a friend'
солда́т 'soldier'	**солда́тский** 'soldierly'	**по-солда́тски** 'in a soldierly manner', 'like a soldier'
това́рищ 'comrade'	**това́рищеский** 'comradely'	**по-това́рищески** 'in a comradely manner'

Его́ сужде́ния всегда́ бы́ли пове́рхностными и *по-де́тски* **наи́вными.**
His judgements were always superficial and childishly naive.

Он кра́тко, *по-солда́тски* **отве́тил на все мои́ вопро́сы.**
He answered all my questions briefly, like a soldier.

NOTE In some instances adverbs with and without the **по-** prefix exist side by side:
дру́жески/по-дру́жески

The second group consists of adverbs formed in the same way from adjectives indicating nationality. These usually have the meaning of 'in a particular language', although they can also mean 'in a way associated with a particular nationality':

англи́йский	English	по-англи́йски	in English
неме́цкий	German	по-неме́цки	in German
ру́сский	Russian	по-ру́сски	in Russian
францу́зский	French	по-францу́зски	in French

Вы говори́те *по-ру́сски*?
Do you speak Russian?

У нас таки́е стра́нные диало́ги: она́ задаёт вопро́сы *по-англи́йски*, а я отвеча́ю *по-францу́зски*.
We have these strange dialogues: she asks questions in English, and I reply in French.

Хозя́йка до́ма оказа́лась втя́нутой в дли́нный разгово́р, и он ушёл *по-англи́йски*, не попроща́вшись.
His hostess was involved in a long conversation and he left without saying good-bye.

NOTE | **уходи́ть/уйти́ по-англи́йски** *literally* 'to leave in an English manner' means 'to leave without saying good-bye'.

The third group of these adverbs is formed from *soft adjectives* of the *second group* (*see* **6.3**). In use and meaning they are similar to the first group of adverbs with a **по-**prefix:

Noun	Adjective	Adverb
волк	**во́лчий**	**по-во́лчьи**
'wolf'	'relating to wolves'	'in a wolf-like manner'
ко́шка	**коша́чий**	**по-коша́чьи**
'cat'	'relating to cats'	'in a cat-like manner'
челове́к	**челове́чий**	**по-челове́чьи**
'man', 'human being'	'relating to human beings'	'in a human way'

В его́ расска́зах зве́ри ча́сто говоря́т *по-челове́чьи*.
In his stories animals often speak like humans.

С волка́ми жить
—*по-во́лчьи* выть.
When in Rome, do as the Romans do. (*Literally*, When living with wolves, howl like a wolf.)

NOTE | When referring to the social or spiritual, as opposed to the biological properties of a human being, the adverb **по-челове́чески** is used:

Мне её *по-челове́чески* жаль.
From a human point of view, I'm sorry for her.

Adverbs belonging to the final group have an ending identical to the *dative singular neuter* of the adjectives or pronouns from which they are formed. They have various meanings:

по-друго́му	differently	по-но́вому	in a new way
по-пре́жнему	as before	по-ра́зному	variously
по-мо́ему	in my opinion	по-сво́ему	in my/your/his/her/our/ their own way

Дава́йте поду́маем, как э́то сказа́ть *по-друго́му*.
Let's think how we might say this differently.

Страна́ стреми́тельно меня́ется, и придётся научи́ться жить и рабо́тать *по-но́вому*.
The country's changing rapidly, and we'll have to learn how to live and to work in a new way.

***По-мо́ему*, они́ при́няли пра́вильное реше́ние.**
In my opinion they've made the right decision.

Э́тот фильм *по-сво́ему* интере́сен, но мно́гим он не понра́вится.
In its own way the film is interesting, but a lot of people won't like it.

In some contexts **по-ра́зному** can serve as the equivalent of 'it depends' or 'it varies':

—Как реаги́рует ме́стная администра́ция на ва́ши тре́бования?
—*По-ра́зному*, но в о́бщем у нас с ней о́чень хоро́шие отноше́ния.

—How does the local administration react to your demands?
—It depends (*or* It varies), but on the whole our relations with them are very good.

9.1.3 Adverbs of time

The following are the principal *adverbs relating to time*:

сейча́с	now, immediately, just a minute	тепе́рь	now
тогда́	then, at that time	пото́м, зате́м	then, after that
позавчера́	the day before yesterday	вчера́	yesterday
сего́дня	today	за́втра	tomorrow
послеза́втра	the day after tomorrow	накану́не	the day before

For the pronunciation of **сего́дня**, *see* **1.5.5** and **7.3.1**.

ра́но	early	по́здно	late
давно́	a long time ago, for a long time (referring to a continuing action)	неда́вно	recently
до́лго	for a long time (referring to an action in the past or the future)	ско́ро	soon
сра́зу	immediately, at once	неме́дленно	immediately
зара́нее	in advance, beforehand	постоя́нно	constantly
всегда́	always	ещё	still, yet
уже́	already		

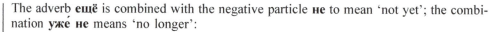

The adverb **ещё** is combined with the negative particle **не** to mean 'not yet'; the combination **уже́ не** means 'no longer':

Он *ещё не* **сдал все экза́мены.**
He has not yet passed all his examinations.

Э́та програ́мма устаре́ла, и я её *уже́ не* **испо́льзую.**
This programme is out of date, and I no longer use it.

In combination with a *perfective* verb in the *past* tense **уже́** can serve as the equivalent of the English *pluperfect* ('had done'), indicating that one action was fully completed before another took place:

Я *уже́* **уе́хал отту́да, когда́ разрази́лся сканда́л.**
I had already left when the scandal broke out.

For more on the use of perfective verbs in a sequence of events, *see* **5.4.1**.

Ещё can have the meaning of 'yet (another)', 'more':

Что вы *ещё* **хоти́те?**
What else would you like?

Вот *ещё* **оди́н челове́к, кото́рый хоте́л бы изуча́ть ру́сский язы́к.**
Here's another person who would like to learn Russian.

Further examples of adverbs of time are given in **21.1**.

9.1.4 Adverbs of place

The following are the principal *adverbs* used to indicate *place*:

здесь, тут	here	там	there
сюда́	here (motion), hither	туда́	there (motion), thither
отсю́да	from here, hence	отту́да	from there, thence
везде́	everywhere	всю́ду	everywhere
повсю́ду	everywhere	бли́зко	near
далеко́	far	ря́дом	adjacent, next to, next door
вверху́	above	наверху́	upstairs
вверх	upwards	наве́рх	upwards, upstairs (motion)
све́рху	from above, from upstairs	внизу́	below, downstairs
вниз	downwards, downstairs (motion)	сни́зу	from below, from downstairs
впереди́	in front, ahead	вперёд	forwards
наза́д	backwards	сза́ди	from the back
сбо́ку	from/on one side	сле́ва	from/on the left
спра́ва	from/on the right		

For the use of **наза́д** in the time expression (тому́) наза́д 'ago', *see* **21.1.9**.

до́ма	at home	домо́й	home(wards)

Examples of adverbs indicating place are given in **21.2**.

9.1.5 ## Indefinite adverbs

Four series of indefinite adverbs, corresponding to the four series of indefinite pronouns described in **7.6**, are formed from the following question words:

где?	where?	**как?**	how?
когда?	when?	**куда?**	where to?, whither?
откуда?	where from?, whence?	**почему?**	why?, for what reason?
зачем?	why?, with what aim?		

где-то	**где-нибудь**	**где-либо**	**кое-где**
как-то	**как-нибудь**	**как-либо**	**кое-как**
когда-то	**когда-нибудь**	**когда-либо**	**кое-когда**
куда-то	**куда-нибудь**	**куда-либо**	**кое-куда**
откуда-то	**откуда-нибудь**	**откуда-либо**	
почему-то	**почему-нибудь**	**почему-либо**	
зачем-то	**зачем-нибудь**	**зачем-либо**	

There are no adverbs in the **кое-** series formed from **откуда, почему** or **зачем.**

In general terms the usage of these series is equivalent to that of the corresponding series of indefinite pronouns as described in **7.6**. With the **-то** series reference is to something specific, the identity of which is unknown or indifferent to the speaker; the **-нибудь** and **-либо** series refer to something indefinite, and the **-либо** tends to be preferred with a *negated* verb or after a *comparative*; the **кое-** series indicates a small quantity of places or occasions:

Я *где-то* забыл свой зонт.
I've left my umbrella somewhere.

Она *когда-то* работала у нас.
At one time she did work for us.

Он *почему-то* всегда опаздывает.
For some reason he's always late (there is a specific reason, but the speaker does not know what it is).

Он всегда *почему-нибудь* да опаздывает.
He's always late for some reason or other (but not necessarily the same reason each time).

Не беспокойтесь: *как-нибудь* разберёмся.
Don't worry, we'll sort it out somehow.

Может, сходим *куда-нибудь* после обеда.
Perhaps we might go somewhere after lunch.

У себя на даче он чувствовал себя очень комфортно - комфортнее, чем *где-либо*.
He always felt at ease at his dacha, more at ease than anywhere else.

Зима в этом году теплее, чем *когда-либо* на моей памяти.
This year the winter has been warmer than at any time that I can remember.

Из-за метели движение транспорта в городе парализовано, и *кое-где* отключено электричество.
Because of the snow-storm traffic in the city has ground to a halt and here and there (*or* in some places) electricity has been cut off.

There are, however, some additional points to consider:

(i) Especially in informal language **как-то** and **как-нибудь** are sometimes used to refer to time, i.e. they can be synonyms of **когда-то** and **когда-нибудь** respectively:

> **Приезжа́йте *как-нибудь* ле́том, и мы вам пока́жем все достопримеча́тельности го́рода.**
> Come and see us some time in the summer, and we'll show you all the sights of the city.

(ii) Adverbs of the **-либо** series, and especially **когда-либо**, are used in a clause following on from a *superlative* adjective:

> **Это са́мая интере́сная кни́га, кото́рую я *когда-либо* чита́л.**
> This is the most interesting book I have ever read.

For more on superlative adjectives, *see* **6.8.4** and **6.8.5**.

(iii) The meanings of **кое-как** do not correspond to those of the other pronouns and adverbs in the **кое-** series; it can usually be translated into English as either 'only just (manage to do something)' or 'any-old-how, in a slapdash manner':

> **От ка́ждого ку́рса ну́жно бы́ло вы́ставить баскетбо́льную кома́нду. *Кое-как* и мы собра́ли во́семь челове́к.**
> Each year had to put up a basketball team. We just about managed to assemble (a squad of) eight people.

> **В шко́ле он учи́лся *кое-как*, с дво́йки на тро́йку.**
> He didn't bother about studying when he was at school and just about scraped by.

Other adverbs

A large number of *adverbs* fit into none of the other categories. The most important of these are listed here:

> **о́чень**   very

Unlike its English equivalent, **о́чень** can be used to qualify not only an *adjective* or an *adverb*, but also a *verb*:

> ***О́чень люблю́* слу́шать, когда́ Евтуше́нко чита́ет свои́ стихи́.**
> I really like hearing Evtushenko reading his poetry.

> **та́кже**   also
> **то́же**   also

Although both these adverbs can be translated as 'also', they are not generally interchangeable. **Та́кже** is used when extending a list and is often combined with the conjunction **а** 'and', while **то́же** is used when making comparisons:

> **На́ше аге́нтство предлага́ет пое́здки по всей Росси́и. Мы *та́кже* организу́ем авто́бусные ту́ры в По́льшу и Че́хию.**
> Our agency offers trips to all parts of Russia. We also organise coach tours to Poland and the Czech Republic.

> **Она́ свобо́дно владе́ет францу́зским, испа́нским, *а та́кже* разгово́рным ру́сским языко́м.**
> She has a fluent command of French, Spanish and also colloquial Russian.

На Камча́тке кли́мат о́чень суро́вый; на Сахали́не он помя́гче, но зимо́й там *то́же* о́чень хо́лодно.

In Kamchatka the climate is very severe; on Sakhalin it is gentler, but in winter it gets very cold there as well (just like Kamchatka).

Она́ свобо́дно владе́ет францу́зским, испа́нским, а та́кже разгово́рным ру́сским языко́м. Её брат *то́же* немно́го говори́т по-ру́сски.

She has a fluent command of French, Spanish and also colloquial Russian. Her brother also speaks a little Russian.

вме́сте	together	да́же	even
ина́че	otherwise	кста́ти	by the way
наоборо́т	on the contrary	опя́ть	again
почти́	almost	сли́шком	too (excessively)
так	so		

The comparative and superlative forms of adverbs

Comparative and *superlative* forms of *adverbs* exist only for those adverbs formed from *adjectives*. The *short comparative* of an *adverb* is identical in form to the short comparative of the adjective from which it is derived:

У себя́ на да́че он чу́вствовал себя́ о́чень комфо́ртно - *комфо́ртнее*, чем где-ли́бо.

He always felt at ease at his dacha, more at ease than anywhere else.

For the formation of the short comparatives of adjectives, *see* **6.8.1**.

For examples of the short comparative of adverbs, *see* **21.9.1-4**.

A *long comparative* can be formed by placing **бо́лее** before the adverb. This form must be used with adverbs formed from adjectives with no short comparative and is preferred with many other adverbs of four or more syllables:

В сове́тские времена́ де́ти проводи́ли ле́тние кани́кулы *бо́лее организо́ванно*.

In Soviet times children spent their sunmmer holidays in a more organised fashion.

For the use of **ме́нее** with adverbs, *see* **21.9.6**.

A *superlative* form can be created by using the *comparative* and the *genitive pronoun* forms **всех** (if the reference is to people) or **всего́** (in other contexts):

Лу́чше всех у нас в семье́ поёт ма́ма.

In our family the one who sings the best is mother.

Лу́чше всего́ она́ поёт украи́нские наро́дные пе́сни.

What she sings best are Ukrainian folk songs.

Ле́гче всего́ нача́ть с са́мого нача́ла.

It will be easiest to begin at the very beginning.

Some of these forms have become set expressions:

пре́жде всего́ 'above all', 'first and foremost'

9.2 Prepositions

9.2.0 Introduction

Prepositions are words placed before *nouns* or *noun phrases* to provide additional information about the meaning and function of the noun. In principle, it is possible for a noun in any case to follow a preposition, and nouns in the prepositional case are used only after prepositions. Several prepositions can be followed by nouns in more than one case, depending on the precise meaning of the preposition; sometimes the different meanings of prepositions when used with different cases are totally unrelated. For this reason, whenever the use of prepositions is discussed in this book, the case required is indicated in brackets after the preposition, e.g. **за** (+ instr.), meaning that in the context being described, **за** is followed by the *instrumental* case.

In Russian a preposition can *never* be followed by a *verb*.

Prepositional usage is discussed in detail at various points in **Part B**. In particular:

Prepositions indicating *time* are discussed in **21.1**.

Prepositions indicating *place* (location, destination and origin) are discussed in **21.2**.

Prepositions indicating *cause* are discussed in **21.4**.

Prepositions indicating *purpose* are discussed in **21.7**.

The use of the preposition **y** (+ gen.) in constructions indicating possession is discussed in **14.3**.

In this section, therefore, attention will be focused only on those issues not covered elsewhere in the book.

9.2.1 Prepositions followed by the nominative

In general, prepositions are not used with the *nominative* case. Exceptionally, two prepositions can be followed by the nominative, but both are used only in a very restricted range of expressions:

в (во)
за

The preposition **в (во)** is followed by the noun **лю́ди** and nouns denoting occupations and professional or social status and is used in certain constructions relating to joining the profession or acquiring the status concerned. It is only ever followed by nouns in the *plural*:

**Сего́дня состоя́лась встре́ча студе́нтов с кандида́том *в депута́ты*
Госуда́рственной Ду́мы.**
Today students had a chance to meet one of the candidates standing for election to the State Duma.

По́сле оконча́ния университе́та она́ пошла́ *в актри́сы*.
After finishing university she went off to become an actress.

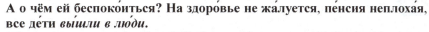

А о чём ей беспоко́иться? На здоро́вье не жа́луется, пе́нсия неплоха́я, все де́ти *вы́шли в лю́ди.*

What's she got to worry about? There's nothing wrong with her health, she doesn't get a bad pension and all her children have made their way in the world.

The preposition **за** is followed by the nominative only in the phrase **что за**, used in questions and exclamations:

А э́то что *за шту́ка*?
What sort of thing is this (meant to be)?

Что *за ерунда́*: ничего́ не поня́тно!
What sort of nonsense is this? I can't understand any of it.

For more on this construction, *see* **17.3.2**.

9.2.2 Prepositions followed by the accusative

The main prepositions followed by the *accusative* are:

в (во)	into, to	**за**	behind (motion), (in exchange) for
на	onto, to	**о (об, обо)**	against, onto
по	until (up to and including)	**под (подо)**	under (motion)
про	about, concerning	**сквозь**	through
че́рез	across, after (a certain time)		

9.2.3 Prepositions followed by the genitive

The main prepositions followed by the *genitive* are:

без (безо)	without	**вдоль**	along
вме́сто	instead of	**вне**	outside
внутри́	inside	**во́зле**	alongside
для	for (the benefit of)	**до**	as far as, until, before
из (изо)	out of, from	**из-за**	from behind, because of
из-под	from under	**кро́ме**	besides, apart from
ми́мо	past	**относи́тельно**	concerning, in relation to
напро́тив	opposite	**о́коло**	around, about
от (ото)	(away) from	**по́сле**	after
про́тив	against	**ра́ди**	for the sake of
с (со)	from (the top of)	**среди́**	among
у	at, near, beside		

In addition, there are a number of prepositional phrases, made up of preposition + noun, all of which are followed by the genitive:

в тече́ние during
за счёт at the expense of, by means of

9.2.4 Prepositions followed by the dative

The main prepositions followed by the *dative* are:

благодаря́	thanks to	**вопреки́**	despite, contrary to
к (ко)	to(wards)	**навстре́чу**	in the direction of
по	along, according to	**согла́сно**	in accordance with

9.2.5 | ## Prepositions followed by the instrumental

The main prepositions followed by the *instrumental* are:

за	behind (location)	**ме́жду**	between
над (надо)	above	**под (подо)**	under (location)
пе́ред (передо)	in front of, (just) before	**с (со)**	with

9.2.6 | ## Prepositions used with the prepositional

в (во)	in (location)	**на**	on (location)
о (об, обо)	about, concerning	**по**	after
при	adjoining, at, in the presence of, in the lifetime of		

NOTE | Both **о (об, обо)** (+ prep.) and **про** (+ acc.) mean 'about', 'concerning'; the former is the more widely used, while the latter is more characteristic of informal language.

9.2.7 | ## The pronunciation of prepositions

All *one-syllable* and many *two-syllable prepositions* have no stress of their own and are always pronounced as a single unit with the following noun or the first word of the following noun phrase. It is important, therefore, not to make any sort of pause between a preposition and the following word, even or especially when the preposition consists of a single consonant:

в Москву́ (vmɑskvú)	to Moscow
с бра́том (zbrátəm)	with (my) brother
под Москво́й (pədmɑskvój)	just outside Moscow

For the signs used to indicate the pronunciation of unstressed vowels, *see* **1.4.4**.

For the use of **под** to mean 'just outside', 'near (a city)', *see* **21.2.12**.

In some circumstances, the single stress for the unit made up of the preposition and the following word can fall on the preposition. It has to be said that such instances are increasingly coming to be regarded as anomalous and are often optional alternatives or even obsolescent; there are, however, a few cases where stress on the preposition is still preferred.

When a numeral follows a monosyllabic preposition, especially **за**, **на**, **по**, and when the numeral is itself not immediately followed by a noun, the tendency is to put the stress on the preposition:

Е́сли хоти́те, возьми́те *по́ два*.
If you want, take two each.

Я уезжа́ю дня *на́ два*.
I'm going away for about two days.

For the use of **по** (+ acc.) in constructions relating to distribution, *see* **19.1.4**.

For information on the placing of the numeral after the noun to indicate an approximate quantity, *see* **19.4.2**.

Other frequently used instances include:

за́ город	out of town (motion)	за́ го́родом	out of town (location)
на́ ночь	for a night,	на́ пол	on(to) the floor
	before going to bed	на́ бок	sideways, to the side

Я не могу́ до него́ дозвони́ться: он, наве́рно, *за́ го́родом*.
I can't get through to him on the phone; he's probably out of town.

Я *на́ ночь* не пью кре́пкий чай.
I don't drink strong tea before going to bed.

Я здесь ни при чём: стака́н сам упа́л *на́ пол* и разби́лся.
This has nothing to do with me; the glass fell on the floor and broke all by itself.

Stress on the preposition is often found in set phrases:

брать/взять кого́-нибудь за́ руку	to take someone by the hand
доста́вка на́ дом	home delivery
как снег на́ го́лову	like a bolt from the blue
пропа́вший бе́з вести	missing in action

9.2.8 The fleeting vowel

The three prepositions consisting of a single consonant and some other prepositions ending in a consonant have a *fleeting vowel* which appears mostly before certain consonant clusters. Forms containing a fleeting vowel are indicated in brackets in the lists above.

With the prepositions **в, к, с** the forms with the fleeting vowel are used:

(1) Before a sequence of two or more consonants, the first of which is either identical to or the voiced/unvoiced partner of the consonant that makes up the preposition (this rule applies to **в** and **с** only):

во́ время	during	со ско́ростью	with a speed (of)
во Фра́нции	in France	со зри́телями	with the viewers
во вто́рник	on Tuesday	со свои́м . . .	with one's own . . .

Also:

во Вьетна́ме   in Vietnam

(2) Before the quantity words **мно́гое, мно́гие** 'many'; before forms of the first person pronoun beginning **мн-**; before forms of the pronoun **весь** 'all' beginning **вс-**:

во мне	in me	ко мне	to me
со мной	with me	во мно́гих	in many . . .
ко мно́гим	to many . . .	со мно́гими	with many . . .
во всех	in everyone	ко всем	to everyone
со все́ми	with everyone		

NOTE — Forms without the fleeting vowel are also found before the quantity words **мно́гое, мно́гие**.

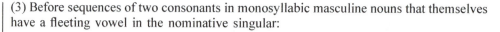

(3) Before sequences of two consonants in monosyllabic masculine nouns that themselves have a fleeting vowel in the nominative singular:

лёд	ice	со льдо́м	with ice
рот	mouth	во рту́	in the mouth

(4) In some other set combinations:

во дворе́	in the yard	во и́мя	in the name (of)
во избежа́ние	for the avoidance of	во ско́лько?	at what time?

With the prepositions **без, из, от, над, перед, под** the fleeting vowel occurs much less frequently. It tends to be preferred before forms of the first person pronoun beginning **мн-** and is sometimes found before **мно́гое, мно́гие**, before forms of the pronoun **весь** beginning **вс-** and before some other sequences of consonants:

надо мно́й	above me	передо мно́й	in front of me
подо мно́й	beneath me	под мно́гими/ подо мно́гими	beneath many
без всего́/ безо всего́	without everything	подо льдо́м	under the ice

The preposition **о** has variant forms **об**, which is used before a vowel, and **обо**, which is used before forms of the first person pronoun beginning **мн-** and before forms of the pronoun **весь** beginning **вс-**:

об А́нглии	about England	об одно́м	about one
об э́том	about this	обо мне́	about me
обо всём	about everything		

9.2.9 Prepositions requiring special comment: за (+ acc.)

When it is not used in contexts relating to time or place (see **21.1.14, 21.2.14**), the basic meaning of **за** (+ acc.) is 'for' in the sense of 'in exchange for'. It is used in contexts of buying or selling items for a particular sum, paying for something and of being rewarded or punished for something:

Похо́жий дом продаётся на сосе́дней у́лице *за сто ты́сяч*.
A house like this is on sale in the next street for a hundred thousand.

Ива́н купи́л у моего́ сосе́да велосипе́д *за ты́сячу* рубле́й.
Ivan bought a bicycle off his neighbour for one thousand roubles.

Ско́лько вы заплати́ли *за биле́т*?
How much did you pay for your ticket?

В про́шлом году́ ей был присуждён специа́льный приз *за ли́чный вклад* в разви́тие росси́йского телеви́дения.
Last year she was awarded a special prize for her personal contribution to the development of Russian television.

Его́ оштрафова́ли *за наруше́ние* па́спортного режи́ма.
He was fined for breaking the passport regulations.

When 'for' means 'for the benefit of', the Russian equivalent is usually **для**:

Для студе́нтов есть специа́льная столо́вая.
There's a special refectory for students.

9.2.10 | **Prepositions requiring special comment: по (+ dat.)**

Apart from its use in contexts relating to place (see **21.2.16**), one of the most important meanings of **по** (+ dat.) is 'according to':

> *По мои́м часа́м уже́ де́сять.*
> According to my watch it's already ten o'clock.

> *По расписа́нию* по́езд до́лжен был прибы́ть два часа́ наза́д.
> According to the timetable the train should have arrived two hours ago.

> *По твои́м глаза́м* ви́жу, что не говори́шь всю пра́вду.
> I can tell by your eyes that you're not telling the whole truth.

> Здесь мы игра́ем стро́го *по пра́вилам.*
> Here we play strictly by the rules.

По (+ dat.) is also used with reference to means of communication:

> Пришли́те нам подтвержде́ние *по фа́ксу.*
> Send us confirmation by fax (*or* Fax us confirmation).

> Я не обсужда́ю таки́е те́мы *по телефо́ну.*
> I don't discuss such things on the telephone.

Another use of **по** (+ dat.) is to define categories:

> Я купи́л хоро́ший уче́бник *по социоло́гии.*
> I bought a good sociology textbook

> Они́ рабо́тают над спра́вочником *по ру́сской грамма́тике.*
> They're working on a handbook of Russian grammar.

> Чемпиона́т Росси́и *по футбо́лу* обы́чно начина́ется в ма́рте и завершае́тся в конце́ октября́.
> The Russian football championship usually starts in March and comes to a conclusion at the end of October.

> В 2000 г. Жоре́с Алфёров был удосто́ен Нобеле́вской пре́мии *по физи́ке.*
> In 2000 Zhores Alfërov was awarded the Nobel prize for physics.

> Он в тече́ние не́скольких лет был дека́ном *по рабо́те* с иностра́нными студе́нтами.
> For several years he was the Dean reponsible for foreign students.

> Он специали́ст *по микрохирурги́и* гла́за.
> He's a specialist in optical micro-surgery.

9.2.11 | **Prepositions requiring special comment: с (+ instr.)**

The basic meaning of the preposition **с** (+ instr.) is 'with' in the sense of 'accompanying, together with':

> Она́ обы́чно прихо́дит на таки́е мероприя́тия *с му́жем.*
> She usually comes to events like this with her husband.

For the use of **с** (+ instr.) to refer to multiple persons in contexts where English would use 'and', *see* **7.1.6**.

The preposition **c** (+ instr.) is not used in contexts relating to the instrument with which something is accomplished:

Посу́ду из-под молока́ сле́дует мыть снача́ла *холо́дной*, а зате́м *горя́чей водо́й*.
Crockery that has had milk in it should be washed first with cold water and then with hot.

For more examples, *see* **3.5.1**.

9.3 Conjunctions

9.3.0 Introduction

Conjunctions are words used to link either whole clauses or individual words and phrases within the framework of a single sentence. There are two kinds of conjunctions: *co-ordinating* and *subordinating*.

9.3.1 Co-ordinating conjunctions

Co-ordinating conjunctions join units of equal weight, whether they are words, phrases or whole clauses. The following are the main co-ordinating conjunctions used in Russian:

и 'and'	**а** 'and', 'but'
но 'but'	**зато́** 'but', 'on the other hand'
в то вре́мя как 'while'	**и́ли** 'or'
не то ... не то indicates uncertainty	**то ли ... то ли** indicates conjecture
	то ... то indicates alternating actions

9.3.2 The use of и, а, но, зато́, в то вре́мя как

The conjunctions **и** and **но** correspond to English 'and' and 'but' respectively:

В университе́те я изуча́л ру́сский язы́к *и* литерату́ру.
At university I studied Russian language and literature.

Ве́чером он обы́чно сиди́т до́ма *и* смо́трит телеви́зор.
In the evenings he usually stays at home and watches television.

Зи́мы у нас ста́ли тепле́е, *и* о́чень ре́дко па́дает снег.
Winters have got warmer here, and we very have little snow.

NOTE | In general, all conjunctions are preceded by a *comma*. Commas are not, however, used before **и**, except when it joins two clauses, each of which has an *explicit* grammatical subject (as in the third of the above examples).

For the use of **и** to indicate emphasis, *see* **20.3.3**.

Его́ выступле́ние на съе́зде бы́ло кра́тким, *но* содержа́тельным.
His speech at the congress was short, but full of content.

Ве́чером он обы́чно до́ма, *но* сего́дня я почему́-то не могу́ до него́ дозвони́ться.
In the evening he's usually at home, but today I can't get through to him on the phone for some reason.

The equivalent of 'both … and' is usually **и … и**:

> **У него́ широ́кий круг друзе́й _и_ в Москве́ _и_ в Петербу́рге.**
> He has a wide circle of friends in both Moscow and St Petersburg.

In formal written language, however, **как … так и** is also found:

> **На́ша па́ртия по́льзуется большо́й подде́ржкой как в Москве́, так и Санкт-Петербу́рге.**
>
> Our party enjoys great support both in Moscow and in St Petersburg.

The normal equivalent of 'not only … but also' is **не то́лько … но и**:

> **Её произведе́ния публику́ются _не то́лько_ в Росси́и, _но и_ во мно́гих страна́х Центра́льной и Восто́чной Евро́пы.**
> Her works are published not only in Russia, but also in many Central and East European countries.

The use of the conjunction **a** is rather more complicated, since it can correspond to either 'and' or 'but', depending on the context. It always contains an element of contrast, but to a lesser degree than that indicated by **но**:

> **В суббо́ту я уе́хал к роди́телям, _и_ в воскресе́нье мы отме́тили день рожде́ния па́пы.**
> On Saturday I went to visit my parents, and on Sunday we celebrated father's birthday. [Here there is no contrast: the events of Sunday are a logical development of those of Saturday.]

> **В суббо́ту я весь день занима́лся в университе́тской библиоте́ке, _а_ в воскресе́нье мы с подру́гой е́здили за гриба́ми.**
> On Saturday I spent all day working in the university library, and on Sunday my girlfriend and I went out into the country to collect mushrooms. [Here there is a degree of contrast between the events of Saturday and Sunday, but the two days' events still make up a coherent way of spending a weekend, which is why 'and' is used in the English translation.]

> **В суббо́ту мы уе́хали на да́чу, _но_ пришло́сь в тот же ве́чер верну́ться в го́род из-за плохо́й пого́ды.**
> On Saturday we went to the dacha, but we had to come back the same evening because of the bad weather. [Here there is a stronger contrast between the two events described; the change in the weather means that the plans for the weekend have to be changed.]

The following give further further examples of the use of **a**:

> **С сёстрами он говори́л по-ру́сски, _а_ с ма́терью по-тата́рски.**
> He spoke Russian with his sisters and/but Tatar with his mother.

> **Через полчаса́ приду́т го́сти, _а_ ты ещё не привела́ себя́ в поря́док.**
> Our visitors will be here in half an hour and you're still not ready.

The conjunction **a** is also used to introduce a positive contrast to a previous negative:

> **Мы приезжа́ем не в понеде́льник, _а_ во вто́рник.**
> We are arriving not on Monday, but on Tuesday.

For the use of **a** with **та́кже**, _see_ **9.1.6.**

For the use of **a** to link sentences, _see_ **23.2.2.**

For the use of **a** in the phrase **а то**, *see* **21.6.3**.

The conjunction **зато**, used either on its own or after **на**, means 'yet', 'but on the other hand':

> **При тако́м ремо́нте жилы́е ко́мнаты не тро́гают, (***но***) зато́ меня́ют кро́влю и обновля́ют систе́му отопле́ния.**
> With a refurbishing of this sort they don't do anything to the living accommodation, but on the other hand they do re-roof the property and renew the heating system.

The conjunction **в то вре́мя как** means 'while', used in a contrastive sense:

> **У «По́чты Росси́и» са́мая больша́я сеть отделе́ний по всей Росси́и, *в то вре́мя как* комме́рческие структу́ры рабо́тают преиму́щественно в кру́пных города́х.**
> The Russian Post Office has the largest network of branches throughout Russia, while commercial structures work mainly in large cities.

9.3.3 ### The use of the conjunctions **и́ли, не то … не то, то ли … то ли, то … то**

The conjunction **и́ли** means 'or':

> **Что важне́е для студе́нта – учёба *и́ли* рабо́та?**
> What is more important for a student – study or work?

> **Ремо́нт бу́дет зако́нчен за́втра, *и́ли* в ху́дшем слу́чае послезавтра.**
> The repair will be carried out tomorrow or, at the worst, the day after.

'Either … or' is **и́ли … и́ли** (less often **ли́бо … ли́бо**):

> **Туда́ мо́жно добра́ться *и́ли* на метро́ *и́ли* авто́бусом.**
> You can get there either by metro or by bus.

> **Не понима́ю: *и́ли* он о́чень у́мный, *и́ли* ему́ про́сто повезло́.**
> I don't understand it; either he's very clever or he was simply lucky.

The conjunctions **не то … не то** and **то ли … то ли** both suggest uncertainty; the former suggests neither quite one thing nor another, while the latter introduces an element of conjecture:

> **Я купи́л себе́ но́вую маши́ну, то́лько цвет непоня́тный, *не то* се́рый, *не то* серебри́стый.**
> I've bought myself a new car, but I can't work out what colour it is; it's somewhere between grey and silver (*or* it's not exactly grey and it's not exactly silver).

> **По́сле распа́да Сове́тского Сою́за она́ эмигри́ровала *то ли* в Герма́нию, *то ли* в Изра́иль.**
> After the collapse she emigrated; I think she went either to Germany or to Israel.

The conjunction **то … то** indicates alternating actions:

> **Пого́да здесь переме́нчивая: *то* идёт дождь, *то* сия́ет со́лнце.**
> The weather's changeable here; one minute it's raining, the next the sun is shining.

9.3.4 **Subordinating conjunctions**

Subordinating conjunctions always join two clauses to make up a single sentence. They are so called because the clauses they introduce (*subordinate clauses*) can never stand alone, but can appear only in conjunction with a *main clause* as part of a *complex sentence*.

The use of subordinating conjunctions is described in detail in **Chapter 21**.

The following are the most widely used subordinating conjunctions in Russian:

(1) Subordinating conjunctions of time:

когда́	when (**21.1.5**)
до того́ как	before (**21.1.11**)
пре́жде чем	before (**21.1.11**)
по́сле того́ как	after (**21.1.11**)
пока́	while (**21.1.14**)
с тех пор как	since (**21.1.16**)
как то́лько	as soon as (**21.1.16**)
(до тех пор), пока́ ... не	until (**21.1.16**)

(2) Subordinating conjunctions of place:

где	where (**21.2.13**)
куда́	where (to), whither (**21.2.14**)
отку́да	where from, whence (**21.2.15**)

(3) Subordinating conjunction of manner:

как	how (**21.3.4**)

(4) Subordinating conjunctions of cause and consequence:

потому́ что	because (**21.4.6**)
потому́ как	because (**21.4.6**)
та́к как	because, since (**21.4.6**)
поско́льку	because, since (**21.4.6**)
и́бо	for (**21.4.6**)
так что	so that (**21.4.7**)

(5) Subordinating conjunction indicating conditions:

е́сли	if (**21.5**)

(6) Subordinating conjunction indicating a concession:

хотя́	although (**21.6.3**)

(7) Subordinating conjunction of purpose:

что́бы	in order to/that (**21.7.3**)

(8) Subordinating conjunctions introducing indirect speech:

что	that (**21.8.2**)
что́бы	introduces indirect commands (**21.8.2**)
бу́дто	that (implies doubt) (**21.8.2**)
я́кобы	that (implies disbelief) (**21.8.2**)

(9) Subordinating conjunctions used in comparisons:

чем	than (**21.9.2**, **21.9.4**)
тем бо́лее, что	all the more because, especially as (**21.9.4**)
как as (**21.9.8**)	

NOTE   The conjunction **что́бы** contains the particle **бы**, which is used to form the conditional (*see* **4.10**); just as **бы** is combined with a finite verb in the past tense, so if **что́бы** is used with a finite verb, that verb will always be in the past tense as well.

9.3.5

'Matching' adverbs and conjunctions

One feature of Russian is that *subordinating conjunctions* are often buttressed by *adverbs* in the *main clause* that match the conjunction in meaning and usually in form as well. Matching pairs of adverbs and conjunctions include the following:

тогда́, когда́
там, где
туда́, куда́
отту́да, отку́да
так, как

сто́лько, ско́лько	as much as
насто́лько, наско́лько	to the extent that
посто́льку, поско́льку	in so far as

Мы подпи́шем контра́кт то́лько *тогда́*, *когда́* у нас бу́дет по́лная информа́ция по всем вопро́сам.
We will sign the contract only when we have full information on all questions.

Я хоте́л бы жить *там*, *где* меня́ никто́ не зна́ет.
I'd like to live where nobody knows me.

Е́сли бу́дете поступа́ть *так*, *как* я вам рекоменду́ю, никаки́х пробле́м не бу́дет.
If you do as I recommend, there won't be any problems.

Я зна́ю об э́том *сто́лько*, *ско́лько* и вы.
I know as much about it as you do.

Ва́ши пробле́мы интересу́ют меня́ *посто́льку*, *поско́льку* они́ влия́ют на о́бщую атмосфе́ру в коллекти́ве.
Your problems interest me in so far as they affect the overall atmosphere in the group.

Used on its own, the phrase **посто́льку поско́льку** means something like 'not bad', 'up to a point' or even 'it depends':

—**У вас хоро́шие отноше́ния с зарубе́жными партнёрами?**
—***Посто́льку поско́льку.***

—Do you get on well with your foreign partners?
—Up to a point. (*or* 'It depends.')

9.3.6 Prepositional phrases with conjunctions

In Russian two clauses are often joined by a *prepositional phrase* (a preposition followed by the appropriate form of the *neuter demonstrative pronoun* **то**) and a conjunction. This can correspond to the English use of a preposition followed by the -ing form of verb. The most frequent conjunction used in this way is **что**, although others that occur include **чтобы** (in hypothetical contexts) and **почему**:

> **Её критиковáли *за то, что* в свои́х ромáнах онá не затрáгивала**
> **социáльные тéмы.**
> She was criticised for not touching on social topics in her novels.

> **Начнём *с того́, что* изберём председáтельствующего.**
> We'll begin by electing someone to take the chair.

> **Они́ настáивают *на том, чтобы* это усло́вие бы́ло включено́ в контрáкт.**
> They are insisting on this condition being included in the contract.

> **Им сле́довало бы задýматься *над тем, почемý* нормáльные лю́ди**
> **прибегáют к таки́м мéрам.**
> They should stop and think about why normal people resort to such measures.

9.4 Particles

9.4.0 Introduction

Particles are additional words providing information that supplements or supports that provided by the main elements of a sentence. Some particles have a very specific grammatical or semantic function, while others are used in a less easily defined manner.

9.4.1 Particles with a very specific grammatical or semantic function

The particles used when answering questions are **да** 'yes' and **нет** 'no'. For more on their use in this function, *see* **17.1.4**.

The *particle* **да** is also used with third person verb forms to create an imperative. This usage is mostly characteristic of church language, but one phrase in common use is:

> **да здрáвствует!**
> long live!

> **Да здрáвствует дрýжба мéжду нáшими стрáнами!**
> Long live the friendship between our countries!

NOTE   The opposite of **да здрáвствует** is **доло́й** 'down with', which is followed by a noun in the *accusative* case:

> **Доло́й смéртную казнь!**
> Down with the death penalty!

The particles **вот** and **вон** are used when pointing out; the former, which is much more frequent, points to something or somewhere near and is often combined with **здесь** 'here', while the latter points to something far from the speaker and can be combined with **там** 'there':

> *Вот* мои́ очки́, я иска́л их весь день!
> Here are my glasses, I've been looking for them all day!

> Они́ лежа́ли *вот здесь*, под э́той газе́той.
> They were lying right here, underneath this newspaper.

> *Вон* Мавзоле́й Ле́нина, но, ка́жется, вход в него́ закры́т.
> There's Lenin's Mausoleum, but I don't think you can get in.

> Мо́жно е́хать на пя́том авто́бусе; остано́вка *вон там*, на той стороне́ у́лицы.
> You can go on the number five bus; the stop's over there, on the other side of the street.

For the use of **вот** as a sentence filler, *see* **23.3**.

Some particles are used to form parts of the verb system:

For the use of the particle **пусть** to form the third person imperative, *see* **4.9**.

For the use of the particle **бы** to form the conditional, *see* **4.10**.

For the use of the particle **-ка** with the imperative, *see* **18.2.1**

For the use of the particle **ли** in direct questions, *see* **17.1.2**.

For the use of the particle **ли** in indirect questions, *see* **21.8.3**,

For the use of the **negative** particle **не**, *see* **15.1**.

For the use of particles in indirect speech, *see* **21.8.2**.

9.4.2   Other particles

Other frequently used particles include the following:

ведь 'surely', 'you know'	**же** adds emphasis or can indicate contrast
ну 'well (now)'	**-то** adds emphasis
уж adds emphasis	

The use of these particles is a complex matter of idiom, and the translations and indications given here are only approximate.

For information on the use of particles to provide emphasis, *see* **20.3.3**.

For information on particles used as sentence fillers, *see* **23.3**.

In addition, the particles **да** and **вот** can be used for expressive effect:

> *Да* ты с ума́ сошла́! В тако́й моро́з в одно́й ку́рточке!
> Are you totally out of your mind? Going out in this cold weather in just a jacket!

> *Вот* так пра́здник! Ни горя́чей воды́, ни электри́чества!
> A fine holiday this has turned out to be! No hot water and no electricity!

Notes on the pronunciation and spelling of particles

The following particles are *enclitic*, that is, they have no stress of their own, but form a single stress unit with the *preceding* word:

бы, -ка, же, ли, -то

Of these, **ли** always follows the first stressed word of the clause or sentence in which it appears.

The particle **не** is *proclitic*, that is, it forms a single stress unit with the *following* word.

The particles **-ка** and **-то** are always joined to the preceding word with a hyphen. Other particles are always written as separate words.

10

Word formation

10.0 | Introduction

An important feature of the structure of Russian is the use of various word-forming devices to create new words on the basis of those that already exist. The most important of these are *prefixes* and *suffixes*, although sometimes new words are created by removing suffixes or by combining two words into one. Since the meanings of the various prefixes and suffixes are fairly consistent, it is often possible to work out at least the approximate meaning of an unknown word by breaking it up into its individual word-forming components. (Note the words 'fairly' and 'approximate': this is a useful, but not an infallible tip!)

As with aspects of the verb, whole books have been written on Russian word formation, and in this chapter it is possible only to touch on those issues that are likely to be of most concern to learners. There are sections on the noun (**10.1**), the adjective (**10.2**) and the verb (**10.3**), while section **10.4** deals separately with the question of verbal prefixes.

10.1 | Formation of nouns

10.1.1 | Diminutives and augmentatives

Most Russian nouns have a variant form, created by the addition of a suffix, which is conventionally known as the *diminutive*. This form is often used with specific reference to size, but it can also indicate a particular emotional attitude to the object in question; the attitude is often one of affection or attachment, although sometimes it may be one of contempt.

In some instances the diminutive has partly or wholly detached itself from the noun from which it was originally formed and has acquired a separate meaning. Examples where this has happened are noted in the lists below.

With some nouns it is possible to add a different suffix to form an *augmentative*. These normally refer to (large) size, but this too can be combined with the expression of an emotional attitude. In general, augmentatives are much less widely used than diminutives.

The use of diminutives and augmentatives to indicate emotional attitudes is discussed in **16.1**.

It can occasionally happen that the addition of a diminutive or an augmentative suffix changes the declension type of the original noun. In such instances the grammatical gender of the noun remains unchanged.

10.1.2 ## Diminutive suffixes for masculine nouns

The main diminutive suffixes for masculine nouns are **-ик**, **-ок/-ёк/ек**, **-ец** and **-чик**.

The suffix **-ик** is never stressed. Examples include:

дом	house, block of flats	до́мик	*especially* a small individual house
за́яц	hare	за́йчик	
ковёр	carpet	ко́врик	*also* mat
ломо́ть	slice	ло́мтик	
мост	bridge	мо́стик	*also* captain's bridge
нож	knife	но́жик	*especially* penknife
сад	garden	са́дик	*also* kindergarten (informal)
стол	table	сто́лик	*especially* restaurant *or* café table
час	hour	ча́сик	
шар	sphere, globe, balloon	ша́рик	

The suffix **-ок/-ёк/-ек** is usually, though not always, stressed. Before this suffix the consonants **-г**, **-к**, **-х** change to **--ж-**, **-ч-**, **-ш-** respectively. Some nouns ending in **-н** or **нь** change the final consonant to **-ш-**. Examples include:

глаз	eye	глазо́к	*also* peep-hole
друг	friend	дружо́к	
знак	sign	значо́к	badge
конья́к	brandy, Cognac	коньячо́к	
ко́рень	root	корешо́к	*also* counterfoil
ко́фе	coffee	кофеёк	
круг	circle	кружо́к	*also* club
ого́нь	fire	огонёк	
пету́х	rooster, cock(erel)	петушо́к	
реме́нь	strap, belt	ремешо́к	strap (e.g. of a watch)
стари́к	old man	старичо́к	
чай	tea	чаёк	
шум	noise	шумо́к	
горо́х	peas	горо́шек	
оре́х	nut	оре́шек	
челове́к	man, human being	челове́чек	

The following are among the nouns that form the diminutive with the **-ец** suffix:

моро́з	frost	моро́зец
хлеб	bread	хле́бец

The following are among the nouns that form the diminutive with the **-чик** suffix:

блин	pancake	бли́нчик
карма́н	pocket	карма́нчик
па́лец	finger	па́льчик
стака́н	glass	стака́нчик

The vast majority of nouns have only one diminutive forms, but the following are exceptions in having two alternative forms:

брат	brother	бра́тец, бра́тик (used only to refer to children)
вопро́с	question	вопро́сик, вопро́сец
год	year	го́дик, годо́к
стул	chair	сту́льчик, сту́лик

10.1.3 Diminutive suffixes for feminine nouns

The most widely used diminutive suffix for feminine nouns is -ка. Before this suffix the consonants -г-, -к-, -х- change to -ж-, -ч-, -ш- respectively and -ц- changes to -ч-. Examples include:

вода́	water	во́дка	vodka (only! *see* 10.1.5)
голова́	head	голо́вка	*also* head of any small object
доро́га	road	доро́жка	path
дочь	daughter	до́чка	
ель	fir tree	ёлка	*also* Christmas tree
кни́га	book	кни́жка	
нога	leg, foot	но́жка	*also* leg of item of furniture
пло́щадь	square (in city)	площа́дка	any small area
пти́ца	bird	пти́чка	
река́	river	ре́чка	
рука́	arm, hand	ру́чка	*also* handle, pen
стрела́	arrow	стре́лка	*also* hand (of a clock)
тётя	aunt	тётка	

Some feminine nouns have a diminutive form with the suffix -ица:

вещь	thing	вещи́ца	
часть	part	части́ца	particle

Some nouns with a stem ending in two consonants have a diminutive with the suffix -очка; this suffix is the one normally used for nouns ending in a consonant + ка:

звезда́	star	звёздочка	
ка́рта	card, map	ка́рточка	[as in креди́тная ка́рточка credit card]
ло́дка	boat	ло́дочка	
тря́пка	rag, piece of cloth, duster	тря́почка	

10.1.4 Diminutive suffixes for neuter nouns

Many neuter nouns have a diminutive ending in -ко or -ико. Before these suffixes -к- and -ц- change to -ч-; -х- changes to -ш-:

блю́дце	saucer	блю́дечко	
молоко́	milk	молочко́	
о́блако	cloud	о́блачко	
се́рдце	heart	серде́чко	
у́хо	ear	у́шко́	*also* eye (of a needle)
я́блоко	apple	я́блочко	
яйцо́	egg	яи́чко	*also* testicle
колесо́	wheel	колёсико	

лицо́	face	ли́чико
плечо́	shoulder	пле́чико

Another suffix found with neuter nouns is **-це/-цо/-ецо**; the third variant of the suffix is used after a sequence of two consonants:

зе́ркало	mirror	зе́ркальце
сло́во	word	словцо́
письмо́	letter	письмецо́

NOTE The noun **блю́дце** 'saucer' is in origin a diminutive form of **блю́до** 'dish'.

A small number of neuter nouns have a diminutive with the suffix **-ышко**:

го́рло	throat	го́рлышко
зерно́	grain, kernel	зёрнышко
крыло́	wing	кры́лышко

10.1.5 Secondary diminutive suffixes

With some nouns it is possible to add a further suffix, thereby creating a *secondary diminutive* form:

друг	friend	дружо́к	дружо́чек
сын	son	сыно́к	сыно́чек
тётя	aunt	тётка	тётенька

In general, these forms have a significantly stronger emotional content than the primary diminutives and they should be used with some degree of caution. For more on this, *see* **16.1**.

There are, however, some secondary diminutives that are used either exclusively or more frequently than the primary forms (the latter, where they exist, are indicated below in brackets):

мину́та	minute	мину́точка (мину́тка)
секу́нда	second	секу́ндочка
сестра́	sister	сестри́чка (сестри́ца)

It is particularly important to distinguish the following pair of nouns and their respective diminutives:

вода́	water	води́чка (води́ца)
во́дка	vodka	во́дочка

10.1.6 Augmentative suffixes

Augmentative forms are used much less frequently than *diminutives*. The suffixes used are **-ище** (for masculine and neuter nouns), **-ища** (for feminine nouns) and **-ина** (for masculine and feminine nouns). Before these suffixes the consonants **-г-, -к-, -х** change to **-ж-, -ч-, -ш-** respectively:

волк	wolf	волчи́ще
кула́к	fist	кулачи́ще
борода́	beard	бороди́ща
жара́	heat (wave)	жари́ща

| дом | house, block of flats | доми́на |
| рыба | fish | ры́бина |

Suffixes indicating someone who carries out an action

The suffix most frequently used to form a noun indicating the person who carries out the action denoted by a verb is **-тель**:

води́ть	to lead, to drive	води́тель	driver
жить	to live	жи́тель	inhabitant
избира́ть/избра́ть	to elect	избира́тель	elector
изобрета́ть/изобрести́	to invent	изобрета́тель	inventor
люби́ть	to love	люби́тель	lover (e.g. of art), amateur
писа́ть/написа́ть	to write	писа́тель	writer
рожда́ть/роди́ть	to give birth	роди́тель	parent
стро́ить/постро́ить	to build	строи́тель	builder
учи́ть/научи́ть	to teach	учи́тель	teacher
чита́ть/прочита́ть	to read	чита́тель	reader

The pair of verbs **спаса́ть/спасти́** 'to save' is unusual, in that it serves as a base for two nouns with different meanings; one is formed from the *imperfective* and the other from the *perfective*:

| спаса́тель | rescue worker | | спаси́тель | saviour |

Some nouns formed in this way indicate an object, rather than a person:

выключа́ть/выключить	to switch off	выключа́тель	switch
дви́гать/дви́нуть	to move	дви́гатель	engine, motor
предохраня́ть/предохрани́ть	to protect	предохрани́тель	safety catch, fuse
ука́зывать/указа́ть	to point out	указа́тель	index

Other suffixes that can be used to form nouns indicating someone who carries out a particular activity are **-ник**, **-чик** and **-щик**. These are mostly used with nouns not formed directly from verbs:

защи́та	defence	защи́тник	defender
мя́со	meat	мясни́к	butcher
поля́рный	polar	поля́рник	explorer of the polar regions
рабо́та	work	рабо́тник	worker, employee
ремесло́	trade, craft	реме́сленник	craftsman, artisan
совреме́нный	contemporary (adjective)	совреме́нник	contemporary (noun)
уча́стие	participation	уча́стник	participant
учи́ться	to learn	учени́к	pupil
груз	load	гру́зчик	loader, porter, docker
лета́ть	to fly	лётчик	pilot
перебега́ть/перебежа́ть	to run across	перебе́жчик	defector
боле́ть	to be ill; to support (a sports team)	боле́льщик	supporter

| гардеро́б | cloakroom | гардеро́бщик | cloakroom attendant |
| регули́ровать | to regulate, to control | регулиро́вщик | policeman controlling traffic |

Some of the following nouns denote instruments, rather than or as well as people:

| гра́дус | degree (temperature) | гра́дусник | thermometer |
| счёт | bill, account | счётчик | a counting device, meter, someone who counts |

10.1.8 Suffixes indicating inhabitants, members of nationalities or other forms of status

The suffix **-ец** is widely used to indicate inhabitants of towns and cities in Russia and elsewhere, as well as nationality and ethnic affiliation. Nouns with this suffix normally have a *fleeting vowel*:

Воро́неж	Voronezh	воро́нежец	
Влади́мир	Vladimir	влади́мирец	
Екатеринбу́рг	Ekaterinburg	екатеринбу́ржец	
(Санкт-)Петербу́рг	St Petersburg	(санкт-)петербу́ржец	
Я́рославль	Iaroslavl	яросла́вец	
Ло́ндон	London	ло́ндонец	
Пеки́н	Beijing	пеки́нец	
Аме́рика	America	америка́нец	American
Герма́ния Germany; неме́цкий German		не́мец	German
Испа́ния	Spain	испа́нец	Spaniard
Ита́лия	Italy	италья́нец	Italian
Кана́да	Canada	кана́дец	Canadian
Кита́й	China	кита́ец	Chinese person
Шотла́ндия	Scotland	шотла́ндец	Scot
Чечня́	Chechnya	чече́нец	Chechen

For more on the fleeting vowel, *see* **2.5.1**.

For more on the use of small letters to indicate inhabitants and members of nationalities and ethnic groups, *see* **1.5.7**.

The suffix **-анин/-янин/-чанин** is widely used to form nouns indicating the inhabitants of towns and cities in Russia, Ukraine and Belarus:

Ирку́тск	Irkutsk	иркутя́нин
Ки́ев	Kiev	киевля́нин
Минск	Minsk	минча́нин
Петрозаво́дск	Petrozavodsk	петрозаводча́нин
Росто́в-на-Дону́	Rostov-on-Don	ростовча́нин

The same suffix is used, albeit less often, to forms nouns indicating inhabitants of other cities or indicating nationality:

Пари́ж	Paris	парижа́нин
Ри́га	Riga	рижа́нин
Рим	Rome	ри́млянин

А́нглия	England	англича́нин	Englishman
Арме́ния	Armenia	армяни́н	Armenian
Да́ния	Denmark	датча́нин	Dane

This suffix can also form nouns indicating inhabitants of more general locations, members of religious faiths and persons possessing a particular social or other kind of status:

го́род	city, town	горожа́нин	city-/town-dweller
село́	village	сельча́нин, селя́нин	village-dweller
		гражданн́н	citizen
		дворяни́н	nobleman
		крестья́нин	peasant
		мусульма́нин	Muslim
Христо́с	Christ	христиа́нин	Christian

NOTE When it declines, the noun **Христо́с** loses the **-ос**: genitive **Христа́**, dative **Христу́** etc.

For the declension of nouns ending in **-анин/-янин/-чанин**, *see* **2.11.3**.

Some nouns indicating the inhabitants of some Russian, Ukrainian or Belarusian towns and cities or indicating nationalities are formed with other, often unpredictable suffixes; some nouns indicating nationalities have no suffix at all:

Москва́	Moscow	москви́ч	
Оде́сса	Odessa	одесси́т	
Пермь	Perm	пермя́к	
По́льша	Poland	поля́к	Pole
Гре́ция	Greece	грек	Greek
Фра́нция	France	францу́з	Frenchman
Шве́ция	Sweden	швед	Swede

10.1.9 Suffixes used to form feminine nouns

Nouns indicating inhabitants of a place, national or ethnic affiliation or social status normally have separate *masculine* and *feminine* forms. Some nouns indicating occupations also have a separate feminine form. The feminine forms are created either by replacing one suffix with another or by adding a feminine suffix to the masculine form.

To form the feminine equivalent of nouns indicating nationalities and ending in **-ец** the suffix is normally removed and replaced with **-ка**:

америка́нец	American	америка́нка
шотла́ндец	Scot	шотла́ндка

NOTE The feminine equivalents of nouns indicating the inhabitants of Russian cities and ending in **-ец** are rare and can be difficult to form. To indicate a female inhabitant of St Petersburg **петербу́рженка** is the preferred form, but words formed with other suffixes may also be encountered.

With nouns in **-анин/-янин/-чанин** the feminine equivalent is formed by removing the last two letters of the masculine suffix and adding **-ка**:

ростовча́нин	inhabitant of Rostov-on-Don	ростовча́нка
англича́нин	Englishman	англича́нка	Englishwoman

With other nouns indicating inhabitants of a place or national or ethnic affiliation the feminine suffix **-ка** is usually added to the end of the masculine form; in a few instances **-ка** replaces the masculine suffix:

москви́ч	Muscovite	**москви́чка**
швед	Swede	**шве́дка**
поля́к	Pole	**по́лька**

With a few nouns indicating national or ethnic affiliation the feminine in **-ка** is not formed directly from the masculine:

грек	Greek	**греча́нка**
кита́ец	Chinese man	**китая́нка**
коре́ец	Korean	**корея́нка**
францу́з	Frenchman	**францу́женка**

NOTE A certain amount of care is required with some of these forms, since the 'expected' feminine form exists, but with a different meaning:

гре́чка	(an informal term for) buckwheat
коре́йка	(a form of) smoked ham

For more on nouns indicating citizenship or ethnic affiliation, *see* **12.5.1**.

With nouns denoting someone who carries out an action the suffix **-ница** is added to nouns ending in **-тель**; the feminine equivalent of nouns ending in **-ик** is formed by replacing the final two letters with the suffix **-ица**:

писа́тель	writer	**писа́тельница**
учи́тель	teacher	**учи́тельница**
убо́рщик	cleaner	**убо́рщица**
учени́к	pupil	**учени́ца**

The suffix **-ша** is added to nouns with the suffixes **-арь**, **-ер**, **-ёр**, **-ир** and to a few other nouns, while the suffix **-ка** tends to be used with nouns falling into none of the above categories:

вахтёр	janitor, person who guards the entry to a building	**вахтёрша**	
касси́р	cashier, person who sits at a cash-desk	**касси́рша**	
секрета́рь	secretary	**секрета́рша**	
аспира́нт	post-graduate student	**аспира́нтка**	
спортсме́н	sportsman	**спортсме́нка**	sportswoman
студе́нт	student	**студе́нтка**	

It is important to note that there are restrictions on the use of feminine nouns describing someone who has a particular occupation or profession. This question is discussed in detail in **12.6.2**.

10.1.10 Other nouns formed from verbs

Many verbs have nouns formed from them with the suffix **-ание** (verbs with an infinitive in **-ать**), **-яние** (verbs with an infinitive in **-ять**) or **-ение** (other verbs). Nouns formed from *second conjugation* verbs have the same changes of consonant as occur in the *past passive participle*.

For more on these changes of consonant, *see* **4.12.4**.

Many of the nouns formed in this way function as pure *verbal nouns*, that is, they indicate the action denoted by the verb:

изуча́ть/изучи́ть	to study	изуче́ние	study(ing)
кури́ть	to smoke (tobacco)	куре́ние	smoking
оформля́ть/ офо́рмить	to register, to legalise	оформле́ние	registration, legalisation
раска́иваться/ раска́яться	to repent	раска́яние	repentance
созерца́ть	to contemplate	созерца́ние	contemplation
употребля́ть/ употреби́ть	to use	употребле́ние	use
чита́ть/прочита́ть *or* проче́сть	to read	чте́ние	reading,

The use of these verbal nouns is particularly characteristic of formal written language. For more on this use, *see* **23.1.4**.

Many of these verbal nouns have acquired more concrete meanings:

вводи́ть/ввести́	to lead in, to bring in	введе́ние	introduction (e.g. to a book)
дви́гать/дви́нуть	to move	движе́ние	movement, traffic
предлага́ть/ предложи́ть	to offer	предложе́ние	offer; sentence (grammatical)
приглаша́ть/ пригласи́ть	to invite	приглаше́ние	invitation
содержа́ть	to contain	содержа́ние	contents (e.g. of a book)
сокраща́ть/ сократи́ть	to abbreviate	сокраще́ние	abbreviation
убежда́ть/убеди́ть	to convince	убежде́ние	conviction, belief

Nouns belonging to this group can occur in all types of writing and speech.

NOTES
(i) It will be noticed that the nouns **чте́ние** and **движе́ние** are not formed directly from the corresponding verbs.

(ii) The noun used to indicate the physical contents of, for example, a tin is **содержи́мое**.

Some nouns are formed from verbs without the addition of a suffix. This means of forming nouns is particularly characteristic of prefixed forms of certain verbs in common use. Many nouns formed in this way have concrete meanings more or less closely linked to the normal meaning of the verb:

входи́ть/войти́	to enter (on foot)	вход	entry
выходи́ть/вы́йти	to go out (on foot)	вы́ход	exit
доходи́ть/дойти́	to get as far as	дохо́д	income

запуска́ть/запусти́ть	to launch (e.g. a rocket)	за́пуск	launch
пропуска́ть/ пропусти́ть	to let through, to omit	про́пуск	pass, omission
приговáривать/ приговори́ть	to sentence	пригово́р	sentence (in court)
расскáзывать/ рассказáть	to tell, to narrate	расскáз	short story

10.1.11 Other suffixes used to form abstract nouns

The *suffix* **-ость** is widely used to form abstract nouns from adjectives; these nouns are always *feminine*:

глу́пый	stupid	глу́пость	stupidity
молодо́й	young	мо́лодость	youth(fulness)
но́вый	new	но́вость	(item of) news
ре́дкий	rare	ре́дкость	rarity
сме́лый	bold, courageous	сме́лость	boldness, courage
ста́рый	old	ста́рость	old age

Other **suffixes** that can be used to form **abstract** nouns from various parts of speech include **-ство, -ба, -нь, -изна**:

бе́гать	to run	бе́гство	flight, escape
брат	brother	бра́тство	fraternity
де́ти	children	де́тство	childhood
боро́ться	to struggle, to wrestle	борьба́	struggle, wrestling
стреля́ть	to shoot	стрельба́	shooting
боле́ть	to be ill	боле́знь	illness
жить	to live	жизнь	life
бе́лый	white	белизна́	whiteness
круто́й	steep	крутизна́	steepness

10.1.12 Making one noun out of two words

There are numerous nouns in Russian that are put together out of two recognisably separate elements. In most instances the elements are linked by the vowels **о** (after hard consonants) or **е** (after soft consonants or **ц, ж, ш**) and sometimes the noun ends in a suffix of one sort or another:

бронь 'armour' + носи́ть 'to carry'	броненóсец 'battleship'
верте́ть 'to spin' + летáть 'to fly'	вертолёт 'helicopter'
рукá 'hand', 'arm' + писáть 'to write'	ру́копись 'manuscript'
о́бщий 'general', 'common' + жить 'to live'	общежи́тие 'hostel'
ого́нь 'fire' + туши́ть 'to extinguish'	огнетуши́тель 'fire extinguisher'
пра́во 'right', 'law' + наруше́ние 'infringement'	правонаруше́ние 'crime, infringement of the law'
пыль 'dust' + сосáть 'to suck'	пылесо́с 'vacuum cleaner'
сам 'oneself' + гнать 'to chase', 'to distil'	самого́н 'home-distilled vodka', 'hooch'
сам 'oneself' + летáть 'to fly'	самолёт 'aeroplane'
тёплый 'warm' + ходи́ть 'to go'	теплохо́д 'motor vessel'

Another device for creating one noun out of two words is to preface a noun with the abbreviated form of an adjective. These formations were particularly characteristic of bureaucratic and journalistic writing in the Soviet period, but the device has survived and several such forms are in more or less common use:

де́тский сад	kindergarten	детса́д
медици́нская сестра́	nurse	медсестра́
полити́ческая корре́ктность	political correctness	политкорре́ктность
полити́ческий заключённый	political prisoner	политзаключённый
профессиона́льный сою́з	trade union	профсою́з

The status of the abbreviated forms varies: **детса́д** normally occurs only in informal language, but in the other instances the abbreviated version is in practice the only form in general use.

In the following instances the first part is not really capable of being expanded into a full adjective:

авиабиле́т	air ticket
автовокза́л	(long-distance) bus station

Another type of word formation that was characteristic of the Soviet period is the so-called 'stump compound'. These are words put together from a part (usually the first syllable or first two syllables) of two or more other words; a typical example is **генсе́к**, formed from **генера́льный секрета́рь** 'general secretary'. Many such forms have disappeared or have become restricted to specialised contexts, but among those still in common use are the following:

вое́нный комиссариа́т military recruitment office	военкома́т
избира́тельная коми́ссия electoral commission	избирко́м
компромети́рующий матери́ал compromising material	компрома́т
во́инские подразделе́ния специа́льного *назначе́ния* special forces	спецна́з
Министе́рство здравоохране́ния Ministry of Health	Минздра́в
универса́льный магази́н department store	универма́г

In a number of instances a noun is formed from a phrase usually consisting of noun + adjective; the original noun is dropped and a noun-forming suffix (usually -ка but sometimes -ник) is added to a shortened form of the adjective. These formations are widely used in informal language, but in more formal contexts the full form is preferred:

креди́тная ка́рт(очк)а credit card	креди́тка
ма́нная крупа́ semolina	ма́нка
минера́льная вода́ mineral water	минера́лка

моби́льный телефо́н mobile telephone	**моби́льник**
футбо́льная ма́йка football shirt, tee-shirt	**футбо́лка**
чита́льный зал reading room	**чита́лка**
«Вече́рняя Москва́» (Moscow's evening newspaper)	**«Вечёрка»**
Госуда́рственная публи́чная библиоте́ка и́мени М.Е. Салтыко́ва-Щедрина́ M.E. Saltykov-Shchedrin State Public Library (in St Petersburg)	**Публи́чка**

10.2 Formation of adjectives

10.2.0 Introduction

To form an adjective from a noun it is necessary to add a suffix to which adjectival endings can be added. The three main suffixes used are: **-н-**, **-ск-** and **-ов-/-ев-/ёв-**. In addition, there are certain suffixes (**-енький**, **-оватый**) which are used to form adjectives from other adjectives.

10.2.1 The suffix -н-

The suffix **-н-** is by far the most widely used of the three suffixes used to form adjectives from nouns. Certain consonants undergo changes before this suffix:

к ~ ч
г ~ ж
х ~ ш
ц ~ ч
л ~ ль

As a rule, the adjective has the same meaning as the noun. Exceptions are indicated where appropriate:

автомоби́ль	car, motor vehicle	**автомоби́льный**	
ба́рхат	velvet	**ба́рхатный**	
верёвка	string	**верёвочный**	
во́здух	air	**возду́шный**	
война́	war	**вое́нный**	military
восто́к	east	**восто́чный**	
де́рево	tree, wood (the material)	**деревя́нный**	wooden
за́пад	west	**за́падный**	
луна́	moon	**лу́нный**	
молоко́	milk	**моло́чный**	
се́вер	north	**се́верный**	
трамва́й	tram	**трамва́йный**	
у́лица	street	**у́личный**	
шко́ла	school	**шко́льный**	
юг	south	**ю́жный**	

In some instances the stress is on the ending, which means that the *nominative singular masculine* ends in **-ой** (see **6.1.2**):

день	day	дневно́й	
зуб	tooth	зубно́й	
ночь	night	ночно́й	
пи́во	beer	пивно́й	
река́	river	речно́й	
рука́	arm, hand	ручно́й	*also* tame

10.2.2 The suffix -н- with a soft ending (-ний)

The combination of the suffix **-н-** and a soft ending (**-ий**) is characteristic of adjectives formed from *nouns, adverbs* or *prepositions* relating to *time* or *place*. These adjectives belong to the *first group* of *soft adjectives*, described in **6.2**.

Adjectives formed from nouns relating to time:

ве́чер	evening	вече́рний
у́тро	morning	у́тренний

But cf. **дневно́й**, **ночно́й** listed in **10.2.1**.

весна́	spring	весе́нний
зима́	winter	зи́мний
ле́то	summer	ле́тний
о́сень	autumn	осе́нний
суббо́та	Saturday	суббо́тний

But **воскресе́нье** Sunday **воскре́сный**

Adjectives formed from adverbs relating to time:

вчера́	yesterday	вчера́шний	yesterday's
сего́дня	today	сего́дняшний	today's
ны́не	today, nowadays	ны́нешний	today's, present
за́втра	tomorrow	за́втрашний	tomorrow's
всегда́	always	всегда́шний	usual, invariable
тепе́рь	now	тепе́решний	present, of today
тогда́	then	тогда́шний	

Adjectives formed from nouns relating to place:

зад	back (part of something), buttocks	за́дний	back, rear
перёд	front (part of something)	пере́дний	front
верх	top	ве́рхний	upper
низ	bottom	ни́жний	lower

Adjectives formed from adverbs or prepositions relating to place:

здесь	here	зде́шний	
тут	here	ту́тошний	
там	there	та́мошний	
вне (+ gen.)	outside	вне́шний	external
внутри́ (+ gen.)	inside	вну́тренний	internal

10.2.3 · **Adjectives formed with the suffix -ск-**

The suffix **-ск-** is particularly characteristic of adjectives formed from geographical names:

Аме́рика	America	**америка́нский**	American
А́нглия	England	**англи́йский**	English
Великобрита́ния	Great Britain	**(велико)брита́нский**	British
По́льша	Poland	**по́льский**	Polish
Росси́я	Russia	**росси́йский**	Russian
		ру́сский	Russian

For the difference between **росси́йский** and **ру́сский**, *see* **12.5.2**.

Москва́	Moscow	**моско́вский**
(Санкт-)Петербу́рг	St Petersburg	**(санкт-)петербу́ргский**

NOTE · The form **(санкт-)петербу́ржский** is also possible, but is less widely used. Forms with the prefix **Санкт-** are characteristic of formal language and are used, for example, in the official titles of St Petersburg institutions such as **Санкт-петербу́ргский госуда́рственный университе́т** St Petersburg State University.

Ло́ндон	London	**ло́ндонский**
Пари́ж	Paris	**пари́жский**
Байка́л	Lake Baikal	**байка́льский**
Кавка́з	Caucasus (mountain range)	**кавка́зский**
Камча́тка	Kamchatka (peninsula)	**камча́тский**
Нева́	River Neva	**не́вский**

The same suffix is also used with adjectives formed from *surnames*:

Горбачёв	**горбачёвский**
Пу́шкин	**пу́шкинский**
Толсто́й	**толсто́вский**

Other adjectives with the **-ск-** suffix include the following:

янва́рь	January	**янва́рский**
апре́ль	April	**апре́льский**
октя́брь	October	**октя́брьский**

and all other adjectives formed from the names of the months;

арифме́тика	arithmetic	**арифмети́ческий**	arithmetical
Би́блия	Bible	**библе́йский**	biblical
брат	brother	**бра́тский**	fraternal
де́ти	children	**де́тский**	childlike, childish
капитали́ст	capitalist	**капиталисти́ческий**	
люби́тель	lover (e.g. of music), amateur	**люби́тельский**	amateur
роди́тель	parent	**роди́тельский**	
солда́т	soldier	**солда́тский**	

Some of the adjectives with this suffix have the stress on the ending:

Дон	(river) Don	донско́й	
го́род	city, town	городско́й	
мо́ре	sea	морско́й	marine

10.2.4 Adjectives formed with the suffix -ов-/-ев-/-ёв

The suffix **-ов-/-ев-/-ёв** is the least widely used of the three word-forming suffixes discussed here. Examples include:

бана́н	banana	бана́новый	
бро́нза	bronze	бро́нзовый	
ма́сса	mass (large amount or quantity)	ма́ссовый	
образе́ц	model (for imitation)	образцо́вый	model, ideal
оре́х	nut	оре́ховый	
осётр	sturgeon	осетро́вый	
рис	rice	ри́совый	
свине́ц	lead	свинцо́вый	
сире́нь	lilac (tree)	сире́невый	
со́я	soya	со́евый	
чере́шня	cherry	чере́шневый	
ви́шня	(morello) cherry	вишнёвый	
рубль	rouble	рублёвый	
бе́рег	shore	берегово́й	
быт	daily life	бытово́й	everyday, social
гру́ппа	group	группово́й	
звук	sound	звуково́й	
мозг	brain	мозгово́й	
час	hour		
часы́	clock, watch	часово́й	*also* sentry
пи́ща	food	пищево́й	
речь	speech	речево́й	

10.2.5 Adjectives belonging to the second group of soft adjectives

The adjectives belonging to the *second group* of *soft adjectives* (described in **6.3**) are all formed from animate nouns:

Бог	God	Бо́жий
челове́к	man, human being	челове́чий
вдова́	widow	вдо́вий
бара́н	ram	бара́ний
бык	bull	бы́чий
верблю́д	camel	верблю́жий
волк	wolf	во́лчий
коро́ва	cow	коро́вий
ко́шка	cat	коша́чий
лиса́	fox	ли́сий
медве́дь	bear	медве́жий
пти́ца	bird	пти́чий
соба́ка	dog	соба́чий
щу́ка	pike	щу́чий

These adjectives, and especially those formed from nouns denoting animals, can be used in a wide range of possessive and descriptive functions:

> **Здесь храм *Бо́жий*: на́до вести́ себя́ прили́чно.**
> This is God's temple; you must behave properly.

> **У него́ *во́лчий* аппети́т.**
> He has the appetite of a wolf.

> **Я отку́да-то слы́шу *коша́чье* мурлы́канье.**
> From somewhere I can hear the purring of a cat.

The following adjectives are used in a number of set expressions:

Зако́н Бо́жий	Religious Instruction (subject in school)
«Пти́чье молоко́»	a well-known brand of chocolates [the allusion is to bird's milk as something exquisite and rare]
соба́чий хо́лод	intense cold
(как) по щу́чьему веле́нью	as if by magic

10.2.6 Nouns from which two or more adjectives are formed

There are several Russian nouns from which more than one adjective can be formed. In such instances the different adjectives will have diferent meanings:

боль	pain, ache	**больно́й**	sick, ill, sore, (as a noun) patient
		болево́й	relating to pain
век	century	**веково́й**	centuries old, ancient
		ве́чный	eternal
друг	friend	**дру́жеский**	friendly
		дру́жественный	friendly, cordial (official)
		дру́жный	harmonious, unanimous
мир	world; peace	**мирово́й**	world(-wide)
		ми́рный	peaceful
		мирско́й	secular, lay
серебро́	silver	**сере́бряный**	(made of) silver
		серебри́стый	silver (coloured)
си́ла	strength, force, power	**си́льный**	strong
		силово́й	relating to power or the use of force
стекло́	glass	**стекля́нный**	(made of) glass
		стеко́льный	relating to the production of glass
чу́до	miracle	**чуде́сный**	miraculous, wonderful, marvellous
		чу́дный	wonderful, marvellous
		чудно́й	strange, cranky

язы́к	tongue, language, tribe	языково́й	linguistic, relating to language
		язы́ческий	pagan

10.2.7 Adjectives formed from phrases

In many instances it is possible to form a single adjective from a phrase. The majority of these consist either of an *adjective + noun* or a *numeral + noun*.

When adjectives are formed from an *adjective + noun*, the two parts of the adjective are linked by the vowel **o** (**e** after a soft consonant):

бе́лая голова́	white head	белоголо́вый	white-haired, fair-haired
Ве́тхий Заве́т	Old Testament	ветхозаве́тный	Old Testament
кра́сное лицо́	red face	краснолицый	red-faced
кру́пный масшта́б	large scale	кру́пно-масшта́бный	large-scale
нау́чная фанта́стика	science fiction	нау́чно-фантасти́ческий	science-fiction
ру́сский язы́к	Russian language	русскоязы́чный	Russian-speaking
сре́дние века́	Middle Ages	средневеко́вый	medieval

NOTE The example **нау́чно-фантасти́ческий** is unusual because it has two stresses and is normally hyphenated, rather than being written as one word.

Adjectives of this type are frequently formed from geographical names:

Да́льний восто́к	Far East
дальневосто́чный	far eastern
За́падная Украи́на	Western Ukraine
западноукраи́нский	West Ukrainian
Ти́хий океа́н	Pacific Ocean
тихоокеа́нский	Pacific

When adjectives are formed from a *numeral + noun*, the numeral is usually in the *genitive case* form:

две ноги́	two legs	двуно́гий	two-legged
два смы́сла	two senses	двусмы́сленный	ambiguous
два то́ма	two volumes	двухто́мный	in two volumes
два этажа́	two storeys	двухэта́жный	two-storeyed
три часа́	three hours	трёхчасово́й	three hours long
два́дцать пять лет	twenty-five years	двадцатипятиле́тний	twenty-five years old

10.2.8 Adjectives formed from other adjectives

The suffix **-енький** fulfils a similar function for adjectives as the various diminutive suffixes do for nouns, that is, they indicate either small size or a particular emotional attachment. In most instances, therefore, they do not have a different translation from that of the adjective from which they are derived. In practice, adjectives with this suffix tend to be formed only from adjectives indicating colour and a few other widely used adjectives indicating a subjective quality:

краси́вый	beautiful	**краси́венький**
кра́сный	red	**кра́сненький**
коро́ткий	short	**коро́тенький**
чи́стый	clean	**чи́стенький**

There are two special cases to note:

| ма́лый | small, little | **ма́ленький** |

Here, adjectives with the **-енький** suffix are in general use; **ма́лый** tends to be restricted to set phrases or to titles such as:

| Ма́лая А́зия | Asia Minor |
| Ма́лый теа́тр | (name of a theatre in Moscow) |

In the following instances the adjective with the suffix has a different meaning:

| хоро́ший | good | **хоро́шенький** | pretty |

Rather less widely used are the *augmentative* suffixes **-ющий**, **-енный**:

| холо́дный | cold | **холодню́щий** | |
| здоро́вый | healthy | **здорове́нный** | fine, strapping |

For more on the use of these diminutive and augmentative suffixes, *see* **16.1.5**.

The suffix **-ватый** attenuates the meaning of the original adjective; it can thus correspond to the English '-ish':

глу́пый	stupid	**глупова́тый**	fairly stupid
кра́сный	red	**краснова́тый**	reddish
стра́шный	terrible, frightening	**страшнова́тый**	quite frightening

10.3 Formation of verbs

10.3.0 Introduction

Any newly created verb in Russian, other than those created by the addition of a prefix (*see* **10.4**), must belong to one of the four *productive* classes of verbs described in **4.6**, although in practice some of these classes are more productive than others.

10.3.1 Verbs ending in -овать

The overwhelming majority of newly created Russian verbs belong to the class of verbs with an *infinitive* ending in **-овать** and *non-past* endings in **-ую**, **-уешь**, etc.

For the conjugation of verbs belonging to this class, *see* **4.6.2**.

The suffix used to form the infinitive of these verbs can take the following forms: **-овать/-евать**, **-изовать**, **-ировать**, **-изировать**. Many verbs in this class that have entered the language very recently are *bi-aspectual*, that is, the same form is used for both *imperfective* and *perfective* aspects; bi-aspectual verbs are indicated in the lists below with the abbreviation **нсв/св**.

Examples of verbs ending in **-овать**:

арестова́ть (нсв/св)	to arrest
бастова́ть/забастова́ть	to go on strike
диктова́ть/продиктова́ть	to dictate
коронова́ть (нсв/св)	to crown
про́бовать/попро́бовать	to try
расшифро́вывать/расшифрова́ть	to decipher
рискова́ть/рискну́ть	to risk

The infinitive ending **-евать** occurs after soft consonants and after the consonants **ж**, **ц**, **ш**, **ч** in accordance with the spelling rule given in **1.5.2**:

ночева́ть/переночева́ть	to spend the night
танцева́ть/станцева́ть	to dance

Examples of verbs ending in **-изовать**:

организова́ть (нсв/св)	to organise
парализова́ть (нсв/св)	to paralyse
характеризова́ть/охарактеризова́ть	to characterise

NOTES

(i) Some perfective verbs ending in **-овать/-изовать** have an imperfective partner in **-овывать/-изовывать** (as in the example **расшифро́вывать/расшифрова́ть**).

(ii) Although the verbs **арестова́ть** and **организова́ть** are bi-aspectual, there are imperfective partners **аресто́вывать** and **организо́вывать** respectively; these are not normally used in the present and future tenses.

Examples of verbs ending in **-ировать**:

бойкоти́ровать (нсв/св)	to boycott
игнори́ровать (нсв/св)	to ignore
инвести́ровать (нсв/св)	to invest
иллюстри́ровать (нсв/св)	to illustrate
плани́ровать/заплани́ровать	to plan
редакти́ровать/отредакти́ровать	to edit
цити́ровать/процити́ровать	to quote

Examples of verbs ending in **-изировать**:

госпитализи́ровать (нсв/св)	to hospitalise
модернизи́ровать (нсв/св)	to modernise
приватизи́ровать (нсв/св)	to privatise
символизи́ровать (нсв/св)	to symbolise
стабилизи́ровать (нсв/св)	to stabilise

10.3.2 Verbs with an infinitive ending in -ить

It is sometimes possible to form from a noun a second conjugation verb with an infinitive ending in **-ить**.

For the conjugation of second conjugation verbs with an infinitive ending in **-ить**, *see* **4.6.4**.

Examples of verbs formed in this way include the following, most of which tend to be restricted to the more informal levels of language:

партиза́н	partisan	партиза́нить (нсв)	to fight with the partisans
пылесо́с	vacuum cleaner	пылесо́сить (нсв)	to vacuum
сигна́л	signal, alarm	сигна́лить/ просигна́лить	to signal (*especially* to hoot a car horn)
сканда́л	scandal, scene	сканда́лить (нсв)	to create a scene
тира́н	tyrant	тира́нить (нсв)	to behave like a tyrant towards, to oppress
транжи́р	spendthrift	транжи́рить/ протранжи́рить	to squander
хулига́н	hooligan	хулига́нить (нсв)	to behave like a hooligan

10.3.3 Verbs formed from adjectives

There are two types of verbs formed from adjectives. *Intransitive* verbs with an infinitive ending in **-еть** are formed from a wide range of adjectives. These are *first conjugation* verbs and they belong to the type described in **4.6.1(c)**.

Transitive verbs with an infinitive ending in **-ить** are formed from a more restricted range of adjectives. These are *second conjugation* verbs of the types described in **4.6.4**.

For the difference between transitive and intransitive verbs, *see* **4.13.1**.

Examples of intransitive verbs with an infinitive ending in **-еть**:

бе́дный	poor	бедне́ть/обедне́ть	to grow poor
бе́лый	white	беле́ть/побеле́ть	to turn white, to show up white
бле́дный	pale	бледне́ть/побледне́ть	to turn pale
бога́тый	rich	богате́ть/разбогате́ть	to become rich
кра́сный	red	красне́ть/покрасне́ть	to turn red, to blush
ле́вый	left	леве́ть/полеве́ть	to move to the left (politically)
ста́рый	old	старе́ть/постаре́ть	to grow old
тёмный	dark	темне́ть/стемне́ть	to grow dark
тре́звый	sober	трезве́ть/отрезве́ть, протрезве́ть	to sober up

Examples of transitive verbs with an infinitive ending in **-ить**:

бе́лый	white	бели́ть/побели́ть	to paint white, to whiten
молодо́й	young	молоди́ть/омолоди́ть	to make someone look younger
тре́звый	sober	трезви́ть/отрезви́ть	to sober someone up
чёрный	black	черни́ть/зачерни́ть очерни́ть	to blacken [*literally*] to blacken [*figuratively*]

10.4 Verbal prefixes

10.4.0 Introduction

Attaching a *prefix* to a *verb* serves one of two functions. In the first place it can create the *perfective* partner of an unprefixed *imperfective* without changing the meaning of the verb; examples of this are given in **4.2.3**. The second function is to change both the *aspect* and the *meaning*; in the great majority of these cases new pairs of imperfective and perfective verbs with the same prefix are created according to the patterns described and illustrated in **4.2.4**. This use of verbal prefixes is an important part of the Russian system of word formation; it corresponds in large measure to the creation of the so-called 'phrasal verbs' in English (such as 'go out', 'take in' or 'put up with') and, as with phrasal verbs in English, some of the distinctions of meaning that result from this process are quite subtle.

The following prefixes are used to create new verbs: **в(о)-, вз(о)-/вс-, воз(о)-/вос-, вы-, до-, за-, из(о)/ис-, на-, недо-, о/об(о), от(о)-, пере-, пре-, под(о)-, пред(о)-, при-, про-, раз(о)/рас-, с(о)-, у-**.

The spelling (**о**) indicates that a *fleeting vowel* (see **2.5.0**) appears before some forms of certain verbs.

For more on the distribution of forms in **-з** and **-с**, *see* **1.5.6**.

Some of the above prefixes have either a single or a very limited range of meanings: the prefix **недо-** always conveys the idea of an action carried out to an insufficient degree; the prefix **в(о)-** usually conveys the idea of movement into (if not literally, then figuratively). Other prefixes, such as **за-, о/об(о)** or **с(о)-**, have a wide range of meanings that do not necessarily have any obvious link between them; one consequence of this is that it is sometimes possible to find the same verb used with the same prefix in two different meanings. Almost all prefixes, though, have at least one fundamental spatial meaning which is revealed when they are used with *verbs of motion*.

For more on verbs of motion, *see* **22.1, 22.2**.

In many instances there is a match between the prefix and the preposition most widely used in conjunction with the verb in question, as in the following example:

> Она́ *вошла́ в* ко́мнату.
> She came into the room.

10.4.1 The prefix в(о)-

With the meaning of movement into **в(о)-** is used with *verbs of motion*, but also with a number of other verbs:

входи́ть/войти́	to go in, to come in (on foot)
въезжа́ть/въе́хать	to drive in, to enter (by vehicle)
вбега́ть/вбежа́ть	to run in
вводи́ть/ввести́	to bring in, to introduce
вме́шиваться/вмеша́ться	to interfere in
впуска́ть/впусти́ть	to let in
вставля́ть/вста́вить	to insert
вступа́ть/вступи́ть	to enter, to join (e.g. a political party)

With the following verb the meaning is understood figuratively:

включа́ть/включи́ть	to include, to switch on

10.4.2 **The prefixes вз(о)-/вс-, воз(о)-/вос-**

The basic meaning of **вз(о)-/вс-** is movement upwards:

всходи́ть/взойти́	to rise (e.g. the sun)
взлета́ть/взлете́ть	to take off (of an aeroplane)

When it is used with the following verbs, the meaning is more one of agitation:

взбива́ть/взбить	to whip (cream)
взрыва́ть/взорва́ть	to blow something up

The prefix **воз(о)-/вос-** has basically the same range of meanings, but it tends to be used in more figurative contexts:

возбужда́ть/возбуди́ть	to arouse, to incite
возвыша́ть/возвы́сить	to raise (up)
возмуща́ть/возмути́ть	to anger, to outrage
возника́ть/возни́кнуть	to arise, to spring up, to appear
воспи́тывать/воспита́ть	to bring up, to educate
восхища́ться/восхити́ться	to admire, to be captivated by

With some verbs this prefix can convey the meaning of returning, restoring:

возвраща́ть(ся)/возврати́ть(ся), верну́ть(ся)	to return
восстана́вливать/восстанови́ть	to restore

10.4.3 **The prefix вы-**

The basic meaning of the prefix **вы-** is movement out:

выходи́ть/вы́йти	to go/come out of, to leave (on foot)
выбега́ть/вы́бежать	to run out from
выноси́ть/вы́нести	to carry/bring out (physically), to endure
выбра́сывать/вы́бросить	to throw out
вынима́ть/вы́нуть	to take out
выпи́сывать/вы́писать	to write out, to subscribe to
выступа́ть/вы́ступить	to appear (in public), to perform, to make a speech

With some verbs this prefix can convey the notion of an action carried out exhaustively:

выска́зываться/вы́сказаться	to have one's say
высыпа́ться/вы́спаться	to have a good sleep, to sleep one's fill

The following useful verbs do not really fit into either of the above categories:

выи́грывать/вы́играть	to win
выключа́ть/вы́ключить	to switch off

For information on the stress of perfective verbs with the **вы-** prefix, *see* **4.2.4**.

10.4.4 The prefix до-

The basic spatial meaning of the prefix до-, when it is combined with *verbs of motion*, is movement as far as:

доезжа́ть/дое́хать	to travel as far as
доноси́ться/донести́сь	to carry (of a sound)

In the following verb the meaning is figurative:

доноси́ть/донести́ на (+ acc.)	to denounce someone

The prefix до- is combined with a wide variety of verbs to convey the meaning to finish off an action:

допи́сывать/дописа́ть	to finish writing
достра́ивать/достро́ить	to finish building
дочи́тывать/дочита́ть	to finish reading

A closely related meaning, found with a few verbs, is that of topping up:

долива́ть/доли́ть	to top up with (a liquid)
допла́чивать/доплати́ть	to have to pay a bit extra

There are certain *reflexive* verbs with the prefix до- that have the meaning of doing the action until the desired result is achieved:

дога́дываться/догада́ться	to guess the right answer
догова́риваться/договори́ться	to come to an agreement
дожида́ться/дожда́ться	to wait until the person arrives
дозва́ниваться/дозвони́ться	to get through (on the telephone)
дока́пываться/докопа́ться	to dig down until you find what you are looking for (*literally and figuratively*)

With other reflexive verbs the same prefix can convey the meaning of carrying out an action to the point where there are unpleasant consequences:

допева́ться/допе́ться (до хрипоты́)	to sing (until you are hoarse)
допи́ться (св) (до чёртиков)	to drink (to the point of seeing little pink elephants (*literally*, small devils)
доигра́ться (св)	to land oneself in trouble

10.4.5 The prefix за-

When used with *verbs of motion* and other verbs indicating displacement, the prefix за- often has the meaning of movement behind:

заходи́ть/зайти́	to go behind

Verbs of motion with the prefix за- often convey the meaning of calling in somewhere:

заходи́ть/зайти́	to call in, to drop in

In a number of expressions the prefix за- can convey the idea of movement into; used in this way, this prefix implies the application of a certain amount of energy and a movement that continues far inside the implied or expressed container:

забива́ть/заби́ть гол	to score a goal
забра́сывать/забро́сить ша́йбу	to score a goal (in ice-hockey)

засо́вывать/засу́нуть ру́ки в карма́н	to thrust one's hands into one's pocket

The prefix **за-** can also convey the idea of closing or wrapping up:

завора́чивать/заверну́ть	to wrap up (a parcel)
завя́зывать/завяза́ть	to tie up (a parcel)
закрыва́ть/закры́ть	to close, to shut
запира́ть/запере́ть	to lock
застёгивать/застегну́ть	to button up

The prefix **за-** is combined with some reflexive verbs to convey the idea of carrying on an activity for too long or getting carried away with an activity:

завира́ться/завра́ться	to get carried away with one's lies
загова́риваться/заговори́ться	to get carried away talking
заси́живаться/засиде́ться	to sit too long (e.g. over food and drink or at a meeting)
зачи́тываться/зачита́ться	to become (too) absorbed in one's reading

The connotations of the following verb are slightly different:

заду́мываться/заду́маться	to become pensive, to ponder over

Another meaning often conveyed by the prefix **за-** is that of beginning an action. For the most part **за-** is used in this sense to form a *perfective* partner of an unprefixed *imperfective* verb:

говори́ть	to talk	заговори́ть	to start talking
пла́кать	to cry, to weep	запла́кать	to start crying
ходи́ть	to go (on foot), to walk	заходи́ть	to start walking up and down

There are, however, a few instances of *imperfective/perfective* pairs:

заболева́ть/заболе́ть	to fall ill
зажига́ть/заже́чь	to ignite, to set fire to
засыпа́ть/засну́ть	to fall asleep

In addition to the above, there are a large number of verbs where the prefix **за-** fits into none of the above categories; in many of these the prefix does not itself have an easily identifiable meaning and in some instances may no longer be perceived as a prefix:

заблуди́ться (св)	to lose one's way
заблужда́ться (нсв)	to be mistaken
забыва́ть/забы́ть	to forget
зава́ривать/завари́ть	to brew (tea)
зави́сеть (св) от (+ gen.)	to depend on
загора́ть/загоре́ть	to sunbathe, to acquire a tan
зака́зывать/заказа́ть	to order (goods or in a restaurant)
заключа́ть/заключи́ть	to conclude
заменя́ть/замени́ть	to replace, to substitute
занима́ть/заня́ть	to occupy, to borrow
занима́ться/позанима́ться	to study
запи́сывать/записа́ть	to write down, to record
запреща́ть/запрети́ть	to forbid
заполня́ть/запо́лнить	to fill in (a form)
запомина́ть/запо́мнить	to memorise, to remember

заставля́ть/заста́вить	to force, to compel
защища́ть/защити́ть	to defend
заявля́ть/заяви́ть	to declare, to state

10.4.6 The prefix из(о)/ис-

The prefix **из(о)/ис-** is often associated with the general idea of movement outwards, often conceived figuratively:

избега́ть/избежа́ть	to avoid
избира́ть/избра́ть	to elect (to high office)
извлека́ть/извле́чь	to extract, to gain (e.g. benefit)
издава́ть/изда́ть	to publish, to make (a sound)
исключа́ть/исключи́ть	to exclude, to expel, to rule out

With some verbs the prefix **из(о)/ис-** can convey the meaning the exhaustion of resources or covering the whole surface of something; with these meanings **из(о)/ис-** can either form a *perfective* partner of an unprefixed *imperfective* or form *imperfective/perfective* pairs:

| тра́тить | to spend | истра́тить | to spend up |
| ходи́ть | to go (on foot), to walk | исходи́ть | to walk the length and breadth of |

| испи́сывать/исписа́ть | to fill up with *or* to cover with writing |

10.4.7 The prefix на-

The prefix **на-** can convey the idea of motion onto; examples with *verbs of motion* are rare, but more frequently encountered instances include:

нажима́ть/нажа́ть (на кно́пку)
to press (a button)

накле́ивать/накле́ить (ма́рку на конве́рт)
to stick (a stamp on an envelope)

наступа́ть/наступи́ть на (+ acc.)
to step on, to tread on

When used with some *reflexive* verbs, the prefix **на-** can convey the idea of carrying out an action to the point of satisfaction; some of these verbs occur only in the *perfective*:

наговори́ться (св)	to talk enough
наеда́ться/нае́сться	to eat one's fill
налюбова́ться (св)	to admire to one's heart's content

In the following verb the connotation is slightly different:

| напива́ться/напи́ться | to get drunk |

There are some miscellaneous verbs with the prefix **на-**:

набира́ть/набра́ть	to pick up (speed), to dial
намека́ть/намекну́ть	to hint
нареза́ть/наре́зать	to cut, to slice (bread or cheese)
настра́ивать/настро́ить	to tune (a radio or a musical instrument)
находи́ть/найти́	to find

10.4.8   The prefix недо-

The prefix **недо-** always conveys the idea of insufficiency:

недооце́нивать/недооцени́ть	to underestimate
недоса́ливать/недосоли́ть	to undersalt

10.4.9   The prefix о/об(о)

When used with *verbs of motion*, the prefix **о/об(о)** conveys the meaning of movement around:

обходи́ть/обойти́	to walk around
облета́ть/облете́ть	to fly around, to orbit

This prefix can also convey the idea of the comprehensiveness or thoroughness of an action:

обходи́ть/обойти́
to go round (e.g. all the shops in search of something)

опи́сывать/описа́ть
to describe

опра́шивать/опроси́ть
to ask a large number, to carry out a survey of opinion

осма́тривать/осмотре́ть
to examine, to inspect (from all angles)

The prefix in the form **о-**, when used with certain *reflexive* verbs, can indicate an accidental mistake:

огова́риваться/оговори́ться	to make a slip of the tongue
опи́сываться/описа́ться	to make a slip of the pen
ослы́шаться (св)	to mishear
ошиба́ться/ошиби́ться	to make a mistake

On the other hand, the prefix in the form **об-** can be used with certain verbs to imply deliberate deception:

обма́нывать/обману́ть	to deceive
обве́шивать/обве́сить	to give short weight to
обсчи́тывать/обсчита́ть	to shortchange

The prefix **о/об(о)** is sometimes used to form *transitive* verbs from *adjectives*:

оглуша́ть/оглуши́ть	to deafen
осложня́ть/осложни́ть	to complicate

The reflexive verb **обходи́ться/обойти́сь**, when used with **без** (+ gen.), means 'to do without'.

10.4.10   The prefix от(о)-

The spatial meaning of the prefix **от(о)-** is movement away from:

отходи́ть/отойти́	to move away from
отстава́ть/отста́ть	to fall behind, to be slow (of a clock or watch)
отступа́ть/отступи́ть	to retreat

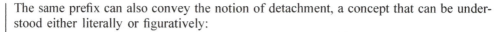

The same prefix can also convey the notion of detachment, a concept that can be understood either literally or figuratively:

отви́нчивать/отвинти́ть	to unscrew
отку́сывать/откуси́ть	to bite off
отпи́ливать/отпили́ть	to saw off
отвыка́ть/отвы́кнуть	to get unused to
отгова́ривать/отговори́ть	to dissuade
отка́зывать(ся)/отказа́ть(ся)	to refuse
откла́дывать/отложи́ть	to postpone
отменя́ть/отмени́ть	to cancel

The prefix от(о)- can also convey the idea of responding:

отвеча́ть/отве́тить	to answer
отзыва́ться/отозва́ться	to respond, to react
отклика́ться/откли́кнуться	to respond (e.g. to a shout or an appeal)

10.4.11 The prefixes пере-, пре-

The spatial meaning of the prefix пере- is movement across:

переходи́ть/перейти́	to go across (on foot)
переезжа́ть/перее́хать	to travel across, to move house
переплыва́ть/переплы́ть	to swim across, to travel across (by boat)
пересека́ть/пересе́чь	to cross (e.g. a frontier)

The prefix пере- also has the meaning of dividing, cutting through, sometimes understood figuratively:

перепи́ливать/перепили́ть	to saw through
перереза́ть/перере́зать	to cut through
перебива́ть/переби́ть	to interrupt

This prefix can also convey the idea of excess; in this sense it is the opposite of недо-:

переоце́нивать/переоцени́ть	to over-estimate
перепла́чивать/переплати́ть	to pay too much
перестара́ться (св)	to try too hard, to get carried away

The prefix пере- is used to express the idea of redoing an action:

переде́лывать/переде́лать	to redo
переду́мывать/переду́мать	to change one's mind
перезва́нивать/перезвони́ть	to phone back
перепи́сывать/переписа́ть	to rewrite

This prefix can sometimes convey the idea of outdoing:

перекри́кивать/перекрича́ть	to out-shout
перехитри́ть (св)	to outwit

With some verbs that are both *reflexive* and *imperfective* only, the prefix пере- indicates a repeated action that goes backwards and forwards between two participants:

перебра́сываться (нсв)	to throw backwards and forwards
перепи́сываться (нсв)	to exchange letters, to correspond

With certain verbs the prefix **пере-** conveys the idea of extending the action to all possible objects:

перечисля́ть/перечи́слить	to enumerate, to list in full

The meanings of the prefix **пре-** overlap with those of **пере-**; in particular, it can convey the ideas of cutting through and exceeding, often understood figuratively:

прегражда́ть/прегради́ть (путь)	to bar (the way)
прекраща́ть/прекрати́ть	to cease
превыша́ть/превы́сить	to exceed

10.4.12 The prefix под(о)-

The first spatial meaning of the prefix **под(о)-** is movement or position under:

подкла́дывать/подложи́ть	to put under (in a horizontal position)
подставля́ть/подста́вить	to put under (in a vertical position)
подпи́сывать/подписа́ть	to sign, to put one's name to
подчёркивать/подчеркну́ть	to underline

With many verbs of motion and some other verbs, **под(о)-** conveys the meaning of movement up to, approaching:

подходи́ть/подойти́	to approach, to go up to
подвози́ть/подвезти́	to give someone a lift
пододвига́ть/пододви́нуть	to bring something nearer

A third spatial meaning conveyed by this prefix is movement upwards or from below; this can be either literal or figurative:

подбра́сывать/подбро́сить	to throw up in the air
подде́рживать/поддержа́ть	to support
поднима́ть/подня́ть	to raise
поднима́ться/подня́ться	to rise, to go up(wards)

The prefix **под(о)-** can convey the notion of adding a small quantity:

подбавля́ть/подба́вить	to add (a small amount)
подогрева́ть/подогре́ть	to warm something up
подса́ливать/подсоли́ть	to add a little salt

A further meaning of this prefix is that of doing something furtively or illegally:

подде́лывать/подде́лать	to forge (banknotes or documents)
поджига́ть/подже́чь	to burn down
подкупа́ть/подкупи́ть	to bribe, to subborn
подска́зывать/подсказа́ть	to prompt, to whisper the answer
подслу́шивать/подслу́шать	to eavesdrop, to 'bug'

10.4.13 The prefix пред(о)-

The prefix **пред(о)-** normally has the meaning of anticipation:

предви́деть (нсв)	to predict
предполага́ть/предположи́ть	to assume, to presuppose
предупрежда́ть/предупреди́ть	to warn

However:

предлага́ть/предложи́ть	to offer, to propose
представля́ть/предста́вить	to present, to introduce (people)

10.4.14 The prefix при-

When used with verbs of motion and with certain other verbs, the prefix **при-** conveys the idea of arrival or (less often) approaching:

приходи́ть/прийти́	to come, to arrive (on foot)
приезжа́ть/прие́хать	to come, to arrive (by vehicle)
приноси́ть/принести́	to bring (on foot)
приземля́ться/ приземли́ться	to land
приближа́ться/ прибли́зиться	to approach
призыва́ть/призва́ть	to summon, to call up (for military service)
привлека́ть/привле́чь	to attract

The same prefix can convey the idea of attaching one thing to another (sometimes figuratively):

привя́зывать/привяза́ть	to tie (something to something else)
присоединя́ть/присоедини́ть	to join, to unite
пришива́ть/приши́ть	to sew on (e.g. a button)
припи́сывать/приписа́ть	to ascribe

The prefix **при-** can also convey the meaning of adding:

прибавля́ть/приба́вить	to add
припи́сывать/приписа́ть	to add (something to a written text)
пристра́ивать/пристро́ить	to build on (horizontally)

With certain verbs this prefix can convey the notion of doing something either tentatively or only partially or for a short time:

приболе́ть (св)	to be off-colour, to feel unwell
привстава́ть/привста́ть	to half-rise (e.g. from a sitting position)
приле́чь (св)	to lie down (for a short time)
приостана́вливать/ приостанови́ть	to stop (something for a time), to suspend
приса́живаться/присе́сть	to sit down (for a short time), to perch on the edge of one's seat

With reflexive verbs formed from verbs indicating watching or listening, the prefix **при-** suggests attentiveness; the prefective verbs often contain the additional meaning of acting in response to the observations made:

прислу́шиваться/прислу́шаться к (+ dat.)
to listen attentively, to pay heed to

присма́триваться/присмотре́ться к (+ dat.)
to watch attentively, to size someone up

10.4.15 The prefix про-

The prefix **про-** has two spatial meanings. With *verbs of motion* and a number of other verbs it can indicate movement through:

проходи́ть/пройти́	to go through (on foot)
проника́ть/прони́кнуть	to penetrate
пропуска́ть/пропусти́ть	to let through
протека́ть/проте́чь	to leak through

The other meaning, found only with verbs of motion, is movement past:

проходи́ть/пройти́	to go past (on foot)
проезжа́ть/прое́хать	to drive past

The prefix **про-** also has the meaning of omission, often through inattentiveness:

проба́лтываться/ проболта́ться	to let the cat out of the bag, to spill the beans
прогу́ливать/прогуля́ть	to miss (classes), to be absent from work
проезжа́ть/прое́хать (свою́ остано́вку)	to miss (one's stop)
прозева́ть (св) (свою́ о́чередь)	to miss (one's turn through inattentiveness)
пропуска́ть/пропусти́ть	to omit

The prefix **про-** can also convey the idea of failure:

прои́грывать/проигра́ть	to lose (a game)
пропива́ть/пропи́ть (все де́ньги)	to drink away (all one's money)

When used with a *direct object* indicating time or distance, verbs with the prefix **про-** emphasise either the time an action was continued for or the distance covered during an action:

пробега́ть/пробежа́ть (две́сти ме́тров)	to cover (200 metres, running)
прожива́ть/прожи́ть (где́-то со́рок лет)	to live (somewhere for 40 years)

There are some useful verbs with the prefix **про-** that do not fit into any of the above categories:

проводи́ть/провести́	to conduct (e.g. a meeting or an experiment)
продава́ть/прода́ть	to sell
просыпа́ться/просну́ться	to wake up

10.4.16 The prefix раз(о)/рас-

The prefix **раз(о)/рас-** can convey the meaning of 'dispersal', 'distribution':

расходи́ться/разойти́сь	to disperse (intransitive)
разгоня́ть/разогна́ть	to disperse (transitive)
расступа́ться/расступи́ться	to part, to make way
раздава́ть/разда́ть	to give out, to distribute
распределя́ть/распредели́ть	to distribute, to allocate

The same prefix can also convey the idea of dividing up (into many pieces):

разбива́ть/разби́ть	to break into pieces, to smash
разводи́ться/развести́сь	to get divorced
разделя́ть/раздели́ть	to divide up
разреза́ть/разре́зать	to cut up, to slice up (into many pieces)

The prefix **раз(о)/рас-** can be used to indicate the idea of reversing an action; this applies in particular to two groups of verbs, those connected with tying or closing and those referring to certain mental processes:

развя́зывать/развяза́ть	to untie
раскупо́ривать/раскупо́рить	to uncork, to open (a bottle)
расстёгивать/расстегну́ть	to unbutton
разду́мать (св)	to decide not to do something, to change one's mind
разлюби́ть (св)	to stop loving
разочаро́вывать/разочарова́ть	to disenchant, to disappoint
расхоте́ть (св)	to stop wanting
разоружа́ть/разоружи́ть	to disarm [transitive]

With some verbs the prefix **раз(о)/рас-** suggests an action carried out thoroughly:

разраба́тывать/разрабо́тать	to work out, to elaborate, to develop
расспра́шивать/расспроси́ть	to question, to ask all about
рассма́тривать/рассмотре́ть	to examine (thoroughly)

With a number of *reflexive* verbs the prefix **раз(о)/рас-** indicates an action that gradually gains in intensity or which is carried out with some vigour; these verbs are *perfective* only:

разговори́ться	to start talking freely *or* fluently
распла́каться	to burst out crying
рассмея́ться	to burst out laughing
расхохота́ться	to burst out into uproarious laughter

10.4.17 The prefix с(о)-

With *verbs of motion* and with some other verbs, the prefix **с(о)-** has the meaning of movement downwards:

сходи́ть/сойти́	to come down (on foot)
сноси́ть/снести́	to bring down, to demolish
спры́гивать/спры́гнуть	to jump down
спуска́ться/спусти́ться	to come down, to descend

With a large number of verbs the same prefix has the meaning of 'removal' (especially from a surface):

сбра́сывать/сбро́сить	to shed, to throw off
сбрива́ть/сбрить	to shave off
сверга́ть/све́ргнуть	to overthrow
смыва́ть/смыть	to wash off
снима́ть/снять	to take off, to remove
стира́ть/стере́ть	to rub off, to erase

With some *reflexive verbs of motion* and with a number of other verbs, the prefix **c(o)**- conveys the meaning of congregating or uniting:

сходи́ться/сойти́сь	to congregate, to come together
собира́ть/собра́ть	to collect
свя́зывать/связа́ть	to tie together
соединя́ть/соедини́ть	to unite

With a small number of verbs the prefix **c(o)**- conveys the idea of copying:

снима́ть/снять	to photograph, to film
спи́сывать/списа́ть	to copy

With some reflexive verbs the prefix **c(o)**- can suggest a mutual action (one that is not usually repeated):

сдружи́ться (св)	to become friends
созва́ниваться/созвони́ться	to have a conversation on the telephone

With some verbs that are used only in the *imperfective* the prefix **c(o)**- can indicate accompanying or carrying out an action together; in this meaning the prefix always appears in the form **co**-:

сопровожда́ть (нсв)	to accompany (e.g. on a journey)
сочу́вствовать (нсв)	to sympathise

There are some useful verbs that do not fit clearly into any of the above categories:

сбыва́ться/сбы́ться	to come true
сдава́ть/сдать	to give up, to hand in, to take (imperfective)/ to pass (perfective), an examination
сдава́ться/сда́ться	to give in, to surrender
сде́рживать/сдержа́ть	to restrain
скрыва́ть/скрыть	to hide
содержа́ть (нсв)	to contain, to maintain, to keep

10.4.18 The prefix y-

When used with verbs of motion and with some other verbs, the prefix **y**- has the meaning of going away or removal:

уходи́ть/уйти́	to go away (on foot)
уезжа́ть/уе́хать	to go away (by transport)
уноси́ть/унести́	to take away, to carry away
уклоня́ться/уклони́ться	to evade
убира́ть/убра́ть	to clear away, to tidy up
удаля́ть/удали́ть	to remove

The same prefix is used to form *transitive* verbs from *adjectives* and (less often) *nouns*:

улучша́ть/улу́чшить	to improve
упроща́ть/упрости́ть	to simplify
ухудша́ть/уху́дшить	to make worse
удочеря́ть/удочери́ть	to adopt (a daughter)
усыновля́ть/усынови́ть	to adopt (a son)

The prefix **y-** can convey the meaning of an action carried out in a way that makes things convenient or comfortable:

        уса́живаться/усе́сться   to sit comfortably
        устана́вливать/установи́ть   to establish, to set up, to install
        устра́ивать/устро́ить   to organise, to arrange

The prefix **y-** can imply the accomplishment of an action only after some difficulty:

        убежда́ть/убеди́ть   to convince
        угова́ривать/уговори́ть   to persuade

11

Agreement

11.0 **Introduction**

It is an important principle of Russian grammar that every ending, whether on a noun, an adjective, a pronoun, a numeral or a verb is there for a reason, and that these endings convey information that is often vital and always helpful in enabling the listener or the reader to understand what is said or written. There are two factors that between them determine the ending of each element within a sentence: the first is *government*, which basically concerns the rules for selecting which case to use. The basic principles relating to the use of the cases were given in **Chapter 3**; information concerning the use of cases after prepositions is given in **9.2**, and more detailed information relating to specific functions is given in **Part B**.

The second factor is *agreement*: the endings of certain words are determined by the word either that they qualify or to which they refer. There are two contexts where agreement is particularly important: the first is within the *noun phrase* (that is, two or more of *pronoun + numeral + adjective + noun*); the second is *agreement* between the *grammatical subject* of a sentence and the *verb*.

11.1   Agreement within the noun phrase

11.1.1   The general rule

The general rule for *agreement* within the *noun phrase* is simply that *pronouns, adjectives* and the *numeral* **один** 'one' always agree with the noun they qualify in number, gender and case:

> **Вчера́ ве́чером я познако́милась с одно́й о́чень интере́сной писа́тельниц***ей***.**
> Last night I met a certain (*literally*, one) very interesting (female) writer.

Here the noun **писа́тельница** is *feminine, singular* and in the *instrumental case* after the preposition **с** (meaning 'with'). Consequently, both the numeral **один** and the adjective **интере́сный** have the *singular feminine instrumental* ending:

> **Обы́чно в э́то вре́мя я рассыла́ю вс***ем*** сво***и́м*** ста́р***ым*** друзья́м новогодние поздравления.**
> Usually at this time (of year) I send out New Year greetings to all my old friends.

Here the noun **друг** is *masculine, plural* and in the *dative case* as the *indirect object* of the verb **рассыла́ть**. Consequently, the pronouns **весь** and **свой** and the adjective **ста́рый** all have the *plural dative* ending (remember that pronouns and adjectives do not distinguish gender in the plural).

An adjective that simultaneously qualifies two singular nouns will tend to agree with the nearer:

> **В университе́те я изуча́ю *ру́сский язы́к* и литерату́ру.**
> At university I'm studing Russian language and literature.

The only circumstances when adjectives do not agree in number, gender and case with the nouns they qualify is after the numerals **два**, **три**, **четы́ре** in the *nominative* or the *accusative* case. Here it will be recalled that a noun used after these numeral is in the *genitive singular*. If, however, the noun is qualified by an *adjective*, the adjective is in the *genitive plural*. With *feminine* nouns, the adjective can be in either the *genitive plural* or the *nominative plural*.

For examples and more detailed information, *see* **8.2.2**.

11.1.2 Apposition

A *noun* or *noun phrase* that is in *apposition* is one that is placed adjacent to a noun or pronoun in order to expand on or qualify its meaning. Nouns or noun phrases in apposition must be in the same case as the nouns or pronouns to which they refer:

> **На́ша цель – познако́мить вас с Санкт-Петербу́рг*ом*, са́м*ым* краси́в*ым* го́род*ом* Росси́и.**
> Our aim is to familiarise you with St Petersburg, Russia's most beautiful city.

Here the phrase **са́мым краси́вым го́родом** is in apposition to **с Санкт-Петербу́ргом** and must therefore be in the same case, here the *instrumental*.

Sometimes words or phrases in apposition are introduced by **как** 'as', 'in the capacity of':

> **Позво́льте *мне*, как са́м*ому* ста́р*ому* челове́ку в э́той компа́нии, предложи́ть тост за здоро́вье всех прису́тствующих.**
> Allow me, as the oldest person in this company, to propose a toast to the health of everyone present.

> **Я восхища́юсь Маяко́вск*им* как поэ́т*ом*.**
> I admire Maiakovskii as a poet [though not necessarily as a playwright].

NOTE When **как** means 'such as', 'for example', it is followed by the *nominative* case:

> **Я восхища́юсь таки́ми поэ́тами, как *Пу́шкин* и *Маяко́вский*.**
> I admire poets such as Pushkin and Maiakovskii.

11.1.3 Names of works of literature, commercial enterprises, railway stations and geographical locations

An exception to the rule about apposition occurs with names of *works of literature, commercial enterprises* and *railway stations*: these are normally in the *nominative* case, provided that they are preceded by a *defining term*, which takes on the ending required by the grammatical context; examples of such defining terms include **рома́н** 'novel', **ОАО (откры́тое акционе́рное о́бщество)** 'PLC', **ста́нция** 'station'. In the written language the defining term may sometimes take the form of an abbreviation, while the name itself will be placed in inverted commas:

> **Э́то, ка́жется, цита́та *из рома́на «Война́ и мир».***
> I think this is a quotation from the novel *War and Peace.*

> **В про́шлом году́ наш городско́й теа́тр поста́вил че́ховскую *пье́су «Три сестры́».***
> Last year our local theatre put on Chekhov's play *Three Sisters.*

> **Годово́е о́бщее собра́ние акционе́ров *ОАО «Газпро́м»* состоя́лось 29 ию́ня 2007 го́да.**
> The Annual General Meeting of the shareholders of Gazprom PLC took place on 29 June 2007.

> **Я обы́чно покупа́ю проду́кты *в магази́не «Седьмо́й контине́нт».***
> I usually do my food shopping in (the shop) *Sed'moi kontinent* [*The Seventh Continent*].

> **По́езд сле́дует *до ста́нции «Комсомо́льская».***
> This train goes as far as Komsomol'skaia station.

The same principle applies to *names of geographical locations*, except that declension tends to occur when the place is well known and the name is grammatically simple:

> **Я отпра́вился *в г. Бе́лая Кали́тва.***
> I set off for (the town of) Belaia Kalitva.

But

> **Наш по́езд прибы́л на коне́чную ста́нцию в *г. Москву́.***
> Our train has arrived at our terminus in Moscow.

NOTES

(i) In these examples the preposition **в** is followed by the *accusative* case; the abbreviation **г.** stands for **го́род** 'town', 'city'.

(ii) With names of towns and some other geographical terms, English uses a construction with 'of'; in Russian, however, the two nouns are placed in apposition:

> **го́род Бе́лая Кали́тва**   the town of Belaia Kalitva

Names belonging to all these categories are normally declined if the defining term is *not* present:

> **Вы когда́-нибудь чита́ли *«Война́ и мир»?***
> Have you ever read *War and Peace?*

> **Каки́е права́ есть у акционе́ров *«Газпро́ма»?***
> What rights do the shareholders of Gazprom have?

> **Наш по́езд сле́дует то́лько *до «Комсомо́льской».***
> Our train is only going as far as Komsomol'skaia.

> **Ци́фры говоря́т, что в тече́ние го́да ка́ждый четвёртый жи́тель *Бе́лой Кали́твы* обраща́лся к услу́гам ско́рой по́мощи.**
> Figures show that in the course of a year a quarter of the inhabitants of Belaia Kalitva contacted the emergency medical services.

Agreement between subject and verb

General principles

When a *finite verb* is in the *present* or the *future* tense, agreement with the subject in the nominative case is by *person* and *number*:

> **Почему́ *ты* всегда́ встаёшь так ра́но?**
> Why do you always get up so early?

Here the grammatical subject is the *second person singular pronoun* **ты** and consequently, the verb has the ending for the *second person singular, present tense*.

> **Мои́ *роди́тели* приду́т попо́зже.**
> My parents will come a bit later.

Here the grammatical subject is the plural noun **роди́тели**; this is a *third person plural* subject and consequently, the verb has the ending for the *third person plural, future tense*.

When a *finite verb* is in the *past* tense, agreement with the subject in the nominative case is by *number* and *gender*:

> **Я вы́шла за́муж в 1995 г.**
> I got married in 1995.

Here the subject is *first person singular* and *feminine* (in the first and second person singular the grammatical gender is determined by the sex of the speaker or the addressee respectively; here the speaker can be assumed to be a woman since the phrase **вы́йти за́муж** is used only of a woman getting married). Consequently, the verb has the *feminine singular past tense* ending.

For more on the different verbs corresponding to English 'to get married', *see* **12.7**.

The second person pronoun **вы** is always used with a plural verb, even when it is used in formal address to one person:

> **А́нна Ива́новна, пра́вда, что *вы* одна́жды *ви́дели* Ста́лина?**
> Anna Ivanovna, is it true that you once saw Stalin?

For more on formal and informal ways of addressing people, *see* **13.1** and **13.4**.

The pronoun **кто**, whether used as an interrogative or as a relative pronoun, is always used with a verb in the *(masculine) singular* form, even when reference is clearly to more than one person or to a woman:

> **Лу́чше дове́рить э́то де́ло тем, *кто* уже́ *накопи́л* како́й-то о́пыт в э́той сфе́ре.**
> It's best to entrust this matter to those who have already gained some experience in this area.

> **Для тех, *кто рожа́л* пе́рвый раз, проводи́лись специа́льные ле́кции.**
> Special lectures were available for those who were about to give birth for the first time.

11.2.2   Sentences without a grammatical subject

Russian has a large number of *impersonal* constructions, that is, constructions where a *grammatical subject* in the *nominative* case is impossible. In such constructions there is no subject for the verb to agree with, and accordingly it takes on the 'default' form, which is the *third person singular* (*neuter singular* in the *past tense*).

In some of these constructions it is the verb itself that is impersonal:

> **Бы́ло четы́ре часа́, и уже́ *темне́ло*.**
> It was four o'clock and already getting dark.

> **Мне *удало́сь* вы́яснить, каки́е докуме́нты нужны́.**
> I've managed to find out what documents we need.

> **Хоте́лось бы знать побо́льше о его́ пла́нах.**
> One would like to know a bit more about his plans.

In other constructions the place of the verb is taken by an *impersonal predicate form*. These can either take the form of an adverb, such as **хо́лодно, интере́сно** or **хорошо́**, or they can be the *modal predicate forms* **мо́жно** 'one may', 'it is possible'; **нельзя́** 'it is forbidden', 'it is impossible'; **на́до** 'one must'. These forms themselves never change, but in tenses other than the *present*, they are used with the appropriate form of the verb **быть**:

> **Вчера́ *бы́ло* о́чень хо́лодно.**
> It was very cold yesterday.

> **Интере́сно *бы́ло* бы знать его́ то́чку зре́ния по э́тому вопро́су.**
> It would be interesting to know his opinion on this question.

> **Хорошо́ *бы́ло* бы уе́хать куда́-нибудь на юг на па́ру неде́ль.**
> It would be nice to go off to somewhere in the south for a couple of weeks.

> **Ремо́нт кварти́ры уже́ *нельзя́ бы́ло* откла́дывать на пото́м.**
> The refurbishment of the flat could be put off no longer.

> **На́до *бы́ло* сказа́ть об э́том зара́нее.**
> You should have told us about this in advance.

For more on adverbs, *see* **9.1**.

For more on the use of modal predicate forms, *see* **Chapter 18**.

11.2.3   Difficult cases: number

Two *singular* subjects joined by **и** or by **с** (+ instr.) will normally be used with a verb in the *plural*:

> **Росси́я и Украи́на *подписа́ли* но́вый догово́р о поста́вке га́за.**
> Russia and Ukraine have signed a new agreement on gas deliveries.

> **Брат с жено́й *провели́* Но́вый год в А́встрии.**
> My brother and his wife spent New Year in Austria.

This does not apply, however, when a phrase introduced by **с** (+ instr.) is not part of the subject:

> **Мой брат *уе́хал* в Аме́рику с подру́гой.**
> My brother went off to America with a girlfriend.

In English, some collective nouns, such as 'family' or 'government' can be used with either a singular or a plural verb: 'the government has decided' *or* 'the government have decided'. In Russian, this possibility does not exist: collective nouns are grammatically *singular* and must be used with a *singular* verb:

> ***Прави́тельство реши́ло**, что приорите́тной зада́чей в бу́дущем году́ бу́дет борьба́ с инфля́цией.*
>
> The government has decided that its main priority next year will be the battle against inflation.

> **На́ша *семья́* обы́чно *встреча́ет* Но́вый год до́ма.**
>
> Our family usually see(s) in the New Year at home.

> **Наконе́ц-то! В пе́рвый раз в э́том сезо́не на́ша *кома́нда одержа́ла* побе́ду.**
>
> At last! For the first time this season our team has/have managed to win a game.

The one exception to this is the noun **большинство́** 'majority', which, when used with a noun in the *genitive plural*, is frequently used with a plural verb:

> **Подавля́ющее *большинство́ други́х се́кторов* эконо́мики *бу́дут* весьма́ привлека́тельными для инвести́ций.**
>
> The overwhelming majority of the other sectors of the economy will be extremely attractive for investing in.

11.2.4 Difficult cases: numerals and quantity words

When the subject of a sentence consists of or contains a *numeral* or another quantity word, such as **мно́го**, **ма́ло** or **не́сколько**, the verb can be in either the (*neuter*) *singular* or the *plural*. In many instances it is difficult to give hard-and-fast rules, but factors favouring the *plural* are: (i) placing the subject *before* the verb; (ii) an *animate* subject; (iii) the presence of a verb that indicates *activity* on the part of the subject. Conversely, factors favouring the use of the *singular* are: (i) placing the subject *after* the verb; (ii) an *inanimate* subject; (iii) the presence of a verb that does *not* indicate *activity* on the part of the subject. The singular is also more likely to be used when the subject contains a preposition such as **о́коло**.

Examples with *plural* agreement:

> **133 челове́ка в яку́тском посёлке Арты́к две неде́ли *остаю́тся* без тепла́.**
>
> 133 people in the Yakut settlement of Artyk have been left without heating for two weeks.

> **Ране́ния *получи́ли* не́сколько челове́к, среди́ них дво́е военнослу́жащих из континге́нта ООН.**
>
> Several people were wounded, including two soldiers serving in the UN contingent.

NOTE | Here the plural is used, even though not all three factors mentioned above are present.

Examples with *singular* agreement:

> **Здесь *бу́дет постро́ено* де́сять ты́сяч но́вых домо́в.**
>
> Ten thousand new houses are to be built here.

В э́том райо́не *прожива́ет о́коло семи́ ты́сяч* челове́к.
About seven thousand people live in this district.

The (*neuter*) *singular* is always used when the subject is an expression relating to time or to someone's age:

Бы́ло четы́ре часа́, и уже́ темне́ло.
It was four o'clock and already getting dark.

В январе́ э́того го́да ему́ *испо́лнилось со́рок лет*.
In January of this year he turned forty.

Where the subject consists of or contains a numeral form that is unambiguously in the *nominative plural* (for example, **ты́сячи** 'thousands' or **мно́гие** 'many (people)', the verb will always be in the *plural*:

Мно́гие предпочита́ют об э́том не ду́мать.
Many people prefer not to think about that.

11.2.5 **Difficult cases: gender**

In general, gender agreement between subject and verb does not cause problems. In the vast majority of instances there is an automatic match between the grammatical gender of any noun that is the subject of a sentence and the gender of a verb in the past tense. The only circumstance where this does not always apply is when a *masculine* noun is used to refer to a woman. Most masculine nouns used in this way are terms indicating a profession, such as **врач** 'doctor' or **профе́ссор** 'professor', for which there are no feminine equivalents. When this occurs, various patterns of agreement are possible, but the one that occurs most frequently and is most widely recommended is for any adjective used *attributively* with the noun to be *masculine*, but for any past tense verb to be in the *feminine* form:

Наш но́вый врач рекомендова́ла нам побо́льше занима́ться спо́ртом.
Our new (woman) doctor has recommended us to do more sport.

For more on masculine nouns indicating occupations and the absence of feminine equivalents, *see* **12.6.2**.

For more on attributive adjectives, *see* **6.0**.

Part B

Functions

12

Establishing identity

12.0 Introduction

The principal document that confirms the identity of a Russian citizen is known, rather confusingly, as a **па́спорт** 'internal passport', 'identity document'. Russians who travel abroad will also have a **заграни́чный па́спорт** or **загра́нпа́спорт** 'passport'. Many Russians will have an additional identity document, which may be issued by an employer or by some official body, and which is known as an **удостовере́ние** 'identity document'. Students have a **студе́нческий биле́т** 'student card'. As Bulgakov wrote in his novel **«Ма́стер и Маргари́та»**:

> **Нет докуме́нта, нет и челове́ка.**
> If there's no document, then there's no person either.

12.1 Russian names

12.1.0 Introduction

Those who read Russian novels, especially in translation, are sometimes heard to complain about the apparent complexity of Russian names. It is true that the variety of names by which any individual Russian can be addressed is slightly larger than would be the case in English-speaking countries, but the complexity is more apparent than real: all Russian names follow a standard pattern and the range of possibilities is determined by a few specific rules of grammar and etiquette.

In this section we discuss the formation of Russian names. How these forms are used in addressing people is dealt with in **13.4**.

All Russians have *three* names: a *forename* (**и́мя**), a *patronymic* (**о́тчество**) and a *surname* (**фами́лия**). The forename is bestowed individually, the patronymic is normally derived from the name of the holder's father, and the surname, as elsewhere, is passed down through the family. The names are usually given in the order: **и́мя – о́тчество – фами́лия**, but in some formal and official contexts the order can be changed to **фами́лия – и́мя – о́тчество**. The following are examples of Russian names in the order **и́мя – о́тчество – фами́лия**:

Андре́й Па́влович Ивано́в
Лев Никола́евич Толсто́й
Светла́на Па́вловна Ивано́ва
Со́фья Андре́евна Толста́я

NOTE | In written texts of all types, Russian names often appear in the form of two initials followed by the surname, for example, **Л.Н. Толстой, С.П. Иванова**. When these are read out, the normal convention is to say the name in full; if the forename and patronymic are not known, just the surname should be read out.

12.1.1 Russian forenames

Most (though not all) Russian forenames come in several different versions, of which *two* are particularly important.

The first of these is the *full* or *formal version*: this is the version given on birth certificates and in passports or other identity documents.

The second is the *familiar* or *informal* version that is used in a wide range of social contexts, for example, between friends, siblings and in addressing children. Although the familiar version is derived from the full version, the link between them is in some cases not immediately transparent.

NOTE | Although the relationship between the full and the familiar versions can in some respects be compared to the relationship between English 'Robert' and 'Bob', there is an important difference: in English, the decision to use a familiar version is usually a matter of personal preference; in Russian there are circumstances where the use of the familiar version is more or less obligatory. These are discussed in **13.4.1**.

The following tables give the full and familiar versions of the principal Russian forenames:

Male forenames

Full name	*Familiar version*
Алекса́ндр	Са́ша, Шу́ра, Са́ня
Алексе́й	Алёша, Лёша
Анато́лий	То́ля
Бори́с	Бо́ря
Валенти́н	Ва́ля
Васи́лий	Ва́ся
Ви́ктор	Ви́тя
Влади́мир	Воло́дя, Во́ва
Генна́дий	Ге́на
Григо́рий	Гри́ша
Дми́трий	Ди́ма, Ми́тя
Евге́ний	Же́ня
Ива́н	Ва́ня
Константи́н	Ко́стя
Михаи́л	Ми́ша
Никола́й	Ко́ля
Паве́л	Па́ша
Пётр	Пе́тя
Серге́й	Серёжа
Ю́рий	Ю́ра

Female forenames

Full name	Familiar version
Алекса́ндра	Са́ша, Шу́ра
Анастаси́я	На́стя
А́нна	А́ня
Валенти́на	Ва́ля
Гали́на	Га́ля
Да́рья	Да́ша
Евге́ния	Же́ня
Екатери́на	Ка́тя
Еле́на	Ле́на
Лари́са	Ла́ра
Любо́вь	Лю́ба
Людми́ла	Лю́да
Мари́я	Ма́ша
Наде́жда	На́дя
Ната́лья	Ната́ша
О́льга	О́ля
Светла́на	Све́та
Со́фия	Со́ня
Татья́на	Та́ня

NOTE Some familiar names can be formed both from a male and a female name – for example, Ва́ля (from Валенти́н and Валенти́на), Же́ня (from Евге́ний and Евге́ния), Са́ша and Шу́ра (from Алекса́ндр and Алекса́ндра).

Many names tend not to have separate familiar forms; these include the following:

Male names: Андре́й, Дени́с, И́горь, Макси́м, Оле́г

Female names: А́лла, Окса́на, Тама́ра

Additional expressive versions of forenames can be formed from the familiar version using the diminutive suffixes described in **10.1.2** and **10.1.3**. These can be illustrated by the following:

Во́ва – Во́вочка – Во́вик – Во́вчик
А́ня – А́нечка – А́ннушка – Аню́та – Ню́ша – Ню́ра

Although it is useful to be able to recognise these forms, their use carries with it significant connotations and nuances of attitude. Learners are therefore advised that they should be very sure of their ground before attempting to use them.

For more on the use of these forms, *see* **16.1.4**.

In general the full, familiar and expressive versions of Russian forenames all decline predictably according the patterns given in **Chapter 2**. The following specific points may be noted, however: the name **Па́вел** has a fleeting vowel, **Любо́вь**, when used as a forename, has no fleeting vowel.

For more on the fleeting vowel, *see* **2.5**.

12.1.2 **Patronymics**

The *patronymic* is derived from the forename of the bearer's father, using different suffixes for the male and female versions. The patronymic is always derived from the full version of the forename.

Patronymics are formed as follows:

1 If the forename ends in a *consonant*, the *male* version is formed by adding **-ович** and the *female* version by adding **-овна**:

Ива́н	Ива́нович	Ива́новна
Пётр	Петро́вич	Петро́вна
Па́вел	Па́влович	Па́вловна

NOTE | If the forename contains a *fleeting vowel*, this is removed before forming the patronymic.

2 If the forename ends in **-ей**, the final letter is removed and **-евич** is added to form the *male* version and **-евна** to form the *female* version:

Алексе́й	Алексе́евич	Алексе́евна
Серге́й	Серге́евич	Серге́евна

3 If the forename ends in **-ий**, the final two letters are removed and **-ьевич** is added to form the *male* version and **-ьевна** to form the *female* version:

Анато́лий	Анато́льевич	Анато́льевна
Ю́рий	Ю́рьевич	Ю́рьевна

4 If the forename ends in **-ь**, the final letter is removed and **-евич** is added to form the *male* version and **-евна** to form the *female* version:

И́горь	И́горевич	И́горевна

5 If the forename ends in **-а** or **-я**, the male version is formed by removing the last letter and adding **-ич**; the female version is formed by removing the last letter and adding **-инична** (if the ending is stressed) or **-ична** (if the ending is unstressed):

Кузьма́	Кузьми́ч	Кузьми́нична
Ники́та	Ники́тич	Ники́тична
Илья́	Ильи́ч	Ильи́нична

In all but the most formal levels of spoken language, patronymics are shortened in pronunciation:

Миха́йлович	Миха́лыч	Миха́лна
Никола́евич	Никола́ич	Никола́вна
Серге́евич	Серге́ич	Серге́вна
Алекса́ндрович	Алекса́ндрыч	Алекса́нна
	(*or* Алекса́ныч	
	or Са́ныч)	
Па́влович	Па́лыч	Па́лна

In informal speech some combinations of name and patronymic can be reduced even further:

Алекса́ндр Алекса́ндрович   Сан Са́ныч
Па́вел Па́влович   Пал Па́лыч

For more information on the use of the patronymic in addressing people, *see* **13.4.2** and **13.4.3**.

The following points may be noted here:

1   The patronymic may be combined only with the full form of the forename.

2   Because all citizens of Russia are required to have a patronymic, these can be formed, where necessary, from non-Russian names:

Альфре́д Рейнго́льдович Кох
Серге́й Кужуге́тович Шойгу́
Шами́ль Вялиу́ллович Ха́йров
Ири́на Муцу́евна Хакама́да

3   Although it is normal practice to form the patronymic automatically from the forename of the bearer's father, there is no actual legal requirement to do so, and in appropriate circumstances (for example, when someone is adopted) a patronymic may be bestowed or even changed.

12.1.3   **Russian surnames**

Most Russian *surnames* belong to one or other of the following patterns:

1   Surnames ending in **–ов(а)/-ев(а)/-ёв(а)** or **-ин(а)/-ын(а)**: this is the most frequently encountered pattern. Surnames following this pattern have *masculine*, *feminine* and *plural* forms:

Masculine	*Feminine*	*Plural*
Бурми́стров	Бурми́строва	Бурми́стровы
Кузнецо́в	Кузнецо́ва	Кузнецо́вы
Серге́ев	Серге́ева	Серге́евы
Ми́шин	Ми́шина	Ми́шины
Пти́цын	Пти́цына	Пти́цыны

The declension of these surnames is given in **2.12.1**.

2   Surnames that take the form of adjectives. These too have separate *masculine*, *feminine* and *plural* forms:

Masculine	*Feminine*	*Plural*
Бе́лый	Бе́лая	Бе́лые
Петро́вский	Петро́вская	Петро́вские
Садо́вничий	Садо́вничая	Садо́вничие
Толсто́й	Толста́я	Толсты́е

For more on these surnames, *see* **6.4.2**.

3 Surnames (other than those following patterns (1) and (2)) ending in a consonant, in -й or in -ь. The *masculine* and *feminine* forms are indentical in the *nominative*, but while the masculine forms decline according to the patterns given in **2.6**, the feminine forms are indeclinable; the plural forms tend to be avoided:

Абрамо́вич	Швец
Борисе́вич	Ковту́н
Шевчу́к	Воробе́й
Третья́к	Го́голь

NOTE It is important to distinguish surnames ending in **-о́вич** or **-е́вич** from male patronymics that may be similar in appearance. The surnames differ from the patronymics in two ways: (i) the stress in the nominative is always on the second last syllable; (ii) in the nominative, the feminine is identical to the masculine.

For more on the declension of these surnames, *see* **2.12.2** and **2.13.1**.

4 Surnames ending in **-a** or **-я**. These normally decline following the patterns described in **2.9**. The plural forms are not used:

Гли́нка
Ку́чма

5 Surnames ending in **-o** (including Ukrainian surnames ending in **-ко, -енко**). These are *indeclinable*:

Жива́го
Стижко́
Шевче́нко

For more on indeclinable surnames, *see* **2.13.1**.

NOTE On getting married, Russian women may either keep their maiden name or adopt their husband's surname. The practice of joining the two names with a hyphen is rare. The Russian for 'maiden name' is **де́вичья фами́лия**.

12.2 Foreign names

In general, Russians do not 'russify' foreign names. Instead, the preferred option is to transliterate or to transcribe the name according to the principles given in **1.6.5** and **1.6.6**. If the result fits into one of the declension patterns described in **Chapter 2**, the name will be declined accordingly; if not, it will be *indeclinable*. This principle applies to both *forenames* and *surnames*:

John Dunn   Джон Данн

Both parts can be declined according to the pattern given in **2.6.1**:

Я разгова́ривал с Джо́ном Да́нном.
I was talking to John Dunn.

Marie Dunn   Мари́ Данн

Both parts are *indeclinable*, following the rules given in **2.13.1**:

Я разгова́ривал с Мари́ Данн.
I was talking to Marie Dunn.

Anna Smith   **А́нна Смит**

The forename can be declined according to the pattern given in **2.7.1**; the surname is indeclinable following the rules given in **2.13.1**:

Я разгова́ривал с А́нной Смит.
I was talking to Anna Smith.

It may be useful to note the following points about foreign names:

1   It is not customary to create informal or expressive versions of foreign forenames.

2   Although some choose to adopt one, presumably from a desire to appear more 'Russian', in general, foreigners are neither required nor expected to have a patronymic.

3   Names originating in languages other than English are transliterated or transcribed according to the rules applicable to that language. This can produce forms that are not immediately recognisable to English speakers:

French:	**Гюго́**	(Victor) Hugo
	Дюма́	Dumas
German:	**Гёте**	Goethe
Italian:	**Толья́тти**	Togliatti
Chinese:	**Ма́о Цзе-ду́н**	Mao Zedong (Mao Tse-tung)

4   There is an exception to the general practice of not 'russifying' foreign names. Female forenames ending in a consonant may sometimes have two forms: a form derived by direct transcription/transliteration and ending in a consonant, and a form ending in **-а** or **-я**, which may be adjusted to be identical with a similar-sounding Russian forename. The former is used in official documents, such as visas, but the latter tends to be preferred in ordinary conversation:

| Louise | **Луи́з** | **Луи́за** |
| Margaret | **Ма́ргарет** | **Маргари́та** |

12.3 Talking about people's ages

12.3.1 Saying how old you are

When talking abut someone's age, the person in question is normally indicated by a *pronoun*, *noun* or *noun phrase* in the *dative*.

The normal way of asking about someone's age is as follows:

Ско́лько тебе́ лет?
How old are you?

Ско́лько лет ва́шей до́чери?
How old is your daughter?

NOTE | If the person is indicated by a pronoun, this will normally be placed before **лет**; a noun or a noun phrase normally follows **лет** (as in the above examples).

The answers to these questions may be:

> **Мне пятьдеся́т во́семь (лет).**
> I'm fifty-eight (years old).

> **Мое́й до́чери два́дцать оди́н (год).**
> My daughter's twenty-one (years old).

For the different forms of the noun used with these numerals, *see* **8.2.1**, **8.2.2** and **8.2.3**.

In the *past* tense, the *neuter singular* form of **быть** is used.
In the *future* tense, the *third person singular* of **быть** is used:

> **Ей *бы́ло* всего́ *два го́да*, когда́ роди́тели отда́ли её в я́сли.**
> She was only two years old when her parents put her into a nursery.

> **На́шему го́роду ско́ро *бу́дет ты́сяча лет*.**
> Our city will soon be a thousand years old.

Although this construction is mostly used with reference to people and animals, it can sometimes be used, as this last example shows, to refer to inanimate objects.

When referring to a change in someone's age, the verb **исполня́ться/испо́лниться** is used:

> **В октябре́ *ему́ испо́лнится восемна́дцать* (лет): зна́чит, он смо́жет получи́ть права́ и води́ть маши́ну.**
> In October he will be eighteen (years old); he'll be able to get a driving licence and start driving a car.

The most frequently used means of indicating an approximate age is to put the numeral after the noun:

> **Мне бы́ло *лет де́сять*, когда́ меня́ пе́рвый раз взя́ли на рыба́лку с ночёвкой.**
> I was about ten years old when I was first taken on an overnight fishing trip.

To indicate an approximate age *above* a certain limit, a construction with the preposition **за** (+ acc.) can be used (the words **год/лет** are omitted):

> **Ему́ *за три́дцать*.**
> He's over thirty.

To indicate an approximate age *below* a certain limit, a construction with **нет и** is used; the numeral indicating the age is in the *genitive* and the words **год/лет** are usually omitted:

> **Ей *нет и двадцати́* (лет).**
> She isn't yet twenty.

12.3.2 Talking about age using adjectives

The age of a person can also be indicated using an *adjective*. These adjectives are mostly formed from the combination *numeral + noun*. They can be illustrated by the following examples:

двухме́сячный	two-month-old
девятиме́сячный	nine-month-old
двухле́тний	two-year-old
двадцатиле́тний	twenty-year-old
двадцатипятиле́тний	twenty-five-year-old
сорокале́тний	forty-year-old

Он жени́лся на *двадцатиле́тней* **студе́нтке.**
He married a twenty-year-old student.

For more on the formation of these adjectives, *see* **10.2.7**.

NOTE The adjective corresponding to 'one-year-old' is **годова́лый**. Adjectives formed from numerals ending in **оди́н** 'one' (e.g. **два́дцать оди́н** 'twenty-one') are problematic and best to be avoided.

12.3.3 Other ways of talking about age

The following *prepositional* constructions are used when talking about age:

в (+ acc.)	at the age of
в во́зрасте (+ gen.)	at the age of
с (+ gen.)	from the age of
до (+ gen.)	up to the age of
к (+ dat.)	by the age of

Он научи́лся игра́ть в ша́хматы *в четы́ре го́да.*
He learned to play chess at the age of four (*or* when he was four).

Она́ овдове́ла *в во́зрасте тридцати́ двух лет.*
She was widowed at the age of thirty-two.

В бале́тную сту́дию принима́ют *с пяти́ лет.*
They accept (children) at ballet school from the age of five upwards.

Он дирижи́ровал орке́стром *до восьми́десяти лет.*
He continued to conduct the orchestra up to the age of eighty (*or* until he was eighty).

Она́ сохраня́ла я́сность мы́сли и бо́дрость ду́ха *до глубо́кой ста́рости.*
She remained clear-headed and cheerful until well into her old age.

К сорока́ года́м **он полысе́л, обзавёлся брюшко́м и оста́вил свои́ революцио́нные иде́и.**
By the time he was forty, he had gone bald, acquired a paunch and abandoned his revolutionary ideas.

12.4 Addresses

12.4.1 Postal addresses

Traditionally, addresses on Russian envelopes were written in the reverse order from that normally used in English-speaking countries, that is, starting with the largest unit and ending with the smallest; the recipient, usually in the *dative* case, came at the end. Now, however, the Russian Post Office recommends following international practice, starting with the recipient and listing the address working from the smallest unit to the largest. The recipient still tends to be indicated in the dative, although names of organisations are more likely to be in the *nominative*. It is reasonable to assume that for the time being both systems are being used, and they can be illustrated by the following examples:

Traditional system

Postcode + republic or region	**185014 р. Карелия**
City, town or village	**г. Петрозаводск**
Street name	**ул. Гоголя**
Street number + flat number	**д. 21, корп. 3, кв. 46**
Recipient (in the dative)	**Касьянову Глебу Сергеевичу**

NOTE | Lines 3 and 4 could be combined if space allowed. The abbreviation **корп.** (**корпус** 'block') is used to distinguish between several buildings that share the same street number.

New system (personal recipient)

Recipient (in the dative)	**Касьянову Глебу Сергеевичу**
Street name + street and flat numbers	**ул. Гоголя, д. 21, корп. 3, кв. 46**
City, town or village	**г. Петрозаводск**
Republic or region	**р. Карелия**
Postcode	**185014**

If the recipient is an organisation

Name of organisation (in the nominative)	**Клуб юных моряков «Парус»**
City, town or village	**пос. Солнечное**
District	**Сестрорецкий р-н**
Republic or region	**Ленинградская обл.**
Postcode	**197720**

NOTE | Because the second address is located in a large village, no street name or number is needed, but an extra administrative layer (**райо́н** 'district') is required.

The following abbreviations are used in postal addresses:

к.	ко́мната	room
кв.	кварти́ра	flat
корп.	ко́рпус	block
д.	дом	house, building
б-р	бульва́р	avenue

пер.	переулок	alley
пр.	проспект	avenue
ш.	шоссе	highway, road
ул.	улица	street
пл.	площадь	square
п/я	почтовый ящик	PO box
пос.	посёлок	large village, settlement
дер.	деревня	(small) village, hamlet
с.	село	village
г.	город	town, city
р-н	район	district
обл.	область	region
р.	республика	republic

Two abbreviations that are used regionally are:

а.	аул	village (in the Caucasus)
х.	хутор	village (in Cossack areas)

The following terms are also useful in indicating addresses:

до востребования	poste restante
почтовый индекс	postcode

If a letter is intended for a person other than the addressee, a construction with **для** (+ gen.) is used:

Мишиной С.А (для Даши).
Dasha c/o S.A. Mishina.

`12.4.2` ## Finding one's way

When indicating how to get to a particular location the following terms may be used:

станция	(metro or railway) station
остановка	(bus or tram) stop
светофор	traffic lights
перекрёсток	road junction, crossroads
въезд	entry (for vehicles)
двор	yard, back courtyard
подъезд	entry (to a block of flats), stairway
этаж	floor, storey
дверь	door
вход со двора	the entrance is located in the back courtyard
домофон	entry-phone
кодовый замок	a lock with an entry code

NOTE

The term **первый этаж** corresponds to (British) English 'ground floor'; similarly, **второй этаж** corresponds to 'first floor', and so on.

Скажите таксисту, что вход в подъезд не с улицы, а со двора. Въезд во двор сразу за перекрёстком. У нас третий подъезд. Домофон не работает. В подъезде кодовый замок. Код 345. Поднимайтесь на лифте на девятый этаж, квартира 36, это вторая дверь направо.

Tell the taxi driver that the entrances to the building are in the back courtyard, not in the street. There's an entry for vehicles just past the crossroads. Our flat is on the third staircase. The entry-phone isn't working, but there is a lock with an entry code. The code is 345. Take the lift to the ninth (eighth) floor. Our flat is number 36; it's the second door on the right.

12.4.3 **Registration**

Each indivdual in the Russian Federation is supposed to be officially registered at a specific address, which is indicated by a stamp in his/her **па́спорт** (see **12.0**). The term now officially used for this procedure is **регистра́ция**, but the older word **пропи́ска** is still in common use. The verbs used in relation to this process are:

регистри́ровать/зарегистри́ровать	to register (someone)
пропи́сывать/прописа́ть	to register (someone)
регистри́роваться/зарегистри́роваться	to be registered
пропи́сываться/прописа́ться	to be registered
прожива́ть	to reside (at), to be resident (at)

—**По како́му а́дресу вы** *прописаны (зарегистри́рованы)*?
—**Я** *пропи́сан* **по а́дресу: Санкт-Петербу́рг, Садо́вая, три́дцать четы́ре, кварти́ра два́дцать пять, но я там** *не прожива́ю.*

—What address are you registered at?
—I'm registered in St Petersburg, at 34 Sadovaia, flat 25, but I don't actually live there.

На вре́мя учёбы ба́бушка *прописа́ла* **его́ у себя́.**
While he was a student, he was registered at his grandmother's (address).

У меня́ вообще́-то нет моско́вской *регистра́ции*: **я** *пропи́сана* **в Ряза́ни.**
I don't have a registration for Moscow; I'm officially registered as living in Riazan'.

NOTE | As these examples may suggest, there is often a considerable gap between the requirements of officialdom and the demands of real life.

12.5 **Citizenship and nationality**

12.5.1 Гражда́нство and национа́льность

In Russian, a very clear distinction is normally made between the following two concepts:

гражда́нство	citizenship, nationality
национа́льность	ethnic identity

In Soviet times the *национа́льность* was a part of every citizen's identity; it was shown in the **па́спорт** (see **12.0**) and usually had to be indicated on official forms. Alhough this tends no longer to be the case, the concept of *национа́льность* remains very relevant in the Russian multi-ethnic context.

NOTE | In the lists that follow the *masculine* form is placed to the *left* of the slash (*/*) and the *feminine* form is placed to the *right*.

The following terms are seen as relating to *национа́льность*:

In the context of Russia

евре́й/евре́йка	Jew
калмы́к/калмы́чка	Kalmyck
ру́сский/ру́сская	Russian
тата́рин/тата́рка	Tatar
чече́нец/чече́нка	Chechen

In other contexts

валли́ец/валли́йка	Welshman, Welshwoman
катало́нец/катало́нка	Catalan
цыга́н/цыга́нка	Roma
шотла́ндец/шотла́ндка	Scot

Кто вы по национа́льности?
What is your ethnic identity?

Я тата́рин.
I am a Tatar.

The following terms refer specifically to *гражда́нство*:

брита́нец/брита́нка	citizen of Great Britain
россия́нин/россия́нка	citizen of Russia

Како́е у вас гражда́нство?
What is your nationality *or* citizenship?

Я брита́нец *or* **Я гражда́нин Великобрита́нии.**
I am British *or* I am a citizen of Great Britain.

Many terms can be used in either sense:

америка́нец/америка́нка	American
армяни́н/армя́нка	Armenian
италья́нец/италья́нка	Italian
не́мец/не́мка	German
украи́нец/украи́нка	Ukrainian
финн/фи́нка	Finn
францу́з/францу́женка	Frenchman/Frenchwoman

For more on the suffixes used, *see* **10.1.8** and **10.1.9**.

12.5.2 Росси́йский and ру́сский

It will be noticed from the preceding section that Russian has separate terms for the concept of 'Russian', depending on whether reference is to *гражда́нство* or *национа́льность*. The noun **россия́нин/россия́нка** and the associated adjective **росси́йский** refer to Russia as a state and a political unit, and hence, to the concept of Russian citizenship; the term **ру́сский**, which is both noun and adjective, refers to Russian language, culture and ethnicity. It has to be said that the distinction has been important only since 1991 and is not universally observed; it can also be difficult on occasion to work out which term is more appropriate. Nevertheless, the following collocations give some indication of how the two terms are used:

российский флаг	Russian flag
российский президент	Russian president
российский спортсмен	Russian sportsman
российская а́рмия	Russian army
российская исто́рия	history of Russia
российское гражда́нство	Russian citizenship
российское руково́дство	Russia's leaders
ру́сский язы́к	Russian language
ру́сский хара́ктер	Russian character
ру́сский фолькло́р	Russian folklore
ру́сский худо́жник	Russian artist
ру́сская литерату́ра	Russian literature
ру́сская ку́хня	Russian cooking
ру́сская наро́дная му́зыка	Russian folk music
ру́сское хлебосо́льство	(traditional) Russian hospitality

In international contexts the language factor often plays the key role in defining a person or an object as **ру́сский**:

ру́сские фи́льмы	Russian films
ру́сские газе́ты	Russian(-language) newspapers

12.6 Occupations

12.6.1 Talking about one's occupation

The following questions can be used to ask about somebody's occupation:

> **Кто вы по профе́сии?**
> **Кака́я у вас профе́ссия?**
> **Чем вы занима́етесь?**
> **Кем вы рабо́таете?**

All these can be translated as:

> What do you do for a living?

Answers might be:

> **(По профе́ссии) я инжене́р.**
> (By profession) I'm an engineer.

> **Я рабо́таю бухга́лтером.**
> I work as an accountant.

In these contexts **занима́ться** and **рабо́тать** are used with the *instrumental* case. For more information, *see* **3.5.5** and **3.5.7**.

Other terms used in relation to employment include:

до́лжность	position
зва́ние	rank (e.g. in the armed forces)
слу́жба	service (e.g. in the armed forces)
рабо́тник	worker (someone who works in a particular place)
рабо́чий	worker (member of the working class)

сотру́дник	someone who works for a particular organisation, official, employee
служи́ть	to serve (e.g. in the armed forces or in government service)
зараба́тывать/зарабо́тать	to earn
подраба́тывать/подрабо́тать	to moonlight
подхалту́ривать/подхалту́рить	to moonlight

Её муж сле́дователь, *слу́жит* в прокурату́ре. На *слу́жбу* хо́дит в шта́тском.
Her husband's an investigator for the prosecutor's office. He goes to work in civilian dress.

Госуда́рство обя́зано забо́титься о *рабо́тниках* бюдже́тной сфе́ры.
The state has an obligation to take care of those who work in the public sector.

***Сотру́дник* аэропо́рта проверя́л все поса́дочные тало́ны.**
An airport official was checking all the boarding cards.

В тру́дные для семьи́ го́ды она́ *подраба́тывала* перево́дами и ча́стными уро́ками.
When times were difficult for her family, she earned a bit of extra money doing translations and giving private lessons.

Мно́гие столи́чные студе́нты *подхалту́ривают* в массо́вках на «Мосфи́льме».
Many Moscow students earn a bit extra by working as extras for Mosfilm.

12.6.2 Occupation and gender

As was noted in **10.1.9**, some, but not all nouns indicating holders of jobs or members of professions have separate *masculine* and *feminine* nouns. From this point of view these nouns can be divided into several categories.

1   Nouns with only a *masculine* form, which is used for both men and women. This is the largest group and is found particularly widely in relation to 'high-prestige' professions:

архите́ктор	architect
водола́з	diver
врач	doctor
гео́лог	geologist (the same applies to all other nouns ending in -олог)
депута́т	deputy (in a parliament)
космона́вт	cosmonaut
лётчик	pilot
мини́стр	minister
офице́р	officer (in the armed forces) (the same applies to all ranks in the armed forces)
пе́карь	baker
профе́ссор	professor
режиссёр	(film) director
сле́сарь	metal worker, locksmith, repair man
строи́тель	builder
фи́зик	physicist

2 Some nouns have separate *masculine* and *feminine* forms with equal status; the use depends solely on the sex of the person concerned:

актёр/актри́са	actor
официа́нт/официа́нтка	waiter/waitress
певе́ц/певи́ца	singer
танцо́р/танцо́рка, танцо́вщица	dancer
танцо́вщик/танцо́вщица, балери́на	ballet dancer

3 In some instances, the *feminine* form is restricted to informal language, while in formal language the *masculine* is used to refer to both sexes:

воспита́тель/воспита́тельница	teacher (e.g. in a kindergarten)
преподава́тель/преподава́тельница	teacher (in a college or university)
продаве́ц/продавщи́ца	salesperson
учи́тель/учи́тельница	teacher (in a school)
худо́жник/худо́жница	artist

4 In the following cases the *feminine* form, though widely used in informal language, may be perceived as derogatory:

касси́р/касси́рша	cashier
секрета́рь/секрета́рша	secretary

NOTES

(i) Only the masculine form **секрета́рь** would be used to refer to someone who holds high office in a political party or an academic institution.

(ii) Other feminine forms ending in **-ша** or **-иха** are unreservedly derogatory and should be avoided.

5 Some nouns have only a *feminine* form:

акуше́рка	midwife
го́рничная	(chamber)maid
медсестра́	nurse
ня́ня	nanny
пра́чка	laundrywoman

NOTE

The term **медбра́т** 'male nurse' is possible in theory, but very rare in practice.

6 There is one 'asymmetric' pair:

машини́ст	locomotive driver
машини́стка	typist

For information on the question of grammatical agreement when masculine nouns are used to refer to a woman, *see* **11.2.5**.

12.7 Talking about marital status

Talking about marital status in Russian is complicated by the fact that different words are used, depending on whether you are talking about a man, a woman or a couple. The following are the main terms found in this context:

муж	husband
жена	wife
супру́г/супру́га	spouse (used more often than the English equivalent)
жени́х	bridegroom, fiancé
неве́ста	bride, fiancée
жени́ться (нсв/св) на (+ prep.)	to get married (of a man)
выходи́ть/вы́йти за́муж за (+ acc.)	to get married (of a woman)
пожени́ться (св)	to get married (of a couple)
быть жена́т(ым) на (+ prep.)	to be married (of a man)
быть за́мужем за (+ instr.)	to be married (of a woman)
жена́тый	married (of a man)
заму́жняя	married (of a woman)
холостя́к	bachelor
незаму́жняя же́нщина	unmarried woman

For more on the use of the instrumental long form and the short form of adjectives such as жена́т(ый), *see* **14.1.4**.

сва́дьба	wedding
брак	marriage
супру́жество	matrimony, wedlock
жени́тьба	marriage (referring to a man)
заму́жество	marriage (referring to a woman)
ЗАГС	register office
гражда́нский брак	unofficial marriage, civil partnership
расписываться/расписа́ться (в ЗА́ГСе)	to get married (at the register office) [*literally*, to sign the register], to take the plunge

For more on the acronym **ЗАГС**, *see* **2.14.1**.

разво́д	divorce
разводи́ться/развести́сь	to get divorced
разведённый	divorced
расходи́ться/разойти́сь	to split up

In recent years some terms borrowed from English have started to be used, especially in the mass media:

бойфре́нд	boyfriend
партнёр	partner

Он жени́лся на двадцатиле́тней студе́нтке.
He married a twenty-year-old student.

Она́ вы́шла за́муж за иностра́нца.
She married a foreigner.

Он жена́т на изве́стной писа́тельнице.
He's married to a famous writer.

Она́ за́мужем за сотру́дником нало́говой инспе́кции.
She's married to someone who works at the tax office.

Они́ пожени́лись в про́шлом году́.
They got married last year.

В тече́ние двадцати́ лет они́ жи́ли в *гражда́нском бра́ке*, но в про́шлом году́ они́ наконе́ц *расписа́лись*.
For twenty years they lived together (in a civil partnership), but last year they finally took the plunge and got married.

Наско́лько я зна́ю, он *разведён*.
As far as I know, he's divorced.

Да, то́чно. Они́ *развели́сь* два го́да наза́д.
Yes, that's right. They got divorced two years ago.

13

Establishing contact

13.1 ## Formal and informal address

Russian has two *second person pronouns* that correspond to English 'you': **ты** and **вы**. Their use is determined by the following rules and guidelines.

When addressing more than one person, only the *plural* pronoun **вы** can be used.

When addressing one person the *singular* pronoun **ты** is used when addressing a child, an animal, a member of one's family or a person with whom one is on informal terms; it is also the form used in prayers. In other circumstances, that is, when addressing an adult with whom one is not on informal terms, the pronoun **вы** is used.

For the rules of agreement between the pronoun **вы** and the verb, *see* **11.2.1**.

In transactions between adults **вы** is the default form, and the switch to **ты** is usually by mutual agreement. The person initiating the switch may say:

> **Дава́йте перейдём на «ты».**
> Let's switch to 'ty', shall we?

It is hard to give absolute rules for the use of **ты** and **вы**, since much depends on circumstances and on individual habits and preferences. In general, the younger people are, the more quickly they will switch to **ты**, and, other things being equal, two people of the same sex may switch more rapidly than two people of different sexes. The use of **ты** and **вы** between adults is supposed to be equal and mutual, but the practice of addressing inferiors with **ты** and superiors with **вы** is found in many hierarchical situations.

The use of many of the greetings and forms of address dealt with in the later sections of this chapter are closely linked to the use of **ты** and **вы**.

For the occurrence of capital letters with the pronouns **Вы** and **Ваш** when they are used in letters to address one person, *see* **1.5.7**.

13.2 ## Greetings

13.2.1 ### The greeting здра́вствуй /здра́вствуйте

The greeting **здра́вствуй /здра́вствуйте** is a useful all-purpose greeting that corresponds fairly closely to the English 'hello'. It can be used at any time of the day and in a wide variety of situations. **Здра́вствуй** is used when speaking to someone one would address with **ты**; otherwise, **здра́вствуйте** is used:

> *Здра́вствуйте*, сади́тесь. Начина́ем уро́к.
>
> Good morning. Sit down. Let's get on with the lesson (in school).

> *Здра́вствуйте*, уважа́емые радиослу́шатели.
>
> Hello, listeners.

> —*Здра́вствуйте*, Джейн.
> —*Здра́вствуйте*, Бори́с Бори́сович. Как вы пожива́ете?
> —**Спаси́бо, неплóхо, а вы?**

> —Hello, Jane.
> —Hello, Boris Borisovich. How are you?
> —Not bad, thank you. And how about you?

> —*Здра́вствуйте*, Ири́на Алексе́евна.
> —*Здра́вствуй*, Ко́ля. Что у тебя́ но́венького?
> —**Мне ма́ма купи́ла соба́ку.**

> —Hello, Irina Alekseevna.
> —Hello Kolia. What news have you got?
> —Mummy's bought me a dog.

For the pronunciation of **здра́вствуй(те)**, *see* **1.2.6**.

For more on the names and forms of address, *see* **13.4** and **13.5.2**.

13.2.2 Informal greetings

The most widely used informal greeting is **приве́т**, which can be used when greeting a single person or a group. Also found, though less often, are **здоро́во**, which contains a strong element of familiarity and which is more characteristic of male speech, and **салю́т**.

> *Приве́т*, Ла́ра, как у тебя́ дела́?
>
> Hi, Lara. How are things?

> —*Здоро́во*, мужики́. Игра́ давно́ начала́сь? Како́й счёт?
> —*Приве́т*. Мину́т пять наза́д. Пока́ по нуля́м.

> —Hi lads, has the game been going long? What's the score?
> —Hi. About five minutes. It's still nil-nil.

Приве́т can also be used both in speech and writing with the meaning 'regards', 'best wishes':

> —*Переда́йте приве́т* роди́телям и ба́бушке.
> —**Непреме́нно переда́м.**

> —Pass on my regards to your parents and your grandmother.
> —I most certainly will.

The verb **передава́ть /переда́ть** is often omitted:

> Ну что ж, счастли́вого пути́! *Приве́т* жене́. В сле́дующий раз приезжа́йте вме́сте.
>
> Well, then, have a pleasant journey. Regards to your wife. Next time the two of you must come.

Приве́т из Вене́ции! Тут мно́го воды́, ло́док и тури́стов.
Best wishes from Venice! There's a lot of water, a lot of boats and a lot of tourists.

Приве́т от Воло́ди.
Regards from Volodia.

13.2.3 Other greetings

The following greetings are specific to a particular part of the day; they are slightly more formal than **здра́вствуйте**:

до́брое у́тро	good morning
до́брый день	good day, good afternoon
до́брый ве́чер	good evening

До́брое у́тро, Никола́й Ива́нович. Как пожива́ете?
Good morning, Nikolai Ivanovich. How are you?

До́брый ве́чер. Начина́ем наш вы́пуск с обзо́ра гла́вных собы́тий дня.
Good evening. We begin our bulletin with a round-up of the main events of day.

The verb **приве́тствовать** is now slightly obsolete, but it is still used on formal and ceremonial occasions:

Мы ра́ды *приве́тствовать* вас в на́шем го́роде.
We are delighted to welcome you to our city.

Добро́ пожа́ловать means 'welcome' and for the most part is used in formal situations or on signs; it is often followed by the prepositions **в** or **на** (+ acc.).

А вот и го́сти. *Добро́ пожа́ловать*! Проходи́те, раздева́йтесь.
Here are our guests. Welcome! Please come in and take off your coats.

Добро́ пожа́ловать в Москву́!
Welcome to Moscow!

13.2.4 Saying goodbye

The most widely used and most neutral way of saying goodbye is the phrase **до свида́ния**. Less widely used are the extended version **до ско́рого свида́ния** and its shortened informal version **до ско́рого**.

Всего́ (вам) до́брого, **всего́ хоро́шего** are slightly more formal and often used as a reply to **до свида́ния** in order to avoid repetition.

Пока́ is particularly common in informal situations, especially among younger people; it is normally used only with people you would address with **ты**.

Будь здоро́в (здоро́ва), **бу́дьте здоро́вы**, **быва́йте здоро́вы** are now restricted to informal situations. Although they are sometimes favoured by older people, these phrases are becoming obsolete.

Проща́й(те) is used when parting for a long time or forever.

Счастли́во is used when saying goodbye to someone who is leaving. Alternatively, if you are leaving, you may say **счастли́во остава́ться** to those who are staying behind.

Споко́йной но́чи or **до́брой но́чи** 'good night' are used when parting late at night or when going to bed.

If you know when you are next going to meet, this can be indicated using **до** (+ gen.):

до за́втра	see you tomorrow
до сле́дующей неде́ли	see you next week

In other circumstances **до встре́чи** 'until we next meet' can be used.

13.2.5 Polite enquiries and responses

The following polite enquiries can be used to follow up a greeting:

Как пожива́ешь?/Как пожива́ете?
Как живёшь?/Как живёте?
Как (твои́/ва́ши) дела́?
Как у тебя́/вас дела́?

The following versions are more familiar in tone:

Как дели́шки?
Как здоро́вье?
Как жизнь?
Как живётся-мо́жется?

All of the above can be translated as 'How are things?'

In response, the following answers might be given, all introduced by **Спаси́бо** 'Thank you':

хорошо́	fine
норма́льно	OK, not bad
непло́хо	not bad
ничего́	OK, not too bad
та́к себе	so-so
лу́чше всех	great (this is more familiar in tone)

If things really are too bad for any of the above, a humorous answer is:

—**Как дела́?**
—**Как са́жа бела́…**

—How are things?
—Really bad. (*Literally*, As soot is white, i.e. the reverse of how things ought to be.)

13.2.6 Greetings and salutations for special occasions

Russian has a wide range of greetings and salutations used for special occasions, many of which have no real equivalent in English. Most of these follow one of two patterns.

The first pattern uses the construction **поздравля́ть/поздра́вить с** (+ instr.); the recipient of the salutation, if indicated, is in the *accusative*:

> *Поздравля́ю тебя́ с днём рожде́ния!*
> I wish you all the best on your birthday *or* Many happy returns on your birthday!

> Дорого́й па́почка, *поздравля́ем тебя́ с* Днём защи́тника Оте́чества!
> Dear father, we salute you on Defenders of the Fatherland Day.

NOTE | **День защи́тника Оте́чества** (23 February) is a special day devoted to those who are serving or who have served in Russian or Soviet armed forces.

In less formal contexts the verb tends to be omitted:

> **С днём рожде́ния тебя́!**
> Many happy returns of the day!

Other frequently used salutations include the following:

> **(Поздравля́ю/Поздравля́ем):**

с Но́вым го́дом	Happy New Year
с Рождество́м Христо́вым	Happy Christmas
с Па́схой	Happy Easter
с Днём све́тлого Христо́ва Воскресе́ния	Happy Easter (more formal)
с Днём Побе́ды	(used on Victory Day, 9 May)
с (Междунаро́дным) же́нским днём	(used on International Women's Day, 8 March, a national holiday in Russia)
с Днём учителя	(see Note (i) below)

NOTES | (i) In Russia, it is the custom for all professional groups to have their own special day (which does not, alas, mean an extra day off work). **День учи́теля** 'Teachers' Day' is 5 October.

(ii) On Easter Sunday, it is the custom for Orthodox believers to greet each other with the following exchange:

> —**Христо́с воскре́с(е)!**
> —**Вои́стину воскре́с(е)!**

> —Christ is risen!
> —He is risen indeed!

The verb is not used in the following greetings:

с пра́здником	(a useful all-purpose greeting that can be used on any national or other holiday)
с лёгким па́ром	(a greeting often made to someone who has just taken a shower, although it is more properly reserved for those who have taken a steam bath in a **ба́ня** (a traditional Russian bathhouse))

In circumstances where it is appropriate to return a salutation, this can be done by saying:

Взаи́мно!	And the same to you!

The verb **поздравля́ть/поздра́вить с** (+ instr.) also means 'to congratulate':

> *Поздравля́ю/поздравля́ем вас с рожде́нием до́чери.*
> Congratulations on the birth of your daughter!

The second pattern uses a *noun phrase* in the *genitive*. This is understood as being the object of the verb **жела́ть/пожела́ть** 'to wish', although the verb itself is usually omitted; examples include:

Счастли́вого пути́	Have a good journey
До́брого пути́	Have a good journey
Прия́тного о́тдыха	Enjoy your holiday
Прия́тного аппети́та!	(said to someone who is eating or about to start eating)
Ни пу́ха ни пера́!	Good luck!

NOTE
This last phrase, which literally means 'Neither fur nor feather', is used to wish someone good luck before an ordeal such as an examination or a performance on stage. The correct reply, which is perfectly polite in this context, is:

> **К чёрту!**   Go to the devil!

13.3 Making introductions and giving names

13.3.1 Introducing yourself

Older Russians are likely to introduce themselves either with their full name or with their surname alone:

> **Разреши́те предста́виться: Генна́дий Петро́вич Козодо́ев.**
> Allow me to introduce myself: I am Gennadii Petrovich Kozodoev.

The following phrases all correspond to the English 'Pleased to meet you':

> **о́чень прия́тно**
> **прия́тно познако́миться**
> **я ра́д/ра́да (мы ра́ды) познако́миться.**

> **Рад познако́миться. Горбунко́в.**
> Pleased to meet you. (I am) Gorbunkov.

Younger people tend to use only their forenames even in formal introductions:

> —**Дава́йте познако́мимся: меня́ зову́т Михаи́л.**
> —**Поли́на.**
> —**О́чень прия́тно.**

> —Let's introduce ourselves: I am (called) Mikhail.
> —I am Polina.
> —Pleased to meet you.

13.3.2 Introducing people to each other and to a third party

When introducing people to each other or introducing somebody to a third party the following phrases are used:

знако́мьтесь	may I introduce you?
познако́мьтесь	may I introduce you?
разреши́те вам предста́вить (+ acc.)	allow me to introduce you to
разреши́те вас познако́мить с (+ instr.)	allow me to introduce you to

Джон, *разреши́те вас познако́мить с* мои́м колле́гой Воло́дей Сема́ковым.
John, allow me to introduce you to my colleague Volodia Semakov.

Э́то моя́ сестра́ Гали́на, а э́то мой шве́дский друг А́ндерс, – *познако́мьтесь.*
May I introduce you? This is my sister Galina and this is my Swedish friend Anders.

13.3.3 ## Asking for someone's name

To ask for someone's name the question word **как**, *literally*, 'how', is used. The most usual way to ask someone's name is to use the *third person plural*, *present tense* of the verb **звать** 'to call' (**зову́т**) and the *accusative*:

Как вас/тебя́ зову́т?
What is your name?

Как зову́т твою́ сестру́?
What is your sister called?

In more informal language the verb can be in the *infinitive*:

Как тебя́ звать?
What's your name?

If you want to enquire about a specific part of someone's name, a construction with the preposition **по** (+ dat.) can be used:

Как вас *по и́мени-о́тчеству*?
What is your name and patronymic?

NOTE

и́мя-о́тчество is frequently used as a single compound noun, as in the above question. In this usage both parts of the noun decline.

The following illustrate another pattern for asking about a specific part of someone's name:

Как ва́ше и́мя-о́тчество?
What is your name and patronymic?

Как фами́лия э́того актёра?
What is that actor's surname?

With other types of name the pronoun **како́й** tends to be used:

про́звище	nickname
кли́чка	nickname, name of an animal
ник	nickname (of Internet user)

***Кака́я* кли́чка у э́той ло́шади?**
What is the name of that horse?

13.3.4 **Giving one's name**

The normal way of giving one's name echoes the question given at the beginning of the previous section:

> **Меня́ зову́т Ива́н.**
> I am called Ivan.

> **Её зову́т Лари́са Петро́вна.**
> She is called Larisa Petrovna.

Although the name is normally given in the *nominative*, in informal language it can be put in the *instrumental*:

> **Ме́ня зову́т Ива́ном.**
> I'm called Ivan.

> **Её звать Лари́сой.**
> She's called Larisa.

To refer to a specific part of someone's name, a construction with the preposition **по** (+ dat.) can be used:

> **Был на на́шем ку́рсе оди́н студе́нт *по фами́лии* Бре́жнев.**
> We had a student in our year called Brezhnev (*or* whose surname was Brezhnev).

13.3.5 **Titles and names of places or other objects**

The word **назва́ние** is normally used to indicate the name of an inanimate object, including geographical names, names of institutions, and the titles of books, films and works of art. The verb associated with this noun is **называ́ться** 'to be called':

> **Как *называ́ется* дере́вня, в кото́рой мы ви́дели вчера́ чуде́сную деревя́нную це́рковь?**
> What is the name of the village where we saw a wonderful wooden church yesterday?

> **Как *бу́дет называ́ться* э́та но́вая организа́ция?**
> What's this new organisation going to be called?

> **Как *называ́лись* э́ти два самолёта, кото́рые просла́вились в возду́шных боя́х за Брита́нию?**
> What were the names of those two aeroplanes that became famous during the Battle of Britain?

Another, more informal way of asking about the name of an inanimate object is to use the phrase: **как назва́ние**:

> ***Как назва́ние* того́ лека́рства, что ты мне дава́ла на про́шлой неде́ле?**
> What is the name of that medicine you gave me last week?

When answering the question, the name of the object is usually given in the *nominative*:

> **Э́та дере́вня *называ́ется* Та́мбицы.**
> The village is called Tambitsy.

The noun **назва́ние** is used in the following patterns and phrases:

име́ть назва́ние	to have the name
носи́ть назва́ние	to bear the name

| дава́ть/дать назва́ние | to give the name |
| под назва́нием | under the name |

—Как называ́ется ва́ша земля́? – спроси́л капита́н испа́нского корабля́.

—Юката́н! – отве́тил вождь ме́стного пле́мени, что на тузе́мном языке́ означа́ло «не понима́ю». С тех пор полуо́стров *но́сит назва́ние* Юката́н.

—'What is your land called?' asked the captain of a Spanish ship.

—'Yucatán!' answered the the leader of the local tribe, using a phrase which in the local language meant 'I don't understand'. Since then the peninsula has been called (*literally*, borne the name) Yucatán.

Назва́ние «Война́ и мир», кото́рое *дал* Толсто́й своему́ рома́ну, ста́ло предме́том диску́ссий на до́лгие го́ды.

The name *War and Peace*, which Tolstoy (chose to) give his novel, was the subject of controversy for many years.

Фигури́сты испо́лнили но́вый та́нец *под назва́нием* «Матрёшки».

The figure-skaters performed a new dance called (*literally*, under the name) 'The Matrioshkas'.

For the use of inverted commas in titles, *see* **1.5.8**.

13.4 Addressing friends and acquaintances

13.4.0 Introduction

Although Russian has several different forms that can be used to address friends and acquaintances, the most important are the *familiar* form of the *forename* and the *full forename* + *patronymic*.

For the structure of Russian names, *see* **12.1**.

13.4.1 Using the forename

The *familiar* version of the *forename* is the normal form of address used between friends or, within the family, between siblings and by adults when speaking to children. It is used more generally by older people when speaking to children and is, for example, the form used by teachers when speaking to their students. Although there is no absolute rule about this, the familiar form of the forename is normally combined with the pronoun ты:

На́дя, иди́ домо́й, ба́бушка прие́хала!
Nadia, go home! Your grandmother's arrived.

Ко́ля, приве́т! Как у тебя́ дела́?
Hi, Kolia, how are things?

Серёжа, здра́вствуй! Сто лет тебя́ не ви́дела. Как пожива́ешь?
Hello, Seriozha, I haven't seen you for ages. How are you getting on?

In appropriate circumstances the more *expressive* forms of the forename can be used:

Приве́т, *Ната́шка*. Меня́ в а́рмию забира́ют. Про́воды в суббо́ту. Придёшь?

Hi, Natasha! I've been called up into the army. The farewell party is on Saturday. Are you coming?

For more on forenames and their familiar and expressive forms, *see* **12.1.1** and **16.1.4**.

When addressing someone using a familiar form that ends in **-а** or **-я**, it is possible to shorten the name by dropping the final vowel. This shortened form, which is characteristic of more informal levels of language, is used particularly frequently when the name is repeated:

> **Коль, не зна́ешь, ско́лько вре́мени?**
> Kolia, do you happen to know what time it is?

> **Тань, а Тань, иди́ сюда́!**
> Tania, Tania, come here!

13.4.2 Use of forename + patronymic

The combination of *full* version of the *forename + patronymic* is the default form of address among adults. It is used in most circumstances where English speakers would use 'Mr'/'Mrs'/'Ms' + surname and in some instances where English speakers might switch to the forename. In particular, it is used between colleagues in offices and institutions (and especially when addressing a superior); by pupils and students when addressing their teachers and lecturers, and more generally when addressing older people. It is always combined with the pronoun **вы**:

> **Пётр Петро́вич, зайди́те, пожа́луйста, ко мне в кабине́т. У меня́ есть не́которые вопро́сы по ва́шему отчёту.**
> Piotr Petrovich, would you mind stepping into my office. I've got some questions about your report.

> **А́нна Серге́евна, вы уже́ прове́рили на́ши сочине́ния?**
> Anna Sergeevna, have you marked our essays yet?

13.4.3 Other forms of address

Traditionally, the *full* form of the forename was not widely used as a form of address, except when speaking to foreigners (since foreign names do not as a rule have *familiar* forms; *see* **12.2**). In recent years, however, it has become more acceptable as an intermediate form in circumstances when the use of *forename + patronymic* seems too formal, but where the use of the familiar form of the forename is too informal, for example, between colleagues. It can be combined with either **ты** or **вы**. One situation where this form can be widely heard is on television, when, for example, newsreaders are talking on air to correspondents on location:

> **Репорта́ж с ме́ста собы́тий ведёт наш корреспонде́нт Алекса́ндр Курга́нов.**
> —*Алекса́ндр? Алекса́ндр*, вы слы́шите меня́?
> —Да, *Татья́на*, я слы́шу вас хорошо́.

> For a live report from the scene of the events we are going over to our correspondent Aleksandr Kurganov.
> —Aleksandr? Aleksandr, can you hear me?
> —Yes, Tat'iana, I can hear you loud and clear.

In Soviet times the titles **господи́н** 'Mr' and **госпожа́** 'Mrs' were combined with the *surname* only when addressing foreigners. Since 1991, however, these titles have started to be used more widely, although they can still sometimes carry ironic or even derogatory overtones. Nevertheless, in formal circumstances it is now generally acceptable to address someone whose name and patronymic you do not know using the form **господи́н/ госпожа́** + surname:

> *Господи́н Петро́в*, вы не могли́ бы запо́лнить для нас э́ту анке́ту.
> Would you mind filling in this form for us, Mr Petrov?

On the other hand, the form **това́рищ** 'comrade' + surname, which was used in Soviet times, has now largely died out, although **това́рищ** followed by the name of the rank is still used when addressing a superior officer in the armed forces or the police.

Surname alone is used by teachers and lecturers when addressing their students and also when addressing those lower in rank in the armed forces and other strictly hierarchical institutions:

> *Ивано́ва*, к доске́! Докажи́ нам, пожа́луйста, теоре́му Пифаго́ра.
> Ivanova, please step up to the blackboard and demonstrate for us the proof of Pythagoras's theorem.

Patronymic alone is sometimes used in informal contexts. It indicates familiarity and can be combined only with **ты**. It cannot be used by younger people to indicate respect towards their elders:

> *Миха́лыч*, когда́ за гриба́ми пое́дем? Ты обеща́л!
> Mikhalych, when are we going to look for mushrooms? You did promise!

For the 'reduced' form of the patronymic, *see* **12.1.2**.

13.4.4 Referring to someone not present

When referring in Russian to someone with whom one is on formal terms, it is perfectly normal to use the formula *forename + patronymic*. If the person referred to is a man, the name, especially in informal language, is often treated as a single unit, with only the patronymic being declined; here too the patronymic is normally spoken in the reduced form:

> *Я то́лько что был у Ива́н Ива́ныча*.
> I've just been to see Ivan Ivanovich.

Referring to someone by *title + surname* is fairly rare. On the other hand, reference by surname alone is much more frequent and is acceptable in a wide range of contexts:

> *Ты слы́шала? Филимо́нова из отде́ла ка́дров родила́ дво́йню!*
> Have you heard? Filimonova from personnel has had twins.

> *Бритви́хина и Столяро́ва вы́звали в декана́т.*
> Britvikhin and Stoliarov have been summoned to the Dean's office.

The formula *full forename + surname* (which is virtually never used as a form of address) was until recently used mainly to refer to sportspeople and performers in the world of the arts and show business. In the last few years its usage has been extended to others in the public eye, such as politicians:

> *В фи́льмах Леони́да Гайда́я снима́лись лу́чшие оте́чественные актёры: Ю́рий Нику́лин, Андре́й Миро́нов, Анато́лий Папа́нов.*
> The films of Leonid Gaidai featured the best Russian/Soviet actors: Iurii Nikulin, Andrei Mironov, Anatolii Papanov.

NOTE The adjective **отéчественный** is derived from **отéчество** 'homeland', 'fatherland' and is frequently used in journalism and other similar types of language. Its meaning, depending on the time frame to which it refers, is either 'Russian' or 'Soviet'.

13.5 Addressing strangers

13.5.1 Introduction

When addressing strangers, Russians prefer, if possible, to use a form of address. There are various such forms in use, many of which have no real equivalent in English.

13.5.1 Addressing an individual

The forms used most frequently to address someone who is not known to the speaker are **молодóй человéк** 'young man' and **дéвушка** *literally*, 'girl'. These terms, which are perfectly polite and can be used to address anyone from late teens to early middle-age (and even beyond), are widely used in the street; they are the preferred forms for addressing waiters, shop assistants and others with whom one may come into casual contact:

Молодóй человéк, это не вы урони́ли блокнóт?
Excuse me (young man), was it you that dropped this notebook?

Дéвушка, покажи́те мне вон ту кýртку с капюшóном, что слéва на витри́не.
Would you mind showing me that jacket there with the hood, the one on the left in the window?

A problem arises with people who are too old to respond gracefully to **молодóй человéк** or **дéвушка**. Forms such as **мужчи́на** 'man', **жéнщина** 'woman' and **дáма** 'lady' are quite frequently heard, but they can cause offence and are best avoided. There are periodic attempts to revive **сýдарь** 'sir' and **судáрыня** 'madam', but these have never caught on and their use is likely to be seen as quaint or ironic. The best solution is probably to use an indirect way of attracting someone's attention, such as **прости́те** 'excuse me' or **бýдьте любéзны** 'please', 'would you mind?':

Прости́те, это не вы урони́ли блокнóт?
Excuse me, was it you that dropped this notebook?

Бýдьте любéзны, передáйте за проéзд: за двои́х до Рáменского.
Excuse me, would you mind passing this fare up to the driver? It's for two people going as far as Ramenskoe.

Дя́дя 'uncle' and **тётя** 'aunt(ie)' are used informally to address people of an older generation and, along with the more familiar **дя́денька** and **тётенька**, are used by children addressing adults:

Дя́денька, а вы прáвда фóкусник?
(Uncle), is it true you're a conjuror?

Addressing a group

Announcements made in Russian to a group of people normally begin with a form of address containing a noun which identifies the audience. This is normally preceded by the plural adjective **уважа́емые** 'dear', *literally*, 'respected', 'esteemed'. Examples of these forms of address, which are given with notional translations since they do not have English equivalents, include the following:

уважа́емые (теле)зри́тели	dear viewers
уважа́емые колле́ги	dear colleagues
уважа́емые пассажи́ры	dear passengers
уважа́емые слу́шатели	dear listeners

Уважа́емые пассажи́ры, начина́ется поса́дка на самолёт, сле́дующий по маршру́ту Росто́в – Волгогра́д ре́йсом 2458.
Flight 2458 (from Rostov) to Volgograd is now ready for boarding.

A greater degree of intimacy is suggested by the formula:

дороги́е друзья́	dear friends

The Russian equivalent of 'ladies and gentlemen' is **Да́мы и господа́**, although the presence of the above formulae means that it is used less often than the corresponding English phrase.

At the end of a lecture or a speech it is polite to say:

Спаси́бо за внима́ние	Thank you for your attention.

Writing letters and telephoning

Writing letters

The normal practice is to begin ordinary letters with the adjective **дорого́й** (**дорога́я**, **дороги́е**) 'dear' followed either by the name(s) of the people being addressed or by an appropriate noun, such as **друг** 'friend':

Дорого́й Ва́ня!	Dear Vania
Дорого́й друг!	Dear friend

The adjective **ми́лый** (**ми́лая**, **ми́лые**) 'dear' can also be used, especially when writing to close friends or relatives:

Ми́лая Та́нечка!	Dear Tania
Ми́лая ма́мочка!	Dear Mum

Relatively formal letters can end with the formula:

и́скренне Ваш (твой)	Yours sincerely
с наилу́чшими пожела́ниями	With best wishes

For the occurrence of capital letters with the pronouns **Вы** and **Ваш** when they are used in letters to address one person, *see* 1.5.7.

More informal ways of ending letters are:

всего́ до́брого	all the best
всего́ хоро́шего	all the best

всего́ наилу́чшего	all the very best
кре́пко жму ру́ку	*literally*, I shake your hand firmly (mostly used by men)
(обнима́ю и) целу́ю	*literally*, (I embrace and) kiss you (mostly used by women)

In formal and official letters the name of the recipient is preceded by the adjective **уважа́емый** *literally*, 'respected', 'esteemed' *or* **глубокоуважа́емый** 'highly respected/esteemed':

Уважа́емый Ива́н Петро́вич!	Dear Ivan Petrovich
Глубокоуважа́емый господи́н Си́мпсон!	Dear Mr Simpson

Formal letters can end with one of the following salutations:

С уваже́нием	Yours faithfully, Yours sincerely
И́скренне Ваш	Yours sincerely

NOTE | Textbooks generally recommend putting an exclamation mark after the greeting at the beginning of a letter, although a comma can also be used.

Using the telephone

Алло́ (less frequently **алё**) is used to establish initial contact after picking up the telephone. A more formal way of answering the telephone is to say **слу́шаю (вас)** *literally*, 'I am listening to you'. **Да** 'yes' is sometimes used, but is less polite; it tends to be used more often when the connection has been lost and re-established.

Алло́, вас пло́хо слы́шно. Перезвони́те, пожа́луйста.
Hello, I can't hear you properly. Can you phone me back?

—*Слу́шаю вас.*
—*Алло́*, Михаи́л Моисе́евич? До́брый день. Это Цветко́ва из «Вече́рней газе́ты».
—Чем могу́ быть поле́зен?

—Hello.
—Hello, is that Mikhail Moiseevich? This is Tsvetkova from the *Vecherniaia gazeta*.
—How can I help you?

NOTE | In Russian there is no problem about combining **алло́** with a greeting such as **до́брый день** or **здра́вствуйте**.

The courtesy formulae in the buiness-related calls are normally reduced to a minimum:

—Такси́ «Тро́йка». *Слу́шаю вас.*
—Бу́дьте любе́зны, нам маши́ну на два́дцать два три́дцать.
—Пожа́луйста, ваш а́дрес, куда́ пое́дем и на чьё и́мя зака́з.
—Берёзовый бульва́р, 33, кварти́ра 11, на железнодоро́жный вокза́л, фами́лия Дубро́вин.
—Зака́з при́нят.

—Hello, Troika taxi service.
—Can I order a taxi please for 10.30 this evening?
—Can you give me your address, the destination and the name of the customer?
—33 Beriozovyi Bul'var, flat 11, going to the railway station, and the taxi's for Dubrovin.
—Your taxi is ordered.

To ask to speak to somebody the following formulae can be used:

пригласи́ть (*or* позва́ть) к телефо́ну
мо́жно
нельзя́ ли

All three can be followed by the name of the person in the *accusative*; the second and third can also be followed by a verb in the *infinitive*. To ask who is calling, the following sentence is used:

(А) кто его́/её спра́шивает?   Who is calling?

The following sentence can be used to offer to take a message:

Что ему́/ей переда́ть?   Can I give him/her a message?

—Алло́, сало́н причёсок.
—Бу́дьте добры́, *пригласи́те к телефо́ну Станисла́ва Ю́рьевича.*
—У него́ сейча́с клие́нт. Перезвони́те попо́зже.

—Hello, hairdressers.
—Hello, can I speak to Stanislav Iur'evich, please?
—I'm afraid he's with a customer. Can you ring back later?

—Слу́шаю вас.
—Здра́вствуйте, *мо́жно Ни́ну?*
—Одну́ мину́точку. *А кто её спра́шивает?*
—Э́то Вале́рий, она́ зна́ет.

—Hello.
—Hello, can I speak to Nina, please?
—Just a minute, Who's calling?
—It's Valerii. She's expecting me to phone.

—Алло́, Макси́м?
—Нет, э́то его́ оте́ц.
—До́брый ве́чер, а *нельзя́ ли с Макси́мом переговори́ть?* Э́то Па́вел, его́ одноку́рсник.
—Макси́ма нет. *Что ему́ переда́ть?*
—Попроси́те, пожа́луйста, что́бы он мне перезвони́л на моби́льник. Он зна́ет но́мер.

—Hello, is that Maksim?
—No, it's his father.
—Would it be possible to speak to Maksim? This is Pavel from the university.
—Maksim's not here. Can I give him a message?
—Would you mind asking him to phone me back on my mobile? He's got my number.

NOTE | As the first example shows, Russian businesses are not always as informative as they might be when they answer the telephone.

There are two ways of telling someone that they have got a wrong-number:

> **Вы оши́блись (но́мером).**
> **Вы не туда́ попа́ли.**

A typical message left on an answering machine (**автоотве́тчик**) might be:

> **Здра́вствуйте, с ва́ми говори́т автоотве́тчик. Оста́вьте, пожа́луйста, ва́ше сообще́ние по́сле звуково́го сигна́ла.**
> Hello, this is an answering machine. Please leave a message after the tone.

Other useful telephone-related words and phrases include the following:

звони́ть/позвони́ть (+ dat.)	to telephone (someone)
звони́ть/позвони́ть из автома́та	to phone from a call-box
дозва́ниваться/дозвони́ться	to (succeed in) getting through
перезва́нивать/перезвони́ть	to ring back
брать/взять тру́бку	to pick up the phone
ве́шать/пове́сить *or* класть /положи́ть тру́бку	to hang up
набира́ть/набра́ть но́мер	to dial a number
моби́льный/со́товый телефо́н	mobile telephone, cellphone
моби́льник	mobile (informal)
посыла́ть/посла́ть (отправля́ть/ отпра́вить, ски́дывать/ски́нуть) те́кстовое сообще́ние *or* СМС (эсэмэ́с, эсэмэ́ску)	to send a text message
вводи́ть/ввести́ но́мер в па́мять	to put a number into the memory
заряжа́ть/заряди́ть телефо́н	to charge up a telephone

14

Being, becoming and possession

Being and becoming

Using the verb *быть*

The verb that corresponds most closely to the English 'to be', as used in sentences of the type 'X is/was/will be Y', is **быть**. When it is used in this function, **быть** has no *present tense* forms. In writing, the missing verb is normally indicated by a dash (–), especially when both *subject* and *complement* are *nouns*:

> **Ма́ло кто зна́ет, что мой брат – изве́стный актёр.**
> Not many people know that my brother is a famous actor.

> **Эльбру́с – са́мая высо́кая гора́ в Евро́пе.**
> El'brus is the highest mountain in Europe.

> **Спаси́бо, что ты всё так бы́стро сде́лал. Ты – настоя́щий геро́й!**
> Thanks for doing everything so quickly. You are a real hero.

> **Два́жды два – четы́ре.**
> Twice two is four.

The dash is not used when the subject is the *pronoun* э́то or when the complement is an *adjective*; it tends to be omitted when the subject is a *personal pronoun*:

> **Э́то, ка́жется, ва́ши ключи́.**
> I think these are your keys.

> **Запо́мни золото́е пра́вило би́знеса: клие́нт всегда́ *прав*.**
> Remember the golden rule of business: the customer is always right.

> **Она́ моя́ двою́родная сестра́.**
> She is my cousin.

For more on the present tense of **быть**, *see* **4.8**.

For the formation of the future tense of **быть**, *see* **4.4.1**.

For the formation of the imperative of **быть**, *see* **4.9.1**.

For the formation of the imperfective gerund of **быть**, *see* **4.11.1**.

14.1.2　Noun complements of *быть*

As was noted in **3.1.3** and **3.5.3**, the complement of **быть**, if it is a noun, is in some circumstances in the *nominative* case and in other circumstances in the *instrumental* case. The general rules for the use of the two cases are as follows:

In the present tense only the nominative is possible. Examples are given in the previous section.

With all other forms of **быть** except the past tense, the instrumental is normally used:

Future tense

> Уже́ я́сно, что в ближа́йшие го́ды инфля́ция *бу́дет серьёзной пробле́мой* для росси́йского прави́тельства.
> It's already clear that in the next few years inflation will be a serious problem for the Russian government.

Imperative

> Профе́ссор, у меня́ к вам про́сьба: *бу́дьте мои́м нау́чным руководи́телем.*
> Professor, I've a favour to ask you. Would you agree to be my supervisor?

Conditional

> Е́сли *бы ты был президе́нтом Росси́и*, как бы ты вёл борьбу́ с корру́пцией?
> If you were president of Russia, how would you manage the battle against corruption?

Infinitive

> Не обяза́тельно *быть проро́ком*, чтобы предсказа́ть, чем э́то всё ко́нчится.
> You don't have to be a prophet to predict how it will all end.

Gerund

> Он на́чал свою́ карье́ру, ещё *бу́дучи студе́нтом.*
> He began his career while he was still a student.

For more on the use of the imperative in requests, *see* **18.3.1**.

For more on the use of the gerund, *see* **21.10**.

With the past tense of **быть** there is a tendency to prefer the *instrumental*:

> Когда́ я *был студе́нтом*, я *был чле́ном* трёх о́бществ, но *чле́ном па́ртии* я *не́ был.*
> When I was a student, I was a member of three societies, but I was never a member of the party.

> Но мы когда́-то *бы́ли друзья́ми.*
> But at one time we were friends.

The *nominative*, however, is normally used if the *complement* refers to a permanent state:

> **На́ша ба́бушка *была́ краса́вица*, к ней мно́гие сва́тались.**
> Our grandmother was a beauty and many sought her hand in marriage.

14.1.3 Sentences where the complement precedes the subject

In Russian, there is no requirement for the subject of a sentence to precede the verb.

For information on the principles of word order in Russian, *see* **20.1**.

It is thus perfectly possible for a sentence to be constructed according to the following pattern: *complement* (in the *instrumental*) – *verb* – *subject* (in the *nominative*). A much quoted example is the following sentence:

> **Пе́рвым челове́ком в ко́смосе был *Ю́рий Гага́рин*.**
> The first man in space was Iurii Gagarin.

With sentences of this type it is not always straightforward to work out which noun should be in the *nominative* and which in the *instrumental*, but in general the following principles apply:

(1) The noun or noun phrase giving the more important information will come at the *end of the sentence*.
(2) The noun or noun phrase indicating the more temporary state will be in the *instrumental*.

The above sentence follows both those principles: the key information here is that it is Iurii Gagarin (and not someone else) who was the first man in space; Iurii Gagarin was always Iurii Gagarin (a permanent state), but he was only the first man in space for a part of his life (a more temporary condition).

Sometimes either noun or noun phrase can be in the instrumental, but in such instances there will be a subtle difference in meaning between the two sentences:

> **Её *тре́тьим му́жем* был *режиссёр*.**
> Her third husband was a (theatre or film) director [unlike her other husbands].

> **Её *тре́тий муж* был *режиссёром одного́ из моско́вских теа́тров*.**
> Her third husband was (*or* had been) a director at one of the Moscow theatres [but then may have gone on to do other things].

In the first sentence, being the third husband is seen as the more temporary state: the husband was a director before and possibly after his marriage. In the second sentence, being a director at one of the Moscow theatres is the more temporary state: the husband could have given up this specific activity some time before or during his marriage.

14.1.4 Adjective complements

When the complement of **быть** is an *adjective*, different rules apply. In the present tense there are two possibilities:

The *long form* in the *nominative*.

The *short form* (for those adjectives that have short forms).

With other forms of **быть** there are three possibilities:

The long form in the *nominative*.

The long form in the *instrumental*.

The short form (for those adjectives that have short forms).

For information on the short forms of adjectives and on those adjectives that have no short forms, *see* **6.5**. It will be remembered that short forms occur only in the *nominative*.

The long form in the nominative tends to be used to refer to permanent characteristics, especially in present tense sentences:

> **Она́ така́я *спосо́бная*: ка́жется, что уме́ет де́лать всё.**
> She's so talented; it seems there's nothing she can't do.

> **Тут я впервы́е заме́тил, что глаза́ у него́ – *голубы́е*.**
> It was then that I noticed for the first time his eyes are bright blue.

> **Осторо́жно, э́тот гриб *несъедо́бный*!**
> Be careful, this mushroom's poisonous.

The long form in the *instrumental* tends to be preferred when **быть** is in the *future*, the *conditional* or the *infinitive*:

> **Я уве́рен, что его́ но́вая кни́га *бу́дет* о́чень *интере́сной*.**
> I am sure that his new book will be very interesting.

> **Е́сли *бы* он *был* бо́лее *дальнови́дным*, он не стал бы де́лать таки́х заявле́ний.**
> If he were more far-sighted he would not have made statements of that nature.

> **Ка́ждый согласи́тся, что лу́чше *быть бога́тым* и *здоро́вым*, чем *бе́дным* и *больны́м*.**
> Everyone would agree that it is better to be rich and healthy than poor and sick.

When **быть** is in the *past tense*, the long form in the *instrumental* is widely used, but the long form in the *nominative* can be used when it is necessary to make it clear that a permanent quality is being talked about:

> **То́лько тепе́рь она́ поняла́, что её реше́ние *бы́ло ошибочным*.**
> Only now did she understand that her decision had been wrong.

> **В де́тстве ты была́ *непосе́дливой и болтли́вой*.**
> When you were a child you would never sit still or shut up.

> **Кварти́ра, где он жил с семьёй, была́ *больша́я, све́тлая*, с ви́дом на о́зеро.**
> The flat where he lived with his family was large, bright and had a view onto the lake.

When **быть** is in the *imperative*, either the long form in the instrumental or the short form can be used:

> **Бу́дь *мужественным*: ничего́ с тобо́й не случи́тся.**
> Be brave: nothing's going to happen to you.

Води́тели! Пе́рвого сентября́ бу́дьте осо́бенно *осторо́жны* и *внима́тельны*!
Drivers! On 1 September (the start of the school year in Russia) be especially careful and pay particular attention!

For more examples with the short form, *see* below.

The short form tends to be used with reference to a specific occasion or set of circumstances:

Съёмка око́нчена, все *свобо́дны*.
The filming is over. Everyone is free to go.

Большо́е спаси́бо за по́мощь. Я о́чень *благода́рна*.
Many thanks for your help. I'm very grateful.

—Ну что, пойдём у́жинать?
—Я вообще́-то не *го́лоден*.

—Shall we go and have some supper?
—I'm not really hungry.

An extension of this is that the short form can have the meaning of 'too …':

Ты ещё *мо́лод*, что́бы суди́ть люде́й.
You're still too young to judge people.

Э́ти ту́фли мне *велики́*, у вас есть на разме́р ме́ньше?
These shoes are too big for me. Do you have them in a size smaller?

Ру́ки *ко́ротки*!
Says you! (*Literally*, 'Your arms are too short!' It is said in response to a threat to carry out a particular action.)

The short form is normally used when the adjective occurs in conjunction with a dependent phrase, most commonly a noun or pronoun in a case other than nominative or accusative, or a prepositional phrase:

Я не знал, что ты *спосо́бна на тако́й по́двиг*.
I didn't know you were capable of such a great achievement.

Я *в матема́тике не силён*.
I'm not very good at maths.

The short form is used when the complement precedes the subject:

Изве́стны слу́чаи, когда́ роди́телям даю́т гражда́нство, а их де́тям – нет.
Cases are known where parents are granted citizenship, but not their children.

With some adjectives the short form is associated with a particular meaning:

живо́й	alive, lively	**жив**	alive
пра́вый	right (not wrong), just; right (not left)	**прав**	right (not wrong)

The short form of the adjective **хоро́ший** 'good' has the special meaning of 'good-looking', 'attractive':

Она́ была́ так *хороша́*, так мила́ – слов нет!
She was such an attractive and pleasant person that there are no words to describe her.

The short form of the adjective occurs in a number of set expressions:

Бу́дьте добры́	Please be so kind as to
Бу́дьте любе́зны	Please be so kind as to
Будь здоро́в, Бу́дьте здоро́вы	Bless you! (when someone sneezes), Take care (on parting)
Мир те́сен	It's a small world
Я жив, здоро́в	I'm alive and well, I'm still going strong

14.1.5 Synonyms of *быть*

The following verbs are more or less exact synonyms of **быть**. They are found almost exclusively in formal language:

> явля́ться
> представля́ть собо́й

Явля́ться is used with a *complement* in the *instrumental* case, which, where appropriate, can precede both *verb* and *subject*; both *subject* and *complement* are generally *nouns*, although *adjectival complements* are occasionally found, especially in bureaucratic language. **Представля́ть собо́й** is used with a *direct object* in the *accusative case*; both subject and object are normally nouns:

> С 2002 го́да он *явля́ется* чле́ном Сою́за фотохудо́жников Росси́и.
> He's been a member of the Russian Union of Photographic Artists since 2002.

> *Учреди́телем* Моско́вского междунаро́дного кинофестива́ля *явля́ется* прави́тельство Росси́и.
> The official founder of the Moscow International Film Festival is the Russian government.

> Но́вый фильм *представля́ет собо́й* неуда́чную смесь боевика́ и мелодра́мы.
> The new film is an unsuccessful cross between an action film and a melodrama.

The verb **заключа́ться в** (+ prep.) can correspond to the English 'to be' when it has the meaning of 'consist in'; it can also be used with a clause introduced by the conjunction **что**:

> Гла́вное отли́чие Бэ́тмена от други́х супергеро́ев *заключа́ется в отсу́тствии* у него́ сверхъесте́ственных спосо́бностей.
> The main difference between Batman and other superheroes is his absence of supernatural abilities.

> Гла́вная на́ша пробле́ма *заключа́ется в том, что* у нас не оста́лось де́нег.
> Our main problem is that we have no money left.

The verb **быва́ть** means 'to tend to be', 'to be (frequently)'. It is used in all levels of language to refer to something that is repeated either intermittently or regularly, but would not be used to refer to something that is always the case; it is normally used with a complement in the *instrumental*, although an adjectival complement can be in the *short form*:

> Зачасту́ю таки́е диску́ссии *быва́ют* жа́ркими и затя́гиваются до по́зднего ве́чера.
> Quite often these discussions can be heated and can drag on late into the evening.

Used on its own or with **это**, **быва́ет** means 'it happens' *or* 'these things can happen':

> —До́ктор, по́сле удале́ния зу́ба у меня́ воспали́лась десна́.
> —Э́то *быва́ет*. Я назна́чу вам антибио́тики.

> —Doctor, after my tooth was removed, my gum became inflamed.
> —This can happen. I'll prescribe you antibiotics.

> *Быва́ет*, в са́мый разга́р спекта́кля у кого́-нибудь из зри́телей вдруг
> начина́ет звони́ть моби́льник.
> It can happen that at the most exciting point of the play someone's mobile phone
> goes off.

With a negative **быва́ть** can indicate that something cannot or should not be expected
to happen:

> Он прогуля́л все ле́кции, а тепе́рь наде́ется хорошо́ сдать экза́мен.
> *Чуде́с не быва́ет.*
> He missed all his lectures and now hopes to get a good mark in the exam. He
> can't expect miracles.

> Лу́чше не быва́ет.
> It doesn't get any better.

For more on negation with **быва́ть**, *see* **15.1.2**.

The verb **ока́зываться/оказа́ться** means 'it transpired that', 'it turned out to be',
although in practice it can sometimes correspond simply to the English 'to be'; it is
used with a *complement* in the *instrumental*:

> *Ока́зывается*, мы с ним учи́лись на одно́м факульте́те, то́лько в ра́зные
> го́ды.
> It turns out that we attended the same faculty but in different years.

> В конве́рте был како́й-то бе́лый порошо́к, но он *оказа́лся* безвре́дным.
> There was some white powder in the envelope, but it was (*or* turned out to be)
> harmless.

The verb станови́ться/стать

The verb **станови́ться/стать** means 'to become'. It is used with a complement in the
instrumental:

> Никто́ и поду́мать не мог тогда́, что он *ста́нет кру́пным учёным*.
> At that time nobody could ever have thought that he would become a
> distinguished scholar.

> Суде́бные и́ски потреби́телей к производи́телям нека́чественных
> това́ров *ста́ли обы́чным явле́нием*.
> Instances of consumers suing manufacturers of poor quality goods have become
> an everyday occurrence.

> Бло́ги *стано́вятся* всё бо́лее *популя́рными* среди́ молодёжи.
> Blogs are becoming more and more popular among young people.

In many instances and especially in sentences referring to a particular set of circumstances, it is possible to use, instead of **станови́ться/стать** with an adjectival complement,
an intransitive verb formed from an adjective according to the pattern described in
10.3.3:

За э́ти го́ды она́ си́льно *похуде́ла*, а он, наоборо́т, *располне́л*.
In the last few years she has become much thinner, while he, on the other hand, has become fatter.

When it refers to a new state of affairs that has come into being, **стать** functions very much like a perfective partner of **быть** and in many instances it can be translated by 'to be':

Ки́евское «Дина́мо» под руково́дством росси́йского специали́ста Ю́рия Сёмина впервы́е *ста́ло* облада́телем Ку́бка Пе́рвого кана́ла.
Dynamo Kiev, under the guidance of the Russian trainer Iurii Sëmin, have won the First Channel Cup for the first time. (*Literally*, have become the winners … for the first time.)

Впервы́е в исто́рии духо́вное управле́ние мусульма́н возгла́вил этни́ческий ру́сский - им *стал* Али́й Ефте́ев.
For the first time in its history the Religious Council of (Russian) Muslims is to be headed by an ethnic Russian: he is Alii Efteev.

Following the same principle, the Russian version of the television quiz *Who Wants to be a Millionaire?* is called «Кто хочет *стать* миллионе́ром?». Presumably, everybody wants to *be* a millionaire, but not everyone is necessarily willing to do what is required in order to *become* one.

14.2 Existence, presence and location

14.2.1 The use of the verb *быть*

Existence, presence, and location is also often indicated by the verb **быть**:

Была́ одна́ пробле́ма, но мы суме́ли её реши́ть.
There was a problem, but we've managed to solve it.

За́втра я *бу́ду* весь день на совеща́нии.
I'll be at a meeting all day tomorrow.

Здесь когда́-то *была́* ста́рая це́рковь, но её снесли́ в пятидеся́тые го́ды.
There used to be an old church here, but it was demolished in the 1950s.

In the present tense the third person form **есть** is frequently used, especially when the emphasis is on the fact of presence, rather than on the subject of the sentence; **есть** can be used with plural as well as with singular subjects:

В го́роде *есть* то́лько оди́н челове́к, кото́рый мо́жет нам помо́чь.
There's only one person in the town who can help us.

Есть ве́щи, о кото́рых не при́нято говори́ть вслух.
There are certain things that are not mentioned in public.

Тепе́рь моско́вским автомобили́стам *есть* куда́ пожа́ловаться на незако́нную эвакуа́цию их маши́н.
Now there is somewhere where Moscow drivers can complain when their vehicles have been towed away illegally.

14.2.2 **Synonyms of _быть_**

The verbs **бывать** and **оказываться/оказаться** (see **14.1.5**) can also be used in sentences indicating existence, presence or location; the shades of meaning that they convey are the same as those described in **14.1.5**:

> **Он здесь _бывает_ только по вторникам.**
> He is normally here only on Tuesdays.

> **_Бывали_ случаи, когда вслед за разрывом дипломатических отношений объявлялась война.**
> There have been cases when the breaking-off of diplomatic relations has been followed by a declaration of war.

> **Он забивает столько мячей именно потому, что всегда _оказывается_ в нужном месте в нужное время.**
> The reason he scores so many goals is that he's always in the right place at the right time.

The verb **иметься** is used, mostly in more formal types of language, to indicate existence or presence:

> **В распоряжении хакеров _имеются_ программы, идентифицирующие пароли за несколько секунд.**
> There are programs available to hackers that identify passwords in a few seconds.

The verb **находиться** and the past passive participle **расположен** are widely used to indicate location:

> **Моя комната _находится/расположена_ в конце коридора, рядом с ванной.**
> My room is (situated) at the end of the corridor, next to the bathroom.

> **Город Глазго _расположен/находится_ в западной части Шотландии на обоих берегах реки Клайд.**
> Glasgow is located in the West of Scotland, on both banks of the River Clyde.

For more on past passive participles, _see_ **4.12.4**.

The verb **стоять** can be used of buildings, statues and for objects standing vertically:

> **На центральной площади всё ещё _стоит_ памятник Ленину.**
> In the central square there is still a statue of Lenin.

> **На полках _стояли_ словари и книги на славянских языках.**
> On the shelves there were dictionaries and other books in Slavonic languages.

The verb **лежать** can be used with reference to something that can be thought of as lying flat. Following this logic the same verb is used with reference to someone in hospital:

> **В одном из этих конвертов _лежит_ тысячерублёвая купюра.**
> In one of these envelopes there is a bank note for 1,000 roubles.

> **Он не может сегодня присутствовать, так как _лежит_ в больнице.**
> He can't be here today as he's in hospital.

The verb **сиде́ть** is used with reference to specific locations, namely, staying at home or in prison; indeed, **сиде́ть** is sometimes used on its own with the meaning 'to be in prison':

> **Вчера́ я *сиде́ла* до́ма весь день, так что не пыта́йся меня́ уверя́ть, бу́дто ты звони́л не́сколько раз.**
> I was at home all day yesterday, so don't pretend that you tried to phone several times.

> **Я зна́ю, что он *сиди́т* (в тюрьме́), но не зна́ю, за что.**
> I know he's in prison, but I don't know what for.

NOTE   The verbs **име́ться, находи́ться, стоя́ть, лежа́ть, сиде́ть** are *imperfective*.

14.3 Talking about possession

14.3.1 Talking about possession using the preposition y (+ gen.)

The normal way of talking about possession in Russian does not involve a verb corresponding to the English 'to have'; instead, a construction indicating *location* is used: the verb is normally **быть** (in the third person) and the possessor is indicated by means of the *preposition* **y** (+ gen.):

> **Сего́дня я о́чень за́нят, но за́втра *у меня́ бу́дет* мно́го свобо́дного вре́мени.**
> I'm very busy today, but tomorrow I'll have a lot of free time.

> ***У него́* когда́-то *была́* маши́на, но он её про́дал и тепе́рь е́здит то́лько на обще́ственном тра́нспорте.**
> He used to have a car, but he sold it and now travels only on public transport.

In the present tense, the verb form **есть** can either be present or be omitted. It tends to be used when emphasis is on the fact of possession, rather than the possessor or the item possessed:

> ***У меня́* два бра́та и одна́ сестра́.**
> I have two brothers and a sister.

> ***У неё* ру́сые во́лосы и голубы́е глаза́.**
> She has light brown hair and pale blue eyes.

> ***У меня́* эта кни́га уже́ *есть*.**
> I already have that book.

For the use of constructions with **y** (+ gen.) in sentences indicating location proper, *see* **21.2.11**.

The verb form **быва́ть** can be used in sentences indicating possession that is frequent, regular or intermittent:

> **Да́же у изве́стных футбо́льных клу́бов ча́сто *быва́ют* больши́е *долги́*.**
> Even well-known football clubs often have big debts.

The verb име́ть

Russian has an equivalent verb to the English 'to have': this is **име́ть**, a first conjugation verb belonging to the class described in **4.6.1 (c)**. It is used for the most part with a limited group of abstract nouns in what are more or less set expressions:

име́ть в виду́	to have in mind, to mean
име́ть возмо́жность	to have the opportunity
име́ть де́ло с (+ instr.)	to have dealings with
име́ть значе́ние	to have significance, to be important
име́ть ме́сто	to take place, to occur
име́ть на́глость	to have the cheek
име́ть после́дствия	to have consequences
име́ть пра́во	to have the right
име́ть причи́ну	to have a reason
име́ть суди́мость	to have a previous conviction
име́ть честь	to have the honour

Интере́сно бы́ло бы знать, что он *име́л в виду́*, когда́ задава́л э́тот вопро́с.
It would be interesting to know what he had in mind when he asked that question.

Корреспонде́нты ме́стных газе́т гора́здо ре́же *име́ют возмо́жность* зада́ть вопро́с президе́нту.
Correspondents working for local papers have much less opportunity to ask the president a question.

Ва́ши слова́ *име́ют* для меня́ огро́мное *значе́ние*.
Your words are extremely important to me.

Она́ заяви́ла, что договорны́е и́гры в те́ннисе по-пре́жнему *име́ют ме́сто*, но то́лько в мужско́м разря́де.
She stated that fixed tennis matches still did take place, but only in men's tournaments.

***Име́ю честь* предоста́вить сло́во на́шему почётному го́стю.**
I now have the honour of asking our distinguished guest to address us.

For an example of **име́ть пра́во**, *see* **15.4**.

With **возмо́жность** and **причи́на** the construction with **у** (+ gen.) is also possible:

Е́сли *у меня́* бу́дет *возмо́жность*, я обяза́тельно переда́м ему́ приве́т от тебя́.
If I have the opportunity, I will definitely pass on your regards to him.

The verb **име́ть** can be used to indicate possession, but it tends to occur only in more formal or abstract contexts:

Что́бы претендова́ть на э́ту до́лжность, на́до *име́ть* вы́сшее образова́ние.
In order to apply for this post it is essential to have a university degree.

Мно́гие футбо́льные клу́бы, несмотря́ на хоро́шие результа́ты, *име́ют* больши́е долги́.
Many football clubs, in spite of good results, have large debts.

В бра́ке не состоя́л, *дете́й не име́ю*.
I have never been married and have no children (e.g. in a formal statement).

В анке́те, по́мнится, была́ така́я графа́: «*Име́ете ли вы ро́дственников за грани́цей?*»
I remember that official forms used to contain the question: 'Do you have any relatives living abroad?'

14.3.3 The verbs облада́ть and владе́ть

The verbs **облада́ть** and **владе́ть** both mean 'to own', 'to possess' and both are used with an object in the *instrumental*. Their use is normally restricted to formal contexts in which the object possessed has a certain value:

Контро́льным паке́том а́кций э́той компа́нии *владе́ет* госуда́рство.
A controlling share in the company is owned by the state.

До 1867 го́да Аля́ской *владе́ла* Росссия.
Until 1867 Alaska was a possession of Russia.

Султа́н *облада́л* несме́тными бога́тствами и неограни́ченной вла́стью.
The sultan possessed countless riches and unlimited power.

Э́тот челове́к *облада́ет* уника́льной спосо́бностью чита́ть чужи́е мы́сли.
That man has the unique ability to read other people's thoughts.

The phrase **владе́ть (иностра́нным) языко́м** means 'to know a (foreign) language':

Мой колле́га свобо́дно *владе́ет* семью́ иностра́нными языка́ми.
My colleague has a fluent knowledge of seven foreign languages.

15

Negation

Simple negation

The particle не

The normal way to create a straightforward negative sentence is to insert the negative particle **не** before the verb:

> **Рекоменду́ется меня́ть де́ньги в аэропорту́ или в гости́нице.**
> It is advisable to change money at the airport or in the hotel.

> **_Не рекоменду́ется_ меня́ть де́ньги в аэропорту́ или в гости́нице.**
> It is not advisable to change money at the airport or in the hotel.

> **Тепе́рь я зна́ю, что де́лать.**
> Now I know what to do.

> **Тепе́рь я _не зна́ю_, что де́лать.**
> Now I don't know what to do.

> **Звони́ домо́й ка́ждый день.**
> Phone home every day.

> **_Не звони́_ домо́й ка́ждый день.**
> Don't phone home every day.

This rule applies to **быть** 'to be', but only when it is used in the way described in **14.1.1**, that is, in sentences indicating equivalence. In present tense sentences, where there is no verb present, the particle **не** is placed before the complement:

> **Бою́сь, что его́ но́вая кни́га _не бу́дет_ о́чень интере́сной.**
> I'm afraid his new book won't be very interesting.

> **Е́сли бы вы _не́ были_ кру́пным бизнесме́ном, кем вы хоте́ли бы стать?**
> If you weren't a big businessman, what would you like to be?

> **Мы _не олига́рхи_, мы _не акционе́ры_, мы про́сто норма́льные лю́ди, кото́рые хотя́т жить норма́льной жи́знью.**
> We're not oligarchs, we're not shareholders, we're just ordinary people who want to live an ordinary life.

> **Я в матема́тике _не силён_.**
> I'm not good at maths.

The particle **не** is *proclitic*, that is, it forms a single stress unit with the following word. In a small number of past tense forms the stress moves forward from the verb onto the particle. The most widely occurring example is **быть**, where the negated forms of the past tense are stressed according to the following pattern:

> Masc. **нé был**   Fem. **не былá**   N. **нé было**   Pl. **нé были**

Negation can be reinforced by the adverbs **совсéм**, **совершéнно**, **абсолю́тно** 'absolutely', '(not) at all':

> **Тепéрь я** *совсéм/совершéнно/абсолю́тно* **не знáю, что дéлать.**
> Now I don't know at all what to do; *or* Now I haven't the slightest idea what to do.

15.1.2 Negation of sentences indicating existence, presence, location and possession

When **быть** 'to be' is used in sentences indicating existence, presence, location and possession (that is, those described in **14.2** and **14.3**), special rules for negation apply. An *impersonal construction* is used in which the *noun* or *pronoun* indicating what does not exist or is not present or possessed is in the *genitive* case, and the *verb* is in the *third person singular*, *neuter* in the *past tense*. The present tense form **есть** has a negative equivalent **нет**, which can never be omitted:

> **Я увéрен, что бýдут проблéмы.**
> I am certain there will be problems.

> **Я увéрен, что** *не бýдет проблéм.*
> I am certain there won't be (any) problems.

> **В двадцáтые гóды в Ростóве ужé был университéт.**
> In the 1920s there was already a university in Rostov.

> **В концé девятнáдцатого вéка в Ростóве ещё** *нé было университéта.*
> At the end of the nineteenth century there still was no university in Rostov.

> **Есть примéры э́того явлéния и в Росси́и.**
> There are examples of this phenomenon in Russia.

> **В Росси́и** *нет примéров* э́того явлéния.
> There are no examples of this phenomenon in Russia.

> **Зáвтра у меня́ бýдет врéмя для э́того.**
> I shall have time for this tomorrow.

> **Зáвтра у меня́** *не бýдет врéмени* для э́того.
> I won't have time for this tomorrow.

> **У них дочь.**
> They have a daughter.

> **У них** *нет сы́на.*
> They have no son.

У меня́ э́та кни́га уже́ есть.
I already have that book.

У меня́ *э́той кни́ги* уже́ *нет*.
I no longer have that book.

Particular attention is drawn to the following examples, where this construction is used to indicate absence:

—Мо́жно поговори́ть с Га́лей?
—Can I speak to Galia?

—Да, она́ здесь.
—Yes, she's here.

Or

—Нет, сейча́с *её нет*.
—No, she's not here at the moment.

Or

—Нет, *её нет* до́ма сейча́с.
—No, she's not at home at the moment.

Я был на э́том собра́нии: я всё по́мню.
I was at that meeting. I can remember everything.

***Меня́ не́ было* на э́том собра́нии: я не зна́ю, что там обсужда́ли.**
I wasn't at that meeting. I don't know what was discussed there.

This construction is not found only with **быть**, but also with a number of other verbs when they are used to indicate existence, presence, location or possession:

быва́ть	to be frequently *or* to be regularly
ока́зываться/оказа́ться	to turn out to be
остава́ться/оста́ться	to remain
происходи́ть/произойти́	to happen, to occur
случа́ться/случи́ться	to happen, to occur
существова́ть (нсв)	to exist

В импе́рии *не быва́ет гра́ждан*. Есть то́лько по́дданные импера́тора.
You don't have citizens in an empire. You just have subjects of the emperor.

В его́ маши́не *не оказа́лось ме́ста* для меня́.
(It turned out that) there was no room in his car for me.

В Москве́ *не оста́лось дешёвых рестора́нов*.
There are no cheap restaurants left in Moscow.

Что́бы *э́того не случи́лось*, на́до во́время опла́чивать счета́.
For that not to happen, you have to pay your bills on time.

***Еди́ной моде́ли демокра́тии* про́сто *не существу́ет*.**
A single model for democracy simply doesn't exist.

NOTE   The expression **Его́ не ста́ло** is a somewhat high-flown way of saying 'He has died'.

15.2 Partial negation

15.2.1 Negating only part of a sentence

In the examples given in **15.1** it is the whole sentence that is negated. Where, however, it is only a single word or a specific part of a sentence that requires to be negated, the *negative* particle **не** is placed immediately *before* the word or phrase concerned:

Он приезжа́ет *не в четве́рг*, а в пя́тницу.
He isn't coming on Thursday, but on Friday.

Не ка́ждый уме́ет писа́ть на тако́м прекра́сном ру́сском языке́, как ты.
Not everyone can write such excellent Russian as you.

The position of **не** can affect the meaning of the sentence:

О́чень *не* рекоменду́ю вам меня́ть де́ньги в аэропорту́ или в гости́нице.
I would very much advise you not to change money at the airport or in the hotel.

Я вам *не о́чень* рекоменду́ю меня́ть де́ньги в аэропорту́ или в гости́нице.
I would not particularly/really advise you to change money at the airport or in the hotel.

In the second example only **о́чень** is negated.

Её сего́дня *нет* до́ма.
She's not at home today.

Она́ сего́дня *не до́ма*, а на рабо́те.
She's not at home today, but at work.

In the second example only **до́ма** is negated. When only part of the sentence is negated, *impersonal constructions* of the type described in **15.2** are not used.

15.2.2 'Pseudo-negatives'

In some instances this use of **не** creates set phrases that are negative in form, but not necessarily in meaning:

не раз   (not once, but) several times
не оди́н   (not one, but) several

Мы *не раз* обсужда́ли э́тот вопро́с на заседа́ниях сове́та директоро́в.
We've discussed this question several times at board meetings.

Пережи́в *не оди́н* тяжеле́йший кри́зис, «Спарта́к» вы́жил.
Having come through several extremely serious crises, Spartak has survived.

In **7.3.2** examples were given of the use of the phrase **не тот** to mean 'the wrong ...'; **не** can also be combined with the adverbs **там** 'there' and **туда́** 'thither', 'to that place' to similar effect:

Вы *не там* сиди́те.
You're sitting in the wrong place.

Вы *не туда́* попа́ли.
You've got the wrong number. (*Literally*, You've ended up in the wrong place.)

15.3 Negative adverbs, negative pronouns and the negative particle ни

15.3.0 Introduction

Russian has a number of negative adverbs, negative pronouns, as well as the negative particle **ни**, which correspond to such English negative words as 'nowhere', 'nothing' and 'neither'. In Russian, these words are normally used in conjunction with the particle **не** in what appear to be sentences with a 'double negative'.

15.3.1 Negative adverbs

The following negative adverbs are used in Russian:

никогда́	never
ника́к	in no way, by no means
нигде́	nowhere
никуда́	(to) nowhere
ниотку́да	from nowhere
ниско́лько	not in the slightest
ничу́ть	not in the slightest

Но мы *никогда́ не́* были друзья́ми.
But we were never friends.

Он *ника́к не* реаги́рует на мои́ про́сьбы.
He doesn't react in any way to my requests.

Бы́ло вре́мя, чёрная икра́ *не* продава́лась *нигде́*.
There was a time when black caviar was not sold anywhere.

***Никуда́ не* уходи́те.**
Don't go off anywhere.

Я по́мощи *ниотку́да не* жду.
I'm not expecting help from anywhere.

Его́ *ниско́лько не* смуща́л тот факт, что уже́ два́жды ему́ отка́зывали.
He was not in the slightest embarrassed by the fact that he had already been turned down twice.

Я *ничу́ть не* сомнева́юсь, что он врёт.
I don't doubt in the slightest that he's lying.

15.3.2 Negative pronouns

The main negative pronouns used in Russian are:

никто́	no one
ничто́/ничего́	nothing
никако́й	not any, no

Никто́, **ничто́/ничего́** and **никако́й** decline like the interrogative pronouns **кто**, **что** and **како́й** respectively (*see* **7.4.1** and **7.4.2**); for more on **ничто́/ничего́**, *see* **15.3.3**.

Сего́дня *никто́ не* звони́л.
Nobody phoned today.

Я *никого́ не* **обвиня́ю, но уже́** *никому́ не* **ве́рю.**
I'm not accusing anybody, but I no longer believe anyone.

Ничего́ **здесь** *не* **понима́ю.**
I can't understand anything here.

Я *не* **получи́л от него́** *никако́го* **отве́та.**
I haven't received any answer from him.

Прода́жа таки́х вооруже́ний *не* **ограни́чена** *никаки́ми* **междунаро́дными соглаше́ниями.**
The sale of such weapons is not restricted by any international agreements.

Further examples with **ничто́/ничего́** are given in **15.3.3**.

There are two *negative pronouns* that are used rather less frequently: **ниче́й** 'no one's'.

This declines like the pronoun **чей** (*see* **7.4.2**):

—**Чья э́та соба́ка?**
—*Ничья́.*

—Whose dog is that?
—Nobody's.

The feminine form **ничья́** is also used as a noun with the meaning 'draw' (in sport):

Их после́дняя игра́ ко́нчилась *ничье́й.*
Their last game ended as a draw.

The pronoun **нико́й** is really only used in two set phrases that serve as emphatic negatives:

нико́им о́бразом	in no way whatsoever
ни в ко́ем слу́чае	in no circumstances whatsoever

Госуда́рственные корпора́ции *нико́им о́бразом не* **замеща́ют ча́стный би́знес.**
In no way whatsoever do state corporations take the place of private business.

Телевизио́нная акаде́мия *ни в ко́ем слу́чае не* **должна́ быть политизи́рованной.**
In no circumstances whatsoever should the Academy of Television become politicised.

As the last example shows, when these pronouns are used with prepositions, the preposition is placed between the negative prefix and the rest of the pronoun, and the whole unit is written as three separate words:

Я *ни с ке́м* **не обсужда́л ва́шу пробле́му.**
I haven't discussed your problem with anyone.

Э́тот стиль *ни с че́м* **не спу́таешь.**
You wouldn't confuse this style with anything.

Её сопе́рник *ни при каки́х* **обстоя́тельствах не мо́жет рассчи́тывать на подде́ржку национа́льных меньши́нств.**
There are no circumstances in which her rival can rely on the support of the ethnic minorities.

Я *ни в чьей* помощи не нуждаюсь.
I don't need anyone's help.

More on ничто/ничего

The form **ничто** is used only for the *nominative* case and thus occurs only on the fairly rare occasions when this pronoun is the *grammatical subject* of a sentence:

Ничто здесь меня не интересует.
Nothing here interests me.

Forms in **… что** are also used in conjunction with *prepositions* that take the *accusative* case:

Она *ни за что* не поедет на Дальний Восток!
She won't go to the Far East at any price!

The pronoun is found much more often in the form **ничего**; this is the ending for the *genitive* case, but it is also the form used without exception when the pronoun serves as the *direct object* of a *transitive* verb:

For more on transitive verbs, *see* **4.13.1**.

Мы *ничего* не боимся.
We're not afraid of anything.

Наши дети *ничего* не читают.
Our children don't read anything.

The form **ничего** is also used in impersonal expressions of the type:

Ничего не слышно, *ничего* не видно.
We can't hear anything, we can't see anything. (*Literally*, Nothing is to be heard . . .)

In addition, **ничего** can have the meaning of 'all right, not too bad':

—**Как дела?**
—**Ничего.**

—How are things?
—Not too bad *or* OK.

Фильм *ничего*, смотреть можно.
The film's OK; it's watchable at least.

Ничего (страшного) can be used in reply to an apology:

—**Извините, пожалуйста.**
—**Ничего.**

—I'm sorry.
—That's all right.

For more on the use of **ничего**, *see* **13.2.5** and **16.2.4**.

15.3.4 ## More on negative adverbs and pronouns

It is perfectly possible in Russian to combine two or more negative adverbs and/or pronouns in the same sentence:

Никто́ никому́ ничего́ не до́лжен.
Nobody owes anybody anything.

Я никогда́ никому́ ничего́ подо́бного не говори́ла.
I never said anything of the sort to anybody.

Negative adverbs and pronouns can be used in conjunction with the negative impersonal predicate forms **нельзя́** 'it is forbidden', 'it is impossible' and **невозмо́жно** 'it is impossible':

Во вре́мя дежу́рства никуда́ нельзя́ выходи́ть.
You are not allowed to go anywhere while you are on duty.

Ника́к нельзя́ откры́ть окно́.
It's totally impossible to open the window.

Нигде́ невозмо́жно бы́ло купи́ть чёрной икры́.
It was impossible to buy black caviar anywhere.

For more on impersonal predicate forms, *see* **11.2.2**.

For more on the aspects of infinitive verbs used with **нельзя́**, *see* **5.7.5**.

There are some more or less set phrases where negative adverbs or pronouns are used without the particle **не**. These include:

Я здесь ни при чём.
This has nothing to do with me.

Мы оста́лись ни с чем.
We were left with nothing.

Вы сейча́с нахо́дитесь на доро́ге в никуда́.
At the moment, you're on a road to nowhere.

15.3.5 ## The negative particle ни

When it is used as a negative particle **ни** has two functions. The sequence **ни ... ни** corresponds to English 'neither ... nor':

Я не ем ни ры́бы ни мя́са.
I eat neither fish nor meat.

Она́ не уме́ет разгова́ривать ни с колле́гами ни с ученика́ми.
She doesn't know how to talk either to her colleagues or to her pupils.

Я не хочу́ ни есть ни пить.
I want neither to eat nor to drink.

Его́ нет ни до́ма ни на рабо́те.
He's neither at home nor at work.

The particle **не** is not used when **ни ... ни** is used in certain set phrases of the type:

ни ры́ба ни мя́со	neither one thing nor another
ни с того́ ни с сего́	suddenly, for no obvious reason

Она́ *ни с того́ ни с сего́* реши́ла всё бро́сить и уе́хать рабо́тать в Ита́лию.
She suddenly decided to give everything up and go off and work in Italy.

The other use of **ни** is to make negation more emphatic:

Я *не* зна́ю *ни одного́* сло́ва по-кита́йски.
I don't know a single word of Chinese.

Я *ни ра́зу не́* был на Кавка́зе.
Not even once have I been to the Caucasus.

NOTE	It is important to distinguish these emphatic negatives (which are combined with the particle **не**) from the 'pseudo-negatives' **не оди́н**, **не раз** described in **15.3.2**.

Они́ *не* обрати́ли на меня́ *ни мале́йшего* внима́ния.
They didn't pay me even the slightest attention.

Ни с ме́ста!
Don't move! *or* Stay right where you are!

NOTE	The negative particle **ни** should be distinguished from the reinforcing particle **ни** found in constructions such as:

как бы то ни́ бы́ло   however that might be
что бы ты ни говори́л   whatever you might say

For more on these constructions, *see* **21.6.4** and **23.2.1**.

15.4   The case of the direct object in negative sentences

In **3.3.3** it was noted that the *genitive* is sometimes used instead of the *accusative* for the *direct object* of a *transitive* verb in a *negative* sentence. The choice of case is partly a matter of rules, but partly a matter of preference.

The genitive is always used in conjunction with the emphatic particle **ни**:

Я не зна́ю *ни одного́ сло́ва* по-кита́йски.
I don't know a single word of Chinese.

Они́ не обрати́ли на меня́ *ни мале́йшего внима́ния*.
They didn't pay me even the slightest attention.

The genitive is normally used:

(1) In sentences with a *negative adverb* or the *negative pronoun* **никако́й**:

Я *никогда́* не ем *мя́са*.
I never eat meat.

Я не получи́л от него́ *никако́го отве́та*.
I haven't received any answer from him.

(2) In constructions involving the verb **име́ть**, as well as in some other set phrases such as **игра́ть роль** 'to play a part':

Они́ *не име́ют пра́ва* входи́ть в ваш дом без ва́шего разреше́ния.
They have no right to enter your house without your permission.

Здесь интеллиге́нция *не игра́ет значи́тельной ро́ли*.
Here the intelligentsia does not play a signifcant part.

(3) When the object is **э́то**:

Э́того я не знал.
That is something I didn't know.

The *genitive* tends to be preferred in general statements or when the object is indefinite:

Ты что, *газе́т* не чита́ешь?
You mean to say you don't read newspapers?

Почему́ ты не купи́л *хле́ба*?
Why didn't you buy (any) bread?

The *accusative* is used as follows:

(1) When it is not the whole the sentence, but only a specific part that is negated:

Не ка́ждый соверши́т *тако́й посту́пок*.
Not everyone would do something like that.

(2) In sentences where the negation is apparent, rather than real, for example, 'psuedo-negatives' of the type described in **15.2.2** or genuine double negatives of the type **нельзя ... не** 'it is impossible not to':

Мы *не раз* обсужда́ли *э́тот вопро́с* на заседа́ниях сове́та директоро́в.
We've discussed this question several times at board meetings.

Нельзя́ не почу́вствовать *го́рдость*, когда́ чита́ешь о его́ спорти́вных подвигах.
It's impossible not to feel pride when you read about his sporting achievements.

In most instances not included in any of the above categories either case may be found:

Я реши́л не тра́тить *вре́мя/вре́мени* на оправда́ния.
I am not going to waste time on excuses.

Я не зна́ю его́ *жену́/жены́*.
I don't know his wife.

Мя́со/мя́са мы не еди́м то́лько по бу́дням.
We don't eat meat on weekdays only.

15.5 Negatives of the не́чего, не́когда type

Russian has a special set of negative pronouns and adverbs that are used in sentences corresponding to the English 'there is nothing to do', 'there is nowhere to go':

не́кого	there is no one
не́чего	there is nothing

не́когда	there is no time
не́где	there is nowhere
не́куда	there is nowhere (to go)
не́откуда	there is nowhere (from where)
не́зачем	there is no point

These forms are mostly used with an *infinitive* verb. If there is a *logical subject*, it goes, as in most impersonal sentences, in the *dative*:

Он вдруг по́нял, что ему́ *не́кому передава́ть* о́пыт.
He suddenly realised there was nobody he could pass on his experience to.

Нам здесь *не́чего де́лать*.
There's nothing for us to do here.

Мне *не́когда* тут с ва́ми *расси́живаться*.
I haven't got time to sit around here with you.

Здесь *не́где припаркова́ть* маши́ну.
There's nowhere here to park a car.

Нашей молодёжи ве́чером *не́куда пойти́*.
Our young people have nowhere to go in the evening.

Таку́ю огро́мную су́мму *взять* бы́ло *не́откуда*.
There was nowhere to get hold of such an enormous sum (of money).

Мне *не́зачем е́хать* за грани́цу: у меня́ здесь есть всё, что ну́жно.
There's no point in going abroad; I've everything I need here.

NOTE | These sentences are the negative equivalent of sentences of the following type (already illustrated in **14.2.1**):

> **Тепе́рь *моско́вским автомобили́стам* есть *куда́ пожа́ловаться* на незако́нную эвакуа́цию их маши́н.**
> Now there is somewhere where Moscow drivers can complain when their vehicles have been towed away illegally.

In this case, however, the negative sentences are rather more frequent than those without negation.

When *pronouns* of this type are used with a *preposition*, the preposition is normally placed between the negative prefix and the pronoun, and the whole unit is written as three separate words:

Здесь *не́ с кем* вы́пить.
There's nobody to have a drink with here.

Нам с тобо́й *не́ о чем* говори́ть.
The two of us have nothing to talk about.

Не́чего can also mean 'there's no need to...', 'there's no cause to ...', used in the sense of conveying a reproach:

Кто винова́т, что вы пропусти́ли са́мое интере́сное? *Не́чего* бы́ло уходи́ть так ра́но.
Whose fault is it that you missed the most interesting part? There was no need to leave so early.

Рабо́тать на́до, *не́чего* дурака́ валя́ть!
You need to get on with your work, instead of messing around.

Тут удивля́ться *не́чего*.
There's no cause to be surprised.

Some expressions involving these negative forms have become set phrases:

не́ за что	don't mention it (a fairly formal reply to thanks)
от не́чего де́лать	from want of anything better to do (note that the preposition goes before the entire phrase)
да́льше не́куда	that's the limit, it can't get any worse

—Большо́е спаси́бо..
—*Не́ за что.*

—Thank you very much.
—Don't mention it.

Не́которые полага́ют, что сове́тский челове́к чита́л *от не́чего де́лать*.
Some people think that people in the Soviet Union read because they hadn't anything better to do.

Ситуа́ция до того́ осложни́лась, что *да́льше не́куда*.
The situation's become so complicated that it can't get any worse.

16

Expressing attitudes

16.1 Expressing attitudes using suffixes

16.1.0 Introduction

A very important means by which attitudes are expressed in Russian is the use of certain *suffixes*, especially those attached to *nouns*. These suffixes, which are described in detail in **10.1.1**, are conventionally known as *diminutive* and *augmentative suffixes*, but these terms are somewhat misleading, since in addition to (and sometimes instead of) any connotations of size, they also give information about the attitude of the speaker. It is the use of these suffixes that often makes many people who come into contact with Russian describe the language as being unusually emotional and expressive. At the same time, however, these suffixes are particularly difficult for learners to master, partly because of the great variety of suffixes available and the sometimes unpredictable nature of the way in which they are used, and partly because the connotations they contain and the nuances of attitude that they express are often extremely subtle.

In general terms, suffixes with *positive* connotations, all of which are diminutive suffixes, render things small and/or 'nice' or 'cute'. Suffixes with negative connotations, which can be diminutive or augmentative, on the other hand, make things either smaller or bigger, but also uglier or in some other way less appreciable.

16.1.1 Using diminutive suffixes with positive connotations

In the following examples nouns are used with a *diminutive* suffix that has a positive connotation. In these sentences the suffix is not intended to give information about size, but instead serves to convey a positive feeling from the speaker to the listener, for example, helping to soften a command or a request. For this reason the suffix itself is generally untranslatable, although sometimes its effect may be conveyed in English by other means:

> **Ну, съе́шьте ещё *таре́лочку*!**
> Come on, eat up another plateful, please.

> **Бу́дьте любе́зны, ва́ши *биле́тики*?**
> Can I see your tickets, please?

> **Извини́те, мо́жно вас на *мину́точку*?**
> Excuse me, could I have a word with you?
> *Or* Excuse me, could I see you for a minute?

Прости́те, *огоньку́* **не найдётся?**
Excuse me, you wouldn't happen to have a light, would you?

Запиши́те, пожа́луйста, *телефо́нчик*: **е́сли кран опя́ть потечёт, позвони́те мне.**
Do please write down my phone number. If the tap starts dripping again, feel free to telephone me.

Жизнь на но́вом ме́сте пошла́ гла́дко, и они́ уже́ ста́ли поду́мывать о том, что́бы завести́ второ́го *ребёночка.*
After the move everything was going smoothly and they were starting to think about having a second child.

К ле́ту я равноду́шен: жара́, пыль, комары́... А вот *зи́мушку* **моро́зную люблю́!**
I'm not bothered about summer, with all the heat, the dust and the mosquitoes, but I really love a cold and frosty winter.

Заходи́ за́втра *вечерко́м,* **вы́пьем по** *рю́мочке*!
Call in tomorrow evening for a dram (*or* and we'll have a glass of something warming).

In the following sentences the suffix combines both a positive emotion and a reference to size:

Ду́ет тёплый *ветеро́к,* **и по не́бу плыву́т пуши́стые облака́.**
There's a warm breeze, and fluffy clouds are scudding across the sky.

В пода́ренной су́мочке она́ обнару́жила сере́бряное *коле́чко* **и** *зе́ркальце* **в фо́рме** *серде́чка.*
In the handbag she'd been given she found a silver ring and a small mirror in the shape of a heart.

Смотри́, кака́я заба́вная *соба́чка*!
Look, what a funny little dog!

Наде́ньте малышу́ что́-нибудь на *голо́вку,* **на у́лице уже́ прохла́дно.**
You'd better cover the baby's head; it's quite chilly outside.

16.1.2 ## Using suffixes with negative connotations

In the following examples the *diminutive* suffix **-ишк-** refers to size, but is also used to express a negative or diminishing attitude on the part of the speaker:

Городи́шко, **в кото́рый его́ командирова́ли, оказа́лся се́рым и ску́чным, как ты́сячи други́х провинциа́льных городко́в на э́том све́те.**
The miserable hole that he'd been sent to was as grey and as boring as thousands of other provincial towns on this earth.

А э́тот *зайчи́шка* **отку́да взя́лся? У тебя́ не́ было тако́й игру́шки.**
Where did you find that wretched little hare? That's not one of your toys.

Он бро́сил в чемода́н ста́ренький сви́тер, две па́ры носко́в да ко́е-како́е *бельи́шко.*
He threw into the suitcase an old sweater, two pairs of socks and some underwear.

Augmentative suffixes normally convey both a reference to (large) size and generally negative connotations:

> **Такóй *голосúна* когó хóчешь разбýдит.**
> A voice like that could wake anyone up.

> **С егó *кулачúщами* емý бы бóксом занимáться, а не на скрúпке игрáть.**
> With fists like that he should take up boxing, not the violin!

> **Он сдал ключú от кóмнаты, но такýю *грязúщу* пóсле себя остáвил, – дáже посýду за собóй не помыл!**
> He handed in the keys to the room, but left such a filthy mess behind; he didn't even do the washing up!

> **Сосéдний дом пошёл под снос; стоúт грóхот, *пылúща* . . .**
> They've started to demolish the building next door; there's noise and dust everywhere!

> **Не дышú на меня; от тебя *винúщем* пáхнет!**
> Don't breathe on me; you smell terribly of booze!

NOTES

(i) As the first, second and fourth of the above examples demonstrate, the addition of a diminutive or an augmentative suffix, regardless of the ending, does not affect the gender of the original noun (*see also* **10.1.1**).

(ii) Although the augmentative suffix **-ище** normally has negative connotations, the noun **дружúще**, used as a form of address, expresses both a familiar and a positive attitude:

> **Сто лет тебя не вúдел, *дружúще*!**
> I haven't seen you for ages, mate!

Nouns indicating members of the family

Diminutive suffixes are frequently used to add expressive connotations to nouns indicating members of the family. Not surprisingly, the connotations of these suffixes are almost invariably positive. The following terms might be used when referring to a member of your family:

дочь	daughter	дóчка, дóченька, дочýрка
сын	son	сынóк, сынóчек, сынúшка
мáма	mum, mother	мáмочка, мамýля, мамáша, мáменька
сестрá	sister	сестрúца, сестрúчка, сестрёнка
брат	brother	брáтик, брáтец

> **Нáша *дóчка* ужé перешлá во вторóй класс.**
> Our daughter has already gone into second year (at primary school).

The following terms can be used as affectionate forms of address to members of your family:

женá	wife	жёнушка
муж	husband	муженёк
мáма	mum, mother	мáмочка, мамýля
пáпа	dad, father	пáпочка, папýля
сын	son	сынóк, сынóчек, сынýля
сестрá	sister	сестрúца, сестрúчка
брат	brother	брáтец, братúшка
дéдушка	grandfather	дедýля

ба́бушка	grandmother	бабу́ля
дя́дя	uncle	дядю́шка
тётя	aunt	тётушка

Сыно́чек, сде́лай му́зыку поти́ше, а то сосе́ди опя́ть приду́т жа́ловаться.
Turn your music down (son), or else the neighbours will be coming to complain again.

NOTES

(i)   In this usage the suffix **-ишк-** (**сыни́шка**) has positive connotations.

(ii) **Бра́тец** is often used as a familiar form of address to a male person:

А ты, *бра́тец*, хитёр! Ло́вко приду́мал!
You're a sharp one, mate! I don't know how you thought that one up!

16.1.4   Using suffixes with forenames

It was noted in **12.1.1** that Russian forenames have various different forms, of which the most important are the *full* and *familiar* versions. In addition, it is possible to add a wide range of diminutive suffixes to the familiar version in order to create forms that can express various subtle nuances of connotation. The two most frequently used suffixes are -к- and –очк-/-ечк-, -оньк-/-еньк-. These suffixes normally convey different attitudes: the former expresses close familiarity and even on occasion slight disdain; it is typically used between close friends and siblings. The latter expresses strong affection and love, and might be used by parents when comforting their children or when writing letters to them.

The following tables give the various forms of selected forenames:

Male forenames

Full version	*'Standard' familiar version*	*Version that expresses close familiarity or disdain*	*Version that expresses strong affection*
Бори́с	Бо́ря	Бо́рька	Бо́ренька
Валенти́н	Ва́ля	Ва́лька	Ва́лечка
Влади́мир	Воло́дя, Во́ва	Во́вка	Во́вочка
Григо́рий	Гри́ша	Гри́шка	Гри́шенька
Дми́трий	Ди́ма	Ди́мка	Ди́мочка
Евге́ний	Же́ня	Же́нька	Же́нечка
Ива́н	Ва́ня	Ва́нька	Ва́нечка
Михаи́л	Ми́ша	Ми́шка	Ми́шенька
Никола́й	Ко́ля	Ко́лька	Ко́ленька
Пётр	Пе́тя	Пе́тька	Пе́тенька
Серге́й	Серёжа	Серёжка	Серёженька

Female forenames

Full version	*'Standard' familiar version*	*Version that expresses close familiarity or disdain*	*Version that expresses strong affection*
А́нна	А́ня	А́нька	А́нечка
Валенти́на	Ва́ля	Ва́лька	Ва́лечка
Екатери́на	Ка́тя	Ка́тька	Ка́тенька, Катю́ша

Full version	*'Standard' familiar version*	*Version that expresses close familiarity or disdain*	*Version that expresses strong affection*
Еле́на	Ле́на	Ле́нка	Ле́ночка
Евге́ния	Же́ня	Же́нька	Же́нечка
Мари́я	Ма́ша	Ма́шка	Ма́шенька
Ни́на	Ни́на	Ни́нка	Ни́ночка
Поли́на	По́ля	Поли́нка	Поле́нька
Раи́са	Ра́я	Ра́йка	Ра́ечка
Светла́на	Све́та	Све́тка	Све́точка

Пе́тька, почему́ не звони́шь, стари́к?
Petia, old man, why do you never phone?

Ма́шенька, не на́до волнова́ться. Всё бу́дет хорошо́.
Masha, there's no need to worry. Everything will turn out OK.

Using suffixes with adjectives and adverbs

As was noted in 10.2.7, it is also possible to add *diminutive* and *augmentative* suffixes to *adjectives* and *adverbs* in order to create forms that can express a particular attitude on behalf of the speaker. In many instances the nuances are particularly subtle and difficult to express in translation:

Пока́ по телеви́зору шла рекла́ма, он *бы́стренько* сходи́л на ку́хню и отку́порил буты́лочку *холодне́нького* пивка́.
While the advertisements were on TV he nipped into the kitchen and opened a bottle of nice cool beer.

На сле́дующий день она́ уже́ хва́сталась в шко́ле свои́м *нове́ньким* телефо́ном.
The next day she was already showing off her new telephone in school.

У́тром на своём *ста́реньком* велосипе́де прие́хал дереве́нский почтальо́н; привёз ба́бушке пе́нсию.
In the morning the village postman arrived on his ancient bicycle; he had brought granny her pension.

Нет, купа́ться я сего́дня не бу́ду; вода́ *холодню́щая*!
I have absolutely no intention of bathing today; that water's freezing cold!

Когда́ он появи́лся на заня́тиях, под гла́зом у него́ красова́лся *здорове́нный* синя́к.
He came to lectures sporting a fine black eye.

—Вы́ключи телеви́зор; оте́ц спит.
—Я *тихо́нечко* досмотрю́ фильм и пото́м вы́ключу, мо́жно?

—Turn off the television; your father's asleep.
—Will it be all right if I turn it down now and turn it off after the film?

—Зна́чит, мы договори́лись; встреча́емся за́втра в семь.
—Вот и *чудне́нько*!

—We're agreed, then. We're meeting tomorrow at seven.
—That's great!

16.2 | # Likes, dislikes, loves, hates and preferences

16.2.1 | ## To like and to love: нра́виться/понра́виться and люби́ть/полюби́ть

Нра́виться/понра́виться and **люби́ть/полюби́ть** correspond approximately to the English verbs 'to like' and 'to love'. In general, the latter pair of verbs indicates a stronger feeling than the former.

Люби́ть/полюби́ть is transitive: the grammatical *subject* in the *nominative* case indicates the person experiencing the feeling, while the *direct object* in the *accusative* indicates the object of his or her affection. With **нра́виться/понра́виться** the roles of subject and object are inverted: the grammatical *subject* in the *nominative* denotes what is liked and the *indirect object* in the *dative* denotes the person experiencing the feeling.

The following sentences illustrate the use of these verbs with reference to inanimate objects:

> Я *люблю́* класси́ческую му́зыку.
> I like/love classical music.

> Я *люблю́* зелёные я́блоки.
> I like/love green apples.

> Я *не люблю́* класси́ческую му́зыку/класси́ческой му́зыки.
> I don't like/enjoy classical music.

> *Мне нра́вится* класси́ческая му́зыка.
> I like/am fond of classical music.

> *Мне нра́вятся* зелёные я́блоки.
> I like/am fond of green apples.

> *Мне не нра́вится* класси́ческая му́зыка.
> I don't like (*or* I'm not fond of) classical music.

For more on the use of the accusative and the genitive cases to indicate the direct object of negative transitive verbs, *see* **15.4**.

The perfective verb **понра́виться** tends to be used to indicate an immediate reaction to something:

> Мне о́чень *понра́вились* э́ти зелёные я́блоки.
> I really liked those green apples (when I tasted them).

> Мне *не понра́вился* его́ после́дний фильм.
> I didn't like his last film (when I saw it).

When they are used with reference to living beings, and especially people, **люби́ть/ полюби́ть** and **нра́виться/понра́виться** correspond respectively to the English 'to love' and 'to like':

> Она́ *полюби́ла* его́ с пе́рвого взгля́да.
> She fell in love with him at first sight.

> Он *понра́вился* ей с пе́рвого взгля́да.
> She took an instant liking to him.

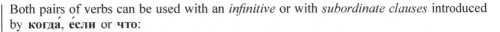
Both pairs of verbs can be used with an *infinitive* or with *subordinate clauses* introduced by **когда́**, **е́сли** or **что**:

> **Я** *люблю́ слу́шать* **совреме́нную му́зыку.**
> I enjoy listening to contemporary music.

> **Ей** *нра́вилось гуля́ть* **в па́рке по́сле у́жина.**
> She used to like going for a walk in the park after supper.

> **В де́тстве она́** *люби́ла, когда́* **ей чита́ли вслух.**
> When she was a child, she used to like being read aloud to.

> **А тебе́** *понра́вится, е́сли* **кто-нибудь начнёт следи́ть за ка́ждым твои́м ша́гом?**
> Would you like it if someone started to watch you at every step?

> **Ему́ не** *нра́вилось, что* **по́сле ка́ждой вечери́нки мать звони́ла роди́телям его́ друзе́й.**
> He didn't like the fact that his mother phoned his friends' parents after every party.

16.2.2 Other ways of talking likes and dislikes

The phrase **быть по душе́** is similar in meaning to **нра́виться** and is constructed in the same way: the grammatical *subject* in the *nominative* denotes what is liked and the *indirect object* in the *dative* denotes the person experiencing the feeling:

> **Нам** *бы́ло по душе́* **тако́е обслу́живание.**
> We liked that level of service.

The following words and phrases express a very strong degree of liking:

обожа́ть (нсв)	to adore, to admire
быть в восто́рге от (+ gen.)	to be delighted with

> **Она́** *обожа́ет* **бале́т.**
> She adores ballet.

> **Своего́ ста́ршего бра́та он** *обожа́л* **и подража́л ему́ во всём.**
> He admired his elder brother and imitated everything he did.

> **Мы** *бы́ли в восто́рге от* **тако́го приёма.**
> We were delighted by the welcome we got.

There are a number of useful words and phrases that use forms derived from **люби́ть**:

влюбля́ться/влюби́ться в (+ acc.)	to fall in love with
влюблён/влюблена́ в (+ acc.)	in love with
влюблённый	lover, person in love (often plural)
любо́вник/любо́вница	lover (sexual partner)
люби́тель/люби́тельница	lover (of an activity), (masculine form only) amateur

> **Роме́о** *влюби́лся в* **Джулье́тту с пе́рвого взгля́да.**
> Romeo fell in love with Juliet at first sight.

> **Они́** *влюблены́* **друг в дру́га.**
> They are in love with one another.

Моя́ сестра́ *влюблена́ в теа́тр*; она́ не пропуска́ет ни одно́й премье́ры.
My sister is in love with the theatre; she never misses a single first night.

Молоды́е *влюблённые* лю́бят гуля́ть по на́бережным Невы́, когда́ в Петербу́рге стоя́т бе́лые но́чи.
Young lovers like to stroll along the banks of the Neva during the White Nights season in St Petersburg.

Ходи́ли слу́хи, что она́ како́е-то вре́мя была́ *любо́вницей* изве́стного поли́тика.
There were rumours that for some time she was the mistress of a famous politician.

Его́ мать – больша́я *люби́тельница* фигу́рного ката́ния.
His mother is a great lover of figure-skating.

Ко́нкурсы для профессиона́лов и *люби́телей* обы́чно прохо́дят разде́льно.
Competitions for professionals and amateurs usually take place separately.

Люби́тель often appears as part of a compound noun denoting someone who practises a particular hobby:

фотолюби́тель	a keen photographer
кинолюби́тель	an amateur film maker
автолюби́тель	someone whose hobby is cars and/or driving.

16.2.3 Talking about preferences

Preferences are indicated using the verb **предпочита́ть/предпоче́сть**. If the item to which something is preferred takes the form of a *noun* or *noun phrase*, this is in the *dative*; if it takes the form of a *clause*, this is introduced by the conjunction **чем**:

Он *предпочита́ет* конья́к во́дке.
He prefers brandy to vodka.

Я *предпочту́* жить в нищете́, *чем* занима́ться нелюби́мым де́лом.
I would prefer to live in poverty than to have to do something I don't like.

The phrase **на мой (твой, ваш**, etc.**) вкус** 'to my (your, etc.) taste' can also be used to express preferences:

Дава́й ку́пим ей в пода́рок ва́зу; вы́бери что́-нибудь подходя́щее, *на твой вкус*.
Let's buy her a vase for a present. You choose something suitable, whatever you prefer (*or* think best).

16.2.4 Indicating approval or acceptance

A reaction of approval or appreciation is normally expressed by one of the following adverbs, all of which can be translated as 'wonderful', 'excellent' or 'great':

великоле́пно
замеча́тельно
здо́рово
отли́чно
превосхо́дно
чуде́сно

—А я уже́ пригото́вил за́втрак.
—Вот и *отли́чно*.

—I've already made breakfast.
—That's great!

—Он сдал все экза́мены на пять и око́нчил университе́т с кра́сным дипло́мом.
—*Превосхо́дно!*

—He got top marks in all his exams and graduated with distinction.
—Excellent!

NOTE   Five is the top mark in all Russian exams. Those graduating with distinction receive a degree certificate with a red (instead of the normal blue) cover.

In informal language a reaction of acceptance, rather than of approval can be expressed by the following forms, all of which mean something like 'OK' or 'it will do':

годи́тся
та́к себе
пойдёт
сойдёт

The last two words can be reinforced by the particle **ничего́**:

—Это съедо́бный гриб?
—*Годи́тся*, клади́ его́ в корзи́ну.

—Is that an edible mushroom?
—It's OK, put it in the basket.

—Фильм был интере́сный?
—*Да та́к себе́.*

—Was the film interesting?
—It was all right, I suppose.

—Ка́жется, я не о́чень хорошо́ закле́ил э́ту дыру́?
—*Ничего́, пойдёт.*

—I don't think I made a very good job of stopping up that hole.
—It's OK; it will do.

—Как ты ду́маешь, нам ну́жно де́лать в кварти́ре вла́жную убо́рку?
—*Ничего́, и так сойдёт.*

—What do you think? Do we need to give the flat a thorough spring cleaning?
—No, it will do as it is.

The adjective **сно́сный** means 'adequate', 'acceptable', 'reasonable', 'not bad':

Пого́да стоя́ла *сно́сная*, и, е́сли оде́ться потепле́е, мо́жно бы́ло гуля́ть у мо́ря.
The weather wasn't too bad, and if you wrapped up warmly, you could go for a walk by the sea.

16.2.5 ## Indicating indifference, disapproval, dislikes and hates

Indifference can be expressed by the adverb **безразли́чно** or the phrase **всё равно́**; in both instances the noun or pronoun denoting the person who experiences the feeling is in the *dative* case:

> *Ему́ бы́ло всё равно́, куда́ идти́.*
> He didn't care where they went.

> **Я не боле́льщик:** *мне безразли́чно, чья кома́нда сего́дня победи́т.*
> I'm not supporting anyone: it's a matter of indifference which team wins today.

Indifference can be indicated more forcefully by using the verbs **начха́ть** (*literally*, 'to sneeze') and **плева́ть/наплева́ть** (*literally*, 'to spit'), both of which are used with the preposition **на** (+ acc.). Since these verbs are used in the infinitive, the logical subject is in the *dative*:

> **Напра́сно мы наде́ялись, что он послу́шает на́шего сове́та.** *Ему́ бы́ло на э́то наплева́ть.*
> Our hopes that he might listen to our advice were in vain. He couldn't care less.

> *А мне начха́ть на то*, **что обо мне поду́мают сосе́ди!**
> I don't give a damn what the neighbours think about me!

To express mild dislikes, the negative forms of the verbs and phrases given in **16.2.1** and **16.2.2** can be used:

> —Ну, как тебе́ моя́ но́вая причёска?
> —Ты зна́ешь, я *не в восто́рге…*

> —What do you think about my new hairstyle?
> —Well, to be honest, I'm not exactly over the moon about it …

For other examples, *see* **16.1.1**.

The verb that corresponds to the English 'to hate' is **ненави́деть/возненави́деть**, while a strong dislike can also be indicated by the following constructions, all of which correspond approximately to the English 'I can't stand':

> я не выношу́
> я не перева́риваю   (*literally*, I can't digest)
> я терпе́ть не могу́
> я на дух не переношу́

> **В лю́дях она́** *ненави́дела* **жа́дность и лицеме́рие.**
> She hated greed and hypocrisy in people.

> **Я челове́к терпели́вый, но не** *выношу́* **одного́ – же́нской исте́рики.**
> I am a patient man, but one thing I can't stand is female hysterics.

> *Терпе́ть не могу́*, **когда́ в маши́не ку́рят.**
> I cannot put up with people smoking in my car.

> **На́ша ба́бушка** *на дух не перено́сит* **рок-му́зыку.**
> Our grandmother cannot abide rock music.

> **Ты опя́ть идёшь на дискоте́ку со свое́й но́вой подру́жкой? Сказа́ть тебе́ че́стно, я её** *не перева́риваю.*
> Are you going to the disco again with that new girlfriend of yours? To be honest, I can't stand her.

The *conditional*, reinforced with the adverb **ещё**, can be used to express disapproval:

> **Неуже́ли ты и э́того не уме́ешь? Ты *бы ещё спроси́ла*, как на́до карто́шку чи́стить!**
> Are you trying to tell me you can't even do that? You might just as well ask how to peel potatoes!

For information on the conditional, *see* **4.10**.

16.3 Wishes and desires

16.3.1 Хоте́ть/захоте́ть and жела́ть/пожела́ть

The main verbs used for expressing wishes and desires are **хоте́ть/захоте́ть** 'to want' and **жела́ть/пожела́ть** 'to wish (for)'.

Хоте́ть/захоте́ть is normally used with an object in the *accusative* case, but the *genitive* tends to be used if the object is abstract:

> **Ма́ма, я *хочу́* вот *э́ту су́мочку*!**
> Mum, I want this bag here!

> **Он всю жизнь *хоте́л* то́лько *одного́ – бога́тства*.**
> All his life he wanted only one thing: riches.

For more on the use of the accusative and the genitive with **хоте́ть/захоте́ть**, *see* **3.3.5**.

Жела́ть/пожела́ть is used with an object in the *genitive* (see **3.3.4**):

> **Мы *пожела́ли* друзья́м *счастли́вого пути́*, и по́езд тро́нулся.**
> We wished our friends a pleasant journey and the train then set off.

Both pairs of verbs can be used with an *infinitive* verb if the wish or the desire concerns only the *subject* of the sentence:

> **Она́ *хо́чет* вы́йти за́муж в э́том году́.**
> She wants to get married this year.

> **Мы *хоти́м* завести́ соба́ку.**
> We want to get a dog.

> **Гость *пожела́л* приня́ть ва́нну и вы́пить ко́фе.**
> The guest expressed a wish to take a bath and have a drink of coffee.

If the wish or the desire concerns anyone other than the subject of the sentence, both pairs of verbs are followed by a *subordinate clause* introduced by the conjunction **что́бы**:

> **Мы *хоти́м, что́бы* на плане́те не́ было войн.**
> We want the planet to be free of war.

> **Хочу́ *пожела́ть всему́ коллекти́ву* а́второв, что́бы э́та кни́га была́, наконе́ц, и́здана.**
> I would like to express to the entire team of authors my wish to see the book finally published (*literally*, that the book be finally published).

For the use of the past tense with **что́бы**, *see* **9.3.4**.

16.3.2   Less categorical desires

The *impersonal reflexive* pair of verbs **хоте́ться/захоте́ться** expresses a less categorical desire than **хоте́ть/захоте́ть** and can imply less intention on the part of the person concerned; it often corresponds to the English 'feel like'. The person experiencing the feeling, if present, is indicated by a noun or pronoun in the *dative*:

> *Ей хо́чется* вы́йти за́муж за киноактёра.
> She wants to marry a film-star.

> *Ей захоте́лось* рома́нтики, чего́-то необы́чного.
> She (suddenly) felt like something romantic, something out of the ordinary.

> Ле́том *хо́чется* загора́ть и купа́ться, а не сиде́ть на ску́чных ле́кциях.
> In summer you feel more like sunbathing and going for a swim than sitting in boring lectures.

For more on impersonal verbs, *see* **3.4.3** and **11.2.2**.

The conditional form of **хоте́ть** has the effect of turning a wish into a polite request:

> До́брый день, моя́ жена́ *хоте́ла бы* получи́ть консульта́цию врача́.
> Good day, I would like to make an appointment for my wife to see the doctor (*literally*, my wife would like an appointment …).

> Я *бы хоте́л* заказа́ть за́втрак в но́мер.
> I would like to order breakfast in my room.

16.3.3   Expressing a desire using the particle бы

The particle **бы** is often used in informal language to indicate a wish. It is usually accompanied by the infinitive:

> Сейча́с *бы вы́пить* кру́жку пи́ва!
> I'd love a glass of beer right now!

> *Пое́хать бы* сейча́с на неде́льку к мо́рю!
> If only we could drop everything and go off to the seaside for a week!

> Тебе́ *бы отдохну́ть* как сле́дует!
> If only you could get a proper rest!

The infinitive, however, can be omitted:

> Сейча́с *бы* кру́жку пи́ва!
> I'd love a glass of beer right now!

> Сейча́с *бы* к мо́рю на неде́льку!
> If only we could drop everything and go off to the seaside for a week!

> Эх, диктофо́н *бы* сюда́: мо́жно бы́ло бы записа́ть расска́з э́того старика́ о войне́.
> If only we had a dictaphone here, we could have recorded the old man's reminiscences about the war.

16.4 Expressing opinions

16.4.1 Indicating your opinion

To ask for someone's opinion the following question formula can be used:

как ты ду́маешь/вы ду́маете?
What do you think?

Как вы ду́маете, мы во́время прие́дем, и́ли нет?
What do you think? Will we arrive on time or not?

To indicate that something is a matter of opinion, the following verbs and phrases can be used:

ду́мать/поду́мать	to think
полага́ть (нсв)	to assume, to suppose
счита́ть/счесть	to consider
мне ка́жется	I think
по моему́ мне́нию	in my opinion (in your opinion, etc.)
(по ва́шему мне́нию etc.)	
по-мо́ему (по-ва́шему etc.)	in my opinion (in your opinion, etc.)
на мой взгляд	in my opinion (in your opinion, etc.)
(на ваш взгляд etc.)	

Ду́маю, что скоре́е всего́ мы опозда́ем.
I think we'll probably be late.

Вы не счита́ете, что всё э́то мо́жно бы́ло бы сде́лать намно́го про́ще?
Don't you think that this could all have been done much more simply?

По на́шему мне́нию, у обвине́ния недоста́точно доказа́тельств.
In our opinion the prosecution does not have sufficient evidence.

По-мо́ему, ты непра́в. Я бы посове́товал тебе́ извини́ться перед ней.
I think you're wrong. I would advise you to apologise to her.

На мой взгляд, лю́ди име́ют пра́во одева́ться, как они́ хотя́т.
In my opinion, people have the right to wear whatever they like.

16.4.2 Indicating agreement and consent

The following formulae can be used in soliciting or giving agreement:

ты согла́сен/согла́сна, вы согла́сны?
do you agree?

я согла́сен/согла́сна, мы согла́сны.
I agree, we agree.

—**Мне ка́жется, пе́рвый приз ну́жно присуди́ть уча́стнику под но́мером три. *Вы согла́сны?***
—*Да, я согла́сен.*

—I think we should award the first prize to contestant number three. Do you agree?
—Yes, I agree.

A slightly less enthusiastic form of agreement can be indicated by using negated forms of the verb **возража́ть/возрази́ть** 'to object':

> *Ты не возража́ешь, е́сли мы вы́ключим телеви́зор?*
> Would you have any objections if we turned the television off?

> —**Мне ка́жется, пе́рвый приз ну́жно присуди́ть уча́стнику под но́мером три. Вы согла́сны?**
> —*Я не возража́ю.*

> —I think we should award the first prize to contestant number three. Do you agree?
> —I've no objections.

For the use of the *negative* to make a question more tentative, *see* **17.1.3**.

The verb **соглаша́ться/согласи́ться** 'to agree' is more frequently used to describe someone's reaction rather than as a means of expressing one's agreement:

> **Мы предложи́ли ей вы́ступить у нас на семина́ре. Поду́мав, она́** *согласи́лась.*
> We invited her to give a seminar. After giving it some thought, she agreed.

Дава́ть/дать согла́сие на (+ acc.) 'to give one's agreement' is used in formal contexts:

> **Настоя́щим** *даю́ согла́сие* **на самостоя́тельный вы́езд мое́й несовершенноле́тней до́чери за преде́лы Росси́йской Федера́ции без сопровожде́ния взро́слых.**
> I hereby give my consent for my daughter, who has not reached the age of majority, to leave the territory of the Russian Federation without being accompanied by an adult.

In informal language the following words and phrases can be used to indicate consent:

хорошо́	good, fine
ла́дно	OK, fine
так и быть	OK
договори́лись	that's agreed, OK

> —**Мо́жно Ната́ше взять твой зонт?**
> —*Ла́дно,* **пусть берёт.**

> —Can Natasha borrow your umbrella?
> —OK, she can borrow it, if she wants to.

> —**Прошу́ тебя́, помоги́ ей с перево́дом.**
> —*Так и быть,* **пусть прихо́дит.**

> —Would you mind helping her with her translation?
> —That's OK. Tell her to come and see me.

> —**Дава́йте сде́лаем так: сего́дня посу́ду мо́ет Ива́н, а за́втра Ли́за.**
> —*Договори́лись.*

> —Let's do it this way. Today Ivan does the washing up and tomorrow it's Liza's turn.
> —OK.

Indicating disagreement

Disagreement can be expressed by using negated forms of **согла́сен** etc. or by using **про́тив** (+ gen.):

Мы соверше́нно *не согла́сны* с таки́м реше́нием!
We are totally opposed to that decision.

Мы бы́ли *про́тив* э́тих бюрократи́ческих нововведе́ний.
We were against these bureaucratic innovations.

In more formal contexts the following formulae can be used to express polite disagreement:

э́то не (совсе́м) так
it's not (quite) like that

у меня́ друго́е/ино́е мне́ние
I am of a different opinion

я приде́рживаюсь друго́го/ино́го мне́ния
I am of a different opinion

позво́льте с ва́ми не согласи́ться
perhaps I might be so bold as to disagree with you

Что каса́ется заключе́ния коми́ссии по да́нному де́лу, то я *приде́рживаюсь ино́го мне́ния*.
As regards the conclusion reached by the commission looking into this matter, I am afraid that I am of a different opinion.

The following are used in informal language:

как бы не так!	nothing of the sort, not a bit of it, don't you believe it!
ничего́ подо́бного!	nothing of the sort, not a bit of it, don't you believe it!

Ты ду́маешь, он призна́л свои́ оши́бки? *Как бы не так*!
Do you think he owned up to his mistakes? Nothing of the sort!

Expressing certainty, uncertainty, possibility or doubt

Expressing certainty, probability and possibility

The following words and phrases are widely used to indicate certainty:

коне́чно	of course
(само́ собо́й) разуме́ется	of course
безусло́вно	certainly, definitely
несомне́нно	undoubtedly
вне вся́кого сомне́ния	beyond any doubt
обяза́тельно	definitely

All except the last of these come into the category of *вво́дные слова́* (see **23.2.1**) and are separated off from the rest of the sentence by commas:

Почему́ бы тебе́ не пое́хать с на́ми в дере́вню? Обеща́ю: бу́дет рыба́лка, ночно́й костёр на берегу́ о́зера, и, *коне́чно*, уха́ с во́дочкой.
Why don't you come with us to the country? I can promise you there'll be fishing, a camp fire by the lake and, of course, fish soup and vodka.

Он, *безусловно*, **специалист в э́той о́бласти, но я бы посове́товался с ке́м-нибудь ещё.**

He's certainly a specialist in this field, but I would get a second opinion.

Благодарю́ вас за письмо́. Я *обяза́тельно* **Вам отве́чу, как то́лько что-нибудь вы́ясню относи́тельно Ва́шего вопро́са.**

Thank you for your letter. I'll definitely reply once I have some information concerning your question.

For the use of the capital letter with the pronouns **Вы** and **Ваш**, *see* **1.5.7**.

The following adverbs and phrases are widely used in informal language to indicate certainty:

наверняка́	definitely
желе́зно	sure thing!
как пить дать	you (can) bet (your life on it)!

Телефо́н не отвеча́ет; они́, *наверняка́*, **уже́ уе́хали.**

Nobody's answering the telephone; they must definitely have left.

—**Придёшь за́втра на трениро́вку?**
—*Желе́зно.*

—Are you coming to the training tomorrow?
—I sure am!

—**Как ты ду́маешь, она́ доло́жит ше́фу о на́шем опозда́нии?**
—**Доло́жит,** *как пить дать*!

—Do you think she'll report us to the boss for being late?
—You can bet your life on it.

The following words and phrases, all of which come into the category of *вво́дные слова́*, express different degrees of probability:

по всем приме́там	by all appearances
по всей ви́димости	by all appearances, it must be the case that
должно́ быть	it must be the case that
похо́же на то	it looks like it
по-ви́димому	apparently
пожа́луй	perhaps, probably
вероя́тно	probably
наве́рное, наве́рно	probably
скоре́е всего́	probably

У нас вчера́ на весь день не́ было горя́чей воды́; *по всей ви́димости*, **где́-то меня́ли тру́бы.**

We'd no hot water all day yesterday; they must have been changing the pipes somewhere.

—**Бою́сь, что магази́н уже́ закры́т.**
—*Похо́же на то.*

—I'm afraid the shop's already shut.
—It looks like it.

—Ты не зна́ешь, кто э́то сейча́с с на́ми поздоро́вался?
—*Скоре́е всего́*, кто́-то из мои́х студе́нтов.

—Do you know who that was who just said 'hello' to us?
—It's probably one of my students.

NOTE In Russian cities hot water is usually supplied centrally from district heating stations (ТЭЦ = теплоэлектроцентра́ль).

For more examples of *вво́дные слова́* expressing probability, *see* **23.2.1**.

16.5.2 Expressing uncertainty and doubt

The following words and phrases can express uncertainty:

ка́жется	it seems, I think
мо́жет быть	perhaps
возмо́жно	possibly
вро́де (бы)	it seems, I think

All except the last come into the category of *вво́дные слова́*:

Что́-то я нева́жно себя́ чу́вствую. *Ка́жется*, у меня́ температу́ра.
I'm not feeling too good. I think I've got a temperature.

Мо́жет быть, она́ уже́ не вернётся сюда́.
Perhaps she won't come back here again.

—Ты не забы́ла вы́ключить телеви́зор?
—*Вро́де* нет.

—Did you forget to turn the television off?
—I don't think so.

In informal contexts мо́жет быть is often reduced to its first element:

Мо́жет, я ещё прие́ду сюда́ о́сенью.
I might come again in the autumn.

The Russian verb corresponding to the English 'to doubt' is **сомнева́ться** (нсв). This can be used with the preposition в (+ prep.) or by a clause introduced by что:

Они́ почему́-то *сомнева́ются в* на́шей че́стности.
For some reason they have doubts about our honesty.

Я *сомнева́юсь*, что она́ сдаст э́тот экза́мен.
I doubt whether she'll pass the exam.

The following words and phrases can also be used to indicate doubt:

вряд ли	it's unlikely
навря́д ли	it's unlikely
маловероя́тно	it's improbable
тру́дно сказа́ть	it's difficult to say
нельзя́ с уве́ренностью сказа́ть	it's impossible to say with certainty

Он бо́лен и *вряд ли* поя́вится на рабо́те на э́той неде́ле.
He's ill and is unlikely to come back to work this week.

Маловероя́тно, что здесь произойдёт что-нибудь интере́сное.
It's unlikely that anything interesting is going to happen here.

Тру́дно сказа́ть, что ху́же - трёхчасово́й пи́сьменный экза́мен и́ли у́стный экза́мен пе́ред коми́ссией.
It's difficult to say what's worse, a three-hour written exam or an oral exam in front of a committee.

16.5.3 'It depends'

Russian has no direct equivalent of this useful means of expressing uncertainty or being evasive. The verb **зави́сеть** corresponds to the English 'to depend', but unlike the English verb it can never be used on its own, but only in conjunction with the preposition **от** (+ gen.):

—**Вы пое́дете за́втра с на́ми за́ город?**
—*Зави́сит от пого́ды.*

—Are you going to the country with us tomorrow?
—It depends (on the weather).

The prepositional phrase **смотря́ по** (+ dat.) is similar in meaning:

—**Вы за́втра пое́дете с на́ми за́ город?**
—*Смотря́ по пого́де.*

—Are you going to the country with us tomorrow?
—It depends (on the weather).

Смотря́ can also be followed by a question word, such as **кто** 'who', **что** 'what', **когда** 'when', **где** 'where' or **как** 'how':

—**Вы лю́бите игра́ть в ка́рты?**
—*Смотря́ с кем.*

—Do you like playing cards?
—It depends (who with).

—**Вы лю́бите выезжа́ть на приро́ду?**
—*Смотря́ куда́.*

—Do you like visiting the countryside?
—It depends (where).

The following can all serve as equivalents of 'it depends' when it means something like 'it varies according to the circumstances':

когда́ как	
быва́ет по-ра́зному	*also* it varies
посто́льку поско́льку	*also* up to a point

—**Вам ча́сто прихо́дится рабо́тать по вечера́м?**
—*Когда́ как.* or *Быва́ет по-ра́зному.*

—Do you often have to work in the evenings?
—It depends (sometimes I do, sometimes I don't).

For an example with **посто́льку поско́льку**, *see* **9.3.5**.

17

Asking questions

17.1 ## Neutral yes/no questions

17.1.0 ### Introduction

A neutral yes/no question is one that makes no assumptions about which answer is required. In Russian there are two ways of asking a question of this type: either by changing the intonation of the sentence or by using the interrogative particle **ли**.

17.1.1 ### Asking questions using intonation

Almost any statement can by transformed into a question by raising the intonation on the relevant word:

> **Ива́н вчера́ *купи́л* слова́рь?**
> Did Ivan buy a dictionary yesterday?

> **Ива́н вчера́ купи́л *слова́рь*?**
> Was it a dictionary that Ivan bought yesterday?

> ***Ива́н* вчера́ купи́л слова́рь?**
> Was it Ivan who bought a dictionary yesterday?

The focus of the question, if it is not the verb, tends to be placed at the end of the sentence:

> **Ива́н купи́л слова́рь *вчера́*?**
> Was it yesterday that Ivan bought the dictionary?

Raising the intonation is the normal means used to indicate a question in a sentence that contains no verb:

> **Вам пло́хо?**
> Are you feeling unwell?

Счёт уже́ два-два?
Is the score already two-two?

Опя́ть не́чего пить?
Is there nothing to drink again?

Questions formed with the particle ли

The *particle* ли is *enclitic* and normally follows the first stressed word of the sentence. In most situations this will be the *verb* or another predicate word, but if some other element forms the focus of the question, this can be placed first instead:

Купи́л ли Ива́н слова́рь?
Did Ivan buy the dictionary?

Мо́жно ли есть э́ти я́годы?
Can you eat these berries?

Здесь ли выдаю́т анке́ты?
Is it here that you can get application forms?

В ту ли сто́рону мы идём?
Are we going in the right direction?

NOTE | When the focus of an English question is on some part of the sentence other than the verb, this is often indicated by using the formula 'Is/was it … that'. In Russian, the same effect is normally achieved by changing the word order of the sentence, as is shown in the above examples. *See also* **20.3.1**.

For more on enclitic particles, *see* **9.4.2**.

For the use of the particle ли in indirect questions, *see* **21.8.3**.

Negative questions

Asking a negative question in Russian does not necessarily make assumptions about the answer. A negative question may still be neutral, but will usually be more tentative or more polite than an ordinary question. For this reason negative questions are often used when asking strangers for information:

Не хо́лодно ли вам?
Are(n't) you cold?

Ты *не возража́ешь*, е́сли я вы́ключу телеви́зор?
Would you have any objections if I turned the television off?

Не ска́жете, как дойти́ до автовокза́ла?
Could you tell me how to get to the bus station?

Прости́те, э́то *не вы* урони́ли блокно́т?
Excuse me, was it you that dropped this notebook?

17.1.4 ## Answering yes/no questions

The Russian answers to yes/no questions are:

да   yes
нет   no

The answer can be expanded by repeating the verb or whichever other word forms the focus of the question:

—Ива́н вчера́ купи́л слова́рь?
—*Да, купи́л.*
—*Нет, не купи́л.*

—Did Ivan buy a dictionary yesterday?
—Yes, he did.
—No, he didn't.

—Здесь ли выдаю́т анке́ты?
—*Да, здесь.*

—Is it here that you can get application forms?
—Yes, it is.

17.2 # Asking loaded questions

17.2.0 ## Introduction

A loaded question is one that expects a particular answer. Russian has several ways of asking loaded questions.

17.2.1 ## Negative loaded questions

Because *negation* is often used in Russian to make a question tentative or polite, *negative loaded questions* are somewhat less frequent than in English. They do, however, occur and can be illustrated by the following:

Не его́ ли мы ви́дели вчера́ на приёме в посо́льстве?
Didn't we see him at the embassy yesterday, at the reception?

Одну́ мину́точку, а *нет ли* тут како́го-нибу́дь подво́ха?
Just a minute, isn't there some sort of catch here?

A negative question formed with a *perfective infinitive* verb produces what amounts to a suggestion or an invitation:

Не *позвони́ть ли* Джо́ну?
Why don't we phone John?

А не *вы́пить ли* нам коньячку́?
Why don't we have a brandy?

17.2.2 ## Loaded questions with ра́зве and неуже́ли

The question particles **ра́зве** and **неуже́ли** are widely used to form *loaded questions*. Both mean something like 'Can it really be the case that …?', but they are not interchangeable because they imply different attitudes on the part of the speaker. **Ра́зве** suggests that the speaker doubts or disbelieves the statement in question; **неуже́ли**, while not implying disbelief, suggests that the speaker is surprised or disappointed. Sentences introduced by **ра́зве** or **неуже́ли** can be translated into English in a variety of ways, but sentences with **ра́зве … не** or **неуже́ли … не** often correspond to English negative questions:

> *Ра́зве* он уже́ вы́шел на пе́нсию?
> Has he really retired? *or* Surely he's not retired yet?

> А *ра́зве* сего́дня *не* пя́тница?
> Isn't today Friday?

> А *ра́зве* вход *не* беспла́тный?
> Isn't there free entry? *or* I thought entry was free.

> *Неуже́ли* тебе́ бы́ло тру́дно позвони́ть?
> Was it really so difficult for you to telephone?

> *Неуже́ли* уже́ ничего́ нельзя́ измени́ть?
> Is it really impossible to change anything?

In informal language **неу́жто** can be used instead of **неуже́ли**:

> *Неу́жто* и впрямь не́ было биле́тов?
> Are you telling me there were really no tickets?

17.2.3   Tag questions

Tag questions are those where the question is asked in a supplementary phrase added on to the end of a statement, as in English 'aren't you?', 'isn't it?'. They usually, though not always, assume a particular answer.

In spoken Russian the tag **что́ ли** is used very frequently to turn a statement into a question. It does not necessarily assume a particular answer and has no direct equivalent in English; in dialogue it can imply an element of reproach, while elsewhere it can convey the notion of uncertainty or the suggestion of a possible answer:

> —У меня́ неприя́тности на рабо́те.
> —Ты опя́ть опозда́л, *что́ ли*?

> —I'm having problems at work.
> —Were you late again?

> На́до что-то пригото́вить на обе́д: свари́ть щи, *что́ ли*?
> We need to prepare something for dinner. Shall I cook some *shchi*?

The tag **что́ ли** is often reinforced by using **что** after the first word of the sentence:

> Никто́ не берёт тру́бку. Да что они́ там, огло́хли, *что́ ли*?
> No one's answering the phone. Have they all gone deaf or something?

The following Russian tags correspond to the English 'aren't you?', 'isn't it?', 'don't we?', etc. Unlike the English equivalents, the form does not depend on the structure of the original statement:

> не так ли?
> не пра́вда ли?
> так?
> пра́вда?
> скажи́?

Это ва́ша запи́ска, *не так ли*?
This is your note, isn't it?

Отли́чный сего́дня денёк, *не пра́вда ли*?
It's a lovely day today, isn't it?

Когда́ набира́ешь код го́рода, ноль не ну́жен, *так*?
When you're dialling the area code, you leave the zero out, don't you?

Ты ведь не идёшь на ле́кцию, *пра́вда*?
You're not going to the lecture today, are you?

Здо́рово они́ сего́дня игра́ли, *скажи́*?
They played really well today, didn't they?

Some tag questions are a request for further information:

—Ты хорошо́ во́дишь маши́ну?
—Непло́хо, *а что*?

—Are you a good driver?
—Not bad. Why?

—Э́то ва́ша маши́на?
—Моя́, *а в чём де́ло*?

—Is this your car?
—Yes, it is. Why do you want to know? *or* What's the problem?

—Ты за́пер вчера́ за собо́й дверь?
—Да, *а что тако́е*?

—Did you lock the door behind you yesterday?
—Yes. What's happened?

17.3 Asking questions using question words

17.3.0 Introduction

Questions that do not require a yes/no answer are introduced by special *question words* that are normally placed at the beginning of the sentence. The question (or *interrogative*) words that are used in Russian can be divided into *pronouns*, *quantity words* and *adverbs*.

17.3.1 Interrogative pronouns

The following *interrogative pronouns* are used in Russian:

кто?	who?
что?	what?
чей?	whose?
како́й?	which?, what sort of?
кото́рый?	which?

For the declension of **кто** and **что**, *see* **7.4.1**.

For the declension of **чей**, **како́й** and **кото́рый**, *see* **7.4.2**.

Кто́ е́дет за́втра на экску́рсию?
Who's going on the excursion tomorrow?

От кого́ э́то письмо́?
Who's the letter from?

Кем был постро́ен э́тот дворе́ц?
Who was this palace built by?

Что ты ему́ сказа́ла?
What did you say to him?

Чем бу́дем заправля́ть сала́т – расти́тельным ма́слом или майоне́зом?
What are we going to dress the salad with – oil or mayonnaise?

Из чего́ постро́ено э́то зда́ние?
What is this building made of?

На како́й остано́вке вы выхо́дите?
Which stop are you getting off at?

Каки́е языки́ вы зна́ете?
What languages do you know?

Како́е моро́женое предпочита́ешь – с шокола́дом и́ли с оре́хами?
What kind of ice cream do you prefer – with chocolate or with nuts?

As a question word **кото́рый** is nowadays used mostly with the set phrases:

Кото́рый час?   What time is it?
В кото́ром часу́?   At what time?

For more on the use of **кото́рый** in time expressions, *see* **19.2.1** and **19.2.5**.

17.3.2   More on кто and что

The interrogative pronouns are often used with the *neuter demonstrative* э́то:

Како́й замеча́тельный портре́т – *кто э́то?*
What a remarkable portrait. Who is it?

Я никогда́ не про́бовал ничего́ подо́бного – *э́то что?*
I've never tried anything like that before. What is it?

Ты слы́шала шаги́? *Кто э́то был?*
Did you hear footsteps? Who was it?

Ты слы́шала шо́рох? *Что э́то бы́ло?*
Did you hear a rustling noise? What was it?

Questions of this type can be made more emphatic by the introduction of the demonstrative pronoun **тако́й**; this pronoun will be *masculine singular* when used with **кто** and *neuter singular* when used with **что**:

Како́й стра́нный портре́т – *кто э́то тако́й?*
What a strange portrait. Who (on earth) is it?

Я никогда́ не про́бовал ничего́ подо́бного – *что э́то тако́е?*
I've never tried anything like that before. What (on earth) is it?

Кто and такой can also be used with a personal pronoun, in which case the gender of такой depends on the sex of the person being addressed or referred to:

>—Прости́те, а *кто вы така́я*, что́бы здесь распоряжа́ться?
>—А *вы кто тако́й*?

>—Excuse me, who do you think you are, going round giving orders like that? (addressed to a woman)
>—And who do you think you are? (addressed to a man)

For more on the demonstrative pronoun э́то, *see* **7.3.2**.

For more on the demonstrative pronoun тако́й, *see* **7.3.3**.

For more on grammatical agreement with кто, *see* **11.2.1**.

A question corresponding approximately to the English 'what sort of?' can be asked using **что за** (+ nom.):

>*Что э́то за ры́ба* (така́я)?
>What sort of fish is that?

>*Что она́ за челове́к*?
>What kind of a person is she?

This construction can sometimes be used as a pointed way of trying to identify someone or something:

>*Что э́то за тип* в тёмных очка́х?
>Who is that character in the sunglasses?

17.3.3 The interrogative quantity word

There is only one interrogative quantity word:

>**ско́лько?**   how much?, how many?

For the declension of ско́лько, *see* **8.6.3**.

>*Ско́лько* у них дете́й?
>How many children do they have?

>*За ско́лько* вы купи́ли э́тот шарф?
>How much did you buy that scarf for?

17.3.4 Interrogative adverbs

The following *interrogative adverbs* are used in Russian:

когда́?	when?
где?	where?
куда́?	where to?, whither?
отку́да?	where from?, whence?
как?	how?
наско́лько?	to what extent?
почему́?	why? (for what reason?)
отчего́?	why? (from what cause?)
заче́м?	why? (for what purpose?)

Когда́ вы уезжа́ете?
When are you leaving?

Где нахо́дится го́род Сара́нск?
Where is (the town of) Saransk?

Куда́ идём по́сле рабо́ты?
Where are we going after work?

Отку́да у вас таки́е све́дения?
Where did you get that information from?

Как вы гото́вите борщ?
How do you make *borshch*?

Наско́лько хорошо́ он владе́ет англи́йским?
How well does he know English?

Почему́ э́тот файл не открыва́ется?
Why won't this file open?

Почему́ отмени́ли экску́рсию?
Why have they cancelled the trip?

Отчего́ у тебя́ тако́й мра́чный вид?
Why are you looking so gloomy?

Заче́м ты вы́ключил свет?
Why did you turn the light off? *or* What did you turn the light off for?

Заче́м вы прово́дите э́тот опро́с?
Why are you carrying out this survey? *or* What are you doing this survey for?

17.3.5 More on как

The interrogative adverb **как** corresponds to the English 'what?' in a number of frequently asked questions:

Как вас зову́т?
What's your name?

Как называ́ется ваш но́вый рома́н?
What is the name of your new novel?

Как по-ру́сски бу́дет «elephant»?
What's the Russian for 'elephant'?

Как ты ду́маешь? сто́ит смотре́ть э́тот фильм, и́ли нет?
What do you think? Is it worth seeing this film or not?

For more on asking about names, *see* **13.3.3** and **13.3.5**.

On the other hand, **отку́да** corresponds to the English 'how?' in the following question:

Отку́да я зна́ю?
How should I know?

For more information on rhetorical questions, *see* **17.4.2**.

17.4 **Rhetorical questions**

Introduction

Rhetorical questions are phrases and sentences that are constructed in the form of a question, but that are not intended to obtain information. They can be used for a variety of purposes.

17.4.1 **Expressing the speaker's attitude**

Rhetorical questions can be used to indicate the speaker's attitude towards a particular situation. Perhaps the largest number express irritation or frustration:

Как вы сме́ете говори́ть со мной таки́м то́ном!
How dare you speak to me in that tone of voice!

Как тебе́ не сты́дно!
You should be ashamed of yourself! (*Literally*, How are you not ashamed of yourself?)

Ты *что*, с ума́ сошёл (*что ли*)?
Have you gone raving mad?

Приде́рживайте дверь, *ско́лько* мо́жно говори́ть!
Hold the door. How many times do I have to tell you!

Да ско́лько мо́жно повторя́ть – не брал я си́ней па́пки!
How many times do I have to say it: I didn't take the blue folder!

Опя́ть в кварти́ре барда́к - *на что* э́то похо́же!
The flat's in a total mess again. I've never seen anything like it! (*Literally*, What does it look like?)

Оди́н прогу́л и два опозда́ния за неде́лю - *куда́* э́то годи́тся!
In the single week you were late twice and failed to turn up at all once. That's totally unacceptable! (*Literally*, What use is that?)

Како́го чёрта/како́го дья́вола ты здесь болта́ешься!
What the devil are you hanging round here for?

Мы́слимое ли де́ло, простоя́ть два часа́ на моро́зе в наде́жде на авто́граф.
It doesn't bear thinking about (*literally*, Is it something that can be thought about?): standing two hours in the freezing cold hoping to get someone's autograph!

Ну *како́й* из тебя́ Дед Моро́з!
What sort of Father Christmas do you think you'd make!

NOTE   Дед Моро́з, *literally*, 'Grandfather Frost' is the Russian equivalent of Father Christmas. A Soviet invention, he normally appears, accompanied by **Снегу́рочка** 'the Snow Maiden', at New Year, rather than at Christmas.

Rhetorical questions can also be used to express admiration or to express wishes:

И *отку́да* у неё то́лько си́лы беру́тся!
Just where does she get her strength from!

Кому́ не хо́чется прокати́ться зимо́й на ру́сской тро́йке!
In winter who wouldn't like to go for a ride in a Russian *troika*!

For more on the noun **тро́йка**, *see* **8.6.1**.

17.4.2 Rhetorical questions in dialogue

As part of a dialogue rhetorical questions can be used to solicit sympathy or solidarity:

Вы мо́жете себе́ предста́вить? Стою́ на перро́не с газе́той в руке́, а мой по́езд уже́ ушёл.
Can you imagine it? I was standing on the platform with a newspaper in my hand and my train had already left!

Пришли́ санте́хники, перекры́ли во́ду – и пропа́ли на весь день! *Как вам э́то понра́вится?*
The plumbers came, cut off the water and then disappeared for the rest of the day. What do you think of that!

По́верите ли, до сих пор при ви́де каче́лей мне де́лается ду́рно.
Can you believe it? Even now the very sight of a swing makes me feel queasy.

Он обы́грывал да́же гроссме́йстеров, *не ве́ришь?*
He's even managed to beat grand masters. Can you believe it?

Она́ ещё и прете́нзии предъявля́ет, *вида́ли?*
And now she has the nerve to complain! Have you ever heard of (*literally*, seen) such a thing!

Other rhetorical questions can express a challenge to the other speaker:

—А *кто вы така́я*, чтобы здесь распоряжа́ться?
—*А вы кто тако́й*, чтобы мне ука́зывать?

—Who do you think you are, going round giving orders?
—And who do you think you are, telling me what to do?

—Как ты мо́жешь тако́е говори́ть!
—*А что, не так?*

—How can you say such things?
—Are you suggesting what I'm saying is untrue?

—Переста́нь безде́льничать. Ты всю неде́лю проваля́лся на дива́не.
—*Ну и что?*

—It's time you got up and did something. You've spent all week lying on that sofa.
—And your point is?

—Кака́я пого́да бу́дет за́втра?
—*Отку́да я зна́ю?*

—What's the weather going to be like tomorrow?
—How should I know?

Requests in the form of a rhetorical question

A rhetorical question is a useful way of making a very polite (or a sarcastic) request:

> *Ты не хо́чешь* помы́ть посу́ду?
> You wouldn't like to wash the dishes, would you?

> *Не могли́ бы вы* прикры́ть дверь? Здесь сквозня́к.
> Would you mind closing the door? There's a draught here.

> *Вам не тру́дно* включи́ть свет?
> Would you be kind enough to turn the light on? *or* (if being sarcastic) Would it be an imposition for you to turn the light on?

> *Вы не подади́те* мне очки́?
> Would you be good enough to pass me my glasses?

> *Нельзя́ ли* немно́го погро́мче?
> Could you turn the volume up a little?

> *А мо́жно* чуть поти́ше?
> Would you mind turning it down a bit?

For more on making requests, *see* **18.3**.

18

Obligation, instructions, requests, advice and permission

18.1 Talking about obligation and necessity

18.1.1 Using на́до, ну́жно and необходи́мо

Obligation or necessity can be indicated in a wide range of contexts and all levels of language by using the *impersonal predicate* words with an *infinitive* verb:

> на́до
> ну́жно

> *На́до* крича́ть гро́мче: тебя́ никто́ не слы́шит.
> You need to shout louder. Nobody can hear you.

> *Ну́жно* ка́ждый день выпива́ть пять стака́нов воды́.
> You/one should drink five glasses of water a day.

> *На́до бы́ло* ду́мать об э́том ра́ньше.
> You should have thought of that earlier.

> *Е́сли бу́дет ну́жно*, мы вам позвони́м.
> If need arises, we'll phone you.

The person on whom the obligation or necessity falls can be indicated by a *noun* or *pronoun* in the *dative*:

> *Тебе́ на́до* сде́лать рабо́ту над оши́бками.
> You need to do some work on these mistakes.

> *Мне ну́жно бу́дет* поду́мать над ва́шим предложе́нием.
> I shall have to give some thought to your proposal.

The *impersonal predicate form* необходи́мо is similar in meaning to на́до and ну́жно, but is characteristic of more formal levels of language:

> Е́сли вы направля́етесь за грани́цу по ча́стным дела́м, то за ви́зой *вам необходи́мо обрати́ться* непосре́дственно в посо́льство или ко́нсульство соотве́тствующей страны́.

If you are travelling abroad on private business you need to apply directly for a visa to the embassy or consulate of the appropriate country.

For more on impersonal predicate forms, *see* **11.2.2**.

18.1.2 Using должен, обязан and следует

The following tend to be used when talking about a duty or an obligation:

должен/должна/должно/должны
обязан/обязана/обязано/обязаны
следует

The first two behave like *short adjectives* and agree with a *grammatical subject* in the *nominative* case. The third is an *impersonal verb*; the person on whom the obligation falls, if present, is in the *dative*:

Я *должен* вам напомнить, что ключи от номера нужно будет сдать до двенадцати часов.
I have to remind you that room keys must be handed in before twelve.

Вы *обязаны* закончить работу к пяти часам.
You are required to finish work by five o'clock.

Вашим детям *следует* проводить больше времени на свежем воздухе.
Your children ought to spend more time in the fresh air.

Должен can have the meaning of 'it ought to be the case that …':

Попробуй заменить батарейку, приёмник *должен* заработать.
Try replacing the battery, then your radio should come on.

Она там жила пять лет, и поэтому *должна* знать лучшие рестораны города.
She lived there for five years, so she ought to know which are the best restaurants in the city.

Они *должны были* приехать два часа назад. Видимо, где-то задержались в пути.
They should have been here two hours ago. They must have been held up somewhere on the way.

For more on short adjectives, *see* **6.5.1**.

For more on impersonal verbs, *see* **11.2.2**.

For the use of the phrase должно быть to indicate probability, *see* **16.5.1**.

18.1.3 Using приходиться/прийтись

The *impersonal verb* приходиться/прийтись is widely used to express necessity through force of circumstances; the person subject to the necessity, if indicated, is in the *dative*:

На кухне опять течёт кран: *придётся* вызвать сантехника.
There's a tap dripping in the kitchen again. I'll have to get a plumber to look at it.

Иногда́ помога́ют колле́ги, но о́чень ча́сто *прихо́дится* всё де́лать *самому́*.

Sometimes my colleagues help, but very often I end up having to do everything myself.

Из-за нелётной пого́ды *Аэрофло́ту пришло́сь* отмени́ть бо́лее пяти́десяти ре́йсов.

Because of the bad weather Aeroflot had to cancel over fifty flights.

Indicating lack of obligation

The negative forms **не на́до, не ну́жно, не до́лжен** and **не сле́дует** are generally used to indicate that something is forbidden or inadvisable (*see* **18.2.4**). To indicate that something is not obligatory, the negative form **не обя́зан** can be used:

Вы *не обя́заны* отвеча́ть на э́тот вопро́с.

You're not obliged to answer that question.

Another way of conveying the same information is to say that someone has permission not to do something. This is done by using either the verb **мочь** or the *impersonal predicate* form **мо́жно**:

Вы *мо́жете не отвеча́ть* на э́тот вопро́с.

You don't have to answer that question.

Мо́жно *не переводи́ть* э́то после́днее предложе́ние. Я и так всё по́нял.

You don't have to translate that last sentence. I understood everything perfectly well.

Infinitive verbs used in these sentences are *imperfective* (though the *perfective* is occasionally found with **не до́лжен** and **не обя́зан**). For more on the use of aspects in these sentences, *see* **5.7.5**.

Instructions and prohibitions

Issuing instructions and prohibitions using the imperative

The *imperative* form of the verb is the one most widely used for issuing instructions or prohibitions:

Неме́дленно *прекрати́те* э́то безобра́зие!

Stop this misbehaviour immediately!

Отойди́те отсю́да.

Move away from here.

Помолчи́, тебя́ никто́ не спра́шивает.

Be quiet, nobody's asking you.

Кто́-нибудь *принеси́те* воды́.

Would somebody bring some water.

Подожди́те секу́ндочку.

Wait a second.

Пусть он *возьмёт* такси́ и сро́чно *е́дет* домо́й.

He'd better get a taxi and go home as a matter of urgency.

Не влезай: убьёт!
Danger! Don't climb (this pylon)!

Ни в коем случае *не выходите* из машины.
Don't get out of the car under any circumstances.

Не смей спорить со мной.
Don't dare to argue with me.

An instruction can be made less peremptory by attaching the particle **-ка** to the imperative:

Подождите-ка секундочку.
Wait a second.

For the formation of the imperative, *see* **4.9**.

For the use of aspects with the imperative, *see* **5.6** and **5.7.2**.

18.2.2 Using the infinitive to issue an instruction or a prohibition

The infinitive is used for instructions and prohibitions in a number of specific situations. These include the following categories:

(1) The armed forces and certain other very formal contexts:

Прекратить огонь!
Stop firing!

Встать! Суд идёт.
All rise! The court is in session.

Military-style commands can sometimes be heard in everyday situations:

Мама сказала, ты отлично сдала экзамены. Молодец, *так держать!*
Your mother tells me you got top marks in the exam. Well done, keep it up!

Играть низом, к своим воротам не *прижиматься*!
Keep the ball down and keep moving upfield.

(2) Official signs and notices:

Не курить!
No smoking!

(3) On labels and packaging and in instruction manuals:

Внимание, перед включением в сеть *удалить* предохранительные прокладки.
Warning: remove all protective packing before connecting to the mains.

Открывать с противоположной стороны.
Open from the other end.

Перед употреблением *взбалтывать*.
Shake thoroughly before taking.

(4) In recipes:

> **Куски́ ры́бы** *посоли́ть, посы́пать* **пе́рцем,** *обваля́ть* **в муке́ и** *обжа́рить* **на сковороде́.**
> Season the pieces of fish with salt and pepper, coat them in flour and fry them in a frying pan.

NOTE The imperative can also be used in recipes.

For more on the infinitive, *see* **4.1**.

For the use of the imperfective aspect with the infinitive when it indictates a prohibition, *see* **5.7.5**.

18.2.3 ### Other ways of giving instructions

The following verbs can be used in relation to giving orders:

прика́зывать/приказа́ть	to order (someone to do something)
веле́ть (нсв/св)	to order (someone to do something)
распоряжа́ться/распоряди́ться	to arrange (for something to be done), to see (that something is done)

First person forms of **прика́зывать** are associated with military and bureaucratic language.

The person required to carry out the order (if indicated) is in the *dative* and these verbs are usually used with an infinitive, although they can also be followed by a clause introduced by **что́бы**:

> *Прика́зываю* **вам в пятидне́вный срок** *прибы́ть* **в расположе́ние ча́сти.**
> You are ordered to return to your unit within five days.

> **Ре́ктор** *приказа́л объедини́ть* **э́ти две лаборато́рии в связи́ с реорганиза́цией.**
> In connection with reorganisation, the rector (of the university) ordered that the two laboratories be merged into one.

> **По́мню, когда́ я подра́лся с однокла́ссником, учи́тельница** *веле́ла* **мне** *привести́* **в шко́лу мать.**
> I remember that when I had a fight with a classmate, the teacher ordered me to bring my mother into school.

> **Я** *распоряжу́сь, что́бы* **вам вы́писали про́пуск.**
> I'll arrange for you to be given a pass.

Some instructions can be issued without any verb:

> **Сми́рно!**
> (Stand to) Attention!

> **Стоп!**
> Stop! [e.g. on roadsigns]

> **Мальчи́шки, а ну** *марш* **на у́лицу! Не́чего до́ма сиде́ть в таку́ю пого́ду.**
> Right, boys, quick march outside! You can't sit around the house in weather like this.

18.2.4 Other ways of issuing prohibitions

The verb corresponding to the English 'to forbid' is **запреща́ть/запрети́ть**. It is normally used with an infinitive and the person who is being forbidden to do something is in the *dative*. In official and semi-official contexts, and especially on notices, the verb is often in the *passive*:

Врачи́ *запрети́ли* ему́ кури́ть.
The doctors have forbidden him to smoke.

В слу́чае пожа́ра по́льзоваться ли́фтом *запреща́ется*.
In the event of fire it is forbidden to use the lift.

Стоя́нка *запрещена́*.
No parking.

For more on the formation of passive verbs, *see* **4.14**.

The *negative predicate* form **нельзя́** can also be used to indicate that something is forbidden:

Здесь *нельзя́* кури́ть.
You can't smoke here.

—А без па́спорта мо́жно де́ньги обменя́ть?
—Нет, *нельзя́*.

—Can you change money without a passport?
—No, you can't.

The *negative predicate* forms **не на́до, не ну́жно, не до́лжен, не сле́дует** convey something between a prohibition and a strong recommendation not to do something:

—Мо́жно откры́ть окно́?
—*Не на́до*, здесь и так хо́лодно.

—Can I open a window?
—No, don't; it's cold enough in here as it is.

Вы *не должны́* забыва́ть, что Москва́ и оста́льная Росси́я – это далеко́ не одно́ и то́ же.
Don't forget that Moscow and the rest of Russia are far from being one and the same thing.

***Не сле́дует* сли́шком серьёзно относи́ться к его́ угро́зам.**
You shouldn't take his threats too seriously.

In informal language an expressive element can be added to a prohibition by using the imperative forms **не взду́май, (то́лько) попро́буй**:

***Не взду́май* выходи́ть без ша́пки в тако́й моро́з.**
Don't even think of going out without a fur hat in this cold weather.

***То́лько попро́буй* ещё раз э́то сде́лать!**
Just try doing that again!

For the use of aspects in sentences indicating prohibition, *see* **5.1.1**, **5.7.3** and **5.7.5**.

18.3 Making a request

18.3.1 Making a request using the imperative

Unlike English, Russian makes very frequent use of the *imperative* for making a request. What distinguishes a request from an instruction is the inclusion of various courtesy formulae:

пожа́луйста	please
бу́дьте добры́	please (be so kind as to)
бу́дьте любе́зны	please (be so kind as to)
е́сли вас не затрудни́т	if it is no trouble
не сочти́(те) за труд	if it is no trouble
сде́лай(те) одолже́ние?	would you do me a favour?

The first of these is the most frequent and can be used in more or less any circumstances. The others add an extra degree of courtesy and formality, although the last can also be used in relatively informal situations:

Предъяви́те, пожа́луйста, ва́ше удостовере́ние?
Could you please show me your ID?

Верни́ мне, пожа́луйста, кни́гу: она́ библиоте́чная.
Can you please let me have the book back? It belongs to the library.

Бу́дьте добры́, переда́йте соль.
Would you mind passing me the salt?

Е́сли вас не затрудни́т, прикро́йте окно́. Сквозня́к.
If it's no trouble, would you mind closing the window? There's a draught.

Не сочти́ за труд, сбе́гай в магази́н: у нас ко́нчился са́хар.
If it's no trouble, would you mind running to the shops? We've run out of sugar.

Сде́лай одолже́ние, отпра́вь вот э́ти пи́сьма.
Would you do me a favour and post these letters for me?

Sometimes the presence of a noun with a *diminutive suffix* can have the effect of softening the force of an instruction and turning it into a request:

Позвони́те мне вечерко́м.
Could you phone me in the evening?

Возьми́те ещё кусо́чек то́рта.
Do please take another piece of cake.

For more on the use of diminutive suffixes, *see* **16.1.1**.

Occasionally, the context alone is sufficient to make it clear that a statement is a request, not an instruction:

Скажи́те, где тут вы́ход?
Excuse me, where is the exit?

When in doubt, however, it never does any harm to use **пожа́луйста** or one of the other politeness formulae mentioned above.

Making a request using проси́ть/попроси́ть, про́сьба, умоля́ть

The verb **проси́ть/попроси́ть** means 'to ask someone to do something'; the person being asked is in the *accusative*, and the verb can be followed by an *infinitive* or a clause beginning with **что́бы**. This verb can also be combined with a sentence containing an *imperative* verb of the type described in the previous section:

> Я *прошу́* вас задержа́ться ещё на не́сколько мину́т.
> Would you mind staying back for a few minutes?

> Уважа́емые пассажи́ры, убеди́тельно *про́сим* вас не открыва́ть оста́вленные без присмо́тра су́мки и паке́ты, а сообща́ть о них в мили́цию.
> We kindly request all passengers not to open any bags or parcels left unattended but to inform the police.

> Я *прошу́*, что́бы к прихо́ду ма́мы посу́да была́ помы́та.
> Will you please make sure that the washing up has been done by the time your mother gets home?

> *Прошу́* вас, задержи́тесь ещё на не́сколько мину́т.
> Would you mind staying back for a few minutes?

For the use of the form of address **уважа́емые пассажи́ры**, *see* **13.5.2**.

The verb **умоля́ть** can be used for strongly felt requests:

> *Умоля́ю* тебя́, откажи́сь от э́той зате́и!
> I beg you, please give up that idea!

> Она́ *умоля́ла* сы́на не уезжа́ть.
> She pleaded with her son not to move away.

Impersonal requests (e.g. on signs) can be made using the noun **про́сьба** 'request':

> *Про́сьба* не кури́ть.
> You are kindly requested not to smoke.

This noun can, however, be used in other contexts as well:

> У меня́ к тебе́ (есть) одна́ *про́сьба*: ты не мог бы одолжи́ть мне а́нгло-ру́сский слова́рь на па́ру дней?
> I have a favour to ask you. You couldn't lend me an English–Russian dictionary for a few days, could you?

> На её *про́сьбу* говори́ть поти́ше никто́ не отреаги́ровал.
> No one reacted to her request for people to speak more quietly.

For the use of questions as a means of making a polite (or a sarcastic) request, *see* **17.4.3**.

Exhortations

The *imperative* form **дава́й(те)** can be used either with a *first person plural* verb or with an *infinitive* to suggest beginning an action jointly with the person(s) being addressed. The form **дава́й** is used when speaking to someone who would be addressed using the pronoun **ты**; otherwise, **дава́йте** is required. An accompanying *finite* verb will be *perfective*; an accompanying *infinitive* will be *imperfective*:

Я ви́жу, ты о́чень уста́л. *Дава́й сде́лаем* **перерыв на не́сколько мину́т.**
I can see you're very tired. Let's have a break for a few minutes.

Дава́йте вы́пьем **за здоро́вье на́ших госте́й,**
Let's drink to the health of our guests.

Дава́йте проводи́ть **таки́е опро́сы ежего́дно.**
Let's carry out these surveys every year.

Дава́йте ду́мать, **как нам лу́чше организова́ть рабо́ту над э́тим проéктом.**
Let's think about how best to organise the work on this project.

NOTE | When a toast is being proposed, a construction with the preposition за (+ acc.) is used, as in the example above.

For the use of **пошли́** and **пое́хали** in exhortations, *see* **22.1.8**.

18.3.4 Apologising and making one's excuses

One special type of request is an apology, in which someone asks to be forgiven for some error or misdeed. The two forms used most frequently either to express an apology or as the equivalent of 'excuse me' when used as a politeness formula are:

извини́(те)
прости́(те)

They are mutually replaceable in most situations, but the latter tends to occur in more formal contexts (i.e. letters and speeches) or to apologise for something more serious. They can be reinforced either with **пожа́луйста** 'please' or with the more expressive **ра́ди бо́га** 'please do' (*literally*, 'for God's sake'):

Извини́те, **мо́жно Ната́шу к телефо́ну?**
Excuse me, could I speak to Natasha, please (on the telephone)?

Прости́те, **а кака́я сле́дующая остано́вка?**
Excuse me, what is the name of the next stop?

Извини́те, пожа́луйста, **нет ли у вас ру́чки? Моя́ что́-то не пи́шет.**
Excuse me, please, but would you happen to have a pen? Mine doesn't seem to be writing.

Извини́те **меня́** *ра́ди бо́га* **– я не хоте́л вас оби́деть.**
Do please forgive me – I didn't mean to offend you.

Я зна́ю, что я поступи́л нехорошо́. Е́сли мо́жешь, *прости́.*
I realise that I acted wrongly. Forgive me, if you can.

In the spoken language the exclamation **винова́т!** (masculine only) 'sorry!' can be used:

—**Прости́те, вы положи́ли зонт на мою́ газе́ту.**
—*Винова́т!*

—Excuse me, you've put your umbrella on my newspaper.
—Sorry!

The first person singular form **извиняюсь** can sometimes be heard instead of **извини(те)** in informal contexts, although many people consider it inappropriate (because it seems to pre-empt being excused):

> **Я извиняюсь, это не ваша газета?**
> Excuse me (*literally*, I excuse myself), isn't this your newspaper?

For the correct response to an apology, *see* **15.3.3**.

The Russian words used for talking about being sorry in the sense of expressing regret are:

сожалеть	to regret
к сожалению	unfortunately
жаль	I'm (you are, we are, etc.) sorry [less formal than the others]

> **Мы искренне *сожалеем* о том, что произошло, и приносим свои глубокие извинения.**
> We are sincerely sorry about what happened and would like to express our profound apologies.

> **К (моему глубокому) *сожалению*, я не смогу приехать на Ваш юбилей.**
> I am (extremely) sorry that I won't be able to come to your (special) birthday party.

> **Мне *жаль*, что так получилось, но вы не огорчайтесь: вам всего двадцать, у вас ещё всё впереди.**
> I'm sorry that it turned out like that, but don't be upset: you're only twenty and you've got your whole life ahead of you.

NOTE In this context **юбилей** (*literally*, 'jubilee') refers to a special birthday, associated with a round figure, such as a thirtieth, fortieth or fiftieth.

18.4 Giving advice

The following verbs and impersonal predicate forms can be used with an infinitive when giving advice:

советовать/посоветовать	to advise
рекомендовать/порекомендовать	to recommend
полезно	it is useful *or* beneficial to
вредно	it is harmful to
лучше	it would be better to

> ***Советую* вам записаться на приём к психиатру.**
> I'd advise you to seek an appointment with a psychiatrist.

> **Если вы собираетесь с нами в экспедицию, мы настоятельно *рекомендуем* вам сделать все необходимые прививки.**
> If you're planning on coming on the expedition with us, we strongly recommend that you have all the necessary vaccinations.

> **При хронической бессоннице выпивайте на ночь полстакана горячего молока с мёдом, а вот острую и жирную пищу есть не *рекомендуется*.**
> If you suffer from chronic insomnia, you should drink last thing at night half a glass of hot milk and honey, and spicy or fatty foods should be avoided.

Вам *поле́зно* отдохну́ть не́сколько дней, лу́чше за́ городом.
It would be a good idea to take a few days off, preferably in the country.

***Вре́дно* пить кре́пкий ко́фе на́ ночь.**
It's harmful to drink strong coffee last thing at night.

Тебе́ *лу́чше* не ввя́зываться в э́тот спор.
It would be better if you don't get involved in that argument.

The particle **бы** can also be used with the *infinitive*:

Тебе́ *бы сходи́ть* к врачу́.
You ought to go and see the doctor.

The *conditional* can be used to make statements that come somewhere between a request and a piece of advice:

Ты *бы* поча́ще *звони́л* домо́й.
You should phone home more often.

Ты *бы* поме́ньше *кури́ла*.
You shouldn't smoke so much.

For the formation of the conditional, *see* **4.10**.

18.5   Giving permission

The *impersonal predicate* form **мо́жно** is normally used for asking and giving permission; it can be used on its own or with an *infinitive*:

—*Мо́жно зада́ть* вам оди́н вопро́с?
—Да, коне́чно, *мо́жно.*

—Can I ask you a question?
—Yes, of course you can.

—*Мо́жно заплати́ть* креди́тной ка́рточкой?
—К сожале́нию, *нельзя́.*

—Can I pay with a credit card?
—No, I'm afraid you can't.

NOTE | The negative form of **мо́жно** is **нельзя́**. For the use of **нельзя́** in prohibitions, *see* **18.2.4**.

For extra politeness the phrase **с твоего́/ва́шего разреше́ния/позволе́ния** 'with your permission', 'if you don't mind' can be used:

***С ва́шего разреше́ния*, я откро́ю окно́.**
With your permission (*or* If you don't mind), I'll open the window.

19

Using numbers: talking about times, dates and quantities

19.0 **Introduction**

This chapter focuses on the use of numbers and other words indicating quantity in various activities, such as counting and simple arithmetic (**19.1**), telling the time (**19.2**) and indicating the date (**19.3**); it will also examine how to talk about approximate or imprecise quantities, using either numerals (**19.4**) or other words that can indicate quantity (**19.5**).

19.1 **Counting and doing simple arithmetic**

19.1.1 **Counting**

In counting, the numeral **один/одна/одно** is often replaced with the word **раз** (*literally*, 'once'):

> **Внима́ние, поднима́ем:** *раз-два,* **взя́ли!**
> Ready to start lifting? One, two, up she goes!

> *Раз*-**два-три-четы́ре-пять, вы́шел за́йчик погуля́ть …**
> One, two, three, four, five, a hare went out for a walk … (the start of a well-known child's counting rhyme; it is sometimes used, for example, when testing microphones).

Оди́н, etc. tends to be used when counting out specific objects or people:

> **Ско́лько здесь жела́ющих пое́хать на экску́рсию?** *Оди́н,* **два, три …**
> How many people here want to go on the excursion? One, two, three …

Оди́н (in the masculine form) is also used when counting down:

> **Пять, четы́ре, три, два,** *оди́н,* **пуск!**
> Five, four, three, two, one, launch!

19.1.2 Doing simple arithmetic

When simple arithmetical operations are being described, there is normally a choice between two constructions. In the first the operation is described as producing a result equal to a particular number:

> **Семь *плюс* два́дцать два *равно́/равня́ется* двадцати́ девяти́.**
> *Literally*, Seven plus twenty-two equals/is equal to twenty-nine.

> **Два́дцать де́вять *ми́нус* семь *равно́/равня́ется* двадцати́ двум.**
> *Literally*, Twenty-nine minus seven equals/is equal to twenty-two.

> **Двена́дцать, *умно́женное на* во́семь, *равно́/равня́ется* девяно́ста шести́.**
> *Literally*, Twelve multiplied by eight is equal to ninety-six.

> **Две́сти де́сять, *делённое на* де́сять, *равно́/равня́ется* двадцати́ одному́.**
> *Literally*, 210 divided by ten is equal to twenty-one.

NOTE **Равно́** and **равня́ется** 'equals', 'is equal to' are both followed by a numeral in the *dative* case. With addition and subtraction, the construction can be simplified by using **бу́дет**, which is followed by the *nominative*:

> **Семь *плюс* пять *бу́дет* двена́дцать.**
> Seven plus five is (literally, will be) twelve.

In the second construction, the operation takes the form of a *condition*; the verb describing the operation is normally in the *infinitive* and the *conjunction* **е́сли** is usually absent.

For more on conditions, *see* **21.5**.

> **К двадцати́ двум *приба́вить* ты́сячу *бу́дет/полу́чится* ты́сяча два́дцать два.**
> *Literally*, If you add a thousand to twenty-two the result will be 1,022.

> **Из двадцати́ девяти́ *вы́честь* семь *бу́дет/полу́чится* два́дцать два.**
> *Literally*, If you subtract seven from twenty-nine the result will be twenty-two.

NOTE In more informal language **отня́ть** may be used instead of **вы́честь**.

> **Ты́сячу *умно́жить на* ты́сячу *бу́дет/полу́чится* миллио́н.**
> *Literally*, If you multiply a thousand by a thousand, the result will be a million.

> **Два́дцать одну́ ты́сячу *раздели́ть на* сто *бу́дет/полу́чится* две́сти де́сять.**
> *Literally*, If 21,000 is divided by 100, the result will be 210.

19.1.3 Another way of talking about multiplication

In more informal language there is a third option that can be used when talking about multiplication. In this the number being multiplied is indicated by a special *adverb* form. Such adverb forms exist for all numbers from *two* to *ten*: **два́жды, три́жды, четы́режды, пя́тью, ше́стью, се́мью, во́семью, де́вятью, де́сятью**:

> **Два́жды два – четы́ре.**
> Twice two is four.

Три́жды семь – два́дцать оди́н.
Three times seven is twenty-one.

Пя́тью пять – два́дцать пять.
Five fives are twenty-five.

Се́мью во́семь – пятьдеся́т шесть.
Seven eights are fifty-six.

NOTES
(i) These are the forms used when reciting multiplication tables in school.

(ii) The forms from five to ten are indentical in spelling to the *instrumental* form of the corresponding *cardinal* number. The stress, however, is on the initial, rather than on the final syllable.

For more on the endings of cardinal numbers, *see* **8.1**.

The adverbs **два́жды**, **три́жды** and (to a lesser extent) **четы́режды** are also used more generally to correspond to English 'twice', 'three times' and 'four times'; the equivalent of 'once' is **одна́жды**, which often has the meaning of 'at some time (or other)':

Тако́е в исто́рии страны́ случа́лось лишь *одна́жды*, ещё до войны́.
That's happened only once in the history of the country, and that was before the war.

Мы *одна́жды* встре́тились на конфере́нции слави́стов.
We met once at a conference of Slavists.

Полива́йте э́ти цветы́ *два́жды в неде́лю*.
Water these flowers twice a week.

Её дед – знамени́тый лётчик, *Три́жды* Геро́й Сове́тского Сою́за.
Her grandfather is a famous pilot, who was three times made a hero of the Soviet Union.

NOTE
To indicate the period in which an action is repeated a certain number of times, a construction with **в** (+ acc.) is used (as in the second example).

19.1.4 Distribution

The idea of distribution is expressed in Russian by means of a construction using the preposition **по**. This construction corresponds approximately to English constructions with 'each', although the Russian is used more widely.

With the numeral **оди́н/одна́/одно́** or with a noun in the singular (including in this context **ты́сяча, миллио́н, миллиа́рд**) **по** is followed by the *dative*:

Принима́йте э́то лека́рство *по одно́й* табле́тке три ра́за в день.
Take this medicine in doses of one tablet three times a day.

Все те, кто даст пра́вильный отве́т на э́тот вопро́с, полу́чат *по ты́сяче* рубле́й и *по биле́ту* на га́ла-конце́рт.
Everyone who answers this question correctly will receive 1,000 roubles and a ticket for the special concert.

With all other numerals **по** is followed by the *accusative*:

> **По пятна́дцать.**
> Fifteen all (score in lawn tennis).

> **Дед расска́зывал нам, что перед бо́ем солда́там выдава́ли *по сто грамм(ов)* во́дки для хра́брости.**
> Grandfather told us that before a battle the soldiers were given 100 grams of vodka (each) for courage.

For the use of the genitive plural forms **грамм**, **гра́ммов**, *see* **2.7.4**.

> **Перед отпра́вкой они́ получи́ли *по три апельси́на на ка́ждого*.**
> Before setting out they received three oranges each.

As the second example demonstrates, the recipients of a distribution can be indicated by the use of a construction with **на** (+ acc.). Similarly, those who contribute can be indicated by a construction using **c** (+ gen.):

> **На пода́рок молодожёнам скла́дывались *по пятьсо́т рубле́й с челове́ка*.**
> Everyone contributed 500 roubles (a head) towards a wedding present for the young couple.

19.2 Telling the time

19.2.1 Asking what time it is

In Russian, there are two ways of asking the question 'What time is it?' and these can be used interchangeably:

> **Кото́рый час?**
> **Ско́лько вре́мени?**

19.2.2 Telling the time: a whole number of hours

If the answer to the question asked in **19.2.1** involves only a whole number of hours, the relevant numeral is used with the noun **час** in the appropriate case. To indicate 'one o'clock' **час** is normally used on its own, without the numeral:

час	one o'clock
два часа́	two o'clock
четы́ре часа́	four o'clock
пять часо́в	five o'clock
во́семь часо́в	eight o'clock
пятна́дцать часо́в	15.00 hours, 3 p.m.
два́дцать два часа́	22.00 hours, 10 p.m.

NOTE   The 24-hour clock is widely used in Russia, especially in any official context. In particular, it is used in timetables of all sorts, for radio and television schedules, and to indicate the starting and finishing times of public events.

There are no direct equivalents of 'a.m.' and 'p.m.' in common use in Russian. Instead, the part of the day can be indicated by the use of the appropriate noun in the *genitive* case. The nouns used and the approximate segment of the day that each one indicates are as follows:

у́тра	morning (5 a.m.–midday)
дня	day, afternoon (midday–5 p.m.)
ве́чера	evening (5 p.m.–midnight)
но́чи	night (midnight–5 a.m.)

Therefore, times of the day can be indicated as:

два часа́ дня	2 p.m., two o'clock in the afternoon
два часа́ но́чи	2 a.m., two o'clock in the morning

The terms corresponding to 'midday' and 'midnight' are **по́лдень** and **по́лночь** respectively.

Sometimes an *ordinal* number is used with **час** to refer to an unspecified time in the first part of the *following* hour; thus, **тре́тий час** means 'some time after two o'clock':

> Был *тре́тий час* но́чи, когда́ нас разбуди́ли сире́ны пожа́рных маши́н.
> It was some time after two in the morning when we were woken up by the sirens of the fire engines.

19.2.3 Telling the time the 'traditional' way

There are two ways of telling the time when both hours and minutes are involved: these can be referred to as the 'traditional' way and the 'digital' way. Both are in common use.

When telling the time the 'traditional' way reference is made to the *following* hour. With times up to and including the half-hour, the hour is indicated using an *ordinal* number:

де́сять мину́т второ́го	ten (minutes) past one
два́дцать мину́т тре́тьего	twenty (minutes) past two
два́дцать две мину́ты пя́того	twenty-two minutes past four
два́дцать пять (мину́т) седьмо́го	twenty-five (minutes) past six

NOTE The noun **мину́та** 'minute' is always present, except after **два́дцать пять**, when its presence is optional.

The quarter is indicated by **че́тверть** and the half-hour by **полови́на**; the latter is often abbreviated to **пол-** in more informal language:

че́тверть восьмо́го	a quarter past seven
полови́на деся́того, полдеся́того	half-past nine

For times between the half-hour and hour, a *cardinal* number is used to indicate the hour; the minutes are indicated using **без** (+ gen.):

без пяти́ двена́дцать	five (minutes) to twelve
без трёх мину́т три	three minutes to three
без одно́й мину́ты два	one minute to two
без двадцати́ час	twenty (minutes) to one
без че́тверти семь	a quarter to seven

NOTE | With this construction the noun **мину́та** tends to be omitted, except for numbers between one and nine (excluding five).

When this method is used, a precise number of hours is indicated by the adverb **ро́вно**:

> **ро́вно де́вять часо́в**   nine o'clock precisely

19.2.4   Telling the time the 'digital' way

The 'digital' method of telling the time originated in military and bureaucratic circles, but because it is grammatically much simpler, it has come to be widely used in ordinary speech and is a perfectly acceptable alternative to the 'traditional' method. According to this method the time is given as if reading from the face of a digital clock:

> **Моско́вское вре́мя *пятна́дцать часо́в, три́дцать мину́т*. В эфи́ре но́вости.**
> Moscow time is 15.30 hours [*or* half-past two (p.m.)]. Here is the news.

> **То́чное вре́мя *оди́н час, два́дцать две мину́ты*.**
> The exact time is 1.22.

In less formal contexts, however, **час** and **мину́та** tend to be omitted, except that, as with the 'traditional' method, 'one o'clock' is indicated by **час**:

> **семь два́дцать пять**   7.25, twenty-five past seven
> **оди́ннадцать со́рок**   11.40, twenty to twelve

> **Сейча́с уже́ час пятна́дцать.**
> It's already 1.15 (*or*, a quarter past one).

The 'zero' in times between one and nine minutes past the hour is indicated by **ноль**; an exact number of hours is indicated by **ноль ноль**:

> **шестна́дцать ноль пять**   16.05 hours, five past four (p.m.)
> **двена́дцать ноль ноль**   twelve hundred hours, twelve o'clock precisely

Although it is by no means obligatory in informal contexts, the 24-hour clock does tend to be used quite frequently with the 'digital' method of telling the time.

19.2.5   Talking about the time at which something happens

In addition to the general question word **когда́?** 'when?', there are various phrases that can be used to ask at what time something happens, happened or will happen:

> **В кото́ром часу́?**
> **В како́е вре́мя?**
> **Во ско́лько?**

The last of these is considered a little more informal than the others.

> ***В кото́ром часу́* начина́ется спекта́кль?**
> At what time does the performance begin?

> ***В како́е вре́мя* вы ча́ще всего́ быва́ете до́ма?**
> At what time do you tend most often to be at home?

> ***Во ско́лько* отправля́ется твой по́езд?**
> What time does your train leave?

The phrase **В какое время (суток)** tends to be used with reference to segments of the day, rather than to precise times:

> *В какое время суток вы предпочитаете работать?*
> During what part of the day do you prefer to work?

When whole hours are involved or when telling the time using the 'digital' method, a construction with the preposition **в** (+ acc.) is used to indicate at what time something happens (happened, will happen):

> **Магазин открывается** *в восемь* **часов.**
> The shop opens at eight o'clock.

> **Поезд отправляется** *в девятнадцать ноль ноль* **с Московского вокзала.**
> The train departs at 19.00 hours (*or* at 7 p.m. exactly) from the Moscow station.

> **Полное лунное затмение начнётся** *в два часа двадцать одну минуту.*
> The full lunar eclipse will begin at 2.21.

> **Наш самолёт приземлился в Лондоне** *в двадцать тридцать пять.*
> Our plane landed in London at 20.35.

If **ровно** is used, it is placed *before* the preposition:

> **Наш поезд отправляется** *ровно в семь часов.*
> Our train departs at exactly seven o'clock.

The construction with the preposition **в** (+ acc.) can be used when telling the time the 'traditional' way, but only for times before the half-hour:

> **Сегодня я вышел из дома** *в десять минут* **девятого.**
> Today, I left home at ten past eight.

> **Встретимся на выходе из метро** *в четверть* **пятого.**
> Let's meet at the exit from the metro at a quarter past four.

In informal language it is possible to omit the preposition **в**:

> **Сегодня я вышел из дома** *десять минут девятого.*
> Today I left home at ten past eight.

To indicate half-past the hour the preposition **в** is used, but it is followed by the *prepositional* case:

> **Я кончаю работу** *в половине* **шестого.**
> I finish work at half-past five.

If, however, the abbreviated form **пол-** is used, this is unchanged:

> **Мы договорились встретиться** *в полвосьмого.*
> We arranged to meet at half-past seven.

Since it is not normally possible to put two prepositions together in Russian, the construction with **в** cannot be used for times between the half-hour and the hour. The easiest way to solve the problem is to resort to the 'digital' method, where the problem does not arise, but if the 'traditional' method is preferred, the time is indicated without the use of any additional words:

> **Он подъехал на своём мотоцикле к её дому** *без четверти шесть.*
> He arrived at her house on his motorcycle at a quarter to six.

19.2.6 Talking about time zones

Russia is spread over eleven time zones, of which the most important is the Moscow time zone, partly because it includes a substantial part of European Russia, but also because all rail and air timetables throughout the country use Moscow time. The phrase that indicates that Moscow time is being used is **по моско́вскому вре́мени**; in written sources this is sometimes abbreviated to **мск**. Other useful phrases are:

по ме́стному вре́мени	local time
по Гри́нвичу	Greenwich Mean Time

За́пуск косми́ческого корабля́ был произведён в два́дцать оди́н час, три́дцать мину́т *по моско́вскому вре́мени*.
The launch of the spacecraft took place at 21.30 hours Moscow time.

Прибы́тие ре́йса из Ло́ндона ожида́ется в 15.30 *мск*.
The flight from London is expected to arrive at 15.30 Moscow time.

Мы вы́летели из Ло́ндона в четы́рнадцать три́дцать пять *по ме́стному вре́мени*.
We left London at 14.35 local time.

Землетрясе́ние произошло́ в ноль часо́в, два́дцать одну́ мину́ту *по Гри́нвичу*.
The earthquake took place at 00.21 hours Greenwich Mean Time.

19.3 Talking about the date

19.3.1 The day of the month

The normal way of asking the question 'What is the date today?' in Russian is:

Како́е сего́дня число́?

To which the answer might be:

Сего́дня два́дцать девя́тое. *Or* **Сего́дня два́дцать девя́тое число́.**
Today is the twenty-ninth.

If the name of the month is given, this is in the *genitive* case and **число́** is always omitted:

Сего́дня пе́рвое сентября́.
Today is the first of September.

For the use of small letters with the names of the months, *see* **1.5.7**.

19.3.2 Adding the year

The year in Russian is expressed using an *ordinal* number + the noun **год** 'year'. In writing, the noun is usually abbreviated to **г.** The numeral **одна́** is normally omitted before the word **ты́сяча**:

Ты́сяча восемьсо́т со́рок восьмо́й год (1848 г.)	1848
Двухты́сячный год (2000 г.)	2000
Две ты́сячи седьмо́й год (2007 г.)	2007

When the date is given in full, the year is in the *genitive* case:

Сего́дня пятна́дцатое а́вгуста *две ты́сячи седьмо́го го́да.*
Today is the fifteenth of August 2007.

NOTE When dates are written out using figures, the European order (day, month, year) is adopted. There is a tendency to use Roman numerals to indicate the month:

15 viii 2007   15 August 2007

19.3.3   Talking about the date on which something happens

When the exact date of an event is given, the whole of the date is in the *genitive* case:

Пу́шкин роди́лся *шесто́го ию́ня ты́сяча семьсо́т девяно́сто девя́того го́да.*
Pushkin was born on 6 June 1799.

Всео́бщая деклара́ция прав челове́ка была́ при́нята *деся́того декабря́ ты́сяча девятьсо́т со́рок восьмо́го го́да.*
The Universal Declaration of Human Rights was adopted on 10 December 1948.

When only the month and year are given, the former is indicated using the preposition **в** (+ prep.), while the latter is in the genitive:

В Москве́ я был пе́рвый раз *в а́вгусте ты́сяча девятьсо́т шестьдеся́т восьмо́го го́да.*
The first time I was in Moscow was August 1968.

If only the month or only the year is given, the preposition **в** (+ prep.) is used:

Наско́лько я по́мню, они́ пожени́лись *в ию́не.*
As far as I remember, they got married in June.

Очередны́е ле́тние Олимпи́йские и́гры пройду́т в Ло́ндоне *в две ты́сячи двена́дцатом году́.*
The next summer Olympics will take place in London in 2012.

For the use of the prepositional form in **-у́**, *see* **2.7.2.**

In spoken Russian it is a common practice, whenever there is no danger of ambiguity, to abbreviate the year to the last three, or more usually, the last two digits:

Она́ живёт в Москве́ на у́лице *Девятьсо́т пя́того го́да.*
She lives in Moscow, in 1905 Street.

Семна́дцатый год стал перело́мным в исто́рии Росси́и.
1917 was a turning point in Russian history.

В со́рок пе́рвом году́ её муж ушёл доброво́льцем на фронт.
In 1941 her husband left for the front as a volunteer.

19.3.4 | **Decades and centuries; BC and AD**

Individual decades within a century are indicated using an *ordinal* number and the plural noun **го́ды**:

> *Девяно́стые го́ды* ста́ли эпо́хой больши́х переме́н для мно́гих стран Центра́льной и Восто́чной Евро́пы.
> The (19)90s were a period of great change for many countries in Central and Eastern Europe.

To indicate that something happened in a particular decade, a construction with the preposition **в** (+ acc.) is normally used:

> Э́тот та́нец был осо́бенно популя́рен *в семидеся́тые го́ды*.
> This dance was especially popular in the (19)70s.

NOTE
> The word for 'decade' is **десятиле́тие**; the word **дека́да** means a period of ten days:
>
> Проездны́е биле́ты поступа́ют в прода́жу в после́дней дека́де предыду́щего ме́сяца.
> (Monthly) season tickets go on sale during the last ten days of the preceding month.

Centuries are indicated using an *ordinal* numeral and the noun **век** (usually abbreviated in writing to **в.**). To locate an event within a particular century a construction with the preposition **в** (+ prep.) is used:

> Крепостно́е пра́во в Росси́и бы́ло отменено́ *в девятна́дцатом ве́ке*.
> Serfdom in Russia was abolished in the nineteenth century.

If the century is indicated using figures, *capital Roman* numerals are invariably used:

> Успе́нский собо́р был постро́ен во второ́й полови́не *XV в.* (пятна́дцатого ве́ка).
> The Cathedral of the Dormition (in the Moscow Kremlin) was built in the second half of the fifteenth century.

To indicate that a date is before Christ (before the Christian era) the phrase **до на́шей э́ры** (abbreviated to **до н.э.**) is used; **до рождества́ Христо́ва** is also possible, but is much less frequent. If it is necessary to specify a date as AD (the Christian era) the phrase **на́шей э́ры** (abbreviated to **н.э.**) can be used:

> По да́нным архео́логов пе́рвые поселе́ния появи́лись на э́том ме́сте приблизи́тельно в пе́рвом ве́ке *до н.э.*
> According to work carried out by archaeologists, the first settlements appeared here somewhere around the first century BC.

For other time expressions, including those that do not involve numerals, *see* **21.1**.

19.4 | **Talking about approximate quantity using numerals**

19.4.1 | **Talking about approximate quantity using adverbs**

The following *adverbs* can be used to indicate approximate quantity:

приме́рно	about, approximately
приблизи́тельно	about, approximately
где́-то	about, somewhere in the region of, something like

These have the advantage of flexibility in that they can be used in more or less any grammatical context. The first two are more characteristic of formal language, while the third is more likely to be found in informal contexts:

> **Ру́сский язы́к на на́шем факульте́те изуча́ют** *приме́рно* **сто два́дцать челове́к.**
> Russian is studied in our faculty by approximately 120 students.

> **Курс а́кций упа́л** *приблизи́тельно* **на два́дцать пу́нктов.**
> The price of the shares fell by about twenty points.

> **В о́тпуске он пробы́л** *где́-то* **неде́лю, но не вы́держал безде́лья и верну́лся к рабо́те.**
> He spent about a week on holiday, but couldn't stand the idleness and came back to work.

> **Сре́дний за́работок на́ших сотру́дников –** *где́-то* **два́дцать ты́сяч рубле́й в ме́сяц.**
> The average salary of those who work here is about 20,000 roubles a month.

19.4.2 Talking about approximate quantity: placing the numeral after the noun

It is also possible to indicate approximate quantity by placing the numeral *after* the relevant noun. This is a particularly useful construction with numerals that are, grammatically speaking, relatively simple:

> **Ему́, наве́рно, бу́дет** *лет со́рок пять.*
> He'll be about forty-five, I reckon.

For more on how to talk about people's ages, *see* **12.3**.

> **Подожди́** *мину́т пять*, **а пото́м попро́буй ещё раз.**
> Wait for about five minutes and then try again.

When this means of expressing approximation is used with a prepositional construction, the preposition is placed *after* the *noun* and *immediately before* the *numeral*:

> **Я уезжа́ю** *дня на́ два.*
> I'm going away for a couple of days or so.

19.4.3 Talking about approximate quantity using prepositions

The preposition used most frequently to indicate approximate quantity is **о́коло** (+ gen.):

> **В мое́й колле́кции** *о́коло двадцати́* **довое́нных плака́тов.**
> I have about twenty pre-war posters in my collection.

> **Я ждал его́ на вокза́ле** *о́коло пятна́дцати мину́т.*
> I waited for him at the station for about fifteen minutes.

Also used sometimes is the preposition **с** (+ acc.). This tends to be used mostly in combination with the nouns **деся́ток, полсо́тни, со́тня**, which indicate respectively the quantities of ten, fifty and one hundred:

В холоди́льнике мы обнару́жили *с деся́ток* яи́ц, кусо́к сы́ра и буты́лку пи́ва.
In the fridge we discovered about ten [*or* about a dozen] eggs, a piece of cheese and a bottle of beer.

С *полсо́тни* книг из свое́й библиоте́ки он разда́л студе́нтам.
He took about fifty books from his collection and gave them out to his students.

For more on **деся́ток, полсо́тни, со́тня**, *see* **8.6.1** and **19.4.4**.

NOTE   Because it is not normally possible in Russian to combine two prepositions, о́коло (+ gen.) and с (+ acc.) cannot be used in contexts where quantity is expressed by a phrase including a preposition. In the third example in **19.4.1**, о́коло can be used to replace где́-то, but it would be impossible to substitute о́коло for приблизи́тельно in the second example:

В о́тпуске он пробы́л *о́коло* неде́ли, но не вы́держал безде́лья и верну́лся к рабо́те.
He spent about a week on holiday, but couldn't stand the idleness and came back to work.

19.4.4   Talking about approximate quantity using nouns formed from numerals

The nouns **деся́ток** and **со́тня** are frequently used in the plural to indicate large, but imprecise quantities:

Я был в Росси́и *деся́тки* раз, но ни ра́зу не стал же́ртвой преступле́ния (тьфу, тьфу).
I've been to Russia dozens of times and have never once been the victim of crime (touch wood).

На́шу переда́чу ежедне́вно слу́шают *со́тни ты́сяч* люде́й.
Hundreds of thousands of people listen to our programme every day.

NOTE   Making the gesture of pretending to spit over one's shoulder and saying тьфу, тьфу (i.e. imitating the noise of spitting) is the Russian equivalent of touching wood.

19.4.5   Talking about the upper and lower limits of an approximate quantity

The upper and lower limits of an approximate quantity are normally indicated by two numerals joined by a hyphen. This can be combined with other means of expressing approximation such as где́-то or placing the numeral after the noun:

В прода́же уже́ есть *пять-шесть* хоро́ших словаре́й.
There are already five or six good dictionaries available.

На конфере́нции бы́ло *где́-то два́дцать пять-три́дцать* представи́телей стран За́падной Евро́пы.
At the conference there were somewhere in the region of twenty-five to thirty representatives of West European countries.

За сезо́н э́тот напада́ющий непреме́нно забива́ет *мяче́й пятна́дцать-два́дцать*.
That forward can be guaranteed to score something like fifteen to twenty goals a season.

19.5 Talking about imprecise quantities using forms other than numerals

19.5.1 Talking about large quantities using мно́го, мно́гое, мно́гие

The word used most widely to indicate an imprecise large quantity is **мно́го** 'much', 'many', 'a lot'. This can be used on its own or with a noun in the *genitive singular* (if it denotes an uncountable substance) or the *genitive plural*. It can also be followed by an *adjective* in the *genitive singular neuter* form. **Мно́го** does not decline and when used with a noun can be used only in contexts that require the *nominative* or the *accusative* case without a preposition:

> **Я о́чень *мно́го* слы́шал о вас.**
> I've heard a lot about you.

> **Таки́е ве́щи занима́ют *мно́го вре́мени*.**
> These things take up a lot of time.

> **Она́ *мно́го раз* была́ в Москве́.**
> She's been to Moscow many times.

> **Я узна́л от него́ *мно́го интере́сного*.**
> I learned from him much that was interesting.

For expressions that can be used to replace **мно́го** in cases other than the nominative or the accusative or after a preposition, *see* **19.5.2**.

Мно́гое 'much', 'a great deal' can be used on its own or with a construction using the preposition **из** (+ gen.), but it is not followed directly by a noun. It declines like an adjective in the *neuter singular* and can be used in all cases:

> **Мно́гое *из* того́, чему́ я научи́лся в а́рмии, я уже́ успе́л забы́ть.**
> I've already managed to forget much of what I learned when I was in the army.

Мно́гие 'many (of)' can be used on its own or it can be followed directly by a noun or by a construction using the preposition **из** (+ gen.). It usually implies 'many of some larger group' (which may or may not be mentioned explicitly), and when used on its own normally refers only to people. It declines like an adjective in the *plural* and can be used in all cases:

> **Мно́гие *счита́ют*, что поли́тика – э́то гря́зное де́ло.**
> Many people think that politics is a dirty business.

> **У *мно́гих москвиче́й* есть твёрдая ве́ра в то, что мир конча́ется за преде́лами кольцево́й автодоро́ги.**
> Many Muscovites have the firm belief that the world comes to an end beyond the city's outer ring-road.

> **Я уже́ име́л удово́льствие познако́миться *со мно́гими из его́ друзе́й*.**
> I have already had the pleasure of meeting many of his friends.

19.5.2 **Talking about large quantities using other expressions**

Нема́ло 'quite a lot', 'a fair number/amount' is similar in meaning and usage to **мно́го**, although the quantity suggested may be slightly smaller:

> **В после́днее вре́мя у нас бы́ло *нема́ло пробле́м* с програ́ммным обеспече́нием.**
> Recently we've been having a fair number of problems with software.

The following words and expressions can be used instead of **мно́го** after a preposition or in contexts requiring a case other than the nominative or the accusative, although they are also used more generally. The third and fourth of these tend to found in more formal language:

большо́е коли́чество	a great quantity, many
огро́мное коли́чество	an enormous quantity, very many
мно́жество	a great number, many
(це́лый) ряд	a (great) number, many

> *Без большо́го коли́чества де́нег* **вам тру́дно бу́дет жить в Ло́ндоне.**
> Without a lot of money you'll find it difficult to live in London.

> **Я получи́л от него́ письмо́ *с огро́мным коли́чеством вопро́сов*.**
> I've received a letter from him with a great many questions.

> **Э́тот стра́нный фено́мен уже́ породи́л *мно́жество тео́рий*.**
> This strange phenomenon has already prompted a great many theories.

> *На ря́де предприя́тий* **ме́неджеры ещё не осво́или нове́йшие ме́тоды управле́ния.**
> In a number of businesses the managers have yet to come to terms with the latest management practices.

> *Це́лый ряд европе́йских университе́тов* **тепе́рь предлага́ет ку́рсы но́вого ти́па на сте́пень маги́стра.**
> Many European universities are now offering master's courses of the new type.

The following words and expressions also indicate a large, but unspecified quantity. They tend to occur in more informal types of language:

ку́ча	heaps (of)
тьма́	multitudes (of), hordes (of)
у́йма	masses (of)
не перече́сть	you can't keep count (of), there's no end to

> **Дела́ у неё пошли́ в го́ру; на одно́й то́лько прода́же компа́кт-ди́сков она́ зарабо́тала *ку́чу де́нег*.**
> Her business has really taken off; she's made a heap of money just from selling compact discs.

> **На конце́рт под откры́тым не́бом пришла́ *тьма́ наро́ду*.**
> The open-air concert was attended by hordes of people.

> **Я наде́юсь, что ты никуда́ не торо́пишься; у меня́ к тебе́ *у́йма вопро́сов*.**
> I hope you're not rushing off anywhere; I've got masses of questions to ask you.

> **Дочь губерна́тора была́ необыкнове́нно краси́ва, и *покло́нников* у неё к двадцати́ года́м бы́ло *не перече́сть*.**
> The governor's daughter was extraordinarily attractive, and by the time she was twenty there was no end to the number of her admirers.

19.5.3 Talking about small quantities using мáло, немнóго

Мáло 'not much', 'few', 'little' can be used on its own or with a noun in the *genitive singular* (if it denotes an uncountable substance) or the *genitive plural*. It can also be followed by an adjective in the *genitive singular neuter* form:

> **В послéднее врéмя я *мáло* читáю, а всё бóльше смотрю́ телевизор.**
> Recently, I haven't been reading much and have been watching television more and more.

> **Éсли мóжно, зайдите ко мне зáвтра; у меня́ сейчáс *мáло врéмени*.**
> If you can, call in and see me tomorrow; I haven't got much time at the moment.

> **Сдéлать карьéру здесь ему́ бýдет слóжно; у негó *мáло друзéй* среди начáльства.**
> It will be difficult for him to get on here; he has few friends among the bosses.

> **Я былá на егó лéкции, но узнáла *мáло интерéсного*.**
> I went to his lecture, but I learned little that was interesting.

The connotations of **мáло** are often negative, and sometimes it can mean 'too few', 'too little', 'not enough':

> **Пять ты́сяч рублéй? Этого, я дýмаю, бýдет *мáло*.**
> 5,000 roubles? I don't think that's going to be enough.

Мáло can be combined with a question word. The most widely used combination is **мáло кто** 'not many people'; when it functions as the subject of a sentence, the verb is in the *singular*:

> ***Мáло кто знáет* об этом.**
> Not a lot of people know about that.

Немнóго and the more informal diminutive form **немнóжко** 'some', 'a bit', 'a little' can be used on their own or with a following noun. In the latter environment they are mostly used with nouns denoting uncountable substances. The connotations of **немнóго** and **немнóжко** are usually neutral or positive:

> **Подождите *немнóжко*: дождь скóро пройдёт.**
> Wait a little; this rain will soon pass over.

> **Я прочтý вáшу статью́ в суббóту, когдá у меня́ наконéц бýдет *немнóго свобóдного врéмени*.**
> I'll read your article on Saturday, when I'll finally have a little free time.

> **Этот суп стáнет вкуснéе, éсли в негó добáвить *немнóжко сóли*.**
> This soup will taste better if you add a bit of salt to it.

Немнóго and **немнóжко** can be used with ordinary and comparative adjectives with the meaning of 'a little', 'to some extent':

> **Он никогдá не встаёт рáньше двенáдцати; в этом отношéнии он действительно *немнóжко стрáнный*.**
> He never gets up before twelve; in this respect he is indeed a little strange.

> **Онá *немнóго молóже* меня́ – дýмаю, лет на семь-вóсемь.**
> She's a bit younger than I am, by about seven or eight years, I reckon.

Ма́ло, немно́го and **немно́жко** do not decline and can be used with a following noun only in contexts requiring the *nominative* or the *accusative* case without a preposition.

For expressions that can replace **ма́ло, немно́го** and **немно́жко** in cases other than the nominative or the accusative or after a preposition, see the following sections.

19.5.4 Talking about small quantities using не́сколько, не́который

Не́сколько 'several', 'a few', 'some', is usually followed by a noun in the *plural*. When **не́сколько** is in the *nominative* or the *accusative* case, any following noun and/or adjective is in the *genitive plural*. When it is in the *genitive*, *dative*, *instrumental* or *prepositional* case, then any accompanying noun and/or adjective is in the *same case*.

For the declension of **не́сколько**, *see* **8.6.3**.

> **В ко́мнате стоя́л большо́й стол и** *не́сколько деревя́нных сту́льев.*
> In the room there was a large table and a few wooden chairs.

> **Я уже́** *не́сколько раз* **объясня́л ему́, почему́ нельзя́ употребля́ть таки́е слова́.**
> I've already explained to him several times why he's not allowed to use words like that.

> **В** *не́скольких областя́х* **вы́падет снег и́ли пройдёт дождь со сне́гом.**
> In a few regions there will be snow or sleet.

In the singular **не́который** 'some', 'a certain' is used with **вре́мя** 'time' and with other abstract nouns:

> **Че́рез** *не́которое вре́мя* **он по́нял, в чём была́ его́ оши́бка.**
> Some time later he realised where he had made his mistake.

> **В её прису́тствии я всегда́ испы́тываю** *не́которую нело́вкость.*
> When I'm in her presence I always feel a certain awkwardness.

The plural form **не́которые** means 'some', 'a few of some larger group' (which may or may not be mentioned explicitly). It can be used on its own or it can be followed directly by a noun or by a construction using the preposition **из** (+ gen.). When used on its own it refers only to people:

> *Не́которые* **критикова́ли его́ за чрезме́рную осторо́жность, но я с э́той то́чкой зре́ния не согла́сен.**
> Some people criticised him for being excessively cautious, but I don't agree with that point of view.

> **По́сле распа́да Сове́тского Сою́за** *не́которые эмигра́нты* **реши́ли верну́ться в Росси́ю.**
> After the collapse of the Soviet Union, some émigrés decided to return to Russia.

> *С не́которыми из её книг* **я уже́ знако́м, но есть и таки́е, кото́рых я не чита́л.**
> I'm familiar with some of her books, but there are others that I haven't read.

NOTE | Не́который declines like an adjective.

For more on the declension of adjectives, *see* **6.1**.

19.5.5   ## Talking about small quantities using чуть, чуть-чуть, чу́точку

The adverb **чуть** 'just', '(very) slightly' is often used to qualify adjectives and other adverbs:

> **За перекрёстком рестора́н «Гава́на», а *чуть* да́льше наш дом.**
> After the crossroads there is the Havana restaurant and our block is just beyond that.

The phrase **чуть не**, when used with a verb, means 'almost', 'nearly' and refers to involuntary actions:

> **Когда́ он сказа́л мне, что собира́ется жени́ться, я *чуть не* упа́л со сту́ла.**
> When he told me that he was going to get married, I nearly fell off my chair.

The phrase **чуть ли не** means 'almost', 'just about' and is used in a wide variety of contexts:

> **Он приходи́л ко мне *чуть ли не* ка́ждый день.**
> He used to come and see me just about every day.

> **Рубль сейча́с укрепля́ется и стал *чуть ли не* са́мой надёжной валю́той.**
> The rouble is now getting stronger and has become just about the most reliable currency.

Чуть-чу́ть and **чу́точку** are more emphatic forms of **чуть**, but they can also be used on their own or with nouns denoting uncountable substances to indicate a very small amount:

> **Вы не могли́ бы диктова́ть *чуть-чу́ть/чу́точку* поме́дленнее? Мы не успева́ем запи́сывать.**
> Could you dictate just a little bit more slowly? We can't keep up with you (*literally*, we don't have time to write it down).

> **Подви́ньтесь *чуть-чу́ть/чу́точку* – тогда́ бу́дет ме́сто и для меня́.**
> If you move up a tiny bit, there'll be room for me as well.

> **Суп непло́х, но я бы доба́вил *чуть-чу́ть/чу́точку* со́ли.**
> The soup's not bad, but I would add just a tiny bit of salt.

19.5.6   ## Talking about small quantities using other words and expressions

The following words and expressions can be used instead of **ма́ло** or **немно́го** after a preposition or in contexts requiring a case other than the accusative, although they are also used more generally:

ма́ленькое коли́чество	a small quantity
небольшо́е коли́чество	a small quantity
не́которое коли́чество	a certain quantity

> **Гла́вный недоста́ток э́того уче́бника – сли́шком *ма́ленькое коли́чество* приме́ров и упражне́ний.**
> The main problem with this textbook is that it has too few examples and exercises.

> **Она́ ме́лко наре́зала лук и обжа́рила его́ *в небольшо́м коли́честве* ма́сла.**
> She cut the onion up small and fried it in a little oil.

Для э́того тре́буется *не́которое коли́чество* де́нег.
For that you need a certain amount of money.

The following words and phrases also indicate an unspecified small quantity:

го́рстка	handful (of)
ку́чка	handful (of)
кот напла́кал	very little, precious little
раз-два и обчёлся	very few, you can count on the fingers of one hand

По́сле до́лгих лет молча́ния у него́ оста́лась всего́ лишь *го́рстка* почита́телей.
After the long years of silence he only had a handful of admirers left.

Несмотря́ на дождь и хо́лод, на пло́щади собрала́сь *ку́чка* сторо́нников одного́ из кандида́тов.
In spite of the rain and the cold, a handful of supporters of one of the candidates gathered in the square.

Де́нег у них остава́лось *кот напла́кал*.
They've got precious little money left.

Хоро́ших специали́стов у нас по э́той ча́сти *раз-два и обчёлся*.
You can count on the fingers of one hand the number of good specialists we have in this area.

20

Focus and emphasis

Principles of word order in Russian

Russian and English compared

The word order in an English sentence simultaneously fulfils two functions. In the first place it has a *structural* function: in a normal English sentence the *subject* comes *before* the verb; if there is an *object*, that will come *after* the verb. This makes it possible to interpret the following sentence unambiguously: 'John invited Mary.' 'John' comes before the verb and can only be the subject; 'Mary' comes after the verb and can only be the object. Therefore, it was John who did the inviting and Mary who was the person invited.

The second function relates to the *flow of information*: the word order of the above sentence tells us that this is a piece of information about John and what he did: that he invited Mary, either as opposed to inviting some other person or as opposed to forgetting to tell her about the event.

In Russian, the word order does not have to fulfil a structural function: the distinct case endings mean that the *subject* does not need to be identified by being placed *before* the verb, and the *object* does not have to be placed *after* the verb. The difference can be illustrated by the following pairs of examples:

> John invited Mary.
> Mary invited John.
>
> **Ива́н пригласи́л Мари́ю.**
> **Мари́ю пригласи́л Ива́н.**

Changing the word order in the English sentences changes who invited whom: in the second example Mary did the inviting and John was the person invited. In both Russian sentences Ivan did the inviting and Mariia was the person invited. Indeed, as we shall see, the word order *object–verb–subject*, illustrated by the second sentence, is by no means unusual.

Because Russian word order does not fulfil a structural function, it is often described as 'free', but this is somewhat misleading: Russian word order does fulfil a function relating to *focus*, *emphasis* and the *flow of information*, and changing the word order of a Russian sentence will change the meaning and more often than not will affect the most natural way of translating the sentence into English. To take the above examples, if the first sentence can be translated as:

Ivan invited Mariia.

the most appropriate translation of the second might be:

Mariia was invited by Ivan.

Or

It was Ivan who invited Mariia.

20.1.2　The basic principle of Russian word order

The basic principle underlying the word order of a Russian sentence is that the most important information comes at the *end of a sentence*. In other words, what often happens is that the first part of a sentence sets the scene, so to speak, by presenting the *topic* of the sentence (often in the form of information that is already known or given); the concluding part of the sentence tells us what is being said about the topic, usually in the form of new information.

NOTE　As it is used in this context, *topic* is not to be confused with *grammatical subject*. The topic of a sentence can be the grammatical subject, but it can equally well be the *direct object* or, indeed, any other constituent of the sentence.

This principle can be illustrated by the following sequences of sentences:

A　**Пётр Пе́рвый счита́ется основа́телем росси́йского вое́нно-морско́го фло́та. Пётр та́кже заложи́л осно́вы росси́йского судострое́ния.**
Peter I (the Great) is considered the founder of the Russian navy. It was also Peter who laid the foundations of the Russian ship-building industry.

B　**Пе́рвые росси́йские вое́нные корабли́ в Росси́и бы́ли постро́ены в Воро́неже. Осно́вы росси́йского судострое́ния заложи́л Пётр Пе́рвый.**
The first Russian warships were built in Voronezh. It was Peter the Great who laid the foundations of the Russian ship-building industry.

In each of the above sequences the second sentence provides information about Peter the Great laying the foundations of the Russian ship-building industry, but the information is presented in a different order. In sequence A, the subject (**Пётр** 'Peter') comes first, and the object (**осно́вы росси́йского судострое́ния** 'the foundations of the Russian ship-building industry') comes at the end. In sequence B, however, the object comes at the beginning of the sentence and the subject comes at the end.

The explanation for this lies in the context provided by the first sentence in each sequence. In sequence A, the first sentence concerns the activities of Peter the Great; he thus becomes the topic of the second sentence, with the new information being that in addition to founding the Russian navy, he also laid the foundations of the Russian ship-building industry. Hence, Peter the Great (here the grammatical subject of the sentence) comes first and the reference to the foundations of the ship-building industry comes at the end. In sequence B, the first sentence relates to the building of ships; here, therefore, it is 'the foundations of the Russian ship-building industry' that is the topic of the second sentence, and the new information is that these foundations were laid by Peter the Great, and not by some other Russian ruler.

The following examples provide further illustrations and demonstrate other possibilities for the word order in a Russian sentence:

> **Перехо́дный 2008 год бу́дет непросты́м для США.** *Стране́ ну́жен ли́дер,* **но си́льных люде́й** *нет.*
> The transitional year of 2008 will be difficult for the USA. The country needs a leader, but there are no strong people around.

> **В ма́е 1953 го́да Э́дмунд Хи́лллари и Те́нсинг Но́ргей пе́рвыми взошли́ на Эвере́ст.** *С тех пор на высоча́йшей то́чке земно́го ша́ра* **побыва́ло бо́лее 1200 челове́к из 63 стран ми́ра.**
> In May 1953 Edmund Hillary and Tensing Norgay were the first people to reach the summit of Everest. Since then, over 1,200 people from 63 countries have reached the highest point on the planet.

In the second sentence of the first example, the word **страна́** 'country' provides the link between the two sentences and it comes in first place, although it is, in the Russian construction, the dative complement of the short adjective **ну́жен** 'is needed', 'is required'. In the second clause of the second sentence, the most important information is the absence of strong people; this information is provided by the negative verb form **нет** which comes at the end of the sentence.

In the second example, the link between the two sentences is provided by both the time and the place, and these elements are placed at the beginning of the second sentence. The most important information in this sentence is the number of people who have climbed Everest since Hillary and Tensing, and this information (the subject of the sentence) comes at the end.

Another illustration of the way in which information flows in Russian is provided by sentences that begin with a date or another construction indicating when an event happened. Here the most important information in the sentence is provided not by the verb, but by the subject of the sentence, that is, the noun or noun phrase referring to the event. For this reason the normal order of elements is: *date–verb–subject*:

> **22 ию́ня 1941 го́да** *начала́сь Вели́кая Оте́чественная война́.*
> The Great Patriotic War broke out on 22 June 1941.

> **В 1905 году́** *произошла́ Пе́рвая Ру́сская револю́ция.*
> The first Russian revolution took place in 1905.

> **В январе́ у них** *родила́сь* **дочь.**
> They had a daughter in January.

NOTE Russians normally distinguish between **Втора́я мирова́я война́**, that is, the Second World War, which began in September 1939, and **Вели́кая Оте́чественная война́**, which began with the German invasion of the Soviet Union in June 1941.

For more on talking about dates, *see* 19.3.

20.1.3 More principles of Russian word order

In addition to the above, there are some general principles of Russian word order that apply to specific elements within a sentence.

Adjectives and *pronouns* are normally placed *before* the nouns they qualify:

> **Поздравля́ю вас с *Но́вым* го́дом!**
> I wish you a happy New Year!

> **Я хочу́ купи́ть себе́ *но́вые* джи́нсы.**
> I want to buy myself some new jeans.

> **То́лько что вы́шел *како́й-то но́вый* спра́вочник по грамма́тике *ру́сского* языка́.**
> A new handbook of Russian grammar has just been published.

In written Russian, it is sometimes possible to place an entire adjectival phrase in front of a noun:

> **В Герма́нии откры́лся *пе́рвый в ми́ре* по́лностью автоматизи́рованный рестора́н.**
> The first fully automated restaurant in the world has opened in Germany.

Occasionally, an adjective is placed after a noun in order to convey special emphasis:

> **Челове́к он был *ре́зкий*, но *справедли́вый*.**
> He was a man who was harsh, but fair.

For the use of short comparative adjectives after the noun they qualify, *see* **21.9.1**.

Numerals are also placed *before* the nouns they refer to:

> **Ему́ *со́рок пять лет*.**
> He is forty-five years old.

A numeral placed after the noun it refers to indicates approximate quantity. For examples, *see* **19.4.2**.

Adverbs are normally placed immediately *before* the words they qualify, whether these are *verbs*, *adjectives* or other *adverbs*:

> **Она́ *по-пре́жнему ча́сто* звони́ла своему́ *уже́* взро́слому сы́ну.**
> She telephoned her already grown-up son just as frequently as before.

> **Эта *поначалу* безу́мная иде́я *о́чень бы́стро* преврати́лась в *абсолю́тно* чёткий план.**
> This initially insane idea has turned very quickly into an absolutely lucid plan.

Adverbs that are perceived as qualifying a whole sentence can be placed at the beginning:

> **Внешне* но́вый «Форд» похо́ж на ста́рую моде́ль.**
> On the outside the new Ford is similar to the old model.

Adverbs in Russian are not placed at the end of a sentence as often as their English counterparts are, but this word order does occur if it is an adverb that is supplying the most important information:

**Я не большо́й покло́нник её тала́нта, но до́лжен призна́ться, что
сего́дня она́ выступа́ла *о́чень хорошо́*.**
I am no great admirer of her talent, but I have to admit that today she performed
very well.

Small words, especially unstressed pronouns, tend to be tucked away in the middle of
a sentence:

—Ме́жду про́чим, он сде́лал *мне* предложе́ние.
—И что, ты *его́* приняла́?

—By the way, he's proposed to me.
—And so, have you accepted him?

Relative pronouns normally follow the nouns or pronouns to which they refer:

Хо́чешь уви́деть *маши́ну, на кото́рой* мы прое́хали через всю Росси́ю?
Do you want to see the car that we travelled across Russia in?

Не верь *тому́, что* он бу́дет сейча́с говори́ть.
Don't believe what he's about to tell you.

In more informal varieties of Russian, however, it is sometimes possible for a relative
pronoun (especially **кто** or **что**) to come at the *beginning* of a sentence, with the reference (usually a pronoun) coming at the beginning of the second clause. This construction
is mostly used for making generalised statements:

А *кому́* не интере́сно, *те* пусть не смо́трят.
Those who don't find it interesting, don't need to watch.

***Кто* не рабо́тает, *тот* не ест.**
Those who don't work, don't eat.

Participial phrases, which can be used in place of relative clauses in the most formal
levels of written Russian, also tend to follow the nouns or pronouns that they qualify:

**В Росси́и постепе́нно формиру́ется слой гра́ждан, *де́лающих ста́вку на
индивидуа́льный вы́бор и ли́чную отве́тственность*.**
Russia is gradually acquiring a section of society that is willing to rely on
individual choice and personal responsibility.

**Ми́фом явля́ются и представле́ния о «культу́рной про́пасти», *я́кобы
разделя́ющей Росси́ю и Евро́пу*.**
The notion of a 'cultural gap' that supposedly divides Russia from Europe is
also a myth.

It is, however, by no means unknown for a participial phrase to precede the noun it qualifies; this word order also allows the same noun to be qualified by a relative clause:

**Он был из тех ре́дких, *зна́ющих челове́ческую психоло́гию*
руководи́телей, кото́рые уме́ют привле́чь люде́й на свою́ сто́рону.**
He was one of those rare leaders who understood human psychology and who
was therefore able to persuade people to support him.

For more on the use of participles, *see* **23.1.3**.

20.2 Active and passive verbs

20.2.1 Active and passive verbs

When a verb is in the *active* voice, the performer of the action or the main participant in the state is the *subject* of the verb. The recipient of the action, if there is one, is the *direct object*:

> **Ива́н пригласи́л Мари́ю на ве́чер.**
> Ivan invited Mariia to the party.

> **Профе́ссор Попо́в написа́л о́чень интере́сную кни́гу о совреме́нном русском рома́не.**
> Professor Popov has written a very interesting book about the modern Russian novel.

Both these sentences give us information about the subject: they tell us something about what Ivan and Professor Popov did. Sometimes, it is necessary to give information about the recipient of the action, and one way of doing this is to use a *passive verb*. When a passive verb is used, the recipient of the action is the *subject* of the verb. The performer of the action, if mentioned, is referred to as the *agent*; in Russian, the agent of a passive verb is in the *instrumental* case:

> **Ока́зывается, Мари́я была́ приглашена́ на ве́чер Ива́ном.**
> It transpires that Mariia was invited to the party by Ivan.

> **Са́мая интере́сная кни́га о совреме́нном ру́сском рома́не была́ напи́сана профе́ссором Попо́вым.**
> The most interesting book on the modern Russian novel was written by Professor Popov.

For information on the formation of passive verbs, *see* **4.14.1**.

20.2.2 Using and avoiding passive verbs

In Russian, it is not necessary to use a *passive* verb in order to give information about the recipient of the action. The same effect can often be achieved by using an *active* verb, but placing the *direct object* at the beginning of the sentence:

> **Ока́зывается, Мари́ю пригласи́л Ива́н.**
> It transpires that Mariia was invited by Ivan.

> **Са́мую интере́сную кни́гу о совреме́нном ру́сском рома́не написа́л профе́ссор Попо́в.**
> The most interesting book on the modern Russian novel was written by Professor Popov.

It follows from this that passive verbs are not used as frequently in Russian as they are in English, and that the most natural means of translating into English a Russian sentence where the object precedes the verb is often by means of a passive construction (as in the above two examples). Often there is a choice in Russian between the two types of construction, but passive verbs tend to be preferred in sentences where no agent is mentioned:

> **Э́тот собо́р был постро́ен в шестна́дцатом ве́ке.**
> This cathedral was built in the sixteenth century.

Эта книга *была написана* на русском языке и только потом *переведена* на английский.
This book was written in Russian and only later translated into English.

In the first of the above examples it would be possible to use an active verb in the third person plural, but this usage should be avoided when referring to actions caried out by nameable individuals (as in the second example):

Этот собор *построили* в шестнадцатом веке.
This cathedral was built in the sixteenth century.

For more on this use of the third person plural active verb, *see* **7.1.5**.

Passive verbs also tend to be preferred in those sentences where there are additional elements referring to time and/or place:

Мария была приглашена *в числе первых*.
Mariia was one of the first to be invited.

Эта книга *была переведена* на английский *в начале прошлого века* одним из братьев автора.
This book was translated into English at the beginning of the last century by one of the author's brothers.

Passive verbs tend to be characteristic of more formal types of language:

На вывозимые произведения искусства *установлена* экспортная пошлина в размере 100 процентов их стоимости.
Exported works of art are subject to a customs duty of 100 per cent of their value.

Ниже *приводится* перечень искусства, выдающих свидетельства на право вывоза произведений искусств за границу.
Below is published a list of those institutions that issue export certificates for works of art.

20.3 Other forms of emphasis

20.3.1 The pattern: 'It was Ivan who invited Mariia'

It was noted above that one of the ways of translating the following Russian sentence into English was:

Марию пригласил Иван.
It was Ivan who invited Mariia.

Sentences of this type are known as 'cleft sentences': they are very common in English, but have no direct equivalent in Russian. The change of emphasis introduced by the English construction is achieved in sentences following the above pattern by using the *object–verb–subject* word order, but where this is inappropriate, other forms of indicating emphasis can be used.

20.3.2 **Indicating emphasis using и́менно and как ра́з**

One of the main functions of the adverb **и́менно** is to indicate emphasis in a similar way to English 'cleft sentences':

> *И́менно так* у нас происхо́дит процеду́ра голосова́ния.
> That is how our voting system works.

> **Тру́дно перечи́слить всё, что сде́лал Пу́шкин для ру́сской культу́ры.
> Так, *и́менно с Пу́шкина* начина́ется совреме́нный ру́сский
> литерату́рный язы́к.**
> It is difficult to enumerate everything that Pushkin did for Russian culture. It is
> to Pushkin that the modern Russian literary language traces its origins.

Как ра́з can also be used to add emphasis to a specific word or part of a sentence:

> А я *как ра́з* собира́лся вам звони́ть.
> I was just on the very point of phoning you.

> *Как ра́з* на моло́чные проду́кты у меня́ аллерги́я.
> It is precisely to milk products that I have an allergy.

20.3.3 **Indicating emphasis using particles**

Various particles can be used to indicate emphasis. In many instances the degree of emphasis indicated is smaller than is the case when **и́менно** is used, and the emphasis is not always indicated in translation.

One particle that can indicate strong emphasis is **вот**; in this function it tends to be used with question words and to appear at the beginning of a sentence:

> *Вот* кто нас вы́ручит!
> That's who is going to save our bacon!

> *Вот* как на́до чи́стить ры́бу.
> That's how to clean fish.

> *Вот* куда́ де́нежки улета́ют.
> That's where our money's going to.

The particle that is perhaps the most widely used for indicating emphasis is **-то**; this is always joined to the preceding word with a hyphen:

> *Наконе́ц-то!* Пе́рвый раз в э́том сезо́не на́ша кома́нда одержа́ла
> побе́ду.
> At last! For the first time this season our team has managed to win a game.

> *Вообще́-то* здесь нельзя́ кури́ть.
> You shouldn't really smoke here.

> Но *они́-то* и есть на́ши гла́вные сопе́рники.
> But these are the people who are our main rivals.

> Е́сли Аме́рика не хо́чет ссо́риться с Росси́ей, то уж *нам-то* заче́м?
> If America does not want to quarrel with Russia, then why (on earth)
> should we?

It will be noted that in the last two examples **-то** is combined with the particles **и** and **уж** respectively.

Further examples of the use of **и** and **уж** are provided by the following:

> —**Тут напи́сано: «Перед употребле́нием взба́лтывать».**
> —**Что я *и* де́лаю.**

> —It says here that you should shake (the bottle) before use.
> —Which is (exactly) what I do.

> **Э́то не так *уж* и пло́хо!**
> It's not all that bad!

Another particle that can be used to indicate emphasis, especially after question words, is **же**:

> **Когда́ *же*, наконе́ц, почи́нят лифт?**
> So when will they finally get round to repairing the lift?

> **Так чего́ *же* ты хо́чешь?**
> But what on earth do you want?

> **Я *же* тебе́ говори́л!**
> I told you so.
> *Or* Didn't I tell you?

20.4 Definite and indefinite

20.4.0 Introduction

Because Russian has neither *definite* nor *indefinite articles*, it has to resort to other means to indicate whether a noun is definite or indefinite. Often this can be done using the word order of a sentence, although there are some occasions when a qualifier (a *pronoun* or the *numeral* **оди́н**) can be used to clarify whether a noun is definite or indefinite.

20.4.1 Using word order to indicate whether a noun is definite or indefinite

In general, there is a strong tendency for indefinite nouns to be placed after the verb and towards the end of a sentence:

> **Ря́дом с мои́м до́мом есть *кинотеа́тр*. И в э́том кинотеа́тре нахо́дится *ма́ленькое кафе́*, где я ча́сто пью ко́фе с друзья́ми.**
> Next to my house there is a cinema. And in the cinema there is a small café where I often meet my friends for coffee.

> **В Москве́ открыва́ется *вы́ставка* совреме́нной францу́зской жи́вописи.**
> An exhibition of modern French painting is opening in Moscow.

> **Она́ была́ до́ма одна́, когда́ в дверь постуча́ли. На поро́ге стоя́л *прия́тный молодо́й челове́к* с блокно́том в руке́.**
> She was at home alone when someone knocked at the door. On the doorstep was a pleasant young man with a notebook in his hand.

Conversely, *definite* nouns, which often form a link with the previous sentence(s), will tend to come at or near the beginning of a sentence:

В Москве́ открыва́ется вы́ставка совреме́нной францу́зской жи́вописи. *Вы́ставка* пройдёт в Госуда́рственном музе́е им. А.С. Пу́шкина.
An exhibition of modern French painting is opening in Moscow. The exhibition will take place in the Pushkin Museum.

Она́ была́ до́ма одна́, когда́ в дверь постуча́ли. *На поро́ге* стоя́л прия́тный молодо́й челове́к с блокно́том в руке́.
She was at home alone when someone knocked at the door. On the doorstep was a pleasant young man with a notebook in his hand.

20.4.2 Using qualifiers to indicate indefinite nouns

The pronouns **како́й-то** (if referring to something specific) and **како́й-нибудь** can be used to indicate an *indefinite* noun:

Моя́ жена́ опя́ть забы́ла перча́тки в *како́м-то* кафе́.
My wife has gone and left her gloves in a café again.

—Тебе́ звони́ли с рабо́ты.
—Кто звони́л?
—Не зна́ю. *Како́й-то* мужчи́на.

—Somebody phoned from work for you.
—Who was it?
—I don't know. It was a man.

По доро́ге домо́й купи́ *каку́ю-нибудь* газе́ту с програ́ммой на неде́лю.
On the way home buy a newspaper with the week's (television) programmes in it.

For more on the difference between **како́й-то** and **како́й-нибудь**, *see* **7.6.2** and **7.6.3**.

The numeral **оди́н** can also correspond to the English indefinite article:

В нача́ле восьмидеся́тых годо́в *оди́н* студе́нт устро́ился ночны́м сто́рожем в *оди́н* из моско́вских музе́ев.
At the beginning of the 1980s a student was taken on as a night-watchman in a Moscow museum.

20.4.3 Using pronouns to indicate definite nouns

The demonstrative pronoun **э́тот** can be used to indicate that a noun is definite:

Ря́дом с мои́м до́мом есть кинотеа́тр. И в *э́том кинотеа́тре* нахо́дится ма́ленькое кафе́, где я ча́сто пью ко́фе с друзья́ми.
Next to my house there is a cinema, and in the cinema there is a small café where I often meet my friends for coffee.

The demonstrative pronoun **тот**, when used to qualify a noun used with the relative pronoun **кото́рый**, often corresponds to an English definite article. For an example, *see* **7.5.1**

21

Establishing contexts and connections

21.1 Time

21.1.1 Talking about when something happened/happens/will happen: parts of the day

To indicate a part of a day the relevant noun is used in the *instrumental* case: **у́тром** 'in the morning', **днём** 'during the day', **ве́чером** 'in the evening', **но́чью** 'in/during the night'. Russian has no noun that corresponds to English 'afternoon', and the equivalent of 'in the afternoon' is either **днём** or **по́сле обе́да** 'after lunch':

> *У́тром* вы бу́дете ходи́ть на заня́тия, а *по́сле обе́да* вы свобо́дны.
> You will attend classes in the morning and in the afternoon you are free.

> А что вы собира́етесь де́лать *ве́чером*?
> And what are you going to do in the evening?

> Я обы́чно занима́юсь *днём*, но к экза́менам могу́ гото́виться и *но́чью*.
> I usually work (study) during the day, but before exams I can work at night as well.

The phrase **с утра́** means 'early/first thing in the morning':

> Перево́д ещё не гото́в, позвони́те за́втра *с утра́*.
> The translation's not ready yet; phone first thing in the morning.

If an event occurs regularly at a particular time of day, the preposition **по** (+ dat.) can be used; **по** is followed by a noun in the plural:

> *По утра́м* мы ходи́ли за гриба́ми.
> In the mornings we used to go mushroom hunting.

> Нам пришло́сь перее́хать из-за сосе́дей; *по нача́м* то сканда́лы, то му́зыка на по́лную гро́мкость.
> We had to move because of our neighbours; at night they were always either shouting at each other or playing music at full volume.

21.1.2 **Talking about when something happened/happens/will happen: days of the week**

To indicate an event that happened or will happen on a particular day of the week, the preposition **в** (+ acc.) is used:

> **Я уе́ду *в сре́ду*.**
> I'm leaving on Wednesday.

> **Она́ прие́хала *в воскресе́нье*.**
> She arrived on Sunday.

If an event occurs regularly on a particular day of the week, the preposition **по** (+ dat.) can be used; **по** is followed by a noun in the plural:

> **Я предпочита́ю не рабо́тать *по суббо́там*.**
> I prefer not to work on (a) Saturday.

> **Я обы́чно принима́ю *по пя́тницам*, но на э́той неде́ле вы мо́жете зайти́ ко мне *в четве́рг*.**
> I normally see (students) on Fridays, but this week you can call in and see me on Thursday.

For the use of small letters for days of the week, *see* **1.5.7**.

For information on telling the time and indicating dates, *see* **19.2** and **19.3**.

21.1.3 **Talking about when something happened/happens/will happen: seasons of the year**

The names of the seasons are:

весна́	spring
ле́то	summer
о́сень	autumn
зима́	winter

The *instrumental* case is used when talking about the seasons of the year:

> ***Ле́том* я обы́чно провожу́ суббо́ту-воскресе́нье на да́че.**
> In summer I usually spend the weekend at my dacha.

> **Сове́тую вам посети́ть наш го́род и́ли *весно́й* и́ли *о́сенью*.**
> I recommend that you visit our city either in the spring or autumn.

21.1.4 **Other words and phrases used to indicate the time when something happened/happens/will happen**

The following words and phrases are used to indicate specific times:

вчера́	yesterday
сего́дня	today
за́втра	tomorrow
позавчера́	the day before yesterday
послеза́втра	the day after tomorrow

на про́шлой неде́ле	last week
на э́той неде́ле	this week
на бу́дущей неде́ле	next week
в про́шлом ме́сяце	last month
в э́том ме́сяце	this month
в бу́дущем ме́сяце	next month
в про́шлом году́	last year
в э́том году́	this year
в бу́дущем году́	next year

The following words and phrases are used to indicate an unspecified time:

ско́ро	soon
неско́ро	not for a long time yet
давно́	a long time ago
неда́вно	recently
на днях	recently, the other day (in the past), soon, any day now (in the future)

когда́-то, не́когда, в своё вре́мя all mean 'once', 'at some time (in the past)', the first is the most widely used:

Мы *ско́ро* узна́ем всю пра́вду об э́том.
We'll soon find out the whole truth about this.

Су́дя по всему́, поя́вится он тут *неско́ро*.
It looks as if he won't be here for a long time yet.

Мы познако́мились *давно́*; мо́жно сказа́ть, что мы ста́рые друзья́.
We met a long time ago; you could say that we're old friends.

Мы совсе́м *неда́вно* перее́хали в Ло́ндон и ещё пло́хо ориенти́руемся в го́роде.
We moved to London only very recently and still don't know our way round the city.

Мы встре́тились *на днях*, и тогда́ он был в отли́чном настрое́нии.
We met the other day and then he was in an excellent mood.

***Не́когда* на э́том ме́сте стоя́ла це́рковь.**
There was once a church on this spot.

Он *в своё вре́мя* был чемпио́ном ми́ра.
At one time he was a world champion.

For another meaning of **давно́** and **неда́вно**, *see* **21.1.13**.

For more on **когда́-то**, *see* **9.1.5**.

For another meaning of **не́когда**, *see* **15.5**.

21.1.5 **Talking about when something happened/happens/will happen using the conjunction когда**

When the time of an event is indicated by an entire clause, the conjunction когда́ is used; this is used for events in the past or in the future, for single events or repeated occurrences:

Когда́ я учи́лся в шко́ле, у меня́ всегда́ бы́ли хоро́шие отме́тки по матема́тике.
When I was at school, I always got good marks for maths.

Жена́ уже́ спала́, *когда́* я пришёл домо́й.
My wife was already asleep when I got home.

Когда́ пого́да плоха́я, я стара́юсь не выходи́ть из до́ма.
When(ever) the weather is bad, I try not to leave the house.

Когда́ придёт, обяза́тельно скажу́ ему́.
When he arrives, I'll definitely tell him.

NOTE | If the event takes place in the future, the verb must be in the *future tense* (as in the last example).

When the sentence refers to an event in the future, the conjunction **когда́** is sometimes omitted in informal language:

Оте́ц вернётся – сама́ расска́жешь.
When father gets back, you can tell him for yourself.

Купи́, откро́й, зажги́ горе́лку;
Вскипи́т – и налива́й в таре́лку.
Buy (it), open it, light a hotplate;
When it boils, pour it into a bowl. [From an advertisement for tinned *borshch*.]

21.1.6 **Before and after**

The prepositions that are used most commonly when placing one event relative to another are до (+ gen.) 'before' and по́сле (+ gen.) 'after':

Мне лу́чше звони́ть *до обе́да*.
It's best to phone me before lunch.

По́сле двух я всегда́ на ме́сте.
I'm always here after two o'clock.

Пе́ред (+ instr.) means 'immediately before':

Всегда́ мо́йте ру́ки *пе́ред едо́й*.
Always wash your hands before eating.

Sometimes **ра́ньше** (+ gen.), which literally means 'earlier than', can correspond to English 'before'; it is used when stressing the earliest time at which something can or should happen:

Ра́ньше вто́рника меня́ здесь, наве́рно, не бу́дет.
I probably won't be here before Tuesday.
Or Tuesday is the earliest I am likely to be here.

рáньше is the comparative of рáно 'early'. For more on using comparatives, *see* **21.9**.

По (+ prep.) can mean '(immediately) after'; like the English 'upon', it is used only with nouns that are formed from verbs and tends to be characteristic of more formal styles:

> *По окончáнии университéта онá поступúла в аспирантýру.*
> After finishing her first degree she embarked on postgraduate studies.
> cf. **окáнчивать/окóнчить** 'to finish', 'to graduate from'

For more on nouns formed from verbs, *see* **10.1.10**.

21.1.7 When one event occurs before or after another

Where one event occurred (or will occur) *before* another, the construction за (+ acc.) ... до (+ gen.) is used:

> *Он приéхал в Áнглию за два гóда до войны́.*
> He came to England two years before the war.

On the same principle, where one event occurred (or will occur) *after* another, the construction чéрез (+ acc.) ... пóсле (+ gen.) is used:

> *Онá уéхала из Росси́и чéрез пять лет пóсле револю́ции.*
> She left Russia five years after the Revolution.

21.1.8 Indicating that something will occur after the elapse of a period of time

To indicate that something happened or will happen after the elapse of a period of time, either чéрез (+ acc.) or спустя́ (+ acc.) can be used:

> *Он приéхал на шесть недéль, но уéхал чéрез три дня.*
> He came for six weeks, but left after three days.

> *Я вернýсь чéрез час.*
> I'll be back in an hour.

> *Они́ поженúлись и спустя́ год (or год спустя́) уéхали жить в Гермáнию.*
> They got married and a year later went to live in Germany.

Unusually, **спустя́** can come either before or after the noun to which it refers.

21.1.9 The equivalent of 'ago'

To indicate that something happened at a particular time in the past, the adverb (томý) назáд 'ago' is used:

> *Он ушёл буквáльно две минýты назáд.*
> He left literally two minutes ago.

> *Пéрвые троллéйбусы появúлись на ýлицах Москвы́ бóлее чем сéмьдесят лет томý назáд.*
> The first trolleybuses appeared on the streets of Moscow more than seventy years ago.

21.1.10 Talking about before and after using adverbs

The equivalent of English 'before' when used as an adverb is **ра́ньше**; the equivalents of 'afterwards' are **по́зже** and, more informally, **попо́зже** or **пото́м**:

На́до бы́ло сказа́ть об э́том *ра́ньше*.
You should have mentioned this before.

Разберёмся во всём э́том *по́зже*.
We'll sort all this out afterwards.

Расскажу́ тебе́ об э́том *пото́м/попо́зже*.
I'll tell you about it afterwards.

21.1.11 Talking about before and after using conjunctions

Sometimes clauses joined by a conjunction are used to indicate that one action happened before or after another. The Russian conjunctions used in this sense are **до того́ как** or **пре́жде чем** 'before' and **по́сле того́ как** 'after'. If the subject in both halves of the sentence is the same, the conjunction **пре́жде чем** can be followed by an *infinitive*:

***Пре́жде чем* вы́сказать своё мне́ние по э́тому вопро́су, я хоте́л бы поблагодари́ть председа́тельствующего за приглаше́ние вы́ступить на э́той конфере́нции.**
Before expressing my opinion on this question I would like to thank the chairman for the invitation to speak at this conference.

Or Before I express my opinion …

***До того́ как* он стал нача́льником, я ча́сто приглаша́л его́ на кру́жку пи́ва.**
Before he became the boss, I often used to invite him out for a glass of beer.

Я по́нял и́стинный смысл её слов то́лько *по́сле того́, как* она́ уе́хала.
I understood the true meaning of her words only after she (had) left.

NOTE | A comma should normally be placed before **как** or **чем** (as in the third example above), but can be omitted when the conjunction begins the sentence (as in the first two examples).

These conjunctions are not used anything like as frequently as their English equivalents, and especially in more informal contexts it is probably better to try to avoid them if at all possible. Sometimes this can be done by using a noun with a preposition:

Я *до за́втрака* вообще́ ни на что́ не спосо́бен.
Before I've had breakfast I'm totally incapable of anything.

То́лько *по́сле оконча́ния* университе́та вы осознае́те, как здо́рово быть студе́нтом.
Only after you've graduated will you understand how great it is to be a student.

A similar effect can sometimes be achieved by looking at an event from a different point of view, making it possible to use the more frequent conjunction **когда́** 'when':

Да́же *когда́* я ещё учи́лся в шко́ле, я то́чно знал, кем я хочу́ стать
Even before I left school I knew exactly what I wanted to be.
(*Literally*, Even when I was still at school …)

21.1.12 Duration: completed actions

To indicate the duration of time spent on an action the *accusative* case is used without a preposition:

> **Я жил в э́том до́ме *пять лет*.**
> I lived in this house for five years [but now no longer do so; see below, **21.1.13**].

> **Вам придётся стоя́ть *два часа́* за биле́том.**
> You'll have to queue for two hours to get a ticket.

> **Он *три часа́* расска́зывал мне о свои́х приключе́ниях в А́фрике.**
> He was telling me about his adventures in Africa for three hours.
> *Or*, He spent three hours telling me about his adventures in Africa.

Normally, the verb in such sentences is in the *imperfective* aspect, but *perfective* verbs with the prefixes **по-** or **про-** can sometimes be used. The former usually indicates a short duration as part of a sequence of actions, while the latter stresses the length of time an action or event lasted for:

> **По́сле после́дней ле́кции я *позанима́лся два часа́* в библиоте́ке, а пото́м пошёл домо́й.**
> After the last lecture I worked for a couple of hours in the library and then went home.

> **Он *прожи́л три́дцать лет* в сосе́дней кварти́ре, но за всё э́то вре́мя ни ра́зу со мной не поздоро́вался.**
> He lived in the next flat for thirty years, but in all that time never once said hello to me.

To indicate an unspecified duration, the adverbs **до́лго** 'for a long time' and **недо́лго** 'for a short time', 'not for long' can be used:

> **Он допи́л ко́фе, а пото́м *до́лго* смотре́л в окно́.**
> He finished his coffee and then spent a long time looking out of the window.

> **Мы *недо́лго* жи́ли в Пари́же; там всё сли́шком до́рого.**
> We didn't live in Paris for long; everything's too expensive there.

21.1.13 Duration: continuing actions

If an action started in the past and is still continuing, the same construction is used, but the verb is in the *present* tense:

> **Я уже́ *пять лет живу́* в э́том до́ме.**
> I've been living in this house for five years (and still do).

If the action is still continuing, unspecified duration is expressed by the adverb **давно́** 'for a long time'; **неда́вно** 'not for long', 'since recently' is occasionally used, but is less common:

> **Вы *давно́* ждёте?**
> Have you been waiting long?

> **Я здесь *неда́вно*.**
> I haven't been here long.

For other uses of **давно́** and **неда́вно**, *see* **21.1.4**.

21.1.14 **Other constructions relating to duration**

When the stress is on the length of time it took to complete something, the preposition **за** (+ acc.) is used:

> **Я написа́л кни́гу *за шесть ме́сяцев*.**
> I wrote the book in six months
> *Or*, It took me six months to write the book.

This construction is used in order to stress what has been achieved in a particular period of time:

> **За после́дние два го́да в на́шем го́роде постро́ено 3 000 но́вых домо́в.**
> In the last two years 3,000 new houses have been built in our city.

It can also indicate a negative outcome:

> **За вре́мя дежу́рства ничего́ суще́ственного не произошло́.**
> Nothing significant occurred during my period on duty.

A preposition that is close in meaning to **за** is **в тече́ние** (+ gen.) 'during', 'in the course of':

> **В тече́ние пяти́ лет о́бласть по́лностью перейдёт на цифрово́е веща́ние.**
> Within five years our region will have fully gone over to digital broadcasting.

В тече́ние is also used when talking about continuing states of affairs, repeated actions or actions that fail to occur over a particular period of time:

> **В тече́ние э́той неде́ли бу́дет преоблада́ть о́блачная пого́да.**
> During (the course of) this week the weather will be mostly cloudy (*literally*, … cloudy weather will prevail).

> **В тече́ние двух ме́сяцев я не замеча́л, что мой компью́тер заражён ви́русом.**
> For two months I failed to notice that my computer was infected with a virus.
> *Or*, It took me two months to notice …

To talk about the intended duration of an action or event, the preposition **на** (+ acc.) is used:

> **Я уезжа́ю *на па́ру дней*.**
> I am going away for a few days.

> **Он прие́хал *на шесть неде́ль*, но уе́хал че́рез три дня.**
> He came for six weeks, but left after three days.

When one action or event is taking place against the background of another, the preposition **во вре́мя** (+ gen.) 'during' is used:

> **Во вре́мя войны́ он служи́л в вое́нной разве́дке.**
> During the war he worked in military intelligence.

If the background event lasted for several years, then **в го́ды** (+ gen.) 'during (the years/ period of)' can also be used:

> **В го́ды перестро́йки она́ рабо́тала корреспонде́нтом в газе́те «Комсомо́льская пра́вда».**
> During the perestroika period she worked as a correspondent for *Komsomol'skaia pravda*.

If two actions or events taking place at the same time are described in whole clauses, these can be joined by the conjunction **пока́** 'while':

Пока́ **я был бо́лен, сестра́ навеща́ла меня́ ка́ждый день.**
While I was ill, my sister visited me every day.

Пока́ **я здесь, мо́жно задава́ть мне вопро́сы в любо́е вре́мя.**
While *or* For as long as I am here, you can ask me questions at any time.

In the first of these examples it would be equally possible to use **когда́**; **пока́** emphasises that the two actions are simultaneous, corresponding to the English 'for as long as'.

21.1.15 'From'/'to', 'until': using prepositions

The preposition used most frequently to indicate the starting point of an action is **с** (+ gen.):

Я бу́ду здесь *с понеде́льника.*
I'll be here from Monday onwards.

Наш магази́н рабо́тает *с семи́ часо́в.*
Our shop is open from seven o'clock.

The preposition used to indicate the finishing point of an action is **до** (+ gen.), which in addition to meaning 'before' also has the meaning of 'until':

Подожди́те *до четверга́:* **тогда́ я всё объясню́.**
Wait until Thursday, then I'll explain everything.

The phrase **вплоть до** has the meaning of 'right up until':

Вплоть до **конца́ жи́зни он писа́л стихи́, кото́рыми восхища́лись миллио́ны.**
Right up until the end of his life he was writing verse that was admired by millions.

In formal language, and especially in official documents, **по** (+ acc.) is sometimes used with the meaning 'until'. Unlike **до**, which can be ambiguous, **по** always has the meaning of 'up to and including':

Настоя́щий докуме́нт действи́телен с 25-го октября́ *по 31-е декабря́*
This document is valid from 25 October and up to and including 31 December.

21.1.16 'Since'/'as soon as'/'until': using conjunctions

The equivalent of the conjunction 'since', when used to indicate the starting point of an action, is **с тех пор, как**:

С тех пор, как **я прие́хал сюда́, я ни ра́зу не боле́л.**
Since I moved here, I haven't been ill once.

NOTE | The same rule for punctuation applies as for **до того́(,) как** (*see* **21.1.11**).

The Russian equivalent of 'as soon as' is **как то́лько**:

Как то́лько **я вошёл в ко́мнату, я по́нял, что меня́ не жда́ли.**
As soon as I entered the room, I realised that they had not been expecting me.

When 'until' is used as a conjunction, the Russian equivalent is **пока́**, with the negative particle **не** used before the verb in the clause that **пока́** introduces:

> *Пока́ я не получи́л твоё письмо́*, я да́же не знал, в како́й стране́ ты тепе́рь рабо́таешь.
> Until I received your letter, I didn't even know what country you were working in now.

The conjunction **пока́** can be reinforced by the phrase **до тех пор**:

> Я не уйду́ отсю́да *до тех пор, пока́ не* получу́ отве́ты на все мои́ вопро́сы.
> I will not leave here until (such time as) I receive answers to all my questions.

NOTE

When **пока́** and **как то́лько** refer to events taking place in the future, the verb that follows them is in the *future perfective* form:

> *Как то́лько вода́ закипи́т*, доба́вьте морко́вь и вари́те 10 мину́т на ме́дленном огне́.
> As soon as the water boils, add the carrots and let them simmer for ten minutes on a low heat.

> Не уходи́те, *пока́ я не верну́сь*.
> Don't go until I get back.

21.2 Place

21.2.1 Talking about location: the prepositions в (+ prep.) and на (+ prep.)

The most widely used prepositions for talking about location are **в** (+ prep.) and **на** (+ prep.). The basic meaning of **в** (+ prep.), when it is used to indicate location, is 'in(side)':

> Я оста́вил ключи́ *в столе́*.
> I've left my keys in my desk.

> И́менно *в э́той ко́мнате* я написа́л все свои́ кни́ги.
> It was in this room that I wrote all my books.

The basic meaning of the preposition is **на** (+ prep.) 'on (the surface of)':

> Я оста́вил ключи́ *на столе́*.
> I've left my keys on the table.

> Он лежа́л *на траве́*, обду́мывая свои́ пла́ны на бу́дущее.
> He lay on the grass, thinking over his plans for the future.

In addition, these prepositions are used with a wide range of other locations. These are discussed in **21.2.2–21.2.10**.

21.2.2 Town, cities, districts and regions

For locations in these categories the preposition **в** is used:

> *В го́роде Москве́ и в Моско́вской о́бласти* температу́ра днём бу́дет 23–25 гра́дусов.
> In the city of Moscow and in the Moscow region the temperature through the day will be 23–25 degrees.

Таки́е ве́щи мо́жно купи́ть то́лько *в Пари́же, Ло́ндоне или Нью-Йо́рке*.
You can only buy things like that in Paris, London or New York.

21.2.3 Countries

The preposition **в** is also used with **страна́** 'country' and with the names of almost all countries:

Е́сли вы хоти́те улу́чшить свой ру́сский, то на́до поучи́ться *в Росси́и или в како́й-нибудь друго́й стране́*, где ещё говоря́т по-ру́сски.
If you want to improve your Russian, you need to study in Russia or in some other country where people still speak Russian.

В А́нглии в университе́те у́чатся три го́да, а *в Шотла́ндии* обы́чно четы́ре.
In England people study at university for three years, but in Scotland it's usually four (years).

The preposition **на** (+ prep.) is used with the names of some countries that are also islands, notably **Кипр** 'Cyprus', **Ку́ба** 'Cuba', **Ма́льта** 'Malta'; **в** (+ prep.) is used with **Великобрита́ния** 'Great Britain' and **Ирла́ндия** 'Ireland':

На Ки́пре почему́-то о́чень мно́го ру́сских.
For some reason there are a lot of Russians in Cyprus.

В Великобрита́нии сохраня́ется фунт сте́рлингов, тогда́ как *в Ирла́ндии* уже́ перешли́ на е́вро.
In Great Britain the pound sterling has been retained, while in Ireland they have already switched to the euro.

NOTE | Before 1991 **на** was traditionally used with **Украи́на** 'Ukraine', but when the country gained its independence, the Ukrainians launched a campaign to encourage a switch to **в Украи́не** 'in Ukraine'. Now both forms are possible: **в** is normally preferred in Ukraine, while **на** still tends to be used in Russia. The use of **на Украи́не** is likely to cause offence to some Ukrainians.

На is used with the noun **ро́дина** 'homeland':

Занима́я до́лжность посла́, он сохраня́л конта́кты с полити́ческими си́лами *на ро́дине*.
While working as an ambassador, he kept up his contacts with political forces at home.

NOTE | In Soviet times **Ро́дина** was usually spelled with a capital letter; this is now found much less frequently and tends to be restricted to particularly high-flown contexts.

21.2.4 Islands, peninsulas and mountain ranges

На is used with the names of most islands, peninsulas and mountain ranges:

На Камча́тке кли́мат о́чень суро́вый; на Сахали́не он помя́гче, но зимо́й там то́же о́чень хо́лодно.
In Kamchatka (peninsula) the climate is very severe; on Sakhalin (island) it is gentler, but in winter it also gets very cold there.

В ка́честве тележурнали́ста он неоднокра́тно быва́л *на Кавка́зе*.
As a television journalist, he's been to the Caucasus several times.

There are, however, some exceptions, where **в** is used instead:

в Крыму́	in the Crimea
в А́льпах	in the Alps

For the use of **в/на** with islands that are also countries, *see* **21.2.3**.

Other geographical terms

To indicate location with reference to the world **в** is used with **мир**, but **на** is used with **свет**:

Его́ го́лос зна́ют *во всём ми́ре*.
His voice is known everywhere in the world.

На све́те мно́го стран, где лю́ди живу́т в бе́дности.
There are many countries in the world where people live in poverty.

NOTE | The phrase **в све́те** means 'in the light of':

В све́те после́дних археологи́ческих откры́тий мы мо́жем сказа́ть, что в деся́том ве́ке здесь уже́ бы́ло городско́е поселе́ние.
In the light of the latest archaeological discoveries we can say that in the tenth century there was already an urban settlement here.

В is used with terms indicating geographical or climatic zones, such as **пусты́ня** 'desert', **степь** 'steppe', **тайга́** 'taiga', **ту́ндра** 'tundra':

Он чу́вствует себя́ до́ма везде́, будь э́то *в ту́ндре, в тайге́, в степи́* или да́же *в пусты́не*.
He feels at home everywhere, whether it's in the tundra, the taiga, the steppe or even the desert.

На is used for points of the compass:

На се́веро-восто́ке страны́ ожида́ется о́блачная пого́да с небольши́ми дождя́ми, а на ю́ге бу́дет со́лнечно.
In the north-east of the country it is expected to be cloudy with occasional rain, while in the south it will be sunny.

Ей и в го́лову не приходи́ло, что *на За́паде* всё мо́жет быть по-друго́му.
It never even occurred to her that in the West things might be different.

NOTE | Capital letters are generally used in Russian when a point of the compass is used to denote a geopolitical entity.

Locations that can be perceived in terms of a building or some other closed and covered space

For locations that would be thought of in terms of buildings or other enclosed spaces the preposition **в** is normally used:

В шко́ле я учи́лся о́чень хорошо́, но *в университе́те* мне ста́ло ску́чно, и я ушёл по́сле второ́го ку́рса.

At school I did very well, but at university I started to get bored and left after the second year.

Не рекоменду́ется меня́ть де́ньги *в аэропорту́* или *в гости́нице*; курс всегда́ лу́чше *в ба́нках и обме́нных пу́нктах*.
It's not advisable to change money at the airport or in a hotel; the rate is always better at banks and *bureaux de change*.

Извини́те, но *в теа́тре* нельзя́ кури́ть.
I'm sorry, but you're not allowed to smoke in the theatre.

There are, however, a number of locations that seem to belong to this category, but with which, for no obvious reason, **на** is used. These include:

вокза́л	(main line) railway station
ста́нция	(underground, local railway or radio) station
факульте́т	faculty
ка́федра	department (at a university)
по́чта	post office
почта́мт	main post office
заво́д	factory (heavy industry)
фа́брика	factory (light industry)
предприя́тие	enterprise, works, factory
да́ча	dacha, country cottage

Что́бы перейти́ на кольцеву́ю ли́нию, на́до бы́ло вы́йти *на ста́нции «Ки́евская»*.
To change onto the Circle line you should have got off at Kievskaia station.

Он был на тре́тьем ку́рсе аспиранту́ры и *на ка́федре* появля́лся то́лько тогда́, когда́ назнача́лась встре́ча с нау́чным руководи́телем.
He was a third-year postgraduate and only turned up in the department when he had an appointment with his supervisor.

В тече́ние мно́гих лет он рабо́тал *на автозаво́де* в Москве́.
For many years he worked at a car factory in Moscow.

With **кварти́ра** 'flat' and **ку́хня** 'kitchen' either **в** or **на** can be used; when the emphasis is on the actual interior space, as opposed to the location in general, as in the first example, **в** is more likely to be used:

Мысль о том, что *в кварти́ре* в её отсу́тствие побыва́ли посторо́нние, была́ неприя́тной.
The thought that during her absence strangers had been in her flat was not a pleasant one.

Мо́жно оста́вить ва́ши ве́щи у меня́ *в/на кварти́ре*.
You can leave your things in my flat.

Мой муж *в/на ку́хне*, гото́вит у́жин.
My husband's in the kitchen making supper.

21.2.7 | ## Locations that can be perceived as open spaces

The preposition **на** is used with many locations that might be thought of as open spaces. Nouns that come into this category include: **рынок** 'market', **стадион** 'stadium', **остановка** '(bus or tram) stop', **улица** 'street' and **площадь** 'square':

> **Проду́кты я обы́чно покупа́ю *на ры́нке*; там недо́рого.**
> I usually buy food at the market; it's not expensive there.

> **Матч Росси́я – А́нглия состои́тся за́втра *на стадио́не «Локомоти́в»*.**
> The match between Russia and England takes place tomorrow at the Locomotive stadium.

> **Вы выхо́дите *на сле́дующей остано́вке?***
> Are you getting off at the next stop?

> **У неё шика́рная кварти́ра *на Тверско́й у́лице*.**
> She has a posh flat in Tverskaia Street.

> **Мы договори́лись встре́титься *на Кра́сной пло́щади*.**
> We arranged to meet in Red Square.

NOTE | The phrase **на у́лице** often means 'outside', especially in the context of a city:

> **В аэропорту́ «Шереме́тьево» они́ удиви́тельно бы́стро прошли́ па́спортный контро́ль и тамо́жню и че́рез де́сять мину́т уже́ бы́ли *на у́лице*.**
> At Sheremet'evo Airport they got through passport and customs surprisingly quickly and after ten minutes were already outside.

The preposition **в** is used with **парк** 'park', **сад** 'garden' and **переу́лок** 'narow street', 'alley':

> **Ле́том они́ обы́чно встреча́лись *в па́рке* у фонта́на.**
> In summer they used to meet near the fountain in the park.

> **Е́сли вы интересу́етесь экзоти́ческими расте́ниями, сто́ит побыва́ть *в Ботани́ческом саду́*.**
> If you're interested in exotic plants, it's worth visiting the Botanic Gardens.

> **Мы у́жинали вчера́ в ма́леньком рестора́не, кото́рый нахо́дится *в одно́м из переу́лков* Арба́та.**
> We ate last night in a small restaurant, which is in one of the narrow streets of the Arbat.

With **двор** 'yard' both **в (во)** and **на** are found, although there is a difference in meaning. **Во дворе́** is used when talking about a particular yard, and especially the courtyard of a block of flats; **на дворе́** usually means simply 'outside':

> **В ле́тние вечера́ де́ти игра́ли *во дворе́* большо́го до́ма.**
> In summer evenings children used to play in the courtyard of the large house.

> **Кака́я сейча́с пого́да *на дворе́*?**
> What's the weather like outside just now?

For the use of **во** (instead of **в**), *see* **9.2.8**.

21.2.8 Means of transport

For locations that are a means of transport, both **в** and **на** are used, but with a difference in meaning. **В** is used when emphasis is on the interior of the form of transport, while **на** is used when the emphasis is on the vehicle as a means of getting from one place to another:

> Вла́сти рабо́тают над зако́ном, кото́рый запреща́ет поцелу́и *в метро́* и други́х обще́ственных места́х.
> The authorities are working on a law that will ban kissing in the underground and other public places.

> Си́дя *в маши́не* ря́дом с му́жем, она́ мо́лча кури́ла и смотре́ла в окно́.
> Sitting in the car next to her husband, she was quietly smoking and looking out of the window.

> Мо́жно е́хать *на метро́* до ста́нции Университе́т и пото́м *на любо́м трамва́е* до остано́вки «Черёмушкинский ры́нок».
> You can go by underground to University Station and then by any tram as far as the Cherёmushki market stop.

> Я́сно, что *на маши́не* никто́ не е́здил не́сколько дней.
> It is clear that nobody had driven the car for several days.

21.2.9 Organisations of various sorts

When the location is the name of an organisation, **в** is used:

> В сове́тские времена́ он служи́л *в КГБ*, но тепе́рь он рабо́тает *в Министе́рстве иностра́нных дел*.
> In Soviet times he worked for the KGB, but now he has a job in the Ministry of Foreign Affairs.

> *В мили́ции* мне зада́ли не́сколько вопро́сов и соста́вили протоко́л.
> The police asked me several questions and drew up an official report.

21.2.10 Locations where the noun denotes a function or activity

If the noun used to indicate a location denotes the fuction or activity that takes place there, then **на** is used:

> *На рабо́те* я пью то́лько ко́фе – что́бы не засыпа́ть *на совеща́ниях*.
> At work I only drink coffee so as not to fall asleep at meetings.

> Я познако́мился с жено́й в Москве́ *на студе́нческом ве́чере*.
> I met my wife in Moscow at a student party.

> Вчера́ ве́чером я был *на чуде́сном конце́рте*.
> Yesterday evening I was at a wonderful concert.

> *На заня́тиях* я аккура́тно конспекти́рую слова́ преподава́теля, но пото́м всё равно́ ничего́ не понима́ю.
> In classes I take careful notes of what the lecturer says, but afterwards none of it makes sense.

NOTE | When the preposition **в** (+ prep.) is used with nouns belonging to this category, it refers to the *content* of the event or activity rather than the location:

> *В мое́й рабо́те* нет ничего́ интере́сного: я всё вре́мя перевожу́ бесконе́чные ску́чные докуме́нты.
> There's nothing interesting in my work; I spend my whole time translating interminable boring documents.

> *В сего́дняшнем конце́рте* мы бу́дем игра́ть му́зыку Чайко́вского и Му́соргского.
> In today's concert we will be playing music by Tchaikovsky and Musorgskii.

21.2.11 Location using the preposition y (+ gen.)

The basic meaning of the preposition **y** (+ gen.), when used to indicate location, is 'close to', 'adjacent to':

> Он стоя́л *у окна́* и смотре́л вдаль.
> He was standing by the window looking into the distance.

> Она́ ждала́ меня́ *у вхо́да* в теа́тр.
> She was waiting for me at the entrance to the theatre.

The preposition **y** is used when the location takes the form of a noun or a pronoun indicating a person:

> Извини́те за опозда́ние; я был *у врача́.*
> I'm sorry I'm late; I've been at the doctor's.

> Она́ живёт *у роди́телей.*
> She lives with her parents (i.e. at her parents' place).

> *У нас* отключи́ли отопле́ние. Мо́жно, я переночу́ю *у тебя́?*
> They've turned our heating off. Can I spend the night at your place?

The following construction with **y** is often used in conjunction with a second prepositional phrase to indicate a location owned by or otherwise closely connected with the person concerned:

> Мо́жно оста́вить э́ти ве́щи *у меня́ на кварти́ре.*
> You can leave these things in my flat.

> *У сестры́ на рабо́те* есть беспла́тный буфе́т и са́уна, но рабо́та у неё вре́дная.
> My sister has a free canteen and sauna at work, although on the other hand her work is quite dangerous.

> *У нас в Росто́ве* снег уже́ раста́ял.
> In Rostov (where we live *or* come from) the snow has already melted.

21.2.12 Location using other prepositions

A number of other prepositions can be used to indicate location. These include **за** (+ acc.), **за** (+ instr.), **пе́ред** (+ instr.), **под** (+ instr.), **над** (+ instr.), **при** (+ prep.).

За (+ acc.) is used when indicating the distance between two locations:

> На́ша дере́вня нахо́дится *за шестьдеся́т киломе́тров* от це́нтра Москвы́.
> Our village is 60 kilometres away from the centre of Moscow.

За шестьдеся́т киломе́тров от Москвы́ мото́р вдруг загло́х.
Our engine died (when we were) 60 kilometres away from Moscow.

В (+ prep.) can be used with the same meaning, but is more likely to be found in formal contexts, especially in the written language:

Э́та гости́ница не о́чень удо́бная, так как нахо́дится *в пяти́ киломе́трах от вокза́ла.*
This hotel is not very convenient, as it's 5 kilometres away from the station.

The basic meaning of **за** (+ instr.) is 'behind' or 'beyond':

Он е́хал в пе́рвой маши́не. *За ней* сле́довал джип с охра́ной.
He was travelling in the first car. Behind it followed a jeep with the bodyguards.

Вы ви́дите ста́рый до́мик, вон там *за реко́й*?
Can you see that little old house over there, beyond the river?

За (+ instr.) is used in a number of useful set phrases:

за грани́цей	abroad
за рубежо́м	abroad
за преде́лами	beyond the boundaries of, outside
за столо́м	at table
за́ городом	out of town, in the country
за бо́ртом	overboard
за кули́сами	backstage

Она́ вдруг реши́ла, что в Росси́и жить тру́дно, а *за грани́цей* бу́дет гора́здо лу́чше.
She suddenly decided that living in Russia was difficult and that it would be a lot better abroad.

***За преде́лами* Росси́и э́та пробле́ма никого́ не интересу́ет.**
Outside Russia nobody's interested in this problem.

Они́ сиде́ли *за столо́м* и е́ли како́е-то блю́до из мя́са.
They were sitting at the table eating some meat dish.

Я не могу́ дозвони́ться до него́: он, наве́рно, *за́ городом* на да́че.
I can't get through to him on the phone; he must be at his dacha in the country.

The meaning of **пе́ред** (+ instr.), when it refers to a location, is 'in front of':

***Пе́ред вокза́лом* была́ больша́я пло́щадь, где стоя́л па́мятник Ле́нину.**
In front of the station was a large square with a statue of Lenin.

The most usual meaning of **под** (+ instr.) is 'under(neath)':

Я всегда́ пря́чу ключ *под э́тим больши́м ка́мнем.*
I always hide the key under this big stone.

With names of towns **под** (+ instr.) has the meaning of 'just outside', 'very close to'. The same preposition is also used for the location of battles:

Он живёт где́-то *под Москво́й*.
He lives somewhere just outside Moscow.

Он был тяжело́ ра́нен (в би́тве) *под Сталингра́дом*.
He was badly wounded at (in the battle of) Stalingrad.

The preposition **над** (+ instr.) means 'above', 'over':

Мы лете́ли пря́мо *над го́родом*, но из-за плохо́й пого́ды ничего́ не́ было ви́дно.
We flew right over the city, but because of the bad weather we couldn't see anything.

The most usual meaning of **при** (+ prep.), when used to refer to a location is 'attached to', 'adjacent to':

При *университе́те* есть музе́й и карти́нная галере́я.
Attached to the university is a museum and an art gallery.

При also has the meaning of 'in the presence of':

Она́ не хоте́ла разгова́ривать об э́том *при сы́не*.
She didn't want to talk about it in the presence of her son.

21.2.13 Other ways of talking about location

A number of advebs can be used to indicate location. These include:

здесь	here
тут	here
там	there
бли́зко	near(by)
далеко́	far, distant, a long way away
ря́дом	close by, adjacent, next door
впереди́	ahead
сза́ди	behind

Здесь (*or* Тут) все места́ за́няты.
All the places are taken here.

Я не пое́ду с тобо́й в дере́вню. *Там* не́чего де́лать
I won't go with you to the village. There's nothing to do there.

Вокза́л совсе́м *бли́зко*; мо́жно идти́ пешко́м.
The station's very near; you can go on foot.

Она́ *далеко́* живёт, где́-то в друго́м конце́ го́рода.
She lives a long way away, somewhere at the other end of the town.

Гости́ница была́ на гла́вной у́лице го́рода. *Ря́дом* был банк, а пото́м ряд магази́нов.
The hotel was on the main street of the town. Next to it was a bank and then a row of shops.

Я о́чень хорошо́ по́мню, как мы е́хали на откры́тие съе́зда: *впереди́* была́ милице́йская маши́на с мига́лкой, за ней пять-шесть авто́бусов с делега́тами, и *сза́ди* ещё одна́ маши́на с мига́лкой.
I can remember very well how we travelled to the opening of the congress: in front was a police car with a flashing light, then five or six buses with the delegates and behind was another car with a flashing light.

Бли́зко, **далеко́** and **ря́дом** can be used in combination with prepositions, as follows:

бли́зко к (+ dat.) *or* **бли́зко от** (+ gen.)   close to
далеко́ от (+ gen.)   a long way from, far from
ря́дом с (+ instr.)   next (door) to

Кре́пость была́ совсе́м *бли́зко к грани́це*.
The fortress was very close to the frontier.

Она́ стоя́ла так *бли́зко от меня́*, что я чу́вствовал за́пах её духо́в.
She was standing so close to me that I could smell her perfume.

Я бы ходи́л в бассе́йн поща́че, но мы живём сли́шком *далеко́ от* спорткомплекса.
I would go to the swimming baths more often, but we live too far away from the sports facilities.

За нали́чными далеко́ идти́ не на́до: *ря́дом с гости́ницей* есть банк.
You don't have to go far for cash. There's a bank next door to the hotel.

The conjunction used to indicate location is **где**:

Я никогда́ не́ был в го́роде, где есть так мно́го хоро́ших рестора́нов.
I have never been in a city where there are so many good restaurants.

21.2.14 Talking about destinations

There is a close correlation between the preposition used to indicate destination and that used to indicate location. Where location is indicated by **в** (+ prep.), the equivalent destination is indicated by **в** (+ acc.):

Не бу́дем входи́ть *в э́ту ко́мнату*; там спит моя́ до́чка, и я не хочу́ её буди́ть.
We won't go into that room; my daughter's asleep there and I don't want to wake her up.

Тур *в Ло́ндон* сто́ит два́дцать ты́сяч рубле́й.
A package-tour to London costs 20,000 roubles.

На бу́дущей неде́ле меня́ здесь не бу́дет; мне на́до бу́дет съе́здить *в Росси́ю* на па́ру дней.
I won't be here next week; I've got to go to Russia for a couple of days.

Обы́чно я хожу́ *в университе́т* пешко́м.
I usually walk to the university.

Е́сли не прекрати́тся э́тот шум, я позвоню́ *в мили́цию*.
If this noise doesn't stop, I'll phone the police.

Where a location is indicated by using **на** (+ prep.), the equivalent destination is indicated by **на** (+ acc.):

Официа́льная делега́ция во главе́ с премье́р-мини́стром вы́летела сего́дня *на Ку́бу*.
An official delegation, led by the prime minister, left for Cuba today.

Он уе́хал *на За́пад* в 1974 г. и верну́лся в Росси́ю то́лько в конце́ восьмидеся́тых.

He left for the West in 1974 and returned to Russia only at the end of the 1980s.

Мо́жете заходи́ть ко мне *на рабо́ту* в любо́е вре́мя.

You can call in and see me at work any time you like.

Where a location is indicated by using **y** (+ gen.), the equivalent destination is indicated by **к** (+ dat.):

Он подошёл *к окну́* и посмотре́л на у́лицу.

He walked up to the window and looked at the street.

Заезжа́й *ко мне* на рабо́ту к пяти́. Я бу́ду гото́в.

Drop in (*literally*, to me) at work around five. I'll be ready by then.

For the use of **ко** instead of **к**, *see* **9.2.8**.

NOTE | In sentences of the last type, both the person and the place are treated as destinations.

Where a location is indicated by using **за** (+ instr.), the equivalent destination is indicated by **за** (+ acc.):

Сейча́с со́лнце зайдёт *за э́то о́блако.*

The sun's about to go behind that cloud.

В воскресе́нье съе́здим куда́-нибудь *за́ город.*

On Sunday we'll go somewhere out of town (*or* in the country).

Ка́ждый год миллио́ны росси́йских гра́ждан выезжа́ют *за грани́цу* на о́тдых, на рабо́ту и́ли учёбу.

Each year millions of Russian citizens go abroad on holiday, for work or to study.

У́жин гото́в. Приглаша́ю вас *за стол.*

Supper's ready. Please come and sit at the table.

Where a location is indicated by using **под** (+ instr.), the equivalent destination is indicated by **под** (+ acc.). However, this usage is restricted to when the preposition has the literal meaning of 'under':

Положи́ ключ *под э́тот ка́мень.* Там его́ никто́ не найдёт.

Put the key under this stone. No one will find it there.

The remaining prepositions used to indicate location do not have corresponding constructions to indicate destination.

The following adverbs are used when talking about destination:

сюда́	(to) here, hither
туда́	(to) there, thither

Иди́ *сюда́.* Мне на́до поговори́ть с тобо́й.

Come here. I want to talk to you.

***Туда́* я не пое́ду ни за что!**

I won't go there at any price!

The conjunction that is used when talking about destination is **куда́**:

> **Его́ сейча́с нет**, **но я не зна́ю**, *куда́* **он пошёл.**
> He's not here at the moment, but I don't know where he's gone.

Talking about starting points

Just as there is a close correlation between the construction used for location and destination, so there is a similar correlation between the preposition used to indicate location and that used to indicate the starting point of a journey or an action. Where location is indicated by **в** (+ prep.), the starting point is indicated by **из** (+ gen.):

> **Он встал и доста́л** *из я́щика* **стола́ каку́ю-то квита́нцию.**
> He got up and took a receipt from the desk drawer.

> **Они́ улете́ли** *из Москвы́* **в сре́ду.**
> They left (*or* flew out of) Moscow on Wednesday.

> **Не подлежа́т вы́возу** *из Росси́и* **стари́нные кни́ги, и́зданные до 1926 го́да.**
> Old books published before 1926 cannot be exported from Russia.

> **Де́ти обы́чно возвраща́ются** *из шко́лы* **в четы́ре часа́.**
> The children usually get back from school at four o'clock.

Where a location is indicated by **на** (+ prep.), the starting point is indicated by **с** (+ gen.):

> **Мно́гие ру́сские уе́хали** *с Ки́пра* **по́сле экономи́ческого кри́зиса 1998 го́да.**
> Many Russians left Cyprus after the economic crisis of 1998.

> **Поезда́** *с ю́га* **обы́чно прибыва́ют и́ли на Ку́рский и́ли на Каза́нский вокза́л.**
> Trains from the south usually arrive (in Moscow) either at the Kursk or the Kazan' stations.

> **Мне ста́ло пло́хо, и я ушёл** *с конце́рта* **в антра́кте.**
> I started to feel unwell and left the concert during the interval.

Where a location is indicated by **у** (+ gen.), the starting point is indicated by **от** (+ gen.):

> **Он отошёл** *от окна́* **и сел за стол.**
> He moved away from the window and sat down at the table.

> **Я то́лько что** *от Ка́ти* **- она́ передаёт тебе́ приве́т.**
> I've just come from Katia's; she sends you her regards.

In a similar fashion **из-за** (+ gen.) and **из-под** (+ gen.) correspond to **за** (+ instr.) and **под** (+ instr.) respectively:

> **Сейча́с со́лнце вы́йдет** *из-за о́блака.*
> The sun's about to come out from behind a cloud.

> **Доста́ньте ключ** *из-под э́того ка́мня* **и откро́йте дверь.**
> Get the key from under that stone and open the door.

Out of the set expressions using **за** (+ instr.) listed in **21.2.12 из-за** is used normally only with **граница**, **рубеж** and **стол**:

> **Она вернулась *из-за границы* на прошлой неделе.**
> She returned from abroad last week.

> **В этом журнале часто печатались новости науки *из-за рубежа*.**
> This journal often used to publish items of science news from abroad.

> **Он встал *из-за стола* и подошёл к окну.**
> He got up from the table and went over to the window.

NOTE | The preposition **из-под** (+ gen.) is also used to indicate what were or would be contents of an empty container:

> **В раковине лежала чья-то немытая посуда и пустая бутылка *из-под молока*.**
> In the sink were someone's unwashed dishes and an empty milk bottle.

For another use of **из-за**, *see* **21.4.1**.

The following adverbs are used when talking about starting points:

отсюда	from here, hence
оттуда	from there, thence

> ***Отсюда* открывается прекрасный вид на весь город.**
> From here you get a splendid view over the whole city.

> **Родом он из России, но он уехал *оттуда* ещё в молодости.**
> He is from Russia, but he left there while he was still young.

The conjunction used when talking about starting points is **откуда**:

> **Он, наконец, приехал в ту страну, *откуда* эмигрировали его родители в начале прошлого века.**
> He had finally arrived in the country from where his parents had emigrated at the beginning of the last century.

21.2.16 | Other ways of talking about place

When talking about the point actually reached in a journey, the preposition **до** (+ gen.) is used:

> **Этот поезд следует только *до станции «Комсомольская»*.**
> This train only goes as far as Komsomol'skaia station.

> **К вечеру первого дня мы доехали *до Смоленска*, где мы решили переночевать.**
> By the evening of the first day we had reached Smolensk, where we decided to spend the night.

To indicate the distance between two places **от** (+ gen.) **...** **до** (+ gen.) is used:

> ***От центра города до университета* будет около пяти километров.**
> It'll be about 5 kilometres from the centre of the city to the university.

To indicate motion along the surface of something, the preposition **по** (+ dat.) is used. The motion can be in one direction, more than one direction or in no particular direction at all:

> **Скажи́те, пожа́луйста, каки́е тролле́йбусы иду́т *по Не́вскому проспе́кту*?**
> Could you tell me please which trolleybuses run along Nevskii Prospekt?

> **Я о́чень люблю́ ра́но у́тром ходи́ть *по переу́лкам* Арба́та.**
> I am very fond of wandering through the narrow streets of the Arbat in the early morning.

> **Е́сли хоти́те, мы мо́жем организова́ть для вас экску́рсию *по го́роду*.**
> If you want, we can organise a tour of the city for you.

The phrases **по доро́ге**, **по пути́** mean 'on the way (to)':

> **По доро́ге домо́й я заходи́л к сестре́.**
> On the way home I called in at my sister's.

> **Нам с ва́ми, ка́жется, *по пути́*.**
> It looks as if we're going the same way.

To indicate the notion of across, over or from one side to the other of a location, the preposition **че́рез** (+ acc.) is used:

> **Пе́рвый мост *че́рез ре́ку* был постро́ен в двена́дцатом ве́ке.**
> The first bridge across the river was built in the twelfth century.

> **Она́ ничего́ не могла́ разгляде́ть *че́рез тёмные стёкла* маши́ны.**
> She couldn't make anything out through the tinted windows of the car.

Че́рез also corresponds to English 'via':

> **Э́тот авто́бус идёт до университе́та *че́рез це́нтр* го́рода.**
> This bus goes to the university via the city centre.

21.3 Manner

21.3.1 Talking about manner using adverbs

The most common way to indicate the manner in which an action is carried out is by using an *adverb*. Adverbs are usually placed immediately before the verb indicating the action concerned:

> **Она́ *внима́тельно* чита́ла его́ письмо́.**
> She read his letter carefully.

> **Президе́нт *чётко* заяви́л, что он не собира́ется баллоти́роваться на тре́тий срок.**
> The president has stated clearly that he will not stand for a third term.

> **Она́ *о́чень хорошо́* зна́ла, почему́ происхо́дят переме́ны в её жи́зни.**
> She knew very well why changes were taking place in her life.

For more on questions of word order involving adverbs, *see* **20.1.3**.

For more on adverbs generally, *see* **9.1**.

Talking about manner using a qualifier plus noun

Another way of talking about manner is to use a *qualifier* (an *adjective* or a *pronoun*) with a *noun* in the *instrumental case*:

> После коро́ткой па́узы он продо́лжил свою́ речь *бо́лее споко́йным го́лосом*.
>
> After a short pause he continued his speech in a calmer voice.

> Он посмотре́л на неё *печа́льным взгля́дом*, поверну́лся и пошёл прочь.
>
> He looked at her with a sad expression, turned round and walked away.

This construction is widely used with nouns such as **о́браз**, **путь**, **спо́соб** that have the general meaning of 'way', 'manner', 'fashion':

> Ситуа́ция сложи́лась *таки́м о́бразом*, что после́дние три дня они́ проводи́ли почти́ всё своё рабо́чее вре́мя вме́сте.
>
> The situation has turned out in such a way that for the last three days they have spent most of their working time together.

> Э́та пробле́ма *не́которым о́бразом* каса́ется и меня́.
>
> This problem also affects me in some ways [*or* to some extent].

> Он никогда́ никому́ не дава́л взя́ток, и всегда́ де́йствовал то́лько *зако́нным путём*.
>
> He never bribed anyone and always acted legally (*or* in accordance with the law).

> Э́ту зада́чу мо́жно реша́ть *двумя́ спо́собами*.
>
> This problem can be resolved in two ways.

For another use of **таки́м о́бразом**, see **23.2.1**.

Also used in this way is the noun **поря́док**, although here the phrase is more usually used with the preposition **в** and is in the *prepositional* case. This construction tends to be found in formal and bureaucratic language:

> Уте́рянный па́спорт объявля́ется недействи́тельным, а оформле́ние но́вого осуществля́ется *в обы́чном поря́дке*.
>
> A lost passport is declared invalid and a new one is issued in the usual way.

Talking about manner using an abstract noun and the preposition c (+ instr.)

It is also possible to talk about manner using the *preposition* **c** followed by an *abstract noun* in the *instrumental case*. This construction is used much more frequently than the corresponding English equivalent:

> Я *с больши́м удово́льствием* слу́шаю му́зыку Чайко́вского.
>
> I greatly enjoy listening to Tchaikovsky's music
> (*literally*, I listen with great pleasure …).

> Он отве́тил *с досто́инством*, что пришёл по о́чень ва́жному де́лу.
>
> He answered with dignity [*or* solemnly] that he had come on a very important matter.

Он реаги́ровал на все на́ши предупрежде́ния *со свое́й обы́чной беззабо́тностью.*
He reacted to all our warnings in his usual carefree manner.

For the use of **со** instead of **с**, *see* **9.2.8**.

21.3.4 Talking about manner using как

The conjunction used when talking about manner is **как**:

Сде́лайте так, *как* я сове́тую, н никаки́х пробле́м не бу́дет.
Do as I advise and there won't be any problems.

Ситуа́ция сложи́лась не так, *как* мы ожида́ли.
The situation had not turned out in the way that we expected.

Он не звони́л так ча́сто, *как* она́ хоте́ла бы.
He didn't telephone as often as she would have liked.

Он говори́л споко́йно, *как* челове́к, кото́рый зна́ет це́ну свои́м слова́м.
He spoke calmly, in the manner of a man who knows the value of his words.

NOTE | In this usage a comma is normally placed before **как**. It is particularly important to distinguish **так, как** (as in the above examples) from the conjunction **так как** 'since' (*see* **21.4.6**).

For more uses of **как** as a conjunction, *see* **11.1.2** and **21.9.8**.

21.4 Causes and consequences

21.4.1 Talking about general causes: the prepositions из-за (+ gen.) and благодаря (+ dat.)

The two prepositions used most frequently to indicate the general cause of an action or event are **из-за** (+ gen.) 'because of' and **благодаря́** (+ dat.) 'because of', 'thanks to'. The former is used for causes of a negative outcome, while the latter is mostly used when the outcome is positive:

Из-за плохо́й пого́ды наш самолёт опозда́л бо́лее чем на два часа́.
Because of the bad weather our plane was delayed for more than two hours.

То́лько *благодаря́ твое́й по́мощи* мне удало́сь сде́лать всё во́время.
It was only because of [*or* thanks to] your help that I was able to get everything done on time.

21.4.2 Talking about general causes: the preposition по (+ dat.)

The preposition **по** (+ dat.) can be used with the noun **причи́на** 'reason' to indicate the cause of an action or event; this usage tends to be found in more formal types of language:

Она́ сего́дня отсу́тствует *по уважи́тельной причи́не.*
She is absent today for a valid reason.

По причи́не отсу́тствия кво́рума голосова́ние не состоя́лось.
The vote failed to take place for lack of a quorum.

Причи́на is used in the plural in the phrase **по техни́ческим причи́нам** 'for technical reasons'. This is often used in Russian as a euphemism in order to avoid having to give a more precise explanation for some undesirable turn of events:

> **Мероприя́тие отменя́ется** *по техни́ческим причи́нам*.
> The event is cancelled for technical reasons.

По is used with *abstract nouns* to indicate the inadvertent cause, usually of some unfortunate event:

> **Прости́те, я пропусти́л ва́шу ле́кцию** *по рассе́янности*.
> I'm sorry, I missed your lecture out of absent-mindedness.

> *По доса́дному недоразуме́нию* **письмо́ не́ было отпра́влено**.
> As a result of some annoying misunderstanding, the letter was never sent.

21.4.3   Other prepositions indicating general cause

The following prepositions and prepositional phrases are also used to indicate general cause. They are more likely to occur in the written than in the spoken language:

ввиду́ (+ gen.)	because of, owing to, in the light of (normally used in the context of something undesirable)
в результа́те (+ gen.)	because of, owing to, as a result of
в си́лу (+ gen.)	because of, owing to
всле́дствие (+ gen.)	because of, owing to, as a consequence of

> *Ввиду́ угро́зы* **террористи́ческих а́ктов в аэропо́ртах уси́лены ме́ры безопа́сности.**
> In the light of the threat of terrorism, security at airports has been strengthened.

> *В результа́те реши́тельных де́йствий прави́тельства* **рейтинг президе́нта вы́рос на де́сять проце́нтов.**
> As a result of the decisive actions of the government, the president's popularity has gone up by 10 per cent.

> **Возмо́жно,** *в си́лу и́менно э́тих обстоя́тельств* **она́ ушла́ с юриди́ческого факульте́та.**
> It is possibly because of these particular circumstances that she withdrew from the Faculty of Law.

> *Всле́дствие после́дних собы́тий на Бли́жнем Восто́ке* **пото́к тури́стов в э́тот регио́н ре́зко сократи́лся.**
> As a consequence of the recent events in the Middle East, there has been a sharp decline in the number of tourists visiting the region.

21.4.4   Talking about the direct physical cause of a state or action

The preposition most frequently used when talking about the direct, physical and involuntary cause of a state or an action is **от** (+ gen.):

> **В нача́ле двадца́тых годо́в мно́гие крестья́не в э́той о́бласти у́мерли** *от го́лода*.
> At the beginning of the 1920s many peasants in this region died of hunger.

Подумав о возможных последствиях своего поступка, он побледнел *от страха.*
Having thought about the possible consequences of his action, he went pale from fear.

Её глаза всё ещё были мокрыми *от слёз.*
Her eyes were still wet from the tears.

Здесь проехать нельзя. Дорогу развезло *от дождей.*
You can't get through here. The road's been made impassable by the rain.

The preposition **с** (+ gen.) is similar in meaning to **от**, but its use is characteristic of informal language. **С** is often used in figurative statements and in set expressions; when it is used with a masculine noun, this normally takes the ending in **-y** (*see* **2.7.1**):

Он рассказал нам такой смешной анекдот, что мы чуть не умерли *со смеху.*
He told us such a funny joke that we almost died of laughter.

For more concerning the stress on the preposition, *see* **9.2.7**.

21.4.5 Talking about the conscious motive for an action

The preposition used when talking about the conscious motive for an action is **из** (+ gen.):

Я пришёл сюда *из чистого любопытства.*
I came here out of pure curiosity.

Они это делают нарочно, *из вредности*, **чтобы осложнить нашу работу.**
They do it deliberately, out of malice, to make our job more difficult.

21.4.6 Talking about cause using conjunctions

Russian has several conjunctions that indicate cause and that correspond to the English 'because', 'as', 'since', 'for'. These are **потому что, потому как, так как, поскольку, ибо. Потому что, потому как** and **ибо** are normally used in the middle of a sentence to join two clauses, while **так как** and **поскольку** can be used either at the beginning or in the middle of a sentence. **Потому как** is characteristic of informal language, while **ибо** tends nowadays to be found only in very formal language. **Поскольку** occurs widely, but is perceived by some to be characteristic of bureaucratic or journalistic language:

Я не могу звонить ему сейчас, *потому что* **уже поздно.**
I can't phone him now because it's too late.

Я не мог отвечать, *потому как* **не знал языка.**
I couldn't answer since I didn't know the language.

Так как **тебя не было, мы решили подождать несколько минут.**
Since you weren't here, we decided to wait for a few minutes.

Я не пойду с вами в кино, *так как* **я уже смотрел этот фильм.**
I won't go with you to the pictures since I've already seen the film.

Поскольку вы не вовремя сдали документы, будет задержка в выдаче вашей визы.

Since you did not hand in your documents on time, there will be a delay in the issue of your visa.

Он вынужден был уйти в отставку, *ибо* того требовала профессиональная этика.

He was obliged to resign, since his professional ethics left him no choice.

NOTE When **так как** appears in the middle of a sentence, the comma is always placed before **так**. With **потому что** the comma normally precedes **потому**, but it can be placed before **что** if the two elements of the conjunction are separated or if **потому** is given particular emphasis; in the latter case it tends to be reinforced by a word such as **именно** or **как раз** 'precisely':

Именно потому, что этот фильм вызвал столько споров, мы пригласили его авторов в студию.

(It is) precisely because this film has stirred up so much debate (that) we have invited those who made it into the studio.

21.4.7　Talking about consequences

When talking about an action that is consequent on another action or state of affairs, **поэтому** 'therefore', 'that's why' can be used:

Он не очень доверял современным технологиям, и *поэтому* редко пользовался компьютером.

He didn't much trust modern technology and therefore rarely used a computer.

Я хочу, чтобы наша страна процветала, чтобы все жили хорошо. Именно *поэтому* я пришёл в политику.

I want our country to prosper, for everyone to live well. That's why I went into politics.

The expression **вот и** can be used to indicate the consequence of an undesired action or state of affairs:

Я вчера подхватил простуду, *вот и* сижу дома.

I caught a cold yesterday and that's why I'm stuck at home.

For more on the emphatic particles **вот** and **и**, *see* **20.3.3**.

The conjunction that indicates consequence is **так что** '(and) so':

У меня завтра экзамен, *так что* сегодня придётся весь день зубрить.

I've an exam tomorrow, so today I'll have to spend all day swotting.

21.5　Conditions

21.5.0　Introduction

One form of connection is where an outcome or an event depends on the fulfilment of a particular condition. In such situations there are two types of conditions. *Open conditions* are those that are capable of being fulfilled, while *unreal conditions* are those that are incapable of being fulfilled because the situation envisaged by the condition is purely hypothetical.

The means normally used to express this form of connection is the *conditional sentence* which consists of two halves: the outcome indicated in one half of the sentence depends on the fulfilment of the condition indicated in the other half. In Russian, the two halves of the sentence are usually joined by the conjunction **е́сли** (*see* **9.3.4**), which corresponds to the English 'if'.

The following are examples of *open conditions*:

>   If it doesn't rain tomorrow, we will go for a walk.

>   If you know the answer to that, you are cleverer than I thought.

In the sentences above the possibility of it raining tomorrow or of the addressee knowing the answer is each case is real.

The following are examples of *unreal conditions*:

>   If it weren't raining, we might go for walk (but it is, so we can't).

>   If you had been here at the right time, you would have found out the right answer (but you weren't, so you didn't).

Here the possibility of it not raining at the time when the sentence is spoken or of the addressee being present when the right answer was revealed no longer exists.

21.5.1   Open conditions

The majority of *open conditions* refer to contingencies that may or may not arise in the future. For this reason the verb form that is most commonly used is the *future perfective*:

>   **Е́сли *дашь* мне очки́, я *прочита́ю* тебе́ его́ письмо́.**
>   If you pass me my glasses, I'll read you his letter.

>   **Е́сли я не *сдам* экза́мен за́втра, *придётся* пересдава́ть его́ о́сенью.**
>   If I don't pass the exam tomorrow, I'll have to take it again in the autumn.

If the contingency is one that may occur regularly, the *future imperfective* is used:

>   **Е́сли вы постоя́нно *бу́дете опа́здывать*, то у вас *бу́дут* серьёзные пробле́мы.**
>   If you persist in being late, (then) you will have serious problems.

NOTES

(i)   The particle **то** is often used to join the two halves of a conditional sentence (cf. English 'then').

(ii)   In sentences referring to the future, the future tense is used in both halves of the sentences (unlike in English).

Where the contingency relates to the present or the past, the *present* or *past* tenses are used, as in English:

>   **Е́сли Ма́ша *рабо́тает* в вече́рнюю сме́ну, она́ *у́жинает* в столо́вой.**
>   (present tense)
>   If Masha is on the evening shift, she has her evening meal in the canteen.

>   **Да́же е́сли он и *сказа́л*, куда́ ухо́дит, он, наве́рное, *совра́л*.**
>   (past tense)
>   Even if he did say where was going to, he was probably lying.

Where the result of the condition being met is a command, instruction or recommendation, it is indicated by the use of the *imperative*:

> **Éсли всё в поря́дке, *распиши́тесь* здесь.**
> If everything is in order, sign here.

The *infinitive* is often used with **éсли** if the subject is not a specific person or persons:

> **Éсли *приня́ть* во внима́ние все обстоя́тельства, то получа́ется, что он всё-таки был прав.**
> If you take/one takes into account all the circumstances, it turns out he was right after all.

21.5.2 Unreal conditions

With *unreal conditions* the *conditional* (*see* **4.10**) is used in both halves of the sentence:

> **Бы́ло бы о́чень прия́тно жить в Гла́зго, если бы кли́мат тут был полу́чше.**
> It would be very pleasant living in Glasgow if the climate were a bit better (but see note (ii) below).

> **Éсли бы дождя́ не́ было, мы могли́ бы пойти́ гуля́ть.**
> If it weren't raining, we might go for a walk.

> **Éсли бы ты рассказа́л мне всё, я бы помо́г тебе́.**
> If you had told me everything, I would have helped you.

NOTES

(i) The particle **бы** normally follows directly after **éсли**; in the other half of the sentence the word order is less fixed, but **бы** is most frequently placed either after the first stressed word or after the verb.

(ii) In English unreal conditions, the verb distinguishes between present and past tense ('would' or 'would have'). In Russian, the verb does not distinguish tenses, but does distinguish between *imperfective* and *perfective* aspects. In many instances the imperfective aspect will correspond to the *present* in English and the perfective will correspond to the *past*, as in the second and third examples above. This is, however, not always the case, and sometimes it is necessary to consider the context to establish whether a Russian sentence refers to the past or the present. For example, in the first sentence above, the English translation given is appropriate if the speaker still lives in Glasgow and here the context is provided by the adverb **тут** 'here'; almost the same sentence could have been said by someone who no longer lives in that city, in which case the adverb would change to **там** 'there' and the translation would be:

> It would have been very pleasant living in Glasgow if the climate had been better.

In unreal conditions **éсли бы** can sometimes be used simply with a noun, where it corresponds to the English 'If it were not for …':

> **Éсли бы не дождь, мы могли́ бы пойти́ гуля́ть.**
> If it were not for the rain, we might go for a walk.

It is important to note that the boundary between open and unreal conditions is much sharper in Russian than it is in English. In English the forms used for unreal conditions can also be used to indicate a condition which is tentative or which is unlikely to be fulfilled, as in the following example:

> If it were to rain tomorrow, we would have to stay at home.

In Russian, the conditional is used only where it is totally impossible for a condition to be fulfilled. Here it is still possible that it might rain, and therefore in Russian this sentence would be treated as an open condition with the verbs in the *future tense*. If it is important to indicate the improbability or the tentative nature of the condition, this can be done with an adverb such as **случа́йно** 'by any chance', **вдруг** 'suddenly', 'by some chance' or **всё-таки** 'after all':

Е́сли за́втра *бу́дет* дождь, *придётся* сиде́ть до́ма.
If it were to rain tomorrow, we would have to stay at home.

Е́сли за́втра *вдруг* пойдёт дождь, придётся сиде́ть до́ма.
If (by some chance) it were to rain tomorrow, we would have to stay at home.

Е́сли за́втра *всё-таки* бу́дет дождь, придётся сиде́ть до́ма.
If (after all) it were to rain tomorrow, we would have to stay at home.

This situation can also arise in indirect speech. The sentence 'He said he would come if he had time' looks like an unreal condition, but the actual words being reported here are 'I will come if I have time' and therefore the condition is, in fact, an open one. In Russian, the future would therefore be used:

Он сказа́л, что придёт, е́сли у него́ бу́дет вре́мя.
He said he would come if he had time.

For more on the tenses in indirect speech, *see* **21.8.4**.

21.5.3 Conditions without е́сли

In both spoken and written Russian it is possible to express *unreal conditions* by using the *imperative* (*see* **4.9**) instead of **е́сли** and the conditional:

Будь ты умне́е, ты бы написа́л жа́лобу, а не стал бы сканда́лить.
If you were cleverer, you would write a letter of complaint instead of shouting and screaming.

Не *умри́* он пять лет наза́д, он был бы сейча́с премье́р-мини́стром.
If he hadn't died five years ago, he would now be the prime minister.

NOTE   On the use of the instrumental with the conditional of **быть**, *see* **14.1.2**.

In spoken Russian and increasingly in the more informal styles of the written language both *open* and *unreal conditions* are expressed simply by placing two clauses together without any conjunction:

Жа́рко пока́жется – откро́й окно́.
If it seems hot, open a window.

Не уве́рен – не обгоня́й.
If you're not sure, don't overtake.
[In Soviet times this helpful piece of road-safety advice was often stencilled on the sides of lorries.]

Не поскупи́лся бы оте́ц на её образова́ние, Ли́за ста́ла бы вели́кой худо́жницей.
If her father hadn't skimped on her education, Liza would have become a great artist.

In more formal styles the preposition **при** (+ prep.) can be used with various abstract nouns to replace a clause with **е́сли**:

> **При жела́нии мо́жно истра́тить на хоро́ший сайт 10 000 до́лларов.**
> Should you wish to do so, you can spend $10,000 on creating a good website.

> **При необходи́мости мо́жно звони́ть в наш моско́вский о́фис.**
> If the need arises, you can phone our Moscow office.

The phrase **в слу́чае** corresponds to the English 'in the event of':

> **В слу́чае пожа́ра по́льзоваться ли́фтами запреща́ется.**
> In the event of fire it is forbidden to use the lifts.

21.6 Concessions

21.6.0 Introduction

Concession can be seen as the reverse of *condition* (**21.5**). Constructions involving concession are used when talking about something that happens *in spite of* a certain set of circumstances.

21.6.1 Making concessions using **несмотря́ на** (+ acc.), **вопреки́** (+ dat.) or **при** (+ prep.)

The prepositional phrase **несмотря́ на** (+ acc.) corresponds to the English 'in spite of', 'despite':

> **Несмотря́ на ваш акце́нт я понима́ю вас без вся́ких проблем.**
> In spite of your accent, I can understand you without any problems.

Несмотря́ на то, что corresponds to the English 'in spite of the fact that' or 'in spite of' when used with the '-ing' form of the verb:

> **Несмотря́ на то, что вы чита́ли его́ рома́ны то́лько в перево́де, вы прекра́сно зна́ете произведе́ния Толсто́го.**
> In spite of the fact that you have read his novels only in translation, you have an excellent knowledge of the works of Tolstoi.
> *Or* In spite of your having read his novels …

Несмотря́ ни на что́ corresponds to the English 'in spite of everything', although only when it is used as a self-contained expression. When it is extended by another clause, **несмотря́ на всё (то), что** is used:

> **Она́, *несмотря́ ни на что́*, ве́рила в све́тлое бу́дущее челове́чества.**
> In spite of everything, she believed in a bright future for mankind.

> **Несмотря́ на всё (*то*), что с ней случи́лось, она́ не потеря́ла ве́ры.**
> In spite of everything that had happened to her, she had not lost her faith.

The preposition **вопреки́** (+ dat.) corresponds to the English 'in spite of', 'contrary to':

> **Э́то всё произошло́ *вопреки́ мои́м жела́ниям.***
> It all happened contrary to my wishes.

The preposition **при** (+ prep.) corresponds to the English 'for' when used in the sense of 'despite':

> **Она поняла́, что её муж, *при всём своём тала́нте*, никогда́ не ста́нет вели́ким писа́телем.**
> She understood that her husband, for all his talent, would never become a great writer.

> ***При всех своих недоста́тках*, она была́ настоя́щим ли́дером коллекти́ва.**
> For all her faults, she was the real leader of the group.

21.6.2 Concessions and reservations: using adverbs

The following *adverbs* and *adverbial phrases* can be used when talking about concessions and reservations:

всё же	still, all the same
всё равно́	still, even so
всё-таки	still, all the same

> **Бу́дет непро́сто, но *всё же* сто́ит попро́бовать.**
> It won't be straightforward, but it's still worth a try.

> **Сто́лько раз мне э́то объясня́ли, но я *всё равно́* ничего́ не понима́ю.**
> It's been explained to me so many times, but even so I don't understand anything.

> **Я не о́чень люблю́ смотре́ть телеви́зор, но не́которые переда́чи *всё-таки* стара́юсь не пропуска́ть.**
> I don't like watching television much, but all the same there are some programmes I try not to miss.

21.6.3 Talking about concessions: using conjunctions

The conjunction **хотя́** corresponds to the English 'although':

> ***Хотя́* он и прости́л её, оби́да оста́лась.**
> Although he had forgiven her, the sense of grievance remained.

> **Мне бы о́чень хоте́лось, чтобы он победи́л, *хотя́* ша́нсов на э́то ма́ло.**
> I would very much like him to win, although the chances of it are not very great.

In informal language, this conjunction can be shortened to **хоть**:

> **На вся́кий слу́чай она́ перекрести́лась, *хоть* и не ве́рила в Бо́га.**
> She crossed herself just in case, even though she didn't believe in God.

The phrase **при (всём) том, что** can also join two clauses with the meaning of 'although':

> ***При всём том, что* у него́ была́ ма́сса ти́тулов и награ́д, держа́лся он скро́мно и да́же незаме́тно.**
> Even though he had heaps of titles and awards, he still conducted himself modestly and even unobtrusively.

The conjunctions **а то** and **ина́че** correspond to the English 'or else':

> **Поторопи́сь, *а то* опозда́ешь.**
> Hurry up or else you'll be late.

Прое́кт до́лжен быть сдан в срок, *и́на́че* мы мо́жем лиши́ться финанси́рования.
The plan has to be submitted by the deadline, or else we might lose the money.

21.6.4 ### Talking about concessions: using a question word + ни

Another way of talking about concessions is to form a clause using a *question word* and the *particle* **ни**. The verb is normally in the *conditional* (*see* **4.10**), especially if the reference is to hypothetical or generalised events:

Куда́ бы ты *ни* пое́хал, от воспомина́ний не убежи́шь.
Wherever you go, you won't escape your memories.

Где бы ты *ни* жил и ско́лько бы ты *ни* е́здил по све́ту, ты никогда́ не забу́дешь Петербу́рг.
Wherever you live and however much you travel round the world, you'll never forget St Petersburg.

Каки́м бы спосо́бным он *ни́* был, он вряд ли спра́вится с э́той зада́чей.
However capable he may be, he's unlikely to cope with this task.
Or Capable as he is …

Что бы он ей *ни* говори́л, она́ всегда́ поступа́ла по-сво́ему.
No matter what he said to her, she still did whatever she wanted.

If the sentence refers to real, rather than to hypothetical events, the appropriate tense can be used:

Как её *ни* отгова́ривали, она́ всё же вы́шла за него́ за́муж.
However much they tried to persuade her, she still married him.

Ско́лько он *ни* забива́ет на трениро́вках, тре́нер пока́ де́ржит его́ в запа́се.
However many goals he scores in training, the manager still keeps him on the bench.

The *future perfective* (see **4.4**) or the *imperative* may be used in generalised statements, usually with a *second person singular* verb:

Что ни ска́жешь, ты всё равно́ не убеди́шь его́.
Whatever you say, you won't convince him.
Or You can say what you like …

Куда́ ни пое́дешь, от свои́х воспомина́ний не убежи́шь.
Wherever you go, you won't escape from your memories.
Or No matter where you go …

Кого́ ни спроси́, все об э́том что́-то слы́шали.
It doesn't matter who you ask, everyone's heard something about it.

For the use of the second person singular in generalised statements, *see* **7.1.5**.

For other uses of the particle **ни**, *see* **15.3.5**.

21.7 Purpose

21.7.1 Talking about purpose using the prepositions для (+ gen.) and на (+ acc.)

To talk about the purpose served by a room or other space, or by a machine, a piece of equipment or similar object, the preposition **для** (+ gen.) is used:

Ме́сто *для куре́ния* на пе́рвом этаже́.
There is a place where you can smoke (*literally*, a place for smoking) on the ground floor.

У него́ в столе́ есть специа́льный я́щик *для секре́тных бума́г*.
He has a special drawer in my desk for secret papers.

Купи́ мне, пожа́луйста, крем *для бритья́* и шампу́нь *для сухи́х воло́с*.
Could you buy me some shaving cream (*literally*, cream for shaving) and some shampoo for dry hair …

For the use of **пе́рвый эта́ж** with the meaning of 'ground floor', *see* **12.4.2**.

The preposition **на** (+ acc.) is similar in meaning to **для**, but it tends to be used when attention is focused on the purpose for which something is intended and in more abstract contexts:

А быва́ет, что лю́дям не хвата́ет де́нег да́же *на хлеб*.
And some people don't even have enough money for bread.

Разреше́ние *на вы́воз* стари́нных книг мо́жно получи́ть в Росси́йской Госуда́рственной библиоте́ке.
You can get permission to export old books from the Russian State Library.

По́сле сле́дующего докла́да бу́дет переры́в *на обе́д*.
After the next talk there'll be a break for lunch.

21.7.2 Talking about purpose using the preposition за (+ instr.)

The preposition **за** (+ instr.) is used in contexts such as going to the shops to buy something, queuing for something or calling in to collect something or somebody:

Мо́жет, я сбе́гаю в магази́н *за хле́бом*?
Should I run out to the shops to buy some bread?

***За биле́том* на э́тот конце́рт придётся стоя́ть (в о́череди) часа́ три, не ме́ньше.**
To get a ticket for that concert you'll have to queue for three hours, if not more.

Мы зайдём *за тобо́й* за́втра в семь часо́в.
We'll come for you tomorrow at seven o'clock.

21.7.3 Talking about purpose using что́бы (+ infin.)

When talking about someone performing an action in order to achieve a particular aim or for a particular purpose, it is usually necessary to use a sentence made up of two clauses joined by the *conjunction* **что́бы**. If the subjects of the two clauses are the same, **что́бы** is followed by the *infinitive*:

For more on conjunctions, *see* **9.3**.

For more on the infinitive, *see* **4.1**.

> **Он встал, *чтобы пожа́ть* ей ру́ку.**
> He got up in order to shake her hand.

> **Чтобы не опозда́ть на рабо́ту, я всегда́ выхожу́ из до́ма ро́вно в во́семь часо́в.**
> In order not to be late for work I always leave home at exactly eight o'clock.

If the subjects of the two clauses are different, **чтобы** is followed by a verb in the *past tense*:

> **Чтобы тебе́ *бы́ло* ле́гче, я перевёл все тру́дные слова́.**
> So that it is easier for you I've translated all the difficult words.

> **Я расска́зываю тебе́ всё это, *чтобы ты знал* всю пра́вду о ситуа́ции.**
> I'm telling you all this so that you know the whole truth about the situation.

It is possible to reinforce **чтобы** with **для того́** or (less frequently) **с тем**:

> **Я расста́вил все ударе́ния в те́ксте *для того́, чтобы* тебе́ ле́гче *бы́ло* чита́ть его́.**
> I've marked all the stresses in the text so that it's easier for you to read it.

> **Весь год она́ брала́ уро́ки ру́сского *с тем, чтобы* ле́том пое́хать в Сиби́рь с этнографи́ческой экспеди́цией.**
> She spent the whole year learning Russian in order to be able to go to Siberia on an ethnographic expedition.

21.7.4 Talking about purpose: omitting чтобы

In short simple sentences where the subjects of the two clauses are the same **чтобы** can be omitted. This construction is restricted to sentences where the main verb is either a *verb of motion* or a verb with a related meaning, such as **останови́ться** 'to stop', **оста́ться** 'to remain'.

For more on verbs of motion, *see* **Chapter 22**.

> **Я *зашёл поздра́вить* тебя́ с днём рожде́ния.**
> I've called in to wish you a happy birthday.

> **—Где нача́льник?**
> **—Он *вы́шел покури́ть*.**

> —Where's the boss?
> —He's popped out for a smoke.

> **Все го́сти разошли́сь, а Ли́за *оста́лась поболта́ть* с на́ми.**
> All the guests left, but Liza stayed behind to have a chat with us.

In more complicated sentences, in sentences where the clause indicating the aim comes first, or in sentences where the infinitive is negated, **чтобы** is used:

> **Мно́гие на́ши сотру́дники с охо́той пое́хали бы за грани́цу, *хотя́ бы на год, чтобы повыша́ть* квалифика́цию.**
> Many of the people who work would happily go abroad, even if only for a year, in order to improve their qualifications.

Она́ была́ о́чень приле́жной, и *что́бы* во́время *сда́ть* рабо́ту, приходи́ла в университе́т да́же в те дни, когда́ у неё не́ бы́ло заня́тий.
She was very conscientious and in order to hand in a piece of work on time would come in to the university even on days when she had no classes.

Она́ вы́шла из ко́мнаты, *что́бы не оказа́ться* в неудо́бном положе́нии.
She left the room in order not to find herself in an awkward situation.

21.7.5 The phrase с це́лью

The phrase **с це́лью** can be used to indicate purpose, especially in more formal levels of language. It can be followed by a *verb* in the *infinitive* or by a *noun* in the *genitive*:

Они́ ста́вили всё но́вые и но́вые усло́вия *с це́лью* затяну́ть перегово́ры.
They kept coming up with more and more conditions with the aim of stalling the negotiations.

Он прие́хал в Москву́ *с це́лью* трудоустро́йства.
He came to Moscow with the aim of finding work.

21.8 Reporting the words of others

21.8.0 Introduction

There are two ways in which the words of others can be conveyed: *direct speech* means quoting the words of others word for word; *indirect speech* means that words are reported rather than quoted. There are two main forms of indirect speech: *indirect statements* and *indirect questions*.

21.8.1 Direct speech

Direct speech is used in ordinary spoken dialogue to create the effect of immediacy:

Зна́ешь, что он мне сказа́л? «Вы молоде́ц! Нам бы бо́льше таки́х, как вы!»
You know what he said to me? 'You've done really well! We could do with more like you!'

In written Russian, direct speech is used mostly, though by no means exclusively, in works of fiction to convey dialogue or the inner thoughts of a narrator. There are two points to note here.

The first is that where a piece of direct speech is followed by a verb indicating the speech act (e.g. **говори́ть/сказа́ть** 'to say', **спра́шивать/спроси́ть** 'to ask' or **отвеча́ть/ отве́тить** 'to answer'), the verb always precedes the subject:

—Ты, ка́жется, всё зна́ешь, – *сказа́л он.*
—It seems you know everything, he said.

The second point concerns punctuation. *Inverted commas* are used when a piece of direct speech is contained within a paragraph; for more on Russian inverted commas, *see* **1.5.8**. When, however, dialogue is set out in paragraphs, *dashes* are preferred:

Он встал и закури́л. «Заче́м я э́то сде́лал?» – *поду́мал он.*
He got up and lit a cigarette. 'What did I do that for?' he wondered.

—Когда́ мы уви́димся? – спроси́л он.

—Я рабо́таю до шести́, – отве́тила она́. – А пото́м я зайду́ в
суперма́ркет.

—When will we see each other again? he asked.

—I am working until six, she answered. And then I'm going to the supermarket.

Indirect statements

When a statement made by someone else is being reported, the verb most commonly used is **говори́ть/сказа́ть** 'to say'. The conjunction corresponding to English 'that' is **что**:

Он *говори́т, что* никогда́ не ест ры́бы.
He says that he never eats fish.

Он *сказа́л, что* придёт по́здно.
He said that he would arrive late.

For an explanation of the different tenses in the English and Russian, *see* **21.8.4**.

In the more formal varieties of Russian there a number of verbs that can be used as near synonyms of **говори́ть/сказа́ть**. These include:

заявля́ть/заяви́ть	to claim, to state, to declare
сообща́ть/сообщи́ть	to announce, to state
утвержда́ть (нсв)	to affirm, to state

Other verbs that can be used to introduce indirect statements include the following:

добавля́ть /доба́вить	to add
ду́мать/поду́мать	to think
крича́ть/закрича́ть	to shout
наде́яться	to hope
объясня́ть/объясни́ть	to explain
отвеча́ть/отве́тить	to answer
полага́ть (нсв)	to suppose, to think
понима́ть/поня́ть	to understand
предполага́ть/предположи́ть	to assume
счита́ть (нсв)	to consider, to think
шепта́ть/прошепта́ть	to whisper

In English, it is sometimes possible to omit the conjunction 'that'; in Russian **что** cannot be left out:

Он сказа́л, *что* понима́ет моё положе́ние.
He said that he understands my position.
Or, He said he understands my position.

When, however, the verb that introduces the indirect speech is in the present tense, it can be placed inside the speech being reported. In the written language, it is separated from the rest of the sentence by commas:

Он, *говори́т*, понима́ет моё положе́ние.
He says he understands my position.

This can be a useful device for avoiding an awkward sequence of clauses introduced by **что**:

> **Я доба́вил, что она́, *наде́юсь,* понима́ет, что я здесь ни при чём.**
> I added that I hoped she understood this had nothing to do with me.

When the speech being reported contains an instruction or prohibition, this can be indicated by using the conjunction **что́бы**:

> **Он сказа́л, *что́бы* я не уходи́л.**
> He said that I should not go away.
> *Or,* He told me not to go away.

For the use of the past tense with **что́бы**, *see* **9.3.4**.

In the examples given so far in this section, the speaker does not express any attitude towards the statements being reported. Sometimes, however, a speaker will want to distance him- or herself from what others have said. This can be done by using the conjunction **бу́дто**:

> **Он утвержда́ет, *бу́дто* он про́жил пять лет в Росси́и.**
> He says (*or* he claims) to have lived in Russia for five years (but I don't really believe him).

Sometimes in the spoken language or in the more informal styles of the written language a similar effect is achieved by using the particles **мол, мол де** or **де́скать**:

> **Он, *мол,* зараба́тывает миллио́н рубле́й в год.**
> He claims to earn a million roubles a year.

> **Она́, мол де, театра́льный режиссёр.**
> She claims to be a theatre director.

> **Он, *де́скать,* никогда́ не рабо́тал в КГБ.**
> He claims he never worked for the KGB.

A stronger degree of disbelief is indicated by the particle **я́кобы**:

> **Он уверя́л, что он, *я́кобы,* не рабо́тал в КГБ.**
> He claimed that he didn't work for the KGB (but nobody in their right mind would believe him).

For more on expressing doubt, *see* **16.5.2**.

21.8.3   Indirect questions

Indirect questions are most commonly introduced by the verb **спра́шивать/спроси́ть** 'to ask'. Instead of a conjunction, the *enclitic particle* **ли** is used; this corresponds to the English 'if' *or* 'whether':

> **Он *спроси́л,* мо́жно *ли* здесь купи́ть проездно́й биле́т.**
> He asked if/whether it was possible to buy a season ticket here.

> **Он *спроси́л,* не зна́ю *ли* я, где ты живёшь.**
> He asked me if/whether I knew where you lived.

For the use of the negative question, *see* **17.1.3**.

For more on the particle **ли**, *see* **17.1.2**.

The particle **ли** invariably follows the first stressed word of the question being reported. Normally, this is the verb, as in the two examples above, but occasionally if some other part of the sentence forms the focus of the question, this can be placed at the beginning of the clause instead:

> **Он спроси́л, *в понеде́льник ли* ты прие́хал.**
> He asked if/whether it was on Monday that you arrived.

It is important to distinguish between 'if' used to introduce an indirect question (where the Russian equivalent is **ли**) and 'if' used to form a conditional sentence (where the Russian equivalent is **е́сли**; *see* **21.5**). It is particularly important not to confuse **е́сли** (in a condition) with **есть ли** (in an indirect question):

> **Я всегда́ спра́шиваю кого́-нибудь, *е́сли* я что-то не понима́ю.**
> I always ask someone if there's something I don't understand. (condition)

> **Она́ спроси́ла, *есть ли* у меня́ ли́шний биле́т.**
> She asked if/whether I had a spare ticket. (indirect question)

As a general rule, where 'if' can be replaced by 'whether', it is being used to introduce an indirect question, and the Russian equivalent will be **ли**.

Other words that can be used to introduce indirect questions include the following:

интере́сно (бы знать)	I wonder, it would be interesting to know
интересова́ться/поинтересова́ться	to ask, to enquire
осведомля́ться/осве́домиться	to enquire (formal)
справля́ться/спра́виться	to enquire

Indirect questions can also be formed using the various interrogative words described in **17.3**:

> **Я спроси́л его́, *с кем* он был вчера́ на приёме.**
> I asked him who he was with at the reception yesterday.

> **Спроси́ его́, *что* ему́ на́до.**
> Ask him what he wants.

> **Тебе́ не интере́сно, *где* я был?**
> Don't you want to know where I have been?

> **Он поинтересова́лся, *ско́лько* сто́ит биле́т до Ри́ги.**
> He enquired how much a ticket to Riga cost.

> **Я не бу́ду тебя́ спра́шивать, *когда́* ты плани́руешь верну́ться домо́й.**
> I am not going to ask you when you intend to return home.

21.8.4 ## Tenses in indirect speech

In some of the examples given in this section the tense of the Russian verbs is different from that of the English equivalents. This is because in English when a verb that introduces indirect speech is in the past tense, this usually leads to changes in the tense of the verbs used with the indirect speech itself:

> He says he will arrive late.
> He said he would arrive late.

He says he understands my position.
He said he understood my position.

I'll ask him if he knows what time it is.
I asked him if he knew what time it was.

In each of those pairs of sentences the actual words used in the original speech are the same:

I will be late.
I understand your position.
Do you know what time it is?

In Russian, this change of tense does not occur. In indirect speech, the tense and the aspect of the verbs are always *exactly the same* as they would have been in the original statement or question:

Он говори́т, что *придёт* **по́здно.**
He says he will arrive late.

Он сказа́л, что *придёт* **по́здно.**
He said he would arrive late.

Он говори́т, что *понима́ет* **моё положе́ние.**
He says he understands my position.

Он сказа́л, что *понима́ет* **моё положе́ние.**
He said he understood my position.

Я спрошу́ его́, *зна́ет* **ли он, кото́рый час.**
I'll ask him if he knows what time it is.

Я спроси́л его́, *зна́ет* **ли он, кото́рый час.**
I asked him if he knew what time it was.

In English, when conditions appear in indirect speech, the application of this rule has the effect of appearing to turn open conditions into unreal conditions (*see* **21.5.2**):

He says that if he doesn't pass the exam tomorrow, he'll have to take it again in the autumn.

He said that if he didn't pass the exam tomorrow, he would have to take it again in the autumn.

In each case, however, the original words spoken were:

If I don't pass the exam tomorrow, I'll have to take it again in the autumn.

In the Russian equivalents of both sentences, therefore, the verbs in the indirect speech would be in the *future perfective*.

The original words were:

Е́сли я не *сдам* **экза́мен за́втра,** *придётся* **пересдава́ть его́ о́сенью.**
If I don't pass the exam tomorrow, I'll have to take it again in the autumn.

The equivalents in indirect speech are:

Он говори́т, что е́сли он не *сдаст* **экза́мен за́втра,** *придётся* **пересдава́ть его́ о́сенью.**
He says that if he doesn't pass the exam tomorrow, he'll have to take it again in the autumn.

Он сказа́л, что е́сли он не *сдаст* экза́мен за́втра, *придётся* пересдава́ть его́ о́сенью.

He said that if he didn't pass the exam tomorrow, he would have to take it again in the autumn.

21.9 Comparisons

21.9.0 Introduction

Constructions indicating comparison are used to indicate that two people, objects or qualities are the same or similar or, alternatively, that they differ from each other in one way or another.

21.9.1 Making comparisons using the short comparative form of adjectives and adverbs

Comparative adjectives and *adverbs* are used when talking about different degrees of the quality indicated by the adjective or adverb concerned. The *short comparative form* of the adjective is mostly used with *predicative* adjectives, that is, those that occur in conjunction with the verb **быть**:

For more on predicative adjectives, *see* **6.0**.

For the formation of the short comparative, *see* **6.8.1**.

Да, ты прав: э́то моро́женое действи́тельно *вкусне́е*.
Yes, you're right; this ice cream really is tastier.

In informal language a short comparative can be used with an *attributive* adjective, but only if the adjective immediately follows the noun. In such instances the adjective is more often than not used with the prefix **по-**:

For the use of the prefix **по-** with the short comparative, *see* **6.8.1**.

Спаси́бо за предложе́ние, но для тако́й зада́чи вам ну́жен челове́к *помоло́же*.
Thanks for the offer, but for that job you need someone younger.

В сосе́днем магази́не есть пи́во *подешёвле*.
There's cheaper beer in the next-door shop.

The short comparative is also used as the comparative form of *adverbs*:

Говори́те *гро́мче*: из-за шу́ма не слы́шно.
Speak louder. I can't hear because of the noise.

Всё, when used with a comparative, corresponds to the English 'more and more':

Снять кварти́ру в столи́це стано́вится *всё доро́же*.
It's getting more and more expensive to rent a flat in the capital.

21.9.2 The second element of the comparison

The second element of a comparison (introduced in English by 'than') is expressed in Russian in two different ways. In a simple sentence, when the person or object being compared is in the *nominative* case and when a *short comparative* is used, the second element is in the *genitive* case:

> **По-мо́ему кра́сные я́блоки *вкусне́е зелёных*.**
> I think red apples are tastier than green ones.

> **Она́ говори́т по-ру́сски *лу́чше меня́*.**
> She speaks Russian better than I do.

When the short comparative follows the noun, the *genitive* can be used if the person or object being compared is in the *accusative*:

> **Я найду́ гости́ницу *почи́ще э́той*.**
> I'll find a hotel cleaner than this one.

In all other types of sentences the second element of the comparison is introduced by the conjunction **чем**. **Чем** can be followed by a noun in any case, by a phrase or by a whole clause:

> **Ду́маю, что э́тот фильм бо́льше понра́вится Ка́те, *чем её му́жу*.**
> I think Katia will like this film more than her husband will.

> **В А́нглии во́дка доро́же, *чем в Росси́и*.**
> Vodka is more expensive in England than in Russia.

> **Она́ говори́т по-ру́сски лу́чше, *чем в про́шлом году́*.**
> She speaks Russian better than she did last year.

> **Он моло́же, *чем вы́глядит*.**
> He's younger than he looks.

In principle, it is possible to use **чем** (+ nom.) instead of the construction with the genitive. To some extent, it is a matter of personal preference, but **чем** is more likely to be used in more complicated sentences, with less widely used comparative forms or in order to avoid ambiguity:

> **Москва́ ста́рше Санкт-Петербу́рга, но мно́гие счита́ют, что Петербу́рг краси́вее, *чем Москва́*.**
> Moscow is older than St Petersburg, but many people think that St Petersburg is more beautiful than Moscow.

> **На́ша ко́мната светле́е, *чем их*.**
> Our room is brighter than theirs.

In the second of these examples **чем** is needed to make it clear that **их** is the *possessive pronoun* and not the genitive plural of the *third person pronoun*:

For **их** as a possessive pronoun, *see* **7.2.2**.

For the declension of the third person pronoun, *see* **7.1.3**.

NOTE | It is normally necessary to insert a comma before **чем**.

21.9.3 Indicating the extent of a comparison

To indicate the extent to which more (or less) of a quality is found in a person or object a construction with the preposition **на** (+ acc.) is used:

Она́ *на два го́да* **ста́рше меня́.**
She's two years older than me.

Доро́га на метро́ занима́ет *на полчаса́* **ме́ньше, чем на авто́бусе.**
The journey by metro takes half an hour less than by bus.

To indicate 'a lot (more)' **гора́здо**, **намно́го** or **значи́тельно** can be used:

Она́ *гора́здо сильне́е* **в хи́мии, чем в матема́тике.**
She's a lot better at chemistry than at maths.

Э́та зада́ча *намно́го сложне́е*, **чем ка́жется на пе́рвый взгляд.**
This task is a lot more complicated than it looks at first sight.

Для америка́нских студе́нтов ру́сский язы́к *значи́тельно трудне́е*, **чем испа́нский.**
For American students, Russian is much more difficult than Spanish.

In informal language, **мно́го** or **куда́** are sometimes used instead of **намно́го**; **куда́** adds an extra degree of expressiveness to the comparison:

Да, э́то уже́ *мно́го лу́чше*.
Yes, that's already a lot better.

Сейча́с у нас усло́вия *куда́ лу́чше*, **чем год наза́д.**
Conditions now are a whole lot better than they were a year ago.

21.9.4 Other uses of short comparative forms

The forms **бо́льше** or **бо́лее** 'more' and **ме́ньше** or **ме́нее** 'less' are, like their English equivalents, used in a wide range of contexts:

Она́ говори́т по-ру́сски лу́чше меня́, но я понима́ю *бо́льше*.
She speaks Russian better than I do, but I understand more.

У меня́ с собо́й *бо́лее* **пятисо́т рубле́й.**
I've got more than 500 roubles on me.

Э́та маши́на сто́ит намно́го *ме́ньше*, **чем я ожида́л.**
This car costs a lot less than I expected.

Е́сли хоти́те похуде́ть, необходи́мо *ме́ньше* **есть и вести́ здоро́вый о́браз жи́зни.**
If you want to lose weight, you need to eat less and lead a healthy life.

NOTES

(i) In this usage **бо́льше** is interchangeable with **бо́лее** and **ме́ньше** with **ме́нее** when they occur in quantity expressions (as in the second example). Otherwise, **бо́льше** and **ме́ньше** are preferred. Only **бо́лее** and **ме́нее** are used to form the *long comparative* (see **21.9.5** and **6.8.2**).

(ii) Like some other words indicating quantity (see **19.5.1** and **19.5.3**), **бо́льше/бо́лее** and **ме́ньше/ме́нее**, when used in this sense, are not found in contexts where they would be required to be in a case other than the nominative or accusative, or where they would occur after a preposition. In most situations, this difficulty can be overcome by reformulating the sentence in such a way as to make the problem disappear. For example, in a context where an English-speaker might say: 'I left the house with less money than I thought', a Russian might prefer:

Ока́зывается, у меня́ с собо́й *ме́ньше де́нег*, **чем я ду́мал.**
Literally, It turns out that I have less money on me than I thought.

The Russian equivalent of 'the more … the more' is **чем** + comparative **…** + **тем** + comparative:

> **Чем** *громче* она́ говори́ла, *тем ху́же* он понима́л смысл её слов.
> The louder she spoke, the less he understood what she was saying
> (*literally*, the worse he understood the sense of her words).

The useful phrase **тем бо́лее (что)** corresponds to the English 'all the more so (because)', 'especially (because)', although it is used more frequently than the English equivalents:

> Она́ не о́чень хоте́ла остава́ться до́ма, *тем бо́лее что* по телеви́зору не́чего бы́ло смотре́ть.
> She didn't particularly want to stay at home especially since there was nothing to watch on television.

> —Не хо́чешь пойти́ в кино́ сего́дня ве́чером?
> —Не о́чень.
> —Идёт како́й-то но́вый боеви́к.
> —Тогда́ *тем бо́лее.*

> —Do you want to go to the cinema tonight?
> —Not particularly.
> —They're showing some new thriller.
> —In that case I want to even less.

21.9.5 Making comparisons using the long comparative form of adjectives

The *long form* of the comparative is used with *attributive adjectives*, that is, those that form part of a single phrase with the nouns they qualify (*see* **6.0**).

For the formation of the long form of the comparative, *see* **6.8.2**.

> Я нашёл для тебя́ *бо́лее интере́сную кни́гу.*
> I've found you a more interesting book.

> Мы оказа́лись *в бо́лее серьёзной ситуа́ции*, чем мо́жно бы́ло предположи́ть.
> We're in a more serious situation than could have been expected.

> На́ша гру́ппа применя́ет *бо́лее то́нкую мето́дику* опро́са обще́ственного мне́ния.
> Our group uses a more subtle method of surveying public opinion.

The long form of the comparative can also be used with *predicative adjectives*. The long form must be used with those adjectives that do not have a *short comparative*.

For adjectives that do not have a short comparative form, *see* **6.8.1**.

> На́ша страна́ сего́дня *бо́лее демократи́ческая*, но ме́нее стаби́льная, чем три́дцать лет наза́д.
> Our country today is more democratic, but less stable than it was thirty years ago.

Бы́ло бы лу́чше, е́сли бы его́ выступле́ния в Ду́ме бы́ли *бо́лее кра́ткими*, но *бо́лее содержа́тельными*.
It would be better if his speeches in the Duma were shorter, but more full of content.

The four *declinable comparative adjectives* – **лу́чший** 'better', **ху́дший** 'worse', **бо́льший** 'bigger' and **ме́ньший** 'smaller' – are used as attributive adjectives:

Лу́чшего учи́теля ру́сского языка́ вам нигде́ не найти́!
You won't find a better Russian teacher anywhere.

К сожале́нию, к *ху́дшему вариа́нту* мы не́ были гото́вы.
Unfortunately, we weren't prepared for the worst alternative.

Бо́льшую часть рабо́ты де́лала секрета́рша, кото́рая приходи́ла в о́фис два ра́за в неде́лю.
Most (*literally*, the greater part) of the work was done by a secretary who came into the office twice a week.

Результа́т игры́ зави́сит в *ме́ньшей сте́пени* от пого́ды, чем от состоя́ния по́ля.
The result of the game depends to a lesser extent on the weather than on the condition of the playing surface.

For more on the four declinable adjectives, *see* **6.8.3**.

NOTES

Except for **лу́чший** these forms are used rather less often than their English counterparts. In particular, **бо́льший** and **ме́ньший** tend to be restricted to abstract contexts or to set expressions such as **бо́льшая часть** 'the greater part', 'the majority' and **в бо́льшей/ме́ньшей сте́пени** 'to a greater/lesser extent'. In other situations it is often preferable to use either a different adjective or a different construction:

По́сле появле́ния пе́рвого ребёнка они́ пересели́лись в *бо́лее просто́рную* кварти́ру.
After the arrival of their first child they moved into a bigger (*literally*, more spacious) flat.

По́сле Но́вого го́да я куплю́ себе́ маши́ну *побо́льше*.
In the New Year I'm going to buy myself a bigger car.

21.9.6 | ## Indicating a lesser degree

To indicate a comparison of a lesser degree **ме́нее** is used with a *long adjective* or with an *adverb*:

Э́та кни́га *ме́нее интере́сная*, чем я ду́мал.
This book is less interesting than I thought.
Or This book is not as interesting as I thought (it would be).

На́ша страна́ сего́дня *бо́лее демократи́ческая*, но *ме́нее стаби́льная*, чем три́дцать лет наза́д.
Our country is more democratic, but less stable than it was thirty years ago.

Они́ перее́хали в *бо́лее просто́рную*, но *ме́нее удо́бную* кварти́ру.
They moved into a bigger, but less comfortable flat.

Они́ понима́ет по-ру́сски *лу́чше меня́*, но говори́т *ме́нее свобо́дно*.
She understands Russian better than I do, but speaks it less fluently.

Indicating 'the same'

The Russian for 'the same' is **тот же (са́мый)**:

For the declension of **тот**, *see* **7.3.1**.

For the declension of **са́мый**, *see* **7.8.2**.

> **Ока́зывается, мы учи́лись в том же (са́мом) университе́те.**
> It turns out we studied at the same university.

NOTE | The use of **са́мый** in this construction is optional.

Тот же (without **са́мый**) is often reinforced by **оди́н и** (cf. English 'one and the same'):

> **Мы ка́ждый раз ста́лкиваемся *с одно́й и то́й же* пробле́мой.**
> Every time we come up against (one and) the same problem.

> **Он прихо́дит ка́ждый день *в одно́ и то же* вре́мя.**
> He arrives every day at (exactly) the same time.

NOTE | The phrase **в то же вре́мя** tends to mean 'at the same time' in the sense of 'and yet':
> **Они́ научи́лись де́лать надёжные и *в то же вре́мя* недороги́е маши́ны.**
> They have learned how to make cars that are reliable, but at the same time inexpensive.

The equivalent of 'the same' in the sense of 'of the same sort as' is **тако́й же**:

> **У меня́ до́ма есть *тако́е же* пла́тье.**
> I have the same dress at home.

The Russian equivalent of 'the same … as' is usually **тот же (самый) … что и**:

> **У меня́ *та же са́мая* информа́ция, *что и* у вас.**
> I have the same information as you (do).

If the comparison involves locations, **где** is sometimes used instead of **что**:

> **Я покупа́ю проду́кты *в тех же магази́нах, где и* все.**
> I buy my groceries in the same shops as everybody else.

The equivalent of 'the same' when it is used adverbially (in the sense of 'in the same way') is often **одина́ково**:

> **Э́ти слова́ произно́сятся *одина́ково*, но различа́ются в написа́нии.**
> These words are pronounced the same, but differ in their spelling.

Indicating similarity

The adjective that corresponds to 'similar (to)' is **похо́жий (на + acc.)**:

> **У нас с тобо́й *похо́жие* интере́сы.**
> We have similar interests.

> **Мой брат о́чень *похо́ж* на меня́.**
> My brother looks very like me.

NOTE | When used *predicatively* (as in the second example), **похо́жий** is almost always in the *short form*.

When introducing a sentence, **похо́же (что)** means 'it looks as if':

> *Похо́же,* его́ сего́дня уже́ не бу́дет.
> It looks as if he won't be here today.

> *Похо́же,* что он нас обману́л.
> It looks as if he's tricked us.

The conjunction that introduces comparisons is **как**:

> Я голо́дный *как* волк.
> I'm as hungry as a lion (*literally*, as a wolf).

> Э́та де́вочка танцу́ет, *как* прирождённая балери́на.
> This girl dances like a natural ballerina.

The conjunction **как** is also used after a clause containing **тако́й** (*see* **7.3.3**) or **так** (*see* **9.1.6**):

> Она́ *така́я же* делови́тая и неутоми́мая, *как и* её мать.
> She's as efficient and as tireless as her mother.

> *Так же как и* в про́шлом году́ наш нового́дний конце́рт состои́тся второ́го января́.
> Just as last year, our New Year concert will take place on 2 January.

For the form of the date, *see* **19.3.3**.

21.9.9 Indicating difference

The adjective **друго́й** means 'different' in the sense of 'another':

> Е́сли тебе́ не нра́вится э́та руба́шка, я могу́ наде́ть *другу́ю*.
> If you don't like this shirt, I can put a different one on.

Ино́й can be used in formal language with the same meaning:

> У меня́ *друга́я/ина́я* то́чка зре́ния на э́тот вопро́с.
> I have a different opinion on this question (e.g. from you).

The adjective **ра́зный** means 'different' (e.g. from each other):

> У них *ра́зные* то́чки зре́ния на э́тот вопро́с.
> They have different views on this question (i.e. from each other).

> В *ра́зных* уче́бниках ты найдёшь *ра́зные* отве́ты на э́тот вопро́с.
> In different textbooks you'll find different answers to this question.

Ра́зный also means 'different' in the sense of 'various', 'all kinds of':

> Здесь продаю́т *ра́зные* сорта́ чёрного и зелёного ча́я.
> They sell different kinds of black and green tea here.

In formal language **разли́чный** also occurs; **разли́чный**, unlike **ра́зный**, has a *short form* (*see* **6.5**):

> Э́ти фе́рмеры применя́ют *разли́чные* удобре́ния – отсю́да и *разли́чные* урожа́и.
> These farmers use different fertilisers and thus obtain different yields.

Эти сочинения абсолютно *различны* как по стилю, так и по композиции.
These works are totally different, both in style and in the manner of composition.

Отличаться от (+ gen.) means 'to differ from'; **различаться** means 'to differ' (e.g. from each other):

Его вторая книга *отличается от* первой тем, что она более серьёзная.
His second book differs from the first in that it is more serious.

Эти слова произносятся одинаково, но *различаются* в написании.
These words are pronounced the same, but differ in their spelling.

The nouns **разница** and **различие** both mean 'difference'. The former is generally more common, but is only ever used in the singular; if a plural form is needed, the latter must be used:

Какая *разница* между его ответом и вашим?
What's the difference between his answer and yours?

Какие *различия* можно найти между английским оригиналом и русским переводом?
What differences can you find between the English original and the Russian translation?

The equivalent of 'unlike', when used as a preposition, is **в отличие от** (+ gen.):

В отличие от тебя я никогда не был в России.
Unlike you, I have never been to Russia.

In other senses, the equivalent of 'unlike' is often **не похожий**:

Он совсем не *похож* на своего брата.
He is quite unlike his brother.

Я не ожидал такого поведения. Это совсем *не похоже* на тебя.
I didn't expect such behaviour. It's most unlike you.

21.10 Indicating context using gerunds

For the formation of gerunds, *see* **4.11**.

21.10.0 Introduction

As was noted in **4.11.0**, the *gerund* is a *verbal adverb*, which means that it is at the same time both a part of the verb and an adverb. Gerunds can on occasion be used in a sentence alongside other adverbs:

Он отвечал неуклюже, *стесняясь, краснея*, но искренне.
He answered awkwardly, nervously, blushing, but sincerely.

More frequently, however, gerunds are used to form complex sentences. In many instances these are similar in meaning to those formed with a *conjunction* and a *finite verb* and described earlier in this chapter (*see* **21.1.5**, **21.1.11**, **21.4.6**, **21.5.1** and **21.6.3**). Unlike clauses formed with a conjunction and finite verb, gerund clauses are normally possible only when the *grammatical subject* of the *main clause* and the *gerund clause* are the same. Gerunds occur rarely in speech, but are widely used in almost all forms of written language.

21.10.1 Using the imperfective gerund without negation

The *imperfective* gerund is used when the actions indicated by the main clause and the gerund clause take place at the same time. Sometimes the clause introduced by the gerund is similar to an adverb in that it describes the manner in which a particular action is carried out:

> *Стара́ясь* не задева́ть ме́бель, они́ протисну́лись в ма́ленькую ко́мнату.
> Trying not to bump into the furniture, they squeezed their way into the small room.

> Приве́тливо *улыба́ясь*, она́ предложи́ла гостя́м снять пальто́ и пройти́ в гости́ную.
> With a smile of greeting, she invited her visitors to remove their coats and go through into the living-room.

In other contexts, a gerund clause is used in place of a subordinate clause of time, reason, condition or concession:

> Он неторопли́во пил ко́фе, вре́мя от вре́мени *погля́дывая* на часы́.
> He drank his coffee slowly, looking at his watch from to time.

> *Понима́я*, что ша́нсов нет, они́ отозва́ли свой иск.
> Since they realise they have no chance of winning, they have withdrawn their case.

> Они́ ви́дели друг дру́га то́лько случа́йно, *ста́лкиваясь* в коридо́ре и́ли в столо́вой.
> They only saw each other by chance, if (*or* when) they met in the corridor or in the canteen.

> —Поня́тия не име́ю, – сказа́ла она́, прекра́сно *зна́я* отве́т на его́ вопро́с.
> —I haven't the slightest idea, she said, although she knew perfectly well what the answer to his question was.

21.10.2 Using the imperfective gerund with negation

The *negated present gerund* usually functions as an adverb, describing the manner in which an action is carried out:

> Он стоя́л, *не зна́я*, что ей сказа́ть.
> He stood there, not knowing what to say to her.

Often it corresponds to the English 'without … -ing':

> Он слу́шал её внима́тельно, *не пребива́я* и *не задава́я* вопро́сов.
> He listened to her carefully, without interrupting and without asking any questions.

Occasionally, it can correspond to the English 'before':

> Проверя́йте сда́чу, *не отходя́* от ка́ссы.
> Check your change before moving away from the cash-desk.

21.10.3 Using the perfective gerund

The *perfective gerund* is normally used when the action denoted by the gerund *precedes* the action indicated by the main verb. For this reason, the relationship between the two parts of the sentence is usually one of *time*:

Взяв её ру́ки в свои́, он стал не́жно целова́ть её па́льцы.
Taking her hands in his, he started gently kissing her fingers.

Прочита́в э́ту статью́, он реши́л неме́дленно написа́ть в реда́кцию.
Having read the article, he decided to write (a letter) to the editor immediately.

Верну́вшись домо́й, он вошёл в ку́хню и поста́вил ча́йник.
Returning home, he went into the kitchen and put the kettle on.

NOTE | In the English equivalents of such gerund clauses, it may sometimes be preferable to use a present, rather than a past tense form.

Sometimes, past gerunds can be used to express conditions:

Как до́лжен поступи́ть граждани́н, *оказа́вшись* в подо́бной ситуа́ции?
How should someone act if they find themselves in a situation like this?

The use of *negated past gerunds* is similar to that of negated present gerunds, except that the action indicated by the gerund is one that would have preceded the action indicated by the main verb:

Он вошёл, *не постуча́в* в дверь.
He came in without knocking at the door.

The main difference between the two gerund forms is one of *aspect*, rather than one of *tense*, and on occasion it is possible to find the perfective gerund used when the actions indicated by the gerund and the main verb appear to be simultaneous. This is when attention is focused on the *totality* or *outcome* of the action indicated by the gerund, rather than on the *process*.

For the use of the perfective aspect to focus on completion, *see* **5.2.4**.

Что ни говори́, она пра́вильно поступи́ла, *вы́йдя за́муж* за Ко́лю.
Say what you like, but she did the right thing when she married Kolia.

Он вы́шел из ко́мнаты, гро́мко *хло́пнув* две́рью.
He left the room, slamming the door behind him.

Here attention is focused not on the process by which one gets married or makes a door slam, but on the state of being married (or, possibly, on the decision to get married) and on the noise made by a door that has been slammed.

For the different constructions corresponding to the English 'to get married', *see* **12.7**.

22

Coming and going

Introduction

Talking about coming and going involves a number of points of grammar where Russian behaves in a way that is very different from English. In the first place, Russian distinguishes between motion on foot and motion by means of transport, a distinction that is extended to carrying, leading or conveying objects, animals or people. Second, Russian has a special grammatical category of *verbs of motion*, where there is a distinction between *unidirectional* and *multidirectional* verbs. Finally, where English uses so-called 'phrasal verbs', such as 'go in', 'come out', 'run through', Russian uses verbs with prefixes.

22.1 Unidirectional and multidirectional verbs of motion

22.1.0 Introduction

There are fourteen pairs of unprefixed verbs that observe the distinction between *unidirectional* and *multidirectional* forms. All unprefixed verbs of motion are *imperfective*.

Various terms can be used to refer to the two groups of verbs: *unidirectional* and *multidirectional*, *determinate* and *indeterminate*, *durative* and *iterative*. The first is adopted here as being the most widely used and being the most transparent in meaning. Those who prefer, however, can refer to them as идти-type and ходить-type verbs (after the first pair of verbs in the following table).

22.1.1 The fourteen pairs of imperfective verbs of motion

	Unidirectional	Multidirectional	Meaning
1	идти́	ходи́ть	to go (on foot), to walk
2	е́хать	е́здить	to go (by transport), to travel, to ride
3	бежа́ть	бе́гать	to run
4	лете́ть	лета́ть	to fly
5	плыть	пла́вать	to swim, to sail
6	лезть	ла́зить	to climb
7	ползти́	по́лзать	to crawl
8	брести́	броди́ть	to wander
9	нести́	носи́ть	to carry (on foot)

	Unidirectional	Multidirectional	Meaning
10	вести́	води́ть	to lead, to take (a person or an animal, on foot)
11	везти́	вози́ть	to take, to transport (by vehicle)
12	гнать	гоня́ть	to chase
13	тащи́ть	таска́ть	to pull, to drag
14	кати́ть	ката́ть	to roll

In the above table verbs in rows 1–8 are *intransitive*; verbs in rows 9–14 are *transitive*. The verbs in rows 1–5 and 9–11 are the most frequently used and the most important.

Information on the conjugation of these verbs is given in the appropriate sections of **Chapter 4**.

For more on transitive and intransitive verbs, *see* **4.13**.

22.1.2 Perfective partners for unprefixed verbs of motion

Perfective partners for *unprefixed verbs of motion* are formed by adding *prefixes*.

To form the perfective partner of *unidirectional* verbs the prefix **по-** is added:

идти́	пойти́
е́хать	пое́хать
бежа́ть	побежа́ть
вести́	повести́
везти́	повезти́

Various perfective partners of *multidirectional* verbs can be formed by adding different prefixes; the most important of these are **с-**, **по-** and **за-**:

ходи́ть	сходи́ть, походи́ть, заходи́ть
е́здить	съе́здить, пое́здить, зае́здить
бе́гать	сбе́гать, побе́гать, забе́гать
вози́ть	свози́ть, повози́ть, завози́ть

NOTE Many of the theoretically possible perfective partners of multidirectional verbs are never used in practice.

The specific meanings and the use of these perfective forms will be described in the following sections.

22.1.3 Talking about motion in one direction

To talk about motion taking place in one direction the *unidirectional* verbs are used. They often, though not always, correspond to the English continuous present (I am going, etc.):

Приве́т, куда́ *бежи́шь*?
Hi, where are you dashing off to?

***Бегу́* в университе́т, опа́здываю на ле́кцию.**
I'm running to the university: I'm going to be late for my lecture.

В да́нный моме́нт я *иду́* по ва́шей у́лице, бу́ду у вас че́рез пять мину́т.
At the moment I'm walking along your street; I'll be with you in five minutes.

Куда́ *ведёт* э́та доро́га?
Where does this road lead to?

Па́пы нет до́ма сейча́с; он *везёт* сестру́ из музыка́льной шко́лы.
Dad's not at home at the moment; he's bringing my sister home from music school (by car).

22.1.4 Talking about motion in more than one direction

Motion in more than one direction or motion in no particular direction is indicated using *multidirectional* verbs:

Отсю́да ви́дно, как над о́зером *лета́ют* ча́йки.
From here you can see the seagulls flying above the lake.

По́сле двена́дцати но́чи городско́й тра́нспорт уже́ не *хо́дит*.
Public transport no longer runs after midnight.

Он уже́ полчаса́ *хо́дит* взад и вперёд по у́лице: ви́димо, кого́-то ждёт.
He's been walking up and down the street for the last half hour; he must be waiting for someone.

Це́лый час мы *по́лзали* с сы́ном по пля́жу – иска́ли мои́ часы́, но так и не нашли́.
My son and I spent a whole hour crawling all over the beach; we were looking for my watch, but we never managed to find it.

В Росси́и они́ *е́здили* на э́той маши́не.
When they were in Russia they travelled around in this car.

Multidirectional verbs also indicate the ability to perform a particular type of action:

Я не уме́ю *пла́вать* и вообще́ бою́сь воды́.
I can't swim and am totally afraid of water.

На́шему сыно́чку всего́ год, а он уже́ *хо́дит*.
Our son's only a year old, but he's already walking.

22.1.5 Talking about repeated or habitual events

Repeated or habitual events usually involve motion in more than one direction and are therefore mostly described using the multidirectional verbs:

Он всегда́ *но́сит* с собо́й моби́льник.
He always carries his mobile phone with him.

В де́тстве мы ча́сто *ла́зили* на э́то де́рево.
When we were children we often used to climb this tree.

Она́ *хо́дит* в клуб ба́льных та́нцев.
She goes to a ballroom dancing club.

По́сле обе́да де́ти ча́сто *бе́гали в парк*.
After lunch, the children would often run to the park.

После обе́да де́ти обы́чно *бе́гали в па́рке*.
After lunch, the children would often run around in the park.

For the use of prepositions indicating location, destination and starting point, *see* **21.2**.

If, however, the repeated or habitual direction being described is specifically in one direction, a *unidirectional* verb will be used:

Часы́ пик – э́то вре́мя, когда́ лю́ди *е́дут* на рабо́ту и́ли с рабо́ты.
Peak hours are the times when people are travelling either to their work or from their work. [In this sentence the journeys to and from work are viewed as separate events.]

22.1.6 Talking about a single event in the past

To describe a single event in the past there are several possibilities with subtle, but clear differences in meaning and use.

The *imperfective past tense* of the *unidirectional* verb is used when attention is focused on the *process* of a single journey in one direction, especially a journey that is in process when something else happens:

Мы *е́хали* к вам снача́ла на метро́, пото́м на электри́чке.
To get to you, we travelled first on the metro and then on a suburban train.

Я как ра́з *вела́* до́чку в са́дик, когда́ случи́лась э́та ава́рия у светофо́ра.
I was taking my daughter to kindergarten when the accident happened at the traffic lights.

NOTE
Russian distinguishes between **по́езд**, a long-distance train, usually with sleeping accommodation, and **электри́чка**, a suburban (electric) train.

The *perfective past tense* of *unidirectional* verbs is used when the focus is on the *beginning* of the action or a *change* in the direction or pace of the motion being described:

—А где Ива́н?
—Он *пошёл* в поликли́нику.

—Where's Ivan?
—He's gone to the polyclinic (i.e. we know he has set off, but not what has happened after that).

Как то́лько загоре́лся жёлтый, она́ сра́зу включи́ла ско́рость и *пое́хала*.
As soon as the light changed to amber, she engaged gear and drove off.

С наступле́нием о́ттепели по Неве́ *поплы́ли* кру́пные льди́ны.
With the arrival of the thaw, large blocks of ice start coming down the Neva.

Соба́ка како́е-то вре́мя бежа́ла за на́ми, но, услы́шав го́лос хозя́ина, *побежа́ла* обра́тно.
The dog chased after us for a while, but hearing the voice of its master, ran back (to him).

Вы́ехав на шоссе́, он *пое́хал* быстре́е.
Once he turned onto the main road, he drove faster.

The *imperfective past tense* of *multidirectional* verbs is used when talking about a *completed round trip*:

> **Это что за паке́ты на полу́? Ты что, *ходи́ла* в магази́н?**
> What are these bags on the floor? Does this mean you've been shopping?

> **В про́шлом году́ мы *е́здили* в Эсто́нию.**
> Last year we went to Estonia.

> **В суббо́ту они́ *води́ли* дете́й на вы́ставку, а в воскресе́нье *вози́ли* их за́ город.**
> On Saturday they took the children to an exhibition and on Sunday took them for a trip into the country.

The *perfective past tense* of *multidirectional* verbs has different meanings according to the *prefix*. Perfectives with the prefix **c-** are also used to describe a single round trip, but they also convey the notion that the trip was unimportant or of short duration:

> **Когда́ оказа́лось, что не́чем заже́чь све́чи , я бы́стренько *сбе́гал* в кио́ск за спи́чками.**
> When it turned out there was nothing to light the candles with, I dashed out quickly to the kiosk for matches.

> **В суббо́ту я *съе́здил* домо́й к роди́телям.**
> On Saturday I took a quick trip home to see my parents.

Perfectives with the prefix **по-** are used to denote an action (motion in more than one direction) that was carried out for a short time, usually as part of a sequence of actions:

> **По́сле рабо́ты я *поплáвала* в бассе́йне, а пото́м пошла́ домо́й.**
> After work, I went for a swim in the baths and then went home.

> **Он не́сколько мину́т *походи́л* по двору́, а пото́м, наконе́ц, отва́жился позвони́ть в дверь.**
> He walked up and down the courtyard for a few minutes, but finally plucked up courage to ring the doorbell.

Perfectives with the prefix **за-** are used to focus on the start of an action (motion in more than one direction):

> **Прочита́в письмо́, он не́рвно *заходи́л* по ко́мнате.**
> Having read the letter, he began to walk nervously up and down the room.

> **Во́зле упа́вшей с де́рева гу́сеницы тут же *забе́гали* муравьи́.**
> When the caterpillar fell from the tree, ants immediately started to run around.

22.1.7 Talking about a single event in the future

The *perfective future* of *unidirectional* verbs can be used when talking about a single event due to take place in the future:

> **Ле́том мы *полети́м* на Сахали́н.**
> We're flying to Sakhalin in the summer.

> **За́втра я *пойду́* в Ру́сский музе́й.**
> I'm going to the Russian Museum tomorrow.

The *present tense* of *unidirectional* verbs is also used to talk about a *planned* event:

> **Я *иду́* на у́лицу – заодно́ могу́ вы́нести му́сор.**
> I'm going out: I can take the rubbish out at the same time.

> **В сле́дующую пя́тницу я *лечу́* в Москву́: племя́нник же́нится.**
> I'm flying to Moscow next Friday; my nephew's getting married.

The *perfective future* forms of *multidirectional* verbs convey the same shades of meaning as the corresponding *past tense* forms:

> **Что я бу́ду де́лать в воскресе́нье? *Попла́ваю* в бассе́йне, *поброжу́* по па́рку, *схожу́* в кино́.**
> What am I going to do on Sunday? I'll go for a swim in the baths, wander round the park for a bit and go to the cinema.

> **Мо́жет, я *сбе́гаю* за хле́бом?**
> Shall I run out and buy some bread?

<h3>22.1.8 Instructions, prohibitions and exhortations</h3>

Instructions relating to coming and going are usually given using the *imperative* of the *unidirectional* verb:

> ***Иди́те* к нему́.**
> Go and see him.

> ***Поезжа́й* на да́чу.**
> Go to the dacha.

> ***Веди́те* её в музе́й.**
> Take her to the museum.

Prohibitions, however, are normally issued using the *multidirectional* verb:

> ***Не ходи́те* к нему́. К нему́ нельзя́ *ходи́ть*.**
> Don't go and see him. You can't go and see him.

> ***Не е́зди* на да́чу. *Не на́до* туда́ *е́здить*.**
> Don't go to the dacha. You shouldn't go there.

> ***Не води́те* её в музе́й.**
> Don't take her to the museum.

The unidirectional verb is used if the prohibition relates an action already in progress:

> ***Не беги́*, у нас ещё есть вре́мя.**
> Don't run, we've still got time.

> ***Не веди́* маши́ну так бли́зко к обо́чине.**
> Don't drive so close to the curb.

The *plural past perfective* forms **пошли́** and **пое́хали** correspond to the English exhortation 'let's go':

> **Все гото́вы? Ну, тогда́ *пое́хали*.**
> Is everybody ready? Right, in that case let's go.

For more on instructions, prohibitions and exhortations, *see* **18.2** and **18.3.3**.

22.2 Prefixed verbs of motion

22.2.0 Introduction

General information on the use of *prefixes* to form new verbs and on the principal meanings of the different prefixes is given in **10.4**. In this section we describe the formation of *imperfective* and *perfective* pairs of *prefixed verbs of motion* and give examples of how these verbs are used when talking about coming and going.

Prefixed verbs of motion do not distinguish between *unidirectional* and *multidirectional* movement.

22.2.1 The formation of imperfective and perfective pairs of prefixed verbs of motion

Perfective verbs are formed by adding a prefix to the *unidirectional* verb. When **идти́** takes a prefix, the *infinitive* changes to **-йти́** and the corresponding *future tense* forms to **-ду́**, **-дёшь** etc.:

войти́	to enter	войду́, войдёшь
подойти́	to approach	подойду́, подойдёшь

However, note the following:

вы́йти	to go out, to come out	вы́йду, вы́йдешь
прийти́	to come, to arrive	приду́, придёшь

For more on the stress of perfective verbs with the prefix **вы-**, *see* **4.2.4**.

Imperfective verbs are formed in some instances by adding a prefix to the *multidirectional* verb. In other instances, the imperfective verb is related to the multidirectional verb, but has either a different *suffix* or a different *stress*.

The following table illustrates the formation of aspect pairs of *prefixed verbs of motion*. Instances where the prefixed form differs from the unprefixed form are given in *italics*:

Imperfective		*Perfective*
-ходи́ть		**-йти́**
входи́ть	to enter	*войти́*
-езжа́ть		**-е́хать**
уезжа́ть	to leave, to go away	уе́хать
-бега́ть		**-бежа́ть**
выбега́ть	to run out	вы́бежать
-лета́ть		**-лете́ть**
прилета́ть	to arrive (flying)	прилете́ть
-плыва́ть		**-плыть**
переплыва́ть	to swim across	переплы́ть
-леза́ть		**-лезть**
слеза́ть	to climb down	слезть
-ползать		**-ползти́**
подползать	to crawl up to	подползти́
-бреда́ть		**-брести́**
забреда́ть	to wander off, to drop in	забрести́

Imperfective		Perfective
-носи́ть		**-нести́**
приноси́ть	to bring (carrying)	**принести́**
-вози́ть		**-везти́**
подвози́ть	to give someone a lift	**подвезти́**
-води́ть		**-вести́**
своди́ть	to bring (people) together	**свести́**
-гоня́ть		**-гна́ть**
загоня́ть	to corral	**загна́ть**
-та́скивать		**-тащи́ть**
выта́скивать	to drag out	**вы́тащить**
-ка́тывать		**-кати́ть**
прока́тывать	to roll (past)	**прокати́ть**

22.2.2 | Examples of prefixed verbs of motion

The following examples illustrate the use of *imperfective* and *perfective* pairs of *prefixed verbs of motion*:

Туда́ *входи́ть* нельзя́.
You can't go in there.

А сюда́ мо́жно *войти́*?
But can I come in here?

Из за́ла суда́ все *выходи́ли* мо́лча.
Everyone was leaving the court in silence.

Когда́ на аре́ну *вы́шли* кло́уны, де́ти захло́пали в ладо́ши.
When the clowns came out into the ring, all the children started to applaud.

Когда́ мы *подлета́ли* к Ло́ндону, мо́жно бы́ло разгляде́ть Те́мзу.
As we were approaching London (in an aeroplane), we could make out the River Thames.

Я поста́вил в саду́ корму́шку для пти́ц, и к ней сра́зу же *подлете́ли* два воробья́.
I set up a bird table in the garden and two sparrows immediately flew towards it.

Мно́гие пти́цы име́ют спосо́бность *уводи́ть* хи́щника пода́льше от свои́х птенцо́в.
Many birds have the ability to lead a predator away from their young.

Пошёл дождь, и роди́тели *увели́* дете́й с игрово́й площа́дки.
It started to rain and the parents removed their children from the playground.

Весно́й мно́гие хозя́йки име́ют обыкнове́ние *выноси́ть* поду́шки на просу́шку.
In spring, many housewives follow the practice of putting their pillows out to air.

Ты не мог бы *вы́нести* му́сор?
Would you mind taking the rubbish out?

It is important to distinguish the *perfective* verbs **заходи́ть**, **сходи́ть**, which are perfective partners of the *multidirectional* verb **ходи́ть**, from the *imperfective* verbs **заходи́ть**, сходи́ть, which are imperfective partners of зайти́ 'to drop in', 'to go behind' and сойти́ 'to come/go down' respectively.

> **Прочита́в письмо́, он не́рвно** *заходи́л* **(св) по ко́мнате.**
> Having read the letter, he began to walk nervously up and down the room.

> **По доро́ге домо́й он иногда́** *заходи́л* **(нсв) в небольшо́е кафе́ на углу́.**
> On the way home he sometimes dropped in to a small café on the corner.

> **Не́чем заже́чь све́чи – придётся** *сходи́ть* **(св) в кио́ск за спи́чками.**
> There's nothing to light the candles with; somebody will have to go to the kiosk for matches.

> **Ката́ться на лы́жах здесь ста́ло опа́сно – на́чали** *сходи́ть* **(нсв) сне́жные лави́ны.**
> It's become dangerous to ski here; avalanches have started to occur (*literally*, come down).

22.2.3 Correlation between prefix and preposition

There is generally a high degree of correlation between the *prefixes* attached to verbs of motion and the *prepositions* used before *nouns* and *pronouns* to indicate destination, point of departure or an object encountered en route. The following are the correlations that occur most often:

Prefix	Preposition (destination)	Prefix	Preposition (point of departure)
при-	в/на	вы-	из
по-	в/на	у-	из
под-	к	с(о)-	с(о)
за-	к		
			Preposition (object encountered en route)
за-	в/на	о/об(о)-	вокру́г 'around'
		про-	ми́мо 'past'/че́рез 'across'/сквозь 'through'
		пере-	че́рез

> **Она́** *прие́хала в* **Росси́ю.**
> She arrived in Russia.

> **Она́** *пришла́ на* **ле́кцию.**
> She came to the lecture.

> **Она́** *уе́хала из* **Росси́и.**
> She left Russia.

> **Он** *вы́полз из* **норы́.**
> It crawled out of the burrow.

> **Он** *подбежа́л к* **арби́тру.**
> He ran up to the referee.

> **Он** *облете́л вокру́г* **све́та.**
> He orbited (*literally*, flew round) the earth.

> **Мяч** *пролете́л ми́мо* **воро́т.**
> The ball flew past (i.e. missed) the goal

Он *перевёл слепо́го* че́рез доро́гу.
He took the blind man across the road.

In a number of instances the *prefix* and the *preposition* are identical:

Он *зашёл за́* угол.
He went round the corner.

Отойди́ от кра́я платфо́рмы: электри́чка идёт.
Move away from the edge of the platform: there's a train coming.

Когда́ мы *въе́хали в* го́род, была́ уже́ глубо́кая ночь.
When we drove into the city, it was already late at night.

Он *доплы́л до* бе́рега.
He swam as far as the shore.

Она́ *слете́ла с* кры́ши.
It (e.g. a bird) flew down from the roof.

Он *внёс* чемода́н *в* дом.
He carried the suitcase into the house.

А за что, со́бственно, Бог *изгна́л из* Ра́я Ада́ма и Е́ву?
And why, exactly, did God expel Adam and Eve from the Garden of Eden?

22.3 Verbs of motion used in figurative expressions and idioms

22.3.0 Introduction

Verbs of motion are used in a wide range of figurative expressions and idioms, which often have nothing obvious to do with movement. When such expressions involve *unprefixed verbs of motion*, then either only the *unidirectional* verb or (less often) only the *multidirectional* verb can be used.

22.3.1 Figurative expressions with unidirectional verbs of motion

The verb **идти́** is used in a number of expressions where it has the basic meaning of 'to take place':

Туда́ входи́ть нельзя́; *идёт* уро́к.
You can't go in there; there's a lesson taking place.

Како́й фильм *идёт* в кинотеа́тре «Ко́смос»?
What film is on the Kosmos cinema?

Сейча́с *идёт* хоро́ший спекта́кль в теа́тре «Ленко́м».
There's a good play on just now at the Lenkom theatre.

The same verb is also used for certain weather phenomena:

идёт дождь   it's raining
идёт снег   it's snowing

The verb **идти́** is also used to convey the idea of something suiting someone or going well with something else:

Э́то пла́тье ей *идёт*.
This dress suits her.

Во́дка хорошо́ *идёт* с солёными гриба́ми.
Vodka goes very well with pickled mushrooms.

Time goes only in one direction, but can seem to go at different speeds:

вре́мя идёт	time is passing
вре́мя бежи́т/лети́т	time flies
вре́мя ползёт	time is dragging

Other examples with unidirectional verbs include the following:

Здесь мы *ведём* учёт дохо́дов и расхо́дов всех отделе́ний.
Here we keep track of the income and expenditure of all departments.

Она́ *ведёт* дневни́к.
She keeps a diary.

Все на́ши пла́ны *летя́т* (к чёрту). (informal)
All our plans are up the spout.

У э́той соба́ки *ле́зет* шерсть.
That dog is losing its fur.

Не *лезь* в дра́ку.
Don't get involved in that fight.

Мы *несём* отве́тственность за э́то.
We have responsibility for this.

Что за ахине́ю ты *несёшь*? (informal)
What rubbish are you talking now?

У меня́ от всего́ э́того кры́ша *е́дет*. (informal)
All this is driving me round the bend.

For the use of **везти́/повезти́** as an impersonal verb in sentences describing someone's luck, *see* **3.4.3**.

22.3.2 Figurative expressions with multidirectional verbs of motion

There are fewer figurative expressions involving multidirectional verbs.

The verb **носи́ть** can mean 'to wear' (on a regular basis):

Молодёжь *но́сит* джи́нсы.
Young people wear jeans.

Я забы́л, что она́ обы́чно *но́сит* очки́.
I'd forgotten that she usually wears glasses.

There is no verb in Russian that corresponds to English 'to be wearing' (on a particular occasion). Instead, prepositional phrases are used:

Сего́дня *на нём* чёрный сви́тер и се́рые брю́ки.
Today he's wearing a black pullover and grey trousers
(*literally*, On him there is …).

На балу́ то́лько она́ одна́ была́ *в кра́сном*.
She was the only person wearing red (*literally*, in red) at the ball.

The *transitive* verb **ката́ть/поката́ть** and the more frequent reflexive verb **ката́ться/ поката́ться** are used to refer to a pleasure trip, usually without a specific destination, taken in some means of transport:

Оте́ц *ката́л* нас на ка́тере.
Our father used to take us out for rides in his boat.

Мо́жет, *поката́емся* на твое́й но́вой маши́не?
Can we go for a spin in your new car?

Шко́льные кани́кулы я обы́чно проводи́л в дере́вне; *ката́лся* на ло́шади, на ло́дке, на мотоци́кле и да́же води́л грузови́к.
I usually spent my school holidays in the country; I would go horse-riding and boating, would ride on a motorbike and even drove a lorry.

Ката́ться/поката́ться is also used in certain set phrases:

ката́ться/поката́ться на конька́х	to go skating
ката́ться/поката́ться на лы́жах	to go skiing
ката́ться/поката́ться на са́нках	to go sledging

22.4 Other issues relating to coming and going

22.4.1 Coming and going

In general, Russian does not distinguish between 'coming' and 'going' when these relate simply to the direction of movement:

Извини́те за опозда́ние, мо́жно *войти́*?
I'm sorry for being late; may I come in?

Туда́ *входи́ть* нельзя́: идёт уро́к.
You can't go in there: there's a lesson taking place.

Когда́ на аре́ну *вы́шли* кло́уны, де́ти захло́пали в ладо́ши.
When the clowns came out into the ring, all the children started to applaud.

Не зна́ю, где он; мо́жет быть, *вы́шел* покури́ть.
I don't know where he is; he may have gone outside for a smoke.

Ти́ше, *идёт* учи́тель.
Be quiet; the teacher's coming.

To correspond to 'coming' in the sense of 'arriving', Russian verbs of motion with the **при-** can be used:

Мы *пришли́* к вам пешко́м, но домо́й от вас пое́дем на такси́.
We came on foot, but we're going home by taxi.

Приезжа́йте поча́ще.
Do come and see us more often.

22.4.2 **Going on foot or by transport**

In general, **идти** and **ходить** are used to refer to movement on foot. To emphasise that movement is on foot and not by means of transport, the adverb **пешком** can be used:

> Мы *пришли* к вам *пешком*, но домой от вас поедем на такси.
> We came on foot, but we're going home by taxi.

When reference is to a journey by means of transport, the verb depends on the means of transport: **ехать** and **ездить** are used for a journey by land transport, **плыть** and **плавать** for a journey on water, **лететь** and **летать** for a journey by air:

> Я *езжу* в университет на сорок седьмом автобусе.
> I go to the university on a 47 bus.
> *Or*, I get the 47 bus to the university.

> Мы *приехали* поездом/на поезде.
> We came by train.

> Мой прадед *ездил* на лошади, мой дед *ездил* на велосипеде, мой отец *ездил* на мотоцикле, а я хожу пешком.
> My great-grandfather rode a horse, my grandfather travelled by bicycle, my father drove a motorbike and I go about on foot.

> Четыре британки намерены на лодке *переплыть* Атлантический океан.
> Four British women are planning to cross the Atlantic in a rowing boat.

> На этот раз мы решили *лететь* самолётом/на самолёте.
> This time we decided to fly.

In general, there is a correlation between *intransitive* and *transitive* verbs of motion according to the following patterns:

> Идти + нести; идти + вести
> Ходить + носить; ходить + водить
> Ехать + везти
> Ездить + возить

> *Пришла* Нина и, как обычно, *принесла* последние новости.
> Nina came and, as usual, brought the latest news with her.

> Максим *пришёл* не один, он *привёл* невесту.
> Maksim didn't come on his own, but brought along his fiancée.

> Брат *уехал* в Петербург и *увёз* мою гитару.
> My brother has gone off to St Petersburg and taken my guitar with him.

When it is the means of transport itself that is the subject of the movement, Russian tends to use **идти** and **ходить** for land or water transport, but **лететь** and **летать** for air transport:

> Туда идёт сорок седьмой автобус.
> The 47 bus goes there.

> Поезд *пришёл* с небольшим опозданием.
> The train arrived a few minutes late.

> В этот пыльный городишко не *заходят* большие волжские пароходы.
> The big Volga steamships do not visit this dusty little town.

Сюда́ *лета́ют* то́лько вертолёты.
You can only get there by helicopter (*literally*, Only helicopters fly there).

Е́хать and **е́здить** or **плыть** and **пла́вать** tend to be preferred if the focus is on the means of transport as a physical object:

Ми́мо нас *прое́хал* како́й-то авто́бус.
A bus has just gone past us.

Я люби́л смотре́ть, как по Во́лге *плыву́т* больши́е бе́лые парохо́ды.
I used to love watching the big white steamships sailing along the Volga.

22.4.3 Talking about coming and going using other verbs

There are numerous verbs that relate in one way to movement, but which do not come into the grammatical category of *verbs of motion*:

гуля́ть	to stroll, to go for a walk
путеше́ствовать	to travel
отправля́ться/отпра́виться	to set off
оставля́ть/оста́вить	to leave, to abandon
покида́ть/поки́нуть	to leave, to abandon
добира́ться /добра́ться до (+ gen.)	to get to
прибыва́ть/прибы́ть	to arrive
возвраща́ться/верну́ться	to return

Гуля́ть is always *intransitive* and is used with a construction indicating location:

По́сле у́жина мы обы́чно *гуля́ем* **с соба́кой в па́рке.**
After supper we usually take the dog for a walk in the park.

A phrase that also corresponds to English 'to go for a walk' is **идти́** or **ходи́ть на прогу́лку**:

На у́лице прекра́сная пого́да. Ты не хо́чешь *пойти́* **на** *прогу́лку*?
The weather's really nice. Do you want to go for a walk?

Путеше́ствовать is used with relation to a fairly substantial journey; it is normally used with the preposition **по** (+ dat.):

Ле́том мно́гие студе́нты *путеше́ствуют по Евро́пе* **автосто́пом.**
In summer many students hitch-hike around Europe.

Оставля́ть/оста́вить and **покида́ть/поки́нуть** are *transitive* verbs that mean 'to leave' with the additional connotation of 'abandoning':

По́сле кровопроли́тных боёв в ию́ле со́рок второ́го го́да сове́тские войска́ *оста́вили* **Севасто́поль.**
After the bloody battles of July 1942 the Soviet forces abandoned Sebastopol.

Он *поки́нул* **э́тот го́род, что́бы уже́ никогда́ сюда́ не возвраща́ться.**
He left the city, never to return to it.

Добира́ться /добра́ться до (+ gen.) tends to imply a certain amount of difficulty in reaching the destination:

Мы *добрали́сь* **до ме́ста назначе́ния уже́ затемно́.**
It was well after dark when we reached our destination.

Прибыва́ть/прибы́ть tends to be used in more formal types of language:

> **Уважа́емые пассажи́ры, наш по́езд *прибыва́ет* на коне́чную ста́нцию.**
> We wish to inform passengers that this train is arriving at its final destination.

Отправля́ться/отпра́виться and **возвраща́ться/верну́ться** require no special comment:

> **За́втра *отправля́емся* ро́вно в семь часо́в.**
> We're setting off tomorrow at exactly seven o'clock.

> **Я слы́шал, что он *отпра́вился* в путеше́ствие по Золото́му кольцу́.**
> I heard he'd set off on a trip round the Golden Ring.

> **Он поки́нул э́тот го́род, чтобы уже́ никогда́ сюда́ не *возвраща́ться*.**
> He left the city, never to return to it.

> **Пе́рвой в ко́смос полете́ла соба́ка – на Зе́млю она́ не *верну́лась*.**
> The first animal in space was a dog, but she never returned to Earth.

NOTE | The **Золото́е кольцо́** 'Golden Ring' is the name given to a tourist route that takes in several ancient towns and cities located to the north-east of Moscow.

23

Communication strategies

23.1 **Choosing what type of language to use**

23.1.1 **Formal and informal language**

In this book we have tended to give advice on how words, phrases and grammatical constructions are used in terms of *formal* and *informal* language. Although this distinction is not always the most appropriate, it is in most circumstances more useful than the distinction between *written* and *spoken* language, since in practice both written and spoken language exist in formal and informal varieties, and formal written language, for example, will tend to have more in common with formal spoken language than it will with informal written language.

Formal written language is used in official documents, such as laws, regulations and contracts, as well as in business letters and scholarly books. Formal language also tends to be used in journalism, sometimes with an admixture of more informal varieties.

Formal spoken language tends to be used in texts that are written out in advance, such as lectures and political or ceremonial speeches. However, elements of formal language may also be preferred in official discussions and negotiations.

Informal spoken language is that which is normally used in ordinary conversation.

Informal written language is used in private letters and (sometimes in a stylised form) in works of fiction. Informal written language may also appear in the lyrics of pop and rock songs and is widely used in various forms of Internet communication.

It follows from this that virtually everyone who learns Russian is going to need some knowledge of both formal and informal language and of the differences between them. And even if many learners will never have to produce documents in formal written language, anyone who has any contact with the written language will at some point have to read and understand texts written in this particular variety.

NOTE | It is important to distinguish between *informal* language and *non-standard* language. Everybody uses informal language in the appropriate circumstances, while non-standard language consists of forms that are disapproved of and avoided by most educated speakers of the language, who consider them to be incorrect or improper. Those who learn Russian will at some point encounter non-standard language, most probably in casual conversation, although there is a whole Internet subculture that is based on the use of non-standard forms for playful effect, including deliberately incorrect spelling. Nevertheless, there are two points to note. The first is that many Russians take the view that non-standard language is something that learners of the language should know nothing about and that it is certainly not something that they ever expect to find learners using themselves. The second point is that non-standard language, like formal and informal language, is a system in its own right, and the use of non-standard language in ways that do not conform to the 'rules' of that system is at best inappropriate and at worst highly embarrassing to all concerned. At the very least, therefore, the deliberate use of non-standard language should be attempted only by those who have an absolute and total confidence in their command of the standard language.

23.1.2 The characteristics of formal language

Formal language, and especially formal written language, is characterised by the following features:

- A preference for long and grammatically complex sentences.
- The widespread use of participles in the long form.
- A tendency to use abstract vocabulary and especially to prefer constructions with verbal nouns over finite verb forms.
- A tendency to avoid the first person singular and a preference for depersonalised constructions and for passive verbs.

23.1.3 The use of participles

The *short forms* of *past passive participles* are found in all types of language, where they are used to form *perfective passive* verbs. All other forms of participles are restricted to formal language and especially to formal written language.

For information on the formation of participles, *see* **4.12**.

For information on the use of the short form of the past passive participle to form perfective passive verbs, *see* **4.14.2**.

Participles are verbal adjectives and phrases containing a participle in the *long form* fulfil a similar function to clauses introduced by a *relative pronoun*.

For more on relative pronouns, *see* **7.5**.

The stylistic limitation on the use of participles and the functional overlap between participial phrases and relative clauses mean that many learners may find that they rarely or never need to use them. Nevertheless, they are a sufficiently important element of formal writing that an ability to recognise them and to interpret them correctly is essential if this type of language is to be properly understood.

The following sentences illustrate the use of participles. Taken from official regulations concerning foreign travel, they show how several participial phrases can be used in one sentence in order to produce convoluted text that can be difficult to unravel and to translate:

> Граждани́н, *дости́гший* восемнадцатиле́тнего во́зраста и *обраща́ющийся* за получе́нием па́спорта в связи́ с *при́нятым* им реше́нием о вы́езде из Росси́йской Федера́ции для прожива́ния в друго́м госуда́рстве, ука́зывает об э́том в своём заявле́нии.

A citizen who has reached the age of eighteen and who requests the issue of a passport in connection with a decision he has made to leave the Russian Federation in order to live in another country, mentions this in his application.

Иностра́нные гра́ждане мо́гут въезжа́ть в Росси́йскую Федера́цию и выезжа́ть из Росси́йской федера́ции при нали́чии росси́йской ви́зы по действи́тельным докуме́нтам, *удостоверя́ющим* **их ли́чность и** *признава́емым* **Росси́йской Федера́ции в э́том ка́честве, е́сли ино́е не предусмо́трено междунаро́дными догово́рами Росси́йской Федера́ции.**
Foreign citizens may enter and leave the Russian Federation provided that they have a Russian visa accompanying valid documents confirming their identity and recognised for that purpose by the Russian Federation, unless different arrangements are provided for under international agreements signed by the Russian Federation.

Министе́рство иностра́нных дел Росси́йской Федера́ции мо́жет офо́рмить и вы́дать па́спорт граждани́ну Росси́йской Федера́ции, *прожива́ющему* **на террито́рии Росси́йской Федера́ции, по его́ ли́чному заявле́нию,** *по́данному* **че́рез** *команди́рующую* **его́ организа́цию,** *зарегистри́рованную* **в Министе́рстве иностра́нных дел Росси́йской Федера́ции в поря́дке,** *устано́вленном* **Прави́тельством Росси́йской Федера́ции.**
The Ministry of Foreign Affairs of the Russian Federation may issue a passport to a citizen of the Russian Federation who is resident on the territory of the Russian Federation in cases where that person submits a personal request through the organisation that is sending him abroad and which is registered with the Ministry of Foreign Affairs of the Russian Federation in accordance with procedures laid down by the government of the Russian Federation.

Not all sentences containing participles are as complicated as those above. Some examples of rather more straightforward sentences are given in the comments on word order in **19.1.3**.

To demonstrate how *participial phrases* fulfil much the same function as *relative clauses*, here is the first of the above examples rewritten with relative clauses replacing the participial phrases; the following version is somewhat more awkward than the original:

Граждани́н, *кото́рый дости́г* **восемнадцатиле́тнего во́зраста и** *кото́рый обраща́ется* **за получе́нием па́спорта в связи́ с реше́нием о вы́езде из Росси́йской Федера́ции для прожива́ния в друго́м госуда́рстве,** *кото́рое он при́нял,* **ука́зывает об э́том в своём заявле́нии.**

Some participles are also used as ordinary adjectives or (less often) nouns. When used in this way they do not necessarily have the same stylistic restriction as they do when used as true participles. Examples include:

блестя́щий	brilliant
веду́щий	leading, presenter (of a television programme)
выдаю́щийся	outstanding
де́йствующий	active, functioning
окружа́ющий	surrounding
отсу́тствующий	absent (also as a noun)
потряса́ющий	staggering, amazing
предше́ствующий	preceding

прису́тствующий	present (also as a noun)
реша́ющий	deciding, decisive
сле́дующий	following, next
смягча́ющий	mitigating
теку́щий	current (e.g. affairs, account)
вооружённый	armed
воспи́танный	well brought up
разочаро́ванный	disenchanted, disappointed
убеждённый	convinced
уме́ренный	moderate
цивилизо́ванный	civilised
ве́рующий	believer, believing
куря́щий	smoker
слу́жащий	white-collar worker
да́нные	data
по́дданный	subject (e.g. of the crown)
подчинённый	subordinate

Тогда́ у него́ появи́лась *блестя́щая* иде́я.
Then he had a brilliant idea.

На *сле́дующий* день он просн́лся с головно́й бо́лью.
The next day he woke up with a headache.

В семидеся́тые го́ды он был *убеждённым* коммуни́стом.
In the 1970s he was a convinced communist.

На пе́рвом этаже́ есть специа́льное помеще́ние для *куря́щих*.
On the ground floor there is a special room for smokers.

У него́ скве́рные отноше́ния со все́ми *подчинёнными*.
He has a dreadful relationship with all his subordinates.

<h2>23.1.4   Other characteristic features of formal language</h2>

The following sentence, already quoted in the section on participles, also provides an illustration of how *verbal nouns* are used in formal language:

Граждани́н, дости́гший восемнадцатиле́тнего во́зраста и обраща́ющийся за *получе́нием* па́спорта в связи́ с при́нятым им *реше́нием* о *вы́езде* из Росси́йской Федера́ции для *прожива́ния* в друго́м госуда́рстве, ука́зывает об э́том в своём заявле́нии.
A citizen who has reached the age of eighteen and who requests the issue of a passport in connection with a decision he has made to leave the Russian Federation in order to live in another country, mentions this in his application.

If we exclude **заявле́ние**, which takes the form of a verbal noun, but which here means a type of document (a written application for something), there are four verbal nouns in this sentence: **получе́ние, реше́ние, вы́езд, прожива́ние**. In principle, each of these nouns could be replaced with a construction involving a verb; here is part of the sentence rewritten with the verbs used instead of nouns:

Граждани́н … кото́рый хо́чет *получи́ть* па́спорт, потому́ что он *реши́л вы́ехать* из Росси́и, чтобы *прожива́ть* в друго́м госуда́рстве …
A citizen … who wants to receive a passport because he has decided to leave Russia in order to live in another country …

For more on the formation of verbal nouns, *see* **10.1.10**.

The following example, taken from a newspaper article written shortly after Vladimir Putin came to power in 2000, illustrates not only the use of *verbal nouns*, but also a preference for other forms of *abstract nouns* and for *passive* and *depersonalised* constructions. It will be noted that these features cannot always be reproduced in the translation:

> Тем не ме́нее в де́йствиях Пу́тина *прослёживается* определённая ло́гика. Пе́рвые его́ шаги́ *напра́влены на реанима́цию* госуда́рства, а и́менно: *подчине́ние* бюрокра́тии, *восстановле́ние управля́емости* страны́, *ослабле́ние* автоно́мных от госуда́рства це́нтров си́лы. Как уже́ *отмеча́лось*, в да́нном слу́чае *речь идёт о реше́нии зада́ч* нове́йшей эпо́хи.
>
> Nevertheless, it is possible to discern a certain logic in Putin's actions. His first steps were aimed at reviving the state, specifically by bringing the bureaucracy to heel, by making the country governable again and by weakening centres of power not under state control. As has already been pointed out, we are talking here about addressing the problems of the most recent era.

For the use of **да́нный** in place of **э́тот** in formal language, *see* **7.3.2**.

23.2 Constructing a text

23.2.0 Introduction

Any text, whether spoken or written, whether in formal or informal language, will consist of a series of individual sentences. This section will examine some of the ways in which individual sentences can be linked to form a coherent text.

23.2.1 Вво́дные слова́: introductory words

Russian has a special category of forms known as **вво́дные слова́** (*literally*, introductory words). In spite of the name, **вво́дные слова́** do not necessarily appear at the beginning of a sentence and may consist either of a single word or of an entire phrase. **Вво́дные слова́** are separated from the rest of the sentence by commas, and they are used to supply information that is additional to what is contained in the main body of the sentence.

Some **вво́дные слова́** fulfil the specific role of linking sentences. These include:

впро́чем	however, on second thoughts
зна́чит	so
ита́к	and so
как бы то ни́ было	however that may be
кро́ме того́	in addition, moreover
к тому́ же	in addition, moreover
одна́ко	however
сле́довательно	therefore
ста́ло быть	therefore
таки́м о́бразом	therefore
тем не ме́нее	nonetheless, nevertheless

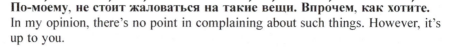

По-мо́ему, не сто́ит жа́ловаться на таки́е ве́щи. Впро́чем, как хоти́те.
In my opinion, there's no point in complaining about such things. However, it's up to you.

Ме́неджеров из стран Евросою́за не так уж мно́го в Росси́и, и они́ иногда́ с трудо́м приспоса́бливаются к росси́йским усло́виям. *Как бы то ни бы́ло*, они́ несу́т с собо́й за́падный подхо́д к де́лу и за́падную организа́цию.
There aren't that many managers from EU countries in Russia, and they sometimes have difficulty in adapting to Russian conditions. However that may be, they do bring with them a Western approach to business and Western organisation.

Вчера́ из-за пого́дных усло́вий бы́ло отменено́ бо́лее двухсо́т ре́йсов. *Кро́ме того́*, из-за тума́на мно́гие ре́йсы бы́ли заде́ржаны на срок до двух часо́в.
Yesterday more than 200 flights were cancelled because of the weather. In addition, the fog meant that many flights were delayed for up to two hours.

Делега́там Съе́зда не разреша́лось разглаша́ть содержа́ние докла́да. *Тем не ме́нее*, по́лный текст вско́ре появи́лся в за́падной печа́ти.
Delegates at the congress were not allowed to reveal the contents of the speech. Nevertheless, the full text soon appeared in the Western press.

Another group of **вво́дные слова́** indicate the extent to which the information being communicated is probable. These include:

коне́чно	of course
(са́мо собо́й) разуме́ется	of course
должно́ быть	it must be case that
наве́рное, наве́рно	probably
по-ви́димому	apparently
пожа́луй	probably, perhaps
ка́жется	it seems
возмо́жно	it is possible that
мо́жет быть	perhaps

NOTE

Both **наве́рное** and **наве́рно** are characteristic of informal language, the former tends to be used in writing and the latter in speech.

Они́, *коне́чно*, име́ют пра́во не согласи́ться с на́ми.
Of course, they have the right not to agree with you.

Здесь нет его́ веще́й, так что он, *должно́ быть*, уже́ уе́хал.
His things aren't here so he must already have left.

Я, *наве́рно*, зайду́ к ней за́втра по́сле рабо́ты.
I'll probably call in and see her tomorrow after work.

Ты, *пожа́луй*, прав; не на́до бы́ло отка́зываться от его́ по́мощи.
You're probably right; we shouldn't have refused his help.

Здесь, *ка́жется*, не за чем остава́ться.
It seems that there's no point in staying here.

Росси́я, *возмо́жно*, **всту́пит в ВТО до конца́ теку́щего го́да.**
It's possible that Russia will join the WTO (World Trade Organisation) before the end of the currrent year.

Сле́дующий конгре́сс на́шей организа́ции состои́тся в Росси́и, *мо́жет быть*, **во Владивосто́ке.**
The next congress of our organisation will take place in Russia, possibly in Vladivostok.

For further examples of **вво́дные слова́** used in this function, *see* **16.5.1**.

Some **вво́дные слова́** make a comment on the nature of the utterance itself. These include:

допу́стим	let us assume
предполо́жим	let us suppose
одни́м сло́вом	in a word
коро́че говоря́	to put it briefly
со́бственно говоря́	strictly speaking
шу́тки в сто́рону	joking apart
кста́ти (говоря́)	by the way
ме́жду про́чим	by the way

Допу́стим, **он придёт. И что бу́дет?**
Suppose he comes. Then what happens?

Одни́м сло́вом, **э́то невозмо́жно.**
In a word, it's impossible.

Со́бственно говоря́, **вы не име́ете пра́ва здесь прису́тствовать.**
Strictly speaking, you don't have the right to be here.

Шу́тки в сто́рону, **дискримина́ция мужчи́н – э́то реа́льная и о́чень серьёзная пробле́ма.**
Joking apart, discrimination against men is a genuine and a very serious problem.

Она́, *ме́жду про́чим*, **заболе́ла и скоре́е всего́ не придёт.**
By the way, she's not well and probably won't come.

The following **вво́дные слова́** indicate the speaker or the writer's attitude to the matter being described:

к сча́стью	fortunately
к сожале́нию	unfortunately

К сча́стью, **мы о́чень хорошо́ понима́ем по-ру́сски.**
Fortunately, we understand Russian very well.

К сожале́нию, **ва́ше заявле́ние не мо́жет быть при́нято, та́к как после́дний срок пода́чи докуме́нтов уже́ истёк.**
Unfortunately, your application cannot be accepted since the final deadline for the submission of documents has already expired.

The following **вво́дные слова́** are used when enumerating points in an argument:

во-пе́рвых	in the first place
во-вторы́х	in the second place
в-тре́тьих	in the third place

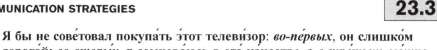
Я бы не сове́товал покупа́ть э́тот телеви́зор: *во-пе́рвых*, он сли́шком дорого́й; *во-вторы́х*, я сомнева́юсь в его́ ка́честве, а *в-тре́тьих*, мо́жно найти́ бо́лее совреме́нную моде́ль.

I wouldn't advise you to buy that television set. In the first place, it's too expensive; in the second place, I have doubts about its quality and in the third place, you can find a more up-to-date model.

23.2.2 Using the conjunction a

In addition to being used to link clauses (see **9.3.2**), the conjunction **A** is often used at the beginning of a sentence, especially in dialogue. Here it serves the function of alerting the listener to a new topic or to a new development in the existing topic or simply of providing extra emphasis. In this function it is particularly common in questions:

Я счита́ю, что всё бу́дет сде́лано к концу́ ме́сяца. А ты как ду́маешь?
I think everything will be done by the end of the month. What do you think?

—Здесь, пожа́луйста, укажи́те ва́ше и́мя, фами́лию, да́ту рожде́ния, а́дрес, телефо́н.
—*А* заче́м вам вся э́та информа́ция?

—Could you indicate here your first name, surname, date of birth, address and telephone number?
—Why do you need all that information?

The phrase **А вдруг** means 'what if?', 'suppose':

—Она́ должна́ быть здесь часа́м к оди́ннадцати.
—*А вдруг* она́ опозда́ет?

—She should be here by about eleven.
—But what if she's late?

23.3 Discourse words

Discourse words are words and phrases that have little or no meaning of their own, but which are used to structure speech. They can be 'filler words' that give the speaker time to think or to find the right word, or they can be words that make a statement more tentative or more emphatic. Russian has a large number of such words and phrases, and these can have a more or less 'translatable' meaning, depending on the context in which they are used. Their proper usage is a matter of idiom and can be described here only approximately. The learner is thus advised to listen carefully to note how Russians use these expressions in their own speech.

The following is a list of discourse words that are widely used in Russian. Where appropriate, translations are given, but it should be noted that these will not be applicable in many instances:

в о́бщем	in general, on the whole
вот	(a sentence filler)
в при́нципе	in principle
зна́чит	so (often used as a sentence filler)
так	so, well (can be used to gain time)
так сказа́ть	so to speak

| это (са́мое) | the whatsit (used when searching for a word) |
| как его́/её там | the whatever-it's-called, the what's-its-name |

In the following examples, some of the above words and phrases are used with a definite and translatable meaning:

У него́ бы́ло не́сколько крити́ческих замеча́ний, но *в о́бщем* его́ реце́нзия положи́тельная.
He had a few critical comments, but on the whole his review is positive.

***В при́нципе* я согла́сен, но тут есть не́которые спо́рные моме́нты.**
In principle I agree, but there are some unresolved issues here.

Сейча́с выхо́дим из до́ма. *Зна́чит*, бу́дем у вас че́рез час.
We're leaving the house now. That means we'll be at your place in an hour's time.

Э́то лека́рство я про́бую в пе́рвый раз. Э́то, *так сказа́ть*, экспериме́нт.
I'm trying this medicine for the first time. It is, so to speak, an experiment.

In the following examples, the words and phrases listed above are used as discourse words, and in many instances they cannot be directly translated:

***Та-ак*, всё, *в о́бщем*, поня́тно. Я, *зна́чит*, поду́маю, что да́льше де́лать.**
Well, then, I suppose that's all sorted out. I'll have to think now what to do next.

Мне, *зна́чит*, тут твоя́ жена́, *э́то са́мое*, рассказа́ла о ва́шей, *так сказа́ть*, пробле́ме. А вы не про́бовали обраща́ться к *э́тому, как его́ там*, сексо́логу?
Well, I've sort of been, I don't know, told by your wife about your problem, as it were. Have you tried going to one of those, what are they called, sexologists?

—Ты мо́жешь меня́ подвезти́ на вокза́л?
—*В при́нципе* да.

—Can you give me a lift to the station?
—I suppose so.

NOTE | When **так** is used at the beginning of a sentence in order to gain time, the vowel is often extended to double (or even triple) the normal length.

There are three discourse words that are particularly characteristic of the speech of young people. These are:

как бы	sort of
ти́па	like
блин	(emphasises the previous word)

Although it is inevitable that many learners of Russian will hear these words used by their friends and acquaintances, it is as well to know that they come with a serious 'health warning': the use of these expressions is regarded by many Russians as an indication of an inadequate grasp of the language and/or an inability to express one's thoughts in a clear and coherent manner. In particular, **блин**, although it literally means 'pancake', is in this usage a transparent euphemism for an obscenity and is consequently offensive to many Russians.

Index

Note: references are to sections, not to pages

INDEX

INDEX

INDEX

INDEX

INDEX

postal address 12.4.1

predicative adjectives 6.0, 21.9.1

preferences 16.2.3

prefixed verbs: aspect 4.2.3, 4.2.4

    correlation between prefix of verbs of motion and preposition 22.2.3

prefixes: spelling 1.5.6

    verbal prefixes 10.4

prepositional case 3.6, 9.2.6, 21.2

prepositions 9.2

    correlation between prefix and preposition 22.2.3

presence 14.2

present participles 4.12.1, 4.12.3

present tense 4.3, 4.6

probability 16.5.1

process: choice of aspect 5.2.2

    verbs indicating an action that by definition cannot be completed 5.3.4

    verbs that can indicate action in process in English, but not in Russian 5.3.3

    verbs that can indicate action in process in Russian, but not in English 5.3.2

productive classes of verbs 4.6.1–4

professions 12.6

prohibition 5.7.5, 18.2.1, 18.2.4

pronouns 7.0

    demonstrative pronouns 7.2

    indefinite pronouns 7.6

    interrogative pronouns 7.4

    personal pronouns 7.1

    possessive pronouns 7.3

    pronouns relating to totality 7.7

    reflexive pronouns 7.1–2

    relative pronouns 7.5

    using pronouns to indicate definite nouns 20.4.3

pseudo-negatives 15.2.2

public notices 18.2.2–4, 18.3.2

punctuation: comma before *как* or *чем* 21.1.11, 21.1.16, 21.3.4

    comma before *чем* in comparisons 21.9.2

    comma in letter headings 13.6.1

    commas separating off participial phrase 23.1.3

    comma separating two clauses 9.3.2–6

purpose 21.7

    omitting *чтобы* 21.7.4

    using *для* (+ gen.) and *на* (+ acc.) 21.7.1

    using *за* (+ instr.) 21.7.2

    using *чтобы* (+ inf.) 21.7.3

quantity: approximate quantity using numerals 19.4

    imprecise quantity using forms other than numerals 19.5

question words 17.3

    used when talking about concessions 21.6.4

questions: asking questions using question words 17.3

    choice of aspect 5.5.1–2

indirect questions 21.8.3

intonation 17.1.1

loaded questions 17.2

questions formed with the particle *ли* 17.1.2

rhetorical questions 17.4

tag questions 17.2.3

yes/*no* questions 17.1

reciprocal pronoun *друг друга* 7.8.3

reduction of unstressed vowels 1.4.3

    unstressed **а** and **о** 1.4.4

    unstressed **е**, **э** and **я** 1.4.5

reflexive pronoun *себя*: declension 7.1.2

    use 7.1.7

reflexive verbs 4.13.2

registration (at a specific address) 12.4.3

relative clauses *see* clauses

relative pronouns: *кото́рый* 7.5.1

    кто and *что* 7.5.2

    чей and *како́й* 7.5.3

repetition: choice of aspect 5.2.3

requests 18.3, 17.4.3

rhetorical questions 17.4

right: *to be right* 3.1.3, 6.5.1, 14.1.4, 21.5.1, 21.9.1, 23.2.1

    one's right 7.5.3, 10.1.12, 11.1.3

Russian names *see* names

same 21.9.7

seasons of the year 21.1.3

second conjugation: productive class 4.6.4

    unproductive classes 4.7.15–16

second genitive 2.7.1

secondary stress 1.4.8

semelfactive perfectives 5.3.5

short adjectives: endings 6.5.1

    irregular forms 6.5.3

similarity 21.9.8

since 21.1.16

singular: nouns that occur only in the singular 2.1.2

soft adjectives: 6.2–3

soft consonants 1.2.1

    pronunciation 1.2.3

    representation in writing 1.2.4

spelling rules 1.5

    pronunciation of the ending -*го* 1.5.5

    spelling after **ш, ж, ч, щ, ц** 1.5.2

    spelling of certain prefixes 1.5.6

    use of capital letters 1.5.7

    use of the letter *ё* 1.5.1

    use of *е* and *э* 1.5.3

    use of *и* after *г, к, х* 1.5.4

starting point (of movement) 21.2.15

stress 1.4

    importance of stress 1.4.1

    marking of stress 1.4.2

466

INDEX

INDEX

INDEX

Related titles from Routledge

Basic Russian
A Grammar and Workbook

John Murray and Sarah Smyth

Designed for students with a basic knowledge of Russian, this book provides an accessible reference grammar and related exercises in a single volume.

Across more than forty grammar topics it introduces the student to Russian people and culture through the medium of the language used today, covering the core material which the student would expect to encounter in their first year of learning Russian.

Complete with a full key to exercises and glossary, *Basic Russian* is a user-friendly reference grammar suitable for both independent study and class use.

ISBN13: 978–0–415–18318–5 (pbk)
ISBN13: 978–0–415–18317–8 (hbk)
ISBN13: 978–0–203–19831–5 (ebk)

Available at all good bookshops
For ordering and further information please visit:
www.routledge.com

Related titles from Routledge

Intermediate Russian
A Grammar and Workbook

John Murray and Sarah Smyth

Intermediate Russian provides a reference grammar and related exercises in one volume. Varied texts from Russian sources give an insight into contemporary Russian society and culture. Features include:

- texts and exercises reflecting contemporary Russian
- concise grammar explanations
- full exercise key
- detailed index.

Intermediate Russian, and its sister volume, *Basic Russian*, are ideal both for independent study and use in class. Together the books provide a compendium of the essentials of Russian grammar.

ISBN13: 978–0–415–22103–0 (pbk)
ISBN13: 978–0–415–22102–3 (hbk)
ISBN13: 978–0–203–18430–1 (ebk)

Available at all good bookshops
For ordering and further information please visit:
www.routledge.com

Related titles from Routledge

Colloquial Russian
The Complete Course for Beginners

Svetlana Le Fleming and Susan E. Kay

Colloquial Russian is easy to use and completely up to date! Specially written by experienced teachers for self-study or class use, the course offers you a step-by-step approach to written and spoken Russian. No prior knowledge of the language is required.

What makes *Colloquial Russian* your best choice in personal language learning?

- interactive – lots of dialogues and exercises for regular practice
- clear – concise grammar notes
- practical – useful vocabulary and pronunciation guide
- complete – including answer key and special reference section

By the end of this rewarding course you will be able to communicate confidently and effectively in a broad range of situations.

CDs or MP3s to accompany *Colloquial Russian* are available to buy separately. Recorded by native speakers, this audio material will help you perfect your pronunciation and listening skills.

ISBN13: 978–0–415–16140–4 (pbk)
ISBN13: 978–0–415–12683–0 (CDs)
ISBN13: 978–0–415–42702–9 (pbk and CDs pack)

Available at all good bookshops
For ordering and further information please visit:
www.routledge.com

Related titles from Routledge

Colloquial Russian 2
The Next Step in Language Learning

Svetlana Le Fleming, and Susan E. Kay

Do you know Russian already and want to go a stage further? If you're planning a visit to Russia, need to brush up on your Russian for work, or are simply doing a course, *Colloquial Russian 2* is the ideal way to refresh your knowledge of the language and to extend your skills.

Colloquial Russian 2 is designed to help those involved in self-study. Structured to give you the opportunity to listen to and read lots of modern, everyday Russian, it has also been developed to work systematically on reinforcing and extending your grasp of Russian grammar and vocabulary.

Key features of *Colloquial Russian 2* include:

- Revision material to help consolidate and build up your basics
- A wide range of authentic contemporary documents, both written and audio
- Lots of spoken and written exercises in each unit
- Highlighted key structures and phrases, a grammar reference and detailed answer keys
- A broad range of everyday situations

CDs to accompany the *Colloquial Russian 2* book are available to buy separately. Recorded by native speakers this material will help you develop your pronunciation and listening skills.

ISBN13: 978–0–415–26116–6 (pbk)
ISBN13: 978–0–415–30250–0 (CDs)
ISBN13: 978–0–415–45394–3 (pbk and CDs pack)

Available at all good bookshops
For ordering and further information please visit:
www.routledge.com